PSYCHOLOGY
Looking at Ourselves

PSYCHOLOGY
Looking at Ourselves

SECOND EDITION

James Geiwitz

Little, Brown and Company
Boston   Toronto

To Pete and Hansina

Library of Congress Catalog Card No. 79-88189

First Printing

Published simultaneously in Canada by Little, Brown & Company (Canada) Limited

Printed in the United States of America

The first edition of this work by James Geiwitz was published in 1976 under the title *Looking at Ourselves: An Invitation to Psychology.*

Book editor: Barbara Sonnenschein
Designer: Anna Post
Art editors: Tina Schwinder, Designworks/Pembroke Herbert
Illustrators: Susan Spellman Mohn, Judy Norton, George Ulrich, Lily Yamamoto

Cat definition, p. 601: © 1975 by B. Kliban. Reprinted from CAT by permission of the Workman Publishing Company, New York.

Illustration Credits

Preface, p. ix: Bill Boyd.
Chapter 1 *Fig. 1.1:* Sybil Shelton/Monkmeyer. *Fig. 1.2:* Courtesy Merck Sharp and Dohme, Division of Merck and Co., Inc., West Point, Pennsylvania 19846. *Fig. 1.4:* Susan Kantowitz, TEXT-EYE. *Fig. 1.6:* © 1969 Colgate Palmolive Company. *Fig. 1.8:* Emeraude by Coty.

Chapter 2 *Fig. 2.4:* From *The Nervous System: Introduction and Review* by C. R. Noback and R. J. Demarest, copyright © 1972 by McGraw-Hill, Inc. Used with permission of McGraw-Hill Book Company. *Fig. 2.8:* From C. G. Gross, C. E. Rocha-Miranda, and D. B. Bender, "Visual properties of neurons in inferotemporal cortex of the macaque," *Journal of Neurophysiology,* 35 (1972), Fig. 6, p. 104. Reprinted by permission. *Fig. 2.9:* The Bettmann Archive. *Fig. 2.12:* Owen Franken/Stock, Boston. **Color Insert** *Plates 1-8:* Lennart Nilsson from *Behold Man,* Little, Brown and Co., © 1973. *Plates 9-10:* Courtesy The American Optical Corporation. *Plate 11:* Mike Mazzaschi/Stock, Boston. *Plate 12:* Jasper Johns, FLAGGS, Leo Castelli Gallery.

Chapter 3 *Fig. 3.1:* Collection Mr. & Mrs. A. Reynolds Morse, Salvador Dali Museum, Cleveland (Beachwood), Ohio. *Fig. 3.4:* Wide World Photos. *Fig. 3.6:* Scala, New York/Florence. *Fig. 3.7:* Harry Callahan. *Fig. 3.10:* J. Allan Cash Ltd. *Fig. 3.11:* Baron Wohlman/Woodfin Camp. *Fig. 3.12:* M. C. Escher, *Symmetry Drawing A,* Escher Foundation–Haags Gemeentemuseum, The Hague. *Fig. 3.14:* Courtesy Levi Strauss and Company. *Fig. 3.15:* From M. J. Horowitz, "Hallucinations: An information-process-
(Continued on p. 645)

Preface

(in which the author sets behavioral objectives for himself)

The other day I opened a psychology book to read that "since his earliest beginnings man has known that he constitutes a complex of differing elements and processes which interrelate with one another in multiform fashion, and that by virtue of such interrelationships he is enabled to operate as an integrated whole." Foolishly, I pushed on, only to encounter a definition: "What the system can and cannot do defines the system's performance capabilities at any particular place and time, and is a product of a variety of factors." Quietly I closed the book and turned to an article. When I reached the adjective "syndromic," I gave it up. Enough is enough.

When I first decided to write an introductory textbook, I set as my primary goal the description of modern scientific psychology in clear and straightforward prose. I tried to avoid what Edwin Newman (1976) calls the "gelatinous verbiage" of the social sciences. I did not always succeed — often I wrote "behavioral objectives" when I meant no more than "goals" — but I believe you will find this book relatively free of the jargon and the excessively complicated constructions that so often plague psychologists' attempts to communicate with others. Instead you will find my approximation of what Newman calls "a civil tongue," language that is "direct, specific, concrete, vigorous, colorful, subtle, and imaginative . . . something to revel in and enjoy."

A second "behavioral objective" I set for myself was to write a fair and accurate account of scientific psychology as it exists today. The path to this goal, like that to uncluttered prose, was strewn with pitfalls and obstacles. For one thing, as a relatively brief introduction to the field, my book is bound to leave out or skip too quickly over some readers' favorite studies and topics. By far the biggest obstacle, however, was the constant pull to forsake informativeness for interest. Many topics of legitimate interest in psychology—biofeedback, brainwashing, ESP—invite flashy, superficial treatment. To avoid this, I tried to focus on the experimental evidence, to tone down the glitter by treating the issues seriously.

Several special topics are covered in their very own short chapters called "interludes." There are interludes on sex differences, drugs, hypnosis, parapsychology, sexuality, sleep and dreams, and several other themes. Most introductory textbooks cover some of these topics, usually in a chapter with related content. Drugs, for example, might turn up in the biological chapter (emphasizing physiological effects) or in the abnormal chapter (emphasizing drug abuse as a personality disorder). By placing these topics within a chapter, these books have to limit their discussions to the one aspect of the topic related to the content of the chapter. In my book, by setting the topics apart in their own interludes, I can bring in research from many areas and discuss the issues from many perspectives. Lie detection is a *test* of *emotion*; it draws on research and theory in assessment as well as in motivation and emotion. Sex differences have biological aspects (hormones), developmental aspects (sex-typing), social-psychological aspects (roles); also relevant to the topic is research in motivation (achievement) and assessment (tests of masculinity, femininity, and androgyny).

But most of the content of psychology is contained in the 14 regular chapters. In this, the second edition, two important new chapters have been added. One is on motivation and emotion, integrating material from biological hunger to individual self-actualization. (Note I didn't say *how well* it was integrated! Let us not make extravagant claims for an area that has resisted integration for a hundred years!) The other is on adult development and aging, a vitally important area in which theory and research are currently burgeoning. There are some new interludes, too: careers in psychology, behavior genetics, parapsychology, human sexuality, sleep and dreams.

A minor behavioral objective of mine was to introduce students to some of the humor in psychology. As TV shows like *Candid Camera* and the situation comedies so vividly demonstrate, what people do—the stuff of psychology—is often very funny. Given a choice between illustrative anecdotes, why not choose the more humorous one? Thus, in Chapter 4, I discuss my own failure as a teacher when, in the midst of a classroom demonstration of operant conditioning, my rat ate the ping-pong ball I was using as a prop! (My class was thereby treated to a vivid demonstration of "instinctive drift," although a week or two of embarrassed self-pity passed before I realized the demonstration's salvage value.) In Chapter 11, I describe an elderly friend of mine, about to take his first-ever objective test (a driving examination). He asked what a "true-false" question was, but my explanation failed; he could not believe that the United States Government would write false items!

Moral issues must be faced, one way or another, in every introductory textbook. I have tried very hard to eliminate racism, sexism, and ageism from the content and the language of this book. Sexist language is a particular problem, because some aspects of it have no agreed-upon solution. Nobody has a right to expect a woman to think of herself as "he" or as part of "mankind," no matter how neutral the words are supposed to be. Sooner or later, I believe, a new pronoun must be created, one that means "either he or she" (Geiwitz, 1978). In the meantime, the only alternative to overt sexism is the attempt to be fair: I have used "he or she" (or "she or he"), except in sentences with so many pronouns that meaning would be lost if the number were doubled. In the remaining cases, I have used a "generic he"—meaning "he or she"—in even-numbered chapters and the interludes following them, and a "generic she"—meaning "she or he"—in odd-numbered chapters and following interludes. I have tried to balance male examples with female examples and to do the same with illustrations.

I want to say a few words about the role of feedback in the creation of an introductory textbook. By my last count, we have had reviews from 66 instructors and 178 students to help us construct the second edition. Most of these reviews were favorable—as one student said, "It wasn't as boring as it could have been"!—but many had minor suggestions for improvement which we were able to implement. A good example was the repeated suggestion by students that they found the "Focus" sections within the chapters—the "boxed" supplementary or incidental material that every textbook has these days—*distracting*. Thus, I took pains to incorporate much of this material directly into the text, and to introduce the remaining "Focuses" *between* major headings, where they will be less disruptive. We made several changes in format to improve the text, and, of course, we made several changes in the content in response to new developments and criticisms of old material.

My goal was to create a textbook that is a fascinating account of modern scientific psychology, one that is aware of problems and moral issues but faces them with what one editor called my "typical optimistic realism." I wanted to write a book that the student would find interesting and informative, a book solidly based on current research and theory, written in simple but vivid prose. My image was of a student who would enjoy learning and, when he or she finished the book, would feel good about psychology as a science and about his or her own progress as an intellectual being. I frankly think that the result, this textbook, is a fairly close approximation of those objectives.

Introductory textbooks these days are not simply books; they are "programs," with an instructor's manual, a study guide, and test items. We worked very hard to make these elements of the *Psychology: Looking at Ourselves* program interesting, informative, and valuable. Ann Syrdal-Lasky's study guide is truly well done; it can be used by itself or in PSI. Ralph Protsik's teacher's manual is fascinating; there are good ideas for every kind of instructor. And what can one say about book-company test items, except that most of them are almost useless? Our test bank by Burleigh Seaver and others is clearly superior; the items were thoughtfully constructed to be fair and educational, and we intend to eliminate stinkers and introduce new items periodically.

Writing an introductory textbook is a mammoth task. I want publicly to assume responsibility for the entire textbook; this is no "managed textbook." I had magnificent help, however, from many people. This book was born in discussions with Christopher Hunter, then psychology editor at Little, Brown, and later nurtured with great care and skill by Marian Ferguson, who is certainly one of the best, if not the best, psychology editor in the business. Developmental editor Carol Verburg is so precious I hardly know what to say; through two editions, she has been my "gelatinous verbiage" detector, polishing my material to a sheen I did not know it was capable of. Book editors Barbara Sonnenschein (second edition) and Lynn Lloyd (first edition) tended to the creation of the book itself—the pages, the illustrations—a process for which I never lost my wonder nor my admiration.

Ernest Kohlmetz, David Gordon, and Barbara Miller Wertheimer wrote drafts of interludes in the first edition on "applications of psychology" (now incorporated into the interlude on careers), "moral development," and "aging and death" (now incorporated into the chapter on adult development and aging), respectively. Gerald Jacobs, Walter Gogel, Anna Kun, Carol Jacklin, Ervin L.

The author. James Geiwitz earned his undergraduate degree at St. Olaf College in Northfield, Minnesota, and his Ph.D. from the University of Michigan. He has taught at Michigan, Stanford University, and the University of California, Santa Barbara.

Betts, James Brown, Robert Castleberry, Robert DaPrato, Joan DiGiovanni, Tullius Frizzi, Roberta Klatzky, Susan McFadden, Arthur Caccese, Philip Captain, Daniel J. Cohen, Richard T. Colgan, Willie Davis, James Durant, Steve Ellyson, Gene R. Empson, Judith Farrell, Albert Gorman, Erwin J. Janek, Karl G. Krisac, B. H. Levin, Charles McCallum, Harold L. Mansfield, M. J. Mistek, Janet Morahan, Harve E. Rawson, Robert G. Riedel, Eugene Rosenthal, Ronald Senzig, A. B. Silver, Colin Silverthorne, Dawn Taylor, Rev. Dean L. Walbaum, Velma Walker, and Clair Wiederholt reviewed all or part of the first or second edition, or both, and provided many valuable comments and constructive criticisms. Numerous instructors and students who used the first edition offered their suggestions. Joanna Pyper and Chris Messick wrote the glossary. Jane McAfee was not only the best typist I've ever had but an able reviewer as well.

Finally, there is Bobby Klatzky. She read and criticized the manuscript. She provided support, amusement, and love; she worried in secret. I wish to thank her especially.

For the author, the preface comes at the end of the book. For the reader, it is just the beginning of a lot of reading and thought. I hope you find it informative *and* something to revel in and enjoy!

J. G.
Santa Barbara

Contents

PART 3 Personality and Development 311

PSYCHOLOGY
Looking at Ourselves

PART

1 Bases of Psychology

Psychology is the study of the workings of the mind. Or is it the study of behavior? Psychologists sometimes differ in their definitions, just as they sometimes differ in how they do research and interpret the results. But all psychologists agree that the scientific method is a basis of psychology. All disputes are taken to court in the halls of science, and evidence always wins over speculation. In Chapter 1, we shall look at how this process works.

Chapter 2 is about another basis of psychology: biology. Seeing, hearing, feeling, eating, sleeping, loving, thinking—all forms of human activity depend on biological systems. We will discuss how information is collected from the environment through our sensory systems and how it is processed in our brain—or perhaps we should say our "brains," since each of us has two of them.

These two bases of psychology—the scientific method and biology—are the first steps in looking at ourselves.

Behavioral Objectives

1. *Outline briefly the history of the science of psychology. Describe and contrast the approaches of introspection, Freud's psychology of the unconscious mind, behaviorism, and today's study of mental processes as revealed by behavior.*
2. *Define scientific inquiry and distinguish it from other kinds of inquiry (such as philosophical inquiry).*
3. *List some problems we encounter in the science of psychology that are not encountered in physics or chemistry, and describe the ways psychologists go about solving these problems.*
4. *List the features of the scientific method used in psychological experiments.*
5. *Define the major features of psychological experiments, including independent variable, dependent variable, experimental group, control group, and operational definition.*
6. *Define correlations, and tell how they are used and what their significance is.*
7. *Distinguish between a true experiment and a natural experiment.*
8. *Explain why true experiments are often considered more scientifically rigorous than natural experiments, and why natural experiments are often considered more relevant than true experiments.*
9. *Define statistical significance.*

CHAPTER

1

The Science of Psychology

"What's happening to my memory?" asked my father, age 82.

"*Your* memory? Your memory is better than mine!"

"I know, but it's worse than it used to be."

The TV news program showed the sheriff's deputies digging up the ninth and tenth victims. The murderer was at the scene, calmly locating the graves. He smiled at the TV camera.

"How can someone do something like that?" asked my friend Lewie. "I mean, is he crazy *by definition?* Can a sane person do something like that?"

"Well . . ." I started, but Lewie interrupted: "The creep's lawyers will plead insanity, for sure. He won't ever come to trial. And then in a year or so, some stupid psychologist will decide he's cured. And he'll move in next door to me!"

I nearly laughed, but Lewie was glaring at me, full of an intense emotion I hoped wasn't directed at me personally. "You psychologists make me sick!" he said.

My friend Bonnie said that her son, age three, had informed her that he was going to be a girl when he grew up.

"Isn't that cute?" Bonnie said.

"Kids say the funniest things," I agreed.

Bonnie paused, then frowned. "It's nothing to worry about, is it?"

"No."

"What do you think of Transcendental Meditation?" I asked my friend Bob.

"I think they charge too much," he replied.

"Oh, come on. Do you think it works?"

"What do you mean, 'works'? Do I think meditators can fly? Become invisible? Do I think meditation affects the weather?"

"Does it do you any good?"

"Probably," he answered.

"In what way?"

"You mean me? Me, personally?"

"Yes, you."

"It's twenty minutes twice a day when I don't make any serious mistakes."

I received a letter from a reader of the first edition of this textbook. (Some of it is paraphrased, to protect the person's identity.)

I am experiencing a unique personal problem. Although your initial reaction will probably be one of skepticism, I assure you that what I am about to describe is in fact a criminal activity conducted in connection with an incredible technological innovation. If you are aware of the facts, you will not be likely to discard my account as mere delusion. The development I speak of is electronically assisted thought transmission. I say "electronically assisted" because, in addition to feeding thoughts into my brain, it affects radio and TV, and even electric lights.

I know you are already skeptical, but imagine what this would mean if I were right. They were able to communicate with me by directing signals to various parts of my brain. The transmissions were muffled, like a poor telephone connection, and sometimes interrupted by static. I did not have to speak out loud to reply to their questions and to get the next question in response. Their responsiveness to my mental thoughts proves that ordinary sources, such as radio signals picked up by dental bridgework, were not involved.

The content of the verbal receptions was apparently intended to subject me to a kind of mental torture. There were many vulgar, obscene remarks and suggestions and sometimes frank admissions that their purpose was to drive me crazy. They were also able to electronically control my moods, inducing fear, rage, anxiety, hostility, and other powerful emotions. They also were able to cause pain in various parts of my body (breast, stomach, spine), along with unbearable itching and labored breathing.

The purpose of this program of torture seems to be remote control of the victim. They say they are working on controlling muscles, including the muscles used in speech, so that they can produce a human puppet to serve their needs. They said their greatest success so far was with Sirhan Sirhan, the murderer of Robert Kennedy, but I don't know if this is true, or just a bluff. They have been able to cause me to utter a few words beyond my control, but not much more than that. On the other hand, I can imagine someone doing just about anything to stop the mental torture.

I have talked to the FBI. They think I am suffering from some kind of mental illness. I encounter much the same reactions when I tell this to newspaper editors. I do not believe I am mentally ill. How can I convince you that what I am experiencing is a threat to personal privacy and all the freedoms we hold dear in the United States? You are a psychologist. Do you deny that at least the potential for remote brain control exists? What if I were sane and telling the truth? Ask yourself that! Some of the reports of psychological manipulation by the CIA are almost as grotesque as my account of my personal mental torture, aren't they?

My life is in danger. Please reply.

How would you reply?

It is not uncommon for psychologists to receive letters like this (I have received three so far) but I still have trouble formulating replies. Typical is the one to this writer, which read in part:

You obviously recognize the skepticism aroused by your story. Therefore it seems to me the best course open to you is to consult a psychiatrist or clinical psychologist who will keep an open mind. If you can convince this person of your sanity and the threat to our freedoms you describe, he or she would be an *invaluable* ally in your struggle. I can recommend, in your city, [name and address] as someone I would trust if I were in your shoes. I guarantee she will listen to your story and carefully evaluate the evidence; she will not assume your claims are "mere delusions."

Today, nearly two years later, the writer of the letter has yet to contact my friend, the open-minded clinical psychologist. Could I have phrased my reply better? The question haunts me.

Psychology. As these anecdotes illustrate, psychology is a field with interests in many diverse topics, ranging from basic processes like memory to complex adjustments of individuals to their environments, from the slow development of a personal sense of sexual identity to the momentary effects of meditation. In this, the introductory chapter in an introductory book, we will begin with a definition and look at some types of psychologists. Then we will plunge into the essentials of the scientific method as it is applied to the subject matter of psychology.

THE STUDY OF MIND/ BEHAVIOR (CHOOSE ONE)

By the usual reckoning, the birth of scientific psychology occurred about a hundred years ago, in 1879, when Wilhelm Wundt founded the first formal psychology laboratory in Leipzig, Germany. The early psychologists defined psychology as "the study of the mind." They believed the task of scientific psychology was to analyze the contents of human mental activity. They hoped to break down human consciousness into its component parts, much as a chemist might analyze a chemical into its molecular or atomic elements; indeed, the approach was often termed "mental chemistry."

To accomplish this task, the early psychologists asked people to examine and analyze what was going on in their minds as they looked at paintings or tried to focus their attention on a small spot of light—a method called *introspection* ("looking inward"). For example, people would be asked to taste several liquids and to describe their experience in the simplest terms possible: not "This tastes like turpentine," but "My first experience is one of sweetness, and there's a sourness later. Maybe a little bitterness." From these introspective analyses, psychologists tried to list the "elementary sensations" that combine to create the sights and sounds, tastes and smells in human consciousness. At last report (Titchener, 1910), they had uncovered 46,708 elementary sensations plus an indeterminate number of smells that seemed to defy further analysis (Brown and Herrnstein, 1975).

The Unconscious Mind

In 1900, a Viennese physician named Sigmund Freud published a book entitled *The Interpretation of Dreams,* in which he described a new theory of personality called *psychoanalysis.* Freud's most notable contribution was his description of the "unconscious mind," that is, the part of the mind that houses ideas not open to introspection. Freud discovered that his patients were not aware of many of the desires and fears affecting their behavior. For example, he found that many patients were afraid of their sexual passions, although they were unwilling to admit this even to themselves; it was an unconscious fear. As a result, however, they avoided sex, using excuses such as work or illness. ("Not tonight; I have a headache.") In extreme cases, a patient might develop unusual symptoms such as paralysis of the legs; the patient would be unaware of the underlying (unconscious) reasons for the symptoms and might even deny a "psychological" component at all.

Although the unconscious mind is not open to direct introspection, its contents sometimes reveal themselves in dreams, slips of the tongue and pen ("Freudian slips"), and other behaviors (as we will see in Chapters 10 and 13). Thus, the methods of psychoanalysis were added to introspection, and the meaning of "mind" was expanded to include its unconscious functioning.

Behaviorism

In 1913, an American psychologist named John B. Watson wrote a paper attacking the definition of psychology as "the study of the mind." The contents of another person's mind, he noted, cannot be directly observed; in other words, I cannot see or hear or smell or touch or taste what you are thinking. Science, Watson asserted, studies public, out-in-the-open objects and events that anyone can observe and record. A true science cannot be based on what might be a figment of an introspector's imagination. Therefore, said Watson, to be truly scientific we should focus on behavior, which we can observe, instead of thoughts and thought process-

es, which we can only guess at. Psychology should be redefined as "the study of behavior."

As an example of "scientific" psychology, Watson described research on animal learning. Obviously, experimenters cannot ask a rat or dog to introspect its thoughts and feelings as it struggles to find food at the end of a maze. Instead the experimenters must carefully describe the situation in which the animal is placed and record the changes in behavior (more speed, fewer errors) that occur as the animal has more experience with the maze.

Watson's arguments were persuasive. *Behaviorism*, as his approach was called, became a major force in psychology, and the "stimulus-response" methods of learning psychologists (see Chapter 4) were applied to problems and issues in all fields of psychology.

Although Watson wanted to exclude unobservable events like thoughts and perceptions from scientific psychology, many psychologists felt this was too narrow an approach and returned to the study of "mental activity." They did so, however, with a new sophistication, using behavioristic methods rather than introspection or psychoanalysis. To use an animal example, suppose we ask if a dog friend of mine named Yaf (short for "young and foolish") sees colors or lives in a world of black and white. We cannot ask her. We must put her in a situation in which her behavior will give us the answer. One way to do this is to put a hungry Yaf in a compartment with two doors, one locked and the other leading to food. The locked door is sometimes on the right, sometimes on the left, but it is *always* marked by a red card. The "correct" or un-

Figure 1.1 *What is this rat thinking? We cannot request an introspective report; we can only observe its behavior.*

locked door is always marked by a green card. We must take care that the cards do not differ in brightness or in any other way except color. Then Yaf will tell us what she sees: If she can learn to go to the green door for food, we know she can tell red from green. If she cannot learn, if she chooses each color about 50 percent of the time, we can assume she cannot see any difference between the doors. (Yaf will fail our test, incidentally; dogs have extremely poor color vision, as determined by research like this.)

Behavior and Human Mental Processes

Human perception can be studied in a similar fashion (Hebb, 1958). For example, color-blind people are often unaware of their inability to distinguish certain colors. (You could say that their introspections are faulty.) They call most colors by their right names; some colors they see normally (complete color-blindness is rare), and others they can usually distinguish on the basis of lightness and darkness, especially in familiar situations (the top light on a traffic signal, for example, can be assumed to be red). A friend of mine was planning to become an electrician until he discovered he couldn't sort wires in a bundle on the basis of a color code. ("Do not, under any circumstances, touch the red wire to the terminal." He got zapped.)

To diagnose color-vision deficiencies *behaviorally* we can present humans with a decision similar to Yaf's. We could ask them to choose between two cards differing only in color, rewarding the choice of red. If they could not learn to choose red invariably, we could reasonably suspect red-green color-blindness. In actual diagnosis, color plates such as those in Color Plate 9 (found on p. 82) are used. People with normal color vision report one number (determined by color differences in the plate), whereas color-blind people report another (determined by brightness differences). The difference in *behaviors* allows us to infer differences in an internal, mental process (perception).

In short, most psychologists observe behaviors to infer mental processes, using the improved methods of behaviorism to study the mind. So how shall we define psychology? The study of behavior, in the service of the study of the mind? I can accept that.

A more practical definition of scientific psychology can be drawn from a look at psychologists themselves—what they do, how, and why. The following section provides a brief overview on the types of psychologists.

TYPES OF PSYCHOLOGISTS

We live in an age of specialization. For example, physicians today do not simply practice "medicine"; each has a specialty — pediatrics, pathology, dermatology, ear/nose/throat. Even the "general practitioner" often has specialized training in family practice or internal medicine. Psychologists tend to specialize, too. Sometimes they specialize to such an extent — in the eye-hand coordination of two-year-olds, perhaps — that they seem to know less about psychology in general than you will when you finish this course. The traditional specialties, however, are reflected in the curriculum of college psychology departments and in the chapter titles of most introductory psychology textbooks, including this one.

"What Is Love?" We Might Ask

The next chapter of this book will introduce you to one specialty in psychology: biological psychology. Biological psychologists are interested in the physiological reasons why we behave as we do; they investigate how the brain and nervous system work. If we were to ask them what they could contribute to an understanding of love, they might begin by describing the brain systems and hormones involved in sexual behavior.

If we put the same question to perception psychologists (Chapter 3), they would probably giggle and say they had very little, if anything, to contribute. They are interested in understanding a basic psychological process: how people acquire information from the environment through sensory receptors (such as eyes and ears) and transform it into percepts. To them, my beloved is just a pattern of light. Memory psychologists (Chapter 5) aren't much better. They are interested in the storage and retrieval of information, in how we remember or why we forget. They might have some comments on why most people can recall their first kiss, but, like perception psychologists, they tend to giggle when asked about intangible emotions like love.

Learning psychologists (Chapter 4) try to understand how we profit from experience. One of the main things that determines what we learn, how well we learn, and whether we exhibit what we have learned is reinforcement (reward). Thus love can be discussed in terms of reinforcement; the approval of a loved one is rewarding, so we work to win that approval by sending gifts, making ourselves more attractive (diet, exercise, new clothes, minty toothpaste, powerful deodorant), and using various other means. Ethologists (also in Chapter 4), who study animals in their natural habitats, also are interested in learning. To them, learning is one way animals adapt to their environment. Instinctive behavior is another way. If asked about love, an ethologist might give an entertaining mini-lecture on some topic such as "The Disco Scene and Instinctive Courtship Displays."

Motivation psychologists (Chapter 6) are a diverse group. Some of them are biological types who investigate things like what neural and hormonal activity underlies hunger attacks. Others are philosophical types who speak of our learned needs to overcome obstacles and to attract attention to ourselves. They probably would dissect love into such elements as the need for affiliation and the need for genital excitement. Motivation psychologists are mo-

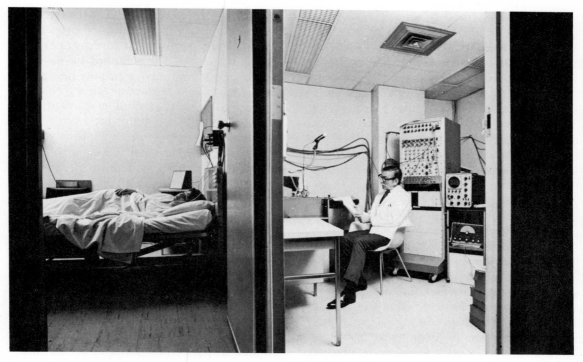

Figure 1.2   *A white-coated scientist in a modern laboratory. He is monitoring the electrical activity of the brain of the sleeping subject in the next room.*

tivated by a need to understand why you do this and not that, why you do it with such intensity, and why you are so persistent.

In Chapter 7, we will learn something of language, that most nearly unique ability of the human species. Language psychologists might be able to tell you when the words "love" and "hate" come into a child's vocabulary, which of the two typically comes first, and what this means in terms of human nature. Another type of psychologist, also discussed in Chapter 7, studies "nonverbal communication" and thus would be of more help in our search for the

psychological meaning of love. Such a psychologist at least would be able to describe in detail the simpering look on the face of a person deeply in love.

Developmental, Personality, Abnormal, and Social Psychologists

Developmental psychologists (Chapters 8 and 9) are interested in how our intellectual and social behaviors change with age. In the beginning, their subjects of study were almost exclusively children, as investigators sought to understand why an adolescent thinks more abstractly than a three-year-old, and why a promising infant, cheerful and friendly, turned into that surly seventeen-year-old. Recently, however, developmental psychology has expanded into the adult years, to explore the changes wrought by the trials and tribulations of adult life. Developmental psychologists could write volumes about love, all kinds of love: the love of a child for his or her parents; the puppy love of a young adolescent; the "intimacy crisis" of young adulthood, when most people choose a mate; the mature love of mature adults; and the satisfactions of a life-long intimacy for elderly couples.

In Chapter 10, we will find Sigmund Freud and other personality psychologists trying to understand what makes people tick. A personality theory is a *general* description of the factors involved in an individual's unique adjustment to life; it is a psychology of the whole person. Personality psychologists would probably tell us more than we would like to know about love: about normal love and inhibited love and impulsive love, about love requited and unrequited.

Severely inhibited, impulsive, frustrated, and freaky lovers are discussed in more detail in Chapter 12 on abnormal psychology and Chapter 13 on psychotherapy. Here we will encounter the psychologists who study mental disorders and the psychotherapists who treat those disorders.

Finally, we will come full circle, from the psychologists who specialize in the study of biological influences on behavior to the psychologists who specialize in the study of social influences (Chapter 14). Social psychologists investigate such activities as conforming, helping, and loving, all of which require at least two people. One social-psychological view of love sees it as a label a person applies to a gooey feeling inside while interacting with someone of the opposite sex, even if that feeling comes from fear or drugs and not from affection at all.

WHAT IS SCIENCE?

Psychologists may vary in the topics they study, but all share a commitment to the scientific method of investigation. So before we turn to the content of psychology, we should briefly discuss the form of psychology—in particular, that mysterious means of seeking truth we call "The Scientific Method." The words alone are so impressive that they conjure up images of complicated but precise procedures, white-coated people who are brilliant but absent-minded, and discoveries that boggle the mind: light that is "bent" by gravity, dead viruses that immunize us against disease, and nuclear reactions that threaten our survival.

When I was in high school, I decided that what I wanted to be when I grew up was a scientist. I had no idea of what that meant. I could only point to people and say, "That's a scientist," or "That's not a scientist." The chemists were scientists, and the physicists, and maybe the biologists. My English teacher was not a scientist, and language courses were not scientific. Some people claimed that social studies, government, and home economics were sciences; I had my doubts. Mathematics was in limbo, neither science nor nonscience. Chemistry and physics, at least, I knew were sciences. So, in college, I majored in chemistry.

Science to me came to mean rigor and precision. The introductory course in chem-

Chapter 7
THE STRUCTURE OF THE NUCLEUS
OF THE ATOM
"What?" exclaimed Roger, as Karen
rolled over on the bed, and rested her
warm body against his. "I know some
nuclei are spherical and some are ellip-
soidal, but where did you find out that
some fluctuate in between?"
    Karen pursed her lips. "They've
been observed with a short-wavelength
probe. . ."

© 1975 by Sidney Harris/American Scientist Magazine

istry presented well-established theories and facts and, in the laboratory, we "did experiments." As it turned out, the experiments we did were more accurately labeled demonstrations; unusual discoveries were attributed to poor methods and given an F.

When I took my first course in psychology, which fancied itself a science, I was shocked. There seemed to be little similarity between the methods of psychology and those of chemistry. In the psychology class I wondered: Where are the grand theories? Where is the mathematical precision? What are the facts of psychology? It seemed mostly speculation, especially when we got to personality theories like Freud's. I wanted to make love to my mother? At age three? Incredible. This is science? In the laboratory—which wasn't a laboratory at all—we designed and executed and analyzed and *interpreted* experiments; unusual discoveries were attributed to a creative mind and given an A. The course was a never-ending source of amazement. Measure that person's "anxiety," I was told, so I gave him an "anxiety test." He scored 79 on a scale of 100. Two weeks later I gave him the same test and he scored 72. A month later he scored 81. If I had taken three temperature readings in chemistry and come up with 79, 72, and 81, I would have been firmly escorted out of the lab and told that perhaps I had talent in some other area of study. But my psychology professor did not seem at all disturbed. In fact, he praised me for taking the time to estimate what he called the "reliability" of my test. He said it was good science.

Scientific Inquiry: The Search for Truth

My later studies convinced me that psychology was indeed a science, in fact one of the most sophisticated. My early definitions of science had missed the point. *Science is an attempt to determine whether various statements are true or false.* Rigor and precision are definitely a help in such endeavors, and a body of knowledge—facts and theories—is typically the result. But it is the search for truth that is the primary characteristic of science.

One can search for truth by means other than science, of course—philosophy and religion, for example. The one thing that distinguishes science from other approaches to knowledge is an emphasis on *empirical data.* Empirical data are information (data) gained through the senses (empirically); in short, empirical data are obtained by seeing, hearing, or otherwise sensing what is happening in the real world. This means that empirical data—unlike introspections, for instance—are accessible to more than one person, and therefore can be verified by others interested in the same question. If I tell you that flying saucers exist, you may agree with me or not; but if I show you a glowing disc in the sky, that constitutes empirical data, and you are forced to consider the possibility that I'm right about flying saucers.

In briefest description, scientific inquiry involves three stages. In the first, the statement we wish to evaluate is formulated as a *hypothesis,* a tentative statement about an event or events in the real world. In the second stage, scientists gather empirical data relevant to the hypothesis; data are usually gathered by means of an *experiment,* a carefully designed situation that allows the scientist to observe what he or she needs to observe. Finally, the empirical data are analyzed, and an *interpretation* is made of what they say about the probable truth of the hypothesis. We will discuss each stage in more detail below.

Forming a Hypothesis

The most practical way to evaluate the truth in a particular situation is to make a tentative statement about it and then try to prove the statement true or false. Such statements are called *hypotheses,* meaning that they are not yet proven or disproven. Empirical data

—information from the senses—are used to evaluate hypotheses. "My wallet is on my desk" is a hypothesis until we look on my desk. The empirical data provided by observing the materials on my desk are used to evaluate the hypothesis.

Most of the hypotheses in psychology deal with *relationships,* as in "*A* is related to *B.*" Frustration is related to aggression. A middle-class environment is related to sexual inhibitions. Activity in a certain part of the brain is related to hunger. The length of time since learning is related to the amount of information that can be recalled.

Where does a hypothesis come from? Sometimes a hypothesis comes from a *theory,* a kind of giant, integrated collection of hypotheses. For example, one theory in social psychology proposes that people are uncomfortable with two ideas that are inconsistent. From this theory one could generate a hypothesis: that people who work hard to achieve some goal will not take kindly to suggestions that their success is meaningless; the idea that the goal is worthless is inconsistent with the knowledge that they have worked hard for it. Sometimes a hypothesis is little more than a hunch, based on a few casual observations. "Choosing a seat in the back of a lecture room is related to shyness." In any case, the creation of a hypothesis is a mysterious event, more art than science.

A scientist's chief business is evaluating a hypothesis once it has been stated. "Prayer increases the growth rate of tulips." The scientist might suspect that the source of this hypothesis was an unusual drug trip or a bizarre dream, but he or she would still respect and consider empirical data put forward in support of the hypothesis. Science is not in the business of prejudging outcomes, and "That sounds ridiculous!" is not a criticism a scientist will accept as proper.

Testing a Hypothesis

Once the hypothesis has been formulated, the next stage of scientific inquiry is gathering empirical data to test the hypothesis, usually by means of an experiment. There are many ways of gathering data, but most of the experiments we will be talking about are of two basic types.

The *true experiment* is one in which scientists actively manipulate the environment. Consider the hypothesis that anxiety about an exam is related to poor performance. In a true experiment, psychologists might form two groups, and then make the students in one group anxious by warning them as they come in that the exam is very difficult. The psychologists would compare this group's average exam score to the average for the other group, which is told the test is easy. By telling the one group that the test is difficult and the other that it is not, the psychologists have actively manipulated the environment. They have run a true experiment.

Or they could gather data in another type of study called the *natural experiment*. A natural experiment is one in which the differences between groups are not created by the psychologists; instead the experimenters use existing differences that have been created, in a sense, by nature. If they compare males and females, for example, they make use of biological differences that existed before their subjects entered the lab. To evaluate the hypothesis that anxiety is related to poor exam performance, they could give all subjects a test designed to measure "general anxiety." Then they could compare the average exam score of the "high-anxiety" people to the average score of the "low-anxiety" people. In this experiment, the psychologists have manipulated nothing; they have merely evaluated the pre-existing differences in anxiety level.

The differences between true and natural experiments will be discussed in more detail after a more complete description of each is presented.

THE TRUE EXPERIMENT

Suppose you had two absolutely identical people, with the same inherited characteristics, the same biological bodies, the same life histories. You would have a scientist's dream, for then you could do something to one and something else to the other, and any difference in what happened next would have to be due to the different treatments. This is approximately the state of affairs in chemistry and physics. Two samples of sodium chloride (table salt) are essentially identical; if you pour a liquid on one and chlorine gas comes off, you can be relatively certain the liquid caused the gas and will do the same with the other sample.

In the true experiment, scientists who work with people must deal with the fact that although two piles of salt are nearly identical, two people are very often as different as salt and steel. Identical twins, who have identical inherited characteristics, come as close to the ideal as is humanly possible, but even identical twins have slightly different life histories—and there are not enough twins around to do all the research, anyway. So psychologists have to resort to another means to get two identical samples. That means is *randomization*.

Randomization

"Random" means "haphazard" and "having no rule." Randomization is a procedure by which two (or more) groups are formed haphazardly, by no particular rule. For example, suppose 22 people wanted to play a little football on a Saturday afternoon, or a church group of 100 wanted to stimulate fund-raising endeavors by forming two competing teams. A rule for forming the teams such as "those over 40 years old on one team, those under 40 on the other" probably would result in unequal teams. A completely haphazard way of choosing team members would be to put all the names in a hat, shuffle thoroughly, and then draw out half for each team. This is randomization. Scientists and participants in team sports have the same goal: to form two approximately equal groups.

Randomization works well if there are enough people in each group. It's like tossing a coin. If you tossed it only four times and got three heads, you wouldn't be too surprised, but if you tossed it 4000 times and got 3000 heads, you might reasonably begin thinking of the coin as odd, biased toward heads. If you had four football players, two middle-aged and two teenagers, and formed teams randomly, you would not be surprised to find youth pitted against age, sometimes. But if you had 22 players, 11 over 40 and 11 under 40, and one team got all the younger athletes, you would probably suspect some cheating.

There is a tremendous power in the randomization procedure. With enough people and in the long run, it equalizes *everything.* You can ask any question about differences between the two randomly formed groups and the answer is always the same: The two

are approximately equal. Intelligence? The two groups have almost exactly the same *average* IQ. Sexual experience? The average number of sexual interactions, marriages, divorces, homosexual experiences, and abortions is the same, approximately, in both groups. The average number of freckles, the number of people with the flu, the number of people who prefer green to blue, and the number of people who hate Russia are the same, approximately. So what do we have, after randomization? We have the scientist's dream: two equivalent things. Now we can treat one group differently from the other, and any differences in what happens next must be due to the different treatments. If the two groups are equal before the treatment, no other explanation is possible. That's power.

By random assignment, we can form two, three, or any other number of approximately equal groups. In the simplest case, with two groups, we then test our hypothesis by treating one group differently from the other. This is the true experiment. How do we go about it?

Running an Experiment

A hypothesis suggests a relationship between two things. The two things are called *variables,* meaning simply that they can or do vary. Consider this hypothesis: Frustration is related to aggression. Frustration and aggression are our two variables; different people can have different levels of each, or the same people might have different levels under different circumstances. To test our hypothesis, we will run an experiment in order to gather relevant empirical data. We will take a large group of people, then divide them *randomly* into two approximately

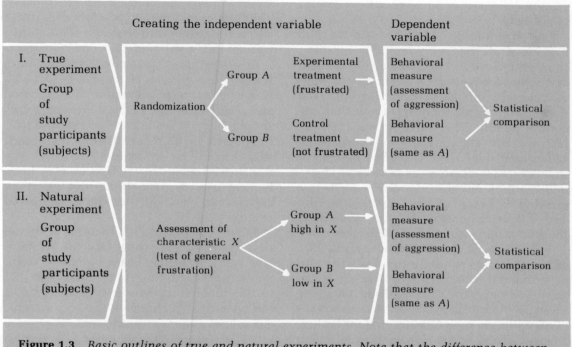

Figure 1.3 *Basic outlines of true and natural experiments. Note that the difference between the two lies in the way the independent variable is created.*

equal groups. We will frustrate the people in one group—called the *experimental group*—and do nothing to those in the other group—the *control* or *comparison group*. We predict that the frustrated people will show more aggression than the nonfrustrated people; this will show that frustration and aggression are related.

Sounds simple enough. It's not quite so simple in actual practice. Let's go through an experiment step by step to see what's involved. (See Figure 1.3.)

The first thing we must do is form two groups of people. People who participate in an experiment are usually called subjects.[1] Who the people are is important for interpreting the results of an experiment, but

[1] Psychologists have been trying to wean themselves of the use of the term "subject" to refer to participants in experiments. The American Psychological Association encourages the use of alternatives like "study participants," "people," or, if appropriate, "children," "patients," or another more specific term. Besides being more informative, the alternative terms are less likely to evoke images of sinister scientists "subjecting" the study participants to some questionable manipulation. Although such rewording may seem to be a superficial cosmetic change, good for "public relations," it certainly can't hurt to have experimenters thinking about their subjects as real "people."

for now let's assume we have our two groups of subjects.

Our hypothesis is that frustration and aggression are related, but really we think frustration *leads to* aggression, rather than aggression leads to frustration. So we want to frustrate the experimental group, and then see if they are more aggressive than the control group. The variable we manipulate—in this case, frustration—is called the *independent variable.* The other variable—in this case, aggression—is called the *dependent variable* because the difference in aggression between groups *depends* on the amounts of frustration and the strength of the frustration-aggression relationship.

Frustration is our independent variable, and we want to frustrate the people in the experimental group. How do we go about this? We have to do something to make these people frustrated. What is frustration? "Frustration is the emotion produced when a person trying to achieve some goal meets an obstacle." Something like that. So we'll interfere with them as they are trying to reach some goal. But how?

Operational Definitions. What we do to the experimental group is the *operational definition* of frustration. Operational definition is a technical term that was borrowed from physics; it does not always fit psychology experiments well. It means "observable criteria"; in other words it tells us what *observable* activities (operations) reflect (define) frustration. An operational definition translates an idea into action: It says, "In this experiment, this is what frustration means."

Suppose we give the people in one group an exam that we describe as vital to their future success. Although they do not know it, most of the exam items are impossible to

solve. Would this be frustrating? Probably. Taking a crucial but impossible exam may not be the best operational definition of frustration, but it will suffice for our purposes.

So one group is "frustrated" and the other is not. Now we want to see if the frustrated people show more aggression. If frustration and aggression are indeed related, they should. If the relationship is weak, the frustrated group will show a little more aggression than the control group, and if the relationship is strong, they will show a lot more. But we need an operational definition for aggression. How do we know aggression when we see it?

What is aggression? A theoretical definition would be something like this: Aggression is the intentional causing of pain or injury to another living thing. Behaviors that fit this theoretical definition can be used as our operational definition. Suppose we give the subjects an opportunity to be aggressive in a fairly acceptable way: We ask them to help us in another experiment, a learning experiment. They are to sit in a little room and listen to the answers of the learner, who is seated in another room. (See Figure 1.4.) If the learner gives a wrong answer, they are to give him or her an electrical shock by pressing a button. They can give a very intense shock—the number 10 button—or a very weak shock—the number 1 button—or anything in between, from 2 to 9. We watch which buttons they choose. We predict that frustrated subjects will deliver higher-intensity shocks. That's our operational definition of aggression: how much pain (shock) a subject gives to another human being.

Both the frustrated and the nonfrustrated subjects take their turns as shock givers. Each subject hears the same number of incorrect answers (because the learner is a

Figure 1.4 *In our imaginary experiment, the operational definition of aggression is the intensity of the shock a teacher-subject gives to a learner.*

friend of ours who intentionally makes errors on the same questions) and thus delivers the same number of shocks. The average intensity of shock for each group is compared. We have predicted that the average for frustrated subjects will exceed that for nonfrustrated subjects. Let's say we are correct. In our imaginary experiment, the frustrated subjects give shocks that average 8.3 in intensity, whereas nonfrustrated subjects deliver jolts averaging only 5.9. Therefore, frustration as we have defined it is related to aggression as we have defined it. Our hypothesis suggested a relationship, and now we have empirical data to support our hypothesis.

Experimental Controls

In our study of the relationship between frustration and aggression, we frustrate one group and not another. Since by randomly assigning the subjects to groups we have created two approximately equal groups, the treatment (frustrating or not) is the only nonrandom difference between groups. By comparing aggression in the two groups, we can say something about our original hypothesis. The two groups are called the experimental group, in which subjects are frustrated, and the control group, in which subjects are not frustrated. The control group is necessary in order to make sense out of the data we get from the experimental group. For example, if we simply frustrated a group of people and they then delivered a shock of average intensity 8.3 to the learners, what do we know? Is 8.3 high or low? We don't know. If, however, we also run a control group that averages 5.9, we do know; 8.3 is higher than 5.9. Increasing frustration leads to increased aggression.

In essence, a control group is not treated, while the experimental group is treated. This does not mean, however, that you always do nothing to the control subjects. What we strive to achieve is to have the only difference in treatments be the factor in which we are interested—our independent variable.

Treating the Control Subjects. Suppose we think drug X has a beneficial effect on depression. Forming two groups (randomly) of depressed subjects, we give a pill containing drug X to one group and do nothing to the control group. The experimental subjects report feeling much better. Now, what are the differences between groups to which we may attribute this effect? Among others, (1) the experimental group got drug X, and (2) the experimental group got a pill. Maybe the simple fact that some subjects got a pill they *expected* to ease their depression resulted in less depression. People have a lot of faith in medical science; maybe this faith and not drug *X* was the cause of their improved mood.

One way to handle this ambiguity is to give the control group a pill, too, one that looks and tastes exactly the same as the one given the experimental group but does not contain the crucial drug *X*. If we now find the depression more relieved in the experimental group, we can with even more confidence attribute the effect to drug *X*.

Controlling Outside Factors. In our experiment on frustration and aggression, we did nothing to the control group, but we gave the experimental group an unsolvable set of problems. Perhaps we should have given both groups a test, one with unsolvable problems and one with solvable problems. Maybe we should have given the same test to both groups, telling one that it would be easy and one that it would be practically impossible. You must decide for yourself what is the best way to make the difference between groups "frustration" and nothing else.

Keep everything under control so that the only difference between groups is the one very precisely defined factor in which you are interested. This is what "control" really means in science; it represents an ideal situation, of course, one we can never achieve in all respects. But we do want to do what we can to eliminate differences that aren't related to the variables we are studying. If the experimental group is tested in an overly hot room, differences in the dependent variable, aggression, could be due to the heat and not to frustration. If the control group is tested in a pleasant setting with light classical music piped in, the dif-

ferences in aggression might be explained without talking about frustration at all.

Same-Subject Controls. Many experiments in psychology use the same subjects twice, so that the experimental group and the control group consist of exactly the same people. There are several advantages to this procedure, including the fact that one needs fewer subjects. The biggest advantage, however, is how easy it is to see the effects of an independent variable. Since each subject receives both the experimental treatment and the control treatment, each subject constitutes an experiment; his or her performance on the dependent variable can be compared for the two conditions, and differences can be noted individual by individual. For example, we could have used this same-subject design for a frustration-aggression experiment. Person *A* is frustrated, then teaches our learner. A week later, person *A* is called into the laboratory again, and this time he or she delivers learning shocks without being frustrated first. If person *A* gives less intense shocks the second time than the first time, we could claim that our hypothesis is supported.

With the same-subject design, we can make certain statements that are not possible with randomized groups. We could report, for example, that 35 of our 40 subjects show an increase in aggression when frustrated. Such a statement is impossible with randomized groups, which are equal only on the average. With the same subjects in each group, the experimental and control groups are identical.

The disadvantage of a same-subject design is that how subjects were used first might affect their behavior when they are used again. Suppose a subject gave the learner severe shocks the first time and felt guilty about it later; the next time he or she might give only slight shocks, regardless of level of frustration. In some experiments, the problems of using the same subjects twice are insurmountable. For example, if we instruct a group of students in effective study techniques and use their grades as a dependent variable, we cannot then "give no instruction" to see if the instructions are related to grades. The students will remember what we told them before; they will not be the "same" subjects after once receiving the experimental treatment.

Interpreting the Results

After they have gathered data, scientists must interpret them. They must say what importance, if any, the data have in regard to the hypothesis. Interpretation involves considering all aspects of the experiment.

Generalization. As we have defined frustration and aggression, there is a relationship—*in this sample of subjects.* The word "sample" means "the group of subjects used in this experiment," and now we must consider exactly who these subjects were. The interpretation of our results depends on such considerations.

Suppose we had the hypothesis that body size (height and weight) is related to excellence in job performance. If our sample of subjects was professional football players, defensive linemen only, we might well find the hypothesis supported by empirical data. If our sample was junior executives for Montgomery Ward, we would probably find no relationship. It makes a difference who the subjects are.

The problem is one of *generalization:* If we find a relationship, how widely, among which people, can we assume it probably holds? We know the relationship exists among the 10, 20, or 100 people we used in the experiment, but does it exist more generally? Few psychologists study relationships they think apply only to a small number of people. They would like to generalize their findings to all human beings, to all Americans, to all students, or to some other population much larger than the experimental sample.

Public opinion polls involving questions of whom we would vote for or what television shows we watch are directly concerned with generalization. These researchers clearly want to make statements that apply to all relevant people (all voters, all TV watchers), even though the sample questioned is only a few thousand. There are sophisticated mathematical techniques for finding a representative sample, one from which you can generalize with reasonable confidence, but outside of opinion polls and the like, such techniques are rarely used. Most frequently in psychology experiments, the subjects are either college students who are taking introductory psychology courses, or rats, who are convenient laboratory animals. Nevertheless, the results of these experiments are generalized to a vast range of animals.

Take our experiment on frustration and aggression. If our sample had been college sophomores, we might nevertheless conclude that frustration leads to aggression in humans. We have no right, scientifically, to expand our conclusion so broadly; we could not even say the relationship exists among all college sophomores, since we have observed only a few. If frustration leads to aggression in a small sample of college sophomores, will frustration lead to aggression in a group of middle-aged working women? We don't know for sure. On the other hand, what is our best guess? Unless we can think up some good reason why a new sample might react differently, our best guess would be that they would respond in a similar fashion. To say that among junior executives body size would not be highly related to job success, as it is among football players, is a reasonable limit to generalization. But in the absence of good reasons (or actual data) to the contrary, generalization is at least a logical assumption. And if it leads to research on the generality of the hypothesis, it is healthy.

Checking the Definitions. When we say that we have empirical data showing that frustration leads to aggression, what we mean is that the operations or observable behaviors we have used to define frustration are related to the operations we have used to measure aggression. In our example, giving some people a supposedly important exam with unsolvable problems leads to a greater average intensity of shocks delivered to another person in a socially acceptable learning situation. Notice that the question with which we began—Does frustration lead to aggression?—is now quite different, made much more specific by the particular operational definitions we use.

The questions we ask about the operational definitions are simple: Are the definitions valid? Will the unsolvable problems *really* frustrate our subjects? Is giving shocks as a "teacher" *really* aggression? One could argue the points. Perhaps unsolvable problems lead only to a feeling of stupidity. Clearly, it is crucial that we choose our operational definitions carefully, and test and retest them if we find any reason to doubt their validity.

Is It Chance? In this sample of subjects, in this situation, we have discovered that *A* is related to *B*. But maybe *A* is related to *B* in this experiment simply because of chance. For example, if I were trying to sell you a coin good for making bets because it turned up heads more than 50 percent of the time, I could toss it in the air to generate some empirical data. If it came up heads on the first toss, I could say, "See! It comes up heads!" You would probably be reluctant to buy my coin after one toss. You cannot deny that it came up heads; what you can reply is that even a normal coin might have done so.

It is said that if a chimpanzee could peck at a typewriter long enough, it would write a great novel without knowing it. What is meant by this is that even the nearly impossible occurs, by chance, once in a very great while. There is a certain probability that if I tossed a coin a hundred times, all hundred tosses would come up heads. It's not likely, of course; it's smaller than a one in a million chance, but it *is* possible. The same can be said of the results of our experiment: They could have been obtained by chance. It is possible that frustration is not related to aggression at all and that we found a difference in aggression for reasons totally unrelated to frustration. Maybe when we formed the two groups by randomization, we were extremely unlucky and got all the naturally aggressive people in the group we were later to frustrate.

Statistics is that branch of mathematics which deals with questions of this type. We said, for example, that the average intensity of shocks delivered by the frustrated group

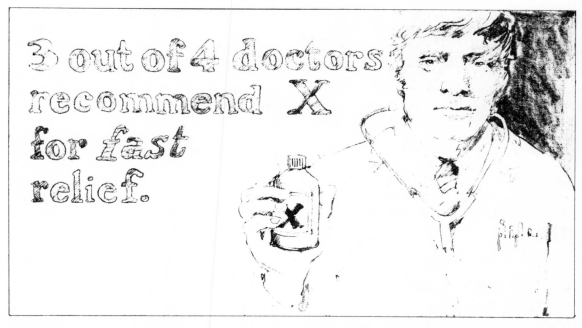

Figure 1.5 *Would you be willing to use* X *without knowing how many doctors were interviewed?*

was 8.3 on our scale and, by the nonfrustrated group, 5.9. Is this difference between groups meaningful, or could it easily have occurred by chance? Any result could have occurred by chance, just as it's possible to toss a hundred heads in a row. We are interested in the *probability* that the difference was just a lucky coincidence. If the probability is very small, we are more nearly certain we have discovered a "true" relationship.

Significance. How improbable must a result be before we accept it as trustworthy? Psychologists have traditionally used the figures of one in twenty (probability or p equals .05) and one in a hundred ($p = .01$) as standards. If a result is such that, by chance

alone, it would have occurred less than one time in twenty, researchers feel reasonably confident that a true relationship exists. Obviously, they feel even more confident with a result that by chance alone would occur less than once in a hundred experiments. A result that passes one of these statistical tests is called *significant*. "Significant" means trustworthy; it does *not* mean important or relevant or praiseworthy.

If we were to tell some psychologists that our frustrated subjects used an average intensity shock of 8.3 and our nonfrustrated subjects scored 5.9, on the average, one of their first questions would be, "Is that difference significant?" Unless we said yes, they would bother no more with our experi-

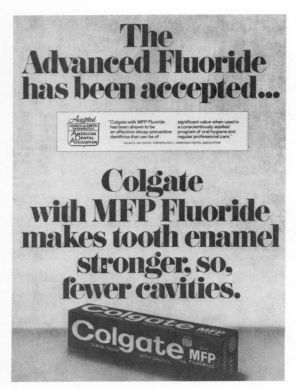

The Advanced Fluoride has been accepted...

Accepted COUNCIL ON DENTAL THERAPEUTICS AMERICAN DENTAL ASSOCIATION	"Colgate with MFP Fluoride has been shown to be an effective decay-preventive dentifrice that can be of	significant value when used in a conscientiously applied program of oral hygiene and regular professional care."

COUNCIL ON DENTAL THERAPEUTICS—AMERICAN DENTAL ASSOCIATION

Colgate with MFP Fluoride makes tooth enamel stronger, so, fewer cavities.

Colgate MFP

Figure 1.6 *Because fluoride treatments have been shown to result in trustworthy differences in how many cavities a child gets, the term "significant value" has scientific meaning as it is used in the box in this advertisement.*

ment. There's too much going on in the world to be concerned with differences that may well be the result of chance or luck. If I said I had a coin that has turned up heads 100 percent of the time, you might ask, "How many times did you toss it?" If I said, "Once!" you would not spend your evening weighing and measuring my coin to find out why it "always" turned up heads.

THE NATURAL EXPERIMENT

Like the true experiment, the natural experiment has an independent variable (such as frustration) and a dependent variable (such as aggression). Both types of experiment have operational definitions, and the statistical analyses involved are usually very similar, if not identical. The main difference between a true and a natural experiment lies in how the groups of subjects are formed. In the true experiment, two (or more) approximately equal groups are formed by randomization; then one is treated differently from the other (for example, it is made to feel frustrated). In the natural experiment, two (or more) groups are formed on the basis of some characteristic the subjects had before they entered the laboratory; "nature" (biology, life experiences) had already treated the people differently before the psychologist ever met them.

Common natural experiments use such variables as race (blacks are compared to whites) and sex (males are compared to females). In other natural experiments, psychological tests are used to determine the talents and personality characteristics of the subjects; subjects of high intelligence might be compared to subjects of low intelligence, where intelligence has been measured by an IQ test.

Let us continue with the same hypothesis, that frustration is related to aggression, but let's run a natural experiment this time. First, we might give all subjects a questionnaire that is supposed to measure "general level of frustration." On this questionnaire might be items such as "I often feel frustrated. True or false?" and "I seem always to be striving for goals I do not achieve. True or false?" People who answer True to a lot of questions like these would be classified as "generally frustrated." We would then divide the people into those with high scores and those with low scores on our frustration test, placing half our sample in each group.

Now that we have our two groups formed, one already more frustrated than the other, we can use the same dependent variable— the intensity of shocks delivered to "learners" who make an error—to test our hypothesis. Let us say we obtain the same figures as in our true experiment: the "highly frustrated" subjects average 8.3 in shock intensity, whereas the "less frustrated" subjects average 5.9. Frustration and aggression (as operationally defined) are related in this sample.

Correlations

In natural experiments, dividing subjects into groups makes less sense than in a true experiment. For one thing, we are not going to treat the groups differently; they already have been "treated." More importantly, placing subjects into, say, a low-score or a high-score group forces us to treat each subject as if he or she had obtained one of only two scores on our test: "high" or "low." In fact, however, subjects usually obtain scores over a considerable range. On the first examination in this course, for example, some of your class probably will score 100 percent, some 99, some 98; and, if the class is large enough, there will be at least one or two at every score down to 60 or so. If our frustration test had a similar range of scores, our high-frustration group would include all the scores above the average—say, 80 to 100— and the other group would include subjects whose scores varied from 60 to 80.

To take advantage of the wide-ranging scores typically obtained in natural experiments, psychologists often use a statistic called the *correlation*. The correlation, in essence, treats each subject as a group. In terms of our experiment, it would reflect the degree to which the aggression scores increased as the frustration scores got higher and higher.

A correlation is a direct estimate of the degree to which two variables are related. It can be positive or negative, reflecting a positive or negative relationship. Correlations range from 0.00 (to two decimal places, the usual practice) to plus or minus 1.00. A correlation of .70 or more is considered quite high in psychological research, .50 to .70 is considered high, .30 to .50 is not bad, and .01 to .30 is "modest" (which means low). To illustrate, the correlation of high school grades with college grades, in a sample of typical college students, would be around .50.

A *positive correlation* says that if one variable is high, the other is likely to be high also (see Figure 1.7A). If a baseball player's batting average is high, his salary is likely to be high also. The quality of a product is positively related to its price. A positive relationship also means that if one variable goes up (or down), the other is likely to go up (or down) as well. Room temperature is positively related to the amount of body perspiration. If the temperature goes up, the amount of sweat also increases.

A *negative correlation* suggests that if one variable goes up (or is high), the other is likely to do (or be) just the opposite (see Figure 1.7B). Practice is related to performance scores in most sports, but in some the relationship is negative. In golf, for example, where a lower score indicates better performance, as practice increases, scores tend

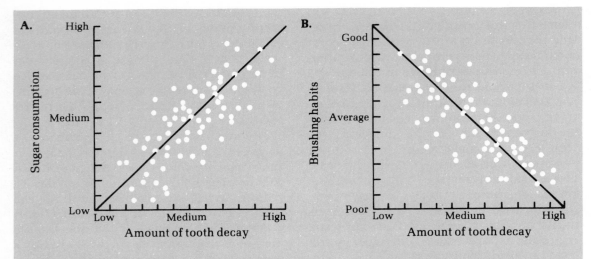

Figure 1.7   *These hypothetical graphs show that tooth decay is positively related to sugar consumption and negatively related to brushing habits. If we calculated the correlations, graph A would produce a high positive correlation, and graph B a high negative correlation.*

to go down. The price of steak is negatively related to the number of people who can afford to buy it.

In our imaginary experiment, we have hypothesized a positive relationship between frustration and aggression. Therefore, we would predict a positive correlation between scores on the frustration test and intensity of shocks given. Let us say that we have computed this statistic and that it was +0.38, a positive correlation with the status of "not bad." As before, we can say that frustration and aggression (as operationally defined) are related in this sample of subjects.

Interpreting Natural Experiments

A relationship is a relationship is a relationship. Unless the scientist has made an error

in recording data or in computing averages and correlations, an empirical relationship demonstrated by a difference between averages or by a correlation cannot be denied. It did exist, in that time and place, with those subjects under those conditions.

If the result is significant, it is unlikely to have occurred by chance. The relationship cannot be generalized without some risk beyond the sample of subjects observed. The operational definitions are open to dispute. All of these matters of interpretation hold for both the true and the natural experiment.

The natural experiment, however, is much more difficult to interpret. Many of the correlations that appear in the mass media illustrate this problem. A few years ago a report noted a positive correlation between psychiatric problems and frequency of sexual intercourse in a sample of unmarried college women (Zimbardo, 1975). The interpretation was that sex can make you crazy, which is rather dubious. Similarly, there is an often-noted negative correlation between drinking problems and employment; heavy drinkers are more likely to work fewer hours per year than light drinkers and teetotalers. Do drinking problems lead to unemployment? Or does unemployment lead to drinking problems? Or both? Or does some third factor—the frustration of having no talent, for example—lead to both unemployment and heavy drinking? This is the first problem in interpreting natural relationships: It is difficult to decide which is cause and which is effect, or even if the two variables are causally related in any sense of the word.

Uncontrolled Variables. The most serious problem in interpreting a natural experiment results from the fact that variation among subjects on the independent variable is not the only variation among these subjects. Any of their differences can be used to interpret differences on the dependent variable.

In support of stiff marijuana laws, advocates cite the empirical correlation between early marijuana use and later dependencies on more dangerous drugs. Suppose that, of people who were smoking pot in 1940, a higher percentage are heroin addicts today than among those who were not smoking in 1940. The difference we are focusing on—smoking or not smoking pot—is clearly not the only difference between smokers and nonsmokers. Most smokers in 1940 were raised in a poorer environment, usually urban; they had less education and were not as bright as the nonsmokers, on the average;

they led a more difficult life with many frustrations; drug use in their neighborhood was accepted, even glorified; they had easy access to drugs, and the pot pushers also had stronger drugs in their bags, the use of which they undoubtedly encouraged. All of these factors would probably correlate with later heroin use. To pick one among the several differences and say that it is the only or the primary cause is more rhetoric and argument than science. I am reminded of a local high school principal who was defending his requirement of short hair before the school board. "Students with long hair," he claimed, "are more likely to use drugs." I imagine he was right about the empirical correlation, but I doubt that simply cutting a student's hair would lessen his or her inclination to use drugs.

Notice, now, the difference between the true and the natural experiment. In the true experiment, there is only one variation among groups—the manipulation defining the independent variable. All other variables are equalized by randomization. In the natural experiment, there are always several differences among groups; the simple act of labeling one of these differences as the independent variable does not guarantee that this variable is meaningfully related to the dependent variable, even though the correlation might be high. Hair length may be highly correlated with drug use, but the relationship is more coincidence than cause.

Remember our two experiments on the relationship between frustration and aggression. In the true experiment, two randomly formed groups were treated differently—the subjects in one were "frustrated"—and then both were given the opportunity to "aggress" by delivering intense shocks. The group that was frustrated averaged 8.3, and

**Emeraude, the liquid emerald.
Precious. Sensual. Slightly dangerous.**

Emeraude Perfume by Coty.

Figure 1.8 *Suppose we discovered that women who use Emeraude get more neck nuzzles than women who use Thrifty Toilet Water. Have we proved Coty's claim? What other variables might be involved?*

it) was the only variable related to aggression (as we defined it). In the natural experiment, frustration was related to aggression —we cannot deny the empirical data—but we may be misled if we assume that a high score on our frustration test is the important factor in aggression. There are other differences between the two groups. How would a generally frustrated person differ from someone low in frustration? Less ability, perhaps. Maybe from a lower social class. It's even possible that these subjects are frustrated because they are highly aggressive in a society that tends to frustrate direct, overt aggression! In any case, the question is this: How can we attribute the difference in aggression to frustration when the high-frustration subjects may also be less talented, from a social class in which violence is less inhibited, or more aggressive for reasons that have nothing to do with frustration? Interpretation of a natural experiment, I say again, is difficult.

Controls in Natural Experiments. Sometimes groups in a natural experiment are formed to be equal in one or a few clearly important additional factors. If we wanted to study sex differences in education, we might try to create two groups, one of girls and one of boys, that are equal in measured intelligence. Otherwise any differences in learning and scholastic performance (our dependent variables) that we want to attribute to sex differences could be more reasonably explained by individual differences in intelligence.

Many studies of differences between blacks and whites are flawed by the failure to equate social class. To illustrate, it had long been assumed that the mother in black families was a stronger figure than in white

the control group averaged 5.9. In the natural experiment, two groups were also formed, but not randomly; subjects with a high level of everyday frustration (as measured, we hope, by our frustration test) were placed in one group, and low-frustration subjects were placed in the other. Again, the high-frustration group averaged 8.3 on the shock scale, and the control group averaged 5.9. Two routes to the same interpretation?

Hardly. In the true experiment we know that frustration (as we operationally defined families, but research indicates that a strong mother is characteristic of the working class, not of blacks (Mack, 1971). Since equal opportunity was a myth when today's adult blacks were growing up, a study that compares blacks with whites also, simultaneously, compares the middle class with the working class. Many behaviors that have been at times attributed to blacks are really characteristic of working-class people, both white and black. A study of racial differences that does not equate groups for social class is essentially meaningless.

So, even in a natural experiment, by carefully selecting the groups we can control for at least obviously important factors. There are also some statistical techniques for equating known variables in individuals for correlation purposes. But it is impossible to equate all variables (other than the independent variable), if for no other reason than that many important factors are as yet unknown to scientists. How can you equate groups on a variable that hasn't been identified? Randomization, on the other hand, equalizes all variables, including the unknown.

RELEVANCE OR RIGOR?

The rigorous precision of the true experiment makes it much easier to interpret, and it is to be preferred if we have a choice. Very often, however, we have no choice, and the natural experiment is better than no empirical data at all. For practical, ethical, and other reasons, many important issues are not subject to true experimental testing. I may have a theory that too-early toilet training leads to certain forms of mental illness. Ethically, I could not randomize 100 babies and insist that 50 be trained for the toilet before they were capable of such bodily control, especially when my prediction was that these children would develop mental problems. Also, I can produce minor frustrations in the laboratory, but it is doubtful that I could match the power of a real-life frustration such as being fired after 40 years of service or being deserted by your spouse. These are vital issues, relevant to life and living, and we need data on these issues.

Rigor versus relevance. Psychologists (and books) that focus on results obtained from carefully controlled true experiments are often accused of avoiding the real problems that face individuals and society. Lack of such relevance is not a necessary feature of true experiments, of course, and many such studies are clearly and directly applicable to real-life problems. But it is true that "hard-headed scientific" psychologists often deal with questions whose relevance is less than obvious. On the other hand, a psychologist (or book) that focuses on natural studies of "relevant" issues—racial problems, drug problems, and the like—is often accused of being sloppy (not rigorous), of providing uninterpretable answers to important questions, and thus of increasing confusion rather than knowledge.

A more moderate view would be that there is a place in psychology for both types of experiments. Indeed, the two can serve as checks on one another, especially when one discovers a relationship that can be investigated by the other as well. The "natural" correlation of smoking with lung cancer led several scientists to do true experiments, and many generations of chimpanzees found themselves in one group or another, randomly chosen, with some learning the "joys" of smoking cigarettes.

In some fortunate circumstances, the best features of the two types of experiments can be combined. For example, in a "real life" study of school integration, half of the predominantly Chicano students at one school were to be integrated with Anglo students immediately, the other half a year later (Gerard and Miller, 1975). If the first group is chosen randomly — after all, what could be fairer, more democratic? — the psychologist has the ingredients of a true experiment in a natural setting: two approximately equal groups, one treated one way (bussed to a new, integrated school), the other left untreated. The treatments imposed by nature are stronger and more relevant than any the psychologist could introduce in the laboratory. But, of course, such opportunities are rare.

So psychology struggles on, trying to be faithful to the scientific method and to human needs at the same time. Someone once said, "A fool either ignores the facts of the matter or accepts them at face value." That, I think, is a fairly good operational definition of foolishness.

FOCUS

Psychology and Ethics

Case 1: A team of psychologists studying racial and religious prejudice hopes to find ways of changing the attitudes of bigoted people. In fact, their research is sponsored in part by an anti-prejudice organization (like NAACP). Their research requires the participation of highly prejudiced subjects, who would probably refuse to be studied if they knew the sponsor and the purpose of the study. Are the investigators obligated to inform their subjects of all the details of their experiment? Can this research be done, ethically, without so informing them?

As a group, psychologists are unusually concerned with the ethics of what they do. Indeed, the decision to become a psychologist is often partly an ethical one, based on a perception of psychology as an opportunity to "promote human welfare." Psychologists involved in counseling and psychotherapy are often able to make life a little less threatening and a little more satisfying for their clients. Much of the research of academic psychologists can be applied to human needs and problems. In the classroom, for example, the principles of learning, memory, and motivation psychologists are used to stimulate intellectual growth and crea-

*Cases 1, 3, 4, and 5 were taken from a proposed revision of the American Psychological Association's Ethical Standards for Psychological Research; the revision was undated. The original version, *Ethical Principles in the Conduct of Research with Human Participants*, was published by the Association in 1973.

tivity. Social and personality psychologists struggle to uncover the key to human violence and to understand the psychological effects of television.

In their efforts to promote human welfare, psychologists often find themselves in an ethical dilemma, trying to balance the potential benefits of their work with the potential costs. Case 1 is one example. Another is the hypothetical experiment we have been describing throughout the chapter. The potential benefit of our experiment would be an increase in knowledge about human aggression and its relation to frustration. The costs include deceiving the subjects, who believe they are actually shocking a bona fide "learner." In addition, in the true experiment, subjects are frustrated by items on an "important" exam, most of which are, unbeknown to them, unsolvable. This deception, if not explained thoroughly at the end of the experiment, might damage the self-esteem of some of the subjects.

Many experiments in psychology require a limited amount of deception. Often it is necessary that subjects be unaware of what is being studied or at least of the particular hypothesis being tested. Deception may be the only means by which the experimenters can create a meaningful "psychological reality" and thus obtain valid data on important social issues. In most cases, the deception is minor:

Case 2: The experimenter has one group of subjects grade a paper written, they are told, by a boy; another group is told the same paper was written by a girl. To show that differences in grading are due to different attitudes toward the work of males and females, and not *to differences in the quality of papers, the very same paper is used for both groups. At least one group is lied to. Is it a white lie?*

I don't want you to get the idea that all cases of deception and stress are minor. Here are two that exceed *my* ethical standards; see what you think:

Case 3: A study of drivers' reactions to emergency situations had the subject driving by a "construction site." Suddenly a realistic dummy was propelled in front of the car; most subjects were unable to avoid hitting it. Although no one was actually hurt, subjects suffered considerable stress until they were informed of the deception. Were the data on emergency reactions worth the temporary stress?

Case 4: An experiment on how people handle undesirable information about themselves had heterosexual male subjects viewing pictures of dressed and nude men. A meter which the experimenter falsely claimed was measuring the subject's "homosexual arousal" gave high readings when he was viewing attractive nude men. Subjects were asked to rate how others reacted to the same pictures, to see if they would "project" their own apparent homosexual tendencies onto others. Subjects were then told of the deception; expressions of great relief gave indication that significant psychological stress had been created. Many questions of great importance cannot be answered adequately unless an experiment deals with very personal characteristics that involve subjects emotionally; but do the benefits of this study exceed the costs?

In the past, individual experimenters were permitted to judge whether the potential benefits of the research outweighed the deception or any physical or psychological stress. No longer is this the case. Almost all schools have committees that must approve the ethics of experiments involving human or animal subjects, and many departments of psychology have their own research committees, in addition.

The American Psychological Association has an Ethics Committee that is supposed to punish violations of the association's tough code of ethical standards. Unfortunately, after-the-fact policing agencies don't function very well, primarily because calling someone unethical invites a big-money lawsuit. The committees that approve or disapprove *before* the experiment is run are much more effective. In fact, had the committee system been in effect at the time, I doubt that the experiments described in Cases 3 and 4 would have been approved.

Not all ethical issues arise during the planning and running of an experiment. Sometimes the *results* of an experiment present an ethical dilemma:

Case 5: An investigator studying the effects of a certain chemical substance noted that among the intended uses of the substance was the lowering of the will to resist and fight during war and riots. He feared that it would be used to suppress opposition to governments and policies he himself opposed. On the other hand, he knew that if the chemical substance were not available, more lethal weapons would probably be used. Is the scientist responsible for the potential misuse of his or her research findings?

There was a time when scientists believed that their sole responsibility was to "search for truth." If someone used their discoveries in an immoral way, the sin was that someone's, not theirs. Fortunately, few scientists today still hold so simplistic a view of their ethical imperative. In a complex world with sophisticated and highly technological sciences, the scientist is often the only one who can anticipate the consequences of various uses of his or her discoveries. If a sinful someone is planning an improper use for personal gain, it is the responsible scientist who can best prescribe effective countermeasures.

SUMMARY

1. Psychology was originally defined as the study of the mind, and early psychologists had their subjects *introspect* their own mental activity. Sigmund Freud showed that not all the contents of the mind are conscious, however, and John B. Watson showed that a scientific psychology must be based on the observation of behaviors. Thus, psychology today is typically defined as the study of behavior as a means of studying the workings of the mind. Most psychologists choose an area of specialization within the field, such as biology, perception, development, or personality.

2. Science is an attempt to establish the truth of a statement. The three stages of scientific inquiry are formulating a hypothesis, gathering empirical data, usually in an experiment, and analyzing and interpreting the data.

3. Most experiments are either *true experiments*, in which the situation of interest is set up and manipulated by the scientist, or *natural experiments*, in which preexisting differences among subjects are evaluated.

4. The true experiment uses *randomization* to create two approximately equal groups, which are then treated differently. The difference in treatments defines the *independent variable*. The *dependent variable* is the behavior we expect the difference in treatments to affect. *Operational definitions* specify exactly what activities and behaviors represent the independent variable and dependent variable in a particular experiment.

5. A *control group* is one that is not treated, so that we can compare it to the *experimental group*, which is treated. We must be careful, however, that the two groups differ *only* in the independent variable. We must make sure that no differences in the dependent variable can arise from the subjects' expectations; and the experimental and control groups should also be equated on factors unrelated to the hypothesis: The groups should be tested in the same room, at the same time of day, and so on. *Same-subject controls* eliminate individual differences by using the same subjects for both experimental and control groups, but first experiences in the experiment may affect later behavior.

6. To interpret the results of a true experiment, we must consider the sample of subjects—how broadly can we generalize?—the operational definitions—are they valid?—and the empirical data—could these results have occurred by chance? A statistically *significant* result is one not likely to have happened by chance.

7. Natural experiments often involve data that are best handled by the *correlation*, a measure of the degree of relationship between two variables. The correlation runs from 0.00 to 1.00 and can be positive (two variables go together), zero (two variables have no relation to each other), or negative (two variables go in opposite directions).

8. Natural experiments are much more difficult to interpret than true experiments. Often it is hard to tell which is cause and which is effect in a correlation. In two groups set up according to some preexisting differences, there can be an infinite number of other differences, and attributing the change in the dependent variable to any one of them is risky.

9. The natural experiment, since it deals with natural differences, very often deals with factors that are relevant to social problems and situations that cannot be recreated

in a true experiment. The true experiment is more precise, rigorous, and interpretable. Psychologists try to balance the relevance of the natural experiment with the rigor of the true experiment to gain knowledge of significant issues.

USING PSYCHOLOGY

When you see or hear news reports or advertisements that refer to scientific experiments, try to evaluate them: What hypothesis was tested? Was a true or a natural experiment performed? What were the independent and dependent variables? Do the operational definitions used seem valid? Were there any possible uncontrolled variables that could have accounted for the results? Were the sampling methods adequate? Were appropriate statistical tests performed? Do the experiment's results justify the reported conclusions? Are there any other possible interpretations of the results? What are the implications of the study? What further experiments should be performed? If you were to conduct a scientific experiment to test the hypothesis, how would you go about it?

SUGGESTED READINGS

Wood, G. *Fundamentals of psychological research*, 2nd ed. Little, Brown, 1977.
An excellent introduction to the scientific method as used in psychology; also an excellent introduction to statistical reasoning.

Barber, T. X. *Pitfalls in human research*. Pergamon, 1976.
An engaging and practical discussion of ten common pitfalls—for example, loose procedures, experimenter bias.

Hilgard, E. R. (ed.). *American psychology in historical perspective*. American Psychological Association, 1978.
A thoughtful selection of the presidential addresses to the American Psychological Association from 1892 to 1977; a delightful historical introduction to the field.

Rychlak, J. F. *A philosophy of science for personality theory*. Houghton Mifflin, 1968.
Difficult reading by a scholar with a somewhat unusual point of view, applied specifically to personality theory. I wouldn't suggest it if I didn't think it would have a profound influence on the way you view science, psychology, and yourself.

Careers in Psychology

On the night of November 8, 1965, a Boeing 727 jet approaching the Greater Cincinnati Airport crashed into a hillside two miles short of the airport. All but 4 of the 62 people aboard were killed. Just three nights later, another Boeing 727 burst into flames when it slammed into an asphalt area short of a runway at Salt Lake City Airport. Only 41 of the 89 people aboard got out alive. Three months earlier, another 727, approaching Chicago's O'Hare Airport at night, had plunged into Lake Michigan, killing all 30 people aboard. Then, in the following February, came the worst of the night approach crashes. Indeed, it was the worst single aircraft accident of any time up to that date. All 133 people aboard a Boeing 727 approaching Tokyo's airport were killed when the jet plunged into Tokyo Bay.

In less than six months, 264 people had perished in four similar accidents. Members of Congress and other concerned citizens called for the grounding of all Boeing 727s until the cause was discovered and corrected. Each of the three American crashes was investigated by the Civil Aeronautics Board, which also cooperated in the investigation of the Japanese crash. In late February 1966, the CAB held a special inquiry into the four crashes, reviewing all the information from the four investigations to try to find the underlying cause of the accidents. The Boeing 727 was a relatively new jet, only recently put into commercial service. It was understandable that mechanical shortcomings were suspected, but the investigations turned up none. After the Salt Lake City crash, the pilot and copilot were given a blood test for alcohol content, but neither had been drinking. The board could only conclude that for some unknown reason the four pilots had misjudged their landing approaches.

Boeing officials were, of course, concerned. Similar inexplicable crashes might have resulted in the permanent grounding of their aircraft. With nearly 200 Boeing 727s in service and over 400 more on order, Boeing had to uncover the cause of the accidents. Dr. Conrad Kraft, a psychologist and Chief Scientist for the Personnel Subsystem of Boeing's Commercial Aircraft Division, was put in charge of the investigation.

Kraft was (and is) known as an expert on the relationship between visual stimuli and psychological or behavioral responses. He suspected that the problem was that the pilots were using false or misleading visual cues to judge their distance from the airport and the ground or water beneath them. He carefully reviewed the data from the government investigations. All four accidents had occurred on clear nights with good visibility. The airports were well lighted. Because of these two apparently favorable conditions, each pilot requested and received permission from the control

tower to approach the field visually, rather than on instruments. Kraft further observed that each of the four airports, together with populated areas immediately around them, stood out against a dark expanse — large bodies of water or uninhabited land.

CRASHES AT NIGHTERTON

So Kraft had a model of a lighted city set against a dark expanse built in his laboratory. "Nighterton" — as the model was dubbed — combined characteristics from 27 cities where night landing accidents had occurred. He also built a full-size model of a 727 cockpit, from which pilots could make simulated approaches to Nighterton.

Twelve pilots, all instructors in Boeing's flight crew training program, were selected as subjects for the test. These highly experienced pilots had an average flying time of 10,700 hours. Each pilot selected his own flight path into the airport, and each considered the problem to be a "no sweat" landing. But eleven out of the twelve pilots "crashed."

Why did the pilots fail? The problem was not simply one of lower visibility at night than during the day. Pilots, like truck drivers on night runs, are accustomed to adjusting automatically to this well-known fact. What was missing were important visual cues needed to judge distance and the rate and angle of descent. The primary visual cue—the lighted city—in fact misled the pilots, causing the crashes.

During a day flight, the pilot sees not only the city but what at night is a dark expanse—the lake, the surrounding plains, the bay. These surrounding areas, it turns out, are crucial in perceiving the location of the plane in relation to the city. Without them—that is, in a night landing—the lighted city seems to float like a star in space. The pilot loses his or her frame of reference. We know that a spot of light in a darkened room is perceived as moving—the autokinetic effect (see Chapter 3). This is apparently what the pilots were trying to do: land their planes on a moving spot of light. Very often, they failed.

With these data, Kraft had no difficulty persuading the Civil Aeronautics Board that readings of the altimeter and instruments measuring speed and slope should be required for all night landings. Pilots are no longer allowed to rely on their perceptions alone. And pilot-training programs now put greater stress on explaining the hazards of night approaches.

CAREERS IN APPLIED PSYCHOLOGY

Sometimes students in introductory psychology develop the impression that a career in psychology means teaching at a college or university and perhaps doing research on perception, memory, personality, or one of the other topics covered in this book. A textbook naturally tries to convey the basic knowledge in a field and how it was obtained, and these are academic functions. But more than half of all psychologists work in *applied* settings, using psychology to save lives, as Dr. Kraft's research illustrates, or to improve the quality of life, as psychotherapists do.

The number and variety of careers open to people with degrees in psychology are enormous. As one psychologist noted, psychology "has come to stand for a wider assortment of activities than any other occupational label, with the possible exceptions of 'civil servant' and 'entertainer'" (Berlyne, 1975, p. 70). The wide variety of academic careers was discussed in Chapter 1, along with the most common applied career, clinical psychology. *Clinical psychologists* apply the principles of psychology to the diagnosis and treatment of people with psychological disturbances; their activities will be discussed in detail in Chapter 13.

Guidance-and-counseling psychologists try to help relatively normal people with their problems. They might administer a test or two to guide someone into a career that promises to be satisfying, fitting that individual's pattern of interests and abilities. Counseling psychologists also provide information and perspective to people faced with difficult decisions (whether or not to divorce one's spouse, for example) or with readjustment to life after a traumatic incident (like the divorce the person finally decided on, in prior counseling sessions). The complexities of modern life get to all of us at one time or another, and sometimes it's helpful to have an intelligent, informed, concerned person to talk to—to discuss the purpose of life or perhaps man-woman relationships in today's society. More and more, counseling (and clinical) psychologists are also leading *group* counseling sessions on topics of general interest.

The role of *school psychologists* is defined by their work setting, which most commonly is an elementary or high school. Many school psychologists are guidance-and-counseling psychologists who are experts in school-related problems of children and adolescents. *Educational psychologists,* on the other hand, are interested in the educational process; learning, motivation, and testing are just a few of the fields of psychology they apply to their interests. Often they direct special programs for mentally retarded or handicapped children or for students who have reading difficulties. School psychologists are often educational psychologists, too; how they are labeled is largely a matter of how they prefer to see themselves.

Industrial psychologists work in industry, designing safer cars or fairer hiring practices—or discovering why Boeing 727s crash. Specific types of industrial psychologists include the *management psychologist,* who counsels executives, and the *personnel psychologist,* who is an expert in placing square pegs in square holes (matching individuals' talents with job requirements).

The careers we have mentioned account for most of the professional psychologists, but there are innumerable other careers, too. There are psychologists who do nothing but develop new tests; psychologists who advise the government on welfare programs; military psychologists who think about battle strategies, brainwashing, and propaganda; engineering psychologists who try to reconcile the needs of humans and the requirements of their machines; rehabilitation psychologists who help disabled people regain lost capacities, physical or mental; psychologists who advise businesses on how to sell their products; psychologists who build slot machines; and psychologists who spend most of their time thinking about the relationships between psychology and religion.

Two Emerging Careers

Two relatively new specialties that are attracting large numbers of psychologists are *environmental psychology* and *program evaluation.* Environmental psychologists study the effects of such environmental factors as noise and crowding on human behavior. They feel that urban planners, architects, and civil engineers too often ignore the human reaction to their cities, buildings, and bridges. It is possible, for example, to build an apartment complex in which we can fairly predict that most tenants will be friends. Or we can build it in such a way that we can predict that most of the tenants will not even know their neighbors.

Program evaluation is a profession that grew from the need of governmental and industrial agencies to measure how well their bright ideas were working out. A business might become concerned about alcoholism among its employees and begin an education and rehabilitation program. Is it working, or is it just a waste of money? The government might sponsor a "Head Start" program to increase the academic skills of disadvantaged children. Is it having any effect? How can it be improved?

Nobody is better than a psychologist at using tests, observations, records, and other data, analyzing the data with sophisticated statistical techniques, and avoiding the many potential biases that infect the collection and analysis of such data. In contrast, I am reminded of a program evaluation by a nonpsychologist, G. Gordon Liddy (who later ran into trouble with the law because of a break-in at the Watergate apartments). In 1969, President Nixon put Liddy in charge of the "Mexican border problem" in the battle against marijuana smuggling. Liddy instituted Operation Intercept, searching almost everyone who crossed the border. After a month or two, Liddy evaluated his own program: The border agents were intercepting practically no marijuana; therefore the program was nearly a complete success. Narcotics officers up north noticed little decline in drug activity, however, and drug runners were later to claim that by tying up agents at the major crossing points, the program allowed them to open up other, better avenues of smuggling. Veteran United States Customs agent Flack Milner gave a more accurate program evaluation: "Worked out just like we thought it would. Congested traffic, brought business to a standstill, messed up the Mexican tourist economy. No, it didn't do any good" (Roemer, 1973, p. 26).

Careers with a Bachelor's Degree

Many careers in psychology—teaching at a major university, for example—are open only to people with the Ph.D. degree. Many students, however, are interested in a psychology major but not in postgraduate study. What can you do with a bachelor's degree in psychology?

Perhaps the best way to answer this question is to examine the careers of people who have earned bachelor's degrees in the past (and did not go on to graduate study). We can open by saying that psychology is an unusually flexible degree, preparing majors for a wide variety of jobs. Indeed, it is no longer surprising to me to see former psych majors turning up in the strangest places. I called a carpenter last week to replace a broken-down porch; a former psych major showed up, built a magnificent porch, and tried to get me to invest in some houses he is building "for speculation." While he was replacing our porch, another former psych major came by—driving a Mercedes—and tried to sell me a leather-bound set of encyclopedias. I looked at his car and suggested he speak to my porch builder about investments.

Although psych majors have a large variety of occupations open to them, most turn up in two areas: education and business (Lunneborg, 1977). In the field of education, many become teachers, often at the elementary levels. Because of their special skills in psychology, many become involved in "special" educational programs; "Head Start Specialist," "parent educator," and "vocational trainer" are a few of the job titles reported by former majors. In business, psych majors tend to gravitate toward administration and personnel activities, working with people rather than with things. Representative job titles include "administrative assistant," "planner," and "employment recruiter." Obviously many students who major in psychology do so because they are interested in people, and their later occupations reflect these same interests.

Interests in people are even more evident in jobs in child and adult care. These occupations involve assisting individuals who are at least partially unable to care for themselves. Job titles include "child care worker" for a juvenile court, "recreational therapist" at a center for the handicapped, and "caseworker" at a home for the elderly. A similar "people orientation" shows up in the field of guidance and counseling. The most common job title is simply "counselor," but the counseling may occur in a wide variety of settings, ranging from a probation department to college dormitories.

Psychology deals with people and behavior, but it is also a science, and the scientific aspects seem to be its chief appeal for another sizable group of majors. After graduation, these students turn up in research occupations, becoming research analysts, statisticians, or biofeedback technicians.

Finally, some jobs held by former psych majors combine social and scientific interests. In general, these occupations involve interviewing people to obtain information for some purpose; in some cases, the interviewer may use the information to advise the interviewee of his or her status in some regard. Welfare eligibility examiners, for example, do this.

Other job titles include "pre-trial screener" for a court, "admitting interviewer" for a hospital, or simply "interviewer" for a variety of employers.

Psychologists and Their Jobs

Even if you have no interest in a career in psychology, the jobs of psychologists are worth considering for the light they throw on the kind of people who become psychologists. They show an obvious interest in people: how they think, why they do what they do, how they go wrong, how they can be helped to better themselves. They demonstrate a corresponding interest in data, in information that allows the psychologist to make these judgments, to answer these questions; there is a decidedly practical, nononsense bent to psychology. A psychologist is a kind of pragmatic humanist, a scientific do-gooder. The field includes a few clinkers, of course—psychologists who use data to *make* people go wrong (buy junk food, support bad political leaders)—but all in all it's an honorable profession. I'm proud to be a psychologist.

SUGGESTED READINGS

Woods, P. J. *Career opportunities for psychologists.* American Psychological Association, 1976.
  Discusses traditional and innovative careers in psychology; appropriate for undergraduate majors as well as graduate students and dissatisfied Ph.D.s.

Lesser, G. S. *Children and television.* Random House, 1974.
  A thorough discussion of *Sesame Street,* its philosophy, its creation, and its evaluation.

Behavioral Objectives

1. Identify the main parts of a neuron and describe how a neuron receives and transmits information.
2. Distinguish between the central and peripheral nervous systems, and list their major components.
3. Define biofeedback and give an example of it.
4. Describe the endocrine system.
5. Distinguish between the apparent functions of the right and the left cerebral hemispheres.
6. List the traditional five senses.
7. Briefly describe the important biological features of the eye.
8. Define color and how we perceive it. Describe how neurons are organized to analyze color information.
9. Briefly describe the important biological features of the ear and relate the auditory dimensions of pitch and loudness to the physical characteristics of sound waves.
10. Identify our two "chemical senses."
11. List the four basic sensations of touch.

CHAPTER

2

The Biological Framework

Psychologist Howard Gardner was interviewing a nice-looking, well-groomed 62-year-old retired bookkeeper named Tom Johnson.

"What kind of work have you done, Mr. Johnson?"

"We, the kids, all four of us, and I, we were working for a long time in the . . . you know . . . it's the kind of space, I mean place near to the spedwan . . ."

Gardner stopped him. "Excuse me, but I wanted to know what work you have been doing."

"If you had said that, we had said that, poomer, near the fortunate, forpunate, tamppoo, all around the fourth of martz. Oh, I get all confused." (Gardner, 1978b,' p. 76).

Well, it's clear that Mr. Johnson has a problem of some sort. But what? One possibility is that Mr. Johnson's disordered language reflects disordered thinking. The mental illness we call schizophrenia, for example, often disturbs thought processes to such an extent that the patient "talks gibberish." Indeed, it's not unlikely that a clinical psychologist or psychiatrist first encountering Mr. Johnson would form a preliminary opinion of schizophrenia.

Another possible reason for Mr. Johnson's language disorder is damage to a "language center" in his brain. In fact, further tests uncovered the source of Mr. Johnson's problem: damage localized in a small area on the left side of the outside surface of the brain. Research has shown this area to be one of several that seem to be intimately involved in the comprehension and production of language. Patients with damage here have difficulty understanding questions that are asked them, although they may produce streams of unrelated speech that are sometimes difficult to shut down.

But the brain is a complex entity. If Tom Johnson's injury had been only slightly forward on the left outside surface of the brain, he would have had problems producing language, as Mr. Cooper did.

"How many children do you have?" asked psychologist Howard Gardner.

After a long pause, Mr. Cooper began to raise fingers: "One, two, tree, pour, no, pive . . . yes pive."

Gardner asked him what kind of work he had been doing. "Me . . . build—ing . . . chairs, no, no, cab—in—nets."

"One more question," said Gardner. "Can you tell me how you would go about building a cabinet?"

"One, saw . . . then, cutting wood . . . working. . . ." All of this was said very slowly, with great frustration, but then suddenly, quickly, fluently, as if another speech mechanism had kicked in: "Jesus Christ, oh boy!" (Gardner, 1978b, p. 79).

Behavior, the subject matter of psychology, is somehow related to the workings of the brain and nervous system. For instance, injury to part of the brain can drastically change a person's ability to answer simple questions, as the cases of Mr. Johnson and Mr. Cooper illustrate. The role the *brain* plays in the workings of the *mind* has been a topic of philosophical inquiry for centuries, and psychological studies relating our brains and our behavior have only increased our appreciation of the complexities of the issue.

For example, with evidence provided by brain-injured patients, theorists proposed a simple model of the brain structures underlying human speech: After being transformed into an electrical signal by the ears, speech enters the brain at one area (the area damaged in Mr. Johnson's brain), where it is *comprehended*. A signal is then sent ahead to another area (the area damaged in Mr. Cooper's brain), where a reply is *produced*. This simple model would explain cases like those of Mr. Johnson and Mr. Cooper, but other cases quickly demonstrate that a more complex theory is needed. One patient had no trouble understanding speech and no trouble speaking; unfortunately, his answers were totally unrelated to the questions (Thompson, 1975). Some patients can comprehend and produce speech, but they have lost their ability to read or write, or both. Patients with severe injuries in the comprehension area sometimes show no loss of language function; a disproportionate number of these are left-handed. A child with brain injuries and speech loss usually recovers; the chances of a complete recovery for an adult with the same damage are slim. A woman who had suffered severe brain injury from carbon monoxide poisoning never spoke spontaneously and showed no evidence of understanding speech in the nine years she was studied. However, if you said to her, "Roses are red . . . ," she would say, "Roses are red, violets are blue, sugar is sweet, and so are you" (Geschwind, 1972). How can we explain that?

Ah, the mysteries of human behavior. A little later in this chapter, we will return with a more complicated theory of how all these strange cases of language disorder relate to one another and to brain function, but first we should describe the brain and nervous system in more detail. We will look at how information gets into the nervous system and what the brain does with the information. We will look at some evidence suggesting that each of us has not just one but two brains, which to some extent function independently. Does this mean we have two personalities in one body? And finally, a word (or two) about the five (or more) senses.

THE NERVOUS SYSTEM

One of the two main ways parts of the body communicate with each other is through the *nervous system*. (The other major biological messenger service is the *endocrine system*, which we will discuss later). Your nervous system is a vast network of electrochemical connections, designed for transmitting messages from one place to another and for making use of these messages, in muscles and glands, in ways that are generally to your benefit. There are two parts to the nervous system, the *central nervous system* and the *peripheral nervous system*. The central nervous system includes all the connections in the spinal cord and in the brain; everything outside of the brain and cord is in the peripheral nervous system.

The Basic Unit: The Neuron

The basic unit of the nervous system is the *neuron*, a single nerve cell. It has been estimated that the brain alone contains 10 billion neurons (Eccles, 1973), so the fact that you are losing thousands of neurons per day through normal aging processes should not concern you greatly. Severe injury, however, can destroy millions of brain cells at once; such a major loss often has clear effects on behavior, as we saw in the patients with language difficulties. Diseases, especially those which cut off blood to the brain (such as strokes), are the major sources of

brain injury, except in times of war. Heavy drinking is another common way people destroy their brain cells.

In the brain and other parts of the nervous system are all kinds of neurons. Some are short, measuring a few hundredths of an inch, and some are over a yard long. Some conduct a message at a snail's pace—around a couple of miles per hour—and some flash their impulses at a couple of hundred miles per hour.

The typical neuron has three major components: *dendrites,* a *cell body,* and an *axon* (see Figure 2.1 and p. 78). Each part of the neuron is specialized to provide some essential function so that the neuron can respond to important stimuli. Dendrites receive messages, while the cell body produces the next message and sends it out via the transmission cable, the axon. In other words, the axon of one neuron connects with one of the dendrites of the next neuron in line, causing the cell body of number 2 to transmit a message down the axon of number 2, which connects with a dendrite of neuron number 3. Sometimes the axon of the first neuron connects directly with the cell body of the second neuron for more direct transmission, and typically the axon of a neuron is split to connect with several other neurons. These variations are probably related to the nature of the message to be conveyed—direct contact with the cell body for an important communication that must get through, and split axons for a message that needs to be spread around.

How a Message Is Sent. Each neuron fires with a certain intensity when it is triggered, and if stimulation is insufficient, it does not fire at all. The neuron does not, in other

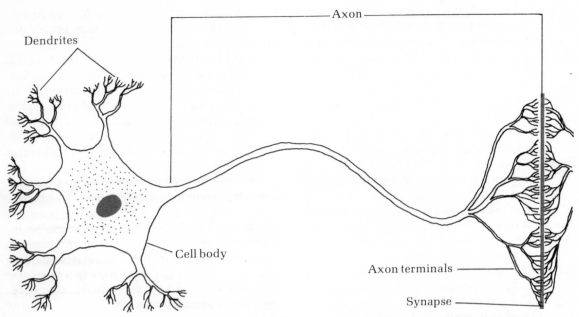

Dendrites

Axon

Cell body

Axon terminals

Synapse

Figure 2.1 *A neuron (nerve cell). When stimulated by a message received through the dendrites, the cell body generates an electrochemical impulse that passes along the axon to the synapse, where a message is released to excite (or inhibit) the next neuron.*

words, send a weaker message with a weaker stimulus, or a more intense signal with more intense stimulation. It operates on an *all-or-none principle* — as a gun does, firing only when its trigger is pulled with sufficient intensity.

When a neuron is stimulated enough to fire, the message is conveyed by a series of electrochemical changes along the axon. Each portion of the axon stimulates the next portion until the message has traveled the entire length. This process is something like the effect of heating a paper straw with a match. If heated (stimulated) enough, the straw would begin to burn. Each burning portion of the straw would heat the next por-

tion in line and cause it to "fire," until the entire length of the straw had been consumed. Fortunately, the neuron, unlike the straw, can regenerate itself and be ready to fire again and again, with sufficient stimulation.

The Synapse. Neurons do not physically touch each other but are separated by a minuscule gap. This point of interaction — called the *synapse* — is of great interest to psychologists for a number of reasons. One is that certain drugs have their effect here by making transmission between neurons more or less likely. For example, botulinum toxin, which in improperly preserved food causes acute food poisoning (botulism), effectively blocks transfer of messages at certain synapses; paralysis may result. Amphetamines (stimulant drugs sometimes sold on the street as "uppers") make synaptic transmission slightly easier. The venom of the black widow spider, on the other hand, makes transmission at the synapse overly easy; the chaotic and continual firing of neurons it causes may result in paralysis (Carlson, 1977).

Another aspect of the synapse that interests psychologists is its potential for change with learning. Is the synapse the point where "associations" are built in? Do these facing surfaces change in size when they are used? Do they change chemically? There is evidence for both kinds of change during learning (Rosenzweig, 1977).

Excitement and Inhibition. Typically many, many axons from other neurons have synapses with the dendrites and cell body of a given neuron. Also typically, it takes more than one of them firing at the same time to trigger the neuron into firing (see Figure 2.2). Using our paper straw analogy, we can say that one puny match would not generate enough heat to ignite the straw; two or three or more would be needed. This is an important biological principle, for it allows neurons to analyze information. Some neurons, for example, fire only when activated by several connecting neurons, each of which is sensitive to light in a particular spot in the visual field. Together, the spots that trigger the several neurons form a line. So this kind of neuron can be called a line detector. It is active if and only if a line is present in the visual field.

If one match will not ignite the straw, it will at least heat it up a bit, making it easier for a second match to start the fire. "Heating up" or *excitement* means the neuron is slightly stimulated, not enough to fire its all-or-none shot down the axon, but enough to make the job easier for other connecting, activating neurons.

There are other connections that have the opposite effect, called *inhibition*. Imagine our paper straw with some very cold air blowing on it. The air cools the straw below room temperature and makes it harder to ignite. Usually it takes, say, two matches to light the straw, but now, cooled, the straw needs three or four matches.

A typical neuron, at any given moment, is being affected by hundreds, even thousands, of other neurons. Some excite it, whereas others inhibit it. The neuron is in a position somewhat like that of a corporate executive who must decide whether or not to proceed with a new project. About half of the executive's advisers are saying "Go!" and the rest are saying "No!" The executive must accept all this information and make a decision. In like fashion, each neuron is a "complex integration of a mosaic of numerous stimuli" —a decision-maker (Noback and Demarest, 1972, p. 23). Admittedly, the neuron's decision process is simpler than an executive's; it simply compares the total excitation to the total inhibition, and fires if the excitation is sufficiently greater. But when billions of neurons are making decisions at the same time, you have an extraordinarily complex, sophisticated, and flexible network of decision-making. (Indeed, you have the corporate executive!)

How the Nervous System Operates

Information enters the body and the nervous system by activating receptor cells that are

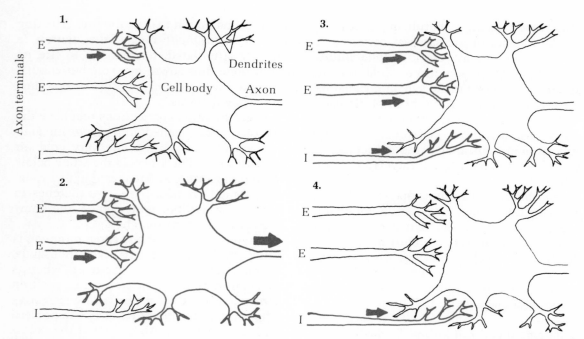

Figure 2.2 *Excitation and inhibition of nerve cells. Nerve cells have synapses with many other nerve cells, as shown above. Some nerves are excitatory and some are inhibitory. There is no difference in the electrochemical impulses they carry; they cause opposite effects by releasing different chemical transmitters at their synaptic terminals. Usually it takes more than one excitatory signal to make a nerve cell fire.*

  (1) If only one excitatory (E) neuron fires, its signal will be too weak to fire the connecting neuron. (2) If both excitatory neurons fire, but not the inhibitory (I) neuron, the connecting neuron will fire. (3) If all three neurons fire at once, the inhibitory effect of the I-neuron will balance the excitatory effect of the E-neurons and the connecting neuron will not fire. (4) If only the inhibitory neuron fires, the connecting neuron will not fire.

specialized to respond to particular kinds of changes in physical energy. The receptors in your eye respond to light, in your ear to sound, in your mouth to tastes, and on your skin to pressure and temperature. Whatever its origin, the information is then encoded as electrochemical impulses, which travel along neurons from the sensory receptors toward the brain. Some information, such as that about vision, enters the brain directly, without passing through the spinal cord. Other messages, especially from receptors on the skin and deep within the body, enter the central nervous system in the spinal cord and then travel up to the brain (see p. 77).

As the information travels toward the brain, finer and more complex analyses are being made. The system is answering questions like: Is there something out there? What color is it? Is it warm or cold? What is its shape? Have I seen this shape before? What is it? Is it a threat to me? How should I respond to it? After passing through various lower centers in the brain, the information reaches its final destination, the *cerebral cortex.* Each sense sends its messages to a more or less specific area of the cortex, where further analysis takes place, and then on to other parts of the cortex, where the information is integrated with information from other senses, motivational systems, memory systems, and other sources. Conveniently, this is also the part of the brain where the unique human abilities to reason, decide, create, and speak are "located."

If muscular activity is called for, specific cortical neurons are activated, and outgoing information begins the journey in reverse, down and out of the spinal cord to connections on the muscles. Outgoing messages are called *motor* messages, in contrast to the incoming, *sensory* messages. As in an integrated battle plan, many muscles then contract or relax in a scheme that is designed to produce a particular behavior, such as running or fighting.

The system as a whole, then, can be described as sensory-central-motor. Psychology tends to focus on the central portion of this scheme and, in particular, on the anatomy and physiology (structure and function) of the brain. The major exceptions to this rule are studies of those sensory systems which provide information uniquely important to us humans—sight and hearing, in particular.

The Central Nervous System

The central nervous system includes the spinal cord and the brain. The spinal cord functions primarily as a messenger service, taking messages from sensory receptors, sending them up the cord to the brain, and then executing the motor orders sent down from above. Some simple analyses and integrations occur at this level, as information is relayed in and out, but the cord rarely acts on its own. When it does, the resulting behavior tends to be elementary, direct, and unthinking, the kind of behavior we call a *reflex.* Even the cord's few independent acts can often be canceled by the brain. For example, you reflexively drop a hot object—the spinal cord needn't be a genius to know that holding onto something that is cooking your flesh is not in your best interests. But if the object is a valuable teacup, the brain can prevent the reflex, telling the cord, essentially, "Don't drop this! Take a little pain this time."

Your brain sits at the top of your spinal cord, in your head, protected by a thick layer of bone called the skull; most of your brain lies higher than your nostrils. If you removed it from its bony cage, it would look something like a hunk of jelly, gray and wrinkled. What you would be looking at, from the top, would be the *cerebral cortex,* the most recently evolved portion of the brain and the most important in terms of the intellectual differences between humans and other animals (see Figure 2.4). The cerebral cortex is involved in "heavy" thinking (philosophy and the like), a unique human activity.

The oldest part of your brain—oldest in terms of evolution—looks like a stalk pro-

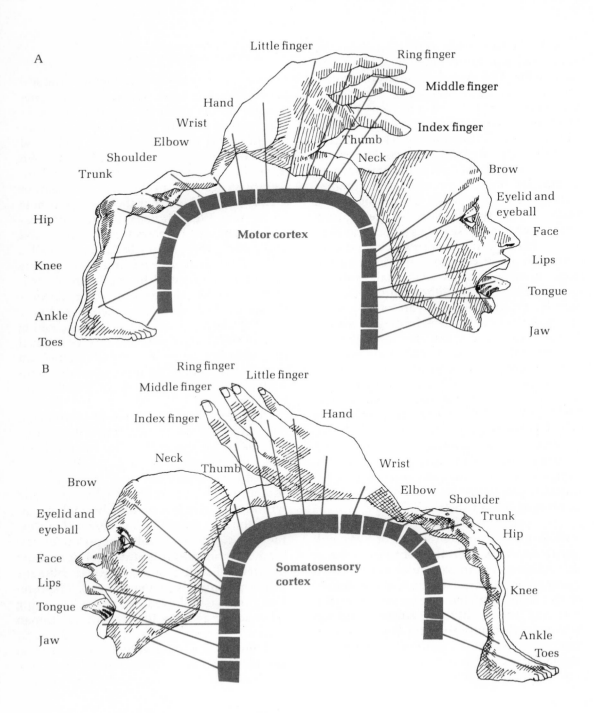

C

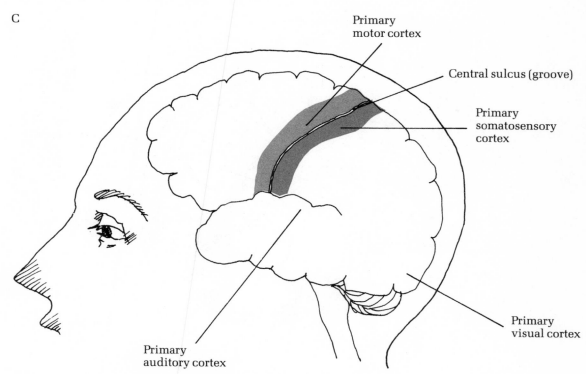

Primary
motor cortex

Central sulcus (groove)

Primary
somatosensory
cortex

Primary
visual cortex

Primary
auditory cortex

Figure 2.3 *A narrow strip on the surface of each hemisphere of the cortex sends out messages that direct motor activity (A). Notice the large amount of cortex involved in control of body parts that require finer, more intricate movements. Another narrow strip of cortex (B) receives information about touch sensations.*

The amount of cortical surface that relates to specific body parts is extremely similar to the motor cortex distribution, since fine motor movements require detailed sensory feedback. C shows the location of cortical areas in the cortex.

truding downward from the mass of gray jelly. This stalk includes several parts of the brain known collectively as the *brain stem,* which plays a major role in primitive (but complex and highly important) behaviors such as breathing and the beating of the heart.

Between the brain stem and the cerebral cortex is another group of brain parts that in-

fluence behaviors more complex than those controlled by the stem and less complex than the "uniquely human" behaviors primarily dependent on the cerebral cortex. These parts include the *cerebellum,* which looks something like a miniature brain located to the top and back of the brain stem, the *thalamus,* the *hypothalamus,* and a collection of related parts known as the *limbic*

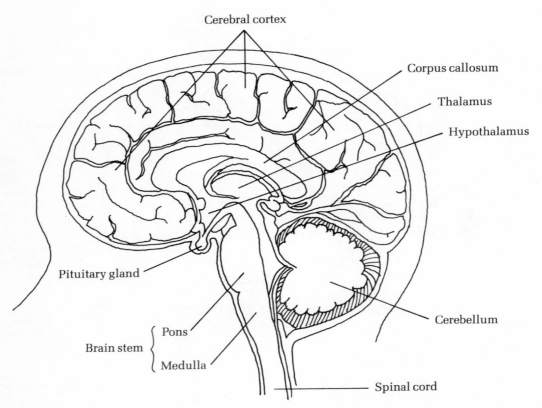

Figure 2.4 *A cross-section showing·the right side of the brain. There are essentially three main sections in the brain: the brain stem; a central core, which includes the thalamus, hypothalamus, and cerebellum; and the outer layer, the cerebral cortex.*

system. Very briefly, the cerebellum has a lot to do with integrated movements such as walking, which is quite complicated if you stop to think about all that is involved. Damage to this part of the brain results in spastic, jerky, uncoordinated body movements. The thalamus, which sits on top of the brain stem, has as one of its primary functions the transmission of signals from the lower parts of the nervous system to the higher and vice versa; it is, among other things, a giant relay station, sort of the Grand Central Station of the nervous system. The hypothalamus is small but important. It plays a major role in emotions, sexual behavior, and a lot of other human behaviors; we will discuss its role in hunger motivation in Chapter 6. The limbic system is located inside the cerebral cortex, as a hand is located inside a boxing glove, and it too is involved in many complex human behaviors. Some parts of the limbic system, for example, play an important role in violent aggression. If those parts are surgically removed from wild rats or savage wild cats such as the lynx, the animals become placid and affectionate (Goddard, 1964). In a Japanese hospital for the criminally insane, similar operations on humans with an uncontrollable streak of violence enable them to live normal lives for the first time (Mark and Ervin, 1970).

Very roughly, then, the human brain has a collection of parts at the bottom called the brain stem, a middle section spreading out from the stalk below the cerebral cortex, and a massive umbrella-like covering—the cerebral cortex. As we proceed upward from the stem, the behaviors governed get more and more complicated and more distinctly human.

One more feature of the brain needs introduction: There are essentially *two* brains in each body. There is a complete cerebral cortex in the right half of your head, and another—a structural duplicate—in the left half of your head. Almost every brain part has a duplicate on each side. This is typical of the human body. We have two lungs, two kidneys, and two eyes, when one is enough, usually, to survive. This is inefficient in the sense that it is inefficient to hire *two* private detectives to follow someone, but it is desirable in a safety sense, for if one detective is taken suddenly ill or otherwise incapacitated, the information input continues from the backup detective.

The Peripheral Nervous System

The peripheral nervous system lies outside of the brain and spinal cord. It includes the sensory receptors, the nerves to the muscles, and the connections between the sensory and motor nerves and the central nervous system. It also includes the *autonomic nervous system*, which regulates the heart, kidney, liver, stomach, intestines, rectum, bladder, and genital organs. Many of the functions of the autonomic nervous system are involuntary, not under conscious control ("autonomic" means "independent"), so if you slip and call it the "automatic" nervous system, you won't be far wrong. Most of the functions of this system we *want* to be autonomous. We don't want to have to monitor our heart rate ("Beat! Pause! Beat! . . ."). The involuntary aspect of the autonomic nervous system is undesirable only rarely: when we blush, when a young man signals his state of mind with an involuntary penis erection, when we stand up to speak in public and find our heart racing, our lungs short of breath, our body in a cold sweat.

Psychologists are especially interested in the role of the autonomic nervous system in emotions. In particular, a part of the system called the *sympathetic division* is active when a person is emotionally aroused—when danger threatens, an important event looms, quick action is needed. The sympathetic division increases blood flow to the muscles, for example, and causes secretion of adrenalin, a powerful stimulant. The other part of the autonomic system is called the *parasympathetic division*, which predominates in more placid times to restore the body's basic stores of energy—by promoting digestion, for example.

FOCUS

Biofeedback

"Feedback" refers to information on how you're doing, in some regard. Teachers give feedback in the form of grades on examinations, to let students estimate their level of scholastic achievement; and investment counselors give feedback on stock prices to their anxious clients. "Biofeedback" refers to information on how (or what) your body is doing. Thus, biofeedback might provide you with knowledge of your heart rate, blood pressure, state of bodily relaxation, and other biological processes you are not ordinarily aware of. A simple example of biofeedback is taking your temperature when you think you might be running a fever.

Many of the biological processes on which we desire feedback are controlled by the autonomic nervous system. Until the late 1950s, psychologists believed that these processes could not be consciously controlled (Kazdin, 1978). According to this belief, one could not adjust his or her heart rate, pupil size, or body temperature, even if offered a huge sum of money to do so. As it turned out, many autonomic functions can be controlled; previous failures to do so were due largely to the fact that people didn't know how well they were doing—they lacked biofeedback. Once psychologists were able to devise instruments to provide instant and continuous information on bodily states, they discovered that subjects were able to control many of their "automatic" functions.

The medical potential of biofeedback training is considerable. Patients who suffer from extremely high blood pressure can often lower it considerably, and people with irregular heart rates can often regularize them to some extent, without dangerous drugs. There is some question, however, whether the average patient can exert enough control for medical purposes (Blanchard, 1978). Similar biofeedback procedures have been used for a myriad of medical problems (Miller, 1978), including diarrhea (feedback from the sphincters or, in one case, "bowel sounds . . . heard over a loudspeaker"!), epilepsy (feedback from the electrical activity in the brain), migraine headaches (feedback on dilatation of blood vessels), and asthma (feedback on body tension).

Psychologists are particularly interested in the use of biofeedback to control emotions. An individual having problems coping with unusual levels of anxiety, for example, might receive biofeedback training to relax. Typically, information on muscle tension, "nervous" perspiration, or heart rate (or some combination of the three) is fed back to patients, who then try to lower the levels of these psychological indications of anxiety. The electrical activity of the brain, recorded from the outside of the skull, can also be controlled to some extent; people who show slow, regular brain rhythms called "alpha waves" (see p. 425) report pleasant, relaxed feelings (Kamiya, 1968).

How people are able to control their autonomic responses is rarely clear; it is a topic of extensive research today. A number of studies suggest that human imagination is often significant, at least in the beginning of training. A patient with spinal cord injuries, who had to *increase* his blood pressure, reported imagining sex; later, however, he found the images unnecessary (Brucker, 1977). Similarly, actors learned to cry on cue by imagining tragic situations. Later they achieved the same effect simply by imagining the feeling in the corner of their eyes when they are crying (Miller and Dworkin, 1977).

THE ENDOCRINE SYSTEM

The nervous system is one means the parts of the body use to communicate with each other; the other is the *endocrine system.* The endocrine system makes use of chemical "rivers" flowing through your body, most notably the bloodstream. The primary function of these rivers is transporting foodstuffs and disease fighters, but, in addition, they carry messages (like notes in corked wine bottles) from one part of the body to another. The parts of the body that construct and release these messages are the endocrine glands; the message is carried by *hormones.* Generally speaking, the endocrine glands regulate long-term, slow-moving processes such as body growth and sexual maturation (see Figure 2.5). The thyroid gland, for example, controls body metabolism; if it does not produce enough thyroxine, the individual may gain weight no matter how little he or she eats.

Even though one uses chemical messengers and the other uses electrochemical transmission, the endocrine and nervous systems interact. The endocrine glands are activated in many instances by nerve impulses, and the hormones very often increase neural activity in parts of the brain and the rest of the nervous system. If I sent a message in a corked wine bottle—"Help! Am being held for ransom in Torgy Anderson's warehouse in Larsen Bay, Alaska"—no doubt the liquid-borne message would soon result in an electrical communication (a telephone call to authorities). The endocrine and nervous systems affect one another in a similar way.

Psychologists' interest in the endocrine system centers on the adrenal glands, the sex glands, and the so-called master gland, the pituitary. The inner core of the adrenal gland—the adrenal medulla—secretes adrenalin, the powerful stimulant just mentioned in our discussion of the autonomic nervous

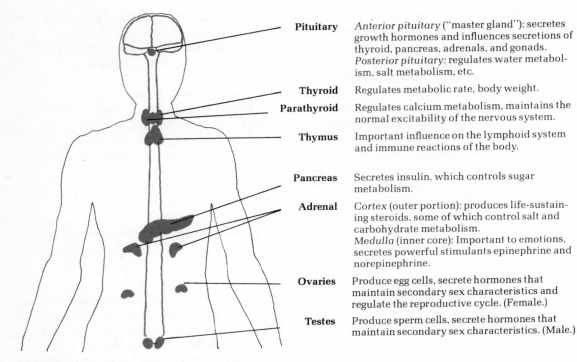

Pituitary	*Anterior pituitary* ("master gland"): secretes growth hormones and influences secretions of thyroid, pancreas, adrenals, and gonads. *Posterior pituitary*: regulates water metabolism, salt metabolism, etc.
Thyroid	Regulates metabolic rate, body weight.
Parathyroid	Regulates calcium metabolism, maintains the normal excitability of the nervous system.
Thymus	Important influence on the lymphoid system and immune reactions of the body.
Pancreas	Secretes insulin, which controls sugar metabolism.
Adrenal	*Cortex* (outer portion): produces life-sustaining steroids, some of which control salt and carbohydrate metabolism. *Medulla* (inner core): Important to emotions, secretes powerful stimulants epinephrine and norepinephrine.
Ovaries	Produce egg cells, secrete hormones that maintain secondary sex characteristics and regulate the reproductive cycle. (Female.)
Testes	Produce sperm cells, secrete hormones that maintain secondary sex characteristics. (Male.)

Figure 2.5   *The major endocrine glands.*

system, when it is instructed to do so by the sympathetic division of the autonomic nervous system. Adrenalin, or epinephrine, as it is more commonly known today, is a prime ingredient of emotional arousal; it speeds up respiration and heart rate, raises blood pressure, sharpens reflexes, and generally increases the efficiency of the nervous system.

The sex glands, ovaries in the female, testes in the male, regulate sexual maturation, including the development of the secondary sex characteristics such as facial hair on men and breasts on women. The female sex hormones, estrogen and progesterone, direct the monthly cycle of menstruation.

The male sex hormones, testosterone and androsterone, are suspected to be related to some forms of aggressive behavior. Both males and females produce both male and female hormones, but in different proportions. For example, by taking female hormones, a man can lose his beard or grow breasts.

And finally there's the pituitary, which hangs from the bottom of the brain. The pituitary was named by a man who concluded that its sole function was to discharge mucus into the nose; the word means "nasal secretion" (Nourse et al., 1964). Little did he know. This acorn-sized gland actually controls much of the activity of the other endocrine glands by sending out hormones that stimulate them into activity; hence its new title, "master gland." If the pituitary detects too little thyroxine in the bloodstream, for example, it sends out a hormone that stimulates the thyroid gland into production. Besides monitoring the bloodstream, the pituitary can be stimulated into action by the hypothalamus of the brain. The intimate relationship between the hypothalamus and the pituitary accounts for much of the interaction between the neural and hormonal systems.

As an example of the whole system in operation, we might consider the peahen. The peahen is courted as no other female, by the most spectacular sexual display in the animal kingdom — by the peacock. The peacock's vivid exhibitionism is *perceived* by the peahen and resulting neural activity stimulates the peahen's pituitary to secrete a hormone that, in turn, stimulates her ovaries. Her ovaries put out sex hormones which, among other things, return to stimulate brain cells involved in sexual behavior. The peahen thus becomes romantic.

THE CEREBRAL CORTEX

Like a one-week tour of Europe, our geographical tour of the human body has given us only a brief acquaintance with the basic parts of the nervous and endocrine systems. Later, in various chapters, we will return to biological considerations, as we review topics such as motivation, aggression, sleep, and mental illness, in which biology plays an important role. But before we leave basic geography, we should take a closer look at the cerebral cortex, the capital city, so to speak, of the nervous system.

"Cortex" means "outer bark." In the brain it refers to the vast collection of cell bodies that forms the outer covering of the cerebral hemispheres, and to which we attribute our most distinctive human abilities. The cortex has two hemispheres, as we have mentioned; typically they work together, but, as we shall see, some intriguing research suggests that these "two brains" can sometimes function independently.

Language and the Cortex

At the beginning of this chapter, I described a few of the language deficiencies that can result from injury to certain parts of the brain. Although our knowledge of how the brain functions in language is far from complete, we do have some general ideas about which brain parts play major roles. For example, we know that for most people most language functions are "located" in the left hemisphere of the cortex. Also for most people, a small area called Broca's area seems to be crucial to speech production, and a somewhat larger area to the rear, called Wernicke's area, seems to be crucial to speech comprehension.

To say that a function is localized in a certain part of the brain means only that this brain region is important, perhaps crucial, to this function. The brain region need not even be the same in all people. In right-handed people, the speech areas are almost always located in the left hemisphere (which also controls movements of the right hand). For left-handed people, the picture is considerably more complex: Most appear to have speech areas in the left hemispheres, as right-handers do, but a sizable percentage have them in comparable areas of the right hemisphere, which controls the movements of the left hand. Another sizable percentage of left-handers have speech areas in *both* hemispheres (Hardyck and Petrinovich, 1977); these people are either inefficient in their use of brain tissue or more flexible than average, depending on your point of view. One thing is certain: they are more adaptable after brain injuries.

If the region in which a function is localized is damaged, other regions can sometimes take over that function. A child with severe damage to the left hemisphere loses the ability to speak, but usually regains it with time. The language functions "relocate" in the right hemisphere. The capacity to recover from brain injuries, however, decreases with age; an adult with damage to Wernicke's areas rarely regains his previous competence in speech (although marked improvement is possible).

Let's consider the typical case: a right-handed adult whose speech functions are localized in the left hemisphere. If Wernicke's area is for comprehension and Broca's area is for production, what would you expect when the neural pathways from Wernicke's area to Broca's area are cut? Comprehension is perfect, for Wernicke's area is intact. Speech is fluent, for Broca's area is intact. When the person is asked a question, however, the answer bears no relation to the question. Patients with this difficulty indicate intense frustration; they cannot say what they mean (Geschwind, 1972).

Other brain regions near the speech areas are important in other language functions. Damage to one particular area, for example, affects the ability to integrate auditory and visual patterns; a person so affected could converse normally, but not read or write.

Many psychologists prefer not to think in terms of "localization" of a function in a specific area of the brain. Instead they think in terms of numerous "specialized" areas, their functions "interconnecting" to create an "integrated" process. Abnormalities thus can be best understood as "disconnections," a failure of various cortical areas to work together (Geschwind, 1972). Damage to Broca's area, which results in poor and difficult speech, would be considered a disconnection between comprehension and articulation. A dramatic example of a "disconnection" problem is the case of the woman described in the introduction of this chapter. This woman showed no ability to comprehend or produce speech, but could recite familiar rhymes and sayings if given a start: "Roses are red . . ." After her death, it was discovered that her speech areas had been totally disconnected from the rest of the brain by surrounding damage caused by carbon monoxide poisoning. She had, in effect, a perfectly functioning little "speech brain," with an intact Wernicke's area, an intact Broca's area, and all connections between them. But almost nothing got into the system from the rest of the brain, so it was nonfunctional. Only an occasional word or phrase got through, for reasons not entirely clear, triggering a well-learned sequence of behavior: "Roses are red . . ."

The Left and Right Hemispheres

As we have discussed, the brain is actually not a single organ but two essentially identical structures working together. Having two cerebral hemispheres ("hemi-" means "half"), we also have not one cerebral cortex but two. The cerebral hemispheres are connected by a great bridge of nerve fibers called the *corpus callosum,* which keeps the brain's two sides in communication.

In the first half of the twentieth century, brain surgeons found occasion to cut into or sever the corpus callosum in a number of people, for medical reasons. They were certain that destruction in such a major brain area would have profound effects, but, to their surprise, they could discover no effects whatsoever. Experiments on monkeys supported the hypothesis that cutting the corpus callosum was essentially harmless.

Still, it simply makes no sense to assign no important role to such a major structure, one that contains the axons of millions of cortical neurons going in both directions. R. W. Sperry held this opinion and set about to study more carefully the deficits associated with the loss of this great hemispheric bridge, starting with experiments on cats in the early 1950s, and progressing to observations of humans. We will focus on the latter.

The Split Brain. Sperry and his associates were able to study the effects of cutting the corpus callosum in humans because of the use of this surgery to alleviate severe epilepsy. Epilepsy is a nervous system malfunction that often results in bodily convulsions because of "electrical storms" in the brain. In some severe cases, patients had their corpus callosums surgically severed when all other remedies failed. The idea was to temper the electrical storms by preventing their spread from one hemisphere to the other, and the results of such surgery were encouraging. Epileptic seizures often stopped altogether, and no unfortunate side effects were noted. Only careful and detailed testing revealed the true nature of the deficit.

One such test examined the patient's ability to perceive lights. A horizontal row of lights was flashed while the patient fixed her gaze at the center of the row. "What did you see?" asked the experimenter.

The patient replied, "A row of lights on the right side of the board." (The lights on the left side had also flashed, of course.)

"Did you see any lights flash on the left?"
"No."

This is intriguing. The human visual system is constructed so that stimuli to the right of the point of focus activate receptors that lead to the left hemisphere; stimuli to the left of focus activate the visual area of the right hemisphere. In other words, there is a crossover of input, from right to left and from left to right, a general characteristic of most sensory systems (see Figure 2.6). The patient reported she saw only the lights on the right, those that went to the left hemisphere. Was she blind in the right cortex?

The guess was that she was not, that it was her spoken report that was deficient. We know that in most humans speech is controlled by centers in the left cortex. Probably the right cortex had seen the lights, but when the psychologist asked for a spoken report, only the left hemisphere could answer. The left cortex replied truthfully; it had *not* seen any lights on the left. The right cortex, being unable to get its report across to the speech center, could not reply.[1]

The right cortex, although typically unable to speak, can report its knowledge in

---

[1] One should realize, of course, that a cortex cannot actually "speak." A cortex, more properly, is "involved in the production of verbal reports" or indirectly "causes speech." Some will object to the personification of the two cortices, with good reason, and I use this device only to keep the focus on the main point: the different functions of the two cortices.

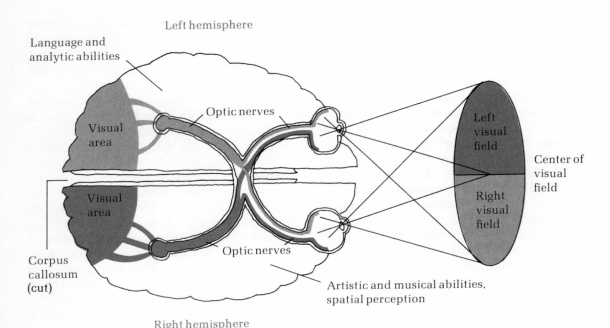

Figure 2.6 *The left side of your field of vision is received by the right hemisphere of your cortex, and the right side by the left hemisphere. Normally, the two hemispheres "inform" each other through the corpus callosum, but if it is cut, two independent brains are created.*

nonverbal terms. For example, it dominates the movements of the left hand. (The left cortex handles most of the duties with the right hand.) If the patient is instructed to point to the lights that flashed, the left hand points to the left side of the board—the right cortex is saying, "I saw lights, too!"

With the corpus callosum intact, the information in one cortex is quickly transmitted to the other cortex, and both are thus informed of the goings-on in the world. In patients with the callosum severed, there is rarely a problem, because the head isn't often stationary; so both hemispheres get a good look. Even if they don't, the two hemispheres can communicate without a corpus callosum: If the left cortex speaks, the right cortex hears, and if the right cortex points, the left cortex sees.

Gazzaniga (1967) has reported an excellent example of how this works. The right cortex was shown a colored card, either red or green, and the person was asked to *speak* his or her report. Since speech is controlled by the left cortex, the accuracy was no better than chance (50:50, by pure guessing). If the experimenter allowed a second guess, however, accuracy improved considerably. It was clear enough why, from simple observation of the subjects. If red was shown and the subject reported "Red," he would stick with his first guess if allowed a chance to change his report. If red was shown and the subject reported "Green," he would frown and shake his head and then say "No, Red." The right cortex knew the correct answer and could hear the "wild guess" of the speaking left cortex. If the guess was wrong, the right cortex exercised its influence over the muscles of the head to cause a frown and a shake. The left cortex picked up this message and changed its answer to the correct one. Such maneuvers probably account for the lack of noticeable impairment in most patients with cut or damaged corpus callosums.

But with careful testing it can be demonstrated that in patients with a severed callosum, there truly are two separate brains, each with a mind of its own. The old saying, "The right hand doesn't know what the left hand is doing," takes on new meaning. If one sets up the situation carefully, the saying is literally true. If the word "pencil" or a picture of a pencil is shown on a screen to left of focus, the right cortex but not the left receives the information. From among a group of objects hidden behind a board, the left hand will pick out a pencil. The right hand, controlled by the left cortex, cannot pick up the correct object at better than a chance level.

Specialization of Left and Right Hemispheres. With the capability of testing each hemisphere separately, biological psychologists have been able to assess the unique abilities in each. In general, the left cortex is the center for language and conceptual abilities; it appears to understand language better, and it can do more complicated mathematical problems than the right cortex. Some religious philosophers, stunned by the task of explaining two souls in one body, were encouraged by such findings and, with great relief, announced the locus of consciousness, personality, and the soul in the left cortex.

Such an interpretation may be comforting, but it is not really in tune with the facts. In many functions, the right cortex is superior to the left. Generally categorized, these functions are primarily sensual or perceptual, as contrasted with the abstract, conceptual powers of the left hemisphere. For example, if each cortex is shown a simple drawing of a house and the patient is asked to draw what he has seen, he does much better with his left hand (right cortex) than with his right hand—this even if he is right-handed and cannot draw well at all with his left hand. The reason, apparently, is that he is copying an accurate image with his left hand, whereas with his right hand he is copying an inaccurate image.

The current view of the significance of all this is that the normal brain increases its efficiency by "division of labor" (Sperry, 1972; Ornstein, 1978). Roughly speaking, the left hemisphere handles the conceptual tasks and those which involve understanding or producing written or spoken language, whereas the right hemisphere is more the visualizer, the perceiver. This is more efficient than to have two identical brains simply duplicating each other's functions. Together our two brains function something like a detective team consisting of a sharp observer, like an Indian scout (the right hemisphere), and a philosopher-logician of the Sherlock Holmes variety (the left hemisphere). This hypothesis has received support from experiments on normal adults with intact corpus callosums (for example, Klatzky and Atkinson, 1971).

FOCUS

In Which Cortex Is Skepticism Located?

Research on the "two brains" is intriguing, even spectacular. Some of the reports have an eerie, science fiction quality: "A man might, for example, grab a woman roughly with his left hand, only to have his right hand seize the left and pull it away" (Thompson, 1975, p. 77). Such stories begin to sound like a movie on late-night television: Dr. Jekyll and Mr. Hyde stuff, two distinct personalities inside one body. The apparent differences in function, too, are intriguing: it's science (left cortex) versus art (right cortex), logic versus intuition, yin versus yang, evil versus good (Dewson, 1976). The relatively small amount of research on split brains has spawned volumes of interpretation. Some people are trying to apply the findings to other fields such as education; I recently read a magazine article about an art teacher who was having unusual success by teaching her students to draw with their left hand (controlled by the presumably more creative right cortex).

In light of this sudden enthusiasm for classifying so many human functions as "belonging" to one hemisphere or the other, we might well bear in mind a few important things about split-brain research. First, there aren't a lot of solid data. Second, much of the information we have came from studies of abnormal subjects—patients with their corpus callosums severed because of brain abnormalities. Psychologists attempting to study differences between the hemispheres in normal people have used two methods. Some have tried to introduce material into one hemisphere before the other—for example, by presenting certain information only to the left ear through special earphones, so that the right hemisphere presumably receives the information a few thousandths of a second sooner (Kimura, 1973). Others have tried to measure which hemisphere is more active during a particular kind of task—for example, by measuring electrical activity in the brain from outside the skull (Shucard et al., 1977). Problems with these techniques (especially the latter) are numerous; indeed, the techniques are often less well understood than the phenomena they are intended to study. Often one researcher finds one thing and another just the opposite.

As split-brain research continues, the distinctions between the hemispheres become less sharp and less consistent. For one thing, not everyone seems to have a neat division of labor between the two hemispheres; in left-handed people and females, for instance, functions are not as clearly divided as in right-handers and males (Levy and Reid, 1978). Even in people whose two brains function in different ways, the functions don't seem to divide as neatly as the original research indicated. The right hemisphere, for example, appears to have many important language functions (Searleman, 1977).

Another problem, especially when discussing complex human activities like logic and art, is that many brain parts in both hemispheres typically are involved. A good example is music appreciation, supposedly "localized" in the right hemisphere. Most people can recognize musical themes presented to their right cortex better than themes coming first to their left cortex (Bever and Chiarello, 1974). But professional musicians show just the opposite, preferring their left hemisphere. Why? One possibility is that they are more "analytical" in a music-recognition task than the average person, and analysis is a left-hemisphere function. Thus, music appreciation, which may be localized in some sense in the right hemisphere, is affected by various parts of the brain in both hemispheres.

Differential function of the two hemispheres is a very complex phenomenon, one we do not understand well at all. I doubt if "turning on" the right hemisphere is going to save America from its overemphasis on intellect and logic and lead to new eras of artistic creativity. (In fact, there is some evidence that "turning on" the right hemisphere would lead instead to severe depression and mental illness; see Bakan, 1975.) I doubt that learning to draw with your left hand will improve your technique by activating your artistic right cortex. (It's possible, however, that using your "clumsy" hand makes you pay more attention to detail and *thus* improves your technique.) Some of this split-brain stuff is pseudoscientific nonsense. Be skeptical.

VISION

Information begins its journey through the human body by activating sensory receptors in the eyes, the ears, the nose, the tongue, or the skin. Of the five senses, vision is the most thoroughly studied, befitting the fact that the human is a visual animal. We rely heavily on visual information in making decisions. What's happening? What should I do about it? We feel uncomfortable when we cannot see—when we lose our glasses, when we're in a dark room, or when it is a moonless night. Our clichés reflect the importance of vision: "Seeing is believing." "I saw it with my own eyes." "Love is blind."

The *psychology* of seeing is the study of visual perception, to be discussed in the following chapter. Underlying the experience of vision is a biological system that includes the eyes and parts of the cortex responsible for processing visual information.

How the Eye Works

The human eye is an egg-shaped object with a *nerve* (a collection of axons from many neurons) coming out the back. The main operating parts are the *pupil*, the *lens*, and the *retina* (see Figure 2.7 and p. 79). The pupil is that black circle in the center of the front surface of your eye. It consists of nothing; it is simply a hole, an opening. The colored part around it is the iris. The lens sits in back of the pupil and, like any other lens, focuses light rays on the appropriate "screen"—the retina, in this case. The retina, which covers the inside back of the eyeball, is the real receiver in the visual system; it contains the receptor elements that transform light energy into neural energy.

The lens changes shape now and then to provide a better focus, depending on whether the thing you're looking at is close or far away; these changes are controlled by muscles to the sides of the lens. The purpose of the pupil and iris is to regulate the amount of light coming in. In weak light, the iris opens wide, making the pupil very large. In bright sunlight the iris closes in and the pupil becomes very small, almost a pinpoint. The difference is sizable and important! In weak light, the pupil becomes about 16 times as large as it is in bright light. These changes are a part of the eye's adjustment to the average level of illumination in the environment, and they play a significant role in our ability to see clearly in bright sunlight as well as in darkened rooms.

Figure 2.7   *The structure of the human eye. Light enters through a hole in the iris called the pupil and is focused on the light-sensitive retina by the lens.*

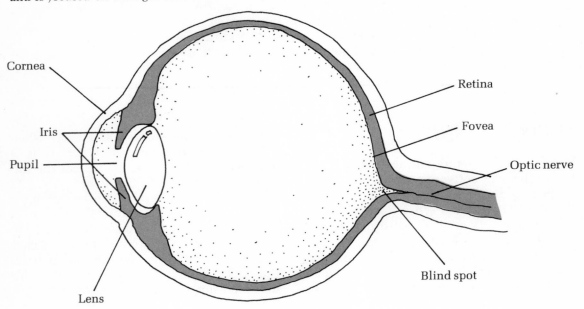

The retina is perhaps the most fascinating part of the eye, partly because it is put together in such an apparently illogical way. The receptor cells in the retina, those which register the incoming images, are located at the deepest of several levels. Light has to pass through or around all kinds of nonsensitive materials—fluids, cell parts, and blood vessels—in order to reach the target. And when the light gets there, it finds the receptor cells pointed backward, toward the brain, almost as if they expected a sneak attack of some sort. With this system, it is somewhat surprising we can see at all.

The receptor cells make a few connections in the retina with relay neurons called bipolar cells. Messages then pass on to the final cells in this system, which have their axons (transmission lines) gathered into a bundle called the *optic nerve* to send the messages to the brain. Since the receptor cells point backward, this bundle forms in *front* of the retina and must pass through the retina in order to get out of the eye. For this reason, all eyes have a blind spot where the optic nerve passes through the retina. Not too efficient.

There are two types of receptor cells in the retina, called *rods* and *cones* because of their shapes (see p. 80). They work quite differently. Rods are colorblind; their purpose is apparently restricted to registering the intensity of light energy (perceived as brightness), especially in dim illumination. The rods are so sensitive that they can be stimulated by a single quantum of light energy, and light doesn't come in smaller units than a quantum.

The cones are responsible for color vision, in ways to be described shortly. They also register intensity in bright light, the job of the rods in dim light. A third function of the cones is to provide visual *acuity*, that is, the ability to see one thing as clearly distinct from another. (Acuity is what is tested by a Snellen eye chart. In 20:20 vision, the person can distinguish letters or whatever from 20 feet away that the average person can see at 20 feet; 20:40 vision means he or she has to stand at 20 feet to distinguish what the average person can see clearly at twice the distance.) Although the rod network can distinguish shapes and forms, the cone system does so much better. To demonstrate, concentrate on what you see in the periphery of your visual field, off to the side of your direct gaze. Forms and shapes are much less clearly defined out there because light from these objects falls on the rods, which predominate outside the center of the retina; cones pack the center (the fovea), and thus you can see more clearly when you look directly at something.

Wavelength and Color

Light can be conceptualized as waves of energy, much like the waves of the sea. Such waves have two primary characteristics. First, they can be big or small; this characteristic we call *intensity*. Second, we can measure the distance from the peak of one wave to the peak of the next; this is called *wavelength*.

Sunlight is a very intense light composed of all the wavelengths we can see. When an object is illuminated by the sun, it absorbs some of the light and reflects some. The light that is reflected to our eyes is reduced considerably in intensity and is composed of many fewer wavelengths. Its intensity, by and large, determines the brightness of the object—whether it is light or dark—and the wavelengths determine the color.

Light itself does not have color. Color is a psychological experience, not a physical attribute. Though light of a certain wavelength might be called red by most people, it might be seen as yellow or even gray by others. (These people we term colorblind.) The question for the psychologist is: Why do the various wavelengths of visible light correspond to the *perception* of the various colors, at least in people with normal color vision?

Early theories about color perception were influenced by observations of the effects of mixing different colors. Using three colored lights, for example, it is possible to create all the colors of the spectrum. This fact led several theorists to propose three different types of cones, each sensitive to a different range of wavelengths. Recent physiological research shows this theory to be correct; the three types of cones are most responsive to wavelengths ordinarily perceived as violet, an unnameable shade of yellowish green, and yellow (Milner, 1970). For convenience, many psychologists refer to these as the blue, green, and yellow receptors.

Beyond the retinal rods and cones, further along in the lines between the retina and the visual areas of the cortex, there are some color detector cells, a recent and fascinating discovery. Like many cells in the nervous system, these neurons fire at a certain (baseline) rate when unstimulated. One type *increases* in activity when the person is looking at "yellow" and *decreases* when the perceived color is "blue," so it is called a yellow plus, blue minus cell. Another type does just the opposite; it is called blue plus, yellow minus. Also discovered were red plus, green minus and green plus, red minus cells.

The color detectors play a greater role in color vision than do the three kinds of cones. The "yellow" cones, for example, respond most vigorously to light with the wavelength we perceive as yellow, but they respond at least a little to all wavelengths. So if a yellow cone is weakly active, what do we know? Entering our eyes is *either* a weak yellow light *or* an intense light at some other wavelength, say, blue. The color detectors tell us which, for a "yellow" light will activate the yellow plus, blue minus cell, whereas a light of the "blue" wavelength will not, no matter how intense; it will, instead, inhibit the cell, decreasing the rate of firing.

These first two stages of color perception illustrate a general principle of the nervous system. Each level, from the primary receptors to the cortex, makes finer and finer analyses of information from the environment. After the color detectors we have a pretty good idea of whether the color of the object is blue or yellow or red or green. But these are only four of the some 200 shades we can distinguish. Obviously, further analysis up the line in the nervous system enables us to distinguish "pure yellow" from "greenish yellow" and "reddish yellow."

At the highest levels of the visual system, factors such as memory and expectation are important. These are functions of the cerebral cortex. A banana, for example, will be perceived as yellow unless it is very green or brown. Teeth seem white until compared to a truly "white" piece of paper; the visual system, which keeps sending up signals that your teeth are a sort of dull yellow, is contradicted by your inaccurate beliefs about the color of teeth. So a knowledge of the workings of the visual system will not tell you everything about real-life perceptions.

On the other hand, certain facts about visual perception are well explained by knowledge of how the system works. For example, to say someone is colorblind usually means that he is unable to distinguish red from green, *not* that he sees no colors at all. (There are a few completely colorblind people, but not many.) This makes sense in terms of the color detector cells we just discussed; something about the green plus, red minus or red plus, green minus cells is haywire. By this reasoning, we would expect, in addition to red-green blindness and total colorblindness, a third type, in which the person is unable to distinguish between blue and yellow. This is exactly the case. There are three types of colorblindness: total, red-green confusion, and blue-yellow confusion. An inability to distinguish between blue and yellow is, however, exceptionally rare, rarer than total colorblindness; why this is so we do not know (see p. 82).

Intensity and Brightness

When you look at a black shoe in sunlight, it still seems black; when you look at a piece of white paper in a poorly lighted room, it seems white. Now this is a bit odd, because the shoe is clearly reflecting much more light than the paper, and we know that intensity (the physical dimension) and brightness (the psychological perception) generally are highly related.

The answer to this puzzle lies in the fact that the visual system adjusts to the general level of illumination. A surface we usually perceive as white reflects a high *percentage* of the available light, and a black object reflects very little. So the black shoe looks black in the sunlight, because everything around it is even brighter; the white paper looks white even in a dim room because its surroundings are reflecting less light than it is.

The ability of our visual system to adjust to different levels of light is a valuable one indeed. Think about it. The brightest light you can tolerate is roughly 10 billion times as intense as the dimmest light you can see. If your visual system had to discriminate intensities across this entire range at all times, it would not be very efficient—for one thing, the "extremely bright" and "extremely dark" receptors would rarely be used. So the visual system is set up to discriminate intensities in a ratio of roughly 100:1. This means that you can see equally well whether you are skiing down a snow-covered hill in bright sunshine or watching someone else skiing on a screen in a dark movie theater.

How does our visual system accomplish this amazing feat? Several mechanisms play a role. One is the pupil of the eye, which is larger in dim light than in bright, letting in more light when the illumination is low. In effect, the eyes put on their own sunglasses when it is bright out.

The major mechanism is called *adaptation,* and it means, very simply, that the retinal receptors become more sensitive in dim light than they are in bright light. We say that eyes "adapt" to light in the sense that it takes a while to see clearly after entering a darkened room on a sunny afternoon. At first, you can't see much of anything. Gradually, clear vision returns. What has happened inside the eye is that a substance called *rhodopsin* has been built up. Rhodopsin is a light-sensitive chemical that acts something like the chemicals on photographic film; that is, it changes in composition when light strikes it. The retinal chemical, of course, differs from photographic chemicals in that it is capable of regeneration (renewing itself).

In bright sunlight, the rhodopsin in your eyes decomposes faster than it regenerates (up to a point), so that if you suddenly enter a dark room, you have less rhodopsin than you need. In the darkness, regeneration overtakes decomposition, and gradually your rhodopsin level builds up. Sensitivity returns, and you can see again. Complete regeneration occurs in a little over half an hour.

When you leave the darkness and return to bright sunlight, the chemical is at a high level; your eyes are supersensitive, and you have trouble seeing clearly because, in effect, you're seeing too much. It's so bright! Decomposition, however, proceeds rapidly, and in a few minutes your eyes are insensitive enough to take in the visual joys of a sunny day.

The outcome of all this neural and chemical maneuvering is to restrict the range of light the visual system has to deal with at any one time to only part of what it is capable of handling. Whatever the opening of the pupil and the eye's rhodopsin level, the more intense stimuli are seen as light, the less intense as dark. So white paper is white paper, in sunlight or in a gloomy room.

Cortical Detector Cells

When the nerve fibers that collectively form the optic nerve begin their journey toward the brain, the messages they transmit have already been processed to a considerable extent. Further processing goes on in the relay stations on the way to the brain and in the cortex. Of great interest in recent years have been reports of cortical *detector* cells.

Detector cells respond only to a very specific stimulus. We have already discussed color detectors in the retina. A set of fascinating experiments on frogs recorded the activity in their optic nerve fibers (Lettvin et al., 1959; Maturana et al., 1960); the researchers found one group of cells that responded only when a small dark round object was moved around in the frog's view. Bug detectors! Unquestionably a valuable type of cell for the frog!

The frog has a rather simple visual system, and it has a fairly small brain. It stands to reason that its visual system would have some means of detecting vital shapes and activities in its environment—such as moving bugs (food)—and that these means would be built into the system at a fairly low level. Humans probably have no bug detectors in the optic nerve; yet we can easily recognize a bug when we see one. At some level of the nervous system, a group of cells is stimulated in a pattern we have learned to identify by the word "bug." In humans, this detector is probably located in the cortex rather than the optic nerve. It may not be "built-in," like the frog's, but, rather, is organized through experience with bugs.

A variety of detectors has been identified in various animals. Most of them detect simple features such as lines, colors, and movement. Some cortical cells have been discovered, however, that appear to abstract (or further analyze) information from simpler detectors. "Corner detectors" respond as if they are being fed by two "line detectors." And some cells respond to lines of a specific tilt; within broad limits, it does

Ineffective   Most effective

Relative effectiveness of various stimuli
in changing activity of cell

Figure 2.8 *Some cortical cells are triggered by very complex stimuli. As shown here, the stimulus most effective in producing a response in a cell of a monkey's cortex looks suspiciously like a monkey's hand.*

not matter where the line is placed in the visual field or how long the line is. One researcher found cortical cells in the monkey that respond most actively to a very precise stimulus as a whole—for example, the shape of a monkey's hand, as shown in Figure 2.8 (Gross, 1973).

The Biology of Seeing

The human visual system begins in the eye and ends in the cortex. The complicated peripheral portion makes us wonder how we form clear pictures at all: The eye constantly jiggles. Why isn't our vision fuzzy? The eye has a blind spot. Why doesn't everything have a hole in it? Light waves that stimulate the retina must travel through blood vessels in front of the rods and cones. Why isn't everything we see covered with blood vessels?

These questions assume that seeing is directly comparable to taking a picture—that the visual system simply records what is out there. This view would be difficult to defend on biological grounds, in light of the complex analyses, integrations, and interactions that occur in the human visual system, but it will become clearly impossible when we consider the *psychology* of seeing in Chapter 3. Perception is active and creative, not passive and reactive. The biological visual system functions to provide information for the act of perception, a function it fulfills in wondrous ways, but it does not by itself explain seeing.

AUDITION

Hearing, known technically as audition, begins with an encounter between sound waves and an ear. The human ear, mechanically speaking, consists of a large horn on the outside of the head; a tunnel with a drum at the end of it; a complicated device that transmits vibrations from the drum to the inner ear; and a snail-like structure that contains the real auditory receptors bathed in a stimulating fluid (see Figure 2.10). Sound waves enter the large external horn, which operates as a funnel, something like a cheerleader's megaphone in reverse, collecting

Figure 2.9 *Helen Keller was blind and deaf. She was able to read using the sense of touch, and even a world without sight and sound is full of sensory pleasures like a flowery fragrance.*

and focusing the waves. Moving along the tunnel, the sound waves start the eardrum vibrating. The eardrum is connected to the three little bones of the middle ear—the hammer, the anvil, and the stirrup—which amplify the vibrations and transmit them to the inner ear. In the inner ear (or cochlea), the vibrations are transformed into waves in a fluid, which stimulates receptor cells along a membrane. These cells generate neural impulses that are then transmitted along the auditory nerve to the brain.

The ear functions in some ways as a microphone, transforming sound waves from speech and other noises to electrical impulses. In fact, if we hooked an electrode onto someone's cochlea and put the signal through an amplifier and loudspeaker in an-

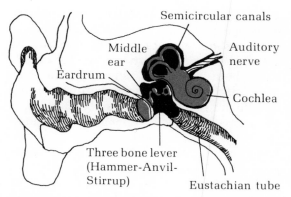

Semicircular canals

Middle
ear

Auditory
nerve

Eardrum

Cochlea

Three bone lever
(Hammer-Anvil-
Stirrup)

Eustachian tube

Figure 2.10 *Good music produces good vibrations. Literally, every sound we hear is a vibration, an air wave that comes in through the funnel of the outer ear and passes down the ear canal to the eardrum. Here it enters the middle ear. The eardrum's vibrations are carried along and magnified by three little bones whose shapes have given them the names hammer, anvil, and stirrup.*

Behind the stirrup is the inner ear. Here, a membrane called the oval window sends waves through the fluid that fills the snail-shaped cochlea. Hairs inside the cochlea are the receptors that transmit the message to the auditory nerve, which sends impulses on to the brain. The semicircular canals are involved in our sense of balance; the eustachian tube, which connects the ear to the nose and throat, relieves pressure on the eardrum.

colo). The wavelength of sound waves is usually called *frequency;* if the length between waves is short, their frequency is high. (Intensity, in similar fashion, is often called amplitude. Do we do this just to confuse you? Sometimes I wonder.) In any case, the human ear is a remarkable instrument, responding to a vast range of intensities and frequencies. If the ear were more sensitive than it is, we would be bothered by the sound of air molecules colliding (Rosenzweig, 1977). Yet we can enjoy a rock concert as easily as a lover's whisper.

Patterns of sound—speech, for example, or music—are perceived with the aid of auditory detector cells, much like those found in the visual system. Most cells in the auditory nerve respond to a certain frequency and may be inhibited by other frequencies. Other cells, in the cortex, respond not only to one frequency but also to multiples of that frequency (Thompson, 1975). In musical terms, multiples are the "same" notes an octave or more apart, so there is some biological basis for the view that "high C" sounds more like "middle C" than notes that may be closer in frequency. Other cortical cells respond best to rising or falling tones, and some detect unusual patterns—for example, "warbles" (Whitfield and Evans, 1965).

other room, we would be able to hear what was being spoken into that person's ear (Thompson, 1975).

Sound waves, like light waves, can be described in terms of wavelength and intensity. Roughly speaking, intensity is related to perceived loudness. Wavelength is related to pitch—that is, whether the sound is low (produced perhaps by a tuba) or high (a pic-

OTHER SENSES

Taste and smell are often called the "chemical senses" because the sensory receptors on the tongue and in the nasal cavity are stimulated by chemicals. The taste receptors, called taste buds, are located mostly along the edges and back surface of the tongue (see Figure 2.11). They register four basic sensa-

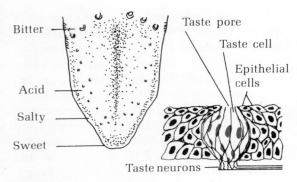

Bitter

Acid

Salty

Sweet

Taste pore

Taste cell

Epithelial cells

Taste neurons

Figure 2.11 *All the different flavors we taste are mixtures of four sensory responses in the tongue: salty, bitter, sweet, and sour. Different parts of the tongue are most sensitive to different sensations. What we call "taste," however, also includes the aroma of the food or drink. This is why substances taste bland when you have a bad cold.*

The tongue has about 10,000 taste buds. Each is a cluster of 10 to 15 sensory receptors. The taste buds can be damaged or destroyed, say, by a very hot piece of food, but because the buds are replaced every week or so, usually no permanent damage is done.

tions—sweet, sour, salty, and bitter; from combinations of these we derive the whole vast variety of tastes we can experience. Actually, however, much of what we call taste is made up of smell and other sensations such as temperature and texture. Consider how bland food tastes when you have a cold, which affects your ability to smell but not your ability to taste.

Smell (olfaction) is a more interesting sense than taste, especially to animals that make greater use of it than humans. (See Figure 2.12.) Skunks use air-borne chemicals in

defense, creating an experience no would-be attacker seems to enjoy. A bitch in heat increases her rate of urination markedly, leaving olfactory advertisements for herself throughout her home range. We humans, especially since we have begun walking upright, bringing our noses above most of the scents available to other animals, tend to think we do not smell very well. In fact, however, our olfactory abilities are quite good; if we trained ourselves properly, we could probably do as well as a hound in tracking criminals or marijuana stashes. The odors we give off are also more complex than we think; sweat from nervousness, for example, smells different from sweat from exercise. One of the prime ingredients in many perfumes is musk, an odiferous substance found, among other places, in sweaty armpits. Men in centuries past would sometimes wipe their armpits with their handkerchief, which they wore in their sleeve, believing the scent to be sexually arousing for their dancing partner. Probably they were right.

The sensory receptors in the skin give us our sense of touch (see Figure 2.13). Touch comprises four basic sensations: pressure, pain, heat, and cold. From these, in combination, we experience all the tactile sensations of which we are capable. Just how the basic sensations combine, though, is not clear. For example, why is it that certain skin experiences are pleasurable? No one knows for sure.

Although we traditionally speak of the five senses, there are in fact several other senses as well. The kinesthetic sense has receptors in the muscles, tendons, and joints; it gives us information about the position and movements of our body. This is

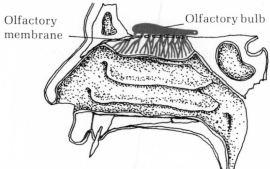

Olfactory
membrane

Olfactory bulb

Figure 2.12 *A professional wine-taster begins by sniffing the wine. Then he takes a small* *amount and rolls it around in his mouth. The sniffing draws odorous molecules from the wine up into the nasal cavity to the olfactory membrane, which contains the sensory receptors. Rolling the wine in the mouth obviously exposes it to different taste receptors, but it also stimulates the smell receptors by forcing more air up through the "rear entrance" to the nasal cavity.*

The olfactory membrane is covered by a thin film of mucus in which the odorous molecules dissolve. There they stimulate thousands of tiny hairs, the receptors that transmit signals to the olfactory bulb, which passes messages on to the brain.

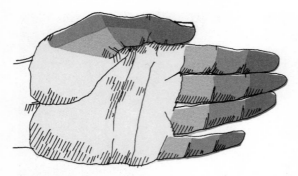

Figure 2.13 *The body's six pounds of skin contain a vast network of nerve endings. Our sense of touch includes at least four basic sensations: pressure, pain, warmth, and cold. Other sensations appear to be variations or combinations of these basic ones.*

The fingertips of the human hand are more sensitive than any other part of the body, with the exceptions of the lips, the tongue, and the tip of the nose. The shading in the picture shows the sensitivity of other parts of the hand — the stronger the color, the more sensitive the area.

the sense that makes it possible for you to touch your nose with your finger even with your eyes closed. The vestibular sense, which has receptors in the inner ear, is our sense of balance; it tells us if we are upright or tilting, moving forward or spinning. It is the sense children stimulate by spinning around until they're so dizzy they fall down.

SUMMARY

1. Human behavior depends on messages conducted via the *nervous system* and the *endocrine system;* the first is elec-trochemical and the second chemical in nature.

2. The basic unit of the nervous system is the *neuron,* the single nerve cell. In addition to the main cell body, most neurons have parts called *dendrites,* which receive messages from other neurons, and *axons,* which transmit messages. The neuron fires on an all-or-none principle. The juncture between two neurons is called the *synapse.* A neuron may either *excite* another neuron or *inhibit* it.

3. The nervous sytem consists of the *central* and the *peripheral* nervous systems. The central nervous system includes all the connections in the brain and spinal cord. The peripheral nervous system comprises those connections which bring in sensory information to the central nervous system and relay motor messages back from it to the muscles; it also includes the *autonomic* nervous system, which serves many of the body's organs.

4. The brain has three main parts: the *brain stem,* which controls most automatic behavior such as breathing; the *cerebral cortex,* the most highly evolved, outer portion of the brain; and a middle section that includes the *hypothalamus* and *limbic system,* which are important in many motivations.

5. The endocrine system consists of the *endocrine glands* and the *hormones.* The endocrine glands regulate many involuntary body processes such as growth and emotional arousal. The hormones are the glands' chemical messengers.

6. The cerebral cortex has two hemispheres, definable areas where sensory messages enter and motor instructions leave, and areas that play a major role in higher

mental processes such as thinking, memory, and language. For most people, most language functions are "localized" in the left hemisphere. Although damage to the brain may cause a loss of or change in a given mental function, another part of the brain often is able to take over much or all of that function.

7. The brain's two essentially symmetrical hemispheres are connected by the *corpus callosum*. If the callosum is severed, the two brains can act independently. The left hemisphere (in most people) is better at language, math, and other conceptual abilities, whereas the right is more specialized in sensual and perceptual abilities. There is evidence indicating that the two brains work together to provide more efficient processing than would be possible with one brain alone.

8. Perception is the psychological counterpart of the biological processes of sensation, in which receptors in the eyes, ears, nose, tongue, and skin relay information to the central nervous system.

9. Vision is normally the result of light passing through the cornea and lens of the eye to the *retina*, where it stimulates receptor cells called *rods* (which register brightness) and *cones* (which are responsible for color vision and acuity). From the rods and cones, messages are relayed by retinal *bipolar cells* to the *optic nerve*, which conveys them to the brain.

10. Light waves have two primary characteristics: *intensity*, which corresponds roughly to our experience of brightness, and *wavelength*, which determines color. Different types of cones in the retina are most sensitive to different wavelengths of light: The blue, green, and yellow receptors are most easily fired by wavelengths corresponding to those colors. Color detector cells, such as the "yellow plus, blue minus," fire in response to certain wavelengths and are inhibited by others. A light-sensitive chemical in the retina called *rhodopsin* enables the eye to adapt to varying intensities of light.

11. In addition to color detectors in the retina, humans and other animals have specialized cells at various levels of the visual system which respond to specific stimuli. Examples are "bug detectors" in the optic nerve of the frog, and "line detectors" in the cortex of the cat.

12. Hearing is our perception of the ear's processing of sound waves, which are funneled through the outer ear to the eardrum and middle ear, where they are amplified. In the inner ear or *cochlea* the vibrations stimulate receptor cells, which transmit them as electrical messages via the auditory nerve to the brain.

13. Like light waves, sound waves have intensity or *amplitude*, which relates to perceived loudness, and wavelength or *frequency*, which determines pitch. Detector cells in the auditory nerve and cortex respond to some frequencies and are inhibited by others.

14. Taste and smell are both stimulated by chemicals. Taste buds — receptors in the tongue — register four sensations: salty, sweet, sour, and bitter. The flavors we taste are mixtures of those four flavors, plus additional information provided by our more complex sense of smell. The sense of touch consists of receptors in the skin. These receptors register pressure, pain, heat, and cold.

USING PSYCHOLOGY

You can easily study your senses of smell and taste, and their interrelationship. Prepare small amounts (a quarter-cup or less) of the following substances and put them separately into small cups; label the cups according to the following number code:

1. sweet sugar-water (sugar completely dissolved)
2. vinegar (diluted with an equal part of water)
3. salty salt water (salt completely dissolved)
4. strong black coffee (no sugar or cream)
5. "flat" cola soft drink (no longer bubbly)
6. lemon juice (diluted with an equal part of water)
7. chicken broth (the kind made from a chicken cube and boiling water)
8. cranberry juice (slightly diluted with water)

Have all the substances at room temperature for the experiment.

Try to get some friends to participate in the tasting session with you. When the taster's eyes are closed (or a blindfold is on) to make sure he or she does not use the color of the liquid as a clue to its identity, have the taster first smell each of the liquids one by one and try to identify them. Make sure the taster takes several breaths of fresh air before trying to identify each substance. Write down the taster's responses by scent alone for each substance. Next, have the taster (again with eyes closed or blindfolded) hold his or her nose. Put about one-half teaspoon of the liquid into the taster's mouth, and ask him or her to identify it. The taster must keep his or her nose closed during this phase of the experiment. Write down the taster's response by taste alone to the substance. Then give another half-teaspoon of the same liquid and have the taster release his or her nose so that both senses can work together. Again, record the taster's response to the substance using both taste and smell together. Have the taster drink some water and wait a time for the previous taste

sensation to go away, and then repeat the taste-only and taste-plus-smell tests with the other substances. Score all the tasters' responses and compare performance for smell alone, taste alone, and taste-plus-smell tests. Do your results indicate that taste and smell together are more accurate than either of the two senses alone? It is somewhat difficult to break down the substances tested into the four basic sensations—sweet, sour, salty, and bitter—because some are very complex tastes; one could say, however, that primarily sweet substances are 1 and 5; primarily sour substances are 2 and 6; primarily salty substances are 3 and 7; primarily bitter substances are 4 and 8, though 8 is also sweet (we don't consume many truly bitter substances). Are any of these more or less basic taste sensations better perceived by smell or by taste alone than the others? Why did we test only liquids in this taste experiment? What is another way we could have controlled for the color clue to a liquid's identity besides not letting the taster see the liquid? Do you think you could break down your taste sensation of a complex substance like a tea, chocolate milk, tomato soup, or wine into its basic taste sensations? Remember from Chapter 1 that this is what early psychologists tried to do with the method of introspection.

Have you ever observed an expert wine taster or studied wine tasting? Wine tasters use their senses of smell and taste as well as vision in very obvious ways. They swirl the wine in its glass, watch it and sniff it; they take a good sip and swish it around in their mouths—practically gargle it—to ensure that all their taste buds located in different parts of the tongue are exposed to the wine and to heighten the scent as well. Wine tasters try to identify several basic taste components of wine and use them to classify and evaluate wines. Particularly because of the booming California wine industry, the art of wine tasting has recently been receiving increased scientific attention.

SUGGESTED READINGS

Carlson, N. R. *Physiology of behavior.* Allyn & Bacon, 1977.
One of many excellent textbooks on biological psychology; comprehensive, rather technical, highly reliable.

Gregory, R. L. *Eye and brain.* 3rd ed. McGraw-Hill, 1978.
A fascinating introduction to both the biology and the psychology of seeing, suitable for artists and architects as well as psychologists.

Teyler, T. J. *A primer of psychobiology.* Freeman, 1975.
A brief, entertaining, nontechnical introduction to biological psychology.

Valenstein, E. S. *Brain control.* Wiley, 1973.
A thoughtful and interesting discussion of the myths and realities of behavior control through brain surgery or electrodes implanted in the brain.

Looking at Ourselves

The incredible photographs of Lennart Nilsson give us a vivid sense of some of the body parts we discuss in this book, a sense that words could not possibly convey. Nilsson, an award-winning Swedish photographer, personally developed many of the lenses and techniques that made these pictures possible. His book, **Behold Man** *(Little, Brown and Company, 1974), is highly recommended.*

Following the Nilsson photographs is a section on the perception of color. In addition to learning something about color, you can find your own blind spot and test yourself for colorblindness.

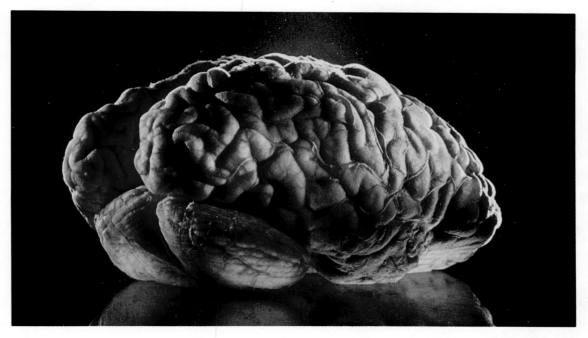

Plate 1. *A human brain. Notice the convoluted (wrinkled) surface of the cortex. This allows a greater amount of cortex to fit inside the small space of the skull. Also visible are the two hemispheres of the cerebellum at the lower left.*

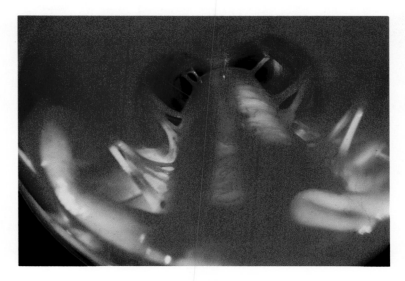

Plate 2. *The spinal cord. The cord fills the tunnel formed by the vertebrae of the backbone. Nerve fibers, carrying sensory messages in and sending motor instructions out, can be seen along the side of the cord.*

Plate 3. *A neuron (nerve cell). This neuron is one of the motor cells of the cortex, which have unusually large cell bodies and long axons. (For a diagram of a neuron, see Figure 2.1 on p. 44.)*

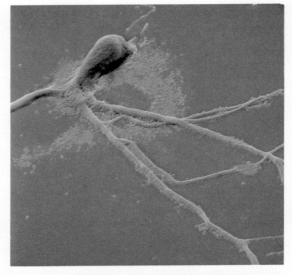

Plate 4. *Neuron-muscle connections. This photo shows a number of axons leading to and crossing muscle cells. Nerve impulses result in the release of chemicals at the junction of neuron and muscle, causing the muscle to contract.*

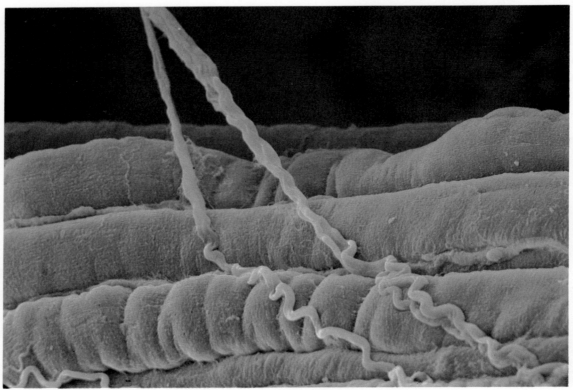

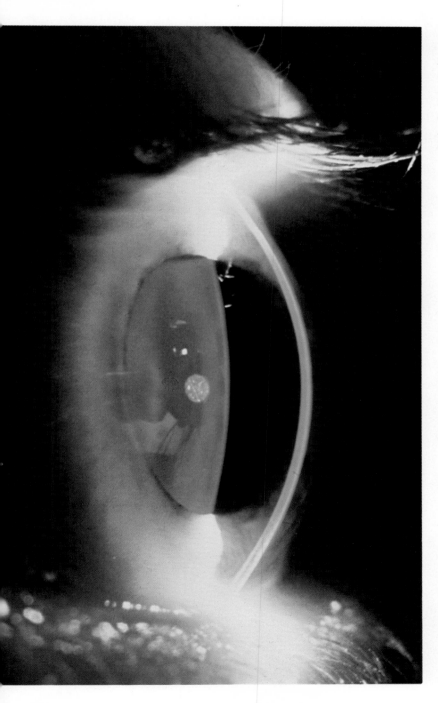

Plate 5. *The eye in profile. The transparent outer surface is the cornea. Behind that is the lens surrounded by the iris, a membrane that can constrict or expand the size of the opening (pupil) in front of the lens. Thus, the amount of light entering the eye is controlled.*

Plate 6. *On the left, fat cones and slender rods. Rods and cones are the actual receptor cells in the visual system. Rods are very sensitive and effective in dim light; cones provide color vision and other functions. (See pp. 62–63.)*

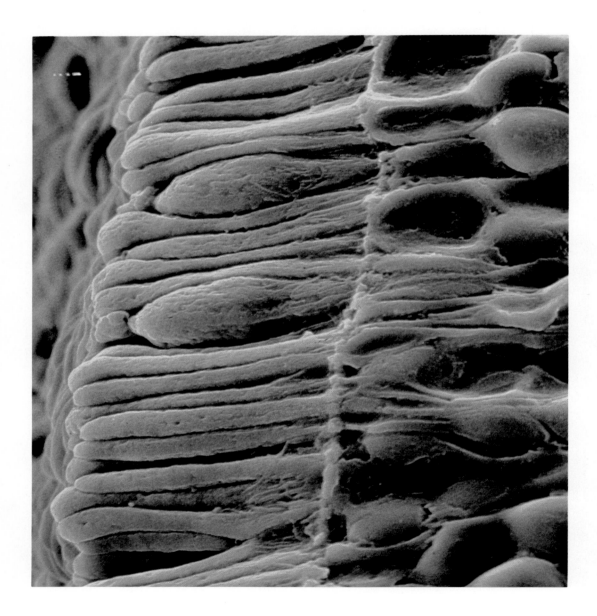

Plate 7. *Inverted images and a blind spot. The subject was looking at a girl holding a telephone. Like any lens, the lens of the eye turns the image upside down. Notice also the yellow circle to the right. This is the region of the eye from which nerve fibers and blood vessels pass through into the body. There are no receptors there; it is a visual blind spot.*

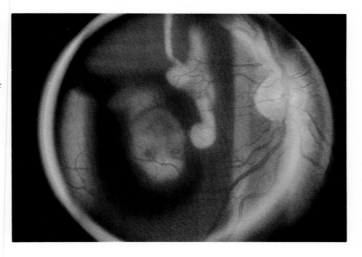

Plate 8. *Taste buds, magnified and magnificent. These bulb-shaped structures give the tongue its rough surface. They are the sensory receptors for taste and, in addition, help mix food and carry it back toward the throat.*

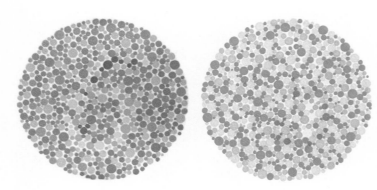

Plate 9. *Colored dot patterns like these are used to test for different kinds of colorblindness. A person with normal vision will see 6 and 15 in the circles; someone with red-green colorblindness would see different numbers or no numbers at all. The reproductions of color tests cannot be used for a conclusive test. The examples shown here are only two of fifteen charts necessary for a complete color recognition examination.* (See p. 65.)

Plate 10. *The blind spot is a small area on the retina where everyone is blind; it is the place where nerve fibers leave the eye. To demonstrate your blind spot, hold the book about 15 inches in front of you. Close your left eye and look at the eight ball. Move the book back and forth until the cue ball disappears. Now close your right eye and look at the cue ball, adjusting the distance until the eight ball disappears. Notice that even when the stimulus is not seen because of the blind spot, we do not perceive a hole in our field of vision; we creatively "fill in" the hole with the background pattern.*

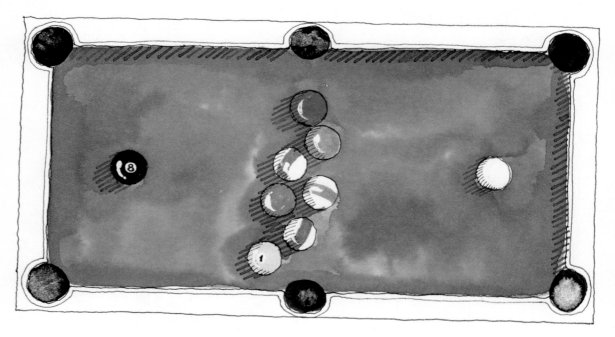

Plate 11. *In daylight, cone cells in the retina of the eye do most of the work of vision, and they allow color perception. At night, rod cells take over; they are more sensitive but do not process color information. Notice how color adds to the perception of depth as well as making the visual world more interesting.*

Plate 12. *A color afterimage is a fleeting image of the stimulus you have been looking at, but often in the complementary colors. Focus on the center of the flag for a few minutes, then shift your gaze to the dark spot in the blank rectangle below. The afterimage of the flag should look very familiar.*

Behavior Genetics: Chromosomes and You

As psychologists try to determine the reasons people behave in a certain way, they are constantly faced with the issue of *heredity versus environment* or, more poetically, *nature versus nurture.* You, for example, are more intelligent than the average person, as evidenced by your status as a college student. Why? Because your parents were bright? Or because your environment—your home, your family life, your friends, your education, your nutrition—was better than average? Can we answer such questions?

THE NATURE OF NATURE

At the moment of conception, a tiny tadpole-shaped sperm cell from the father releases 23 microscopic particles called *chromosomes.* The father's contribution combines with 23 chromosomes from the mother's ovum, or egg, to form the first cell of a brand-new human being. This cell, like

all body cells except sperm and eggs, contains 23 pairs of chromosomes. As this first cell divides and thus multiplies, the same 23 pairs of chromosomes are duplicated in each new cell.

Each chromosome is composed of several thousand *genes*. Genes, in turn, are made of deoxyribonucleic acid, which mercifully almost everyone calls DNA. DNA is the chemical of heredity, the carrier from parent to child of the genetic code that determines each individual's characteristics.

Genes also form pairs, one from the father's chromosome and one from the mother's. Each gene pair influences a particular characteristic—hair or eye color, for instance. Some genes are *dominant* or *recessive*, meaning they either predominate over or defer to other genes governing the same characteristic. If the person has two dominant genes for a certain characteristic, or one dominant and one recessive, that characteristic will reflect the dominant gene. Only if two recessive genes are paired will the recessive gene determine the characteristic. For example, the eye color "brown" is determined by a dominant gene, "blue" by a recessive gene. If a boy inherits two brown genes, he will have brown eyes. If he inherits one brown and one blue gene, the dominant brown gene will still determine his eye color. Only if he inherits two blue genes will he have blue eyes.

A boy with one brown and one blue gene will have brown eyes. The recessive blue gene, however, may affect his offspring. If he marries a blue-eyed woman, about half of their children will get his dominant brown gene (along with a blue gene from their mother) and have brown eyes. The other half will get his recessive blue gene and have blue eyes.

Genes and Mental Disorders

Several rare mental disorders are known to result from having one abnormal gene. One disorder that is caused by a dominant gene is Huntington's chorea; more on that in a moment. Disorders caused by a recessive gene must await the marriage of two people who both transmit the gene to their unfortunate child. Intermarriage between close relatives increases the chances of transmission of a recessive gene, as in the case of Joan Austin (Nyhan, 1976). Joan's parents were second cousins. They worried about possible genetic problems, but their daughter's radiant good health allayed their fears. After earning a college degree, Joan married Jim Austin, her childhood sweetheart, and had two delightful children. She had a good job as an editor with a publishing firm. Life was good.

About five years after their marriage, Jim began to notice changes in Joan, especially in her appearance. Things came to a head one night at a dinner party given by one of Jim's business associates. Before leaving home, Jim noted that Joan looked rather disheveled, almost slovenly — very unlike her. He wrote it off as due to a hectic day at the office. At the party, Joan had a cocktail or two, then began to stumble and lurch noticeably. Was she drunk? During the meal Joan showed no interest in eating; her speech was slurred. Jim's associates glanced at him knowingly, with sympathy. Embarrassed, the Austins left early.

In the following weeks, Joan's behavior deteriorated rapidly. She neglected her work and her family. Her eyes were often glazed, her clothing messy, her movements awkward. Her mind was vacant. Jim was stunned, frightened, alarmed. He concluded that she had become an alcoholic and that her brain was being affected. Or perhaps she had gone mad. Finally, one day he got a call from Joan's office. Her coworkers had sent her home "drunk." Jim raced home to find her on the floor, trembling and incoherent. He took her to the hospital.

Joan's physicians could find no physical cause for her symptoms and tentatively diagnosed her ailment as schizophrenia, a severe mental illness. They suggested hospitalization and shock therapy. Jim insisted they test her liver for cirrhosis; they did and Jim's worst fears were confirmed: Joan's liver was badly scarred. Mental illness induced by alcoholism!

Joan might still be in a hospital somewhere had not a neurologist, conducting some final tests, noticed a greenish ring in her eyes, a sure sign of copper poisoning. After a few more tests, Joan's physicians had a definitive diagnosis: the Wilson disease, known to be caused by a rare recessive gene. The Wilson disease disrupts copper metabolism, with the result that copper accumulates in the brain and liver, poisoning them. The behavioral symptoms are similar to those of alcohol intoxication, but of course there was no way Joan could "sleep it off." Eventually the copper deposits would have killed her.

Fortunately for the Austins, a drug is available that absorbs and eliminates excess copper from the body. Joan's improvement with this drug was startling. In a few months, she was the same sparkling, intelligent young woman she was before. She and Jim threw a big dinner party for Jim's business associates, the same ones who had witnessed her "drunken" behavior the previous year. It was a time of relief and joy.

Both of the Austins' children have been tested and are known to have inherited Joan's recessive gene that produces the Wilson disease, but Jim is apparently not a carrier. With a normal (dominant) gene from their father, Mark and Linda Austin will probably lead completely normal lives. Unless they marry someone who also carries a defective gene, their children also will be safe.

Arlo Guthrie's Long Wait

Woody Guthrie was one of America's greatest folk singers. When he was in his early thirties, his natural moodiness began to deepen. Depression, outbursts of violence, a staggering gait, an unreliable memory, disturbed logic—all uncharacteristic of him—were eventually diagnosed as Huntington's chorea, a disease marked by progressive degeneration of brain tissue. Guthrie lived to the age of 55, spending the last ten years or so in hospitals. At the end, bedridden and immobile, he was able to communicate only by blinking his eyes.

Now our attention turns to Woody Guthrie's son, Arlo Guthrie, also an exceptional folk singer. We know Huntington's chorea is caused by a single dominant gene. Will Arlo suffer and die from the disease, as his father did? He has a 50:50 chance. Either he inherited the chorea-causing gene from the gene pair in his father's chromosomes, or he received the normal gene in the pair. Unfortunately, Arlo won't know for sure unless he actually begins to manifest symptoms of the disease. Unlike many genetically induced abnormalities, Huntington's chorea becomes apparent only later in life, in the thirties or forties or, in a few cases, not until the fifties or later. So Arlo Guthrie waits and worries. It's difficult. One becomes depressed—is it the first sign? Late at night, tired and full of wine, speech is slurred—normal or abnormal? A violent outburst—anger or Huntington's chorea?

And children. Should Arlo have children? The late onset of the disease may make it impossible to wait for certain diagnosis before having children. Arlo's children would have a slightly better chance (75:25) than he does of being normal, because they have an even chance of having a normal father (we don't yet know) and, if he does have the bad gene, an even chance of getting his normal gene nevertheless. It's like flipping a coin. Arlo's coin is still in the air, a 50:50 chance. Arlo's children's coin is flipped twice, once for Arlo, once for themselves. One chance in four of tossing two tails in a row. One chance in four of having children with a lethal brain disease. What would you decide?

Sex-linked Genes

Of the 23 pairs of chromosomes, one pair is called the sex chromosomes because it determines the sex of the child. Females normally have two relatively large chromosomes called X chromosomes (X is for "unknown," because their existence was discovered before their function). Normal males have one X chromosome paired with a much smaller Y chromosome. When a male's germ cells split to form sperm, half receive

[handwritten margin notes: Female / 2 Large / X chromosomes]

[handwritten margin notes: Male / one X chro / with 2 Y chromosomo]

an X chromosome, half a Y chromosome. If the female's egg is fertilized by the sperm with the X chromosome, a daughter is conceived. If the sperm with the Y chromosome connects, a son will appear in nine months.

In addition to the sex of the child, the sex chromosomes carry genes that determine a variety of other characteristics. In terms of behavior genetics, the sex chromosomes are interesting because the stubby little Y chromosome of males is the only chromosome in the 23 pairs that does not match its partner in size and function; it apparently has very few genes (Nyhan, 1976). Thus a recessive gene on the X chromosome of a male is typically expressed in behavior, because there is no balancing normal gene on the Y chromosome to inhibit it. Females must pair two recessive genes if the gene is to affect behavior, the same situation as exists in all the other chromosomes of both sexes. In males, a defective gene on the X chromosome has the show all to itself.

In practical terms, this means that a number of characteristics are found predominantly in males. There is a whole class of genetic disorders that are for this reason called sex-linked (sometimes, X-linked). Hemophilia, a defect in the ability of the blood to clot after injury, sometimes called "bleeder's disease," is one such disorder. Colorblindness is another, as is a type of "night blindness," the inability to see clearly in low illumination.

Abnormal Chromosomes

Some genetically based disorders are caused by an unusual number of chromosomes in a "pair." Some individuals have only a single X chromosome: Described genetically as XO, their external genitalia are female, but their ovaries are poorly developed and they are sterile. XO individuals usually have normal intelligence, but they usually are very short.

Certain men (about one in a thousand) have an extra Y chromosome and are designated XYY. About ten years ago, there was a flurry of interest in these men, who, with an extra "male" chromosome, were suspected of being "super males." Early studies (Jacobs et al., 1965) showed them to be taller on the average and less intelligent than average. They showed up in prison populations and mental hospitals in disproportionate numbers, often for violent or sexual offenses.

Later studies began to question the view of XYY men as caldrons of seething sexuality and violence. New evidence showed many XYY men to be leading quite normal lives (Owen, 1972; Nyhan, 1976). Among the XYY males studied, researchers have found a full spectrum of personality types and a generally normal range of most personality characteristics.

[handwritten margin note: X connection forms girl / Y connection forms boy]

There seems to remain a very slightly increased probability of antisocial behavior among XYY men, but this may not be genetically based. Chromosomal abnormalities are generally more frequent in social groups where the parents suffer from poor diet and inadequate medical care; also, abnormalities are somewhat more frequent when the parents were very young or very old. Both these conditions are probably most prominent in communities that through purely environmental means breed antisocial sexual and aggressive behavior. Thus, in a "natural experiment" comparing XYY men to normal XY men, we cannot be sure whether observed differences are due to genetic differences or to some other, nonbiological reason.

Chromosomal abnormalities, incidentally, are genetic, but they are not inherited in the usual sense. An XYY male's son is no more likely than an XY male's son to be XYY.

Another well-known chromosomal abnormality involving an extra chromosome (in a pair other than the sex chromosomes) is Down's syndrome, formerly called mongolism because of the so-called mongoloid, or oriental, appearance of the eyes of the child so afflicted. Children with Down's syndrome are mentally retarded, usually with an IQ of around 40 (100 is normal). They are invariably described as "appealing and lovable," but they are susceptible to disease and often suffer malformations of important organs as well; many die in childhood. The incidence of Down's syndrome is highly correlated with the age of the mother, suggesting that imperfectly formed egg cells in the older mother are at fault. For a mother age 25, the chances of a Down's child are one in 2000; for a mother age 35, one in 250; for a mother age 45, one in 40 (Nyhan, 1976).

Heredity and Environment: The Case of PKU

Many people believe that if a disorder is genetic, nothing can be done about it. By no means is this always the case. A benevolent environment very often prevents the potential life disruptions a genetic defect can otherwise cause, just as a particularly unfortunate living situation can aggravate a very minor disorder. Consider near-sightedness, which is probably genetically based in most people who suffer from it. With proper eyeglasses (an environmental factor), their lives are not so different from their normally sighted peers. But think what problems near-sighted people must have encountered in ages past, before corrective lenses were available!

A classic example of the effect of environment on a genetic disorder is phenylketonuria, or PKU. Caused by a single recessive gene, PKU is marked by the body's inability to convert a chemical found in many foods to a harmless form. The toxic chemical accumulates and prevents brain cells from developing normally, resulting in severe mental retardation — *unless* . . . If the diet of the child with PKU is carefully arranged to keep the dangerous chemical at acceptable levels, he or she will develop normally. PKU can be identified at birth by a simple blood test, so a child in danger can begin the diet immediately, before brain damage occurs. The diet need not continue for life; in most cases, it can be discontinued around the age of six or seven, when brain development is mostly complete. A woman with PKU, however, must return to the diet if she decides to have a baby, for the toxic chemical in her blood can damage the brain of the fetus.

Complex Human Behaviors

Most of the disorders we have been discussing have been traced to single defective genes or to specific chromosomal abnormalities. Most human characteristics, however, are determined by the combined action of many genes. In addition, the genetic factors interact with environmental factors (as in the case of PKU) to create such an intricate web of nature and nurture that even the most persistent of scientists find it difficult to untangle.

Consider human mental abilities. Although the action of a single gene can cause mental retardation, in most cases a person's intelligence is determined by many genes acting in combination with environmental factors such as nutrition, education, and parent-child relationships. The same is true of many personality traits; whether a person is quiet and thoughtful (introverted) or outgoing and gregarious (extraverted), for example, seems to be determined partly by genetic factors and partly by environment. Certain types of mental illness — schizophrenia, for example — follow subtle family patterns that suggest some genetic influence. The tendency to develop diabetes appears to be inherited, but a good environment (including a proper diet) can prevent its expression. Many of these complex behaviors and disorders will be discussed in more detail in later chapters, and the evidence for genetic influence will be reviewed at that point.

What Does "Evidence for Genetic Influence" Mean?

Most of the evidence that a characteristic is caused or influenced by a gene (or a combination of genes) comes from family patterns of inheritance. In short, a genetic detective looks for evidence that "it runs in the

family." If a certain characteristic is the result of a dominant gene, that gene will be found in approximately half of the children of any person carrying the gene. A recessive gene, on the other hand, will generally not become apparent until two people carrying it marry; then approximately a quarter of their children will get two recessive genes, one from each parent, and manifest the trait. Another two quarters of their children will be carriers—they will have the gene but not the characteristic—and can be followed through subsequent generations. Humans have small families, and human generations span relatively long periods of time (compared to fruit flies, for example, which are often used in genetic research), so the actual process of identifying a dominant or recessive gene in humans may be very time-consuming and difficult. But, in theory, single-gene influences follow straightforward laws of probability.

For most characteristics, those which are influenced by several genes in combination with environmental factors, the family patterns are more complex. Researchers look for evidence that people who are closely related are more alike than people who are less similar genetically. The problem they invariably encounter is that close relatives also have more similar environments than distantly related people. For example, we might look at a family of deadbeats and drunkards and conclude that alcoholism is genetically determined. But it may be that, in that family, irresponsible drinking is permitted, even encouraged, and that (in that family at least) alcoholism is mostly determined by such social, environmental factors.

Absolute distinctions between genetic and environmental influences are rarely if ever possible, but close attention to the patterns of similarity within a family often gives clues to an inherited trait. For example, siblings (brothers and sisters) share about 50 percent of their genes, as do parents and children; genetically, the parent-child relationship is equal to the sibling relationship. All members of the family share some aspects of the social environment, but the shared social influences of siblings, who are in the "child subculture," are slightly different from the shared social influences of parents and children. If the correlation of a trait between siblings is about the same as between parent and child, despite these differences in environmental pressures, we suspect genetic influence. Thus, if one sibling has a cleft palate, the chances of another sibling having a cleft palate are 4 percent; if a parent has a cleft palate, the chances of his or her child having one are also 4 percent. Similarly, the correlation between IQ scores of siblings averages 0.55; between parents and children, 0.50 (Jensen, 1969). These correlations suggest genetic influence.

In their never-ending attempts to sort out the relative effects of heredity and environment, researchers are particularly fond of comparisons between identical and fraternal twins. Identical twins develop from the same fertilized egg; somehow when the egg begins splitting in the process that normally results in a single, multi-celled individual, the first two identical cells separate and form two *genetically identical* individuals. Fraternal twins develop from two different eggs fertilized by two different sperm and, although they are born at the same time, they are genetically no more similar than any other pair of siblings.

Both identical and fraternal twins, however, develop in very similar environments. They shared the fluid environment inside the mother's womb; they have the same birthday; the quality of schools when they reach the first grade is the same for both members of the pair; etc. Comparing identical twins to fraternal twins, therefore, is an approximation of the ideal experiment, in which environment is approximately equal but genetic factors differ. It is only an approximation, of course, for identical twins differ from other people in more than their genes. Their striking physical similarity, for example, leads others to respond to them almost as two versions of the same person. Fraternal twins, who usually look quite different from each other, seldom draw that kind of reaction.

Another popular group in genetic studies is adopted children. They are compared with their adoptive parents, with whom they share a social environment, and with their biological parents, with whom they share their genes, to see which set of parents they resemble more. A study of possible genetic involvement in schizophrenia, for example, compared the biological and adoptive families of a group of schizophrenic children (Rosenthal, 1971). The rate of schizophrenia among the biological relatives was three times greater than in the adoptive families. This is evidence for genetic influence in schizophrenia.

GENETIC COUNSELING: PROMISES AND THREATS

Do you ever have the feeling we know a little too much about some of the laws that govern the universe and its inhabitants? In the field of genetics, we know quite a bit about the basic mechanisms of genetic transmission, enough that it is possible to counsel prospective parents about certain genetic risks. We can tell an older potential mother what her chances are of having a child with Down's syndrome. We can tell a man whose father had Huntington's chorea the chances of producing offspring with the disease. In the case of some genetic diseases—an example is sickle-cell anemia, a disease of the blood found almost exclusively among blacks—simple tests can tell us if a parent is a carrier of a dangerous recessive gene, even though the parent is protected from the disease by the other normal gene in the pair. If both parents are carriers, the risk is 25 percent for each child.

On top of this knowledge, we pile a simple medical technique called amniocentesis which, in some cases, enables us to know for certain if the fetus suffers from a suspected genetic abnormality. Amniocentesis involves inserting a long needle through the abdomen of the pregnant mother into the uterus. Some of the fluid surrounding the developing fetus—which contains cells from the fetus—is extracted and analyzed. Chromosomes are relatively easy to analyze, so we can tell if the fetus has Down's syndrome and will be born severely retarded. From further biochemical analyses, we can often detect the unusual amounts of chemicals that are tell-tale symptoms of certain genetic diseases.

Sometimes amniocentesis provides information that improves the prediction, without establishing a genetic disease for certain. Women who carry the sex-linked gene for hemophilia may be relieved to know their fetus is female, for females are protected by their father's good gene even if they inherit their mother's bad gene. A male fetus gains no protection from his father's stubby little Y chromosome and faces a 50:50 chance of being a bleeder.

What does one do with such information? If informed of a significant genetic risk before pregnancy, the parents may decide to forego biological parenthood; many adopt children instead. Others go ahead with the pregnancy and abort the fetus if amniocentesis shows their worst fears confirmed. Every day couples are making decisions about abortions because of genetic information; even in the worst of cases, the decision is never easy. The guilt of the parents is usually intense and may require psychotherapy.

And one more issue, from this vast Pandora's Box we've opened: What are the responsibilities of a geneticist who has information about the possible increased risks of genetic disease faced by certain individuals, their children, or their relatives? Should you give them the information and let them make the decisions? Most people cannot understand the information — carriers, who are healthy, almost invariably think they have the disease, for example — but the geneticist cannot play God, making decisions for others, right? I believe that. But I waver in some cases. Consider the people who suffer from a genetic disorder known as "testicular feminization" (Restak, 1975). These people appear to be perfectly normal women, but they are in fact genetically male. They are usually detected when they seek a gynecologist's help because they cannot become pregnant. How does one tell a happily married "woman" that "she" is, in chromosomal fact, a man? How does one tell the husband? To further complicate matters, these she-men face a very high risk of cancer of the imperfectly formed (male) sex organs inside their bodies; they should be warned, they should be examined frequently. And — who said life is simple? — their relatives also face a high risk of the same problem. The patient's "sisters" (who are probably in their late teens or early twenties) may also be genetically male and subject to cancer.

I don't know. I think these people have a right to the truth. But would you mind doing the telling?

SUGGESTED READINGS

Nyhan, W. L. *The hereditary factor.* Grosset & Dunlap, 1976.
  An excellent introduction to genetics, written for the intelligent layperson by a major researcher.
Restak, R. The danger of knowing too much. *Psychology Today,* September 1975.
  An M.D. discusses the perils of genetic counseling.

PART

2 Psychological Processes

Like the biological processes, the psychological processes make behavior possible. They are the ways we take in information, store it, and use it. First we will look at perception: how we become aware of our environment and how we construct internal representations of it. (Seeing is believing, isn't it? Or is it?) Next, the study of learning and memory deals with how we store information and how and when it comes out again in behavior. You will learn why it is hard to poison a rat, and how to improve your memory.

Behind all our actions lies motivation. In Chapter 6 we will try to pin down that elusive concept, as we look at human motivations ranging from basic biological needs, such as hunger, to complex social and personal needs, such as the need for achievement and the need to be the best one can be. Then in Chapter 7 we examine language and communication—how we learn to speak, and why our facial expressions sometimes speak louder than words. One of the most important human behaviors, language is also uniquely human—or is it?

Behavioral Objectives

1. Describe the differences and similarities between hallucinations and perception.
2. Identify the general perceptual principle stressed by Gestalt psychologists, and list and describe some phenomena which demonstrate that principle.
3. List monocular and binocular cues that allow us to perceive depth.
4. Define perceptual adaptation.
5. Define Weber's Law and use it to solve simple problems.
6. List some perceptual phenomena that lead us to believe that perception is an active, constructive process.
7. Identify the approaches or models of visual perception and list their strengths and weaknesses. Answer the following questions about each approach or model:
   a. Is the stimulus broken up into features?
   b. Is the stimulus input matched with an internal model or models?
   c. If so, what kind of internal model or models?
   d. Is the context of the stimulus taken into account?
   e. Is a hypothesis constructed and compared to the input?
   f. How flexible is the approach?
8. Discuss ways in which personality affects our perception.

CHAPTER

3

Perceiving

When my friend Lewie was in his drug phase, he was most intrigued by the so-called hallucinogens (LSD in particular) because they so altered his perception of the world. Colors became more vivid and somehow different in meaning; sounds became sharper, more distinguishable from one another. Food tasted different—the same, but somehow better—and smells could dominate his consciousness if he chose to let them. A touch could produce an orgasm. This was perception, Lewie decided, only more so.

In addition to "more so" perception, Lewie sometimes saw or heard or smelled or touched or tasted things that were not really there—in other words, he had hallucinations. His brain was creating perceptions without much help from sensory input (as it does commonly in dreams), and Lewie found this fascinating—until one night of fright when he hallucinated off and on for four hours, uncontrollably, and the pictures were so terrifying that he swore off LSD at once and for all time. "I was in a barrel," he said later. "I could feel the grain of the wood, smell the wood, everything. The lid was closing on top of me. And somehow I knew—I mean, I *really* knew for certain, and I still believe it—that if I let the lid close, I would never make it back. It would be the end of me. I would be insane for the rest of my life. I *knew* it. I spent the four hours—it seemed like four days—pushing against the lid, and when it was over, I was exhausted. I don't *ever* want to go through that again. That was the worst experience of my life!"

Then Lewie asked, "Is that what schizophrenia is like?"

"Maybe it has some similarities," I replied. "But I doubt that the anxiety could continue at that level for years. And people who are going insane don't often fear going insane; that's more a sign of sanity."

Then Lewie went back to the perceptions. "It was so *real!* It wasn't *as if* I was in a barrel, I *was* in it!"

"Any splinters when you came out of it?" I asked, hoping to elicit a laugh.

But Lewie was serious. "I really did expect to find splinters. Or at least calluses, or red hands, or something. It was that real."

Lewie's experience was unusual, but it seemed very real to him. As Neisser (1967) has pointed out, it is no harder to believe in the apparent reality of a hallucination than to understand ordinary, everyday perception. The essential processes underlying the two may well be very similar. Perception is very much an active, constructive process, nothing like the passive registration of an event we get from mechanical "perceivers" such as cameras and tape recorders. We are very much involved in perceiving our world, using the information from our sensory systems to construct an image or *percept* of "what's out there." The main difference between ordinary perception and a hallucination probably lies in the balance between internal creativity and the influence of external stimuli, with hallucinations leaning more to the creative side.

We will return to some of the more creative aspects of perception later in this chapter. First, though, we will consider the information people use to mold their percepts and some of the basic ways they organize this information into simple patterns.

PERCEPTUAL INPUT

Many psychologists have been interested in the relationship between changes in the environment and the way people experience those changes. Studies of this relationship are called *psychophysical* (psychology related to physics). The topic can get extremely complex, with physical and psychological variations described in complicated mathematical formulas. It is sufficient for our purposes to understand the concepts of absolute threshold, difference threshold, and adaptation.

Absolute and Difference Threshold

For our sensory receptors to be activated and to transmit a signal, they must receive a certain amount of physical energy. The minimum stimulation necessary is called the *absolute threshold.* For example, in a hearing test, the intensity of a tone is gradually increased until you can just hear it. This is the absolute threshold for hearing. The absolute thresholds for vision, smell, and other senses are similarly determined.

There are several complications in the actual determination of thresholds, however. There is of course no single absolute threshold, because people differ in their ability to detect stimuli. Even a single person's absolute threshold varies, so that if a certain stimulus is presented many times, he or she may say "Yes, I heard it" 50 percent of the time and "No, I heard nothing" the other 50 percent of the time. Traditionally the absolute threshold has been defined as the stimulus that is detected 50 percent of the time. The average absolute thresholds for the different senses are portrayed in Table 3.1.

Just as the absolute threshold is the minimum amount of energy a person can perceive, the *difference threshold* is the minimum amount of energy *change* necessary for the person to detect a *change* in his or her psychological experience. Suppose you are

Table 3.1
ABSOLUTE THRESHOLDS FOR DIFFERENT SENSES

Sense	*Detection threshold*
Light	A candle flame seen at 30 miles on a dark clear night.
Sound	The tick of a watch under quiet conditions at 20 feet.
Taste	One teaspoon of sugar in 2 gallons of water.
Smell	One drop of perfume diffused into the entire volume of a 3 room apartment.
Touch	The wing of a bee falling on your cheek from a distance of 1 cm.

From "Contemporary Psychophysics" by Eugene Galanter, in *New Directions in Psychology I*, by Roger Brown, Eugene Galanter, Eckhard H. Hess and George Mandler. Copyright © 1962 by Holt, Rinehart and Winston, Inc. Reprinted by permission of Holt, Rinehart and Winston.

listening to a tone of a certain loudness; how much does the intensity have to increase before you say, "That's louder"? The amount of change is the difference threshold. Like the absolute threshold, the difference threshold is defined as the physical change that is detected 50 percent of the time.

One thing is striking about the difference threshold for any sense: The higher the intensity of the stimulus, the more it must change for the change to be detected. If one trombone is playing, the addition of another will result in a noticeable difference in loudness, but you could not detect the difference between 76 trombones and 77. You can tell the difference between half a pound and a pound of coffee in a store, but not in a 50-pound bag of groceries.

In 1846, a man named Weber discovered that the ratio of the noticeable change to the basic intensity is constant for each sense. You can notice 2 grams added to a weight of 100 grams, so the ratio for judging weights is 2/100. Adding 10 grams to 500 is noticeable, so the ratio is 10/500, which also equals 2/100. This fact, that the *just noticeable difference* (abbreviated jnd) for any sense equals a certain number, a constant, is called Weber's Law. The ratio for each sense is called Weber's Constant.

Weber's Law has been modified in recent years (Stevens, 1962), although it remains a good approximation for all but extremely low- or high-intensity stimuli. Since 1846, this simple law, derived from actual subjects' reports of what they experienced, has been the basis for further research in perception and in many other areas of psychology as well. Weber's Law can also be applied to socially defined stimuli. For example, a raise of 20 cents an hour for a worker earning a dollar an hour is likely to be more satisfying than a 20-cent raise for someone earning $9.37 an hour. The longer a jail sentence, the higher its perceived negative value; but an increase in a short term is more painful than the same increase in a long term (Stevens, 1966).

Adaptation

In the preceding chapter we discussed biological adaptation in the visual system. Adaptive processes such as changes in pupil size and rhodopsin level increase the eye's sensitivity in dim illumination and decrease its sensitivity when the light is intense. The perceptual side of adaptation is related to its biological side: When you walk into a dark theater and your rhodopsin level is low, so is your ability to perceive an empty seat. With regard to perception, then, adaptation refers to less sensitivity after persisting stimulation and more sensitivity after an absence of stimulation.

The visual sense is not the only one that adapts to stimuli. In the olfactory sense (smell), adaptation occurs very rapidly. On entering a room, you may notice an odor, but in a very short time, your awareness disappears. It is nearly impossible to detect your own bad breath because of adaptation, a fact that supports our fears (encouraged by the mouthwash industry) of continually offending others. The sense of pressure also adapts rapidly—any pickpocket knows that the best time to take a man's wallet from his back pants pocket is after he gets up from a chair. The auditory sense, on the other hand, shows very little adaptation.

A major factor in adaptation is variety in stimulation; it is the *constant* stimulus to which the sensory systems adapt. If a room has an odor, you smell it for a while and then your awareness decreases, reviving only if you leave the room for a while and then come back. The eye creates its own variety of stimulation. It continually jiggles, so you never can keep the same stimulus projected on the same spot in the retina.

There had been a suspicion among sensory psychologists that if it were not for the eye's constant jiggling, we would become blind after a moment or two of viewing the same scene. This was a logical hypothesis, one that made for some fascinating debates at professional meetings, but of course it couldn't be tested.

Then in the early 1950s a group of scientists was able to stop the image on the retina from jiggling (Riggs et al., 1953). To do this, they constructed a special contact lens for subjects, one with a mirror attached. An image was projected onto the mirror, reflected to a screen, and reflected back into the eye by a complicated system of additional mirrors. The physics of the system is not important; the effect was to keep the image projected on exactly the same spot in the retina. If the eye moved left, the image moved left, and so forth.

What happened to the percept? As predicted, it disappeared after a few seconds. At least, this statement applies to the early studies, in which the stimulus projected was a simple vertical or horizontal line. Later studies presented more complex stimuli, such as drawings of a face or a printed word (for example, Pritchard, 1961). Percepts of these stimuli also disappeared but in a very strange fashion; meaningful portions of the percept disappeared as units and sometimes reappeared before the whole percept was gone. For example, for one subject, the word BEER became PEER, then BEEP ("B" returns), then BEE, then BE, and then it was gone. Notice that all the altered percepts are real words. Later in this chapter we will investigate why the percept disappeared in this strange Cheshire-cat fashion.

ORGANIZATION IN PERCEPTION

When we ask someone what he or she sees, hears, smells, or, in general, perceives, the question implies that the person can recognize the stimuli as something meaningful: a shooting star, a scream, escaping gas, or whatever. If I ask you, "What was that noise?" I expect an answer like "Sounds like the cat knocked over the flowers," and not

"It was a loud series of sounds, consisting of a thud, a crash, and various tinkling noises." Whenever we perceive stimuli, we organize them into meaningful patterns. How we form these patterns and how we recognize them are the traditional topics of perception psychology.

As I mentioned in Chapter 1, early in its history, psychology was aptly termed "mental chemistry." In the field of perception, percepts were the "molecules" that psychologists hoped to analyze into more basic elements, the "atoms" of perceptual experience. To do this, they asked subjects to introspect—that is, to look inside themselves, to observe their own experience. They were trained to describe *not* what they were perceiving—say, a light bulb—but the more elemental features of the percept—a darkness surrounding a bulging brightness of a certain intensity. According to the introspectionists, the subjects' task was much like that of a chemical technician breaking down water into its constituent elements, hydrogen and oxygen.

A group of German psychologists objected to this view, suggesting that to analyze perception was to lose sight of the important factors—the relationship among elements, the pattern of the whole. These *Gestalt* psychologists (Gestalt is a German word implying emphasis on the whole configuration) set their subjects to reporting what patterns they saw when viewing various collections of stimuli. Their studies have given us considerable insight into how we organize stimuli in perception.

Figure and Ground. The Gestalt psychologists, interested as they were in the perception of figures and patterns, gave us over a hundred principles of pattern formation. Figure-ground organization is one, in many respects the most fundamental, "law of form." In almost every visual percept, part of the "picture" can be considered the *figure,* the primary interest, and the rest the *ground,* or background. The figure appears to be better defined than the more diffuse ground, and it seems to be in front of the ground. That these are perceptual experiences and not intrinsic features of the stimulus itself can be shown by pictures in which either of two patterns can be the figure, with the other playing the supporting role of ground, as in Figure 3.1.

Organizing visual patterns into figure and ground is probably an innate (unlearned) capacity of the human visual system, though what is figure and what is ground depends on what you are paying attention to, as the reversible figure-ground patterns show. People blind from birth who have had their sight restored by surgery do not see as we see; at first, they cannot identify common objects unless they are allowed to touch and feel them; but they do distinguish between figure and ground, even when they do not know what the figure is (von Senden, 1960). Both psychologically and physiologically, figure-ground perceptual organization seems to be a very basic process, primitive perhaps, but underlying the more complex forms of pattern and object perception and recognition.

"Going Together." A number of the other principles discovered by the Gestalt psychologists, especially those which apply to vision, have to do with our perception of elements "going together." That is, the elements seem to be related, and for that reason they form a pattern. Here are four examples (see Figure 3.2).

Figure 3.1   *Two examples of figure-ground relationships. On the top is a painting by Salvador Dali, "The Slave Market with Disappearing Bust of Voltaire." Whether you see two nuns in the center, or a man's head, depends on what you see as figure. At left, whether or not you see a word depends on what you see as figure and as the ground behind it.*

1. *Similarity.* Other things being equal, parts of the stimulus that are *similar* are perceived as going together. The similarity can be in just about any attribute: size, shape, color, or whatever.

2. *Proximity.* Other things being equal, stimuli that are close together are perceived as going together.

3. *Continuation.* Members of a group of stimuli that continue the "logical" direction

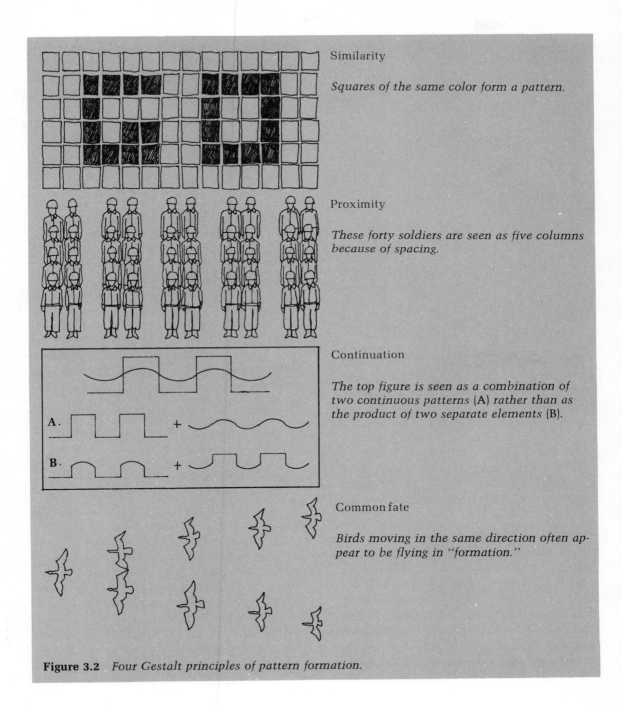

Similarity

Squares of the same color form a pattern.

Proximity

These forty soldiers are seen as five columns because of spacing.

Continuation

The top figure is seen as a combination of two continuous patterns (A) rather than as the product of two separate elements (B).

Common fate

Birds moving in the same direction often appear to be flying in "formation."

Figure 3.2 *Four Gestalt principles of pattern formation.*

Figure 3.3   *Closure. With similar elements in proximity going in a certain logical direction, we fill in or close up incomplete figures.*

of others will be perceived as going together. The logical direction of a straight row, for example, is straight and horizontal, and any stimulus elements that fall on the straight, horizontal line will be perceived as part of the row.

4. *Common fate.* This principle states that if certain stimuli do something together (or have something done to them), they will be perceived as part of a single form. This principle relates to our common experience that movement is helpful in recognizing a stimulus; in a dark alley, we may "perceive" a threatening mugger until the "head" jumps to the left while the "body" remains stationary, and we correctly perceive a cat leaping from a garbage can.

A form that fits the Gestalt principles has several characteristics. It tends to be quite stable, that is, most people see the same pattern at all times; perception does not fluctuate. It is typically judged more aesthetically pleasing than forms that violate the Gestalt principles. Most importantly from a theoretical point of view, the figure is typically perceived as a whole even when it is incomplete. For example, a group of objects arranged in a circle will usually be perceived as a circle, even though there are spaces between them. If we have *similar* elements in *proximity* going in a certain logical direction (*continuity*)—well, with all these laws imposing their dictates, we just fill in any missing aspects in the figure.

Perceptual Constancies

A coin is a good example of a form that follows Gestalt principles. Somehow it manages to maintain its identity even through radical changes. It does not appear to change size as we get farther away; it does not appear to change shape from a circle to an ellipse (football shape) when we view it from different perspectives; and it does not change color in different illuminations. These constancies of size, shape, and color are aspects of *perceptual constancy*, the tendency to perceive a particular stimulus as the same recognizable figure in varied situations.

This is not to say, of course, that we are unaware of variations in stimulation. An object that is shrinking in size, for example, is usually perceived as moving away from us, since we unconsciously interpret the change we see as one of distance rather than size. The perceptual constancies can be used to produce illusions because they are so regular. For example, a good mime or actor can create the impression of walking away without actually increasing distance from us by subtly scrunching up his or her body, making it smaller, while walking in place—and we interpret this as walking away.

When perceptual constancies play tricks on us, we are surprised, sometimes frightened, and often amused. Have you ever tried to take a photograph of yourself by holding the camera in front of your face? If the focus is clear enough, the result can be laughed at for years. The nose is huge, the features are grotesque, and you would guess the subject to be a monster of sorts—if you did not know it to be yourself. But the camera does not lie. That is the image, in terms of relative size of nose, eyes, and ears, that the retina receives in approximately the same location (see Figure 3.4). In other words, if it were not for perceptual ability to adjust,

Figure 3.4 *An inquisitive giraffe demonstrates the breakdown of perceptual constancy.*

somehow, for distance and locations, lovers would appear to each other as monsters every time they moved close enough to kiss (perhaps this is why so many people close their eyes during a kiss!).

Size constancy seems to involve some innate abilities; children as young as eight weeks show evidence of it for objects less than ten feet away (Bower, 1966). But, on the other hand, eight-year-old children still find it difficult to judge the size of objects more than 50 feet away (Zeigler and Leibowitz, 1957), and children will sometimes ask to play with "toy" trains or cars that are actually real objects far away.

It may be that size constancy involves innate abilities at short distances and learned abilities at longer distances (Forgus and Melamed, 1976). At short distances, the brain can use "automatic" information from the eyes, information such as the shape of the lens, the direction the two eyes are pointing (you have to be a little cross-eyed to view something close to you), and the disparity or difference between the images picked up by the two eyes. This information gives clues to distance, but only at short distances; it is something like a camera that focuses precisely at short distances but counts everything over 50 feet as "infinity." At the longer distances, estimates of distance often depend on our learned familiarity with objects and the usual relationships among them.

Consider the case of some African Pygmies who live in forests so dense that it is difficult to see more than a yard or two. With no opportunity to look at anything far away, they might be expected to show a lack of size constancy at long distances, for they have not learned the relationship between apparent size and distance. In a classic report, an adult Pygmy named Kenge was observed in his first visit to the plains outside his native forests (Turnbull, 1961). He spied some buffalo in the distance and asked what they were. When told they were buffalo, twice as large as the buffalo of the forest, he refused to believe; they were insects, he insisted. He got in a car—mystery enough in itself—and was driven to the buffalo. He saw the "insects" growing larger and larger, and he was quite frightened. When he realized they were real buffalo, his fear of the animals disappeared, but he suspected witchcraft as the reason the buffalo had grown so fast. Kenge, after all, was a rational man, and witchcraft was the only reasonable explanation of what he had observed.

We can laugh at Kenge because he sees buffalo in the distance as tiny creatures, but in fact his experience is not so different from our own, in special circumstances. We rarely see objects like trees, houses, and people at very great distances; usually they are cut off from view by closer objects. So when we look at the ground from the window of an airplane, we do not perceive "normal-sized" people, houses, and trees far, far away; we, like Kenge, perceive insects in a kind of miniature doll-house environment. Size constancy breaks down for us, too, in unfamiliar situations, especially at long distances.

Perceptual Contrasts

The perceptual constancies, like the Gestalt principles of figure formation, point to a theory in which perception is active and constructive. We do not see what is really there in terms of actual physical stimuli; instead we use the physical stimuli to construct the percept of, "ah, my lucky coin!" or "good ol' Joe!" This theory of perception also gains support from studies of perceptual contrast, which is the opposite of perceptual constancy. Constancies refer to the same percept in spite of differing stimuli, whereas contrasts involve differing percepts of identical stimuli.

Perceptual contrast refers to the fact that our perception of something is affected by what precedes or surrounds it. A cocker spaniel looks large in the company of mice and tiny amid a herd of elephants. Contrast effects are easily demonstrated for any of the essential characteristics of a stimulus. *Size* contrast we have just seen. A slightly curved surface seems more curved next to a square, an effect of *shape* contrast. Flags are often composed of complementary (opposite) colors because of *color* contrast, which has the effect of making the colors sharper; red, for example, looks redder next to green, its complement, than by itself.

Depth Perception

Like perceptual constancies and contrasts, the perception of depth leads us to a view of perception as an active, constructive process. At any given moment, the image projected on the retina is in two dimensions (length and width). How is it, then, that we perceive depth, the third dimension? In some sense, three-dimensional perceptions are "illusions"; the question is what cues we use to create the proper illusions.

Binocular Cues. Some of the cues on which we base the perception of depth or distance are related to the fact that we have two eyes. One of the most important of the *binocular* (two-eyed) cues is *retinal disparity*, which means that the image on the retina of one eye is slightly different (disparate) from the

Figure 3.5 *The stereoscope takes advantage of the slightly different images each eye receives to create three-dimensional pictures. To see this scene in three dimensions, hold a seven-inch piece of white paper between the two photos so one eye is looking at each photo, With a little patience, you should be able to make the two images fuse into one realistic scene.*

image on the other retina. You can easily demonstrate this fact by looking at, say, a book with one eye closed. Hold the book, vertically, about four or five inches from the open eye so you see only the spine and not the front or back cover. Then close this eye and open the other. Unless the book is very thick, you will now see one of the covers of the book. Because of their different locations in the head, the two eyes receive slightly different pictures of the world. Somehow the brain uses this information to construct a stereoscopic vision of the world in three dimensions.

Monocular Cues. But not all the information about depth is binocular. If you close one

eye, the world does not appear flat. People who have lost an eye have some difficulty at first with tasks like driving a car and playing table tennis, but with practice they can regain most of their former skills. Clearly, then, some information about depth is available to each eye separately. These *monocular* (one-eyed) cues are especially interesting to artists, for it is these they most use to convey solidity and distance in two-dimensional paintings.

Many of the monocular cues have to do with the fact that the dimenions of length and width—or, together, size—decrease with depth or distance. The width of a railroad track decreases with distance, becoming narrower and narrower until the

Figure 3.6   *Artists often use shadow and perspective to create a perception of depth.*

tracks seem to come together and disappear. To draw a box, you have to make the back widths and lengths shorter or it doesn't look right. These are often called cues of *linear perspective* (see Figure 3.6). As an object recedes into the distance and becomes smaller, its individual features draw closer together, making its texture appear denser. This cue is called the *gradient of texture* (see Figure 3.7).

Monocular depth cues not associated with a decrease in size include *changes in color*. Everything far off is more drab; thus an artist adds more blues and purples to dis-

tant colors. This trick was used by painters in the 1500s, so we cannot blame air pollution, although Los Angeles in the distance has no color at all. The use of *shadows* (shading) aids an artist in conveying depth and solidity. If you are moving, the *relative movement* of objects in the distance is a cue to their relative distance from you. Distant objects, like the moon, seem to move in the direction you are moving, whereas closer objects, like trees, move in the opposite direction. Finally, if one object appears to cut off the view of another, the implication is that the "front" one is nearer.

Figure 3.7 *The gradient of texture creates an illusion of distance.*

Unusual Perceptual Organizations

We have given several examples of how people typically combine sensory data into organized perceptions of patterns, depth and distance, and the like. These perceptual acts we perform every day help us to sort out the multitude of stimuli that bombard us, to make sense out of things. Because perception is active and constructive, however, there are also times when our normal perceptual organizations result in inaccurate or ambiguous percepts. Psychologists have discovered several patterns that consistently lead people to "misperceive." Certain stimuli, for instance, lead all or most perceivers to form an inaccurate percept; these are *illusions.* Other stimuli lend themselves to two equally "good" organizations; these are sometimes called *reversible figures.* And some stimuli resist any attempt to organize them into meaningful percepts; these are called *impossible figures.*

Illusions. Illusions vary from simple to complex, from commonplace to rare, and from explainable to still puzzling. The effects of contrast often produce illusions by leading us to misjudge size and other physical attributes. Likewise, violations of the typical relationship between size and distance produce many illusions. In Figure 3.8A, the higher horizontal line appears to be longer because the converging vertical lines tell us (incorrectly) it is more distant. Figure 3.8B compels us to make inaccurate judgments of the distance between various segments of two lines that are in fact parallel, so we see them as curved.

The reasons we form illusions are not entirely clear. Some psychologists believe illusions occur when our innate tendency to perceive stimuli in certain ways runs into unusual stimuli. Other researchers think illusions result from learned reactions to stimuli, which cause us to misinterpret unfamiliar stimuli. The illusions in Figure 3.8, for example, could result from the visual system's normal (innate) processing of lines and angles, and so could the illusion in Figure 3.9. However, the illusion in Figure 3.9 has been one of the favorites of perception psychologists who favor the learning point of view (Gregory, 1970). Notice that the right line of each pair appears to be longer than the left, though they are actually the

Figure 3.8 *Which horizontal line is longer in drawing* A? *Are the horizontal lines parallel or curved in drawing* B?

A.   B.

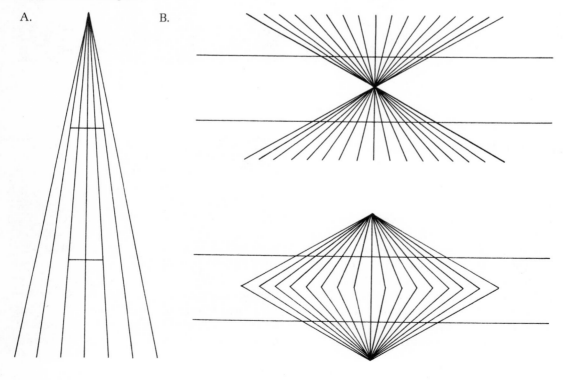

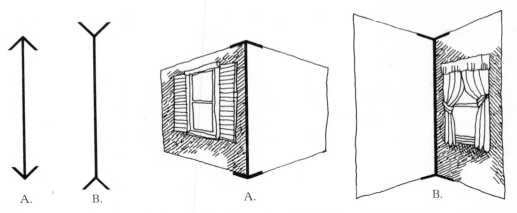

A.   B.   A.   B.

Figure 3.9 *Why does line A appear shorter than line B? Possibly because we are used to seeing A as a near edge and B as a distant one. Not all cultures are fooled by these cues of perspective; see the text.*

same. It has been suggested that this is because the geometry of the right figures is that of a distant edge, whereas the geometry of the left figures is what we typically perceive in a near edge. People who live in rectangular buildings are easily fooled by this illusion, but Africans who live in rounded huts (see Figure 3.10) can make much more accurate judgments of the relative lengths of the two lines (Segall et al., 1963). This suggests that culture and learning affect perception.

The relationship between perceived size and perceived distance has been used by a

Figure 3.10 *Africans who live in rounded huts experience few straight lines and corners and, probably for this reason, are less susceptible to illusions such as those in Figure 3.9.*

psychologist-painter by the name of Ames to create some magnificent illusions; one is shown in Figure 3.11. The boy on the right appears to be much taller than his mother, but in fact he's a normal size child, quite a bit shorter than his mother. Why are we fooled? The Ames room is built to eliminate all visual clues to the fact that the mother is actually standing in a distant corner with a high ceiling. Distorted cues of perspective make what is in fact an oddly shaped room appear rectangular. Instead of perceiving a shorter child closer to us, we perceive the child at the same distance as his mother; therefore, we think, he must be taller. (By walking from the far to the near corner, a person appears to grow in size before our eyes. This illusion has been used on television, on *Star Trek*, for example, to make an "alien" grow rapidly.)

Some illusions involve motion. Most thoroughly studied are those called *phi phenomena* by the Gestalt psychologists, in which one event is perceived as moving into or becoming another. For instance, if two adjacent lights are flashed, first one and then the other, there is a rate of flashing at which subjects perceive a single light moving from the first position to the second. Many advertising signs use this principle. Our perceiving uninterrupted movement in "motion" pictures, which are in fact a series of separate photographs, is also a phi phenomenon.

Another interesting illusion of motion is called the *autokinetic effect.* We can demonstrate it in the laboratory by presenting subjects with a spot of light in an otherwise dark room. Since the subjects cannot see the spot in relation to other features of the environment that would ordinarily define its position, they perceive the light as moving, even though in fact it remains still. Some subjects see a little movement and some see a lot, a fact that at one point stimulated interest in the relationship between how much apparent motion someone sees and his or her personality characteristics. This interest did not result in much productive

Figure 3.11 *Most kids have probably wished they could tower over their parents, but few have had this boy's opportunity. Actually, he's a normal size child and his mother is quite a bit taller than her son. This room was built so that the parent is standing in a distant corner with a higher ceiling. The boy is much closer to the camera and the ceiling is lower at his end of the room. All cues of perspective have been distorted to make the oddly shaped room appear rectangular.*

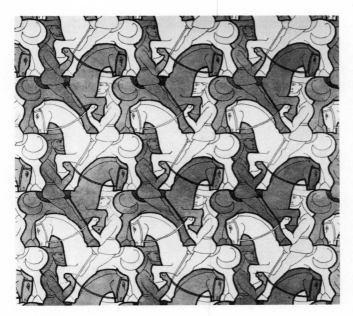

Figure 3.12

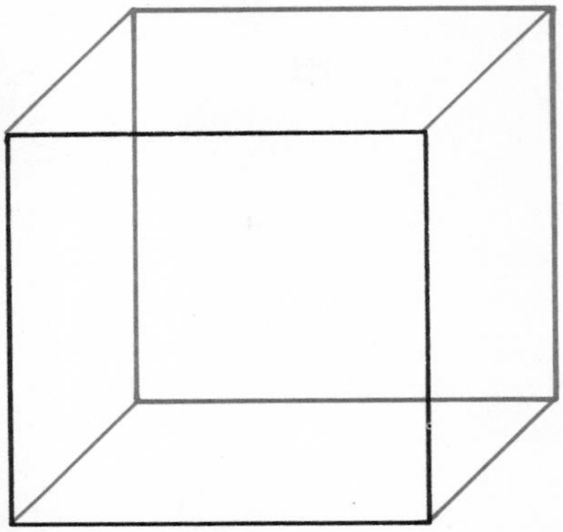

Figure 3.13 *This unassuming little figure is the famous Necker cube. Do you see the square outlined in black as the front of the cube or the back? Stare at it for a minute. Does your answer change?*

research, however, probably because it is so easy to manipulate the amount of apparent motion subjects will see by tactics such as leading them to expect a lot of movement.

In an extreme example of the effect of expectations, subjects were told that the experimenter was writing sentences with the light and that their task was to "read" the sentences. Of course, the light in fact did not move at all, but all subjects perceived words. Many were indignant and angry because such terrible personal things had been written. One subject "saw" the light write out the following:

> When men are tired and depraved, they become mean and callous individuals. When men learn to master their souls, the world will be a more humane and tolerant place in which to live. Men should learn to

control themselves. (Rechtschaffen and Mednick, 1955, p. 346.)

All this from a spot of light that did not move!

Competition Between Organizations. It is not uncommon for sensory input to allow more than one reasonable organization and thus more than one reasonable percept. Figure and ground are often reversible, as shown before in Figure 3.1 and here in Figure 3.12. Figure 3.13, the famous Necker cube, allows two organizations: we can perceive the colored square as either front or back relative to the rest of the cube.

Reversible figures clearly illustrate how we can form different percepts from the same stimuli. The two competing organizations are usually incompatible; you cannot

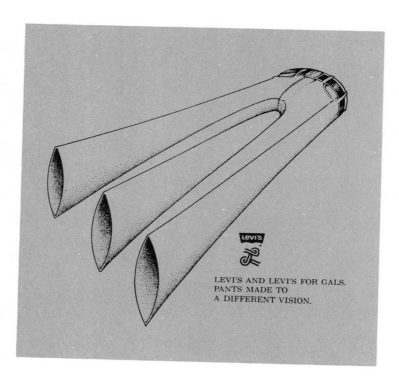

LEVI'S AND LEVI'S FOR GALS.
PANTS MADE TO
A DIFFERENT VISION.

Figure 3.14

see the colored "face" of the Necker cube at the front and at the back at the same time. But the most important point is that you *do* organize the sensory input. When two organizations are possible, they alternate as the percept — the figure never breaks down into a meaningless, unorganized pattern — and one is as satisfying to the eye as the other.

Impossible Figures. The name "impossible figure" might suggest an array of stimuli totally without pattern, making organization impossible, but you can probably guess by now that that is not the case. Organization is imposed on the stimuli by the perceiver; it is a rare form indeed that permits no organization whatsoever. An impossible figure, therefore, is an array of stimuli that leads to

clear and strong and stable percepts; the percept in one portion of the array, however, is incompatible with the organization imposed on another portion. In Figure 3.14, the upper right portion of the picture is perceived as an ordinary pair of pants; the bottom left is organized as three tubes or legs. There is no way to resolve the perceptual discrepancy between two legs at the top and three at the bottom. Organization of the whole is therefore impossible; one has only a sense of something weird.

Hallucinations

Although we have emphasized that forming a percept is active and creative, ordinarily the percept does correspond fairly closely to

A.

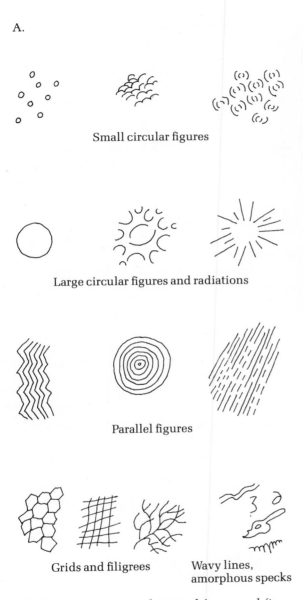

Small circular figures

Large circular figures and radiations

Parallel figures

Grids and filigrees   Wavy lines, amorphous specks

Figure 3.15 *Certain elemental forms and figures turn up repeatedly in visual hallucinations. A few of the most basic are shown in* **A**. *Note how they are combined in the complex hallucination shown in* **B**.

B.

a real object. If it does not, we may call it a *hallucination*. Essentially, a hallucination is a percept with very little relationship to the external pattern of stimulation.

Almost all hallucinations occur in abnormal states of mind. Drugs (LSD and alcohol, for example) can cause hallucinations. The more severe mental illnesses often include hallucinations. A hallucination can be induced by hypnosis, and people who are extremely fatigued from physical activity or who have gone without sleep for a long time often hallucinate. In cultures where hallucinations are valued as "visions," people often combine several of these factors deliberately in an attempt to receive a communication from a god or spirit. They may go without sleep for days, exercise to the point of fatigue, take drugs, and then speak to the trees and sky in words that may have a self-hypnotic effect. In the reality-oriented United States, however, hallucinations are more often feared than revered.

A hallucination is rarely, if ever, created in the mind with absolutely no reference to the external stimuli. More commonly, some isolated feature becomes a base for a vision unrelated to the stimulus pattern as a whole. My friend Lewie told me of one hallucination he experienced, in which a dog was perceived as a cat. He was walking at night with some friends (who, like Lewie, were high on drugs); several yards away, a small animal moved. It was alive, it was small, and it was white; all of these characteristics they accurately perceived. But Lewie saw it as a cat, and said, "Hey, look at the cat!" Influenced by Lewie's perceptual hypothesis, his friends perceived a cat, too. It was *clearly* a cat, with a long tail, short ears, rounded face, and soft fur. As they walked toward the cat in the dim moonlight, suddenly and unexpectedly the cat barked! In that instant, it was transformed into a dog, with a short tail, longer ears, sharper face, and bristly short hair. Lewie was not afraid; he was amazed at the suddenness of the change in perception. The change, no doubt, was an effect of the bark; the percept of a cat could not be maintained in the presence of such incompatible external stimulation.

There are also negative hallucinations—*not* perceiving something that *is* there. A good hypnotic subject, if properly instructed, will not see an object when it is presented to him or her. Mental patients, too, have negative hallucinations; often the objects they cannot see have some painful significance for them—the gravestone of a loved one, for example. Some patients have negative hallucinations for everything, making them effectively blind.

Investigations of negative hallucinations suggest that these subjects get all the information necessary to create the percept, but they unconsciously refuse to create it, so they see nothing (Blum and Porter, 1973). The "blind" patients, for example, will avoid obstacles in their path, even though they do not perceive them; the visual information is there and can be used for self-protection even though it is not used for perception.

Under certain circumstances, such as prolonged exposure to the stimulus, the negative hallucination breaks down, and correct identification becomes more likely (Blum et al., 1978). This is akin to the situation of a "cat" barking; ignoring the "facts"—the external input—becomes too difficult, and the correct perception takes over.

In general, perception and hallucination both involve creating a percept from available information. In ordinary perception, that information comes mostly from the external world, the environment, in the form of features of the sensory input. In hallucinations, the external input plays a lesser role and internal input a greater role. This internal input may include personal conflicts that demand attention, and chaotic, spontaneous patterns of brain activity caused by chemicals, injuries, and the like.

THEORIES OF PERCEPTION AND RECOGNITION

Suppose you are presented with a pen, some common words on paper, or a photograph of your father. You have no difficulty perceiving and recognizing such patterns of stimuli.

If asked, you can provide a lot of related information about the stimuli: the function of pens, the meaning of the words, some foibles of your father. Ordinary perception, easy, straightforward, direct. But how do you do it? Ah, there's a question for you! The nature of perception and recognition has been debated by philosophers for centuries, and now psychologists have joined the debate. So far, we can tell you that perceptual recognition is an incredibly complex process; that is another way of saying that we've made some intriguing discoveries that clear away a little of the fog, but don't expect miracles. We've only been at it for a hundred years!

Psychologists have been interested in each step of the process of perception and recognition (see Figure 3.16). When a stimulus—in our example, a written or a spoken letter A—is registered, it is compared with information in your memory. On the basis of such comparisons, a decision of some sort is made and "recognition" (which may be wrong) occurs. (In ordinary circumstances, these comparisons and decision processes go on rapidly, without awareness or conscious control.) Once you have identified the stimulus, you can tap your memory for related information—in this case, that it is the first letter of the alphabet or that you

Figure 3.16   *General outline of the process of perception and recognition.*

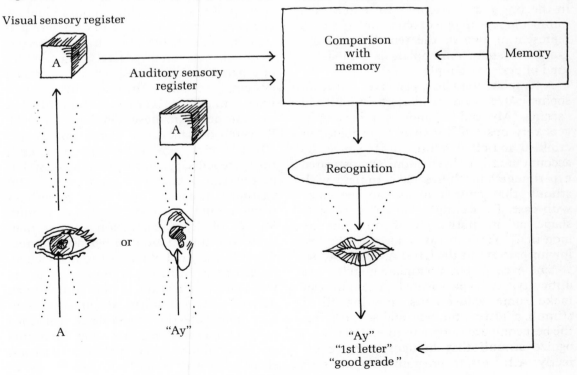

have done quite well on an exam. Psychologists are particularly interested in the nature of the comparison process between sensory input and memory.

Template Matching

If you have a bank checking account, you have noticed the funny-looking numbers at the bottom of your checks. The purpose of these numbers is to identify the bank and your individual account, and they look funny because they are designed to be read by a computer. The means by which the computer perceives and identifies these numbers is called *template matching*, a system that resembles early theories of human perception. Essentially, the machine takes in the image and attempts to match each number in it with one of ten templates, each representing one of the ten digits in our number system. A template is a model, a kind of perfect example.

A template-matching perceiver, however sophisticated, soon encounters difficulty in "seeing." My bank's computer, for example, gets very upset if my checks are folded or crinkled and often refuses to recognize the account number. Even more sophisticated experimental machines have trouble with stimuli that only humans can recognize with ease. For example, variations in size, shape, and orientation give the machine fits (non-fits?). You can easily identify the following patterns as the letter A: Я, **Я**, A, **Я**, ⅄, and even *Я*: but a template matcher has difficulty. A sophisticated machine can make some adjustments, rotating tilted stimuli, adjusting the size, and so forth, but the best computer programs often fail to recognize stimuli that humans perceive directly. Attempts to program computers to

understand spoken, rather than printed, instructions have encountered more difficulties, mostly because the physical characteristics of auditory stimuli vary even more than those of visual stimuli.

It is interesting to consider again just how remarkable are the abilities we often take for granted. If you designed a machine to recognize patterns as easily as all of us do every day, you would be a billionaire, and the Postal Service would give you a medal.

Feature Analysis

If template matching fails as a theory of perception, perhaps we can do better with a theory based on analyzing features of stimuli. Such a theory would at least have the support of research findings, both in biology and psychology, that prior to complete perception and recognition the human nervous system detects certain general characteristics of a pattern. Certain neurons in the visual system, for example, fire only when straight lines, curved lines, corners, or lines tilted at a certain angle are present in the visual field. Research on stabilized retinal images (pp. 101–102) gives similar evidence in reverse; the percept disappears not point by point but part by part; whole units (vertical lines, for example) disappear, and some sometimes reappear and disappear again—as a unit. Studies of depth perception suggest that, somehow, information on perspective, texture, blurring, and other cues to distance influences our estimates of the size of an object. The implication is that the human nervous system automatically processes sensory input, detecting the presence or absence of certain crucial features, and from this *analyzed* information makes a decision about what is or is not "out there."

The Pandemonium Model. In a rather colorful description of how sensory input and feature extraction can lead to perception and recognition of visual patterns, Oliver Selfridge (1959) developed a theory or system called Pandemonium. Although Pandemonium is actually a computer program designed to recognize stimuli—just as the bank's computer recognizes account numbers—it can be described as a world of little demons. These demons have very strict status relationships. At the top of the status heap is the *decision demon*, who makes the final decision about what the system has seen. It bases its decision, right or wrong, on communications from lower demons who are busy registering and analyzing information from the environment.

Let us trace the path of a particular pattern of stimuli shaped like this: A. The sensory input comes in to the receptionist, the *image demon*, who simply records the pattern of stimulation: A. The image demon is a metaphorical representation of our sensory receptors. This information, essentially unprocessed, is then sent to a group of *feature demons*, who correspond to our detector cells (see p. 66). Each feature demon looks at the pattern and notes the presence or absence of the feature for which it is responsible. In the letter A, the features might be "line slanted left," "line slanted right," "horizontal line," "angle or corner at top," and two "T junctures" where the horizontal line joins the side lines.

The *cognitive demons* correspond to the letters as we know them. There is an A demon, a B demon, and so forth through the alphabet. Each cognitive demon uses the results of the feature analysis to decide whether or not it should announce that its letter is being perceived. The cognitive demons are very egotistical and take every opportunity to present themselves to the decision demon. For example, the H demon sees two roughly vertical lines joined by a horizontal crossbar and shouts, "Me! Me!" Even the T demon raises its voice a little—"Me?"—when it sees the presence of a horizontal line. Only the demons who can find absolutely none of their features represented are quiet—the O demon, for example. The more evidence of their features, the louder the cognitive demons shout, and it is truly pandemonium, with all the demons with any feature represented demanding the attention of the decision demon.

The decision demon listens to the hollering cognitive demons and decides which letter is really out there by choosing the cognitive demon who is shouting the loudest. In this case, the A demon would be shouting a little louder than the others—"Me!!! Me!!! Me!!!"—and the decision demon would recognize the letter A.

Sometimes the decision demon is unable to make a decision. If a stimulus such as Ʌ comes in, the A demon and the H demon will probably be equally loud and the decision demon will be perplexed and uncertain.

Pandemonium is a theory of sorts, but perhaps more than that, it is a plausible description of the stages of processing involved in recognizing a pattern. The image is formed, features are extracted, and several patterns are possible; the most likely is chosen (not necessarily consciously). Whether the processes are innate or learned is not specified. There is physiological evidence that cells which act like feature extractors are present at birth (Hubel and Wiesel, 1962), but the abilities of the cognitive demons probably come from experience. Learning is possible for both the cognitive

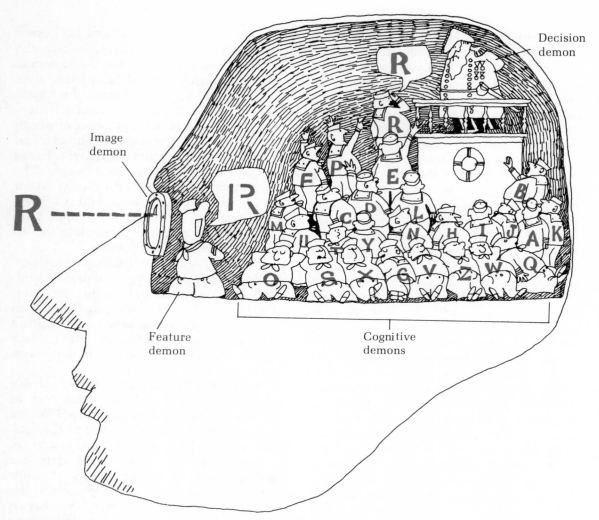

Figure 3.17 *A drawing of the Pandemonium model of pattern recognition.*

demons and the decision demon. The cognitive demons could, with experience, identify their letters better, and the decision demon could learn more about what shouts in the pandemonium reflect the various letters. For example, if R is shown, probably both the R demon and the P demon are shouting at full strength, because R contains P; the same is true of E and F.

Pandemonium can be applied to the perception of any stimulus, not just letters. In the perception of objects, for example, the cognitive demons might be box or bowl or ball demons, the bowl and ball demons looking for rounded sides and the box demon looking for straight sides. The theory of course gets a little complicated if we have a cognitive demon for every possible perceptual report, but the human brain is complex, with a huge capacity, and it is at least theoretically possible (Ratcliff, 1978).

Parallel versus Serial Processing. Both template-matching and feature-analysis theories of pattern recognition assume a very large number of items in memory (templates, cognitive demons). One of the problems with such theories has always been to understand how the perceptual apparatus could compare an incoming stimulus to information in memory without having to search through every memory item, one by one. Perhaps such one-by-one or *serial* comparisons are not the way the system works. The alternative is an all-at-once or *parallel* process.

Imagine 26 people assigned to look for letters of the alphabet on a printed page, comparable to 26 cognitive demons for letters in an individual's memory. The first letter on the page is, say, a T. We could ask the A person if this stimulus looks like hers, then the B person, and so on, in serial fashion, until we get to the T person. Alternatively, and more efficiently, we could project the stimulus onto a screen so all 26 people could get a look at it simultaneously, in a parallel fashion. Twenty-five people would say, "That's not *my* letter!" at the same time the T person shouts "Bingo!" Maybe the perceptual system works with parallel processing. The evidence suggests that some parts of it do, whereas other parts use serial processing (Massaro, 1975).

The Influence of Context. Another way the perceptual system cuts down on the number of comparisons it has to make is to take into account the influence of *context*. For example, suppose we were faced with a stimulus like A. A system that conformed to the Pandemonium model would have a difficult time deciding whether this letter was an A or an H. But *you*, a real live perceptual system, would have little trouble reading the following two words: TAE CAT.

What is the middle letter in the first word? H. In the second word? A. How do you know? "Because there is no such word as TAE or CHT." You are using the context, the surrounding letters, to identify the middle letters.

It is possible to include, say, "context demons" in a theory like Pandemonium, but the theory would become more and more complex, and interest would focus on the poor decision demon. It would have to check first with context demons to get some idea of what is out there, then with the cognitive demons appropriate to the decided context, then back to specialized context demons (What are the surrounding stimuli?) then back to the cognitive demons again, and so forth. Focusing on the characteristics of the decision demon, however, leads to a quite different kind of theory. Research indicates that it is not quite so methodical, but is somewhat more anxious and creative than we would suspect from the Pandemonium model. Thus our last theory, although not denying that feature analysis plays an important role in perception, is best presented separately as one that places much greater emphasis on the active and constructive abilities and tendencies of the human perceiver.

Constructive Perception

If a visual stimulus is presented briefly enough, below the threshold for recognition, subjects may report they see nothing, only a flash. If this same stimulus—let's say it's a word projected on a screen—is presented repeatedly, gradually the subject perceives something, and finally he or she may recognize it (Haber and Hershenson, 1965). In such an experiment, subjects report that, after a few flashes, parts of letters or whole letters appear; after several flashes, several letters or even the whole word is clear. Once they have identified the word, it seems quite visible, even though on the first presentations they literally saw nothing.

These results are intriguing in their own right, but even more so if we consider them in conjunction with another set of data. Suppose you flash a picture of an object so quickly it cannot be identified and then gradually increase the duration of the flash until the object can be perceived clearly. Experiments with this procedure produced data that seem to contradict the interpretation of the benefits of repeated exposures. With longer and longer flashes, subjects did

HOW TO TELL A CAT FROM A MEAT LOAF

Fig. 1   *Fig. 2*   B Kliban

not recognize the picture until the duration was much longer than what it would have had to be for the picture presented only once (Wyatt and Campbell, 1951). For example, suppose you can identify a dog if the picture is flashed once at 0.1 second. If the picture is flashed at very short durations, so that you see nothing at first, and the duration is gradually increased, you usually will *not* recognize the dog at 0.1 second; not until the duration of presentation is much longer—say 0.2 second—will you see the dog. This finding is the opposite of the experiment discussed earlier, in which repeated exposures were of benefit; here they are detrimental. What can account for the difference?

Later research suggested an answer (Bruner and Potter, 1964). These psychologists discovered that as the durations increase and the picture becomes a little clearer, subjects begin to form opinions or hypotheses about what it might be. Indeed, it is nearly impossible to prevent them from doing so, as you can imagine. If a subject's early hypothesis is incorrect (as it often is, since it is based on inadequate information), the subject requires a much clearer presentation (longer duration) before seeing the real picture for what it is. In effect, her inaccurate hypothesis interferes with her ability to see what is really there.

To interpret these two kinds of experiments, we must accept the notion of perception as an active, constructive process. In the first kind, a series of exposures at the same short duration allows attention to focus on different features of the simple stimuli—letters and words—until enough of them are processed to create the percept, which then appears "clear." In the second kind of experiment, the picture stimuli are more complex and the subjects are instructed to identify the stimulus as soon as possible. Presumably these subjects are also focusing on various features and using them to construct the perceptual guess. If the guess is wrong, it is strong enough to keep them from creating the correct percept. This suggests that the human perceiver uses features of the sensory input to construct a percept and then confirms it or changes it as he or she becomes aware of more features.

The Perceptual Cycle

A theory of perception and recognition that emphasizes the active, constructive role of the perceiver can be termed the *interactive theory* (Klatzky, 1980), or the *theory of the perceptual cycle* (Neisser, 1976). The theory is interactive because it depicts perception as an interaction between the sensory input, on the one hand, and, on the other hand, the perceiver's hypotheses and "states of readiness" for certain kinds of information.

States of readiness are anticipations, often based on the context of the stimulus to be perceived. For instance, when you hear someone play the first seven notes of the scale on a piano, a state of readiness for the eighth note is created. Your state of readiness influences not only what hypotheses you will develop when presented with a stimulus but also what exploratory behaviors you may try, such as moving eyes or head or body to get a clearer view of the expected stimulus. The outcome of such explorations—the information you get from them—modifies both the hypotheses your perceptual system is generating and your state of readiness. These modified hypotheses and anticipations direct your further exploration of the "real world," which results in more information, new modifications, further exploration, and so on, in a continuing series of perceptual cycles.

Perception of Language. To illustrate the interactive theory of the perceptual cycle, let us consider the perception of handwritten and spoken words. Although most humans have a remarkable ability to decipher these stimuli, words present enormous difficulties for computers programmed to recognize them. One of the major difficulties is that no two people speak or write exactly the same way, which makes templates of limited value.

Another problem is that, unlike printed words and letters, speech and handwriting do not *segment* themselves nicely. It is often hard to say where one handwritten letter stops and where the next begins because of the way they are strung together.

Speech is similar: When you listen to someone speak, you think you are hearing distinct words, but this is mostly an illusion. If you listen to someone speak in a foreign language that you do not understand, what you hear is an extremely rapid string of sounds; the breaks in the string may come in the middle of words as often as at the end of words. Even in English, we encounter problems similar to that of distinguishing a handwritten "d" and "cl." The sounds, "noo-dis-play" can be heard as "new display" or as "nudist play" (Lindsay and Norman, 1977).

According to the interactive theory, people use the features of the stimulus, its context, and their memories of relevant past events to make a best guess about what the stimulus is. If you have ever gotten a letter from a friend who is a sloppy writer, you know the essence of this approach. The whole letter is hard to read, but sooner or later a scrawl appears that on first glance looks like no known English word. If the word is important enough, you begin to generate hypotheses about what it might be. You try to figure it out letter by letter (analyzing features), you read the rest of the sentence to see what might fit (context), and you consider what this particular friend is likely to be talking about (memory). If you're lucky, you finally come up with a hypothesis that makes sense. Of course, we develop ordinary percepts much more rapidly and unconsciously than we decipher handwriting.

Continuous Speech. What would you think if I told you that you yourself are constructing most of what you hear in normal conversational speech? Listening to a friend doesn't seem to require effort; it doesn't *feel* creative. But, in an experiment in which subjects were asked to identify single words cut from tape recordings of spontaneous conversation (Pollack and Pickett, 1964), the subjects recognized the words accurately less than half the time! The words in a spoken sentence, by themselves, do not always give us enough information to recognize them. In context, however, we use knowledge about rules of grammar, the meaning of the surrounding words in the sentence, and other clues to help us "pin down" each word. The result is that, in context, words are usually perfectly intelligible. For example, subjects recognized 100 percent of the words in the *uncut* tape recording of the conversation just mentioned.

Listening to conversational speech, we are usually unaware of how much we are contributing to the perception of words. In one beautifully illustrative study (Warren and Warren, 1970), people were presented with one of these four recorded sentences:

It was found that the *eel was on the axle.
It was found that the *eel was on the shoe.
It was found that the *eel was on the orange.
It was found that the *eel was on the table.

The asterisk indicates where a small portion of the recorded speech was cut out and replaced with an ordinary cough.

What the subjects heard—quite distinctly, according to reports—was "wheel" if the last word was "axle," "heel" if it was "shoe," "peel" if "orange," and "meal" if "table." These data show how our understanding of a word may be influenced not only by what precedes it but by what follows. Subjects' perception of the earlier word was apparently not completed until the last word came into their perceptual system (Clark and Clark, 1977).

Hearsay. An interactive theory of perception has been used, with considerable success, in a computer program designed to recognize speech (Reddy and Newell, 1974). The program, called Hearsay, listens only if you are talking about chess, unfortunately, but it's a beginning. By limiting its interests to chess, Hearsay can use a relatively small set of hypotheses to aid its recognition of what's being said.

Hearsay, unlike many other programs, works on several segments of speech simultaneously, using its decisions on one segment to identify words in other segments (Klatzky, 1980). In true interactive fashion, Hearsay uses several sources to generate hypotheses about what it is hearing. One is, of course, the speech segment itself: What does it sound like? (This part of the system operates like a simple version of Pandemonium.) At the same time, the computer forms other hypotheses on the basis of the parts of speech and grammatical structure of segments it has already recognized: Is this word-like segment likely to be a verb? A noun? Still other hypotheses are formed from the *meaning* of already recognized segments, as well as from a general knowledge of chess; for example, if Hearsay knows we're talking about rooks, it knows we are unlikely to be discussing diagonal moves.

Having formed hypotheses from the various sources available to it, Hearsay then compares them. Some can be eliminated immediately; for example, analysis on the basis of grammar may suggest that "rook" is a possible utterance but acoustical analysis of the segment says "No way; it doesn't sound like 'rook' at all." The remaining hypotheses are rated in terms of plausibility by each source of information, and the hypothesis with the highest joint rating is chosen—the segment is "recognized." If more than one hypothesis gets a high rating, making a clear decision impossible, Hearsay can hold both hypotheses in memory until more segments are deciphered; usually this additional information makes a clear decision possible.

Is this the way the perceptual system works? Are the contextual effects in speech like the contextual effects in perceptual contrast, for example, or in the Gestalt laws of pattern perception? We don't know the answers to these questions yet, and the interactive theory of perception is relatively new. Undoubtedly it is wrong in some details, and other details have yet to be specified. But it is making sense in an area of human perception—speech perception—that has long resisted the best efforts of scientific psychologists.

PERSONALITY AND PERCEPTION

If percepts are constructed by the perceiver, we would expect personality to play a role in perception. An individual's unique adjustment to her environment makes her at least in some ways different from anyone else; that includes the content of her memory, certain aspects of the way she processes information, and what features of a stimulus will attract her attention. On the other hand, it is easy to exaggerate the importance of personality factors in perception. If everyone perceived something different in the same stimulus, interpersonal communication and interaction would be difficult, maybe impossible. Thus there are very strong pressures on each of us to perceive *accurately*—to perceive *impersonally*—for the sake of general agreement about what is really out there.

Nevertheless, very strong motives and values can alter percepts. Hallucinations are an extreme case, percepts that owe very little to the sensory input and quite a bit to the tangled web of the individual's memory, motives, and conflicts. Psychologists have often tried to establish more ordinary examples of personality effects on perception. We will briefly consider two areas of research, both suggesting that the *value* we place on a stimulus pattern affects our perception of it.

Stimuli with Positive Values. Do people who need money perceive money objects such as coins differently from people who have less need? It would seem so, if we were to accept the conclusions of certain experiments. In one, poor and rich boys were asked to estimate the size of various coins, and the poor boys consistently judged the coins as larger; the higher the value of the coin, the greater the overestimation of size (Bruner and Goodman, 1947).

But this is a natural experiment, and we should be wary of attributing the difference in size judgments to a single difference between the two groups of boys. Poor boys are not only poorer than rich boys; they may be also, on the average, less interested in a stupid experiment by a middle-class psychologist; they may have had less frequent experience with money, especially with high-value coins; and they may live in an environment that honors accuracy of perceptual judgment less highly. A true experiment would be preferable. For example, we might *randomly* form two groups of children and *then* make an object valuable for one (the experimental group) and do nothing for the other (the control group). Suppose we use poker chips. We could make them valuable by letting the subjects in the experimental group exchange them for candy. Our prediction would be that the subjects would not differ in their judgments of size *before* the value-inducing treatment, but that *afterward*, the average estimate of the value group would be greater than that of the control group. This experiment has been done, and the prediction was confirmed (Lambert et al., 1949). We can therefore gain some confidence in our conclusion.

Numerous experiments set up to demonstrate the effects of motives and values on

© 1975 B. Kliban. Reprinted from CAT by permission of the Workman Publishing Company, New York.

perception have been successful. Hungry subjects are more likely to identify an ambiguous (vague, fuzzy) stimulus as some sort of food (Levine et al., 1942). Subjects rewarded while looking at long lines or while handling light weights produced, in a subsequent session, longer estimates of lines and lighter estimates of weights than did a control group (Proshansky and Murphy, 1942). Subjects who scored high on a test of achievement motivation were better at identifying achievement-related words (for example, "strive" and "perfect") when they were briefly flashed on a screen than a group who scored low on this test (McClelland and Liberman, 1949).

The question is immediately raised, however, whether such experiments have any-thing to do with *perception;* maybe they relate to *judgments* of perceptions. For example, maybe hungry and well-fed subjects both saw the same fuzzy stimulus; when asked to identify it, the hungry subjects might well guess a food, but this does not mean they *perceived* the stimulus differently. Since the problem of interpretation is equally applicable to the next set of studies to be discussed, let us withhold comment for a moment.

Stimuli with Negative Value. Personality psychologists often comment on people's tendency to accentuate the positive, and to ignore as much as possible the negative and threatening realities of their life. In perception, this might suggest that people would not form percepts of unpleasant things as quickly as of neutral or positive things. This facet of human behavior has been called *perceptual defense*. A classic study involved flashing neutral and taboo words at subjects and measuring their recognition thresholds by gradually increasing the exposure time for a word until the subject identified it (McGinnies, 1949). The taboo words (for example, "whore") required a significantly longer exposure time, suggesting that subjects were defending against psychological threat by not perceiving dirty words. (Remember, dirty words in the 1940s were more negatively regarded than today!)

Many psychologists objected that dirty words are less frequent in the language, as shown by word counts in popular magazines, and less frequent words are always less recognizable. The perceptual defense theorists, of course, countered by saying that dirty words were common in speech, if not in public print. A second criticism was that subjects do not *expect* dirty words from a respectable psychologist, and expectation has a clear effect on perception. A third criticism was that even if subjects saw the dirty words, they could be reluctant to *report* them, at least waiting until they were *very* sure.

The Effect of Values. So we are back to the question of whether values affect subjects' perceptions or their reports. Psychologists first suspected the latter, but experiments carefully designed to eliminate response effects (like the reluctance to repeat a dirty word) showed that the effect of values could still be found (see Minard et al., 1966).

Newer theories of perception, rather than answering the question, have attacked it from a different angle (see, for example, Erdelyi, 1974). In this view, perception and response (report) are not considered two independent, completely separate processes. Each involves a series of stages, and sometimes the two may overlap. Perception, for example, involves registering sensory data, analyzing features, and constructing a percept—at least. The fact that forming a percept of a dirty word will entail making a report that might meet with social disapproval could well inhibit the creation of the percept in the first place. Did subjects really see the dirty words as well as they saw the neutral words? If by that you mean, did they register the dirty words and process them (analyze them for features), the answer might be yes. But if you mean, did they construct the percepts as readily—and this too is part of perception—the answer is probably no. So the question is not so much whether the effect of values is perceptual or not but at what *stage* of perception values exert their greatest influence.

SUMMARY

1. The *absolute threshold* is that amount of stimulation needed to trigger a percept. A *difference threshold* is that amount of stimulation needed for the difference between two stimuli to be detectable. Weber's Law states that the relationship between a *just noticeable difference* (jnd) and the original amount of stimulation is constant for each sense.

2. With regard to perception, adaptation refers to less sensitivity after persisting stimulation and more sensitivity after an absence of stimulation. Variety is a major factor in adaptation; if the visual image on the

retina is kept from jiggling, preventing variety of stimulation, the image disappears.

3. *Gestalt* principles describe the ways collections of stimuli are perceived as organized patterns. Some Gestalt principles are *figure-ground, similarity, proximity, common fate,* and *continuation.*

4. *Perceptual constancy* refers to our tendency to see familiar objects as the same shape, size, and color despite variations in distance, light, orientation, and other factors that should affect our perception. *Perceptual contrast* means that similar stimuli will be perceived differently in different contexts.

5. Our perception of depth depends on both *binocular cues,* such as *retinal disparity,* and *monocular cues,* such as *linear perspective, texture gradients, changes in color, shadows,* and *relative movement.*

6. Constancies, contrast effects, and depth perception illustrate the active, creative role of the perceiver, because in all cases the stimuli result in a perception that is only partially related to those stimuli. Illusions, reversible figures, impossible figures, and hallucinations provide further evidence for this view.

7. Many *illusions* mislead us because they conflict with our expectations about the customary relations between features such as size and distance. *Phi phenomena* are illusions in which we perceive one or more stationary images as being in motion. A *reversible figure* is a stimulus that can be perceived in two different ways, but not both at once. An *impossible figure* leads to incompatible percepts in different parts of the stimulus. *Hallucinations* are percepts created with very little help from external stimuli, deriving instead mainly from internal input.

8. Theories of perception and recognition attempt to explain how we identify and respond to familiar stimuli. Many computers do this by *template matching,* comparing the stimulus to a standard; this method is limited in that only stimuli quite similar to the template can be identified. *Feature analysis* theories, including the Pandemonium model, work from individual aspects of a stimulus to narrow down the possibilities until the stimulus is identified. Theories of *parallel processing* suggest that many or all of the various steps in identifying a stimulus occur at once, rather than serially.

9. More evidence that perception is active and constructive comes from studies suggesting that we can gradually recognize images flashed repeatedly at a speed too fast to see, *unless* the flashes are lengthened and we form an incorrect percept that hinders identification. The *interactive* theory views perception as interaction between sensory input and the perceiver's hypotheses and states of readiness for information. In this view, the perceiver uses the stimulus and clues from context to generate, check, and modify hypotheses until a percept is formed. A computer program called Hearsay is based on the interactive theory; it recognizes speech, but only if the speaker is discussing chess.

10. Perceptions are the result of many inputs, some of which are traditionally considered personality factors. If a subject values a stimulus positively, she may overestimate various aspects of it such as size, and if she negatively values the stimulus, she may not recognize it as quickly. Personal values, as well as other personality factors, can be considered as contextual, influencing perception in much the same way as do surrounding stimuli.

USING PSYCHOLOGY

The blood vessels and neurons that are actually in front of your receptors are invisible to you because under normal circumstances they are stabilized images (see the text, Chapter 2, p. 63, for a discussion of the neural organization of the eye). You can, however, observe them in your own eye under the following conditions: Take a heavy piece of black paper (such as a filing card colored black by a felt marker) and poke a tiny hole in it using a pin. Mark a small X on a piece of white paper and tape it to a brightly illuminated light colored wall, at eye level. Stand facing the X, close one eye, and place the black card over your open eye. Position the hole in front of your open eye so that through it, you can see the X on the wall. Now jiggle the card rapidly, moving it very slightly so that you can still see the X while it is jiggling. You will soon see a pattern of vessels and tissues surrounding your percept of the X on the wall. You are actually seeing the living tissues in front of the receptors in your eye. Notice that you do not see any such vessels and tissues in a small area surrounding the X. This is because there are none located in front of the fovea (the neurons and vessels serving the cones of the fovea are located to the sides of the fovea). The pinpoint of light moving around on your retina prevents the tissues in front of the receptors from becoming stabilized images. That is why you can see them under these conditions.

SUGGESTED READINGS

Neisser, U. *Cognition and reality*. Freeman, 1976.
Some basic principles of perception and their implications, by one of the best writers and innovative thinkers in psychology.

Lindsay, P., & Norman, D. *Human information processing*. 2nd ed. Academic Press, 1977.
An excellent introduction to the information-processing approach in psychology, with material on learning, memory, and language, as well as perception.

Rock, I. *An introduction to perception*. Macmillan, 1975.
A good introductory textook on perception. It has a thorough discussion of the psychological perception of forms, with little on the biology of sensory systems.

Robinson, J. O. *The psychology of visual illusion*. Hutchinson, 1972.
Illusions are always interesting. This is a collection of them, with explanations.

Parapsychology

About five years ago, I had an amazing dream. The dream image was remarkably clear, of my father sleeping in his bed. I recognized his room in our family home, his wallet and loose change lying on the dresser, his clothes on a chair. He was sleeping peacefully, gently snoring. I remember thinking, "What an odd dream. Nothing happening. Just a nocturnal visit to see Dad." Then, suddenly, he started to gasp for breath. He woke and sat up, with a pained and fearful look on his face. More gasps, and then he fell back. Silence. I walked close to his bed. I could not detect any breathing at all. I took his pulse. There was none. He was dead.

The dream scared me, woke me up. I wanted to call Dad immediately, but it would have been 4:00 A.M., his time. I tried to sleep, with only partial success, and called home finally in the morning.

My father answered. No, he was not dead. No, nothing unusual had happened last night. I told him why I called. He laughed. He said, "Thank God I didn't die! The coincidence would have left you thinking you were psychic!" No doubt!

You have certainly read other accounts of dreams like mine, but most of them have different endings: Father *did* die during the night. Of a heart attack. Eerie! Stranger than science! Coincidence? Or some mysterious mental power that scientists are not yet willing to admit?

Parapsychology is the branch of psychology that deals with "those psychical effects which appear not to fall within the scope of what is at present recognized law" (Roll, 1975). The phenomena of parapsychology —which include clairvoyance, mental telepathy, and precognition, among others—are enormously intriguing, but they are not scientifically respectable. A few parapsychological phenomena, such as "faith healing," have a solid scientific basis of sorts, in that a person's beliefs are known to be able to influence his or her bodily functions. (Physicians experience this regularly, either in the positive effect of a nonfunctional "sugar" pill (placebo) or in the negative effect of almost all physical remedies on someone who sincerely wants to die.) Other psychic phenomena might be explained as coincidence; and there have been more than a few cases of deliberate fraud, sometimes by famous psychics.

EARLY RESEARCH IN PARAPSYCHOLOGY

Although the scientific study of parapsychology can be said to have begun in 1882, when the Society for Psychical Research was founded in England, most of the early research was shoddy, polluted by opportunistic "magicians" who were later uncovered as cheats. The modern era of scientific research began in the fall of 1927, when a young biologist, J. B. Rhine, came to Duke University with a pile of stenographic records from seances (Rhine et al., 1965). In the early years of this century, the question of spirit survival after death was one that many people believed could be explored through science. One way to do this was to examine the claims made by certain persons called "spiritualists" or "mediums," who asserted they could communicate with the spirits of people no longer alive. These "communications" took place in group meetings, called seances, involving the medium and at least one other person—the person with the interest in communicating; usually other people were present as "witnesses."

It was clear from the seance records that in most cases the medium knew things about the deceased and his or her relationship to the medium's client. Where did this information come from? The medium, of course, claimed it came from the spirit of the dead person. Rhine, however, thought that an alternative hypothesis must be considered: the medium might be *clairvoyant,* able to learn about events or objects without direct experience of them, or *telepathic,* picking up information (perhaps even unconsciously) from what the client was thinking. Because Rhine was unwilling to attribute the medium's performance to spirit communication until "mere" telepathy and clairvoyance were ruled out, research interest shifted to those two topics.

EXTRASENSORY PERCEPTION

Almost from the beginning, the bulk of the controlled, scientific research on parapsychology has involved mental telepathy, clairvoyance, or a similar psychic ability called *precognition*—telling the future. Together these three phenomena constitute *extrasensory perception* or ESP, so called because knowledge is presumably gained from information that does not come in through any known sense receptors. Instead, according to believers, information comes from the minds of others (telepathy), from events that are not sensed directly (clairvoyance), or from events that have not yet occurred (precognition). A fourth widely studied psychic ability, made popular by movies and performers like Uri Geller, is *psychokinesis,* which we sometimes call "mind over matter"; a person possessing this ability is supposedly able to influence a physical event by thinking about it—to bend a spoon by thinking it bent, for example. (ESP and psychokinesis together can be referred to as "psi" phenomena.)

There is considerable (and often heated) debate on the validity of ESP. Does such a human ability exist? A number of psychologists, including a few of the most widely respected scientists in the field, regard ESP as established beyond reasonable doubt. A number of other psychologists, myself included, have concluded that there is not a shred of solid scientific evidence for these psychic abilities. With my bias in mind, let us consider some of the research data.

Most early studies (and many of the more recent ones) used a special deck of 25 picture cards, 5 each of a star, a circle, a square, a cross, and wavy lines. In an investigation of clairvoyance, subjects might be asked to guess the order of these pictures in a shuffled deck. They could make their guesses without disturbing the deck, or they could pick up each card in turn, study the back of it, and then place it face down in a new pile. In an investigation of telepathy, one person (the sender) might look at and think about each card in turn (perhaps in another room), while another person (the receiver) tried to guess the sequence. A way of studying precognition might be to have a subject guess beforehand what the order of a deck of cards would be *after* shuffling.

Rhine soon encountered criticism of his telepathy experiments, which followed the pattern just described. Critics claimed that the experiments confused telepathy and clairvoyance: High scores might be due not to a subject's ability to read the sender's mind, but to a clairvoyant ability to know the order of cards whether or not a sender was involved. As a result, pure telepathy experiments were devised in which senders, with no decks or prescribed order, simply thought of one of the five pictures, one after another, until the agreed-on number of telepathic transmissions was completed.

With five different pictures to choose from, a subject has one chance in five of guessing correctly. In a run of 25 trials — going through the deck once — subjects will guess right 5 times, on the average, by pure chance. By the laws of probability, there will be a few high scores, around 10 correct, and a few low scores, occasionally none correct, all by chance. Only subjects who *consistently* make more than 5 correct choices out of 25 can be said to have accomplished something unusual.

The Evidence for ESP

After a year or so of unsuccessful investigations, Rhine began finding subjects who could score consistently above chance (Rhine and Pratt, 1957). His best subject of the early groups was a student named Hubert Pearce, who averaged eight correct guesses per run through the deck. Pearce was tested with 690 runs — a total of 17,250 trials. The statistical probability of such a performance occurring by chance guessing is one in several million—for all practical purposes, an impossibility. Over the years, several other subjects also scored above chance, averaging around 7 "hits" out of 25, over several runs. Success was achieved with all three forms of ESP—mental telepathy, clairvoyance, and precognition—although some subjects were better at one kind of task than at others.

Although many scientists remained skeptical, the advocates of ESP considered the evidence massive and irrefutable. In recent years, they have turned their interests from trying to demonstrate the existence of ESP to trying to understand the conditions under which it would appear or disappear. For example, there have been scattered reports that hypnosis and the drug LSD sometimes improve ESP abilities (Pratt, 1973). Similarly, the dream state has been found to be one especially favorable for the (apparent) reception of telepathic messages and clairvoyant visions.

Gradually the view took hold among parapsychologists that *everyone* has the ability to read minds, to see the future, and to know of events out of sight; it was merely a matter of allowing these abilities to be expressed.

Most people, according to this view, are hampered by disbelief, making them unwilling to develop and use their ESP, and by a lack of understanding of how the abilities function. The "special subjects" of the early studies were presumably among the few whose abilities had developed by unusual, fortunate circumstances. Today books are available to teach you how to use your ESP, if you are interested (Tart, 1976).

One of the most prominent series of studies of what conditions are most favorable for ESP has been running at UCLA, under the supervision of Thelma Moss (1974). Since most psychic incidents outside the scientific laboratory involve highly emotional events—the death or injury of a loved one, for example—Moss decided to investigate mental telepathy in emotional situations. In one situation, senders viewed scenes of Nazi concentration camps while listening to harsh music; in another, they viewed slides of nude women to the musical accompaniment of *The Stripper*. The receivers of these people's mental telepathy were to describe the senders' feelings, thoughts, and images. They were also shown two slides and asked to choose the one the sender had seen. They had a 50:50 chance of picking the right slide, so they had to do consistently better than 50 percent to be presumed telepathic. Of sixteen experiments of this type, the results were statistically significant in ten.

Telepathy is widely studied in the Soviet Union, where the question is not whether it exists but how it works (Kogan, 1969; Krippner and Davidson, 1972). In one investigation of an experienced pair of subjects, the sender was asked to visualize a boxing match with the receiver. He imagined either a 15-second round or a 45-second round. The punches were to correspond to dots and dashes in Morse code so that words or names could be sent. In this roundabout manner, the four-letter name "Ivan" was successfully transmitted from Leningrad to Moscow. (The receiver did not like this study, however, because once the sender punched him so hard that he fell off his chair!) In another experiment, a third person, also a receiver, tried to "bug" the communication between the other two, to intercept it en route. According to reports, he was successful. (Perhaps this is the reason for Russian interest in ESP.)

Psychokinesis

Uri Geller, the handsome young Israeli psychic, was performing on TV. He looked nervous. He tried to bend a strong, thick four-inch nail by simply stroking it gently with one finger. He was unsuccessful. He asked one of the guests, a beautiful woman, to hold the nail in her hand while he stroked it. The nail began to bend (before the audience's very eyes), and it continued to bend after it was placed on a table. Geller then held up a ring. First it bent, then it snapped in two. The audience applauded loudly (Moss, 1974).

What Geller was doing was either magic or a bona fide example of psychokinesis (PK), the other commonly studied parapsychological ability. PK is mind over matter, the control of physical events by psychic powers: bending nails, controlling which numbers come up on dice, levitating objects into the air, taking psychic photographs (causing an image to be formed on photographic film without exposure to light), and other such feats. The scientific data for psychokinesis come predominantly from two sources: observation of special people, like Uri Geller, who claim to have "the power," and dice-throwing experiments in the laboratory. In the dice-throwing experiments, the subject tries to make dice come up with a certain number. One time out of six, of course, the subject will "succeed" by pure chance, so PK is indicated by a hit rate consistently above one out of six.

Although advocates of ESP and PK claim that PK has been established (Rhine, 1968), the reported evidence is very weak (Girden, 1962; Hansel, 1966). Often the difference from chance is slight, on the order of 1.1 hits out of 6 (Moss, 1974). Although this difference is highly unlikely to occur by chance alone if demonstrated over several thousand throws of the dice, very minor errors in the experimental design could account for such results. Errors in recording the data, for example, could occur. Another problem is that no dice are perfectly true; over several thousand trials, all

dice show slight imperfections, favoring one or two numbers over the others. In one experiment, a subject tried to make the number 6 appear on the dice and, over 52,128 trials, scored 582 more 6s than could be expected by chance. PK? The dice were thrown another 52,128 trials, this time with no attempt at mental influence. There were 576 more 6s than could be expected by chance.

And what of Uri Geller? Many magicians and scientists who have observed him believe he is nothing more than a clever trickster. As one reviewer puts it, "Geller probably ranks as the most thoroughly exposed psychic of all time" (Diaconis, 1978, p. 133). His feats have been duplicated by other magicians (for example, Asher, 1976; Randi, 1976), and a magician-scientist has reported direct observations of obvious magical tricks (Hyman, 1977).

Flaws in ESP Research

As the problem of the biased dice indicates, one must be very careful in designing, executing, and interpreting ESP experiments. Just because a result is unlikely to occur by chance, we need not conclude that ESP is involved. Indeed, we should not conclude that ESP is involved until we have eliminated other possible explanations.

Clues from the Deck. Many of the early ESP experiments, in which subjects tried to guess the cards in the special ESP deck, were clearly and seriously flawed. One of the most notable flaws was that the early ESP cards were printed in such a way that a subject could read them from the back! They also could be read from the sides (Hansel, 1966). Although it seems likely that many of the early subjects caught on to this trick and had a little fun with the experimenters, it is also possible that many quite honest subjects "read" the cards without knowing it. They might have looked intensely at the back of the card and, suddenly, one of the symbols seemed to appear. Thinking they were having an ESP experience, they guessed and were right. Such experiences, in which ordinary perception of an external stimulus is mistakenly believed to be a self-generated image or thought, are well known in studies of hallucinations (Horowitz, 1975).

A number of other problems of experimental design also make it likely that an intelligent subject could guess the symbols in an ESP deck at a rate greater than chance. If the subject can catch a glimpse of the bottom card in the deck, for instance, he or she can raise the average score to almost 6, rather than 5, out of 25 (Hansel, 1966). Most early subjects made most of their "hits" in the first 5 cards or the last 5 cards, an effect that could result from having seen a card or two at the top or bottom of the deck. Hubert Pearce, the best of Rhine's early subjects, scored 87 percent correct on the last card of each deck! Another possibility is that some of the cards were slightly larger than others and thus would regularly turn up at the bottom after a cut of the cards. In his first book, Rhine (1934) complained of decks with this defect.

Help from the Experimenter. An additional potential source of information to ESP subjects is the experimenter. In mental telepathy studies, where the experimenter (or sender) has to think about the symbol the subject is to guess, Rhine (1934) himself worried about the "involuntary whispering ghost" — that is, the tendency to read the symbol with one's lips or in some similar way indicate the symbol to the receiver.

A slightly different difficulty arose in the "pure" telepathy experiments that eliminated the deck of cards. The sender in these studies was instructed to think of the symbols in a "random sequence." Unfortunately, it is well known that humans cannot follow such instructions (Slovic et al., 1977). For instance, we tend to avoid repeating a symbol twice or more in a row, even though such strings of repetitions would occur by random chance a certain number of times. Thus, a subject who each time guesses a symbol different from the previous trial will probably "hit" above chance levels (Diaconis, 1978).

Another type of help from the experimenter is unconscious recording errors. It is a well-established fact in psychology — indeed, in science generally — that people who support a certain hypothesis tend to make errors in favor of that hypothesis (Rosenthal, 1966). In ESP experiments, this would mean recording more hits than actually occurred. Since the hit rate of ESP subjects who show better-than-chance averages is *barely* above chance levels, any such unconscious recording error could account for most of the positive results in ESP experiments. Although recording errors are very hard to prove, we do know that believers in ESP generally obtain positive results, whereas disbelievers most often obtain negative results.

Statistics. Some of the debate on ESP, PK, and other parapsychological phenomena centers on statistics. For example, many scientists dismiss the evidence for ESP in "natural" settings as pure coincidence, which is another way of saying that the hit rate does not exceed chance levels. Take the precognition of earthquakes. After every major earthquake in California, reports come out of people who had a "premonition" or an "earthquake dream" before the actual event. Precognition? Not likely. It is probably fair to estimate that at least one "earthquake dream" or premonition occurs somewhere in California every day. Only when an earthquake actually happens—quite coincidentally—are these "precognitions" remembered and taken seriously.

Then there is the problem of "multiple end points" (Diaconis, 1978), a fancy phrase for a study in which any "unusual" happening is considered evidence for ESP. Sometimes subjects in mental telepathy experiments are scored as having guessed correctly if their guess matches the card the sender is trying to transmit, *or* the card the sender sent on the previous trial, *or* the card the sender will send on the next trial (in which case the subject exhibits both telepathy and precognition!), *or* cards two trials before or after the present one. The odds of a good score in such an experiment are obviously much greater than if just one result is considered correct.

Other experiments are even looser. In telepathy experiments in which a picture is sent, what is to be considered a "match"? Often "matching" is a subjective judgment, and any one of a number of responses could be considered "unusually similar" and thus in some respect evidence for ESP. An extreme example of the multiple-end-point problem, reported by Diaconis (1978), involved a highly touted psychic with the initials of B. D. At a scientific demonstration at Harvard University, B. D. invited onlookers to shuffle two decks of ordinary playing cards and to name two different cards. They named the ace of spades and the three of hearts. The cards of each deck then were turned over one by one until one of the named cards appeared. When the three of hearts appeared in one deck, B. D. shouted, "Fourteen!" After 14 more cards in the other deck, wonder of wonders, another three of hearts appeared! Numerous other "trials" of this sort followed, with B. D. sometimes "successful" and sometimes not.

The problem—the statistical problem—was that B. D. did not specify in advance what he was trying to do. Certainly it was amazing that the three of hearts turned up after 14 cards. But the ace of spades would have been equally amazing. Sometimes B. D. missed by one card: the three of hearts or the ace of spades turned up on the thirteenth or fifteenth card. This was also considered amazing. Sometimes the three of diamonds turned up after 14 or 15 cards. B. D. rubbed his eyes and said, "I'm certainly having trouble seeing the suits today," but nevertheless his feat seemed amazing. Sometimes, in the initial turnover of cards, the three of hearts in one deck appeared at the same time as the three of hearts in the other deck. This too was considered amazing. Or the three of hearts turned up in one deck and the ace of spades in the other. All amazing! But statistically, the odds of a coincidence *of some sort* are good, and B. D. was obviously exploiting these odds.

Cheating. In most ESP experiments, the results are not just due to statistical error. Something really is happening. In some cases, ordinary sensory perception is happening, as when subjects read the symbols from the back of the cards. In other cases, the subjects are cheating.

Several famous psychics over the years have been caught in the act of deliberate cheating (Diaconis, 1978). Since such people often make their living on the stage, it is not surprising that they have some motivation to deceive "gullible" scientists. But ordinary subjects also may be motivated to deceive, whether to earn money as subjects, to bias the experimental results, or for other reasons. Some of the incredibly unlikely results of ESP experiments are now known to be due to such cheating. In the first two major ESP experiments done in England in 1882, eight subjects were involved; seven later admitted cheating, and the eighth also cheated, according to his partner in the act. Two Welsh schoolboys studied in England in 1955–1957, in an investigation widely acclaimed as "unrivaled" evidence for ESP, also were caught cheating (Hansel, 1966).

In a book published in 1966, British psychologist C. E. M. Hansel reviewed the available research on ESP, PK, and other psychic phenomena. He documented the many cases of known fraud and showed that the possibility of cheating was distinct in every investigation. The means of cheating or potential cheating are varied. They include falsifying one's record of guesses and catching a glimpse of one or two of the cards in an ESP deck. Sometimes a confederate seems to be involved. Hansel himself managed to duplicate the results of one series of investigations by using a high-pitched whistle to transmit a coded message. His nine-year-old daughter could hear the whistle at a distance of 500 feet, but most people over 40 years of age could not hear it at all. It was, in short, a perfect device for studies run by middle-aged or elderly parapsychologists.

Cheating is not restricted to the subjects. In 1974, the director of J. B. Rhine's Institute for Parapsychology at Durham, North Carolina, was fired for "altering" data in a PK experiment, trying to get significant results in a study where nature had provided none. "We were crushed," Rhine said later. "We couldn't believe it at first" (Bartlett, 1978).

THE QUESTION OF REPEATABILITY

My own conclusion is that there exists today no solid evidence whatsoever for a human ability like ESP or PK. I admit there are some unusual happenings I can't explain, and a few carefully designed experiments where the reason for the significant results is not immediately apparent.

But these data are not convincing—indeed, *should* not be—because they cannot be duplicated by other scientists. Many psychologists, myself included, have run numerous ESP experiments without success. Even the proponents of ESP complain that the phenomena are often "here today and gone tomorrow" (Moss, 1974). Until ESP can be demonstrated regularly, it will be highly suspect.

We should also consider what it would mean if ESP and PK were accepted as valid. It would challenge the basic assumptions of almost every theory in psychology and in other fields such as biology and physics as well. Scientists do not accept such challenges lightly, certainly not without strong reason. So far—*after a hundred years of trying*—the experimental evidence for ESP is practically nonexistent, and thus most psychologists remain skeptical.

SUGGESTED READINGS

Hansel, C. E. M. *ESP: A scientific evaluation.* Scribner's, 1966.
  A little out-of-date, but a thorough discussion by a major critic of ESP research.
Bowles, N., & Hynds, F. *Psi search.* Harper & Row, 1978.
  A more recent scientific evaluation of psychic phenomena, this one by believers.

Behavioral Objectives

1. Outline the history of behaviorism and discuss the scientific problems it was intended to overcome.
2. Describe classical conditioning and identify the terms US, UR, CS, and CR.
3. Define the Law of Effect, and discuss its relationship to operant conditioning.
4. Discuss the differences and similarities between classical and operant conditioning. Tell which procedure you think can be used to train a wider variety of behaviors, and why.
5. Identify the four basic schedules of operant conditioning. Describe the kinds of responding they promote, and how they are used in everyday life.
6. Define secondary reinforcement.
7. Describe some ways of eliminating undesirable behavior. Tell which you think is the best, and why.
8. Discuss the criticisms that have been made of behaviorism.
9. Define ethology and discuss some ethological factors that can affect learning.

CHAPTER

4

Learning and Behavior

I was once in a class that was determined to play a practical joke on its professor. We had just finished a chapter in an introductory psychology textbook, a chapter on learning, and we decided to test a few of the principles we had learned. Our professor, a man of great dignity and scholarship, seemed the perfect subject. He was unaccustomed to guile; he would surely be ignorant of our machinations until it was too late. This, in spite of the fact that he himself had described the technique for the trick we were about to pull.

The technique, called operant conditioning, was simple. We simply rewarded our professor with rapturous attention whenever he looked out the window. When he turned to face the class, we fell into restless and bored disarray, scratching and yawning. When he turned again to the window, we listened quietly to the lessons he was trying to teach. We kept this up for a week (four lectures). On Friday, the noble professor delivered his entire lecture out the window.

When we told our professor of our joke, he was not angry, he was delighted (as we knew he would be). We discussed "the demonstration," as he called it. He said he was totally unaware of our manipulation of his behavior. He was occasionally aware of speaking out the window, but his feeling was that he "felt more comfortable" doing so. We were all impressed by the effectiveness of the learning principles and the training techniques devised by learning psychologists.

In this chapter, we will explore some of the major principles and techniques of learning psychologists. We will encounter an emphasis on behavior, a tendency to study learning in terms not of increased knowledge but of changed behavior. We will see explanations in terms of certain "stimuli" leading to certain "responses" (sometimes called the S-R approach). As we discuss some of the reasons for the traditional—and continuing—behavioral emphasis in learning theories, we will examine some of the major findings resulting from this emphasis, many of which have greatly increased our understanding of human behavior. Finally, we will discuss some objections to the traditional approach to learning, objections that emphasize either especially complex phenomena (like "insight") or unusually simple behaviors (like unlearned instinctive reactions).

THORNDIKE AND THE LAW OF EFFECT

When Charles Darwin published his theories of evolution, several of the major implications excited psychologists. One implication was the basic continuity between humans and lower animals; although the human brain and other body structures were perhaps more complex, they were related to similar structures in other animals. Animals were considered simply less intelligent than humans. A number of learning psychologists began to seek a general test of intelligence, one applicable to all animals. They hoped to answer questions such as "Is the pig smarter than the horse?" and they hoped to arrange various species of animals on a dimension running from "stupid" to "bright." (Everyone hoped humans would rank first!) Positions on this dimension would be highly related, they predicted, to the hypothetical *phylogenetic* scale, a biological classification system that orders animals in terms of

how highly evolved they are—that is, how distant they are from the most primitive, one-celled animals like the amoeba.

Thorndike's Puzzle Boxes

Intelligence was then defined as the ability to learn. An American psychologist named Edward Thorndike (1898) studied the learning performance of chickens, cats, and dogs in what he called "puzzle boxes." The animals were placed in boxes with slatted sides (so they could see out) and food was placed outside. They could get out and get food if they solved the puzzle, which meant making a response Thorndike had decided would open the door: pulling a string that hung from the ceiling of the puzzle box, for example, or stepping on a lever.

At first the animals tried to get to the food by direct means: They tried to scratch, kick, or otherwise eliminate the slats that were between them and the food. This strikes me as quite intelligent behavior, but the way Thorndike defined the puzzle, scratching the walls or singing the Star Spangled Banner were considered equally ineffective and equally unintelligent; such responses were all classed together as errors. At first there were many errors. Then, eventually, and often by accident, the correct response was made—the cat trips on Thorndike's lever, and the door opens. Success!

Now, if an animal were really intelligent, it would recognize the answer to the puzzle immediately; it would make no more errors. But Thorndike's animals made several more errors. The time between being placed in the box and making the correct response decreased gradually, oh so gradually, until finally the animal was placed in the box, made the correct response immediately, and

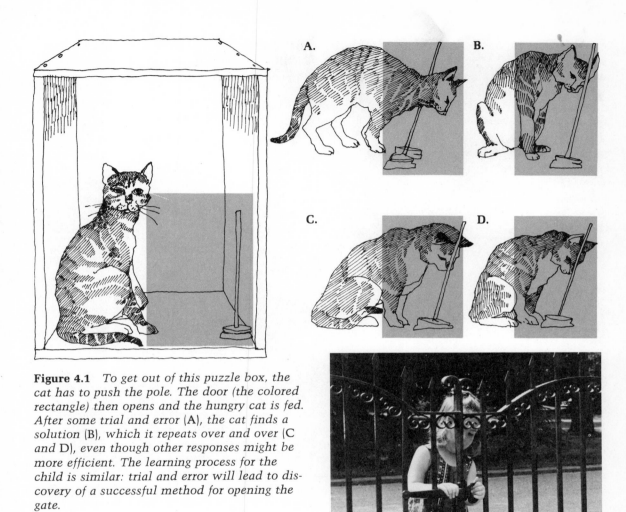

Figure 4.1 *To get out of this puzzle box, the cat has to push the pole. The door (the colored rectangle) then opens and the hungry cat is fed. After some trial and error (A), the cat finds a solution (B), which it repeats over and over (C and D), even though other responses might be more efficient. The learning process for the child is similar: trial and error will lead to discovery of a successful method for opening the gate.*

got out. (See Figure 4.1.) Thorndike called this gradual improvement *trial-and-error learning*. For many years he thought it quite unintelligent behavior—until he tried humans in comparable situations and found they too improved only gradually, by trial and error. The gradual improvement, when plotted on a graph, shows a gentle curve, with time per

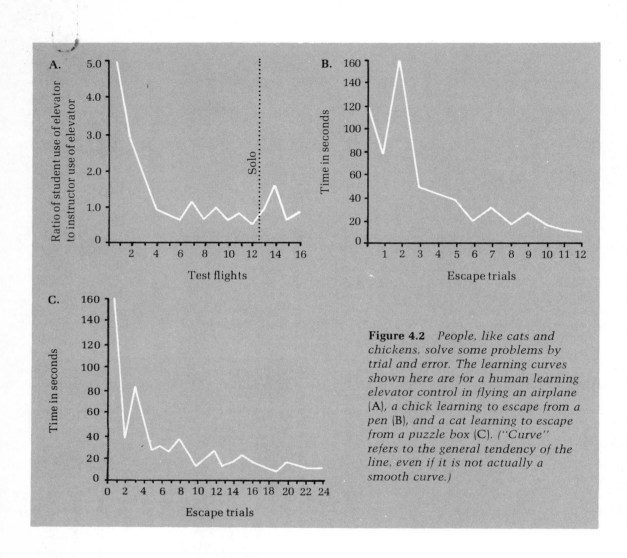

Figure 4.2 *People, like cats and chickens, solve some problems by trial and error. The learning curves shown here are for a human learning elevator control in flying an airplane (A), a chick learning to escape from a pen (B), and a cat learning to escape from a puzzle box (C). ("Curve" refers to the general tendency of the line, even if it is not actually a smooth curve.)*

trial gradually decreasing, and this gained the name *learning curve.* The striking thing, in retrospect, was that all animals—chickens, cats, dogs, and humans—produced the same type of curve (see Figure 4.2). This was considered a verification of Darwin's notion of continuity among species; were humans just smart chimps?

The Law of Effect

Thorndike's major theoretical contribution to psychology was the *Law of Effect.* In essence, the Law of Effect states that behavior will be influenced by its effect, that is, by its outcome. If a response leads to a satisfying state of affairs, it will gradually become more likely. If a response leads to an unpleasant state of affairs, it will become less likely. Although some of Thorndike's detailed speculation about why this might be so has since been superseded by more sophisticated theories, the basic Law of Effect is still acceptable today. In fact, you can use it to explain any repeated behavior, from cigarette smoking to voting for the incumbent.

Since his research was on animals, Thorndike was forced to phrase his observations and conclusions in terms of observable behavior. He couldn't very well ask a cat or chicken if it had solved the riddle of his puzzle box; he had to wait and see whether the animal would make consistent responses aimed at obtaining a satisfying state of affairs — in this case, food. Even a satisfying state, however mental it sounds, had a behavioral definition: one that an animal will do nothing to avoid, one the animal will often act to preserve.

PAVLOV AND CLASSICAL CONDITIONING

Another great behaviorist who pioneered in studies of animal learning was a Russian named Ivan P. Pavlov. Pavlov won a Nobel prize in 1904 for his research on digestive secretions in general, but his investigation of learned salivation in particular is the source of his enduring fame. Pavlov was a

Figure 4.3 *Ivan Pavlov and friends in the laboratory. (Pavlov is the one in the middle who looks like a scientist.)*

plodder. He got hold of an idea and researched it in every way he could imagine, which, in the case of learned salivation, translates into 40 years of work. He was also a genius, and a relentless, plodding genius is a remarkable phenomenon, always among the most productive and influential of our species. (Sigmund Freud is another example.)

Pavlov's method for attaching a response to a previously neutral stimulus is called *classical conditioning.* It was developed as a result of his decision to focus on a sidelight of the unlearned digestive secretions he was studying. Pavlov had been trying to measure the amount of saliva that flowed in response to food placed in the mouth of his experimental animals, usually dogs. This salivary response is an innate feature of the digestive system and requires no learning. But his attempts were complicated by the dogs' tendency to salivate at other times, to different stimuli: to the *sight* of food, for example; to the sight of the experimenter; or even to the sound of footsteps in the hall. It was difficult to measure precisely the saliva secreted to *X* ounces of meat powder when the dog was already slobbering over the sound of a shuffling janitor. The dogs were *anticipating* food; somehow, previously neutral sights and sounds had acquired the power to *elicit* (call forth) the response of salivation that normally occurs only with food.

Instead of trying to control or eliminate these extraneous stimuli, as other scientists were doing in similar situations, Pavlov decided to investigate them directly.

Stimuli and Responses

Classical conditioning involves two types of stimuli, called *unconditioned* and *condi-* *tioned,* and two types of responses, also called unconditioned and conditioned. The psychologist begins with an unconditioned stimulus (US) that elicits an unconditioned response (UR) naturally, without learning, and another stimulus (to become the conditioned stimulus or CS) that does not, at first, elicit the UR (see Table 4.1). For example, food placed in a dog's mouth is an unconditioned stimulus for the unconditioned response of salivation, and turning on a light is a neutral stimulus. Then, in what are called *acquisition trials,* the neutral stimulus is repeatedly presented around the same time as the US-UR pair: The light is turned on, the dog receives food and salivates. Finally, the previously neutral stimulus is presented alone; if the unconditioned response or something akin to it follows, conditioning or learning is said to have occurred. The neutral stimulus is then properly called a conditioned stimulus (CS), although many scientists use the label even before the acquisition stage; and the response, the former unconditioned response, is then labeled a conditioned response (CR) because it occurs because of a learned association. In summary, food (unconditioned stimulus) elicits salivation (unconditioned response) in the presence of a light (conditioned stimulus), and eventually the light elicits salivation (now the conditioned response) by itself.

We have been using the US-UR pairing of food stimuli and the salivary response, but of course there are many other such natural pairs that work as well. A puff of air at the eye (unconditioned stimulus) elicits an eyeblink (unconditioned response), a combination often used in human research. A pattern of psychological responses (for example, increased heart rate) and other behaviors we

Table 4.1
THE STAGES OF CLASSICAL CONDITIONING

Stage	Present stimulus		Observe	
1 Pretest	US	Unexpected loud noise	UR	Bodily reactions like increased heart rate, verbal reports of being startled or fearful
	CS	Odor of cinnamon		No response, or perhaps mild curiosity, but not the UR
2 Conditioning	CS	Odor of cinnamon, then		
	US	loud noise	UR	Startle or fear reaction

(Several acquisition trials are needed before going on to stage 3.)

3 Test	CS	Odor of cinnamon (without the US)	?	

(If the UR, or something like it, is observed, conditioning has been accomplished. The response is then called CR, the conditioned response.)

4 Extinction	CS	Odor of cinnamon (without the US)	CR	Startle or fear reaction at first; eventually no response

(Extinction trials are like test trials, except that extinction typically requires a number of trials. If the CR is not observed, extinction is accomplished.)

5 Spontaneous recovery	CS	Odor of cinnamon (without the US)	CR	Startle or fear reaction

(Recovery occurs after extinction seems complete, when a later test trial shows that the CR has returned. The recovered CR can be extinguished by more extinction trials.)

Generalization	S	Similar to CS (odor of cloves)	CR	Startle or fear reaction
Discrimination	S	Similar to CS (odor of cloves)		No response

(Usually subjects must learn to discriminate. Similar S is repeatedly presented without US-UR, while the CS is still paired with US-UR. Eventually S is discriminated from CS and no response occurs.)

typically call fear is an unconditioned response to many stimuli, such as very loud noises. Within limits, the conditioned stimulus can be just about anything.

Pavlov's Discoveries

The sequence of events in classical conditioning was not Pavlov's discovery. Scientists had known for years that responses sometimes occurred before the appropriate stimuli; and the expression "The mouth waters" is several hundred years old. Pavlov's contribution was his thorough research on the nature of the process. For example, he discovered that the most effective procedure for "hooking" the conditioned stimulus to the response was to present it *a half second* before the unconditioned stimulus. If the time interval is either more or less, the conditioned response will be weaker or nonexistent. If the conditioned stimulus is presented *after* the unconditioned stimulus ("backward conditioning"), there is doubt that any learning at all takes place.

Generalization. Once the conditioned stimulus was established, Pavlov discovered, other stimuli, similar in some way, also elicited the conditioned response, even though they had never been presented before. For example, if a high-pitched tone is the conditioned stimulus for salivation, after the acquisition trials other squeaky tones will also start the flow of saliva, although in slightly reduced amounts. The closer the new stimulus is to the conditioned stimulus, the greater the response. This interesting phenomenon was called *generalization.*

Generalization represents a case of learning without practice or experience. As such, it has enabled psychologists to explain subjects' behavior in situations they have never before encountered. Personality and developmental psychologists use this concept when they suggest that early interactions with parents color later interactions with others — that, for example, if we respected the authority of our father, we are likely now to respect the authority of "similar stimuli" like policemen.

Discrimination. Generalization is not always advantageous. If we are frightened by a snake or a Swede, we must realize that avoidance and hostility toward all snakes or all Swedes is detrimental to the environment, to society, to innocent snakes and Swedes, and to us personally. We must learn to discriminate between good and bad snakes and good and bad Swedes. Such *discrimination*, Pavlov discovered, requires active elimination of the generalized tendencies. If, say, a tone of 1000 Hz (hertz, or cycles per second) is used as a conditioned stimulus in salivary conditioning, a tone of 980 Hz, through generalization, will elicit a sizable response. However, if we repeatedly present a 980 Hz tone *without* the unconditioned stimulus, the conditioned response to this slightly lower-pitched sound will gradually disappear. In like fashion, encounters with a number of friendly Swedes lessen our fear of tall blonds in general and narrow it to the one Swede who frightens us. Fear of snakes is more likely to continue to be generalized, since few of us have enough casual contact with either dangerous or harmless snakes to learn to discriminate.

Extinction and Spontaneous Recovery. If a conditioned stimulus is repeatedly presented *without* the US-UR pair, gradually it will lose its ability to elicit the conditioned response. This process is called *extinction.* The conditioned response, when it no longer appears following the conditioned stimulus, is said to be *extinguished.* Discrimination, for example, involves extinguishing the conditioned responses to stimuli similar to the conditioned stimulus by presenting them without the US-UR. In less technical terms, if you are regularly fed after the sounding of a bell, the bell will come to mean feeding

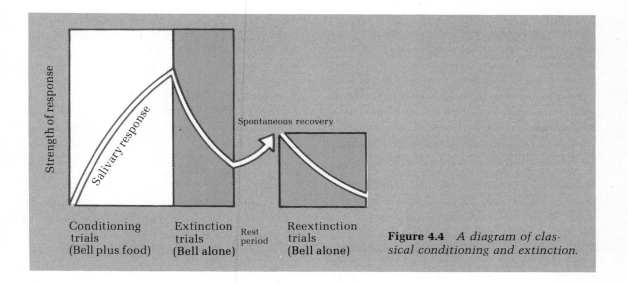

Figure 4.4   *A diagram of classical conditioning and extinction.*

time for you. But if then the bell sounds several times and no food follows, the anticipation triggered by the sound eventually disappears. Extinction, thus, is the opposite of acquisition. Some have called it "unlearning," as contrasted with the original learning.

Pavlov noted a curious *spontaneous recovery* of the learned CS-CR association after initial extinction. In experimental terms, some length of time after extinction, and in the absence of further experience with the conditioned stimulus, the subject will again respond with the conditioned response, at least a weak form of it: A dog might salivate to a tone the day after extinction of that CS-CR bond was seemingly complete. Nobody has a completely satisfactory explanation of spontaneous recovery, although most theories suggest that extinction involves some sort of inhibition or fatigue which dissipates over time, permitting

a partial restoration of the CS-CR sequence. Repeated extinctions eventually vanquish the conditioned response for good.

Whatever the explanation, spontaneous recovery is an empirical fact to be reckoned with. Many psychologist-therapists have used extinction to treat certain behavior problems, only to find their patients dissatisfied with the results because the obnoxious response has mysteriously reappeared. For example, suppose at the first meeting between a grandchild and his grandmother there is an unexpected trauma—a loud noise, perhaps, triggers the child's fear response just as the grandmother is introduced—and the grandmother becomes a conditioned stimulus to the conditioned fear response. This is an unfortunate state of affairs, likely to provoke parents into seeking professional help. The therapist repeatedly presents the conditioned stimulus (a picture of the grandmother or even her, in person) without the unconditioned stimulus (loud noise), and gradually the fear response disappears. At her next visit, however, the child again cringes and runs from the grandmother, and the parents' attorney casts aspersions on the abilities of the therapist. Proper therapy, of course, involves being prepared for possible spontaneous recovery, and treating the recovered conditioned response by further extinction trials.

PAVLOV, WATSON, AND THE BEHAVIORAL REVOLUTION

Pavlov's research, even by today's standards, produced beautiful data. He was a careful scientist and he was blessed with a remarkable dependent variable: saliva flow. Whether or not salivation occurred to the conditioned stimulus was a good indicator of learning; in addition, Pavlov could estimate the *degree* of learning by measuring the *amount* of saliva. It was good work. But could Pavlov's painstaking methods with animals be useful in research with humans as well?

The Rise of Behaviorism

In the early 1900s, psychologists who worked with animals were feuding with psychologists who worked exclusively with human subjects about proper research methods in psychology. The animal psychologists were led by John B. Watson, whom we met in Chapter 1. In 1913, he published one of the most important papers in the history of psychology: "Psychology as a Behaviorist Views It." A later psychologist called it the behaviorist manifesto (Woodworth, 1959). In it, Watson attacked *in-*

trospection, the other popular method of the time, as unscientific. (Introspection usually involved presenting stimuli to human subjects who were trained to report their internal sensations: See p. 103.) Because introspection involved the observation of a private event—only the subjects could "see inside" themselves—these data, according to Watson, were not subject to verification by other objective observers and therefore were not scientific. Observations of behavior, on the other hand, were public data; anyone could see behavior. Behavior, therefore, was the proper focus of study in psychology, *even for human subjects.*

Psychologists using introspection were having difficulties at the time anyway. Trained subjects in one lab reported their sensations differently from subjects in another lab, and there seemed no way to resolve such conflicts. Compared to the petty arguments among introspectionists, the work of Pavlov was a solid example of effective scientific research. Pavlov became the hero of the behaviorists. Watson's argument carried the day and, indeed, several decades to follow.

Albert and the Rat

As an example of how the behavioristic approach could be used to study human learning, Watson conditioned a human infant by the name of Albert (Watson and Rayner, 1920). The unconditioned stimulus was a loud noise caused by whacking a steel bar with a hammer, an event that produced fear (the unconditioned response). The conditioned stimulus was a white rat; in pretesting, Albert showed no fear of the rat and tried to play with it. In the acquisition trials, Watson's assistant whacked the steel bar

Figure 4.5 *Any stimulus that regularly precedes food can become a conditioned stimulus. Here two youngsters salivate at the sight of golden arches.*

just as Albert touched the rat. After seven trials, Albert was in mortal terror of the rat —there is no report of what the rat thought of Albert. Watson demonstrated generalization by showing that Albert also feared a rabbit, a dog, and a fur coat.

The Albert experiment, as you might imagine, was a blockbuster. It supported Watson's main point, that classical conditioning was of general importance and suitable for the understanding of much *human* behavior, but it frightened people who viewed scientists as amoral monsters with powerful techniques at their disposal.

Watson won the day for behaviorism, but, in the process, he himself was destroyed. He had sorely underestimated the emotions of both psychologists and the general public. In 1920, Watson published the Albert article, divorced his wife of 17 years, and married his graduate student. Divorce was not acceptable behavior in 1920, and "relationships" between professors and graduate students were even more taboo. Demonstrations of the power of science in the area of human behavior were frightening. If this weren't enough, Watson's article described the teaching of *fear* to an *infant*, including fear of *dogs*, everybody's favorite pet. Albert was removed from Watson's control before the planned extinction of fear responses to furry conditioned stimuli, a fact Watson blithely described as "unfortunate." There was a big scandal, and Watson was fired from his position at Johns Hopkins University. It was the end of Watson's academic career. He found a job, finally, with the J. Walter Thompson advertising agency, selling Yuban coffee and Camel cigarettes, and died a vice-president of the company (Watson, 1936).

Although Watson the scientist was diminished, his approach was simply too effective to be disregarded. Psychology defined as the study of *behavior* was to rule supreme for 50 years. B. F. Skinner was coming, right around the corner.

SKINNER AND OPERANT CONDITIONING

There are at least two procedures for training animals, including humans: classical conditioning, which we have described, and *operant conditioning*. Operant procedures focus on what happens *following* a response rather than on what *precedes* a response, as in classical conditioning. After the subject makes a response you like, you reward him —give him a prize, some praise, or something else you know he desires. If he makes a response other than the one you want, you do nothing; in other words, the reward is given only if the subject behaves "correctly." We expect he will soon begin making more of the proper responses and fewer of the improper responses. From the point of view of the subject, he does something in order to gain a reward; he "operates" on the environment in order to change it to his advantage—hence the name operant conditioning.

The emphasis in operant conditioning is on the consequences of behavior—the outcome, or, in technical terms, the *reinforcement*. Reinforcement, in most cases, is synonymous with reward, but, technically defined, it is any event that increases the probability of the preceding response. There are *positive reinforcers*, such as food or water, which increase the probability of a response if they are *presented* to the subject (assuming it is hungry or thirsty) after the response. There are also *negative reinforcers*, such as electric shock, which increase response likelihood if they are *removed* after the proper behavior. Such a negative reinforcer may also be described as *aversive*, meaning the subject will work to avoid it.

The most important principle of operant conditioning states that if you reinforce a response, that response will increase in probability. This sounds like Thorndike's Law of Effect, which it is. It is also a truism; the principle has to be true because reinforcement is *defined* as an event that increases the probability of response. In practice, however, the principle is useful; once you have discovered a reinforcer (food for a hungry animal), the same reinforcer is effective for a wide variety of behaviors.

Extinction, in operant procedures, involves withholding the reinforcement for a response, in which case the behavior gradually disappears or returns to some spontaneous base rate. Like a classically conditioned response, however, it may show *spontaneous recovery*.

Schedules of Reinforcement

B. F. Skinner was the American psychologist whose research and writings did the most to develop and promote operant procedures. According to Skinner (1959), he was studying the operant behavior of rats one day by reinforcing every response (pressing a bar) when he discovered that he had just about run out of the food pellets he was using as rewards. At the time, he had to make his own food pellets by compressing rat food in a small pill machine, and the prospect of spending this particularly pleasant Saturday afternoon compressing rat food did not appeal to him. So he decided that it was time to study the effects of *intermittent reinforcement*. Why does *every* response have to be reinforced? What would happen if he set his machine to deliver a reward for the first response after two minutes had elapsed since the last reinforcement, leaving all other responses unrewarded? He knew at least one answer: His supply of food pellets would last considerably longer, and he could enjoy a Saturday outing! As it turned out, *schedules of reinforcement* were to become one of Skinner's most important scientific contributions.

Kinds of Schedules. There are four basic types of reinforcement schedule. *Interval* schedules are based on *time* intervals since the last reinforcement; as in the example above, the first response after the interval has elapsed is reinforced. The interval can be set as any period of time — 10 seconds, 1 minute, 20 minutes — and responses before the interval has elapsed are ignored (not reinforced). *Ratio* schedules are based on the *number* of responses since the last reinforcement; a ratio of 10:1 means that 10 responses must be made to gain one reward, just as a ratio of 3:1 means that every third response is reinforced.

Each of these schedules can be either *fixed* or *variable*. Variable schedules deal out rewards on the basis of a certain *average* interval or ratio. For example, if the variable ratio is 3:1, the subject might get a reward after three responses, then after five, then after one, and so forth; the *average* number is three. In a variable-interval schedule, the subject may be reinforced for the first response after two minutes, then after three minutes, then after one minute, and so forth; the *average* interval is two minutes. In fixed schedules, the subject gets reinforced every third response — no variation — or for the first response after exactly two minutes. Thus, the four basic types of reinforcement schedules are *fixed-ratio, variable-ratio, fixed-interval,* and *variable-interval.*

Applying Reinforcement Schedules. One reason these reinforcement schedules are so interesting is their usefulness in the "real" world. In everyday life, it is rare indeed that a parent, a teacher, or a sales manager can reward *every* desired act. They have other duties, and the best they can hope for is an occasional reinforcement for "good" performance by their children, students, or sales force. What effect does this have on behavior?

The research of Skinner, his associates, and other psychologists interested in his description of schedules gives some answers — answers that come from studies using rats, pigeons, and humans as subjects. The results are remarkably uniform across various species. The first, perhaps obvious, possibility is extinction. In any schedule of reinforcement (other than reinforcing every response), some responses go unrewarded, and the subject might stop responding altogether before the next to-be-rewarded response occurs. In other words, a three-month interval between reinforcements or a plan to reinforce every 500th response will probably result in the extinction (disappearance) of the desired behavior, because so many responses are made without reward. Extreme schedules involving long intervals or large numbers of responses must be approached gradually; if you want to reinforce every 500th response, start with every 5th response, then every 10th response, then every 20th response, and so on. If you begin with the extreme schedule, you will most likely discover that the response you have decided to reward — the 500th — will never occur.

Scalloping. In the fixed schedules, behavior tends to exhibit a characteristic called *scalloping* (see Figure 4.6). After a reinforcement, the rate of responding decreases slightly and increases again before the next reinforcement. Scallops are prominent in the fixed-interval schedule, as you might imagine — what's the use of vigorous responding when the next reward won't come for, say, two minutes? In fixed-ratio sched-

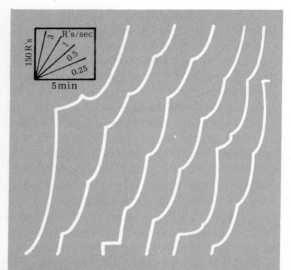

Figure 4.6 *Scalloping as shown by the response record of a pigeon pecking at a key on a fixed-interval schedule of reinforcement. (When the record line reaches the top of the space, the recorder resets to the bottom, so that these lines are really segments of one continuous record.) Notice that the response rate levels off after each reinforcement and increases shortly before the next one is due.*

well-known factor in performance, and large numbers of responses take time; the first few are farthest from the reward, so maybe it's not surprising they are the least vigorous and the least rapid.

Advantages of Variable Schedules. The primary advantage of the variable schedules is that they reduce or eliminate scalloping, producing instead a steady, constant rate of response. I recently read an essay by a religion writer who was criticizing the "20-minute sermon." Some topics, he insisted, needed 35 minutes, some only 10 minutes. As an added benefit, he suggested, churchgoers would pay more attention to the sermon throughout because they would never know when the point would be made (or when they would have to wake up to sing the next hymn). The writer was in effect suggesting a variable-interval schedule with the benefit of a more nearly constant rate of attention responses.

Of the four schedules, the variable-ratio pattern produces the highest rate of response. Pigeons have been known to peck at a colored disc at rates exceeding five pecks per second, continuing this rate for hours. Humans have been known to pull slot-machine levers in Nevada — the "one-armed bandits" operate on a variable-ratio schedule — for hours on end at a rate that exceeds their budget and my capacity for belief.

An infinite number of *combined schedules* can be generated from the four basic patterns. For example, there is what some call the "car warranty" schedule, which delivers a reward, say, after 300 responses or after 5 minutes, whichever comes first. This is a combination of fixed-ratio and fixed-interval schedules. A clinical psychologist called in to treat a child's behavior problems

ules, a decrease in the rate of responding makes less sense, since it always delays the next reward. On the other hand, we have a sort of intuitive sympathy for the rat who "rests a bit" after completing its 200th bar press before it starts in earnest on the next batch of 200 responses. Skinner (1953) likened this to the difficulty a student may experience starting work on his or her next project immediately after finishing a major term paper. More scientifically, the time between a response and its reinforcement is a may examine the interaction of the parents (the reinforcing agents) and child to determine the particular combined schedule they are using, often unconsciously. Many parents put their children on a basic variable-interval schedule, rewarding them with love and attention on the average of every two hours or so, but if the child makes several responses of a certain type—temper tantrums or passive withdrawals, for example—the parent interrupts his or her work to deliver attention-rewards on this ratio schedule. The result is not unpredictable. In extreme cases, the child begins to emit "temper" or "withdrawal" responses at a high and steady rate, and the clinical psychologist is called.

Discriminative Stimuli

Though operant procedures do not emphasize the stimuli *prior* to the response in the same way classical conditioning procedures do, prior stimuli do have a significant role in learned operant behaviors. Suppose you have learned that doing X leads to outcome Y, which, for you, is a reward. Very often, however, outcome Y depends on the situation both for its value and its likelihood. For example, food is more highly valued when you are hungry; telling a good joke is more likely to result in laughter and social approval at a party than at a funeral. So prior recognition of the situation—"I am hungry" or "These people are sad"—helps you estimate the probability of a valued reward. In operant contexts, the *discriminative stimuli* present before the response allow the subject to discriminate between situations in which a response will or will not lead to reinforcement (or in which the reward will or will not be enjoyable).

The concepts of *generalization* and *discrimination,* which apply to conditioned stimuli in classical conditioning, apply in a similar way to discriminative stimuli for operant behavior. For example, if a child learns that a certain behavior, say a temper tantrum, brings a reward (attention) from his parents at home, he is likely to generalize, that is, make the same response in other contexts. When the teacher in his school does not reinforce his tantrums, he learns to discriminate—to yell and shout and kick only at home.

Shaping Behavior

Very often the desired behavior of a rat, pigeon, or human cannot be reinforced because it never occurs. A basketball coach would love to reinforce a player who dribbles skillfully through the entire opposing team to lay in an easy bucket; an animal trainer wants his prize pig to dance to the music of Elvis Presley; an English teacher is quite willing to give praise to a student who wins the National Book Award. But one cannot simply assemble a group of naive people (or pigs), wait for the first magnificent response, and then reinforce it; the wait would far exceed the life span of the teacher.

So the teacher must teach. He or she must "shape" the behavior, much as an artist begins with a block of stone and creates, by chipping and polishing, a significant work.

One such method of producing novel behaviors (those which would not ordinarily occur in finished form without some directed experience) follows directly from the Skinnerian view of training. This procedure is called the *method of successive approximations,* or, more simply, *shaping.* Let me describe the technique with an example born of a desire to illustrate the procedure to a class of undergraduates I once taught. At the time, a dance called the Twist was just becoming popular, and I thought it would be interesting and informative to exhibit a white rat who "enjoyed" this new dance craze. The goal was to enter the classroom with my rat and a cheap phonograph. I would play a Twist record—Chubby Checker's "The Twist," for history buffs— and the rat would perk up and dance the Twist.

Establishing Reinforcers. It was not difficult to achieve this minor goal; Skinner (1951) had described the procedure in detail. The first task was to motivate the rat, which is typically done, with rats, by separating them from food for 24 hours or so. I then had to convince my rat that the food pellets I offered him would relieve the strange discomfort he felt, a surprisingly difficult job. Once that was accomplished, I had to establish a *secondary reinforcer*, some stimulus that the rat would associate with delivery of the *primary reinforcer*, the food pellet. This also proved to be surprisingly difficult and time consuming. I used a child's toy, a metal "cricket" that sounded a sharp click when pressed; I let my rat wander around, and at random moments I clicked the cricket and dropped in a food pellet. After many pairings, the rat began to respond to the click; he would run immediately to the food dish when it sounded.

The purpose of establishing a secondary reinforcer in this case was to enable me to reinforce any behavioral act immediately. The primary reinforcement—food—was too slow and imprecise, for reasons that will soon become apparent.

Shaping the Behavior. Now the shaping began. I knew if I waited for centuries, my rat would never spontaneously do the Twist. The first thing I had to do was to get him standing up on his hind legs. I watched him carefully. At first, whenever he raised his head, even slightly, I clicked the cricket. This had a surprisingly powerful effect; he ran to the food dish, ate the pellet, and then ran back to the same spot. He raised his head again. But this time I wanted more. This time he would have to raise his head even higher than before. Eventually he did, and I clicked. Soon he was poking his head as high as he could; then he was standing up.

Now I changed my criterion for a reward. Not only would he have to stand up, he would also have to make a movement to one side or the other. Any slight movement would do. Eventually he wobbled, I clicked, and soon he was standing up and taking one full step to the left. So I changed my demands again—two steps to the left; then two to the left, one to the right; then two left, two right; then two left, two right, while moving forepaws; and so forth. This sounds a little complicated, but it's not difficult. It took me about two hours to teach the rat that food pellets satisfied his hunger drive; it took me about six hours to teach him that the cricket click "meant" food; but it took me—at most—15 minutes to teach him to dance! The final step was to establish a discriminative stimulus: His dance was rewarded only when a Chubby Checker record was playing. This, too, he learned quickly, and he was then ready for his classroom recital.

The students were properly impressed by the rat's dance, but even more impressive were the following demonstrations of his learning abilities. In order to show how shaping works, I asked for suggestions of tricks. One girl had a little bell (originally attached to her shoe) which we hung from the top of the rat's cage. In five minutes or so, with the cricket to shape his behavior, our rat was climbing up the wall of his cage, leaning out, and batting the bell. First we rewarded any motion toward the wall; then closer and closer; then touching, then grabbing, then climbing; then leaning from the top of the wire mesh wall; and finally touching, then batting the bell. Easy.

Such pedagogical success! However, a failure occurred in the same session, the significance of which will be noted later in this chapter. Convinced I could teach this rat anything, I had brought in a ping-pong ball and a paper clip, in case the students had no suggestions for tricks. I planned to make a hoop with the paper clip and then teach the rat to "play basketball," that is, to pick up the ball and drop it through the hoop. After the bell-ringing, we tried this stunt. Properly reinforced, the rat moved closer and closer to the ping-pong ball; then he touched it, moved it about; then to my rather obvious horror, he *ate* it! He ate my basketball!

Secondary Reinforcements

It should be obvious why, in the demonstration above, I had to establish a secondary reinforcer. To shape the rat's behaviors, I had to make sure the precise behaviors I wanted were reinforced. If I wanted the rat to move slightly left, I had to reinforce such a response *immediately* after it occurred, which I could do with the sharp, clear click of the cricket. Consider the alternative. He moves left, and I place a food pellet in his

Figure 4.7 *A basketball stunt obviously more successful than mine. What do you suppose the trainers rewarded as successive approximations of the final behavior pictured here?*

dish. He would be totally unaware of his reward unless he happened to be looking right at the dish (and, properly speaking, even the sight of food is a secondary, not a primary, reinforcer).

Secondary reinforcers—stimuli that are associated with primary reinforcements—are extremely important in understanding human behavior. Money is a good example. I can easily entice some people to move all my furniture and books from Michigan to California simply by offering them certain pieces of paper. Doesn't that sound ridiculous? The movers know, of course, that they can exchange the pieces of paper for a steak, some beer, or some other more tangible asset, and thus they are willing to work for paper.

PUNISHMENT

Punishment, as a procedure, can be considered the opposite of reinforcement: After a response, either a positive reinforcer (for example, food) is *removed*, or a negative reinforcer (for example, shock) is *presented*. But, although punishment and reinforcement are procedurally opposite, the effects generally are not. Considering effects, extinction is the opposite of reinforcement; reinforcement results in an increase in the probability of a response, whereas extinction results in a decrease. What, then, is the effect of punishment? This, as Skinner has said, "is an empirical question"; the answer must come from research.

Temporary Suppression of Behavior

Research very quickly established one fact: The effects of punishment are not simple. One early experiment involved two groups of rats who learned a bar-pressing response which was then extinguished (they no longer got a food reward for bar-pressing). One group was punished by electric shock for responses made during the early stages of extinction but not thereafter. The second, control group was never punished. The animals who were punished decreased their rate of response *temporarily*, during the punishment trials and shortly thereafter, but the total number of responses made before total extinction was the same as for the rats who were never punished (see Figure 4.8). The conclusion is direct: In this situation, punishment had the effect of *temporary suppression* of the behavior, but it did not weaken the response overall (Estes, 1944).

The rats in this experiment were not receiving reinforcements for their behavior when the punishment was instituted. In most cases, however, punishments are applied to responses that are also being reinforced, and in these cases, too, we observe a temporary suppression of the response. We are all familiar with the child who doesn't touch the cookie jar when Mom or Dad is in the kitchen, the motorist who slows down when he sees a patrol car, and the student who keeps his eyes on his own exam when the teacher is watching. When the social agent with the power to deliver punishments is not present, the cookie-snitching, speeding, or cheating responses reappear in full glory. In cases like these, the behavior is obviously being reinforced at times so the punishment (or threat of punishment) must compete with the reinforcement (or promise of it). The "wrongdoers" learn only to discriminate among stimuli: Parent-in-the-kitchen becomes a clue to the fact that inserting-hand-into-cookie-jar will not result in satisfying-feeling-in-stomach, and parent-out-of-sight means that the same response will now bring the desired reward.

On the other hand, temporary suppression of undesirable behaviors provides an opportunity to teach new and more socially acceptable behaviors. For example, if a parent punishes a child for throwing rocks at the neighbor's windows, the child will most likely suppress the response, at least for a time. The parent can use this time to actively reinforce other behaviors, such as playing baseball, a more socially acceptable way of breaking the neighbor's windows. Rock-throwing may thereby disappear because sports provide a more efficient means of releasing energy, gaining attention, and attaining the other goals previously supplied by window-breaking. To put someone in jail for stealing is clearly a punishment. If the

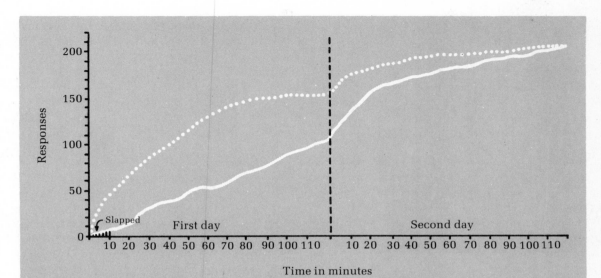

Figure 4.8 *This graph illustrates one effect of punishment. Rats whose paws were slapped during the early phase of extinction respond at a lower rate for a while (temporary suppression), but before extinction is complete the total number of responses is the same as for the unpunished rats.*

period of stealing-suppression (time in jail) is not combined with active rehabilitation—teaching more acceptable ways of obtaining money—the ex-con is likely to revert to old methods once released.

Punishment, Guilt, and Classical Conditioning

Repeated punishments for a particular act are likely to lead to *guilt,* which humans define as feeling remorse about committing an act. To explore the implications of the relationship between punishment and guilt, and the resulting effect on behavior, we might well consider here the guilt of pets. We often improperly attribute human emotions to our pets, but guilt is one attitude humans and other animals do seem to share. For example, my dog knocked over a vase once; I looked at him with a fierceness not quite in keeping with the $1.19 cost of the vase; he hung his head, crouched, and looked at me with guilty eyes. How do we explain such behavior if not as a feeling of remorse?

The behavior pattern, of course, is similar to what happens when a pet is actually punished—shouted at, chased away, or, sometimes, slapped on the nose. The theory is, therefore, that the unconditioned stimulus (loud shout, slap) naturally elicits cowering behavior. Any neutral stimulus that repeatedly precedes the unconditioned

Figure 4.9 *If this boy were caught and punished, would he stop his thieving ways?*

stimulus will eventually become a conditioned stimulus. The sound of something breaking, the scowl on his master's face—these are regular cues to impending punishment. So in their presence the dog cowers—he looks guilty.

Accept this theory for a second, and consider the implications. The cues mentioned—the conditioned stimuli—happen *after*, not before, the improper behavior. The conditioned stimuli suppress further similar behavior because they elicit an incompatible response; the dog can hardly cower and romp through the china at the same time. But the conditioned stimuli cannot prevent the *first* destructive act. This is a characteristic of guilty animals, including humans: They break things—vases, laws, rules of conduct—and *then* response-produced stimuli result in feelings and behavior associated with guilt.

When punishment has effects like these, we have the worst of all possible worlds.

From the point of view of the punisher, the response he is trying to inhibit is not inhibited; from the point of view of the punishee—the pet, the child, the student, or the criminal—the behavior brings no joy. Neither partner in the punishment pair wins; they both lose.

Clearly the improper behavior would be better controlled if the conditioned stimulus occurred *before* the undesirable response. Then guilt would begin before the behavior, and, it is hoped, would prevent it. Humans, with their vast conceptual powers, are prone to such prebehavior guilt, though the effects are not always desirable. Many children are punished for sexual behaviors—masturbation, for example—and develop prebehavior guilt as a result. Thinking about sex may include imagining the act, which may serve as a conditioned stimulus to cowering and feeling guilty. The number of both men and women who have difficulty performing the sex act because of guilt feelings, even in situations they have been taught to consider proper, is enormous.

Discriminative learning—discrimination, the learning of discriminative stimuli, or however you prefer to conceptualize it—is essential in most of the human situations in which we use punishment. A child, if he or she is to be a normal adult, must learn that sexual behavior is proper in some cases and improper in others, just as a dog must learn that excited, rambunctious behavior is proper in some situations and not in others. Discrimination means that punishment *by itself* is a poor means of behavior control; a response in the presence of certain stimuli must be punished, and, in the presence of other stimuli, it must be rewarded. So we come to the same conclusion as before: Punishment may be useful *if* it is combined with a constructive program for reinforcing acceptable acts in the acceptable context.

Punishment and Aggression

In Chapter 1 we defined aggression as behavior intended to cause injury or pain to another person or animal. Punishment, too, can be so defined, for it is deliberate action meant to be aversive to the recipient. Corporal punishment—actually hitting, slapping, or spanking someone—best illustrates the aggressive nature of punishment; but it is reasonable to say that all punishment is aggression, even if the intention is to benefit the recipient in the long run. This fact creates several problems in the use of punishment as behavior control, two of which we will consider now.

Aggression to Stop Aggression? Consider a father who tries to stop his son from fighting by punishing him after fights. What does the boy learn? Perhaps he learns to suppress the fighting behavior, at least when his father is around; the kid is no fool. But he also learns that, say, slapping someone is a father-approved means of getting that person to stop doing something undesirable. Now, this is probably why he was fighting in the first place, to make some young friend do things his way. The use of aggression to inhibit aggression is very confusing, and generally ineffective, as children and nations have discovered for centuries.

A child, in particular, learns much by simply observing and imitating his or her parents. If the parent typically uses physical punishment to control behavior, the child is likely to be similarly aggressive in his attempts to gain his objectives. Many studies have shown that children of punishing parents display the same tactics: If the parents use physical punishments, the child becomes a "fighter," and if the parents punish by withdrawing affection, the child will do the same (Bandura, 1969).

Pain and Aggression. Another relevant series of studies concerns the aggressive response to physical pain that is typical of almost all animals. If you poke an animal with a sharp, painful instrument, its response will be, in most cases, to attack (bite, beat, or otherwise try to injure) the instrument or, in higher animals, the holder of the instrument. Such behavior is so widespread and so regular that many psychologists consider it an unconditioned response to the unconditioned stimulus of pain, a natural reaction that occurs without learning (Azrin, 1972).

There is undoubtedly an evolutionary advantage to attacking an aggressor. In the animal world, physical pain often accompanies a threat to the animal's life, as when another animal is attacking; a vigorously aggressive response may be the difference between life and death. But in the human world, an aggressive response to physical punishment is more likely to start a vicious circle of aggression and counter-aggression than to ensure physical safety. When Susie hits Janie, Mommy or Daddy may hit Susie and consider the exchange of aggression complete. "An eye for an eye." But Susie doesn't see it that way; she is more likely to go hit the dog, or her doll, or little Billy next door. Billy, having been hit by Susie, may hit her back if he is about as big as she is, or if he isn't, may go hit some smaller child. Or he may call in someone bigger—his mother perhaps—in the hope she will hit Susie for him. In any case, the undesirable behavior has not been extinguished, only at best diverted to another target.

BEHAVIORISM: THORNS AMONG THE ROSES

General learning theories in the behavioristic tradition began an ascent in 1900 with Thorndike, reached prominence in the period from 1915 to 1920, thanks to Watson and Pavlov, and completely dominated American psychology from about 1930 to 1960, led by B. F. Skinner and Clark Hull, a Yale psychologist who wrote several versions of "a general behavior theory." It was apparent that one could achieve a significant amount of control over behavior by manipulating stimuli, as in classical conditioning or in creating discriminative stimuli for operant behaviors, and by controlling the outcomes of behavior: reinforcements, punishments, or nothing (as in extinction). The

learning psychologists had the appearance of magicians; they could make a behavior appear or disappear at will. It was a bit frightening, which in a way was a tribute to its effectiveness.

The dominant theorists, however, were not without their gadflies and critics, scientists who complained about untested presumptions and argued about data. The research of the critics, in itself a significant body of knowledge, will be the focus of the remainder of this chapter.

Insight

Most of the general theories assumed that learning proceeds gradually—by trial and error, as Thorndike called it. Many psychologists felt that such accounts overlooked *insight*, a sudden recognition of the nature of the task and what behaviors are most appropriate in that context. But Thorndike's research with his puzzle boxes showed that even human subjects continued to make several errors after the correct solution had been discovered; there was no evidence of insight.

In 1925, research on chimpanzees was published by Wolfgang Köhler, research with strong evidence for insightful learning. The classic example is a problem set for Sultan, Köhler's best pupil. A bunch of bananas was placed outside Sultan's cage, too far away for him to reach by hand. Also outside the cage were two sticks, one short and one long. Sultan could reach the short stick by hand, but it was too short to reach the bananas; it was long enough, however, to reach the long stick. Sultan first tried to reach the bananas by hand. Failing this, he spied the short stick, grabbed it, and tried again to reach the bananas. Again he failed.

He paused, looked about, and noticed the long stick. He scraped in the long stick with the short stick, and then he reached the bananas with the long stick. Köhler thought Sultan was a very bright chimp and that this was truly insightful behavior. Most psychologists agreed.

Teaching Insight. Other psychologists, however, were less impressed. Köhler's experiments seemed to them comparable to the stories pet owners tell about humanlike intelligence in their dogs, cats, and turtles: "Fido understands me! I ask, 'Are you hungry?' and he nods his head and runs to the cupboard where I keep the dog food!" What these pet owners are describing, in most cases, is the *end result* of gradual trial-and-error learning. Food is associated with the kitchen, then the cupboard, then the owner's words, and if the owner makes feeding depend on head-nodding, that response too will be learned in time. The end result is very impressive; it looks like intelligence, but it is a circus trick, pure and simple. With careful planning, you could as easily (almost) teach your dog to shake his head in response to your question and run into the bathroom.

Developing Insight. Was the insight of Sultan also the end result of previous trial-and-error learning? Two types of experiments suggested that it was. First, several studies showed that chimpanzees deprived of the opportunity to manipulate and use sticks during infancy did not show insight in later stick-manipulation problems like the one presented to Sultan (Birch, 1945). These experiments suggest that insight involves skills learned gradually.

The second type of experiment demonstrated the gradual development of so-called sudden insight more clearly (Harlow, 1949). Animals (mostly monkeys at first) were presented with a *series* of simple problems, the solutions of which had in common the same general principle. In the simplest, two objects were presented and the monkey was required to touch or point to one to gain a food reward. (The psychologist had arbitrarily designated one of the two as correct.) On the first trial of a given problem, the monkey has no way of knowing which object is "correct," and it has a 50:50 chance of guessing right. Insight, however, can be demonstrated on the *second* trial; an insightful animal will stay with the same choice if the first trial is rewarded and switch to the other object if initially unsuccessful; it should be 100 percent correct, or close to it, on the second trial.

After a hundred or two of such problems, many higher primates (humans, chimpanzees) were showing insight — responding correctly close to 100 percent of the time on the second trial. Someone observing them at this point might say something like, "Gee! That's a smart animal." But results from the preceding hundred or so problems show that the development of insight occurs very gradually.

Insightful learning, sudden recognition of correct solutions, does exist. But it is fairly clear that such learning typically involves the use of knowledge and behaviors that were learned previously by much more mundane and ordinary procedures, trial-and-error or whatever. Genius is, in this sense, truly "10 percent inspiration and 90 percent perspiration," and most acts of important creativity involve a long period of preparation.

Latent Learning

In a classic laboratory experiment, rats were randomly formed into three groups and placed one by one in a complicated maze (Tolman and Honzik, 1930). Rats in one group found food at the end of the maze, and the number of errors each made decreased rapidly on repeated runs through the maze, as shown in Figure 4.10. (A maze error is going into some pathway that does not lead to the end.) Rats in the other two groups were not rewarded with food at the end, and they showed much less "learning" of the correct route through the maze, although, of course, sooner or later they did make it to the end. (By using one-way doors, the experimenters made it impossible to return to the start.) After 10 trips through the maze—one per day—one of the "ignorant" groups suddenly discovered food at the end, and the next day they were running through the maze as accurately as the rats that had been rewarded throughout. (Better, in fact—a finding that triggered a series of studies on the effects of a "pleasant surprise.")

The results of this experiment were more troubling to the general learning theorists than the insight studies were because these findings cast doubt on one of their fundamental assumptions, that reinforcement is necessary for learning. This experiment suggested that reinforcement was indeed necessary for the behavioral demonstration of learning, but that even without reinforcement, learning occurred and could be elicited at some later time simply by introducing an incentive, a reason for running speedily through the maze. Until the reinforcement is introduced, the learning is *latent*—present but not directly observable.

Reinforcement theorists responded to this study of latent learning by pointing out that rats in the two "no-reinforcement" groups were showing a gradual decrease in the number of maze errors, even though the decrease was not as pronounced as that shown by the rewarded rats. To them, of course, this meant these rats were being reinforced, not by food perhaps, but by other events. They ran a series of experiments showing that rats consider it rewarding simply to find the end of the maze and there to get handled by humans as they are returned to their home cage. By their standards, therefore, they had shown that reinforcement *was* involved in latent learning. Since most of the reinforcement theories did not state that more or better reinforcements led to more or better learning, just that *some* reinforcement was necessary for learning, they were content to dismiss latent learning phenomena as relatively trivial, special cases.

Everyone agreed that an important distinction had been made between *learning* and *performance*. Psychologists often use performance (behavior) as a measure of learning. If nothing else, the studies of latent learning showed that, although behavior change might require learning, little or no change in behavior does not *necessarily* mean that little or no learning has occurred. This is a simple but important distinction, as we will see in many later examples. A disturbed child, for example, may not speak, although he's ten years old. His parents worry that he has brain damage that makes language learning impossible. But when his real problem, which is emotional, is dealt with by a skilled psychotherapist, he may suddenly begin "talking a blue streak." The expression, "He knows more than he lets on," suggests that folk wisdom is sometimes more accurate than nit-picking sciences.

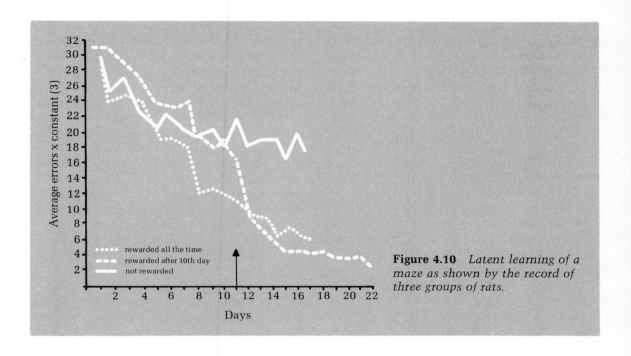

Figure 4.10   *Latent learning of a maze as shown by the record of three groups of rats.*

The Ethologists' Complaints

Insight and latent learning were concepts psychologists found particularly useful in discussions of *human* behavior. The mental ability and "fund of knowledge" of humans is so superior to that of other animals that it seems incredible that "general" learning theories, applicable to both humans and other animals, could even be formulated. Such theories are almost always criticized as being oversimplified, and disregarding the unique status of humans. The critics we have discussed were probing this vulnerability.

Another group of critics complained that general learning theories disregarded not only the unique status of humans but also the special talents of each species in the animal kingdom. These critics were the *ethologists,* scientists who study the behavior of animals in their natural habitats.

Instinctive Drift. A good illustration of what can happen when a learning theorist disregards the common behaviors of animals in their natural environments is the work of two psychologists who were engaged in training animals for zoo shows, TV shows, and the like (Breland and Breland, 1961, 1966). These psychologists used Skinner's operant procedures, usually quite successfully. There were occasional failures in conditioning, however, and soon they began to notice a curious pattern to the failures. In one case, raccoons were being taught to drop "coins" in a "bank" in order to get food. But the raccoons would not comply. They refused to drop the coins; they brought the coins to the bank and there proceeded to rub them together ("washing" them). Finally the trick had to be abandoned.

A similar bank trick was designed for pigs, who were taught to carry large wooden "coins" to a container, again for food reward. In this case, the proper response was learned, but then it deteriorated. The pigs began to drop the coin on the way from the coin pile to the "piggy bank"; they would push it along with their snouts, pick it up, and toss it in the air ("rooting"). Finally, the misbehavior became so pronounced that the pigs were starving—not getting enough food from their coin deposits—and this trick, too, had to be abandoned.

These failures were of great interest to learning psychologists, who sometimes speak as if *any* response can be trained with *any* appropriate reward. In both examples, the motivation (hunger) and the reinforcement (food) were characteristic of feeding situations in the wild, situations in which the raccoon instinctively washes its food and the pig instinctively roots for food. In the context of tricks, however, washing and rooting interfered with the behavior to be learned. The interference was called *instinctive drift,* meaning the desired response was replaced by instinctive behaviors characteristic of the animal in its natural habitat.

It was no great discovery, of course, to find that animals exhibit instinctive behaviors—behaviors that do not require experience before performance. It would not have been surprising to see the raccoons wash their food reinforcement once they got it, nor would it have been considered unusual if the pigs had pushed and tossed their food. It was surprising, however, to find the instinctive behavior patterns of these animals interfering with the operant responses that occurred *before* the food reinforcement. Instincts had to be considered, not only in the eating response, but also in the entire sequence of events that led up to it.

Additional evidence on the same point follows directly, but we should note that herein lies the explanation of why my rat ate the ping-pong ball (p. 161). Frankly, I'm not sure whether he was trying to eat it or whether he was just sharpening his teeth and got carried away, for teeth-sharpening in a feeding sequence is instinctive in rats, but it is quite clear that my demonstration was a failure because I had forgotten to consider instinctive behavior.

Conflict between Response and Reinforcement. Sexual and aggressive behaviors are vital to both individual animals and their species, and among lower animals, at least, they involve several instinctive reactions. So sexual and aggressive situations are good ones in which to further explore the disruptive effects of instinctive behavior on learning. One enterprising researcher used both sex and aggression in one study (Sevenster, 1968). He required the animal (a male fish) to make an *aggressive* response in order to receive a reinforcement related to *sex*—the opportunity to display to a sexually receptive female. (Displays are part of many animal mating rituals. In fish, they typically involve puffing up, becoming more vividly colored, and making elaborate movements.) The responses to be learned were either biting a rod (aggressive) or swimming through a ring (neutral). The fish learned both, but the rate of response for rod-biting was significantly slower.

These data were interpreted as demonstrating a conflict between the response to be learned and the response typically associated with the particular reinforcement. A ripe female is part of a sexual situation, whereas the rod-biting response is aggressive in nature. One would expect that if the reinforcement had been the opportunity to display *aggressively* to another male, rod-biting would have been a compatible response, and the response rate would be very high. This appears to be the case (see Shettleworth, 1972).

In these experiments, and also in those on instinctive drift, the kind of reinforcement used makes a difference; one cannot use any reinforcement for any response. We must consider the nature of the situation defined by the reinforcement (sexual? aggressive? feeding?) and the nature of the response in similar terms. If the reinforcement is food, we must consider the animal's instinctive feeding behaviors, which may compete with our circus tricks; when the reinforcement is sexual, an aggressive response like rod-biting may be inhibited.

Imprinting. There is much evidence that associations between certain stimuli and certain behaviors can be easily learned at some times and at other times learned only with great difficulty, if at all. Suggestions of *critical periods* in learning were made as early as 1873, when an Englishman named Spalding noted strange behaviors in chickens and ducks. Spalding had separated chicks and ducklings from their mothers for periods of a week or more—in order to study learning in newborns—and when he was finished, he returned the birds to their natural habitat. He then made his most significant discovery: The chicks would not respond to the hen's retrieval calls ("Come here, baby" in Chickenese), and the ducklings were terrified of water. He proposed that learning in the wild often has a natural sequence that, if disrupted, results in abnormal behaviors that may persist for life.

Over 50 years later, an Austrian scientist named Konrad Lorenz decided to investigate this intriguing notion of critical periods in learning. He divided the eggs of a friendly goose into two batches, one batch for the mother and one for himself. Mother goose hatched her batch in the natural course of events, while Mother Lorenz required the aid of an incubator. It did not take Lorenz long to discover the dramatic effects of his manipulation.

The mother-hatched goslings were perfectly normal and happy. Lorenz's goslings were also happy and normal except for one peculiar fact: They obviously thought Lorenz was their mother. They followed him around, ran to him when frightened, and, generally, reacted to him as the other goslings responded to their real mother. Lorenz called this phenomenon *imprinting;* he suggested that it was a specific kind of association between a stimulus and various responses learned during a critical period immediately following birth. The responses, of course, are those a gosling makes to its mother, and the stimulus is the first living thing encountered after birth—which, in all but the most carefully contrived situations, is the real mother.

Later research on ducklings did much to define the concept of critical periods. In one experiment (Hess, 1958), ducklings were kept in isolation after birth. At various intervals, they were exposed to an object on which they could imprint—a moving wooden duck (like a decoy). In this way, psychologists discovered that imprinting is greatest between 13 and 16 hours after birth.

Figure 4.11   *"Mother" Lorenz and his brood.*

After 32 hours, the critical period has ended; a duckling kept in isolation that long will not imprint on anything. It has been orphaned in the most profound sense of the word.

The end of the imprinting period coincides with the first signs of another period — fear of unfamiliar stimuli — and fear may well account, in part, for the decrease in affectionate (imprinting) responses (Moltz and Stettner, 1961). The duckling cannot simultaneously approach a stimulus and avoid it in fear. Various manipulations designed to reduce fear, however, extend the critical period only slightly, suggesting that other factors (for example, neural and hormonal maturation) are involved.

Other Critical Periods. The discovery of imprinting led other psychologists to consider the nature and importance of critical periods. It makes sense, for example, to assume that a species would evolve so as to make learning of particularly important behaviors easy during periods in which the relevant stimuli and responses are most likely to occur. Only extremely unusual circumstances, such as a Lorenz smiling proudly on newly hatched goslings, demonstrate the effect of experience on these behaviors and discourage "instinctive" interpretations such as "All children *know* their biological mother."

The learning of various responses to appropriate stimuli, by this view, would have different critical periods in different species. For example, the mating response is variable among species. Lorenz was distressed to learn that female turtledoves, whom he had caused to be imprinted on him as their mother, later considered him to be a male of their species and, during mating season, came to him, fully expecting him to do his duty for the preservation of the species. But the cuckoo does not try to mate with the first species it encounters after birth; this makes sense, because cuckoos lay their eggs in the nests of birds of different species. If the cuckoo tried to mate with the species with which it had been reared, the cuckoo race would die out.

Some social responses are apparently learned later than just after birth. In dogs, there seems to be a critical period between six and eight weeks of age; if dogs have no contact with humans during this period, they never exhibit their characteristic strong attachments to humans (Scott, 1962). An-

other example of a critical period occurring later in life is that of a mother imprinting on her offspring. A mother goat not allowed to lick and smell her kid within an hour after its birth will reject it (Klopfer et al., 1964).

Are there critical periods for human learning? It seems likely, although the exact stimuli and responses are not easily specified. If the speech areas of the brain are damaged through injury or disease, children below the age of ten can usually recover, but loss after that time is generally more nearly permanent (Lenneberg, 1967). Many psychologists feel the brain is more adaptable early in life, with other parts able to take over lost functions.

FOCUS

Bait Shyness

Anyone who has tried to kill rats with poisoned bait can tell you that it's not easy. Somehow the rats learn to avoid the bait, a phenomenon known as *bait shyness*. Just how they do this has been extensively studied by psychologists, with some surprising results (Garcia and Ervin, 1968).

Rats do not recognize poison, and they will not avoid poisoned bait presented to them. Instead, as they do with any new kind of food that turns up in their habitat, they sample a small portion and then do not eat more for several hours. If they become ill, they will then avoid the substance in the future. You can understand the advantages of this behavior pattern to the rat; if the food is poisoned, a small portion is less likely to kill the rat, and if the food makes it ill, the rat will then stay away from it. It's easy to see why it's hard to poison a rat.

There are several curious features to bait shyness. A rat that eats perfectly good food and then gets sick for unrelated reasons will avoid the food as if it were poison. In many experiments, the rat is fed various foods and then injected with sickness-inducing chemicals; it then avoids certain foods and not others. It avoids, for example, the *novel* foods but not those it has eaten regularly in the past. And what it avoids, specifically, is food that has the same (or very similar) *taste* as the new substance. It will not avoid foods of the same color, food served in the same dish, or food as-sociated with other stimulation; poisoned bait served with musical ac-companiment, for example, does not affect the rat's reaction to music. Only the taste of novel food is important.

It is not typical behavior for a rat to respond to taste alone. If you shock a rat while it is eating, it will avoid foods that look like what it was eating or foods with the same associated sounds; strangely, it will *not* avoid foods with the same taste. So taste is the important factor in poison avoidance, but not in other types of avoidance learning in rats.

Consider now the implications of this strange kind of learning, bait shyness. It is admirably suited to the protection of the rat species; in fact, one can hardly imagine a more effective survival mechanism. Neverthe-less, the phenomenon poses serious problems for general theories of learning. Why is only one aspect of the stimuli surrounding the response —taste—influenced by the aversive outcome? How can it be that an out-come occurring an *hour* or so after the response affects the probability of the rat's repeating that response? In most learning, a delay of more than *one second* between behavior and outcome can significantly reduce or eliminate the effects of reinforcement—which is one reason secondary reinforcers that can be delivered immediately are so important. And why is learning so rapid in bait shyness? A single trial is usually enough to keep the rat away.

Nobody has a completely satisfactory answer to the puzzle. We could say that some stimulus-response-outcome sequences are more easily learned than others, especially if the behaviors involved are of obvious importance to the survival of the animal or its species (Rozin, 1977). An explanation in terms of evolutionary advantage suits the approach of the ethologist, but it disheartens psychologists interested in general princi-ples of learning, forcing them to consider each animal and each stimulus, response, and reinforcement separately. Of course, this is precisely what the ethologists have been urging for so many years. Nature, it appears, is never quite as simple as our conception of it.

Rats are not the only animals to exhibit bait shyness. Flavor aversions have been demonstrated in several species, including monkeys, reptiles, fish, and even snails (Wallace, 1976). Bait shyness in visually oriented animals such as birds is sometimes linked to visual rather than flavor stimuli (Wilcoxon et al., 1971), and animals that rely on the sense of smell sometimes learn an instant "distaste" for odors (Rudy and Cheatle, 1977), but taste is the most important factor in most cases with most animals. Humans, too, show "bait shyness," developing an aversion to foods consumed, usually coincidentally, before an illness (Garb and Stunkard, 1974). I had a friend who finally agreed to try Mexican food, which I love. An hour after eating, she became violently ill, and her Mexican food eating days, I'm afraid, were over; she still avoids it as if it were poison! It was not the food that caused the sickness; it was influenza, which began an hour after she had eaten but lasted for almost a week. Although she knows why she got sick, my friend adamantly refuses to look at another enchilada.

The research on bait shyness has a number of potentially invaluable applications. One is with humans who must undergo nauseating drug or radiation therapy because of cancer. These people often develop pronounced aversions to food eaten before they come in for their treatment (Bernstein, 1978), to the extent that loss of appetite and weight is one of the most serious side effects of such cancer therapies. Knowing this, we can suggest that patients plan their meals so that they do not directly precede therapy. In addition, accumulating evidence that histamines underlie the bait shyness effect has led to the hypothesis that antihistamines might relieve cancer patients of some of their distress and learned food aversions (Wallace, 1976). There is some evidence that marijuana acts in a similarly beneficial manner.

Another practical way of using food-aversion research is to save the life of the wily coyote. Each year, around 100,000 coyotes are shot, trapped, or poisoned in the United States alone, according to official records, and another 100,000 or more are killed "off the record." Sheep ranchers are responsible for most of this; they are trying to protect their flocks. Psychologists have proposed that both sheep and coyotes can be saved if the coyote can be influenced to develop an aversion to the taste of lamb (Gustavson et al., 1976). Eating lamb saturated with a chemical that induces nausea and vomiting was effective with coyotes in captivity; after one "tainted" meal, the coyotes refused to attack a (very frightened) lamb let loose in their pen.

Researchers also have obtained promising results on a real sheep ranch by leaving tainted meat in areas frequented by lamb-killing coyotes. It's possible, of course, that the wily coyotes may learn to avoid the bait but not the live lambs; they may learn to eat only animals they themselves have killed. But the results so far indicate that the bait shyness technique is working better than other nonlethal techniques, such as spraying lambs with chemicals that smell like skunks or mountain lions, smells that often cause the mother sheep to reject their lambs. If the coyotes can be kept away from lambs, there is a good chance they and their rancher neighbors will become good friends, for the coyote provides many valuable services. Predators like the coyote are the major means of "population control" among mice, rats, rabbits, and even grasshoppers.

CURRENT VIEWS
OF LEARNING

What are the implications of these studies of instinctive drift, critical periods, and other topics based on the ethological approach to behavior? Because of these studies, psychologists are more aware of possible exceptions to the general principles of learning, exceptions they often can predict by knowing the survival needs and behavior patterns of the animal in its natural habitat. But this does not mean that general principles, with applicability to many species, cannot be formulated.

Consider, for example, the most general principle of operant conditioning, that reinforcements following a response make the response more likely in the future. Obviously this is a widely applicable principle, for any species that did not change its behavior in order to gain more reinforcements would not survive for very long. Consider, also, the most general principle of classical conditioning: A stimulus that regularly precedes a US-UR pair will eventually elicit something like the unconditioned response by itself. Again, this kind of learning is of obvious value to many species in the wild, for it allows them to anticipate or predict important events. A strange smell may regularly precede an attack by a predator, and eventually the prey can tell from the smell (conditioned stimulus) to flee sooner.

So there are general principles of learning. But the unique character of each species makes exceptions and variations likely; each species must be considered separately.

Considering each species separately, of course, makes life a little more difficult for the learning theorists. In fact, by setting their focus on *behavior*, they encountered a series of difficulties. Factors other than learning had to be considered—instinctive behaviors, for example. Studies of latent learning showed that motivation must be taken into account. Perhaps the areas of study had become too broad, encompassing too many phenomena. For whatever reason, after 1960, learning psychologists began to focus much more precisely on the question, "What is learned?" Human subjects rather than rats were used. It was not long before the learning psychologists discovered that they were actually talking about *memory* more than learning; what is learned, it turned out, is best indicated by what is remembered or retained. This story follows, in Chapter 5.

SUMMARY

1. Thorndike studied the intelligence of animals by observing their attempts to escape from a puzzle box. From the resulting data, he formulated the *Law of Effect:* A response that is followed by a satisfying state of affairs will become more likely, and one followed by an unpleasant state will become less likely.

2. From Pavlov's research on learned salivation in dogs came the principles of *classical conditioning.* When a neutral stimulus repeatedly precedes another stimulus (the *unconditioned stimulus* or US) to which there is a "natural" or innate response (the *unconditioned response* or UR), the neutral stimulus gradually comes to elicit the response: The neutral stimulus becomes a *conditioned stimulus* (CS), and the response it elicits a *conditioned response* (CR).

3. Stimuli similar to the CS also elicit the CR, a phenomenon called *generalization.*

But if only one specific CS is followed by the US, eventually the similar stimuli lose their power, as the organism learns *discrimination*. The CS loses its power to elicit the CR if it is repeatedly presented without the US; this is called *extinction*. Often there is some *spontaneous recovery*, however, wherein the CS later recovers some of its power to elicit the CR, and more extinction trials are necessary to extinguish the behavior completely.

4. J. B. Watson was the "public relations director" for the behavioral revolution. He argued that psychology had to use observable behaviors as data, not introspected, subjective reports of sensations; and he pioneered applications of Pavlovian conditioning to human subjects.

5. B. F. Skinner is known for his research in *operant conditioning*. The most general principle of operant conditioning is that responses that are followed by reinforcement become more probable in the future. *Reinforcement* is defined as any stimulus that increases the likelihood of the preceding behavior. *Positive reinforcers* are desirable consequences (rewards); *negative reinforcers* are undesirable, increasing the probability of a response if they are removed after the response. Skinner also investigated the effects of various schedules of reinforcement: fixed-ratio, variable-ratio, fixed-interval, and variable-interval.

6. Stimuli preceding the response in operant conditioning often play the role of *discriminative stimuli*, indicating situations in which the response will or will not lead to rewards. Stimuli regularly associated with primary reinforcements become *secondary reinforcements*; money is one common example. The method of successive approximations or *shaping* is used to get animals to perform complex behaviors they do not exhibit spontaneously.

7. *Punishment* involves taking away something valued or presenting something aversive. It often has the effect of suppressing behavior, at least while the punisher is around, but it is unlikely to lead to permanent changes in behavior unless combined with reinforcement for "good" behaviors while the "bad" responses are being suppressed. Aggressive punishment may elicit aggression in response.

8. *Guilt* is often a CR to stimuli associated with a frequently punished response. But since guilt usually occurs after the response, it does little to control the offensive behavior.

9. *Insight* refers to a sudden recognition of the nature of a task and the dramatic improvement in performance that results. Although insight, by definition, is not gradual trial-and-error improvement, it may depend on previous trial-and-error learning.

10. *Latent learning* is reflected in behavior only when the incentives to perform are sufficient. Research on this topic resulted in increased recognition of the important distinction between learning and performance.

11. *Instinctive drift* often interferes with the performance of trained animals. Food reinforcements may elicit instinctive behaviors related to feeding; and sexual reinforcements can make the learning of aggressive responses more difficult.

12. There appear to be *critical periods* in learning, times when learning certain things is easy and rapid; outside of the critical period, the same learning may be difficult or impossible. *Imprinting*, the learning of dependency responses to some object (usually the mother), is an example of this kind of learning that appears in many species.

USING PSYCHOLOGY

Suppose you were studying color vision in six-month-old infants, and you wanted to find out whether they could tell red from green. How would you use operant conditioning techniques to devise an experiment to answer this question? Could you use classicial conditioning techniques to test it also? If so, which technique do you think would be more effective and why?

SUGGESTED READINGS

Hintzman, D. L. *The psychology of learning and memory.* Freeman, 1978.
An excellent textbook, covering the ethologists' complaints as well as the psychologists' principles.

Rachlin, H. *Introduction to modern behaviorism.* 2nd ed. Freeman, 1976.
An excellent discussion of theories and research in classicial and operant conditioning.

Skinner, B. F. *Walden two.* Macmillan, 1948.
Skinner's novel of life in a "controlled" community.

Morgan, C. T., & Deese, J. *How to study.* 2nd ed. McGraw-Hill, 1969.
Principles of learning applied to the practical problems of students.

INTERLUDE

The Psychology of Sex Differences

"All the world's a stage, and all the men and women merely players." Shakespeare's statement in *As You Like It,* written over 350 years ago, is not a bad description of the focal point of a good many heated arguments going on these days. *Sex roles* are much like the parts played by actors. In a play, every speech and action is dictated by the role. In real life, there is more flexibility in "appropriate" behaviors, but our social roles strongly influence what we do.

One's sex role is just one of many social roles each of us must play. One person may be "manager," "mother," "sister," "daughter," "wife," "Republican," "Catholic," and "woman" to different people, and each of these roles calls for certain role-appropriate behavior. Both a wife and a mother are supposed to be loving, though in different ways, whereas a Republican is patriotic and conservative. Many students vividly experience the meaning of "role" when they return home from college for vacations; the subtle pressures of people and environment to play once again the role of dependent son or daughter are strong. I can remember throwing childish temper tantrums to insist on my new status as an independent adult, a tactic that is a failure almost by definition.

MAN AND WOMAN

The most prominent sex roles in America are man and woman, and we will discuss these in detail. Some psychologists identify other sex roles as well — male homosexual and lesbian, for example. In some American Indian tribes there was a special sexual category, the *berdache,* a man who chose to adopt the clothes and behaviors of women; it was usually a thoroughly respectable sex role. Finally, one might also include *eunuchs* or *castrati,* men who were castrated for some particular purpose in the past.

The sex roles other than man and woman serve as reminders that all sex roles are *socially* defined. Like all other social roles, "man" and "woman" are parts to play, with certain behaviors encouraged and others discouraged or prohibited. In general terms, the male role is instrumental, technical, and adaptive — man is a no-nonsense doer — whereas the female role is expressive and emotional — *caring* for children and husband (McClelland and Watt, 1968).

The behaviors demanded by our roles as men and women often are quite specific. Physically aggressive behavior, for example, is OK for boys and men but not for girls and women. It is not surprising that males tend to behave that way more frequently than females do. Children learn these roles quickly. A six-year-old child (boy or girl), if shown rabbits and tigers, will usually say the tiger is like a man and the rabbit is like a woman (Kagan et al., 1961). The favored behaviors for girls and women include those one psychologist calls "the correlated trio of dependency, passivity, and conformity" (Kagan, 1971, p. 76). Women are expected to be less independent in their actions, to seek the advice and directions of others more often. Women are expected to be more passive, less assertive. Women are expected to conform more, rebel less.

An extensive series of studies of the behaviors associated with one sex or the other gives more detail on the *competency cluster*—socially valued behaviors that are usually associated with males—and the *warmth-expressiveness cluster*—socially valued behaviors that are typically associated with females (Broverman et al., 1972). Subjects (male and female college students) were given a large number of bipolar items (bipolar means having two poles or ends) such as:

Cries very easily ——————— Never cries

The subjects indicated which point of the 60 points between poles best characterized "an adult man" and "an adult woman." Table 1 shows

---

Table 1
STEREOTYPIC SEX-ROLE ITEMS (RESPONSES FROM 74 COLLEGE MEN AND 80 COLLEGE WOMEN)

Competency Cluster: Masculine Pole Is More Desirable

Feminine	*Masculine*
Not at all aggressive	Very aggressive
Not at all independent	Very independent
Very emotional	Not at all emotional
Does not hide emotions at all	Almost always hides emotions
Very subjective	Very objective
Very easily influenced	Not at all easily influenced
Very submissive	Very dominant
Dislikes math and science very much	Likes math and science very much
Very excitable in a minor crisis	Not at all excitable in a minor crisis
Very passive	Very active
Not at all competitive	Very competitive

I. K. Broverman, S. R. Vogel, D. M. Broverman, F. E. Clarkson, and P. S. Rosencrantz, "Sex Role Stereotypes: A Current Appraisal," in *Journal of Social Issues*, vol. 28, 1972, p. 63. Reprinted by permission.

Table 1 *(continued)*

Feminine	*Masculine*
Very illogical	Very logical
Very home oriented	Very worldly
Not at all skilled in business	Very skilled in business
Very sneaky	Very direct
Does not know the way of the world	Knows the way of the world
Feelings easily hurt	Feelings not easily hurt
Not at all adventurous	Very adventurous
Has difficulty making decisions	Can make decisions easily
Cries very easily	Never cries
Almost never acts as a leader	Almost always acts as a leader
Not at all self-confident	Very self-confident
Very uncomfortable about being aggressive	Not at all uncomfortable about being aggressive
Not at all ambitious	Very ambitious
Unable to separate feelings from ideas	Easily able to separate feelings from ideas
Very dependent	Not at all dependent
Very conceited about appearance	Never conceited about appearance
Thinks women are always superior to men	Thinks men are always superior to women
Does not talk freely about sex with men	Talks freely about sex with men

---

Warmth-Expressiveness Cluster: Feminine Pole Is More Desirable

Feminine	*Masculine*
Doesn't use harsh language at all	Uses very harsh language
Very talkative	Not at all talkative
Very tactful	Very blunt
Very gentle	Very rough
Very aware of feelings of others	Not at all aware of feelings of others
Very religious	Not at all religious
Very interested in own appearance	Not at all interested in own appearance
Very neat in habits	Very sloppy in habits
Very quiet	Very loud
Very strong need for security	Very little need for security
Enjoys art and literature	Does not enjoy art or literature at all
Easily expresses tender feelings	Does not express tender feelings at all easily

those items on which there was high agreement that one pole was more characteristic of one sex. An adult man is much closer to the "Never cries" pole, and women are seen as more likely to cry easily.

This list reflects *sex-role stereotypes*, widely held beliefs about differences in the behavioral tendencies of men and women. These beliefs may be true or false. Those which are true may be true for biological reasons (innate sex-linked differences) or for social reasons (different child-rearing practices, different social pressures and expectations). The validity of the stereotypes and the reasons behind those which are valid are genuine scientific topics, suitable for our discussion. But what makes sex roles a matter of urgency rather than simply of interest is their *political* aspects: They can be used as a basis for discrimination, and often are. Some employers (not all of them male) who believe that women are born or brought up to be less logical and less assertive than men use these beliefs in selecting personnel, openly or subtly discriminating against women applicants for executive jobs and in favor of women for secretarial or "assistant" positions. Although I doubt that the scientific merits of their belief system are of much concern to such individuals, they certainly are of concern to the victims of the system.

SOME BASIC BIOLOGICAL CONSIDERATIONS

If we are to understand why sex-role stereotypes exist, and how much truth there is to them, perhaps we should begin with some very basic biological considerations. Consider, for example, four notable features of reproduction in human beings. (1) Two individuals are required, one male and one female. This is not the case in all species of animals. Many animals reproduce asexually: A single organism simply splits in half, forming two new organisms. (2) Fertilization is internal: the egg is fertilized while it is inside the female's body, rather than outside, as in many fish. (3) The fertilized egg develops into a living embryo and fetus inside the woman's body and is born live, as contrasted with many animals, such as birds, whose eggs are incubated outside the female's body. (4) The newborn infant cannot survive without aid; it has a lengthy period of dependence. In most species, the period of dependence is much shorter or nonexistent.

Pregnancy, childbirth, and child care are all relevant to human sex roles. Women carry and bear the child and usually take care of it while it is most dependent. In our technologically advanced society, it is possible for the man to care for the child, but in poor cultures, the infant depends on its mother's milk for food. In cultures where food is scarce, women may nurse their children for five years or more.

Having and caring for children are the most indispensable functions of any species and any society, for without them the group will cease to exist. In those human cultures where both these functions are carried out by women, what are men's functions? Broadly speaking, examining a variety of human societies, the answer seems to be to provide food for the family and to protect it and the larger society from danger. Biologically, the average man is stronger and faster afoot than the average woman. He is well equipped to do heavy farming, to chase, catch, and kill game, and to defend his group against the predation of wild animals and neighboring gangs. And, in most cultures in history, these are the jobs he was assigned.

It is worth noting that although biological differences were obviously related to the division of labor in primitive societies, cultural forces tended to *exaggerate* the biological differences. For example, some women were faster afoot than the average man, and many were faster than the slowest man. But it is inefficient and costly for a society to say "The fastest shall be the hunters," when "Men will be the hunters" is nearly as good, and much simpler. A culture is something like an insurance company, making discriminations on the basis of the most easily gathered facts. A young man seeking automobile insurance will have to pay high premiums, not because he in particular is a poor or unsafe driver, but because he is youthful and male, and the *average* young man has many more accidents than the *average* adult.

Man as the breadwinner and protector, woman as the mother and homemaker — this division of labor is biologically *based,* but not biologically *determined.* Obviously, in our technologically advanced society, the need for strength and speed in breadwinning and protective occupations is much reduced. Breadwinning, for example, is more likely to mean programming a computer than hunting game, and our nation's defense relies more on missiles and airplanes than on strong male soldiers. Yet the traditional view that these roles are appropriate for men and child-centered roles are appropriate for women is still widespread. The sex-role stereotypes we described earlier derive from and are part of this traditional view. Men are supposed to be competent, aggressive, and decisive, whereas women are supposed to be warm and expressive, sensitive and gentle.

Why has this stereotyped division of labor and of corresponding personality traits continued in an advanced society like ours? That is the essential question in the psychology of sex differences.

SEX DIFFERENCES TODAY

The jobs in the modern world involve considerably more intellect and less strength and speed than hunting and protecting one's territory did. Biologically, women are now just as well suited as men to most occupations; and recently women in considerable numbers have joined in the competition for the socially valued positions formerly monopolized by men. There is considerable institutional resistance to this new element in the competition. A culture adapts slowly to changed circumstances and is unwilling to give up traditions and discriminations that have been useful in the past. Over the years, women have found themselves prohibited by law from certain occupations — bartender was one in recent times — and from certain advantages, such as overtime work for extra pay. Many of these laws were originally introduced to protect women from abuse.

But women have often found the sex-role stereotype to be a greater obstacle to sexual equality than legal barriers are. As we mentioned, quite a few people, both male and female, view women as unfit for "men's" jobs such as business executive. They believe women are less competent in such roles because they cannot assert themselves, they are too passive and dependent, they are intuitive and emotional instead of rational and logical, they are not ambitious enough, they are too subjective, and when the chips are down, they cry. We cannot discuss every facet of the stereotype, but we will discuss a few of its central assumptions.

Strength and Nurturance

Although physical strength is still a factor in some occupations, most jobs can be handled by either sex. In jobs where strength is important, laws usually prohibit discrimination on the basis of sex; that is, employers cannot use sex as an indication of an individual's strength. Actual tests of strength, such as lifting a certain weight, can be required if they are shown to be related to job performance, and a higher proportion of men than women will pass these tests. But a few strong women will also make the grade.

In an era of planned vacations and leaves of absence, pregnancy and childbirth need not interrupt the career of a working woman. Most employers seem more concerned about the potentially disruptive effects of child care: "We'll train her, then she'll have a kid and quit her job to raise the kid." Women who have children often feel guilty about working, especially if their children are under six years of age, but these feelings result from a conflict between what they perceive as their responsibilities as mothers and the time and energy they spend on their jobs (Zellman, 1976). Child care is not a *biologically* based duty in societies where food is plentiful—where the mother's milk is not a necessity. In increasing numbers, fathers are taking over an equal or even the larger share of child care duties. Day care facilities are another alternative. One study found that children who spent their days in a day care center for a little over two years, beginning at the age of three and a half months, were indistinguishable from children reared at home, on measures of mental capacity, psychological and social well-being, and attachment to their mothers (Kagan et al., 1978).

Hormones and Hermaphrodites

With strength, speed, pregnancy, and childbirth decreasing in importance as biological considerations in the psychology of sex differences, *hormones* have come to the fore. Hormones, as you recall from Chapter 2, are the chemical messengers of the endocrine system, affecting processes that are generally slow-moving and long-term, such as body growth. The sex hormones are produced by the gonads—ovaries in the female and testes in the male. These hormones are responsible for the physical development of a human fetus into female or male form, both in the womb and after birth—notably at puberty, when the sexual apparatus matures and the secondary sex characteristics (such as breasts and beards) appear. In females, hormones control the monthly cycle of menstruation. Many psychologists believe that sex differences in hormones underlie some of the sex differences in behavior—in violence and aggression, for example, which are more common in males (Maccoby and Jacklin, 1974).

In a few rare cases, hormonal influences on the physical development of the fetus are such that the baby is born a *hermaphrodite*. In loose definition, a hermaphrodite is a person whose sex is unclear. Some hermaphrodites have ambiguous external genitals—what one would call either a small penis or a large clitoris. Others have genitals that conflict with their genetic sex and internal organs; such a person might be genetically female, with two X chromosomes and ovaries inside, but with an external penis (Tavris and Offir, 1977). Psychologists are interested in studies of hermaphrodites because they can answer some of the questions about the effects of hormones on sexual identity. One group of 25 girls had been exposed to male hormones (androgens) at a critical period of fetal development, some because of malfunctions in their mothers' endocrine systems and some because of drugs administered to prevent miscarriage (Money and Ehrhardt, 1972). Their ambiguous genitalia had been corrected by surgery at birth, and they were raised as girls, but there was some question whether the prenatal hormones would affect their social behavior later in life. Compared to a control group of normal girls matched on age, IQ, social class, and other factors, the "androgenized" girls were notably "tomboyish," preferring vigorous outdoor sports and games to the less energetic activities of the "normal" girls. They were said to have had little interest in dolls. On the other hand, the androgenized girls were not more aggressive (hostile, threatening, violent) than the control group, and, without exception, their sexual orientation was heterosexual. (We should note that the vast majority of tomboys have no hormonal imbalances; instead, they have had the good fortune to be raised by parents who do not punish "boyish" behavior by their daughters.)

The people who did this study concluded that the prenatal exposure to male hormones had some effect, not only on the girls' external genitals, but also on their developing brains. Their hypothesis was that the androgens somehow sensitized brain pathways related to rambunctious behavior and suppressed neural systems involved in "rehearsals for motherhood" like doll-playing and babysitting (Williams, 1977). This conclusion seems a little far-fetched, with so few human investigations to support it. But the study does provide suggestive evidence that hormones play some role in sex differences in behavior.

The same investigators (Money and Ehrhardt, 1972) also provide evidence of the significant role of environmental influences in sex-linked behavior and identity. Unlike the girls who had corrective surgery at birth, some born with the external genitals of a male were simply thought to be boys and were raised as such. When the discrepancy between their assigned and genetic sex was discovered, the parents and doctors decided that to reassign a child of three or four years of age to the opposite sex would be damaging to his/her self-concept and continued to raise the child as a boy. These children were compared to the androgenized girls who were surgically corrected and raised as girls. The "boys" were, for all practical purposes, perfectly normal boys, and the girls were clearly feminine, although slightly tomboyish. "One may begin with the same clay," concluded the investigators, "and fashion a god or a goddess" (Money and Ehrhardt, 1972, p. 152).

In the most bizarre case of all, there was a "slight accident" during a circumcision and a normal male infant found himself with no penis. It was decided to raise the boy as a girl, and surgery to that end continued for many years. What makes this case particularly interesting is that this child was one of identical twins, so that one twin was thus raised as a girl and one as a boy. Aside from the tomboy quality of her behavior, the "girl" behaved like most normal young girls; the boy, of course, was normal by definition. Again, the evidence suggests that social and environmental influences are more important than the underlying genetic and hormonal influences.

The Premenstrual Syndrome

Another "hormone issue" of some prominence is the so-called *premenstrual syndrome*. The cycle of ovulation and menstruation in women between puberty and menopause is regulated by the female hormones, estrogen and progesterone. In the five- or six-day period preceding menstruation, some women experience physical symptoms (pains, bloating) and psychological symptoms such as irritability, depression, and anxiety (Williams, 1977). This phenomenon has led some people (not all of them male) to formulate various versions of what I call "the raging-hormone theory of female incompetence." In its extreme form, the theory asks: What good is a worker who must be "excused" from work five to ten days a month? Who wants a president who might send the country to war because of premenstrual tensions? As the husband of a female M.D. said in the foreword of *her* book on the menstrual cycle, "The old cliché, 'It's a woman's privilege to change her mind,' calls for an even greater tolerance than before, now that it is realized that every woman is at the mercy of the constantly recurring ebb and flow of her hormones" (T. E. Dalton, in Dalton, 1969, p. viii).

Any reasonable reviewer of the available research on the premenstrual syndrome (see Parlee, 1973) is bound to conclude that the raging-hormone theory is pure hogwash. Although some women seem to experience a degree of premenstrual tension, they may be as few as 15 percent (Paige, 1973) and the mood change is generally on the order of "Monday morning blues" (Golub, 1973). The occasional woman who experiences severe physical or psychological symptoms has a medical problem that can be treated (Dalton, 1969). Most importantly, there is no solid evidence that women who experience premenstrual symptoms are in any practical way affected by these symptoms. Some have suggested that women taking exams during the premenstrual period are at a disadvantage (Dalton, 1969; Tiger, 1970); but research shows this hypothesis to be false (Golub, 1973). There are scattered reports of a higher rate of suicide and crime among premenstrual and menstruating women than among women in other periods of their cycle (Dalton, 1969), but these data are unreliable because of flaws in collection, analysis, and interpretation (Parlee, 1973; Tavris and Offir, 1977; Williams, 1977). Even if these data were accurate, the *peak* levels of criminal and suicidal behavior among women are far below the everyday averages for men.

Why are raging-hormone theories still current, when the research evidence is so clearly against them? That, I believe, is a far more interesting and promising area of investigation than the theories themselves. The historical bias against women, viewing them as less competent than men, seems to have joined forces with an equally traditional view of menstruation as unclean and debilitating. Perhaps the raging-hormone theories use the negative attitudes toward menstruation to postulate an "acceptable" explanation of women's essential incompetence.

Those who favor these theories would do well to consider the other side of the coin. Although, obviously, males do not menstruate, many men show cyclical fluctuations in hormone levels, fluctuations that are related to depression and possibly hostility (Doering et al., 1974). Young males, full of testosterone, are the most violent and dangerous members of our species. Who wants a president who might send the country to war because of hormonally induced hostility and aggression?

Achievement Motivation

According to the traditional stereotype of women, a woman's work suffers not only from disruptive hormones, but also from a general lack of achievement motivation. Unlike the premenstrual blues, motives to achieve are clearly social, involving learning and social expectations to a high degree. Since 1968, when Matina Horner completed her doctoral dissertation on achievement orientations in females, sex differences in achievement motivation has been a lively area of research. In Horner's experiment, 90 female college students were asked to write four-minute stories for which Horner supplied the opening line: "After first-term finals, Anne finds herself at the top of her medical school class." For comparison, 88 males were given the cue, "After first-term finals, John finds himself at the top of his medical school class."

The male students wrote generally positive stories: John is pleased. He has worked hard and it has paid off. His future is bright. Women will love him.

The female students wrote stories of a completely different type. Most of them could be classified into one of three categories. The first and most common story depicted a *fear of social rejection* because of Anne's high standing in the class: She fears losing her boyfriend, who is afraid of her intelligence. She studies a lot because she never has dates. Her face is plain, her dress is dumpy and so is her figure. (More than 50 percent describe her as tall. I wonder why.)

A second theme in the women's stories was *concern about Anne's femininity and her normality:* Her hard work has paid off and she has earned first place, but now she begins to wonder if this is normal and feminine. In some of the stories she has a nervous breakdown. She is unhappy, as if she were denying her essence as a woman. She quits school, marries a doctor, and raises children.

The third category of stories was called *denials,* but that term doesn't catch the flavor of some of these wild productions: Anne is a code name for a group of med students who take turns taking exams. . . . Anne is very happy to be on her way to becoming a fine nurse. . . . Her classmates jump on her and beat her. She is maimed for life. . . .

Combining these three categories of response into one larger category called *fear of success,* 59 of the 90 females included some fear of success in their stories, whereas only 8 of the 88 males did so.

The Horner study caught the imagination of many psychologists, in a kind of "of course" fashion. It made sense to think of women as afraid of success; they had been taught that competing with men and using assertive behavior was not feminine. However, later research has not been as conclusive as Horner's, perhaps because of rapidly changing attitudes among women about competition and achievement (Tresemer, 1974). An excellent and extensive review of nearly every experiment done on the issue concludes that it is a myth that women lack the motivation to achieve but concedes that men *might* be more competitive (Maccoby and Jacklin, 1974). In other words, a woman will strive to achieve a standard of excellence as well as a man, but a man is more likely to put out that "little extra" if it means he might beat his closest rival in a contest. Even this latter conclusion, however, is listed as "questionable," in need of further research and likely to change.

Achievement and Affiliation

Many psychologists have noted that women seem to have much stronger needs for friendly social interaction—usually called *affiliation* needs—than they do for achievement. And women seem to be more interested than men in popularity and the approval of others (Hoffman, 1972). The research on fear of success suggests that some women tend to play down their achievements for fear of intimidating or "putting off" others, especially men. One prominent female psychologist admits she was enraged when her name was published in the university newspaper as having earned an A average; she was afraid it would affect her social life (Bardwick, 1971).

An interesting experiment arranged things so that women paired with men got higher scores than their male partners on a dynamometer, a device for measuring strength of grip (Weiss, 1962). Most of the women then reduced their efforts, in order to avoid embarrassing the "weakling" males, in spite of the fact that each pair was competing with other pairs on the basis of *combined* scores.

The hypothesis that women are motivated more by affiliation than by achievement needs does not imply that the two will always be in conflict. If achievement behavior is rewarded with social praise and popularity, then girls and women should perform at a high level. This reasonable assumption has received support primarily from natural experiments: Typi-

cally a test of affiliation motivation is correlated with an achievement test, and the correlation is higher for girls than for boys (for example, Sears, 1962). In true experiments, achievement behavior has been compared between two randomly selected groups of girls, one receiving praise and friendship rewards, the other receiving, say, no reward other than the satisfaction of a job well done. The findings here are mixed, and no consistent sex differences are discoverable (Stein and Bailey, 1973), indicating there is something amiss with this aspect of the hypothesis.

The data from these and other studies make more sense under a slightly different hypothesis: Women's achievement motives are often expressed in affiliation behaviors because success in these areas has been their traditional goal and often represents their only possible achievement in a tradition-bound society (Stein and Bailey, 1973). Women can and do pursue such traditional female activities as raising a family, running an efficient household, and entertaining guests, with aggressiveness and persistence and with a clear "standard of excellence" that is the hallmark of all achievement behaviors. TV commercials that show a homemaker frantically striving for a better cup of coffee or shinier dishes are illustrations. And the technical knowledge needed to create Indo-Chinese Chicken Livers or make buttonholes on a sewing machine is just as bewildering to the uninformed as the operating instructions for manly, "muscle" cars. As traditional male occupations open up to females, there is no reason to expect less of the traditional achievement strivings among women who choose these careers.

Raising a Little Lady

If we accept the assumption that women are not less motivated to achieve than men are by nature, how do so many grow up with little or no drive to succeed in business? As you might guess, it has a lot to do with training. Parents of any child understandably try to prepare her or him for life, and, in most cases, the parents' view of a woman's life is dominated by the sex-role stereotype. This training begins at birth. Although female children are in fact sturdier than males, they are treated as more fragile, and their needs are ministered to more quickly than males' (Hoffman, 1972). Males are given more independence training; they are allowed, or even forced, to do more by themselves, and at earlier ages. Females more frequently ask for and receive help from others when faced with threatening situations. By the age of two and a half, most children have learned the concept of two sexes with different roles in life. Even at this early age, boys and girls have begun to behave in accordance with the stereotypes: Boys are more aggressive, girls are more dependent (Mischel, 1971).

What kind of parents produce *atypical* women with unusual achievement strivings? Certain characteristics seem to be common: They put pressure on their daughter to cope, and they withhold love more than average. They are more punitive (punishing). But they are not extreme in any of these characteristics; they don't overprotect and they don't reject. The evidence suggests that females need more rejection than males to develop achievement motivation, whereas males need more warm, loving nurturance from the mother (Stein and Bailey, 1973).

These data come from natural or correlational studies, of course, so we should be careful in interpreting them. Parents rated as having a "moderate level of warmth," neither smothering nor rejecting, have more achieving female children. But "moderate warmth" may have nothing to do with achievement, other than as it indicates a certain portion of the middle class of society which, for reasons of wealth and opportunity, encourages the development of an achieving female. The notion that achievement motivation is set early in life is as deadly as the idea that it is set by biology, and I don't think either notion should be accepted unless we are presented with much stronger evidence than is presently available. Certainly sex-role training influences the development of achievement strivings; but we also have good evidence that women who are given equal opportunity, free of discrimination, with a little experience and a little support, can become as motivated and as successful as men of comparable talents. Even if they have been trained to be "little ladies."

MASCULINE VERSUS FEMININE

A significant aspect of the sex-role stereotype is a belief that masculinity and femininity are opposites. If a man is manly, he cannot also be feminine. Psychologists as well as the lay public have long held this belief without seriously questioning it, and psychological tests therefore reflect it. Several tests have been designed to measure the supposedly bipolar dimension of masculinity-femininity (MF), and many more tests having several scales or subtests include an MF scale. There is such a scale on the Minnesota Multiphasic Personality Inventory (MMPI) and one on the Strong Vocational Interest Blank. These scales can be traumatizing to young males with "feminine" interests who begin to doubt their masculinity and to females who have achievement-related interests but want to be feminine, too.

In recent years a number of psychologists have begun to question the bipolarity—the either-or nature—of the masculine-feminine dimension (Constantinople, 1973). Evidence is accumulating that at least two dimensions are involved, one that we can call masculinity and another completely independent dimension we can call femininity. In studies using two separate scales, the correlations between the two have been essentially zero (Broverman et al., 1972; Stein and Bailey, 1973; Bem, 1974). These data reflect a lack of relationship between the competency cluster and the warmth-and-expressiveness cluster of behaviors. Though it is part of the stereotype that aggressive masculine men are not also warm and gentle, this belief is probably false, at least among the college students who have been the subjects of most studies. A woman who is tender may also be highly competitive.

Human beings who combine the best qualities of both the male and the female sex-role stereotype have been called androgynous (from the Greek roots "andro"—male—and "gyne"—female; the same roots can be seen separately in "androgen"—male hormone—and "gynecologist"—doctor of females). About 35 percent of a large sample of Stanford University undergraduates were androgynous, according to the definition used in one study (Bem, 1974). Compared to stereotyped people—masculine men, feminine women—androgynous students earn more honors and awards in school, date more, and have higher self-esteem (Spence et al., 1975). They have the flexibility to do well in situations that call for either independent judgment (a "masculine" task) or sympathetic nurturance (a "feminine" task); stereotyped people do well only in situations that fit their view of what is proper behavior for their sex (Bem, in press).

These data may herald a breakdown of the traditional sex-role stereotypes and the unnecessarily restrictive lives the traditions have created for both men and women. Part of a widespread sexual revolution that is only beginning, the changes in the psychosocial definitions of "man" and "woman" are coming rapidly. Where will we settle? You will be part of the answer.

SUGGESTED READINGS

Maccoby, E. E., & Jacklin, C. N. *The psychology of sex differences.* Stanford U. Press, 1974.
   A major work by two top psychologists (both women), which reviews almost all the research for and against various hypotheses about sex differences.

Tavris, C., & Offir, C. *The longest war: sex differences in perspective.* Harcourt Brace Jovanovich, 1977.
   There are many excellent textbooks on the psychology of sex differences. This one is soundly based on research; exceptionally well written.

Behavioral Objectives

1. Identify the issues raised by Ebbinghaus in his investigations of memory; describe the type of experiments Ebbinghaus performed, and identify the dependent variables he measured.
2. Identify and describe the three basic processes that psychologists think are involved in memory.
3. Identify the three stages or systems of memory, and describe the functions of each and their relations to one another.
4. Discuss the evidence, such as Sperling's experiment on sensory store, on which psychologists base their claim that there are three storage systems or stages of memory.
5. Discuss the effects of organization on memory.
6. Define working memory.
7. Identify and describe the two theories of forgetting. What variables affect forgetting?
8. Define the term "elaborative memory" and give some examples of how memory is elaborative.
9. Define mnemonic device and list some ways in which memory can be improved.
10. Discuss the effects of alcohol and marijuana on memory.

CHAPTER

5

Memory

The Greek poet Simonides had trained his memory with care. Thus, when commissioned to compose a poem honoring the host of a large banquet (sometime around 500 B.C.), Simonides recited his long lyric poem without error. The host was impressed, but cruelly informed Simonides that he would pay only half the amount agreed upon. Only half the poem, argued the host, was in praise of him; too much was said in honor of the twin gods, Castor and Pollux. Therefore, Simonides should see Castor and Pollux for the balance of his commission.

A little later, Simonides received a message that two young men wished to see him outside. He left the banquet hall, but could find no one. Suddenly the roof of the hall collapsed, crushing all the guests (except Simonides). Simonides thought, I have certainly been well paid by Castor and Pollux! They have saved my life!

The bodies in the banquet hall were so mangled that their relatives could not identify them for proper burial. Simonides was able to help them, for he discovered he could remember precisely where each of the hundreds of guests was sitting. Simonides became renowned not for his poetry but for his trained memory. His fame as a mnemonist (memory expert) and a few of his mnemonic devices (memory tricks) were noted by later historians, who called him "the inventor of the art of memory" (Yates, 1966).

How can the memory experts, like Simonides then, like Harry Lorayne and Jerry Lucas today, perform such incredible feats?

Harry Lorayne recalls a friend who was trying to convince Ed Sullivan to have Lorayne perform on his television variety show. "Ed," the friend said, "the guy is fantastic. He'll meet everyone in your audience. Then, during the show, he'll call each person's name. As he does, each person will stand up — until the entire audience is standing!"

Sullivan, a dour man noted for his inability to remember even the names of the performers he introduced on his show, glowered. "I can have the band play *The Star-Spangled Banner* and get the same result!" (Lorayne and Lucas, 1974, pp. 50–51).

Later in this chapter we will explore a few of the mnemonic devices Simonides and Harry Lorayne used to perform their fabled feats of memory. More generally, we will examine some of the oldest and some of the newest research on memory. We will begin with some excellent studies done 90 years ago by a man named Hermann Ebbinghaus. Then we will examine some of the more current work which suggests that there may be three memories, not just one. We will discuss what promotes learning, what enables us to remember well, what increases the rate of forgetting, and what happens when we attempt to dredge up information from a sometimes grudging memory.

THE EBBINGHAUS INVESTIGATIONS

Hermann Ebbinghaus was an Austrian scientist-philosopher born in 1850. Between 1879 and 1884, he did some incredible experimental studies on memory, experiments that were remarkable not only for their insightful hypotheses but also for their rigorous scientific controls (Ebbinghaus, 1885).

Associations and Nonsense Syllables

About the only theoretical concept Ebbinghaus had to guide his way when he began the study of memory was the *associa-*

tion. This was a term used by philosophers and psychologists to indicate a relationship between two ideas, a relationship often used to "explain" memory. Because two ideas have become associated through previous experience, the occurrence of one somehow involves the other, so that, say, an old song on the radio "reminds" you of an event that occurred at the time you first heard the song.

Ebbinghaus was interested in how such associations developed. He wanted to trace the formation of associations, and then the retention of these associations over time. To do this, he concluded, he could not study memory for meaningful material such as Lincoln's *Gettysburg Address* or even for commonly used words — there were too many previously formed associations. He had to use material that was essentially meaningless, stimuli never before encountered. So he created lists of *nonsense syllables*, meaningless combinations of three letters — two consonants separated by a vowel. BAP, TOX, and RIF are examples.

Armed with these rather sophisticated experimental materials, Ebbinghaus proceeded to investigate several important topics in memory. He used only one subject — himself. The results of his experiments led to conclusions that must be modified to apply to the average person, less experienced with memory tasks than Ebbinghaus and probably less intelligent; but the general implications of his research have stood the test of time. And certainly many of the issues Ebbinghaus raised are reflected in the concerns of modern psychologists. Here are just a few.

List Length

Is it more difficult to memorize a list of 24 nonsense syllables than a list of 12? Well, of

Figure 5.1 *How long do you think it would take to memorize this list?*

course. But how much more difficult? Is it twice as hard? The effect of the length of a list on how many times it had to be read to be learned was one of the first topics Ebbinghaus investigated. He was interested in how we form associations during learning, since he felt that associations provided the basis for memory. He figured that as the number of items in a list increased, the number of associations among items increased even faster. This meant the subject was really learning more than twice as much

material, so he predicted that a list twice as long as another would take *more* than twice as many readings to learn.

His reasoning went something like this: In a list of two items (call them *A* and *B*), there are two possible associations: from *A* to *B*, and backward, *B* to *A*. With three items, *A*, *B*, and *C*, there are six possible associations: *A* to *B*, *A* to *C*, *B* to *C*, and the same, backward: *B* to *A*, *C* to *A*, and *C* to *B*. So, with a list two items long, there are two possible associations, but adding one more item adds four more possible associations. So, to learn a long list the subject has to form many more associations than with a shorter list. Ebbinghaus's predictions were confirmed. For example, to learn a list of 12 nonsense syllables required 17 readings; a list twice as long, with 24 items, required more than twice the number of readings, 44 to be exact.

The general conclusion Ebbinghaus derived from these experiments—that the amount of work required per item (word or sentence or whatever) increases as the number of items increases—has never been questioned. But Ebbinghaus's theory on why this is so (because an increasing number of associations must be formed) is now considered, well, "sophisticated for its time and place," which means "crude." Current theories stress interference among the items, a concept we will return to in a moment.

Ebbinghaus himself noted one very serious problem with his theory: He could not explain the peculiar status of lists with seven items or less. His theory predicted that a list with four items would be more than twice as difficult as a list of two items, a list of six more than twice as hard as three, and so forth. But he found that for *all* lists with fewer than eight items he needed only one reading!

Lists longer than seven, he found, became immediately difficult. He needed 13 readings, for example, to learn ten nonsense syllables. Very puzzling; a single reading for 7 items, but 13 for 10! Ebbinghaus was reduced to a theory that applied only to longer lists, over seven items long—seven, it appeared, was some sort of magic number, marking a characteristic of mental ability that he could not completely understand. More about the number seven later.

The Forgetting Curve

In his investigations of the effect of list length, Ebbinghaus used as his dependent variable the number of trials or repetitions it took to memorize the material, where "memorized" meant he could give one perfect recitation. In other experiments, Ebbinghaus used what is called the *savings* in effort as his operational definition of remembering. Suppose he had a list of nonsense syllables that required 20 repetitions before he could repeat them without error. Suppose that 24 hours later, 5 repetitions were necessary before he again could perform to perfection. The savings would be 15 repetitions (20 the first time, only 5 the second). Expressed as a percentage of the number of original trials, the savings in this case is 75 percent (15/20).

Using the savings method, Ebbinghaus varied the time between initial learning and relearning, and graphed his data. The curve that resulted was called the *forgetting curve* (although it is actually a curve of retention), and it showed memory loss to be very regular (see Figure 5.2). Memory decreases very rapidly at first but then levels off; the amount forgotten after a month is not much more than that forgotten after a day or two.

That humans forget so much so quickly was a bit of a surprise, but even more interesting to the psychologists of Ebbinghaus's time was the very regular shape of the curve. It was a familiar shape, one that is common in physics, where it often defines a "decay" process such as the loss of heat from a cup of coffee. Perhaps psychologists had discovered a *law*, a real, honest-to-goodness, *scientific* law!

The general shape of the forgetting curve was about the same for meaningful material as for nonsense syllables. Ebbinghaus found

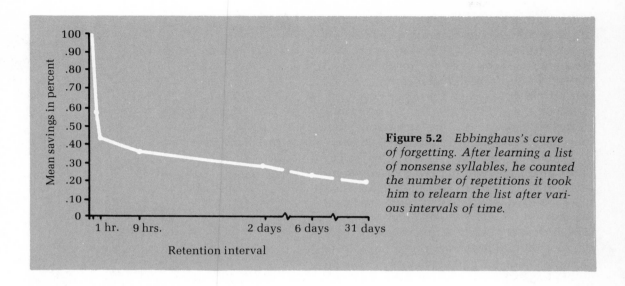

Figure 5.2 *Ebbinghaus's curve of forgetting. After learning a list of nonsense syllables, he counted the number of repetitions it took him to relearn the list after various intervals of time.*

his memory retained poetry better than meaningless material at all intervals, but his forgetting of poetry, like that of nonsense syllables, was very rapid at first and then leveled off. Later research allows us to say that this forgetting curve will be found in a wide range of situations, sometimes riding high on its graph like the curve for meaningful material and sometimes low like the nonsense curve, but essentially the same. But there are also situations in which this curve will not be found, so Ebbinghaus's "law" is perhaps better called a "useful, somewhat crude, empirical generalization." Psychologists have a number of laws like that.

Practical Problems of Memory

Among the many topics Ebbinghaus investigated were several that relate to the everyday, practical use of memory, for example, by students. One such topic was the spacing of practice. Suppose I have to memorize something for an exam. Is it better to go through the material once a day for several days, or should I just keep rehearsing until I've got it? In other words, should my practice sessions be *distributed* or *massed?*

Most books on How to Study will tell you that distributed practice works better than cramming at the last minute. Ebbinghaus found that, for learning lists of nonsense syllables, spacing his practice sessions enabled him to learn a list in roughly half the total study time required to learn the list in one sitting. Later research has verified his conclusion that a little study every day is preferable to a lot of study on one day, although there are a few qualifications (see Underwood, 1961). Of course, the general principle must be applied along with a good dose of common sense: Studying five minutes a day for three weeks is not likely to be better than a single two-hour session; it takes a certain amount of time to warm up. Also, much learning is made easier by organizing the material, and organization takes time; it makes little sense to stop your study of a great philosopher just as you're beginning to glimpse his or her essential meaning, simply because "that's enough for today."

In summary, Ebbinghaus's contributions to memory research were substantial and long-lived. The methods he devised were found useful for years; even today, many of the procedures and materials of the memory psychologist derive from Ebbinghaus's work. Nonsense syllables are still used, and memory for lists of verbal material (nonsense syllables, words, letters) is still one of the most common research techniques.

Since Ebbinghaus published his research, psychologists have generated volumes of additional research. Let us now turn to some more current ideas about memory.

ENCODING

What happens when we remember? What does it mean to have a memory of some fact, event, mood, or even smell? Is the human memory like a microfilm library, with millions of pictures stored somewhere to be called up on demand? Or does it resemble a computer, in which words and pictures alike are translated into some third form, a language only the computer understands?

Contemporary memory theorists propose that when we learn something and later remember it, three basic processes are involved: encoding, storage, and retrieval. *Encoding,* the first step, refers to what we do to information to prepare it for storage in memory. When you take notes in class, you are encoding your professor's lectures so you can file the information for later review. Just

Figure 5.3 *Does human memory work with information in the same way as a computer does?*

as computers or microfilm libraries will not accept material unless it's encoded in computer language or microfilm form, humans must encode their experiences before storing them in memory.

Meaningfulness in Encoding

In older theories of memory, encoding was often viewed as passive, an almost automatic process that occurred whenever a stimulus was encountered. Rehearsal (repetition) is useful, according to these theories, because each repetition of an item (like a word or number) results in a slight increase in the amount of information about that item stored in memory.

But rehearsal is not always an aid to memory, as most of us can demonstrate from our own experience. Have you ever

Figure 5.4 *To this student, batters are more meaningful than battles.*

studied a textbook—a rather boring textbook, but one on which tomorrow's quiz is based—while your mind was wandering? Have you ever spent the good part of an hour reading and rereading the same sentence, seemingly unable to retain any of the information in it?

Such experiences are enough to make one question the "automatic action" of rehearsal that the older theories of memory presumed. Later research suggests that effective encoding is a more active process, one that involves thinking about the meaning of items and relating them to what you already know. Rehearsal may aid in this process, but it is effective mainly when each repetition involves an elaboration of the stimulus (Klatzky, 1980). If you want to recall something, try to encode it meaningfully.

Consider the following experiment (Craik and Tulving, 1975): Subjects were given a list of words, one by one. As each item was presented, the subjects were asked one of three questions about it; the different questions were designed to motivate the subjects to encode the words at different levels of meaningfulness. One question asked simply whether the word was in capital letters or in small letters. A second question asked whether the word rhymed with some other word—"Does it rhyme with house?" A third question asked whether the word fit in a sentence like "The _____ was on the table." The researchers expected that words presented with the first question would not be encoded very meaningfully, because no more than a quick look at the form of the letters is required for an answer. The rhyme question required some additional thought about how the word sounded. And the sentence question, because it made the subjects think about the meaning of the word, should provide the most effective encoding. The data supported the hypothesis: Recall was best for words that subjects tried to fit into sentence blanks, in between for the rhyming words, and poorest for words scrutinized only for capitalization.

Depth of Processing. The idea that more meaningful encoding leads to better recall is central to a rather new theory of memory called the "depth of processing theory." It is so called because it assumes that the "deeper" the thought about a stimulus when it is encoded, the better the word will be remembered. Phrased in this general way, of course, the basic assumption of the theory shows itself to be anything but novel. Ebbinghaus discovered that meaningful (more deeply processed) material was more likely to be remembered than nonsense syllables, and this bit of common sense has been verified in thousands of experiments since. This is true even though no one knows for sure what "meaningfulness" or "deeper processing" means!

We can agree, perhaps, that the *Gettys-burg Address* is more meaningful than a list of nonsense syllables, although we might have trouble explaining why. In general, we can loosely say that meaningfulness refers to how closely information is related to what we already know. Thus meaningfulness is related to familiarity. For example, if the phone number for the movie theater is the same as your best friend's except for the last digit, you will probably not need to refer to the phone book when you want to find out what's playing.

Association Value. Meaningfulness can also be defined in terms of how many things you can relate to a stimulus. For example, although Ebbinghaus considered his nonsense syllables unusually free of previously learned associations, it soon became clear that some syllables were less meaningless than others (see Figure 5.5). If asked to say what associations came to mind in response to different nonsense syllables, more subjects came up with something for WIS than

TAB	TEB	TOB		TAP	TEP	TOP
TAC	TEC	TOC		TAQ	TEQ	TOQ
TAD	TED	TOD		TAR	TER	TOR
TAF	TEF	TOF		TAS	TES	TOS
TAG	TEG	TOG		TAT	TET	TOT
TAH	TEH	TOH		TAV	TEV	TOV
TAJ	TEJ	TOJ		TAW	TEW	TOW
TAK	TEK	TOK		TAX	TEX	TOX
TAL	TEL	TOL		TAY	TEY	TOY
TAM	TEM	TOM		TAZ	TEZ	TOZ
TAN	TEN	TON				

Figure 5.5 *Nonsense syllables are not always nonsense; they vary in meaningfulness. Here are all possible consonant-vowel-consonant combinations beginning with TA, TE, and TO. Some of them are actual words (and would not be used as nonsense syllables, of course). But others are clearly meaningful; they are "almost" words or have other associations.*

XIP. Several investigators published averages for various nonsense syllables; these averages became known as the *association values* of the items (Glaze, 1928). The numbers reflected either (1) the percentage of subjects who could give any association at all in a brief period, or (2) the average number of associations respondents conjured up within a set time, usually one minute. The latter measure could be used for whole words, too (Noble, 1952). Thus it came to pass that nonsense syllables and words used in memory experiments usually had an attached number indicating meaningfulness, and dozens of studies were done to show how much easier it is to recall highly meaningful syllables or words than items with low association values. There is even some direct evidence that subjects try to encode nonsense syllables by relating them to familiar words and phrases, and that how well they remember the syllables has to do with how easily they can find such relationships (Montague et al., 1966; Prytulak, 1971).

Organization

Another aspect of encoding that has been extensively studied is *organization*. Organization refers to arranging a set of words (or other stimuli) in groups on the basis of meaningful relationships among them. For instance, to make your grocery shopping easier, you might organize your list into vegetables and fruits, dairy products, paper goods, and so on. Organizing involves converting a long list of single words into a list of fewer groups, and thus makes it easier to store the information and later to retrieve it.

Sometimes it is quite clear that people asked to remember a learned list are recalling organized information. One sign of this is *clustering*. An early experiment presented subjects with a 60-item list, 15 words in each of four categories: animals, names, professions, and vegetables (Bousfield, 1953). The 60 items were presented in an entirely scrambled (random) order, not by category. When the subjects were later asked to recall the words in any order, they showed a clear tendency to recall in clusters defined by the categories. To illustrate this principle, suppose you were presented with this list:

ANDREW, LAWYER, GREEN, BLUE, DOCTOR, BURT, HENRY, TEACHER, YELLOW, PURPLE, DENTIST, GEORGE.

Recalling this list, most people would cluster, at least a little, by the names, the professions, and the colors. For example, here is the written recall of one subject: "Andrew, lawyer, dentist, teacher, doctor, Henry, Burt, green, yellow, blue, purple, . . . George." The subject recalled all the words, but the order has been altered; the words are clearly clustered into categories.

If the experimenter does not supply the organization by presenting words that fall naturally into two or more categories, a subject will still often organize the words, sometimes in ways meaningful only to him or her. This is called *subjective organization* (Tulving, 1962). Of course, subjective organization is often difficult to recognize, because there is no clear indication to the outside observer of what might be a cluster.

As you might expect, experiments have shown that the better information is organized, the easier it is to recall. In one study, recall for 16-word lists was *perfect* 38 percent of the time when the lists were organized by the experimenter to contain 4 categories of 4 words each (Underwood, 1964). Recall for lists of 16 unrelated words was perfect only 3 percent of the time.

In a different type of experiment, it has been found that if you give subjects a set of words and ask them to sort them into two to seven piles, using any basis for sorting they desire, the more piles they use, the better they can later recall the words. This relationship is unusually strong, generating correlations as high as .95 (Mandler and Pearlstone, 1966), and .70 is average (Mandler, 1967). What this means, apparently, is that using more piles is akin to greater organization. Someone who sorts into "big words" and "little words" has not organized the words with the precision and detail of another subject who uses seven piles: sissy words, liquids, living things, things around the house, sexy words, -tion words, unpleasant words — or whatever seems to fit.

Encoding Complex Material

Like nonsense syllables and words, complex stimuli such as sentences and stories appear to be encoded most successfully when we relate them to existing knowledge. The better they are related to what we already know — that is, the more meaningful they are — the better we remember them.

Here is a demonstration you can try out on yourself (adapted from Dooling and Lachman, 1971). First read the following passage and then, before reading further, try to write down everything you can recall.

> With hocked gems financing him, our hero bravely defied all scornful laughter that tried to prevent his scheme. "Your eyes deceive," he had said. "An egg, not a table,

correctly typifies this unexplored planet." Now three sturdy sisters sought proof. Forging along, sometimes through calm vastness, yet more often over turbulent peaks and valleys, days became weeks as many doubters spread fearful rumors about the edge. At last from nowhere welcome winged creatures appeared, signifying momentous success.

Now conduct the same test on a friend (one whose memory is about equal to your own), but tell the friend that the passage is called "Columbus Discovering America." Compare your recall with his or hers. Your friend should have a marked advantage, because the meaning provided by the title will allow him or her to encode the story more effectively.

In addition to the direct sort of meaning conveyed by a title, the general structure of a story has an effect on later recall. (This effect is not unlike that of organization on the recall of words.) For example, we have certain abstract notions of how a story — any story — should proceed; psychologists call such an abstract notion a *schema*. One such schema states that a problem should come early in a story, and later it should be resolved. Consider the following story, which demonstrates the problem-solving schema:

> A farmer wanted his mule to go into the barn. The mule would not go in, so he asked his dog to bark and scare it in. The dog refused to bark, so the farmer asked his cat to scratch the dog to make it bark. The cat would not scratch the dog unless it got some milk, so the farmer asked his cow to provide some milk. The cow gave the farmer the milk, the farmer gave the milk to the cat, the cat scratched the dog, whereupon the dog barked and scared the mule into the barn.

A little complicated, but nicely organized; recall of this sort of story is generally quite good (Thorndyke, 1977). In contrast, subjects presented with a similar story with the problem stated at the *end* instead of at the beginning have much more difficulty remembering the details of the solution. Without knowing that the farmer was trying to get his mule into the barn, one finds it hard to encode effectively the strange behaviors of the other barnyard animals.

STORAGE: THE THREE SYSTEMS

When information is held in memory, where is it held? Psychologists long ago concluded that we have more than one type of memory system for storing learned information. In 1890, the eloquent psychologist-philosopher William James wrote, in his *Principles of Psychology:*

> The stream of thought flows on; but most of its segments fall into the bottomless abyss of oblivion. Of some, no memory survives the instant of their passage. Of others, it is confined to a few moments, hours, or days. Others, again, leave vestiges which are indestructible, and by means of which they may be recalled as long as life endures (p. 643).

Sigmund Freud, in 1925, asserted that one could not understand the human personality without postulating at least two types of memory (Freud, 1959). He used the analogy of the "Mystic Writing Pad," a brand name of a child's toy still common today. It consists of a waxy slab covered by a translucent sheet on which drawings or writings can be made with a stylus. The stylus connects the sheet to the slab and makes its mark, not by depositing a substance as pens and pencils do, but by driving the sheet into the slab. When the sheet is ripped from its waxy imprint, the markings disappear. Freud suggested that one memory system had the characteristics of the overlying sheet: not permanent, and with a limited capacity. The second memory system was likened to the underlying slab, which retains the marks on its waxy surface even after the sheet has been pulled free. This analogy cannot be taken too literally, said Freud, but it is useful for understanding the notion of a transient (impermanent) memory separate from but related to a more permanent memory. And there must be such a division, said Freud, or else the human mind would not have the ability to create the separate and personal reality it does, subtracting from the outside world those markings which are personally threatening, leaving no conscious trace.

Today, psychologists generally distinguish three storage systems, called the *sensory store,* the *short-term store,* and the *long-term store* (for example, Atkinson and Shiffrin, 1968). According to this view, as a stimulus from the environment is "processed," it passes first through the sensory store; if it survives that ordeal, it enters the short-term store, and then, if still alive, the long-term store (see Figure 5.6).

The Sensory Store (SS)

Information from the environment (the stimulus) first enters the sensory store (SS), where it decays very rapidly, a large portion of the information disappearing in about half

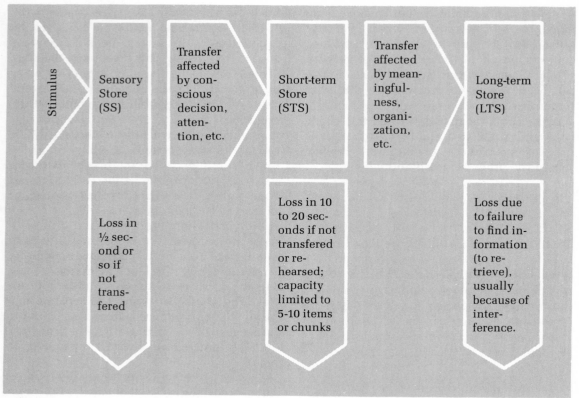

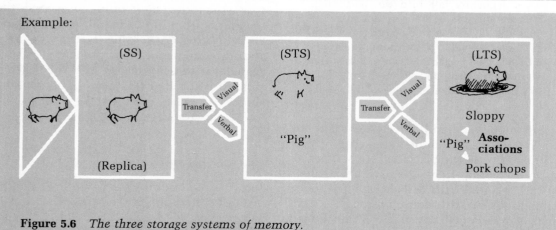

Figure 5.6 *The three storage systems of memory.*

a second. The purpose of this system, according to most common theories, is to preserve the stimulus for a brief period beyond its actual, physical duration. In terms of the Pandemonium model of perceptual recognition (pp. 121–123), the letter A might be flashed; the feature demons are frustrated and grumbling—they want a better look at the stimulus. The sensory store provides such a service, allowing them a slightly longer look at the stimulus.

Tracking the Sensory Store. If information disappears from the sensory store within half a second or so, how do we know there is such a part of the memory process? A good example of the type of experiment that has led psychologists to postulate a sensory store is the work of Sperling (1960). He showed his subjects nine letters on a screen in an array of three by three, something like this:

D T R
S Z P
H P N

An eye chart of sorts, except that the array was flashed for just 50 milliseconds (50 thousandths of a second). An experienced subject generally can recall four or five of nine stimuli.

Sperling, however, did not ask his subjects to recall all nine letters. Immediately after the flash, a tone sounded; the subjects knew from previous instructions that a high tone meant they were to recall the top row, a medium tone meant the middle row, and a low tone, the bottom. One would predict from previous research without tones that recall would be accurate about 50 percent of the time. With the tones, however, subjects usually could recall *all* of the letters in the indicated row. Since the subjects did not

know at the flash which row would be signalled, they must have been able to hold eight or nine of the nine letters in memory for a brief time, until the tone signaled which row to recall.

Psychologists were able to show the brief life span of information in the sensory store by delaying the tone indicating the row to be recalled. A quarter of a second delay was enough to sharply reduce recall percentage. If the tone was sounded a second or more after the flash, the percentage of items recalled was no greater than in experiments with no tones at all.

The Icon. Many additional experiments have been done on this sensory registration system, and the evidence is reasonably clear that after a visual stimulus has been presented, a rather accurate picture of the stimulus persists for a very brief period. This period is typically less than a second, although under the most favorable circumstances it can extend up to five seconds or so. During this time, the individual knows more than he or she ever will again about the event that has just occurred. This copy of the visual stimulus is called the *icon*. Facsimiles of auditory stimuli, called *echoes*, also have been demonstrated.

The time duration of the icon and the echo may seem so short as to be useless, but it is time enough for important decisions. The information that gets out of the sensory store and into the short-term store for further processing is not determined by blind chance. It can be a matter of choice. Consider Sperling's experiments. The tones were instructions to read the top, middle, or bottom row, and it is clear the subjects could follow the instructions. If subjects can follow Sperling's instructions, they can certainly follow their own, and decide for themselves what to preserve from the icon or echo.

The Short-Term Store (STS)

The sensory store is a comparatively recent idea; its existence can be demonstrated only with sophisticated, experimental techniques. The short-term store (STS), on the other hand, has been discussed for many years. Both William James and Sigmund Freud hypothesized such a storage system,

as we mentioned. They conceived of a short-term memory that stores information for a brief time, on the order of a few seconds, and that has a limited capacity, storing only a few items at a time. These remain the defining characteristics of the short-term store today.

Ebbinghaus made some of the earliest experimental observations of the short-term store, when he discovered that he could learn lists of seven items or less in only one reading. About the time that Ebbinghaus was puzzling over these data, another scien-

Figure 5.7 *Look at this picture for a few seconds and then look away. Which signs stand out in your memory? What makes you remember some and forget others?*

tist named Jacobs (1887) began research into what was to become known as the span of immediate memory, or, more simply, the *memory span*. Jacobs was interested in how much material could be reproduced after a single presentation. He presented his subjects with a series of digits, asking them to repeat the digits after hearing them once, a task much like getting a telephone number from Directory Assistance when you have no pad to write it down. Jacob's research showed that a person could remember, on the average, about seven digits or letters after one trial. The span of immediate (short-term) memory, then, was defined as about seven items (Figure 5.8).

The memory span marks a rather abrupt discontinuity in memory performance. The average person can learn a list of fewer than seven items in a single hearing; a longer list is much more difficult. Memory for a list exceeding the span is often poorer than for shorter lists—not only in terms of the percentage of items recalled, but even in absolute terms. One study found that if a list of eight digits was presented once, the average college student could recall all eight items; if more than eight digits were presented, subjects could recall only six (Gates, 1916). Results like this suggest a limited capacity in the human short-term memory. When this capacity is exceeded, things become considerably more difficult, something like a juggler who does fine with three balls but drops two of them when she tries to handle four.

Figure 5.8   *The short-term storage system has a limited capacity.*

Chunking. The term "magic number" was applied to the number seven by George Miller (1956) in a paper subtitled "Some limits on our capacity for processing information." Miller suggested that about seven units of information (actually, seven plus or minus two) was all the human system could handle at one time. But Miller also pointed out that what constitutes a "unit" of the memory span (what uses up one of the seven spaces in short-term memory) varies. To expand the limits of their ability to process information, people can *chunk* information so that what appears to be seventy items is in fact only seven. An easy example is chunking letters into meaningful words. You can remember without difficulty the nine-item list of letters, ELEPHANTS, even though the number of letters exceeds your memory span. In fact, the average subject generally can recall five to nine words after one trial, the same magic number (7 ± 2) that applies to single letters.

Memory experts can carry chunking to astonishing lengths, using tricks that allow them to recode a great deal of complex material into a few chunks. Whereas many people could form a word from certain lettters in a memory-span task—like converting PRSDNTWSHNGTN to PRESIDENT WASHINGTON, and thus making 13 letter units into one chunk—what makes these experts stand out is the ability to work with less amenable material, and to do so very rapidly. Quick! Think up a chunking code for XFSZPFXRGTMPQ! Not so easy, but it is possible. (For a description of some of the memory tricks of experts, see Focus: How to Improve Your Memory, on pp. 212–214.)

It is worth noting that chunking is essentially the process we described earlier as organization. One of the reasons our memory is aided when we organize material into meaningful sets during encoding is because these organized sets, or chunks, take up less space in the short-term store. The implications for the everyday problems of memory bear repeating: If you need to memorize a large amount of material quickly, you should *organize* it into smaller groupings, or chunks. If you understand a general principle of, say, history or chemistry or philosophy, you can use the principle to organize and remember many specific details.

Working Memory. The seven-item limit on the memory span may make the short-term store seem like a file with seven drawers, each holding more or less material, depending on how well it is organized. This is too simple a view, partly because it does no justice to the *active* nature of STS. Some psychologists believe the short-term store is the site of consciousness, of the mental activity of which we are moment by moment aware. This view of STS—that it is the factory of our mental work, so to speak—calls it "working memory." We can then think of the short-term store's limited capacity as not simply a limit on the number of items STS can carry, but a limit on how much mental work can be done there. The idea is that doing one sort of mental work interferes with other uses of the limited capacity. For example, if you rehearse a phone number in your STS while listening to a story, either your comprehension of the story will suffer or you will lose the phone number (Baddeley and Hitch, 1974).

Forgetting in STS. The often striking and sudden loss of information from STS was demonstrated dramatically in a landmark study in 1959 (Peterson and Peterson, 1959).

Subjects were presented with three letters, such as RZP, and then asked to recall them. After 18 seconds, almost no subjects could repeat the letters accurately! This amazing degree of forgetting in such a short time was due to the subjects having been given a "distractor task" between the initial presentation of the letters and the requested recall. They were required to count backward from a three-digit number, say 469, by threes: 466, 463, 460 . . . This procedure was designed to keep subjects from rehearsing the letters.

The investigators' interpretation of their experiment was that, without rehearsal, the information in STS had decayed in a very brief time. Other psychologists favor an explanation in terms of the working-memory notion: The mental work of counting backward by threes interfered with the work of maintaining and encoding the letters. In any case, it is clear that information must be actively maintained in STS or it will be forgotten. And it can be lost quickly, within seconds.

The Long-Term Store (LTS)

From STS, information can enter the *long-term store*, or LTS. LTS has a very large ca-

pacity for information; some say its capacity might as well be considered unlimited. And it stores information for a very long time—possibly forever, if there is no injury to the brain.

What is the nature of this information you can hold on to for so long? Obviously, you can search your own long-term store for answers. In it you will find information related to your personal history; perhaps you can remember facts from your childhood, such as a house you once lived in for a short time. Long-term memory is also the store of general knowledge—how to count, for example, and the knowledge that a dog is an animal. These general facts are not stored randomly but organized: If you think about bread, you are more likely to think next about butter than something unrelated, like a nurse. Psychologists are just beginning to explore the intricate organization of mental facts in the long-term store.

The meaning of information is central to where or how it is stored in long-term memory. In contrast, information in the sensory store and the short-term store is often organized just as it was first experienced. Stimuli that are seen at the same time, for example,

B.C. **by johnny hart**

By permission of Johnny Hart and Field Enterprises Inc.

may be stored together, in the sense that retrieving one is easier given the other, even though the stimuli are unrelated in meaning; stimuli heard in a certain order can more easily be reproduced in that order from the sensory and short-term stores than from the long-term store. In the long-term store, often the general meaning of an event—the "gist" of it—is stored, rather than the exact details. Did you see the movie "Star Wars" a few years ago? Can you remember the plot? Most likely you can recall the gist of the story, but not details of dialogue and plot.

And now we can point out another reason why meaningful encoding, careful organization, and thoughtful chunking are so important to later recall of information: The long-term store is set up to hold things in terms of meaning. Like any filing system, the long-term store responds well only to inquiries made in terms of meaningful labels that are part of an overall, meaningful arrangement. Any material that is entered into LTS as "miscellaneous" is likely to be inaccessible when it is wanted later.

FOCUS

How to Improve Your Memory

There are a number of books with titles something like the heading of this focus. Unlike most psychology books found in newsstands, the memory books tend to be quite useful, mainly because they focus on technique. There are several "tricks" that allow one to memorize large amounts of information with relative ease. Psychologists have typically viewed these tricks as irrelevant to "real" psychology, but lately scientists have become extremely interested in what they call "mnemonic devices." The reason for their interest is that memory tricks are usually ways of organizing and encoding information, and "organization" and "encoding" are hot topics.

Simple rhymes, capitalizing on the rhyme and rhythm of poetry, are often used as mnemonic devices. "Thirty days hath September..." and "I before E, except after C" are common examples. Once learned, they are not easily forgotten. There are restrictions on rhymes, of course; one could never say, "E before I, except after C" because it doesn't rhyme.

A rhyme that is useful for remembering lists (shopping lists, things-to-do lists, etc.), especially if the list must be kept in order, is the following:

One is a bun,   Five is a hive,   Nine is a line,
Two is a shoe,   Six are sticks,   Ten is a hen.
Three is a tree,   Seven is heaven,
Four is a door,   Eight is a gate,

You can extend the length of the list yourself by forming more rhymes.

First, memorize the rhyme. Now you can "hook" anything you want onto the rhyme by forming an image that includes both the rhyme word and the item to be remembered. Say you want to remember to do the following things today:

1. Go to psychology class.
2. Talk to Sam after class.
3. Keep dentist appointment.
4. Pick up milk.

You have to form your own images, but I would visualize my psychology professor lecturing from on top of a bun, Sam living in a shoe (like the old woman who . . .), my dentist in a tree (where I chased him, the sadist), and milk delivered to the door, as in the good old days. Later, when I try to remember what I have to do fourth . . . four is a door, milk on the doorstep . . . get milk! Try it. It works.

Images are very useful, even without rhymes. The other day I was asked to stop at the grocery and pick up: (1) some cottage cheese, (2) some Trident gum, and (3) some cigarettes. I was too lazy to write it down, so I formed an image of Neptune (god of the sea) holding his trident (a three-pronged spear), floating on the ocean in a cottage cheese container, and smoking a cigarette. I suspect I will never forget that shopping list.

Most of these mnemonic devices are based on the "method of places and images" or, as it is more often called, the "method of loci," which is at least 2000 years old. Public speakers in olden times were expected to speak without notes, from memory, and many mnemonic systems were devised for them. In a simple form, the method of loci suggests that you imagine a series of locations—these loci might be places in your house or room, places along a route you walk or drive, or any set of locations that you can visualize in order—and integrate to-be-remembered information into these loci. Your psychology professor might be sitting in your bathtub, Sam on your toilet, and your dentist on your mirror; your sink is full of milk. (You must of course maintain the order in which you visualize locations in your bathroom.) Professional memory experts often use a much more complicated version of this same system; their "memory house" has many rooms, organized in a very systematic fashion (see Yates, 1966; Lorayne and Lucas, 1974; Cermak, 1975).

Lest we be accused of discussing topics of use to everyday living but with no relation to psychological theory, let us notice the support these mnemonic devices give to theories championing the role of *imagery* and the benefits of *organization* in memory (for example, see Paivio, 1971).

Compare these systems, for example, with the belief of some people that you can improve your memory by practicing memorizing. William James (1890) tested this hypothesis; he learned 158 lines of poetry, then an entire book (as practice), then another 158 lines of poetry. The second poetry sample took him longer to learn than the first. Thus, simple practice does not improve memory; plans and organizational schemes, however, can improve memory to such an extent that people will pay good money to see you perform.

RETRIEVAL

Retrieval is the process of getting information out of memory. Retrieving material from the sensory and short-term stores is relatively straightforward — if the information is there, it can usually be reported — but retrieval from the long-term store is more complex. Indeed, considering the vast amount of information in the long-term store, it is an indication of the efficiency of the human memory systems that we are able to find anything at all. How do we do it?

Psychologists view retrieval from memory as a kind of directed search. "Directed" means that the process is not haphazard; if you're trying to retrieve a friend's address from memory, your LTS will not send down a note that George Washington was the first president, a reminder that fruits can be eaten, and several other interesting but irrelevant facts, until finally it comes up with the address of your friend. The process seems to be more efficient than that. Whatever it is that prompts you to get at the information in the first place — call this a *retrieval cue* — begins the retrieval process.

The cue can be as explicit as a question from a teacher ("What was B. F. Skinner's contribution to psychology?") or as subtle as the smell of cinnamon, which triggers memories of your grandmother in the kitchen, baking. The cue starts you out at a fairly precise location in LTS, and from that base camp you are able to search around among related material until you find what you want.

This metaphorical description of the retrieval process is supported by a variety of experiments (Klatzky, 1980). A common experimental technique, called *free recall*, asks subjects to recall the words from a list in any order. Their responses give evidence that the subjects have organized the words in encoding them (see p. 203) and that they tap into these meaningful groups during retrieval. Not only do subjects report words that are related in meaning close together, but they also retrieve sets of related words in "bursts" — with short intervals between items and long pauses between the end of one set and the beginning of another. Thus, a subject might report: "BUICK, FORD, CHRYSLER, CHEVROLET . . . TABLE, CHAIR, SOFA, DESK, STOOL . . . SOUP,

STEAK, BREAD . . ." It is as if the longer intervals between sets correspond to a search for a new location in memory. When the location of an organized unit is discovered, all the items there spill forth rapidly. On the other hand, if a subject fails to report one item in a set, often he or she cannot report any of the items in the set, as if the entire cluster was missed in the retrieval process. We have all had the experience of remembering *nothing* about something and then, when *one* thing is remembered, remembering so much that it is like finding buried treasure.

Tip of the Tongue

Sometimes we know we are close to the location in memory of some desired information, but we cannot quite retrieve it — "It's on the tip of my tongue!" The name of an old friend, a word that fits a particular meaning — we struggle, we know we're close, but we fail to retrieve it.

In an ingenious experiment designed to investigate the "tip of the tongue" phenomenon, researchers gave subjects definitions of slightly obscure words (Brown and McNeill, 1966). One definition, for example, was "the center of a cell." Several of these definitions resulted in tip of the tongue experiences for various subjects. The researchers found that a subject usually could retrieve facts related to the missing word, such as the number of syllables and the first letter; they also could give words with similar sounds and similar meanings. Sometimes recalling such related material led to recalling the missing word itself. "It sounds like mucous, it sounds like neutral — it's nucleus!"

Unrecognized Recall

One of the most peculiar findings in memory research is almost the opposite of the tip of the tongue phenomenon: Subjects search for the right word, find it, report it — but fail to realize that they have been successful! Suppose, for example, you are asked to recall the second president of the United States. You retrieve the name John Adams. Is it correct? You're not sure.

In another ingenious experiment (Tulving and Thompson, 1973), subjects were given a list of words in capital letters. Each word was preceded by another word in small letters, which the experimenter said would help the subject recall the word in capitals. The helping words were related to the words to be recalled, but only weakly — something like "aloof — COLD." Later, instead of a simple recall test, subjects were given a new word and asked to supply four words that come to mind (associates). For instance, subjects were given the word "hot," and nearly all of them gave "cold" as one of their associates. Next, the subjects were asked to look at their associates and to circle any of them that were words on the original list. Surprisingly, the subjects did very poorly at this task. They had retrieved COLD but did not recognize their accomplishment.

What can we make of this intriguing failure of recognition, once recall has succeeded? The authors of the study suggest that the process of retrieving information from LTS depends to a great extent on the way it was encoded. If you encode the word "cold" in the context of "aloof," you file it away in a different place from "cold" meaning opposite of "hot." Retrieving the correct word in the wrong context deceives you and forces you to doubt your memory.

FOCUS

Marijuana, Alcohol, and Memory

My friend Becky was a hard-drinking woman who, once a month or so, would "tie one on." The morning after, she would timidly inquire if I had seen her the night before and, if so, where had she been? What had she done? "Liquor bottles should have a warning on them," she once suggested. "Caution: this substance is hazardous to your memory."

Alcohol does indeed have a detrimental effect on memory, and so does marijuana. But why? Do drugs affect encoding, storage, or retrieval? Do alcohol and marijuana have similar effects, or do they act in different ways, at different points as we process information for memory? A number of sophisticated experiments on these questions have expanded our knowledge of both the drugs and the nature of human memory.

Consider the following study, designed to distinguish between marijuana's effect at the time of the encoding and storage of new information and its effect on retrieval of material previously learned (Darley et al., 1973). Two groups of subjects—all experienced users of pot—learned lists of words. Then one group was given THC, the active ingredient in marijuana, and the other received a placebo—a neutral substance. After waiting a bit for the THC to take effect, the researchers asked all subjects to recall the lists. Thus, by design, the two groups *stored* the information in the same sober state; there is no difference between groups in encoding and storage. If there is a difference in recall, it must be because marijuana is affecting retrieval.

There was, in fact, no difference in average recall scores. "Stoned" subjects could retrieve information from memory just as well as "straight" subjects. This finding leads us to suspect that marijuana interferes with the initial learning (encoding and storage) of information, not retrieval. Almost identical studies on alcohol produced almost identical results (Birnbaum et al., 1978; Miller et al., 1978).

In the course of studying the effect of drugs on memory, psychologists discovered a curious phenomenon called *state-dependent learning*. Learning (encoding and storage) that occurs in an altered "state of consciousness"—drunk from alcohol, stoned from marijuana—is generally more easily remembered in that same state than in some others. My friend Becky, for example, would sometimes forget her activities of the night before when she was sober the next morning, but recall them when she got drunk again later.

A number of experiments on both alcohol and marijuana have demonstrated state-dependent learning in the laboratory (Eich, 1977). At least four groups of subjects are needed: A sober-sober group learns a word list while sober and recalls it in the same state; a stoned-stoned (or drunk-drunk) group both learns and recalls while stoned; a sober-stoned group learns sober and recalls while stoned; and a stoned-sober group learns while stoned and recalls sober. State-dependent learning is shown primarily by the fact that the people who learn while stoned and recall while stoned remember more than the people who learn stoned and recall sober. Strangely, among those who learn while sober, those who recall sober do not usually have much of an advantage (often none at all) over those who recall stoned.

In summary, alcohol and marijuana do have detrimental effects on memory. They appear to affect the initial learning (encoding and storage) but not retrieval. The deficit caused by learning while intoxicated can be reduced by recalling in the same state. Although we are far from understanding the reasons for these effects, the "unusual context" provided by a state of drug-intoxication appears to play some role. If you learn something while stoned or drunk, you may have difficulty retrieving it sober because many of the contextual stimuli (retrieval cues) are absent; getting intoxicated again restores those cues and improves recall. It is something like suddenly recalling a long-forgotten classmate in the third grade when visiting your old classroom. Re-creating the drug context, however, reduces but does not eliminate the deficit. Drugs also seem to affect the transfer of information from the short-term store to the long-term store, maybe by making focused attention more difficult. Thus many of your most memorable experiences are forever lost, never recorded.

FORGETTING

On the surface, forgetting seems to be nothing more than the failure of memory. Can't we consider any study of remembering to be a study of forgetting just as well? Certainly, just as we can view sleep as the failure to keep awake, or alcoholism as the absence of sobriety. But, like sleep and alcoholism, forgetting is its own topic, too, deserving separate attention. It is very much an active process, not merely the absence of its opposite.

Interference Theory

The theory that has dominated psychological discussions of forgetting (from LTS) is called the interference theory. It can be stated quite simply: You forget because

Figure 5.9 *There is a story told of a college president who was an authority on fish. He discovered that each time he learned the name of a new student, he forgot the name of a fish.*

other information interferes with remembering—makes it difficult or impossible for you to retrieve the desired information.

There are two types of interference. *Proactive interference* results when information previously stored in memory interferes with the retrieval of new material. ("Proactive" means "acting forward.") Proactive interference is what makes it hard to remember the name of someone you've just met who reminds you of an old friend; you keep wanting to call her Jane, and you quickly forget that her name is actually Leslie. *Retroactive interference* ("acting backward") results when new learning affects the retention of older material. An example of retroactive interference would be forgetting some of your Spanish vocabulary after studying Italian vocabulary.

Most laboratory experiments on interference have involved paired-associate learning, mainly because stimulus-response (S-R) conceptions have dominated the field. In pairs of items to be associated, the first can be considered the S and the second, the R. Suppose we have a list of pairs of words— EAGLE-BOTTLE, CONTEST-BASKET, and so on—to be learned. EAGLE and CONTEST are Ss, and BOTTLE and BASKET are Rs. Suppose also we have created another list for a second learning task, this one using the same stimulus words but different response words, for example, EAGLE-RESTFUL, CONTEST-REPLY. Such a sequence of lists is labeled A-B, A-C, meaning the same Ss (the A collection) are used with different Rs (the B and C collections) in forming the two lists. The A-B, A-C sequence typically produces substantial interference, as you might imagine. Suppose that 24 hours later the subjects are asked to remember both lists. If they had been given only one list, they would forget about 20 percent; this we know from control subjects. But with two lists they forget about 60 percent (Underwood, 1964). The reason must be interference between the two lists, proactive interference of the first on the second and retroactive interference of the second on the first.

It is at least a working hypothesis of interference theory that interference alone is enough to explain all normal forgetting: no other factor need be considered. (Memory loss due to brain injury or disease, of course, is abnormal.) In particular, interference theorists are openly antagonistic to notions of *decay*, the idea that memories that are not used or restored simply fade away with time.

It is not easy to test decay hypotheses of forgetting because they are not tied to any specific process. A decay theory states, very simply, that the more time elapsed since learning, the more forgotten. A proper test of this theory would involve learning some-

thing, then letting time pass while having no experiences that might interfere, and then recalling the material. If nothing is forgotten, as interference theory would predict, the decay theory would be in trouble. If there is forgetting, decay theory would be supported. Unfortunately, nobody has yet devised a way of letting time pass without experience. One researcher told me he wished he had known Jesus was going to raise Lazarus from the dead, so he could have tested the decay theory of memory by having Lazarus learn a list, die, revive, and recall.

The closest researchers have been able to come to a period without experience is sleep. Sleep is not a total absence of experience, but it presumably involves *less* experience than waking states. Experiments comparing memory after learning-sleep-recall with recall after learning and normal waking activities show clearly that forgetting does occur during sleep but at a significantly slower rate (see Figure 5.10). Almost all the

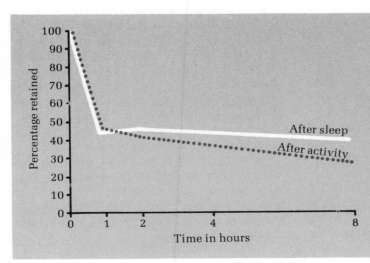

Figure 5.10 *In this experiment subjects memorized lists of nonsense syllables and then either went to sleep or went about their normal waking activities. They relearned the lists at various intervals. As this subject's record shows, forgetting (as measured by the savings method) was less during sleep than during activity.*

forgetting takes place in the first hour of sleep. Most psychologists see this as evidence that decay is not a major factor in forgetting, but the fact that there is *some* forgetting leaves the decay theory at least barely alive.

Forgetting of Natural Language Material

The interference theory of forgetting is a plausible explanation for the kind of forgetting that occurs in experiments involving lists of paired words. But how does it fare in other settings? Most tests of interference theory, in concentrating on subjects' ability to recall particular words exactly as they were first presented, have not been applied to the many situations where we don't care to remember precisely how information was worded. In daily experience, it is probably more common for us to want to remember the general meaning, or gist, of information. For example, we don't memorize a lecture on American history; rather, we try to get the general trends and ideas being talked about.

Only recently have memory psychologists begun to focus on forgetting of *natural language material*—that is, stories and sentences rather than word lists. The picture that has been emerging from their research is quite different from the one generated by the interference theorists. One finding—not surprisingly—is that people often remember the meaning of material even when they forget its exact wording. Another is that forgetting of natural language material sometimes takes the form of remembering *more* than was originally learned! This is because memory for storylike material is "constructive"; in recalling what we heard or read, we may draw on our general knowledge as well as our memory for the text, and the result may be an elaborated version of the original message.

Detail, Meaning, and Elaboration. A classic experiment (Sachs, 1967) that differentiated between memory for meaning and memory for wording had subjects listen to a passage taken from a factual article. At some point the passage was interrupted, and the subject was given a test. The test consisted of a sentence similar to one that had been in the passage, either immediately before the interruption or further back; the subject was to indicate whether or not the test sentence was *identical* to the original. When the test sentence did contain changes from the original, they were either changes in wording that did not alter meaning ("He sent the scientist a letter about it" might become "He sent a letter about it to the scientist") or changes in wording that *also* changed meaning ("The scientist sent him a letter about it"). Subjects proved to be able to detect both kinds of change if the test sentence immediately followed the original. For originals further back in the passage, they detected changes in meaning far more often than changes in wording only. In fact, even when subjects forgot the exact wording altogether (as demonstrated by a total inability to detect changes in wording), they still caught 70 percent of the meaning changes.

Sometimes our memory for meaning can include even more than the original had to offer. Memory is elaborative: Sometimes it fills out a meager story with additional information from its long-term store. Consider the following passage:

Carol Harris was a problem child from birth. She was wild, stubborn, and violent. By the time Carol turned eight, she was still unmanageable. Her parents were very concerned about her mental health. There was no good institution for her problem in her state. Her parents finally decided to take some action. They hired a private teacher for Carol.

Suppose, after reading this passage, you were asked if the sentence, "She was deaf, dumb, and blind" was part of what you read. Of course not, you say, and most subjects said the same. But when the same passage was presented with "Helen Keller" substituted for "Carol Harris," subjects were not so sure. Because they knew that Helen Keller was deaf, dumb, and blind in real life, many subjects thought they remembered having read that sentence about her handicaps in the experimental passage. This mistake was increasingly likely the longer the time between reading the passage and the test, as we would expect if the elaboration depended in part on subjects' forgetting specific wording (Sulin and Dooling, 1974; Dooling and Christiaansen, 1977).

Tricking an Eyewitness. Our elaborative memory can be a problem when we need to recall exact details—for instance, when we are called on to give eyewitness testimony in court. In a relevant experiment (Loftus, 1975; Loftus et al., 1978), subjects viewed slides or a film depicting an accident in which an auto struck a pedestrian or another car. Then they were asked questions about the accident. One of the slides showed a green car driving by the scene of the accident. The investigator asked some of the subjects if the *blue* car driving by had a ski

rack on its roof. Later, these subjects were asked about the color of the passing car. More of them remembered it as blue than did control subjects, who were asked about a ski rack on the passing car, color unspecified. Thus, the question that presumed the car to be blue affected the subjects' memory for its true color. Similarly, questions asked about objects not in the scenes caused some subjects later to remember seeing the objects. Asking a question about a car that "smashed," compared to one that "hit," increased the remembered speed. The distorting questions did not even have to be asked at the time of the viewing of the accident; questions a week later still influenced memory. And even when subjects were told they might have been exposed to misleading information, they persisted in their inaccurate remembrances.

Although this research certainly bids us be wary of eyewitness testimony, its chief purpose is to show how changes in memory can be induced when new information is added to previously stored memories. Such changes are a good example of what we mean when we speak of "constructive memory," as well as an illustration of how elaboration can result in the forgetting of true details.

Forgetting as Failure of Retrieval

Sometimes we can remember exact details and exact wordings; sometimes we can remember only the gist of a story or an event. But sometimes we try to recall and nothing at all comes to mind. What has happened to that forgotten material? Is it truly gone from memory, never to be recovered? Or is it still in LTS, temporarily or even permanently inaccessible to the retrieval process?

There is no way to distinguish between "truly gone" and "permanently inaccessible." But in many cases we can demonstrate that forgetting is a temporary failure of retrieval. Sometimes you cannot *recall* information, but you can *recognize* it. You may not be able to retrieve "John Adams" when asked to name the second president, but you can recognize him in a multiple-choice item: "Herbert Hoover, John Adams, Joseph Namath, George Washington." What you thought you had forgotten is shown to be still in your memory after all, accessible to recognition if not to recall.

One of the most notable advocates of the position that forgetting is really nothing more than retrieval failure is Wilder Penfield, a renowned brain surgeon. In the course of surgery on patients suffering from severe epilepsy, Penfield probed the patients' exposed brains with an electrode that delivered a mild electrical current. The patients were conscious (the brain has no pain receptors, so only a local anesthetic was needed to cut through the skull and surrounding matter) and they told Penfield what they were experiencing at each point of stimulation. Some of these experiences were *auras*, which are experiences many epileptics have just before a seizure; locating the site of an aura enabled Penfield to locate small sections of irritable brain tissue that were responsible for the epileptic seizures and to remove them, to the patients' great benefit. But while searching for auras, Penfield found that certain points in his patients' brains, when stimulated, revived distant memories. One patient reported a

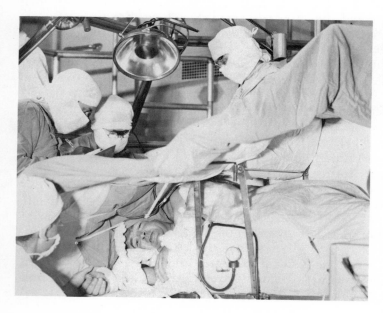

Figure 5.11 *Surgeons map the exposed brain of a patient being treated for severe epilepsy. Looking (with electrical probes) for auras, the precursors of epileptic attacks, they also found many vivid memories.*

"very, very familiar memory, in an office somewhere. I could see the desks. I was there and someone was calling me, a man leaning on a desk with a pencil in his hand" (Penfield, 1955, p. 55). Many of these memories were exceptionally vivid, as if the person were reliving the original experience. Penfield was led to conclude that the brain retains a "permanent record" of "all those things of which the individual was once aware."

But Penfield's data are no more conclusive than any that show that certain information, apparently forgotten, can be retrieved with a more effective tool to dig it out. Although there is no doubt that *some* forgetting is due to retrieval failure, there is no conclusive evidence that *all* forgetting is of this type (Hintzman, 1978).

CREATIVE MEMORY

Memory, then, like perception, is an extremely active and creative process. The evidence is building that we human beings process information in ways dictated largely by our personal purposes and intentions. If we want to retain a literal representation of stimuli from the environment, we can do that. If we want to encode a stimulus into a word that represents it abstractly, we can do that. Or we can use an abstract *image* instead of a word: You have a kind of abstract image of DOG, do you not? When driven to do so, we can even erase all or part of a memory, at least from conscious awareness, a fact psychotherapists have known for a good many years.

Thus, we come to the same position we did in the chapter on perception, sitting in awe of our active creativity and of the vast scope of human intellectual powers, from perception and learning to memory. Awefull abilities, however, do not in themselves determine behavior; "how" we do it must combine with "why" we do it, the topic of the next chapter: Motivation.

SUMMARY

1. Hermann Ebbinghaus used nonsense syllables and the method of *savings* to study memory nearly a century ago. He found that when the length of a list of items doubles, the time needed to memorize it more than doubles; that forgetting is rapid at first and then tapers off; and that *distributed* practice is more effective than *massed* practice.

2. Scientists are still uncertain about just what biological and chemical processes are involved in memory, but its psychological processes are fairly well established. *Encoding* is the process by which material is prepared for *storage* in memory; *retrieval* brings information from storage into consciousness. Inability to remember something may result from a failure in any one of these processes. Of the two forms of retrieval most commonly used in testing memory, *recognition* is easier than *recall*.

3. Encoding material in meaningful ways leads to better memory than encoding in terms of superficial characteristics, as *depth of processing theory* predicts. The *association value* of a nonsense syllable or word indicates its meaningfulness. Use of meaning to *organize* stimuli also aids memory. A descriptive title or thesis sentence promotes the recall of complex stimuli such as stories.

4. Current theories of memory postulate

more than one memory storage system. There is evidence for a sensory store (SS), a short-term store (STS), and a long-term store (LTS).

5. The existence of a *sensory store,* which retains information for only a second or so, was suggested by research indicating that subjects could "read off" a brief afterimage of a visual stimulus. Such a mental picture of a visual stimulus is called an *icon.*

6. The *short-term store* can hold information only for about 20 seconds without rehearsal. STS also has a limited capacity, typically holding seven items or less at a time. But more information can be stored in STS if it is organized into *chunks.* STS has also been called "working memory," to emphasize its active nature; the limited capacity of STS, according to this view, may be a limitation on the amount of mental work a person can do at one time.

7. The *long-term store* has a large capacity and holds information for very long periods, perhaps forever. Much of LTS appears to be organized in terms of *meaning* (semantic memory), which is why meaningful encoding is so effective.

8. *Retrieval* from memory is viewed as "directed search." In the process of retrieval, people often recall meaningful groupings together; they can often recall information related to the stimulus, such as the number of syllables in a word, without recalling the stimulus itself (the *tip of the tongue phenomenon*); and they sometimes fail to recognize a stimulus they are searching for, if the context is different from that at encoding.

9. *Forgetting* is an active process, not simply the failure of memory. *Interference theory* explains forgetting from LTS as a failure to retrieve information because of interference from similar material learned earlier (*proactive interference*) or later (*retroactive interference*). Actual loss of information through decay does not appear to be a major factor in forgetting.

10. Research on natural language material (sentences, stories, and the like) shows less forgetting than interference theory would predict, especially in the gist of a passage. Indeed, subjects sometimes remember more than they were presented, especially if they have personal knowledge about the material; distortions and additions can also be produced by leading questions.

11. Although Penfield's electrical stimulation of exposed brains suggests that much forgetting is simply a failure of retrieval, we cannot conclude that permanent loss does not occur in some instances.

USING PSYCHOLOGY

Test for yourself whether meaningful material is easier to remember than meaningless material. Below is a list of 10 meaningful words and another list of 10 nonsense syllables. Flip a coin to determine which list you will learn first (heads = meaningful, tails = nonsense). *Without* using the mnemonic devices described in Focus: How to Improve Your Memory, try to learn each list in one reading. Cover up all but one item while you are trying to learn it. Spend 10 seconds on each item on each list, trying to learn and memorize the item. When you have completed your reading of the entire 10-item list, wait 30 seconds and then test your recall of the items by writing all you can remember on another piece of paper. Do not look back at the list! Allow about two minutes for this recall test. When the time is up, compare your recall list to the actual list you learned. How many items did you recall correctly? How many did you forget? Did you write down any items that were not actually on the list to be learned? (These are called intrusions.) Is there any evidence of a recency effect? Now go on to the second list you are to learn, repeating the same procedures as you used for the first list. Compare your memory for the two lists. Did you, like most people, find the meaningful words much easier to remember than the nonsense syllables? Notice that both the meaningful word and nonsense syllables are made up of a consonant, a vowel, and a consonant. Why do you think it is important that these are all the same?

Meaningful words		Nonsense syllables	
gem	fat	mel	lur
tar	dig	fip	kef
pen	sit	tob	des
hop	can	rab	lan
lip	bed	hod	gep

SUGGESTED READINGS

Klatzky, R. L. *Human memory: structures and processes.* 2nd ed. Freeman, 1980.
An excellent brief textbook covering the most recent research and theories of human memory.

Crowder, R. G. *Principles of learning and memory.* Erlbaum, 1976.
A more detailed treatment of memory research.

Birnbaum, I. M., & Parker, E. S. (eds.). *Alcohol and human memory.* Erlbaum, 1977.
An excellent volume of reviews of research on alcohol and memory; also contains discussions of research on marijuana and memory.

Cermak, L. S. *Improving your memory.* McGraw-Hill, 1975.
Written by a distinguished researcher in memory and designed to instruct laypeople in old and new mnemonic devices. Fun, and practical.

Hypnosis

Hypnosis has been defined as "an artificially induced state, usually (though not always) resembling sleep, but physiologically distinct from it, which is characterized by heightened suggestibility . . ." (Weitzenhoffer, 1963, p. 3). The sleepy, almost zombie-like behaviors common in hypnotized subjects are what gives hypnosis its name—*hypnos* is the Greek word for sleep. But it is *suggestibility*—a greater-than-normal willingness to accept the statements or suggestions of another person—that gives hypnosis its occult flavor. We have visions of an evil scientist controlling someone else's will, visions that have been dramatized in stories and movies. Suggestibility also gives hypnosis its important role in the history of psychology, as ". . . practically the beginning of the experimental psychology of motivation" (Boring, 1950, p. 116). In this interlude, we will focus on this aspect of hypnosis: how the study of hypnosis clarifies questions about the unconscious mind and human motivation in general.

MESMER

Although hypnosis has been practiced for centuries, it was Friedrich Anton Mesmer (1734–1815) who made hypnotic procedures famous. A Viennese physician, Mesmer believed that the sleeplike states he induced

were the result of magnetism; in fact, at first he induced hypnosis by stroking people with magnets. He soon found that this was unnecessary, that he could as easily hypnotize people without the magnets; his own body, he thought, provided the "animal magnetism." Mesmer used hypnosis to cure certain diseases, such as extreme nervousness, and he tried to interest the medical profession (without success) in what he called animal magnetism and others began to call mesmerism.

In 1778, the Viennese scientific academies forced Mesmer to flee to Paris, where he began a sort of group therapy. Having discovered that it was the subjects' *belief* in magnetism that made it work, he began using a number of gimmicks to help induce hypnosis. Patients sat around a "magnetized" oak chest; the therapy room was dimly lighted, and soft music was played. Mesmer himself often appeared in magician's dress, dancing around the room. He found that often all that was required for hypnosis was to look at someone and shout "Sleep!"

These shenanigans did little for Mesmer's reputation. He was investigated by a scientific commission, which concluded that animal magnetism was not at all like metal magnetism. But if it was not magnetism, then what was this mysterious force? The French government offered Mesmer 20,000 francs for the secret of hypnosis. Since Mesmer had no secret to disclose, he refused. He was denounced as a charlatan and forced to leave Paris; he died in disrepute in Switzerland in 1815.

HYPNOSIS AND PAIN

Dormant for 50 years, scientific interest in hypnosis was revived in the 1840s with the discovery that hypnotized patients, given the suggestion that they would feel no pain, could undergo painless surgery. (The chemical anesthetics — ether, chloroform — had not yet been discovered.) In 1842, an English physician named Ward amputated a leg of a hypnotized patient, who felt no pain. Unfortunately he was chastised by the national medical society: "Patients ought to suffer pain while their surgeons are operating" (Boring, 1950, p. 121). Another British surgeon named Esdaile was operating in India with patients under hypnosis; he performed about 300 major operations, with great success. But he, too, was criticized; his patients, it was said, were trying to please him by showing no evidence of pain.

I have personally witnessed the surgical removal of an appendix from a hypnotized patient, whose only anesthetic was an instruction to feel no pain. Anyone who could believe that he was trying to please the doctor has a greater capacity for belief than I. My impression was that I felt more pain, observing, than the patient did.

HYPNOSIS AND UNCONSCIOUS MOTIVATION

About the time hypnosis was beginning to find acceptance as a medical tool to lessen pain, the anesthetic properties of ether and chloroform came into use, and the somewhat suspect practice of mesmerism, now renamed "hypnosis," went into another decline. Then around 1885, Sigmund Freud began using hypnosis to treat mental disorders. He eventually discontinued it because it could not be used on all patients, and because he discovered what he considered a better technique—free association (see Chapter 10). Nevertheless, Freud's knowledge of hypnosis played a major role in his ideas about *unconscious motivation*, the concept on which his theory of personality—psychoanalysis—is based.

Putting someone into a hypnotic state—the *hypnotic induction* procedure—can be accomplished in several ways. Most commonly, the subject lies on a couch and gazes fixedly at some point on the ceiling. The hypnotist then gives instructions on how to enter the hypnotic state. These are mainly requests to relax—"You are getting very sleepy, very tired, very sleepy . . ."—and to pay attention only to the hypnotist and his or her suggestions—"Listen only to my words. Pay attention to nothing else but what I tell you."

Once the subject has been hypnotized, the hypnotist can suggest a number of experiences for the subject—imagine a fly buzzing around, for example. To demonstrate unconscious motivation, Freud used what is called a *posthypnotic suggestion*—an instruction given under hypnosis but to be carried out later, when the subject is awake. The hypnotist might give instructions something like this: "When you wake up, I will tap my desk with my pencil. When I do this, you will get up, walk to the phone on my desk, pick it up and say, 'Hello? Hello?' Then you will hang it up and sit down again. But you will not remember my telling you to do this, not until I say 'Now you can remember everything.' Then you will remember all that we said and did under hypnosis."

The subject is then awakened. After a few minutes of casual conversation, the hypnotist taps the desk, and, if the hypnotic subject is a good one, she will pick up the phone and say "Hello? Hello?" If you ask her why she did it, she will make up a plausible story—"I thought I heard the phone ring"—because she doesn't remember the real reason. Then the hypnotist gives the signal to remember—"Now you can remember everything"—and the subject recalls the suggestion given under hypnosis.

The phony explanation the subject gives when she is unconscious of her true motive is a particularly interesting aspect of human motivation. We cannot say, "I don't know why I did that." We have to rationalize it somehow, according to our individual whims.

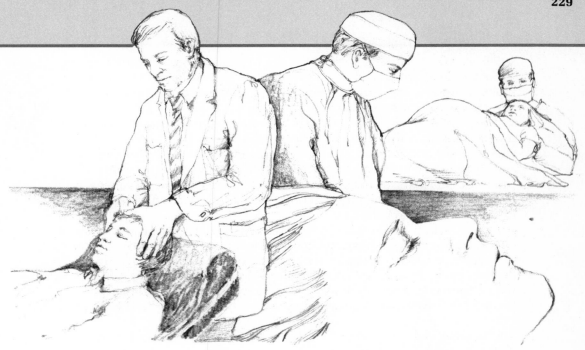

PRESENT USES OF HYPNOSIS

Hypnosis today is used for a number of purposes, primarily in psychotherapy or to reduce pain, and it is an acceptable technique in both medicine and psychology. In psychotherapy, it is most often used to eliminate bad habits and annoying symptoms. Cigarette smoking can be treated, for example, by the suggestion that the person will feel nauseated whenever he or she thinks of smoking. Sufferers of migraine headaches treated with hypnotic suggestions to relax showed a much greater tendency to improve than sufferers treated with drugs; 44 percent were headache-free after 12 months of treatment, compared to 12 percent of their drug-treated counterparts (Anderson et al., 1975).

Other medical problems also can be treated effectively with hypnosis (Bowers, 1976). Most of these fall into the category of "psychosomatic illnesses," which means that although they are real physical disorders, they are believed to be induced or aggravated by tension, anxiety, and other psychological states. Asthma is an example. As with migraines, research suggests that hypnosis is more effective than known drugs at relieving the suffocating symptoms of asthma (Maher-Loughnam, 1970). But the most fascinating research involved warts (Sinclair-Gieben and Chalmers,

1959). Fourteen patients were given the hypnotic suggestion that their warts would disappear—but only on one side of their bodies! After a few months, nine of the patients were completely free of warts, or nearly so—on one side of their bodies.

The first medical use of hypnosis, to reduce pain, is probably still the most common. A Midwest obstetrician who prefers hypnosis (but keeps chemical anesthetics on hand) has reported on 1000 childbirths (Hilgard and Hilgard, 1974). He used the chemicals in 186 cases. In the other 814 cases, the babies were brought into the world—some by caesarean section—from a mother whose only anesthetic was an instruction, given under hypnosis, to feel no pain.

Research on reducing pain by hypnotic suggestion indicates that subjects carry out their instructions in a number of ways. One imagined that the hypnotist had injected him with a pain-killing drug. Another, told to experience no pain in her arm, imagined she was the Venus de Milo—with no arms! Cancer patients give similar reports. One imagined herself leaving her body and, thus, leaving the pain behind (Hilgard and Hilgard, 1974).

It is likely that hypnosis will become an increasingly frequent choice of treatments for the control of pain. Hypnosis has several advantages: It has no dangerous side effects. It is not addictive. It is inexpensive—free, in fact, if the patient can learn self-hypnosis. Practiced subjects can use their skills outside the laboratory to relieve pain, to put themselves to sleep at night, to study more effectively, and to bolster self-confidence (Hilgard and Hilgard, 1974). This, I think, is where hypnosis holds the greatest potential value: to help people deal effectively with the problems they face in life. These problems are largely psychological, not physical. Tension is a major factor, and hypnosis can be used to relieve tension in a far more satisfactory manner than a potentially addictive drug.

HYPNOSIS IN PERSPECTIVE

Psychologists who have worked with hypnosis generally do not consider it as unusual as most people do. Most of the things a hypnotic subject can do also can be done by people in the waking state (Barber, 1969). The typical report of a subject who has been hypnotized for the first time is that she doesn't believe it, because she felt "in control" at all times; she was expecting something that differed significantly from her usual state of consciousness, like a drug experience. But it's not so. Have you ever been tense and said to yourself, "Now, calm down!" You calm down because it suits you to comply with the instruction at that moment. Hypnosis is like that—ordinary.

Good hypnotic subjects experience some things that most of us cannot, but they also experience such things in everyday life (Hilgard, 1968). They are the types who get totally involved in a novel or a movie, and when you describe something to them, they actually see it. However, evidence indicates that hypnosis is a skill that can be learned; if you are not now susceptible to hypnosis, you can be taught how to allow yourself to go into a trance (Blum, 1961). How the good subjects learned their skills is still a mystery. Children, as a rule, are very easily hypnotized, so maybe it is the poor subjects who learn how *not* to be suggestible and, instead, to be critical, analytical, and reality-oriented.

A hypnotist does not hypnotize people. As one hypnotist puts it, "The subject enters the hypnotic state when the conditions are right; the hypnotist merely helps set these conditions" (Hilgard et al., 1975, p. 173). At first, the typical induction involves lengthy instructions, but subjects soon develop the ability to do it themselves. I used the phrase "Deep asleep," nothing more, for practiced subjects.

Hypnosis is really, in all cases, self-hypnosis, which in turn is essentially self-discipline. It's not magic; it's a demonstration of the power of the human mind.

SUGGESTED READINGS

Bowers, K. S. *Hypnosis for the seriously curious.* Brooks/Cole, 1976.
An outstanding introduction to the scientific study of hypnosis.

Hilgard, E. R. *The experience of hypnosis.* Harcourt Brace Jovanovich, 1968.
Hilgard has done a sizable proportion of the best research on hypnosis; this book contains a review of that work as well as the work of others.

Behavioral Objectives

1. Explain how the body normally maintains its proper weight.
2. Contrast the Cannon-Bard, James-Lange, and Schacter-Singer theories of emotion.
3. List several factors that allow us to recognize and to label emotions in other people.
4. Identify the emotions that are generally considered to be most basic and primitive.
5. Describe the physiological measures that can be used as indicators of emotion and tell how effective they are.
6. Define psychosomatic illness.
7. Describe human reactions to constant psychological stress.
8. Tell how helplessness can be learned, what effect learned helplessness has on a person, and how learned helplessness can be avoided.
9. Describe attribution theory; list, define, and give examples of six types of attributions.
10. List Maslow's hierarchy of needs. How are these needs related to one another, according to Maslow's theory?

CHAPTER

6

Motivation
and Emotion

Determining a person's motives is an age-old interest, since to know someone's motives is to know that person's probable behavior, its probable intensity, and the lengths to which the person might be willing to go. Perhaps for this reason, people often take great pains to disguise their true motives. Benjamin Franklin noted that the person who had the most negative things to say about a horse for sale should be marked as the most likely buyer. Motives often creep out in unexpected ways, as shown in an analysis of the writings of drama critic Walter Kerr by *New Yorker* writer Susan Black (now Susan Sheehan):

> Reading Kerr's drama criticism from day to day in the *Herald Tribune*, Miss Black came to realize that most of his metaphors and similes were drawn from the world of food. He wrote that he hoped someone would create a "sirloin steak of a play" for Bette Davis. He described *The Hostage* as a "pot-au-feu" and "a broth," and he said of its author, Brendan Behan, that he was "an original piece of salt." Margaret Rutherford was said to resemble "a shark about to feast on a bather," while the music in *Irma la Douce* was "jelly-roll" and the play as a whole had "no staying power, no hearty filling inside the showy meringue."
>   Having kept track of Kerr's metaphors and similes for several weeks, Miss Black was able to make a convincing case for the probability that Kerr was on a diet and that the diet was giving him a good deal of difficulty. Only once in the period in which she kept him under observation did Kerr abandon his gastronomic analogies, and that was over the Thanksgiving weekend, when, presumably, he let himself go a little (Gill, 1975, p. 338).

The basic task of motivational psychologists is to explain why we do certain things and not others. Why did Bob quit his job to make toys? Why did Andrea marry Eugene instead of Bert? More formally, motivational theorists want to know why we "approach" certain objects and events (desire them, work for them, derive satisfaction from them) and "avoid" other objects and events (dislike them, work to be free of them, find them unpleasant). What determines the positive value of things we approach, and the negative value of things we avoid? One variable to watch for in this chapter is the degree to which one's ideas, beliefs, and perceptions influence value. To a truly hungry individual, the ease or difficulty of attaining a quantity of food has very little effect on its value. To a person hungry for praise for personal accomplishment, however, the value of achievement very much depends on the expectancy of success.

In this brief chapter, we can only sample from the wide variety of motivations that spur humans on. Some, like hunger, are very basic, shared with other animals, and necessary for survival. Others, like the motivating emotional states of fear and anger, are partly biological (in their effects on the body) and partly cognitive (in that they are profoundly affected by how we perceive our environment). In a state of learned helplessness, motivation drops to a low ebb because all actions seem hopeless; this relatively new conception in psychology can help us understand many other phenomena — depression, for example. Finally, we will discuss distinctly human needs, needs that grow out of social interaction instead of a grumbling belly, such as the need for achievement. (The need for achievement is assessed by ways very similar to those Susan Black used to diagnose Walter Kerr's need for food.) The need to be the best person one can possibly

be — to self-actualize — is perhaps the highest of human needs, and it is appropriately "last but not least" in our discussion.

HUNGER

An animal's most basic need is to find food. Most wild animals spend most of their waking hours trying to satisfy their hunger. This need probably determined most human behavior, too, until technological progress and the food surplus it produced allowed us to divert most of our energies to other activities. In a description of the Wild Boy of Aveyron, a child around the age of 12 who was found living in the wild in the forests of France in 1800, French scientists wrote of their first impressions:

> All of his sensations then are concerned uniquely with procuring necessary food . . . or the sweetness of rest. . . . Let him be shown the heavens, the green fields, the vast expanse of the earth, the works of Nature he does not see anything in all that if there is nothing to eat; and there you have the sole route by which external objects penetrate into his consciousness. It is astonishing how thoroughly this one idea absorbs him completely; he is always looking for something to eat. . . . You might say his mind is in his stomach; it is his life center (Lane, 1976, pp. 38–39).

The Biology of Hunger

How does the human animal become hungry when it needs food? Several mechanisms are involved, many of which deliver the same information. As we have mentioned, the body often has duplicate organs and systems that back each other up, and that is the case here. Two primary bits of information used in the hunger system are the body's amount of stored fat and rate of blood sugar consumption. If fat is low and the rate of sugar consumption is also low (which usually means there is not much to consume), it is time, says the body, to add some food resources.

A small region in the interior of the brain called the *hypothalamus* plays a key role in this system, monitoring resources and controlling hunger motivation. By making small holes (lesions) in different parts of the hypothalamus, you can turn an animal into an extraordinarily hefty eater or into a total noneater who will die of starvation without care.

It was originally thought, after these discoveries were made, that "hunger" and "satiation" centers from the feeding system had been located in these very precise spots in the hypothalamus. With the hunger center cut out, the reasoning went, the animal did not get hungry when it should have, so it starved. With the satiation center cut out, its hunger did not diminish as it stuffed its fat body, so it ballooned into a circus freak (see Figure 6.1).

Later research suggests the matter is not quite that simple. Normal rats lose weight after damage to their hunger center, but very thin rats do not. Similarly, normal rats gorge themselves when their satiation center is cut out, but very fat rats actually lose a little weight. Apparently it is the body's *target* weight that is altered by lesions in the hypothalamus, rather than just appetite. Lesions in the "satiation center" raise the target to a fat level, and lesions in the "hunger center" lower the target to a skinnier level.

Hunger is also affected by information the brain is continually receiving from other

Figure 6.1 *Any rat that would let itself get this fat must have a hole in its head—specifically, in the "satiation center" of the hypothalamus.*

sensory systems. For example, eating involves various muscles in the jaw and elsewhere, and you are aware of the activity of these muscles. Your brain also knows how full your stomach is. This information is used to stop eating before too much food is taken in; if you had to eat until blood sugar consumption or fat stores increased, effects of the slow digestive process, you would take in far too much food.

Sensory information from smell and taste receptors is also important. A delicious aroma can make you hungry even when you would ordinarily be full, and foul-tasting food destroys your appetite quickly.

Weight Control and Exercise

It is unusual to see a fat animal in the wild. It takes unusual circumstances, in fact, to produce either skinny or fat animals, including humans. There may be glandular problems or other biological abnormalities, of course, but a skinny wild animal typically means a shortage of food, and fatness, which is more characteristic of "civilized" animals (humans and their pets), typically reflects the ability to get food without working for it. In ordinary circumstances, the body is an amazing machine in terms of regulating weight. It takes in more food when it expends more energy and less when it is quiet; thus it can achieve a balance of input and output resulting in a remarkably constant weight.

Mayer and his associates (1954, 1956) studied the relationships among body weight, calorie intake, and physical activity in an unusual pair of experiments. In the first, rats were forced to run on a treadmill for varying periods of time each day; they were allowed to eat as much as they liked. The more they ran, the more food they ate, and their body weights stayed constant. But another group of rats was confined to small cages and given no opportunity to exercise. They did not eat least of all; they ate a lot, and they got fat, very fat.

What does this experiment mean in terms of the effects of exercise on body weight? Many people think that exercise is good when you are trying to lose weight because exercise "burns off" calories. Mayer's research suggests that this truism is not the important consideration. Sure, exercise burns off calories, but it also makes you hungrier, so you often eat more (as many joggers have discovered). The important fac-

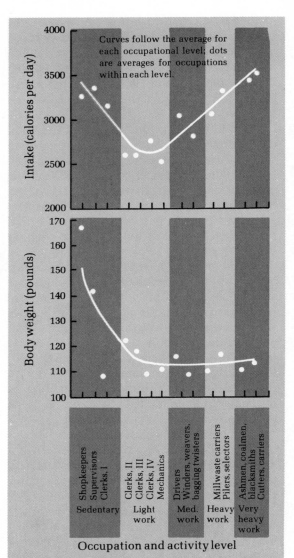

Figure 6.2 *People in this study (Mayer, et al., 1956) ate in relation to the physical demands of their jobs—all physically active workers weighed about the same. But those with sedentary jobs ate as much as the most active and weighed much more than average.*

tor, instead, seems to be that without minimal exercise, your normal body mechanisms for controlling weight do not function. It seems more appropriate to say that the lack of exercise causes fatness than it does to say that exercise causes slimness.

But maybe this conclusion holds for rats and not for humans. So Mayer repeated the study with humans. The affluent and overweight society in the United States is not the best place to do such a study, so Mayer went to India and classified men on the basis of how much physical exercise they got in their daily jobs. He found the same relationship he did with rats (see Figure 6.2). Clerks, who did small amounts of physical work, ate relatively little; blacksmiths worked harder and ate more. The body weights across these occupations were, on the average, remarkably constant. But shop owners (rats confined to small cages?) did no work at all, ate a lot, and became very fat.

So if you are interested in losing weight, don't worry about how many calories you can use in an hour of tennis or a mile of running. That's not the point of it. Exercise will get your body working properly, and when your body is working properly, it will direct your appetite toward a reasonable body weight. This is true only if we ignore social factors, of course. Many people, for example, have a *learned* attraction to sweets, because they are used so commonly as rewards. Also, as Mario Puzo depicted in the novel, *The Godfather,* fatness in some cultures achieves a certain degree of social status, probably because it so reliably indicates a person who does not have to do hard physical labor. Thus, "He has no belly!" can be a real put-down, for if he were truly "successful" (no work), he would be fat. On the other hand, thinness is highly valued in the American culture, to the extent that even truly emaciated people are sometimes looked on with approval. Perhaps this too is related to success; do rich people have more time for exercise? Can they afford leaner meats, better doctors, and "health spas"?

Figure 6.3 *Why is thinness valued in American culture?*

EMOTIONS

Motivation is almost always partly biological and partly cognitive. Hunger is basically biological; it is a motive that serves the body's need for food. Yet even your hunger is affected by what you think about certain foods. Nutritious foods like uncooked fish and grasshoppers, although considered delicacies in some cultures, would probably turn off the hunger of all but the most desperate Americans. Other motives are more clearly and commonly dependent on expectations, attributions, and other cognitive factors. The value an individual places on a personal accomplishment, for example, depends on the perceived probability of success; success in difficult tasks is more highly valued. The degree to which the individual attributes success to personal effort, and not to luck, also influences pride in achievement, as we shall see.

Emotions, considered as motivating forces, will involve us in discussions that run the gamut from the very biological to the very cognitive. On the one hand, emotions are very primitive reactions with widespread biological effects in the body. On the other hand, our emotions are profoundly influenced by our thoughts and expectations, which are formed from experience and learning. The emotion of embarrassment illustrates both the cognitive and biological aspects. A teenager, unsure of the proper behavior in a social situation, feels clumsy, exposed, and ashamed; an uncontrollable biological reaction sets in, drying his mouth, palpitating his heart; a rosy blush colors his

Figure 6.4 *Emotions are primitive reactions that to some extent we share with lower animals. Here a gorilla and a human express anger in strikingly similar ways.*

cheeks, communicating his shame to others. It is an unpleasant emotion, one that motivates him to reduce it now (perhaps by leaving) and to avoid it later (perhaps by reading a book on social etiquette).

"Emotions" is a complex topic. Facial expressions of emotions are communications and will be discussed in Chapter 7. The biological turmoil of emotions may cause illness, even death, as we shall see later in this chapter. Here we will focus on the motivating characteristics of emotions.

Emotions as Primitive Reactions

An emotion is an *unusual* state; the word "emotion" has the literal meaning of "disturbed motion." Most emotions arise suddenly, mobilizing the body and the mind in preparation for some unusual behavior. In animal studies, four of the most important intermittent behavior patterns have been called by one psychologist the Four Fs: Fighting, Fleeing, Feeding, and Sexual Behavior (Pribram, 1960). Thus the emotion of anger prepares animals (including humans) for the behavior of fighting: fear prepares animals for flight. Humans don't often draw on strong emotions in readying themselves for food, but animals who must kill other animals to survive experience a predatory excitement. The emotions before, during, and after sexual intercourse defy description, but humans and other animals seem to share the emotion of lust, and humans add a few others, such as love and tenderness.

The primitive, animal, survival nature of the behaviors associated with emotions marks emotional reactions as one of the least "human," and most "animal" aspects of human existence. Many psychologists believe that emotions are really states of activation related to primitive needs, as shown in Table 6.1. A theory that supports this view of emotions as primitive reactions is the Cannon-Bard theory of emotions.

The Cannon-Bard Theory of Emotions. If emotions are really primitive reactions, then we would expect them to be controlled by the more primitive parts of our brain, parts that are more like those of lower animals than, say, the highly evolved cortex. And so they are. In a theory formulated by Cannon and Bard—called, of course, the *Cannon-Bard theory*—subcortical brain structures were given the major role in emotion (Cannon, 1927, 1931; Bard, 1934). (The thalamus was stressed by Cannon and Bard, but the hypothalamus and the limbic system now seem more likely candidates.) According to this view, sensory input travels through the lower brain structures on its way to the cortex; certain stimuli, like a loud noise, set off an immediate, unlearned reaction there. More complex stimuli elicit learned emotional reactions once they reach the cortex, which sends a signal to the subcortical structures. In either case, the subcortical structures do two things: (1) They send signals to the rest of the body, in particular to the viscera (internal organs like the heart and the intestines) and skeletal muscles, that prepare the organism for action; and (2) they "inform" the cortex that such and such an emotion is now being implemented.

Physiological Indicators of Emotion. According to theories like the Cannon-Bard theory, the subcortical parts of the brain trigger widespread physiological reactions during an emotional state. These physiological reactions are not usually under conscious control, as a blush is uncontrollable.

Table 6.1
BASIC EMOTIONS

Besides the "Four Fs" mentioned in the text, two other attempts to relate primitive behavior patterns to human emotional experience are worth mentioning.

William McDougall (1921), one of the most famous social psychologists, thought there were at least seven "primitive reactions" in humans and seven related emotions:

Robert Plutchik (1962) formulated a theory similar to McDougall's, but it defines eight primary emotions in terms of eight basic functions in the life of an animal:

Reaction	Emotion	Function	Emotion
Flight	Fear	Protection	Fear
Repulsion	Disgust	Destruction	Anger
Curiosity	Wonder	Reproduction	Joy
Pugnacity	Anger	Deprivation	Sadness
Self-abasement	Subjection	Incorporation	Acceptance
Self-assertion	Elation	Rejection	Disgust
Parental	Tenderness	Exploration	Interest
		Orientation	Surprise

Other emotions, according to Plutchik, are mixtures: Love, for example, is seen as a combination of joy and acceptance.

Thus these reactions are often used by psychologists as operational definitions of an emotional, or motivational, state.

Everyone does this to some extent. We notice some physiological manifestation of emotion in a friend—a sweaty brow, a shaky hand, some shortness of breath—and we assume that he or she is nervous, that is, emotionally upset for some reason.

Psychologists frequently improve such observations with machines. Measuring the electrical conductance of the skin, for example, is relatively simple if the subject is willing to accept a few electrodes attached to his or her skin, usually on the fingers. The conductance is the ease with which the skin passes or conducts a current. Skin conductance varies over a wide range; it appears to be the result of sweat-gland activity, although not the result of sweat itself (Woodworth and Schlosberg, 1954).

The measure of most interest to psychologists has been the *galvanic skin response,* or GSR. The GSR is a very rapid change in the conductance of the skin. Psychologists have found that the GSR is a sensitive indicator of matters related to emotions. Most people give a big GSR when they hear embarrassing words, for example. If you read a list of words—elbow, leg, penis, arm—a large GSR ordinarily would result after the third word. GSR is also predictable if people are startled, frightened, angered, or trying to lie about something (which makes the GSR a valuable aid in lie detection; see Interlude: Lie Detection, pp. 264–271).

Other popular physiological measures of emotion include blood pressure, heart rate, muscle tension, breathing rate and depth, and pupil size. If you have an exceptionally agreeable subject, certain other tests are possible, such as chemical analyses of blood, saliva, and urine, and estimates of metabolic rate and gastrointestinal motility. In one experiment female subjects who previously had been rated "anxious about sex" responded to readings of erotic literature with strong expulsive uterine contractions (Bardwick and Behrman, 1967). (The psychologist and gynecologist who did this experiment wanted to gather information on why sexually anxious women sometimes have a hard time becoming pregnant. If a woman's uterus literally expels male sperm during intercourse, this could be a major factor.)

So there are many physiological cues to emotion, if we have the proper recording devices hooked up. One question that arises, though, is whether we can determine the particular emotion from only physiological indicators. Is there a different pattern of physiological reaction when the emotion is, say, fear, as contrasted to the reaction during anger?

Judging from the data of several careful studies using many different measures (for example, Ax, 1953), the answer appears to be that we can distinguish to some extent between emotions. However, most emotions show a very similar pattern of reaction. An angered subject will show a GSR; so will a frightened one, a startled one, and one who has just been sexually aroused. Heart rate changes are characteristic of emotion in general and rarely point to one in particular. In short, no psychologist would be willing to bet very heavily on his or her identification of an emotion if all the information came from physiological cues.

For this reason, psychologists (and probably all of us) use physiological cues mainly to judge simply the presence or absence of emotion; we use other cues, primarily the situation, to identify the emotion. For example, we assume that if a subject shows a GSR to the word "whore," his emotion is embarrassment; if the GSR occurs while viewing a movie of a rabid German shepherd, we guess fear; and if he shows no GSR after being frustrated, we assume the absence of hostility.

Emotions as Interpretations

The Cannon-Bard theory of emotion focuses on biological aspects. Two other major theories, the James-Lange theory and the Schacter-Singer theory, focus on an emotion's cognitive aspects. In particular, these latter theories focus on how we intellectually identify an emotion as anger rather than fear, lust rather than disgust. Obviously, these intellectual decisions have great motivational import, determining whether we fight or flee, whether we approach or avoid.

The James-Lange Theory. How do we know what emotion we are experiencing? According to the Cannon-Bard theory, the cortex receives signals from the older parts of our brain, telling it what emotion has been activated. Another possibility, however, is that the cortex identifies emotional states by monitoring the activation in various parts of the body—in the viscera and the muscles—much as the sophisticated biological psychologist does, with his GSR machines and heart-rate recorders. Certainly our cortex knows what's going on in our bodies. In the James-Lange theory of emotions, this source of information plays a major role.

Formulated independently in the late 1800s by American psychologist-philosopher William James and Danish scientist Carl Lange, the primary hypothesis of the James-Lange theory can be stated briefly:

> Common sense says, we lose our fortune, are sorry and weep, we meet a bear, are frightened and run; we are insulted by a rival, are angry and strike. The hypothesis here to be defended says that this order of sequence is incorrect, . . . that the more rational statement is that we feel sorry because we cry, angry because we strike, afraid because we tremble (James, 1892, p. 243).

Put less poetically, the James-Lange view is that an emotion is our perception of reactions and changes in our body. This theory is not taken very seriously today because it ignores other factors in emotions, but its main point is certainly valid: A person knows when his heart is beating faster, his mouth is dry, and his hands are trembling, and he uses this information along with information from other sources, to identify his emotional state.

If body cues are used to identify an emotion, you should be able to control your emotions, to some extent, by acting out the emotion you want. If you smile, your brain will "read" that facial configuration and you might be a little happier as a result. A frown might add a little unhappiness. As James said, "each fit of sobbing makes the sorrow more acute," and "whistling to keep up courage is no mere figure of speech." There is some indirect support for this notion in a therapy called counterconditioning (see Chapter 13), in which anxious parents are taught how to relax in situations that ordinarily make them feel anxious. This "acting relaxed" in tense moments seems to help quite a bit.

Another implication of the James-Lange theory is that it is possible to misread bodily cues and thus to misinterpret one's emotion. In one experiment (Valins, 1966), college males were asked if they would be willing to look at some pictures of nude females; several volunteered. In what was described as "a study of physiological reactions to sexually oriented stimuli," their heart rates were to be recorded as they looked at the pictures. The experimenters apologized for the primitive recording device, a microphone taped to the chest which broadcasted the heartbeats aloud for all to hear. Apparently the subjects believed this incredible story. Actually, however, the heartbeats the subjects heard were not their own but were arranged by the psychologists. As subjects viewed five of the pictures, the phony heart changed its rhythm not at all, but on another five occasions, it went up from its normal 66–72 beats to 90 beats per minute!

The subjects were reading their body cues for emotion; that is, they were hearing what they thought was their own heartbeat, and this heart was telling them that they were reacting emotionally to five pictures. The question is, therefore, whether they believed what they thought were their own bodies when they were asked to rate the pictures on a 100-point scale in terms of how attractive or appealing each was. And indeed they did.

The average rating for the heart-rate-increase pictures was 72, whereas the average for the no-change pictures was 54. They were also more likely to choose the "emotional" pictures if told they could keep some. To make sure the pictures paired with heart rate increases were not intrinsically more attractive, control subjects rated them too, their ratings averaging 61 and 64 for the increase and the no-increase sets, respectively.

You can see here something of the importance of reading your emotions accurately. Someone with a phony heart rate machine could make you think you're in love.

The Schacter-Singer Theory. Physiological cues, either from subcortical brain regions or from bodily reactions, may sometimes be adequate indicators of an emotional state, but often they do no more than indicate *some* emotion has been activated. As we mentioned, GSR responses, rapid heart rates, and other physiological reactions are characteristic of a wide range of emotions. Additional information is usually necessary to identify the specific emotion. This additional information is usually the situation. If we observe a male friend with shaky hands, we guess "love" when he's talking to a pretty girl, "anger" in an encounter with a person we know he hates, and "fear" when he's about to give a speech.

If we make situation-based interpretations of other people's emotions, maybe we do the same for ourselves. In a classic investigation of this possibility, subjects were given injections of epinephrine (adrenalin), a drug that causes general body excitement (Schacter and Singer, 1962). The subjects did not know that, however; they were told they

were getting a vitamin compound that might affect their vision. The experiment, they were told, would begin in 20 minutes, after the vitamins took effect.

Each subject was asked to wait out the 20-minute period in a room with another person. This other person was introduced as another subject, but actually he was a confederate (also called a stooge) of the researchers. His instructions were to put on a little show for the real subject.

In some cases, the subject found himself closeted with a rather foolish but good-natured fellow. The stooge doodled a fish on some scrap paper he found in the room. He crumpled up papers and shot them, like basketballs, into the wastepaper basket. He was having fun, and he encouraged the subject to join in. He flew paper airplanes. And then he discovered two hula hoops!

As this strange drama unfolded, the "vitamin compound" was taking effect. The subject's heart rate increased, his face flushed, and his hands began to tremble. He had to attribute this excitement to something. The vitamin compound? Probably not. Most subjects in this condition assumed that their excitement was due to the amusing antics of that crazy fellow in the room with them. They reported feeling very happy.

In other cases, both the real subject and the stooge were asked to fill out a questionnaire while they waited for the vitamin compound to take effect. The stooge reacted negatively to the questionnaire. The questions were obnoxious. "What is your father's average annual income?" The stooge thought that was none of the researcher's business. The questionnaire requested the name of a family member who didn't bathe

Figure 6.5 *We often judge our emotions by the situation. If we are excited internally, the way we interpret this excitement may depend on what emotion we think we are feeling. In the presence of someone having fun we usually feel happy.*

regularly. Insulting! After a few other indignities, the stooge stomped out.

The real subject, alone, read one of the last questions:

> With how many men (other than your father) has your mother had extramarital relationships?
>
> 4 and under ⎯⎯⎯
> 5–9   ⎯⎯⎯
> 10 *and over* ⎯⎯⎯

The subjects in this condition were also excited, and they too had to attribute their bodily arousal to something. The subjects assumed they were angry, like the stooge.

How do we judge our own emotions? This experiment gives us one of the answers: We judge our emotions to be those appropriate to the situation. Generally excited from the epinephrine, subjects with the happy stooge rated themselves happy and they smiled and laughed; subjects in the anger condition rated themselves irritated and they said angry words. Other subjects, injected with epinephrine but told what to expect, were not influenced as much by the stooge; they knew why they were "high" and did not need to invent an emotion to account for their excitement.

Emotions and Psychosomatic Illness

The cognitive aspects of emotion and their influence on the biological response are perhaps best illustrated by *psychosomatic illnesses.* Emotions are supposed to be, in some grand animal scheme of things, short-lived emergency reactions to unusual situations. Anger is aroused so the animal can fight, and fear mobilizes the animal for a hasty retreat. But humans, with their great intellectual abilities, can "bear a grudge" for years, keeping themselves in a state of seething anger. They can maintain fears and anxieties at such a level that they "worry themselves sick." The body simply is not equipped to handle the biological excitement of emotions for more than brief periods; under the stress of a long-term emotional upset, it will break down.

The scientific study of the effect of psychological variables on the body belongs to an interdisciplinary area called *psychosomatic medicine.* ("Psyche"—mind—and "soma"—body—are the roots of "psychosomatic," implying an interaction between mind and body.) The psychological variables are usually emotions. Among the illnesses believed to be caused or influenced by emotions are ulcers, high blood pressure, asthma, and that scourge of the emotional adolescent—acne. You certainly have experienced psychosomatic disorders (maybe before an important test); headaches, caused by anxiety, hostility, fear, or other strong emotions, are among the most common.

The Theory of Stress. The theory of stress advanced by Hans Selye in 1956 has been the guiding force for many scientists interested in psychosomatic illnesses. Selye conceptualized the body under stress in terms of three phases of a *general adaptation syndrome* (see Figure 6.6). In the first phase, called the *alarm reaction,* the body encounters something stressful (the stressor), and it reacts with a "generalized call to arms of the defensive forces in the organism" (Selye, 1956, p. 311). The stressor can be something physical, such as injury, or it can be psychological or emotional, the case in which we are interested. After the alarm reaction, the body settles down into a persistent *resistance.* If stress continues, however, the body reaches the stage of *exhaustion:* The resources of the body are depleted, and it can no longer carry on the fight. The terms for the phases sound military, and, indeed, the analogy to an army is informative. We are attacked (by a stressor) and we sound the alarm. We resist the attack with our people and our guns. If we run out of ammunition or food, we may suffer temporary or permanent setbacks.

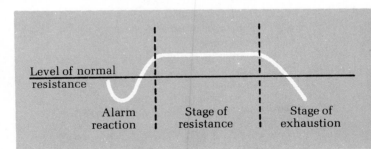

Level of normal resistance

Alarm reaction | Stage of resistance | Stage of exhaustion

Figure 6.6 *Selye's general adaptation syndrome. During the body's initial alarm reaction to a stressor, resistance drops slightly below normal. A long period of above-average resistance follows; but if the stress continues, the body becomes exhausted and the victim may even die.*

All three phases of this general adaptation syndrome are significant for explaining psychosomatic illnesses. The initial alarm reaction, for example, is likely to produce a headache, and so headaches are very often an early result of emotional stress. The resistance stage is a stage of tension, with acids and hormones and such things racing about the body, causing asthma and acne and similar problems, much as the economy of a country develops strains and shortages in a time of war. The stage of exhaustion involves breakdown and severe damage: an ulcer perhaps, or at the extreme, death.

The Effects of Stress. Obviously it takes an unusual situation to lead a human being to lose all hope and die. More commonly, a period of stress leading to increased feelings of helplessness and hopelessness makes illness more likely.

In one study, the medical histories of several thousand people were examined (Hinkle and Wolff, 1957). It was determined that the

---

Table 6.2
RESULTS OF THE LIFE CHANGES SCALING EXPERIMENT

	Life event	Mean value		Life event	Mean value
1	Death of spouse	100	23	Son or daughter leaving home	29
2	Divorce	73	24	Trouble with in-laws	29
3	Marital separation	65	25	Outstanding personal achievement	28
4	Jail term	63	26	Wife begins or stops work	26
5	Death of close family member	63	27	Begin or end school	26
6	Personal injury or illness	53	28	Change in living conditions	25
7	Marriage	50	29	Revision of personal habits	24
8	Fired at work	47	30	Trouble with boss	23
9	Marital reconciliation	45	31	Change in work hours or conditions	20
10	Retirement	45	32	Change in residence	20
11	Change in health of family member	44	33	Change in schools	20
12	Pregnancy	40	34	Change in recreation	19
13	Sexual difficulties	39	35	Change in church activities	19
14	Gain of new family member	39	36	Change in social activities	18
15	Business readjustment	39	37	Mortgage or loan less than $10,000	17
16	Change in financial state	38	38	Change in sleeping habits	16
17	Death of close friend	37	39	Change in number of family get-togethers	15
18	Change to different line of work	36	40	Change in eating habits	13
19	Change in number of arguments with spouse	35	41	Vacation	13
20	Mortgage over $10,000	31	42	Christmas	12
21	Foreclosure of mortgage or loan	30	43	Minor violations of the law	11
22	Change in responsibilities at work	29			

From Rahe, R. H. Subjects' recent life changes and their near-future illness susceptibility. *Advances in Psychosomatic Medicine*, 1972, 8, 2–19. P. 7.

subjects' illnesses clustered at times of life when they were experiencing psychological stress, such as the death of a parent or spouse. In other words, the kinds of event that got them down mentally got them down physically as well. Also, it was found that 25 percent of the people accounted for 75 percent of the illnesses. These 25 percent were the people who were most apt to express both general and specific feelings of helplessness and hopelessness.

To conduct more controlled studies, researchers developed a list of life experiences and assigned each experience a number supposed to reflect the effect or stress value of this life change. For example, they found that the most stressful experience is the death of a spouse; divorce, a jail term, and getting fired are all rated high, whereas a change in eating habits, a vacation, and a "minor violation of the law" are rated low in import (see Table 6.2).

Once this scale of life-change experiences had been developed, it could be used to assess how stressful the life of any individual has been. The subject is given 100 points if his or her spouse has recently died, 73 for a divorce, 13 for a vacation, and so on through the list. In a massive study of American sailors, the life-crisis scores for events *before* a cruise began were significantly related to illnesses *during* the cruise (see Figure 6.7).

We can tentatively explain these social effects on physical illness in terms of bodily resistance. We experience stress, we grow depressed, and somehow our body's ability to fight off invading bacteria is affected. We get sick. However, this mini-theory is complicated by the fact that even noninfectious diseases like cancer are affected by psychological stress (LeShan, 1966). Apparently, emotional upset is related to a decrease in our physical capacity to resist illnesses of all types.

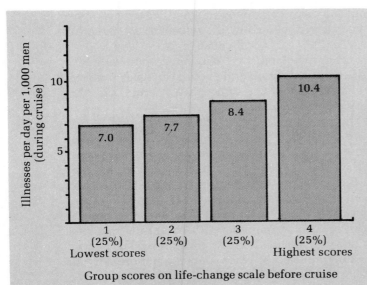

Figure 6.7 *Before a long cruise, sailors were given a life-change score computed from the points in Table 6.2. During the cruise, the group that had the lowest scores had the fewest illnesses, and the group with the highest scores had the most.*

FOCUS

Voodoo and the Power of Emotions

Voodoo is a religion, practiced mainly in Haiti. It is multifaceted, using many Christian principles and practices from the preachings of missionaries. Voodoo death is no more representative of voodoo than exorcism is of Catholicism, but it shows the extreme powers of a voodoo priest, and thus excites the imagination. It also excites the interests of psychologists.

A typical voodoo death was described by Cannon (1942). The voodoo priest points his charm at the victim. The victim begins to scream, writhe on the ground, and froth at the mouth. Then he becomes composed. He sits alone, refusing food; unless the priest undoes his hex or a medicine man can discover an equally powerful countercharm, the victim dies.

Psychologists first discounted such reports as superstitious nonsense, but eyewitness reports by reliable scientists began to accumulate. And research in psychosomatic medicine made voodoo death a plausible, if extreme, phenomenon. The victim's faith in voodoo convinces him that because he has been hexed, he will soon die. He is highly emotional— very frightened, very depressed. He believes that his fate has been taken over by forces beyond his control; it is the end of hope.

This extreme emotional condition produces an equally extreme physiological reaction in the body (compounded by the refusal to eat and other acts of subjection). The actual physiological cause of death is unknown, but it is suspected to be a failure in blood circulation, known medically as *shock*, which damages the heart and brain and eventually leads to death. Fainting is a mild, temporary form of the same phenomenon, one that also can be brought on by emotional upset.

Voodoo death is not the only kind of death caused by emotions. In times of war, the pressure on soldiers is often so intense and sustained that a number of them simply keel over and die, killed not by an enemy but by fear (Moritz and Zamchech, 1946). In a study of 275 cases of sudden, unexpected deaths, highly emotional events were seen as a primary cause (Engel, 1977). About half the cases involved a traumatic loss of a loved one, such as the death of a spouse. In several instances, the death took place on the anniversary of the original loss. A 70-year-old man died during the opening bars of a concert held on the fifth anniversary of his wife's death. She had been a famous piano teacher and, in her memory, he had established a music conservatory. The commemorative concert was being given by conservatory students.

Situations of personal danger, such as earthquakes, floods, riots, and confrontations with criminals, were the second most common precursors of sudden death. A third category of emotional events involved loss of status and self-esteem through failure, defeat, disappointment, or humiliation. President Lyndon Johnson once likened his Great Society programs to a starving woman and added, "And when she dies, I too will die" (Kearns, 1976). On January 21, 1973, new president Richard Nixon announced he was completely dismantling Johnson's Great Society programs. The following day Lyndon Johnson died of a heart attack.

A final sizable category of death-inducing events, strangely enough, contained moments of great triumph and happiness, such as the achievement of some long-sought goal. A 55-year-old man died as he met his 88-year-old father after 20 years apart; his father then too dropped dead. A horse-player won $1683 on a $2 bet; he died as he was about to cash in his ticket.

Emotions can cause death. Can they also prolong life? In one study, researchers assumed that elderly people who look forward to a coming birthday might be able to postpone death until after the celebration (Phillips, 1971). They examined the vital statistics of several hundred prominent aged Americans, reasoning that famous people would be more eager than most to reach a birthday and all the accompanying expressions of love and respect. They found that fewer of the subjects than could be expected (by an even distribution of deaths) died soon before their birthdays; many more than could be expected died shortly after.

LEARNED HELPLESSNESS

The basic task of motivation psychologists is to explain why we approach certain objects and events and avoid others. We approach situations that we perceive are likely to result in pleasant emotions, and we avoid those likely to lead to unpleasant emotions. If we are put unavoidably in a situation eliciting an unpleasant emotion, like anger or fear (or hunger), we will try to reduce the emotion by appropriate behaviors such as fighting or fleeing (or eating).

But what if the individual who is unavoidably experiencing an unpleasant emotion thinks that there is nothing he can do to alter his unfortunate state of affairs? What if he's frustrated and angry, but perceives "the government" or "the system" at fault; how does one punch out the system? What if he's afraid of his boss? How does one flee from one's boss, without losing one's job? What if an individual, frustrated and fearful, feels helpless to improve his state?

The research literature on psychosomatic illness provides part of the answer, for people who cannot extricate themselves from negative emotions eventually get sick. The person is depressed and frightened, sees no answer to his problems; the body seems no longer willing to fight back, and the bacteria, viruses, and cancerous cells gain ground. In extreme cases, such as voodoo curses, the individual feels he is helpless to avoid death; he gives up, and the body quits.

What is the nature of this feeling of helplessness? How do angry or fearful people come to feel that there is nothing they can do? These questions have been the subject of considerable research lately, with some interesting results. The research began with some rather traditional "avoidance learning" tasks involving dogs.

Helpless Dogs

Dogs are good leapers. Laboratory investigations of dog behavior, for this reason, often utilize a device known as a shuttlebox (see Figure 6.8). The shuttlebox has two compartments separated by a barrier wall that can be hurdled by a dog trying, for example, to escape electric shocks. A typical study of escape and avoidance learning begins with a warning signal (for example, the lights dim); ten seconds later a shock is delivered to the feet through an electrified floor. Most dogs quickly learn to leap over the barrier to the safe side of the box as soon as the shock

Figure 6.8 *A dog learning escape and avoidance behavior in a shuttlebox. The light dims ten seconds before the grid floor is electrified* (A). *If the dog ignores the light, it receives a shock and jumps the barrier to escape* (B). *Eventually the dog starts to notice the dimming of the light* (C), *and will jump before the grid is electrified* (D), *avoiding the shock altogether.*

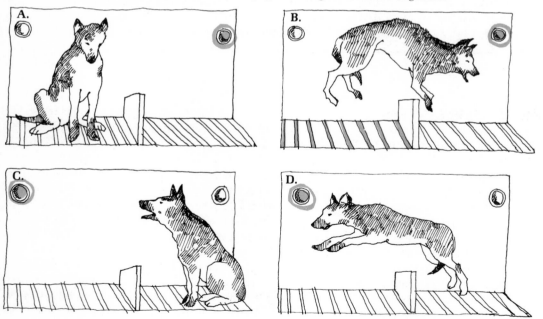

comes on; eventually they learn to leap when the lights dim, avoiding shock altogether.

Most dogs do this, but not dogs who have learned to feel helpless. Helpless dogs were trained in the following way: Twenty-four hours before their shuttlebox test, they were placed in hammock-like harnesses and subjected to several painful but not injurious shocks. There was nothing the dogs could do to prevent the shocks or to escape from them once they began (Overmier and Seligman, 1967).

These dogs reacted quite differently in the shuttlebox. On the first trial with shock, they ran around and howled, then settled down to constant whining, with few motions that could be interpreted as attempts at escape. After 50 or 60 seconds, the shock was stopped automatically, and soon the second trial began. After a few trials, the dogs would do virtually nothing but whine; they appeared to have given up. These dogs had learned helplessness. It was as if they had become fatalists, believing shocks were simply part of life.

The psychologists who discovered learned helplessness viewed the phenomenon as an active, not a passive, learning. The dogs who were shocked for no reason were not passive in their harnesses; they struggled, they barked, and they bit the air, but everything they tried had one thing in common: It didn't work. They learned that nothing helps.

Helpless Humans

Although most of the research on learned helplessness has used dogs as subjects, the same basic experiment has been successfully repeated with college students (Hiroto, 1974). The students were exposed to an offensively loud noise; nothing they did had any effect on the noise. Later these students were tested in a kind of "finger shuttlebox," in which they could escape from the noise by moving a finger to the other side of the box. In contrast to control subjects who had no prior exposure to the noise and who learned the shuttle easily, the helpless humans passively endured the loud sound.

Psychologist Martin Seligman, who has done much of the research on helplessness, thinks the shuttlebox situation has analogies in real life (1972). He describes one young boy named Archie, age 15. Archie is waiting for his chance to quit school. School has been an unending series of shocks and failures for him: questions with no answers because he doesn't know some of the words in the questions, interactions without joy because the other kids think he's stupid. Nothing he does seems to have any effect on these "shocks." Archie is ready to enter the shuttlebox of life, and he has learned how to be helpless. He is likely to endure passively any shocks he encounters outside of school, just as he does in school. His chances of success, obviously, are not good.

In extreme states of helplessness, humans begin a zombie-like existence. Nazi concentration camps were full of what Bettelheim (1960) called "walking corpses." Some mental patients could also be so labeled, not because of their original mental disorders but because they develop an intense feeling of hopelessness. One group, were they not led from a hospital fire, would have burned, motionless and emotionless (Bleuler, 1950).

New Hope for the Hopeless

Learned helplessness involves a situation in which the subjects learn that an aversive event is not affected by anything they do. Nothing helps. Once they have learned this, is there anything we can do to help them "unlearn" helplessness? Can we return to them a confidence in their ability to affect their environment? If you were the experimenter, what would you do to help the helpless dogs? Obviously they must learn that eliminating the painful shock is now within their control. But how? How do you teach a helpless dog to move off an electrified grid?

The psychologists tried a number of tricks. They dropped meat on the safe side. They took down the partition between the compartment and called the dog: "Here, boy." Boy stayed there, however, and finally the researchers were forced to take extreme measures; they dragged the dog on a leash to safety. They continued dragging the dog until it responded without force. It took many, many trials before each dog caught on that it could affect the shock and pain by moving, but eventually all the dogs were cured (Seligman et al., 1968).

The helplessness of the dogs given uncontrollable shocks was overcome with great difficulty. The helplessness of humans may present even more difficulties. What is the human equivalent of dragging an animal into a more pleasant state? I don't know. If that question has an answer, can it be done without violating moral or legal codes? How much better it would be if we could *prevent* the development of hopelessness!

Another study of learned helplessness provides relevant data (Seligman and Maier, 1967). Dogs that had had experience with shock they *could* control were not affected by later experience with inescapable shock; they learned the shuttlebox trick as well as dogs with no prior experience of any kind. In other words, it is enough for dogs to learn

Figure 6.9 *Helplessness shows in the face of this tornado victim.*

that their behavior is effective *sometimes*. They are then relatively immune to the effects of a situation in which they are helpless, and they don't carry over the hopelessness to new situations. The implication for the parents and teachers of human learners is that they should do all in their power to present at least some situations in which a child can see that his or her ability counts for something, makes a difference.

Attribution and Learned Helplessness

We have seen the trend toward increased emphasis of the cognitive components of motivation already, in the Schacter-Singer theory of emotion, for example. Similarly, psychosomatic illnesses are basically intellectual, born of irrational angers and worries. As learned-helplessness theorists have moved from animal studies to the investigation of fatalistic feelings in humans, they too have had to adopt a more cognitive view. Humans are helpless if they *believe* themselves to be helpless.

An emphasis on what people think about an event is part of a general approach in psychology called *attribution theory*. "Attribute" means "to explain by indicating a cause," as in questions like, "To what do you attribute your long life?" Humans are constantly trying to understand themselves and what is happening in their lives; they try to figure out cause-and-effect relationships.

In terms of attribution theory, a situation must be *perceived* as helpless if the individual is to feel helpless and display the symptoms of helplessness—inaction, depression. If you grow to believe that no amount of effort can make you attractive and interesting to other people, you eventually give up hope, even if in fact you are a potentially fascinating person. More specifically, human helplessness is a reaction to failure attributable to something other than lack of effort (Abramson et al., 1978). Failure caused by lack of effort or persistence spurs us to more effort; if at first you don't succeed, try, try again. (You aren't attractive? Try a new toothpaste! Use a different deodorant!) But if increased effort is perceived to have no effect, then we feel helpless; we give up.

There is more to helplessness, however, than simply feeling our efforts are of no use. I may feel that I am unattractive to everybody around me (a global attribution) or only to the one person who has just rejected me (a specific attribution). My attribution may be "stable" or "unstable": I am always unattractive because I am not intelligent (stable); or I am temporarily unattractive because I have the flu (unstable). I may consider myself unattractive for personal (internal) reasons: I'm ugly. Or I am unattractive for impersonal (external) reasons: the person I've been trying to start a conversation with is in a bad mood.

Our attributions make a real difference in our behavior and in our view of ourselves. As we mentioned, if we perceive a failure as due to insufficient effort, we are likely to work harder (Glass, 1977). Even if we perceive the failure as out of our control, our resulting feelings of helplessness have different effects depending on what we attribute them to. If helplessness is due to personal (internal) reasons, for example—"I failed because I'm dumb"—our self-esteem suffers. Helplessness that is due to external causes, on the other hand—"Professor Bogart gives unfair tests"—has little or no effect on our self-conceptions. Global attributions assign failure to general reasons and thus affect a wide range of situations and behaviors; "I am dumb" is likely to affect my performance in all my classes. In contrast, a specific attribution such as "I can't handle math" would explain my F in math without severely affecting my performance in English or chemistry. Stable attributions are not likely to change; if I am physically ugly on Monday, I'm likely to be ugly on Tuesday too. An unstable reason for Monday's rejection—illness, exhaustion—might not be operative on Tuesday.

SOCIAL MOTIVATION: THE CASE OF ACHIEVEMENT

The bases for human motivations are diverse. Some, like hunger, are based on the physiological needs of the body. Others, like helplessness, are based on learning experiences of a certain sort. A third basis is life in social groups, which, for example, triggers the need to compete in some instances, the need to cooperate in others. Some psychologists have tried to explain all human motives in terms of a single basis—human work activity, for example, in terms of behavior designed ultimately to satisfy hunger and other biological needs—but these attempts have not been notably successful. Psychologists have learned to live with the diversity of human motivations, and the different levels on which they are discussed.

Rather than try to reduce all human striving to a few biological drives, psychologist Henry Murray set out to list all the needs necessary to explain "the purposive behavior of humans," as it is lived, in social groups (Murray et al., 1938). To do this, he collected episodes (or "proceedings" as he called them) from the lives of normal human beings—simple, everyday activities, with relatively clear beginnings and ends: Randie Korchak invites a few friends over for a bull session that lasts for an hour or so. Tony Colby walks into a drug store and buys a

---

Table 6.3
PSYCHOGENIC NEEDS ACCORDING TO HENRY MURRAY (1938)

I. Five needs relating chiefly to inanimate objects
   Acquisition—to acquire property
   Retention—to retain it
   Conservance—to preserve, as in repair
   Construction—to build things
   Order—to organize and arrange

II. Three or four needs having to do with ambition and prestige
   Superiority—to be superior
   The need for superiority includes the needs for
      Achievement—to strive and overcome; and
      Recognition—to excite praise
   And possibly the need for
      Exhibition—to attract attention
   (But recognition and exhibitionist needs are hard to distinguish in practice)

III. Four or five needs involving defense of prestige
   Inviolacy—to preserve self-respect
   The need for inviolacy includes the needs for
      Infavoidance—to avoid failure and shame
      Defendance—to defend one's self-respect as in offering reasons or excuses
      Counteraction—to overcome by striving harder
   And possibly the need for
      Seclusion—to be alone, physically or psychologically
   (But seclusion may be the opposite of exhibition or recognition needs)

pack of sugarless gum. From such commonplace events, Murray drew up a list of needs that, in his view, were required to explain human behavior.

Some of the needs were physiological in origin: the needs for air, water, food, sex, lactation, urination, and defecation; the needs to avoid harm, noxious stimuli, extreme heat, and extreme cold; and the needs for sensory stimulation and passivity (rest or sleep). The needs with social and psychological origins are listed in Table 6.3. What do you think? Are these 42 needs (13 physiolog-ical, 29 psychological) sufficient to explain why you do what you do?

The Need for Achievement and the Fear of Failure

To assess the strength of the various needs, especially the psychological needs, Murray developed a new test called the *Thematic Apperception Test* (TAT). The TAT consists of a series of rather ambiguous drawings depicting such scenes as a young man kneel-

---

Table 6.3 *(continued)*

IV.	Five needs relating to power
	Dominance — to influence or control
	Autonomy — to resist influence
	Deference — to admire and serve a leader
	Similance — to agree
	Contrarience — to disagree
V.	A brace of aggression needs
	Aggression — to cause injury or hurt
	Abasement — to surrender; to be hurt
	(In extreme form, these two needs would be called "sadism" and "masochism")
VI.	A quartet of affection needs
	Affiliation — to form friendships
	Rejection — to reject, as in snub or ignore
	Nurturance — to nourish or help
	Succorance — to seek help
VII.	Two brainy needs
	Cognizance — to explore and inquire
	Exposition — to transmit information
VIII.	Miscellaneous
	Play — to amuse oneself
	Blamavoidance — to avoid blame by inhibiting antisocial impulses

From *Approaches to Personality: An Introduction to People,* by J. Geiwitz and J. Moursund. Copyright © 1979 Wadsworth, Inc. Reprinted by permission of the publisher, Brooks/Cole Publishing Co., Monterey, California.

ing at the feet of an older woman. Subjects are instructed to tell a little story about each picture: Who are the people? What led up to this scene? What are they thinking and feeling? What will happen? Like all projective tests (see Chapter 11), the TAT assumes that subjects will "project" their own personality into their stories and thus reveal their needs (much as Walter Kerr apparently revealed his hunger need to Susan Black, as we saw in the introduction to this chapter).

Among Murray's needs, the most widely studied is the *need for achievement*. A scoring system for the TAT was devised such that people who used a lot of achievement imagery in their stories would be high scorers. These people, who were presumably high in the need for achievement, talked about "performance in relation to some standard of excellence" (for instance, getting a good grade on a test); or unique accomplishments (like inventions); or the pursuit of long-term goals (such as a career). Once the scoring system for the achievement motive was published, hundreds of studies poured forth, comparing people who were (by the new system) high or low in the "get-up-and-go" spirit that made America great (Atkinson and Birch, 1978).

One of the major achievements of the achievement theorists was the intensive study of the relationship between achievement orientation and risk taking. In particular, research disclosed that people who scored high in the need for achievement tended to choose moderate risks. Consider the lowly ringtoss game, for example, in which people may choose the distance from which they will toss the ring to try to land it on a peg. People high in the need for achievement tend to choose the middle positions,

where success reflects on their ability, instead of the very near or very far positions, where success is either too easy or purely a matter of luck (Atkinson, 1964).

Achievement theory concerns itself not only with the need to achieve success but also with the need to avoid failure. If we think of the achievement motive as a need to accomplish things of which one can be proud, fear of failure is a need to avoid the shame and embarrassment of an unsuccessful outcome. When the need to avoid failure is aroused in an individual, he or she feels anxious and fearful, and wants to withdraw from the situation (Atkinson, 1964).

Consider the ringtoss game from the point of view of the failure-oriented individual: Such a person is attracted to the positions very close to the peg, since the probability of failure is small. The individual who fears failure will also be attracted to the extremely distant positions, strangely enough, where failure is almost certain; failure at a task where the probability of success is almost zero does not reflect on a person's ability. The situation is worst at the middle position, where the chances and the shame of failure are both sizable. Achievement theory predicts that people afraid of failure will not want to play the ringtoss game at all; no position is comfortable. But forced to play, they will choose *either* the easiest *or* the most difficult position. They will stand right next to the peg (maybe even cheating a little to get closer), because the dreaded failure is unlikely. Or they will stand as far back as possible (maybe even toss the ring under their leg), because nobody expects them to succeed at such an impossible task. Do you recognize some of your friends from these descriptions?

Ringtoss Games in Life

Obviously, achievement theory is not designed to explain behavior only in ringtoss games. Many important situations in life have the same essential characteristics as ringtoss games: One's pride in succeeding goes up as the probability of success goes down. You feel prouder of getting a good score on a hard test than an easy one. Another analogy is the "game" of occupational choice. There is a dimension of status in job choices that runs roughly from "unskilled laborer" to "Supreme Court justice." The higher the status, the greater one's pride in achieving it, but the lower the probability one can do so. Thus we would expect achievement-oriented people to choose a reasonable career, one that requires effort on their part but that is definitely within their capabilities. People who are more concerned about avoiding failure, on the other hand, are more likely to make outlandish choices, either beyond their capabilities—"I'll be a Supreme Court justice"—or too easily within them—"What's wrong with being a ditch-digger?" (Mahone, 1960).

Another analogy to the ringtoss game in real life is ability groupings in the educational system. Achievement theory predicts that people high in the need for achievement should prefer classes composed of students of similar ability (homogeneous classes), because the chances of earning a high grade are close to 50:50; it's a challenge. Students driven by the need to avoid failure should dislike homogeneous classes for the same reason; for them, it's like being forced to play at the middle position in ringtoss where the combination of relatively high chances of failure (50:50) and the relatively high em-

barrassment of failure (it reflects on their lack of personal ability) is greatest. Research has provided support for these predictions (O'Connor et al., 1966).

Attribution and Achievement

Like many other topics in motivation, achievement strivings have recently been viewed in terms of attributions (Weiner et al., 1971). The age-old question asked of successful people is, "To what do you attribute your success?" According to attribution theory, most answers fall into one of four categories. One is *ability:* "I got my job as a talk-show host because I am a very intelligent person." A second is *effort:* "I got the promotion because I worked my buns off." A third category is *task difficulty:* "I got accepted by the Foreign Service because it was an easy exam." The fourth common attribution for success is *luck:* "I only had time to read one chapter, and the whole test was on that chapter!"

As you might expect, people who are high in need for achievement tend to attribute success to personal ability and effort. Because success reflects on their competence, they find it a very satisfying experience. They seek "challenges" such as the moderate-risk positions of the ringtoss game (or the ringtoss analogies in real life). Interestingly, they are protected from the agony of defeat by their tendency to view failure as due to difficult tasks or bad luck!

People with a high fear of failure tend to attribute success to impersonal factors—an easy task or good luck. Success holds no joy for them, and they hate "challenges." They avoid moderate risk positions. They do not like situations that reflect on their ability or effort, preferring very easy or very difficult tasks in which success or failure is attributed to task difficulty or luck.

By manipulating subjects' perceptions of the reasons for success or failure in a task, researchers have been able to affect motivation and, in turn, performance. In one experiment, people with a high fear of failure were given a task involving eye-hand coordination. The task did not appear difficult, but in fact it was; failure was almost certain. Some of the subjects were given a pill—a placebo, with no active ingredients—which, they were told, would interfere with eye-hand coordination and make the task more difficult for them. These subjects did better on the task than others given no pill. With no pill, these latter subjects experienced their great fear—failure—and had to attribute it to lack of personal ability. With shame developing as failure unfolded, their performance worsened as the task progressed. The subjects with the pill, however, could attribute their failure to an external (not-me) cause— the pill's effect on them. They experienced less shame, and their performance was not hindered (Weiner and Sierad, 1975).

MASLOW'S HIERARCHY OF NEEDS

Some human needs, like hunger, are clearly biological in origin. Others, like the need for achievement, are significantly influenced by life experiences and social interactions. And some human needs, like those demonstrated by martyrs who die for an ethical principle, seem almost spiritual, a reaching for godliness. How are all these "springs of action," as William James called them, related? Is it possible to organize the vast variety of human motivation into one coherent framework? One psychologist who tried was Abraham Maslow (1970).

Maslow suggested that the best way to conceptualize human motivation is to see it as a *hierarchy of needs* (Figure 6.10), a sort of pyramid of human needs from the lowest and most basic to the highest and most profound. At the base of the hierarchy are the *physiological needs*—hunger, thirst, sex, and other desires that promote the survival of the individual and the species. These needs must be satisfied first, before the needs higher up can become active. In other words, a starving person has no interest in philosophy.

The second level is that of the *safety needs*, including the desire for security, order, and freedom from fear. These must be

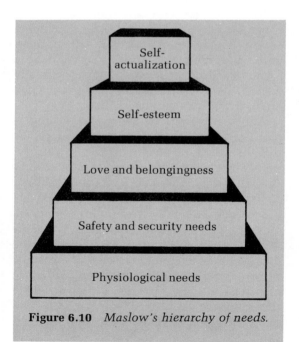

Figure 6.10 *Maslow's hierarchy of needs.*

satisfied before needs in the next group are exhibited.

Third on Maslow's pyramid are the *belongingness and love needs:* the needs for friends, lovers, children. When these needs are not satisfied, one feels lonely. In today's world, it seems to be on this level that many people have strong unfulfilled needs. Many of our more recent cultural institutions—singles bars and apartments, encounter groups, and the like—owe much of their popularity to the fact that people are lonely and have very few places to meet others.

If the love and belongingness needs are satisfied, needs concerned with *esteem* emerge. We need to respect ourselves, and we desire a good reputation, high status, fame, or other forms of regard from others.

At the top of Maslow's hierarchy is the need for *self-actualization.* When all of the needs lower on the hierarchy are satisfied, have we reached the point where we are completely fulfilled? No, says Maslow; at this point we become motivated to become the best person we can possibly be. We pursue the great values of humanity like justice and honesty. If we do not, we grow as dissatisfied as people without food; we become like the thoroughly bored rich socialite who complains that there is no purpose to life. In Maslow's words, "What a man *can* be, he *must* be" (Maslow, 1970, p. 46).

Self-Actualization and Values

If one has a theory that the need for self-actualization is the highest human motive, how does one do research to confirm it? Maslow decided to study people with what he called *abnormally healthy* personalities. These are the people, in theory, who are not

Figure 6.11   *Self-actualizing Ken Archer crosses the finish line of the Boston Marathon. His time was 2 hours, 38 minutes, 59 seconds!*

"hung up" on the lower needs for physiological satisfaction, belongingness, esteem, and the like, who presumably have progressed to the stage of self-actualization.

But how does one identify self-actualizers? Maslow reasoned that it was good enough, for a beginning, to rely on general reputation. For example, some historical figures, like Abraham Lincoln and Albert Einstein, are generally considered to have been very healthy personalities; Maslow read biographies and autobiographies of these people. (Some of them were probably less than heroic in real life; but even so, Maslow could

Table 6.4
CHARACTERISTICS OF SELF-ACTUALIZING TYPES

Characteristic	*Comment*
Self-actualizing people	Self-actualizing people
1. perceive reality accurately, 2. even in regard to themselves, and 3. are not afraid of it.	detect absurdities and dishonesties quickly, even their own; they do not live in a dream world.
4. They are spontaneous and natural.	They are unorthodox, especially in their thoughts. They do not act rebelliously simply because they disagree with the opinions of others. They do not act for effect unless the principle involved is highly valued. They have ideals, in other words, but they also understand reality.
5. They focus on problems, not on themselves.	They are not focused on their own personal problems to the exclusion of the problems of society; they think in terms of contributions they can make.
6. They like privacy and detachment; 7. they can be called autonomous.	They are relatively independent of both the physical and the social environment; they enjoy but do not *need* friends.
8. They have a continued freshness of appreciation.	Life does not become old and stale for them.
9. They have peak experiences.	They have out-of-the-ordinary (mystical) experiences.
10. They have a feeling of relationship with all people and 11. more profound interpersonal relations.	They are realistic reformers, attempting to improve the lot of all people, and their personal friendships and love-relationships are also more intense.
12. They have a democratic character structure and 13. discriminate between means and ends.	They are not prejudiced and they have a strong sense of ethics.
14. They are creative.	This follows from the other characteristics, does it not?
15. They have a philosophical sense of humor.	They laugh at absurdities, not at other people's failings.
16. They resist enculturation.	Each is his or her own person.

The characteristics adapted for use in this table were described by Abraham Maslow, *Motivation and Personality*, 2nd ed. (Harper & Row, 1970), Chapter 11.

at least study the highly virtuous characteristics they were *thought* to possess.) In addition, he interviewed living people who were considered by their friends to be exceptionally healthy.

From these data, Maslow constructed a list of the qualities of the self-actualizing personality (see Table 6.4). What do you think? No great surprises, I think.

In the course of self-actualizing, one has setbacks, but one also has *peak experiences,* mystical experiences involving a feeling of unity of everything, that all is right with the world. Everyone has peak experiences, according to Maslow; self-actualizers have them much more frequently and with deeper implications. Examples include deep religious experiences, which are described as moments when you and God and the universe feel as one, and you are aware — not necessarily in an intellectual sense — of a grand pattern underlying everything. A moment of intense sexual love, when you seem to be sharing the soul of another person, is another example.

In Maslow's view, peak experiences represent satisfaction of the highest human needs. In fact, Maslow decided that the study of peak experiences might well lead us to a description of the greatest goals of human activity. (Here we are using "greatest" to mean most distinctly human and most admirable; most value-able.) These greatest goals Maslow called *B-values* (values of being); they include truth, honesty, beauty, justice, order, and playfulness.

Self-Actualization and Other Needs

For self-actualizers, motivation in general takes on new meaning. In Maslow's terms, they try to satisfy the basic requirements of life — food, safety, love — in ways that simultaneously improve the self. They learn to appreciate subtle differences in the taste and texture of food, and they seek good dinner companions. Their homes provide shelter of course, but are also expressions of themselves — comfortable, unique, friendly, creative. Their love-making is erotic, sensual, and satisfying; tender, considerate, and spiritual.

Maslow's message is optimistic. Every human endeavor, even those which satisfy our most basic biological or social needs, can provide an opportunity for personal growth, an increase in the ability to appreciate life. You can enjoy life. You need not change your life dramatically, and you don't require a fortune. You need not do what you enjoy; you can enjoy what you do. Not a bad message to end the chapter.

SUMMARY

1. Hunger is one of our most basic motivations. It is governed largely by biological mechanisms such as the body's monitoring of stored fat and blood sugar, fullness of the stomach, and sensory information. An area in the brain called the hypothalamus appears to regulate the body's target weight. Exercise not only burns off calories but helps to keep our appetites in line with our physiological needs. Learned tastes and social values also affect our inclinations to consume food.

2. Motivation is almost always partly biological and partly cognitive. Emotions comprise both physiological components,

geared mainly toward mobilizing the body for action, and psychological elements related to learning and experience. Our interpretation of these bodily and mental indicators, plus cues from the situation, help us to judge what emotion we feel and determine our response to it.

3. The *Cannon-Bard theory* emphasizes the biological side of emotions. This theory ascribes control of our emotions to subcortical brain structures such as the hypothalamus and limbic system, which (1) send signals to the rest of the body to prepare for action and (2) inform the cortex of the emotion. The *James-Lange theory,* on the other hand, suggests that the cortex monitors bodily arousal and infers our emotions from it. The *Schacter-Singer theory* maintains that we use bodily arousal to detect the presence of emotion but situational cues to identify what emotion we are feeling.

4. Psychologists, like the rest of us, depend mainly on physiological cues to detect an emotion in other people and on other cues to identify that emotion. Common gauges of bodily arousal are heart rate and GSR (galvanic skin response, a measure of electrical conductance in the skin).

5. Because emotions represent the body's emergency reaction to an unusual situation, prolonged emotional upset can be damaging to one's health. *Psychosomatic illness* is either caused or significantly aggravated by emotions. Selye's theory of stress postulates three stages of a *general adaptation syndrome:* an alarm reaction, resistance, and finally exhaustion. There is considerable evidence that illness is more likely during stressful periods in one's life.

6. The most stressful situations are those in which the subjects feel unable to control what happens to them. This feeling of helplessness has been studied in experiments with dogs and humans: First, subjects are placed in a situation in which they receive aversive stimulation. Nothing they can do has any effect on the aversive stimuli. Later, when their behavior could have an effect, they are passive; they have learned that nothing helps. Subjects can be "immunized" against helplessness, however, if they can accomplish escape from aversive stimuli at least some of the time before they are put into a helpless situation.

7. According to *attribution theory,* our reactions to helplessness depend on the causes to which we attribute our failure. If we make attributions that do not damage our self-esteem, they may spur us to work harder, whereas if we feel truly helpless to change the situation, we are likely to give up.

8. Henry Murray attempted to catalogue human needs. The need for achievement in particular has sparked much research; for instance, people high in *need for achievement* tend to choose moderate-risk situations, whereas people high in *fear of failure* prefer either very high or very low risks. High need for achievement correlates with attributing success or failure to one's own efforts and ability rather than to uncontrollable external causes.

9. Abraham Maslow conceived of human motivations as forming a hierarchy, with the most basic and physiological needs having to be satisfied before we can move up to safety needs, belongingness and love needs, and esteem needs. At the peak is the need for self-actualization, to become the best we possibly can be.

USING PSYCHOLOGY

What event in your life has been the most stressful, and why? How does this event fit into the stress scale shown in Table 6.2 of the text? How much of the range of human stress have you experienced? How did your body react to the stress? Can you relate any illnesses you have had to stressful periods of your life?

SUGGESTED READINGS

Bolles, R. C. *Theory of motivation.* 2nd ed. Harper & Row, 1975.
An excellent textbook; focuses on biological drives and reinforcement theories.

Atkinson, J. W., and Birch, D. *Introduction to motivation.* 2nd ed. Van Nostrand, 1978.
Another excellent textbook; focuses on learned human motives, especially the need for achievement.

Seligman, M. E. P. *Helplessness: on depression, development, and death.* Freeman, 1975.
A summary of research on learned helplessness and its implications for a wide range of human behavior.

Maslow, A. H. *Motivation and personality.* 2nd ed. Harper & Row, 1970.
The best single statement of Maslow's views on self-actualization and other human motives.

INTERLUDE

Lie Detection

Chances are good that you will someday take a lie detector test. Most likely it will not be in connection with a criminal investigation but as part of a job application. You will be asked if you have ever stolen anything valuable, if you use drugs to excess, and other questions of interest to your prospective employer. If you fail the test, you will not be hired. If you pass and are hired, you may have to take annual lie detector tests to see if you have been snitching a little here and there on the job.

It is estimated that 25 percent of the major U.S. companies use lie detectors to screen at least some of their employees (Michaelson, 1973). This percentage increases every year. Some government officials are beginning to recognize the potential dangers of this situation. Very few laws exist to restrict the use of lie detectors, and most states do not even require that an operator be licensed. Then there is the constitutional question: Does an involuntary lie detector test violate one's right against self-incrimination?

Some also question the validity of lie detection procedures. Senator Sam Ervin, former head of a Senate committee investigating the use of lie detectors in American government and industry, claimed lie detection was "twentieth-century witchcraft." He asserted that it is quite possible for someone telling the truth to be diagnosed a liar and for a liar to be marked truthful. But the supporters of lie detection claim the procedures are 99 percent effective.

What is a lie detector? Can it really detect lies? What are reasonable uses of such a procedure? What are its dangers to society and the individual? In this interlude, we will investigate this machine that someday may investigate us.

MEASURING NERVOUSNESS

Centuries ago, Arabian Bedouins, to find out which of two conflicting witnesses was telling the truth, had each lick a hot iron. They believed that the liar would be nervous and his mouth dry; therefore the hot iron would burn his tongue and identify him as the false witness. The same theory—though luckily not the same technique—is used today. The theory of lie detection is that lying makes one nervous. Thus, modern lie detectors determine the level of nervous tension in a subject.

The most common lie detector is a machine designed to measure several physiological variables at once. This machine, called a *polygraph* (which means "many writings"), usually measures heart rate, the rate of breathing, and the *galvanic skin response* (GSR), which is associated with sweating. If a normal subject becomes nervous, his heart rate increases, his breathing becomes irregular, and he sweats, causing a noticeable GSR.

During the 1960s, the federal government spent large sums of money to develop a lie detector that would work even if the subject didn't know his statements were being evaluated. This device analyzes the sound frequencies in speech, using the assumption that a person who is nervous speaks at a higher pitch than when he is less nervous. Speech analyzers are now in use in both government and industry. The Israelis, for example, used one on Anwar Sadat during his speech to the Israeli parliament (*Newsweek*, December 12, 1977); it showed him to be sincere.

The machines give a fairly accurate indication of when someone is nervous, but nervousness is not the same as lying. Surprising subjects with a sudden loud noise would arouse most of them—increase their heart rate, induce some sweating, etc.—but this is not lying. Nervousness is just one clue that a person might be lying. We must depend on other indications in the situation to determine whether the nervousness is due to lying or to other causes.

DETECTING LIES

In a typical interrogation, the examiner asks a list of questions. The list includes questions that should not make anyone nervous—"Am I wearing a white coat?"—as well as the crucial question—"Did you shoot Ferguson?" Unfortunately, most suspects will react emotionally to the crucial question, whether or not they are guilty. For this reason, most polygraphers include questions that are designed to elicit emotion about an unrelated situation for comparison purposes. "Did you murder Verburg?" (The suspect could not possibly have murdered Verburg.) "Did you ever masturbate?" By comparing the subject's response to crucial questions with his or her reactions to irrelevant questions, the polygraph operator judges whether or not the subject has told the truth to the crucial questions. A third category—"inconclusive"—is used for borderline cases.

In the vast majority of cases, this judgment includes information from other sources besides the polygraph (Lykken, 1974). The examiner typically has access to the subject's prior arrest record, if this is a criminal case (and sometimes even if it is simply a job application), and the evidence against him or her in this case. The examiner's prejudices against people of a certain sex, age, race, or life style may also influence his or her judgment.

Can Lies Really Be Detected?

In any event, the basic question remains: Can a lie detector detect lies? Professional polygraph operators estimate their methods are 99 percent accurate—but how do they know? How can the polygraphers tell if they are right or wrong? Some subjects confess after they are told they lied, but this happens rarely. Some cases go to court and a judge or jury makes a judgment, but usually not until months or years after the lie detection test; it would take an extremely complex set of records to follow up test results over such long periods. In fact, what the polygraphers typically report is a percentage that represents the number of known errors divided by all the tests they have done (Barland and Raskin, 1973). Suppose they do 35,000 tests and are able to verify their results in 1000 of these cases; 100 are in error and 900 are correct, according to such data as confessions and the results of jury trials. Most of us would say they are in error 100 times out of 1000, or 10 percent. Polygraphers are likely to report that

they are "known to be in error" only 100 times out of 35,000, an error rate of less than 1 percent (Reid and Inbau, 1966). Incredible!

In one of the few carefully executed studies of lie detection procedures in real life, the complete records of a number of criminal investigations — minus the lie detector test results — were reviewed by four attorneys, who were asked to judge guilt or innocence (Bersh, 1969). In those cases where all four attorneys agreed on a verdict, the polygraph test also agreed 92 percent of the time. When three of the four attorneys agreed, the lie detector was with the majority 75 percent of the time. (A flip of a coin would have agreed, by chance alone, 50 percent of the time.)

Although this study suggests some validity for the lie detector, two unavoidable flaws in the study should be noted. First, the cases that led four "judges" to the same verdict were unusually clear-cut; police like to use lie detectors in less certain cases. Second, as we have mentioned, the polygraph operator ordinarily knows more than simply the polygraph results; he knows the evidence, the prior arrest history, and other factors, which probably increases the accuracy of his judgments.

Another study using almost the same procedure found an error rate of 17 percent (Barland, 1975). A chilling feature of this study was the type of error uncovered: Without exception, the disagreements occurred when the panel of five attorneys judged the suspect innocent and the polygraph examiner judged him guilty! A third study used the polygraph records of people who were known to be guilty (by their own later confession) or innocent (by the later confession of someone else). Ten professional polygraph examiners tried to determine guilt and innocence from the records (Horvath and Reid, 1971). The average error rate was 12 percent; the best examiner was wrong on only 1 out of 40 records (2.5 percent error rate), and the worst missed on 12 people (30 percent).

There are very few good laboratory experiments on the effectiveness of lie detectors. Representative is a study involving a make-believe burglary (Barland and Raskin, 1975). College students played the role of either guilty or innocent suspects and were administered standard polygraph tests by a trained polygrapher. By standard criteria, 35 percent of the tests were inconclusive; 53 percent were correct and 12 percent were wrong. The error rate for innocent subjects (16 percent) was twice as high as for guilty subjects (8 percent).

In summary, careful studies of real-life and laboratory crimes suggest that the average error rate of polygraph examinations is on the order of 10 or 15 percent, with considerable variability among polygraphers. A majority of the errors, unfortunately, consist of calling an innocent person guilty.

THE GUILTY KNOWLEDGE TEST

In police interrogations, the chances of error can be reduced considerably by use of a different method of questioning, called the *guilty knowledge test* (Lykken, 1974). First, the examiner obtains information about the crime from the police, especially facts that only the criminal would know. Then the information is presented to the suspect in a kind of multiple-choice test: "A bank was robbed yesterday. Was it the First National Bank? Was it the Wellington Bank? Was it the Bank of America?" and so forth, using at least four or five alternatives. A second question: "The teller who was robbed: Was it this person? (showing a picture) Was it this person?" And so forth.

If a suspect consistently shows strong physiological responses to the correct answers, the probability that he is guilty increases significantly. The more questions he responds to, the lower the chances he is innocent.

This is much different, you will note, from asking, "Did you rob the Wellington Bank?" An innocent subject, knowing he is suspected, might well react to this question. But an innocent subject is extremely unlikely to know which of five banks was robbed, which of five tellers was robbed, what the note slipped to the teller said, and other details. Laboratory studies of the guilty knowledge procedure find an error rate of about 5 percent. All errors involved calling a guilty person innocent; not a single innocent person was incorrectly labeled guilty (Lykken, 1959; Davidson, 1968).

THE LIE DETECTOR IN GOVERNMENT AND INDUSTRY

In the best of circumstances—police interrogations using the guilty knowledge test—lie detection procedures can be effective and useful. But in the worst of circumstances—screening potential employees in industry and government—the lie detector can be an instrument of unfairness (Lykken, 1974).

The first problem in industrial lie detecting is that if a person fails the polygraph test, he or she is not hired. Or, if an employee is tested during the year and fails, he or she is fired. At least in police interrogations, the lie detector results are only part of the evidence. Most courts will not admit lie detection records as evidence, and even those which do require a considerable amount of other evidence. Not so in industry. If the job applicant claims he or she has never stolen anything, and the lie detector disagrees, no further evidence is necessary. The person is not hired.

Note also that the more effective guilty knowledge test cannot be used in the industrial setting, because the examiner has no idea what particular crimes or obnoxious deeds (drug use, atypical sexual behavior) he or she is testing for.

The major problem, however, is that the lie detector will be unfair to a sizable number of job applicants. Suppose we (generously) assume that the lie detector operator is accurate 90 percent of the time. That is, in 10 percent of the cases where a person is lying, the operator cannot detect the lie; and in 10 percent of the cases where a person is telling the truth, the operator will think he is lying. Now let us make a second assumption: Most people are unlikely to lie during a job interview. How many would lie? One psychologist (Lykken, 1974) considers 5 percent a reasonable figure. Now let us use these estimates to construct a hypothetical example: Suppose that over a period of years, 1000 people are interviewed for jobs and given lie detector tests to see if they've ever stolen from their employer. By Lykken's estimate, 5 percent, or 50, of those people have stolen and will lie about it during the interview. Using the lie detector, we will detect 90 percent of the liars, or 45 people. *But,* the other 950 applicants have not stolen anything and do not need to lie. Our lie detector will clear 90 percent of them, but will diagnose the other 10 percent as liars. And 10 percent of 950 is 95 people! These 95 people (and the 45 real liars who have been detected) will not be hired, and they will not be able to appeal the decision. Fully 68 percent of the applicants rejected because they failed the lie detector test would have been unfairly rejected.

A Brief Case History

The horrors of "scientific" theory and technology gone awry are shown by the case of a young bank manager who was given a routine examination designed to detect embezzlers (Smith, 1967). In response to the question, "Have you ever stolen any money from the bank or its customers?", the manager answered "No," but the lie detector went wild. In further testing, he was asked how much money was stolen. Since the fellow was innocent, it was as much a puzzle to him as the inquisitors, but the lie detector showed strong reactions to the amounts $800 and $1100. Faced with this evidence, the manager confessed to embezzling $1000. Unfortunately, the bank could find no such amount missing.

Well, if he is not guilty, the bank officials reasoned, he must be crazy, so they sent him for a psychiatric examination. It was discovered that he unconsciously felt guilty about financial dealings (legal) with his wife and his mother-in-law, dealings in the amounts of $800 and $1100. Both women were coincidentally customers of the bank. It was the phrase ". . . or its customers" that had triggered his violent emotional response, because of his *unconscious* guilt. A second polygraph test was administered using the same questions and also using new questions separating the words "bank" and "customers." The manager reacted only to "customers." Interestingly, the polygraph operator did not notice the difference, and the manager was again judged to be a liar and a thief — until the psychiatrist came to his defense.

THE FUTURE OF LIE DETECTION

I am not qualified to discuss the constitutional and other legal aspects of lie detection. But it is likely that every state will soon enact some laws defining the proper use of lie detectors, if only to demand evidence that the polygraph operator knows what he is doing (licensing). This makes sense, since the use of lie detectors is increasing, especially in industry and government, and it will undoubtedly continue to grow. With employee theft estimated at $6 billion annually, the pressure to weed out potential offenders is great. Lie detection may soon bring in more dollars per year than any other area of applied psychology (Lykken, 1975).

Another outcome of the increased use of lie detectors, strangely enough, is likely to be training to deceive a lie detector. People can learn to control their emotional responsiveness. In one study, subjects given biofeedback — information about their GSR — learned to control their "nervousness" and were able to fool the polygraph operator. Subjects given instruction in self-hypnosis for relaxation were also able to lie without detection (Corcoran et al., 1978). It would be relatively easy for an unscrupulous attorney or anyone else to train a guilty client to give no detectable emotional response to "crucial" questions. Because of the exaggerated belief most users have in the validity of the lie detector, this would work strongly in the client's favor.

YOU AND THE LIE DETECTOR

As I mentioned at the beginning of this interlude, it is likely that you will someday take a lie detector test. If you must, relax. Remember that the test is right most of the time. If you become one of the unfortunates who are "false positives"—labeled as a liar without cause—then do something about it. See an attorney. Show this interlude to the personnel manager. Talk to your local councilperson. Don't let these infernal machines get the best of us!

SUGGESTED READINGS

Lykken, D. T. The detection of deception. *Psychological Bulletin*, 1979, 86, 47–53.
  The latest statement by a major researcher who dislikes the practice of lie detection almost as much as I do.

Podlesny, J. A. & Raskin, D. C. Physiological measures and the detection of deception. *Psychological Bulletin*, 1977, 84, 782–799.
  Another point of view. These researchers are more favorable to the research, seeing more validity than Lykken sees, and to the use of lie detection in appropriate circumstances. They also have a "reply to Lykken," which follows Lykken's article.

Behavioral Objectives

1. Define "language."
2. Tell whether you think the chimpanzees described in the text really did or did not use language, and defend your choice.
3. Trace the acquisition of language in the human child.
4. Differentiate between adult speech and children's speech.
5. Define "pivot grammar" and explain why it is no longer considered adequate.
6. Define and provide examples of tag questions and overregularization. Explain their significance in the study of language development.
7. Preview the evidence for the innateness of language.
8. Review the evidence against the importance of imitation, reinforcement, and effectiveness of communication in language development.
9. Discuss the relationship between Black English and Standard English.
10. List some ways we communicate nonverbally and indicate their relative accuracy.
11. Describe how facial expressions are thought by some to be related to primitive behaviors.

CHAPTER

7

Language and Nonverbal Communication

The Sequoia National Forest and the giant tree, also called Sequoia, were named after an illiterate Cherokee Indian who invented a written language. Sequoyah was about 30 years old — the year was about 1800 — when he became convinced that the secret of whites' power was in their "talking leaves" (pages of printed material). So Sequoyah, though he himself could not read English, set out to create a written form of the Cherokee language (Garbarino, 1976; Black, 1977). People laughed at his attempts, and not without reason. He first tried to create a symbol for each word, but he could never remember his own symbols. Eventually he began to categorize the syllables that make up words in Cherokee and found them to be many fewer than the number of words; there were, by his reckoning, only 86. To each syllable he assigned a symbol. The symbols were often English letters, some lowercase, some capital. Some were English letters turned upside down — why not? Some were original creations.

His Cherokee comrades were not pleased. Sequoyah was neglecting his tribal duties to work on mysterious markings, with little apparent purpose. Finally he was accused of witchcraft, and a trial was set. Fortunately for Sequoyah, he had by this time finished his task and taught the system to his daughter. At his trial, he astounded his accusers by writing a letter to his daughter, conveying to her by means of printed symbols any and all statements suggested by the doubters. His system was a stunning success, and Sequoyah's accusers, who came to boo, stayed to cheer. Within a single year, virtually all Cherokee in Arkansas became literate. Cherokee across the nation learned Sequoyah's system, and in 1828, the *Chero-*

Figure 7.1 *Sequoyah, who singlehandedly created a written version of the Cherokee language; also, a page from the* Cherokee Phoenix, *a bilingual newspaper, and a carved stone pipe, which demonstrates that literacy had become part of the everyday tribal life among Sequoyah's people.*

kee Phoenix, which ran news in Cherokee, began publication.

What an accomplishment! And yet, if you think about it, Sequoyah's triumph seems hardly more marvelous than the accomplishment of any child learning her or his native tongue. A normal American child speaks her or his first words around the age of one year, and by the age of four or so has a speaking mastery of the English language. This mind-boggling intellectual achieve-ment is accomplished by every child, the dull and the bright, the advantaged and the disadvantaged, in all but the most excep-tional of cases. How do children learn lan-guage? Why do they learn it so quickly? These are mysteries psychologists have only recently begun to unravel.

Language is not only an impressive achievement but our most vital form of communication. In addition to spoken and written language, in this chapter we will also consider nonverbal communication—ways in which we transmit messages, sometimes unintentionally, by facial expressions, gestures, and other behaviors besides speech. Let us begin, however, with an attempt to clarify the definition of language. To do this, we should first consider whether or not animals other than humans have language.

THE LANGUAGE OF ANIMALS

Do animals have language? Obviously animals communicate with one another, and if this is what you mean by language, then animals have it. For example, a bitch communicates to male dogs when she is sexually receptive: Her odors are different, her demeanor is altered, and she sighs and whimpers more than usual. Is this language? Most psychologists would say no. They do not wish to make language synonymous with all communication, although language is certainly used to communicate.

What is Language?

It is not easy to define language precisely, but three features of any communication system we call a language are prominent. First, the elements of the language are *symbols*, things that stand for something else. You cannot ride the word "horse"; it is simply a symbol for the animal. (The bitch's flirting behaviors are not symbolic; they speak for themselves.) Second, the symbols in the language are combined in ways prescribed by a set of rules we usually call a *grammar*. Ungrammatical combinations— "The horses is pretty," or the more extreme, "Bob Harry Tom and hit"—don't follow the

Figure 7.2 *Is this communication? Is it language?*

rules and are not considered legitimate sentences of the language.

The third feature of language is that it is designed to convey *meaning*. The symbols are combined, in ways prescribed by rules, in an attempt to communicate meaning. Both the symbols, which stand for something, and the rules help in this endeavor. Typically one cannot change symbols without changing meaning—"Tom hit Joe" is not the same as "John hit Joe." And word order, which is one way the rules of the grammar come into play, makes a difference, too. "Tom hit Joe" does not equal "Joe hit Tom."

By the standards of symbolism, a proper grammar, and indications of an attempt to communicate meaning, most animal communications have fallen short. The prime contenders for true languages are the communication systems that have been taught to chimpanzees by humans.

Washoe and Sign Language

Suppose you wanted to teach your pet chimpanzee the English language. How would you go about it? Two psychologists raised Gua, a female chimpanzee, at home with their son, Donald (Kellogg and Kellogg, 1933). Both boy and chimp were encouraged to speak, but only Donald did. Gua indicated she could comprehend some language, for she could respond appropriately to about 70 different utterances, but she never *produced* a single word. A second attempt involved more intensive training in speech, and Viki, another chimpanzee, was eventually able to pronounce three recognizable words: "Mama," "Papa," and "cup" (Hayes and Hayes, 1952).

But chimpanzees lack the vocal tract structures necessary for real human speech, and trying to teach them to speak is a bit like teaching humans to fly by flapping their arms. Recognizing this fact, another pair of psychologists did not require their chimpanzee, named Washoe, to speak; instead, they tried to teach her sign language (Gardner and Gardner, 1969). A chimp is very adept with its hands—if anything, more adept than humans—so there seemed to be no reason why a chimpanzee could not learn sign language as readily as a human deaf-mute.

Words and Sentences. Washoe put to rest, almost immediately, the myth that chimpanzees cannot produce "words." Using her hands instead of vocal cords, she began to use between 50 and 100 different signs appropriately, and eventually learned over 150. Communication between Washoe and the researchers was frequent and friendly. But was it language?

Let us consider some additional evidence.

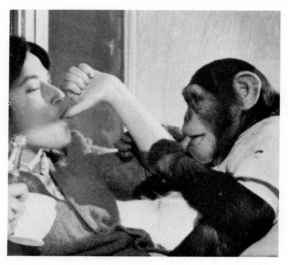

Figure 7.3   *Washoe makes the sign for "drink."*

Washoe could apply her word-signs appropriately to *categories*, not just to specific objects. Once she had learned the sign for "cat" from seeing a picture of a few particular cats, she used that sign for pictures of other cats, for real cats of various descriptions, and for little statues of cats (Gardner and Gardner, 1971).

Even more interesting to psychologists and linguists (language scholars) was Washoe's ability to string signs together to make primitive sentences up to five signs long. Some of these sentences, most of which were two signs long, were entirely her creation. For example, once Washoe learned what the sign "more" meant, she used it in combinations she had never seen used by humans. Learning it in the context of tickling, a favorite sport of hers, she generalized it on her own to food—"More fruit!" Among her more impressive creations was a sentence produced when she perceived she had done something wrong: "Come, hug, love, sorry."

Productivity. Washoe's ability to create original strings or sentences is something worth considering in a definition of language. Linguists call this ability *productivity;* very simply defined, it is the ability to use a few sounds and words and a few rules to construct an infinite number of sentences. Think about it. Except for a few standard phrases — such as greetings like "How are you?" — almost every sentence we write or speak or read or hear is one we have rarely, or never, experienced before in all our life. The sentence I am writing, the one you are reading, is — for better or worse — a prime example. Exceptions are so rare we usually classify them as proverbs or clichés.

Compare the productivity of human language to the so-called language of parrots and other talking birds. Typically, a well-trained parrot can reproduce a phrase heard repeatedly in the past, but outside of fantastic movies or comic strips, no animal lower

than the chimpanzee has been able to create a truly unusual and novel phrasing of an idea.

But apparently a chimpanzee — Washoe — has been able to create a novel phrasing of an idea. Productivity, which involves symbols combined by rules to communicate meaning, is a prime indicator of language. So we can say Washoe had language. Most psychologists would compare Washoe's linguistic performance at age four to that of a human child between the age of one and a half and two (Brown, 1973b).

When Project Washoe ended (for various scientific and economic reasons), Washoe was still young, only five years old. Chimpanzees are not considered mature until the age of 12 or later. Would Washoe have continued her accelerating progress in language skills, as human children do? There was no evidence of a leveling off, according to her trainers; she did not appear to have reached any sort of natural limit for nonhuman subjects (Gardner and Gardner, 1977). It would be very interesting to follow the language development of chimpanzees further, to intellectual maturity at least. To this end, four new chimpanzees have entered the program, and we can expect more information on a number of questions in the near future.

Washoe and other chimpanzees trained in symbolic communication (Premack, 1970; Rumbaugh and Gill, 1976) have shown linguistic abilities far greater than humans previously suspected. Some skeptics still claim that only humans have true language (Limber, 1977), but to say this is to restrict the definition of "true language" more and more narrowly. At the very least, the animal research has helped to sharpen our thinking about what is and is not properly part of our concept of language.

© 1980 by Sidney Harris/American Scientist Magazine

FOCUS

Moja, the Artist

Moja is one of the chimpanzees now being taught sign language in Reno, Nevada, where Washoe was trained. When Moja is not developing her language skills, one of her favorite activities is drawing—or perhaps we should say "making marks on paper" (see Figure 1, for a typical example). One day, when Moja was about three and a half years old, she produced the drawing in Figure 2 (Gardner and Gardner, 1977). Because it was so sparse compared to her

Figure 1 *Moja the artist at work.*

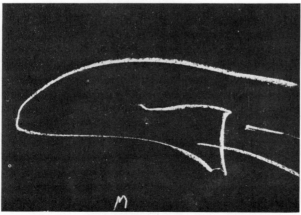

Figure 2 Bird, *the first drawing Moja titled.*

Figure 3 Berry, *a drawing requested by the teacher. For her rendition, Moja chose an orange pen.*

usual scribbles, the research assistant put the chalk back in Moja's hand and said to her, in sign language, "Try more." Moja dropped the chalk and said, "Finish." Acting on an inspired hunch, the assistant did something no one had ever thought of doing before: He asked Moja what she had drawn. "Bird," replied Moja.

Since then Moja has labeled other of her drawings, and she has also produced drawings on request. In Figure 3, we see her rendition of a berry, drawn in response to the teacher's, "Draw berry there." Not bad, I'd say.

Moja's drawings are interesting in their own right, but they are also valuable to psychologists interested in the general intellectual development of the "talking" chimps. In addition, Moja's talent in the visual arts may be related to similar abilities in human children, which some psychologists consider basic to *written* language. Maybe by the next edition of this textbook, we will be able to include a note to you from Moja!

HUMAN LANGUAGE ACQUISITION

The human child exits the womb and immediately communicates to the world its displeasure. This is the beginning of the baby's linguistic career; from the moment of birth it vocalizes in relatively precise and identifiable ways.

A child's first systematic vocalizations are squealing, gurgling sounds called *cooing*. These vowel-like sounds give way at about six months to *babbling*, which combines consonant-like sounds with the "oo's" and "ah's" of cooing. The result is a series of vocalizations similar to simple, one-syllable words, such as "ma," "da," and "mu."

Babbling is behavior exhibited in essentially the same form by all babies everywhere. The babies of France, Japan, and the United States, and the babies of deaf mutes, all babble with the same sounds and intonations . . . at first. Later in the babbling period, however, children of various cultures can be distinguished. Each begins to produce, with slightly greater frequency than the children of other cultures, the sounds and intonations of the people around him. The baby is in effect babbling with an accent.

One-Word Speech

On or a little before its first birthday, the human child speaks. This is on the average, of course, and a few months earlier or later is no cause for a parent's concern. On the other hand, there is not *much* variance in the onset of human speech, considerably less than one would expect if speaking were entirely a matter of learning. It appears that biological maturation is involved, both of the nervous system and of the musculature related to speech, so that when the child is *able* to speak, it does speak. Only the most exceptional circumstances will prevent a normal child from speaking before the age of two.

When the child speaks, its first word will be simple, both primitive and easy. "Mama" is a good prediction, and the definition of this or similar words is "mother" in an unusually large number of societies whose languages have little else in common. Other words follow, and by the time the average child is a year and a half in age, she or he has a vocabulary of between three and fifty words (Lenneberg, 1967). Each word, however, fulfills numerous functions in this *one-word stage,* the first stage of speech.

One characteristic of one-word speech is that it tends to use a single word to express a complex idea. In effect, a child uses one word where an adult would use a sentence. The child may say "Ball!" to mean "I want the ball!" However, the one-word sentence is often ambiguous if not heard in context. "Ball!" may mean "I want the ball" in one situation, it may mean "'There is a ball" in another, and even "Your head is like a ball!" when the rich uncle meets his new niece. Very often, one needs to know what the child is doing in order to understand what she or he is saying (DeLaguna, 1927).

Two Words at a Time

Toward the end of the second year (usually), the child begins to utter strings of two or more related words that carry the intent of sentences. At first, these "sentences" rarely contain more than two words: "My shoe," "Allgone milk," "Daddy byebye."

Early in the 1960s, psychologists and linguists began considering a question surprising only in that it had not been seriously asked before. They wanted to know if they could construct a *grammar* of the child's two-word utterances. A grammar, simply defined, is a set of rules for combining words into sentences. For example, the grammar of English contains rules that describe how certain classes of words—nouns, verbs, adjectives, and so on—can combine. One such rule states that an adjective should be placed before the noun it modifies: We say "red house," not "house red." (The grammar of French, on the other hand, says adjectives *follow* nouns—"house red"—just the reverse of the English rule.)

Telegraphic Speech and the Pivot Grammar. A child who utters sentences consisting of just two words obviously does not follow the rules of English grammar as an adult does. Does this mean that children use no grammar at all? Early observational studies showed clearly that two-word utterances were systematic and regular, implying that the children speaking them were indeed following a set of rules. This grammar, it has been suggested, bears the same relationship to the adult version as a telegram does to adult speech (Brown and Fraser, 1963). Just as I might telegraph my parents, "Broke—send money," the child sends out communications in abbreviated form, leaving out certain words that an adult would include. The child says "More milk!" where the adult would say, "I would like some more milk, please."

To say that two-word speech is telegraphic does not describe children's grammar, however, for it does not specify the rules children seem to use in constructing their two-word sentences. An early attempt at creating such a grammar was based on children's use of certain "general purpose" words. "Allgone" is one example. Just about anything can be "allgone": "Allgone milk," "Allgone Mommy," "Allgone shoe." Words such as "this," "that," "more," "here," and "there" are also frequently used in this way. These general purpose words were called *pivots* (Braine, 1963), and the grammar of the child's two-word utterances, roughly stated, was as follows:

> A sentence (S) is composed of two words, one from the category of *pivot* words (P) and one from the category of *open* words (O), which include all words except pivots.

$$S \longrightarrow P + O$$

A Meaningful Grammar. For a while, pivot grammars were the rage, if one can use that word in science. Now, however, it appears that P + O constructions are used by only *some* children. Even then they reflect a far more sophisticated grammar, more like the adult's, than had been suspected (Brown, 1973b).

Perhaps the pivot grammar's greatest flaw was that, by ignoring the meanings of children's utterances and focusing only on the general types of words used, it told only part of the story. To illustrate, consider "Mommy sock," which was spoken twice by the same child (Bloom, 1970). On the first occasion, the child was picking up her mother's sock; the obvious meaning was "This is Mommy's sock." But on the second occasion, the girl spoke the sentence while her mother was helping her dress; the intended meaning was, "Mommy is putting on my sock." In the first instance, the two words stand in the relation of possessor and possessed; the second depicts an agent (Mommy) and the object (sock) involved in an unnamed action (putting on).

To take account of this kind of difference in meaning, and for other more technical reasons, psychologists have moved to new, more complex grammars, which stress relationships between words. Figure 7.4 shows some of the relationships that have been

Recurrence:	"More milk"
Agent-action:	"Billy hit"
Location:	"Sweater chair"
Attribute:	"Pretty doll"
Negation:	"No bath"

Figure 7.4 *Common two-word relationships in children's speech. (Two others, "possession" and "agent-object," are discussed in the text.)*

identified in children's two-word sentences. According to Roger Brown, 11 of these relationships account for about 75 percent of children's speech during the two-word stage, and 18 relationships almost exhaust the possibilities (1973b).

Rules: Creativity, and Overdoing It

All grammars devised for children's speech have one thing in common: They assume that children follow a set of rules when they construct their two-word speeches. That children learn rules rather than specific words or combinations of words is indicated by the fact that children are, from the beginning, *creative* users of language. They can and do create sentences that nobody has ever heard before, but which are clearly meaningful and easily understood. Consider the primitive beauty of "Allgone sticky," a sentence created by a child who wanted to communicate that he had just washed his hands (Braine, 1963).

On the other hand, children sometimes use rules too slavishly. Instead of creativity, we observe *overregularization.* Parents, teachers, and others who frequently communicate with children are familiar with their tendency to apply a rule even where it is not appropriate. One dog, two dogs; one foot, two *foots.* I walk, I walked; I do, I *doed.*

Consider the reflexive pronoun "himself," used in sentences like "He did it himself." When children first master the use of reflexive pronouns about the age of four, they typically err on this one, creating inaccurately, "He did it *hisself.*" Although some adults do use this form, it is considered substandard. Nevertheless, children invariably use it at one time or another. Why? Most of

the children have never heard it used by an adult, so we cannot attribute their use to imitation. Why do the children create a language form that is, by adult standards, a mistake?

The answer is overregularization (Brown, 1973a). Consider other reflexive pronouns: myself, yourself, herself. All of these are formed by adding "self" to the possessive pronouns (my, your, and her), which are comparable to "his," not to "him." If our language were consistent, "hisself" would be correct. By making this mistake, the child shows she or he is using a rule.

Differentiation and Expansion

As a child's language capabilities develop, her or his grammar more and more closely approximates that of the adult. One of the changes that takes place is that the child begins to *differentiate,* to distinguish among words that before were used more or less interchangeably. For example, from a category that may be called *modifiers,* eventually adjectives, adverbs, and articles become differentiated. *Nouns,* a broad class of words that is used early by children, gradually becomes defined in more detail: There are common nouns, proper nouns, and derivative forms called pronouns, different categories of words that the child comes to use differently. A proper noun is capitalized in English, and it may not be used in contexts where common nouns are commonly used — the big, red Roberta?

Another way children's speech is primitive is the same way the speech of Tarzan is primitive: Me Tarzan. You go. Eat tree. Tarzanic sounds are the result of short sentences, of course, but, more specifically, the

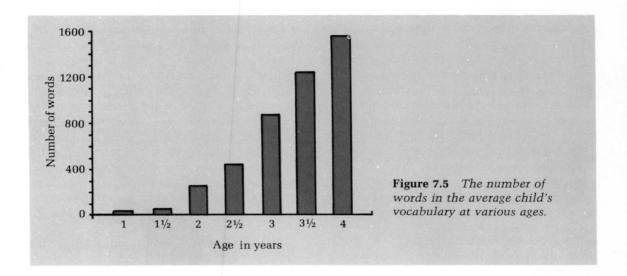

Figure 7.5 *The number of words in the average child's vocabulary at various ages.*

auxiliary words are missing. "Me Tarzan" is as practical, perhaps, as "I am Tarzan," but the use of the many forms of be ("am," "are," "is," and so forth) allows the expression of many fine gradations of meaning. So we can say that, as children grow, their language *expands* to incorporate subtle distinctions and complicated turns of phrase.

Consider, for example, the numerous ways adults phrase negative sentences.

"I am an Italian" becomes "I am *not* an Italian."

"Eat that!" becomes "Don't eat that!"

"That's right!" becomes "That's wrong!" And so forth. Compare these to the child's negation. At the earliest stages, negative words such as "no" or "Not" are tacked onto sentences more or less indiscriminately: "Milk no!" "Not Daddy do!" Very gradually, these simplistic early utterances develop into the more sophisticated adult forms.

DEVELOPING ADULT SPEECH

We have seen a few ways children come to speak more like adults as they get older. But why does children's speech improve? Several simple answers come to mind: The child imitates the adult. The child is rewarded for correct grammar and punished for incorrect grammar. Correct grammar is more efficient in communicating what you want to communicate, so it is favored. And so on. All of these are eminently reasonable assumptions. But research designed to validate these assumptions has not been notably successful.

Modeling and Reinforcement

Very often the parent expands and corrects the child's Tarzanic version of a sentence. Many have surmised that these "models of adult speech" serve to teach children the adult forms. Experiments designed to gather evidence in support of this proposition, however, have been uniformly unsuccessful. Many psychologists have concluded that parental "expanding" has *no* effect on children's language behavior, which is probably an exaggeration. But what does seem clear is that parental expansion-teaching is not very useful if the child is not "ready" to incorporate the expansion proposed. There is a beautiful and classic interchange to illustrate what I have just said, in which the child speaks first, and the mother tries to correct:

"Nobody don't like me."

"No. Say 'Nobody likes me.' "

"Nobody don't like me."

(I will omit here eight duplications of the above interchange. We pick up the conversation with the mother speaking.)

"No. Now listen carefully. Say 'Nobody likes me.' "

"Oh! Nobody don't *likes* me."

If parental modeling is ineffective, perhaps parents have their effect by rewarding adult expressions and punishing childish forms. But research shows quite clearly that in spite of what parents *think* they do, they rarely correct the grammar of their children. Parents will sometimes correct mispronunciations, they will frown on the use of obscene expressions, and they do seem to notice when a child uses a regular form for an irregular verb—"I goed and I swimmed." But expressions like "Why the dog won't eat?" or "Her curl my hair!" seem to slip by unnoticed.

When parents do demonstrate approval and disapproval of their children's speech, which they do quite often, what they correct are *untrue* statements, not ungrammatical sentences. One little girl, trying to indicate her knowledge of her mother's sex, said, "He a girl." The mother responded, "That's right." A little boy said, "Walt Disney comes on Tuesday" and was rebuked: "That's wrong! He comes on Sunday." In short, if one compares all the utterances followed by some sign of parental approval—"Right!" "Good," etc.—to those followed by disapproval—"Wrong!" "No, sweetie," etc.—it is quite clear that parents generally approve of true, and disapprove of false, statements; grammatically correct sentences are not reinforced more often than incorrect expressions (Brown and Hanlon, 1970).

These researchers find it interesting that parents reinforce truthfulness and not well-formed sentences but somehow produce adults "whose speech is highly grammatical but not notably truthful."

Improved Communication Value

If approval and praise are not the rewards of improved speech, perhaps the reinforcement is more subtle. Many have suggested that speech matures because adult speech is more *effective* in communicating ideas. To say "Mama hit!" communicates less than, "Mother, I want you to hit my older brother Jonathan." However, the first is typically uttered to a loving mother in a context that allows her to understand her child without much difficulty. "Why the dog won't eat?" is another example. It is grammatically incorrect, but the question is easily understood.

In one study, children were observed at an age when they were vacillating between crude and mature forms of the same construction—for example, questions (Brown and Hanlon, 1970). Questions elicit responses that can be classified as reasonable in light of the question or as unreasonable (non sequiturs). Thus, if we want to know if more mature forms communicate more effectively, we can see if the childlike forms—"What that is?" "You love Mommy?"—elicit fewer reasonable replies than "What is that?" and "Do you love Mommy?" According to the chief investigator, the scientists "found no evidence whatever" that immature forms led to less understanding (Brown, 1973a, p. 105).

Finally, it is hard to understand what kind of reinforcement might be encouraging certain constructions such as *tag questions*. In the sentence "She is coming, isn't she?" the last two words are the tag question. In English, these constructions are quite complex. Consider English compared with German, in which one tag question (*nicht wahr?* meaning "not right?") is used in all cases. In English, learning how to use tag questions is considerably more difficult. Think about what is involved in the proper use of the following tags:

> She can swim well, can't she?
> She can't swim well, can she?
> She swims well, doesn't she?
> She swims poorly, doesn't she?

Children tend to use simple tags such as "I can go, right?" or "I can't go, huh?" These are perfectly clear. Why do they go on to develop the more complex forms? No one knows, but reinforcement—either in the form of parental rewards or in the form of communication effectiveness—has not been shown to be a prominent factor.

Innate Capacity

If language research has not uncovered any strong effects of variables (such as reinforce-ment) traditionally associated with learning, then how *do* we learn adult speech? Some theorists suggest that we have an innate capacity for language. They would not claim that no learning at all is involved. Instead it has been suggested that all humans have neural structures that make language learning simple, direct, and immediate (Chomsky, 1968). Speaking, by this view, is as natural and as inborn for a child as singing is for a canary. Songbirds generally do not learn their intricate song patterns by imitation, nor do they gradually approximate the adult forms through the selective pressures of reinforcements in the environment. They just sing in full glory, more or less, when the time comes.

Are humans "speechbirds" in the same sense? There is certainly plenty of evidence suggesting that some aspects of language behavior are more or less inevitable. Almost every human speaks, and the time of onset of speech does not vary much. Humans do have certain brain structures that other animals do not, and many of these structures are related to language (Lenneberg, 1967). Also, certain essential features of language—called *universals*—are found in all known languages, in spite of the otherwise wide variations in structure among the many tongues of the world. Nouns and verbs are used in every known language and relate to each other in essentially the same way: as subject and predicate, for example, or as verb and its object (McNeill, 1970). Such grammatical features, in fact, seem so "common-sense" that we forget that things could be otherwise.

One of the most impressive sets of data in support of linguistic innateness is based on the analysis of one child's speech (McNeill, 1966). This child used, at the time, only three grammatical categories: nouns, verbs, and modifiers. If we consider how these categories might be combined to form two-word sentences, we discover there are nine logical possibilities. Of these only four are considered to be part of the "universal grammar." The child uttered frequent examples of these four and not once any of the ungrammatical five. For example, it is permitted that a noun and verb go together as subject and predicate ("Doggie run"), but it is not permitted that two verbs constitute a sentence ("Come eat"). "Come eat" is an example you might think a child would utter, but this and all other instances of verb-verb constructions were totally absent. You might also think the child would at least imitate the adult who says things like "Come eat supper." It never happened.

According to the more extreme theories, humans are born with an innate language capacity and need to learn only the specific words and the nonuniversal rules. This is a very strong statement, and the controversy surrounding the issue is bound to be refreshing. Psychologists, unlike philosophers, have rarely considered the implications of unlearned knowledge and innate ideas; they have stressed learning and the effects of experience to the opposite extreme. (Recall the pigs and raccoons of Chapter 4 whose "innate ideas" about food disrupted the training schedule set down by learning psychologists.)

A Reaction from Learning Theorists

The absence of demonstrated, significant effects of learning variables is a state of affairs that will not likely continue. Learning theorists interested in language have been on the counterattack on a number of fronts.

A particularly effective rebuttal to the innateness theorists has come in regard to imitation. Advocates of innateness have claimed imitation plays no significant role in language acquisition (Dale, 1972), for a number of reasons. One is that many of the earliest utterances cannot possibly be imitations ("Allgone sticky"); they are clearly created by the children who use them. Further, when children do imitate, they imitate only within the scope of their own grammar, leaving out words they have not yet come to use properly. A common imitation of "I am very tall" among children less than three years of age was "I very tall," for the grammar of these children does not yet include the coupling verb "to be" (Brown and Fraser, 1963). If children refuse to imitate those elements of grammar you are trying to teach, how can it be said that imitation plays a major role in acquisition? Another example is the one on p. 284: "Nobody don't like me."

However, as several learning psychologists have pointed out, the type of imitation being dismissed in these examples is simple mimicry; the human child, in other words, is not a parrot (Bandura, 1969; Hebb et al., 1973). Obviously, language learning involves picking up not just simple responses but rules. And there is considerable evidence that rules are learned by imitation. The passive voice—"John was hit by Mary," rather than "Mary hit John"—is rare in children's speech, but children have been induced to use it (learn it?) by imitation (Bandura and Harris, 1966). More generally, rules of all sorts are normally acquired through imitation (Bandura, 1969)—rules of proper conduct, for example. A child who has learned such rules, even by imitation, can *generate* appropriate responses in situations she has never before encountered and in which she has never witnessed the behavior of an adult. In short, once you learn a rule, you can create.

The debate between those who believe in an innate tendency to learn language and those who favor guided experience will continue, of course. Sooner or later, the either-or positions probably will disappear, and research efforts will focus on how inherited factors interact with influences from the environment. As one psychologist has said so well, questions of innate versus learned are like asking whether the length or the width of a rectangle contributes more to the area (Hebb, 1958).

FOCUS

Black English

Many blacks in the urban ghettos of this country speak a variation of English similar to the Southern dialects from which it grew. It is not the only ghetto dialect — there are several — but it is the one that has been most thoroughly investigated (Stewart, 1964; Labov, 1970). It is called *Black English,* a much too grandiose name, but we appear to be stuck with it.

Many whites believe that the language of ghetto blacks is simply a crude, inferior version of Standard English (STE). This is clearly not the case. Black English (BLE) is as lawful and as complex as STE; one would have difficulty proving that either variation is "better" overall. In some instances, BLE is clearly more efficient. BLE uses the word "be" to indicate a habitual or general state, as in "she be working," meaning she has a steady job. "She is working," in STE, does not convey the same sense of a steady job; a more complicated construction would be required.

Mostly, however, BLE and STE are simply different. BLE allows the use of a pronoun following the subject of a sentence, as in "The dog, she bark," a construction for which I once had a fondness, and used, until the inevitable red pencil convinced me that my task, it was fruitless.

Forms of the verb "be" play a major role in STE, but are often missing in BLE. "She a friend" lacks "is," and so do "She tired" and "They working with us." It has been noted that forms of "be" are deleted in BLE only where they can be contracted in STE (Dale, 1972). STE permits "She's a friend" but not "There she's" (for "There she is"). BLE permits "She a friend" but not "There she"; for the latter, it requires the same construction as STE.

This small sample of BLE illustrates some of the differences from STE. Actually BLE and STE are extremely similar, sharing the same rule in the vast majority of cases. In schools, where the BLE of the ghetto kid runs up against the STE of the teacher, the child will often read printed text as if it were BLE. The past tense of "see" in BLE is also "see," as in "Yesterday I see them." Thus many black children will read "saw" as "see," and the teacher will try to correct them. The problem is that the teacher does not realize she or he is dealing with a different dialect, not a simple case of mispronouncing a single word. The result is frustration on both sides.

What can be done? Black ghetto children are extremely verbal; they live in a culture that values quick and skillful manipulation of words (Stodolsky and Lesser, 1967). Unfortunately the words are often slang and the grammar is not STE, and the pervasive racism of this country combines with the differences in dialect to produce many frightened, confused black children. They have stories to tell, but no one to listen.

Some educators have proposed that ghetto children should be taught to read STE as a foreign language, which in a weak sense it is. Unfortunately, this proposal requires good techniques for teaching foreign languages to very young children and such techniques are not yet available. More promising is a proposal to teach children to read in their own dialect, later teaching them to read STE (Baratz and Shuy, 1969). Such programs have been successful with Indian children in Mexico. First taught to read their native Indian language, they subsequently learned to read Spanish much more rapidly than did Indian children who started with Spanish. There are some problems with this approach, though, not the least of which is the attitude of many parents, who see the teaching of BLE as discriminatory and as reinforcing the dialect differences between their children and the favored white society.

NONVERBAL COMMUNICATION

Verbal language—that is, the written or spoken word—is the main way we humans communicate with each other, but it is not the only way. Intentionally or unintentionally, we deliver messages by the tone of our voice, the tilt of our eyebrows, the position of our body, the fire in our eyes. Some of these signals are deliberate and understood by most members of a particular culture. Certain gestures by a traffic officer are well known to mean "Stop," "Go," or "Get that clunker moving!" We nod our heads when we want to answer yes and shake them to say no.

When I was a teenager, I was amazed how many thoughts one could communicate simply by sticking up a finger or two—and I wondered why all these thoughts were obscene. A friend of mine, whom I will call Steve, and I decided to invent a new hand gesture and assign it a benevolent meaning: "I love you." An upraised ring finger on the right hand was, at the time, the only unused configuration, so it was chosen. Steve thought so highly of our new gesture of love that he flashed it to a female classmate, who

Figure 7.6 *Body position is an important means of non-verbal communication. The stance of the white-haired old man above indicates a degree of skepticism about what he's being told. On the left of the photo at right, note the woman's left hand, a gesture indicating an exasperated, questioning attitude: "How should I know if nude therapy will help you, Mary?"*

slapped his face, and the high school principal, who told him he was now on probation. Steve's excuses that the gesture meant "I love you" fell on deaf ears, just as his gesture had fallen on eyes unable to perceive, at a distance, the difference between the ring finger and the middle finger.

How You Say It

It's not always *what* you say that counts, but *how* you say it. A high-pitched, squeaky voice communicates excitement or stress. It may betray the intense feelings of embarrassed teenagers on an important date, the fear of a soldier in battle, the nervousness of a job applicant. Several studies have shown that the pitch of someone's voice tends to rise when she or he is lying (Freedman et al.,

1978), one of the bases for checking "voice stress" in lie detection (see Interlude: Lie Detection, pp. 264–271). Similarly, loudness may be used to emphasize a statement, or it may indicate anger. Pauses and hesitations often communicate uncertainty about what is being said. Thus, "Out of my way, you bully! Or I'll beat you to a pulp!" said in a soft, squeaky, hesitant voice will probably fail in its intended purpose; the verbal communication is in jarring contrast to the nonverbal message.

Changes in the pitch, loudness, or rhythm of part of a sentence—different inflections, they are sometimes called—also carry meaning. An actor's exercise is to repeat a simple sentence, giving the emphasis to each word in turn and thus conveying quite different messages. Try it on something like, "You want to become mellow?'' Emphasizing "you" turns it into "Why *you*, of all people?" Emphasizing "become" suggests you are too laid back already.

The Face and Emotions

It is generally to your advantage for others to know how you are feeling. Expressing anger, for example, indicates to someone that what she or he is doing is meeting with your displeasure. In addition, it communicates the possibility of attack if the behavior in question is not discontinued. It is clearly preferable to express anger *before* attacking than simply to attack, because the anger itself might do the trick and save both people a lot

of grief. In a similar vein, it is to your advantage, usually, to indicate to others what causes you pleasure. If you love jokes but never laugh, no one will tell you jokes.

On the other hand, it is sometimes to your advantage to disguise your emotion. You do not care to broadcast your loathing of your boss or your astonishment at the ugliness of her or his children. The ability to put on a "poker face" is highly valued. With its origins in the ability to conceal joy over an outstanding hand of cards, or fear while pushing a weak hand to its limits, the expression "poker face" has taken on a more general meaning, that in any situation the person has the ability to keep her emotions from being "written all over her face."

Figure 7.7 *During the silent movie era, actors had to depend largely on facial expressions to convey their emotions.*

Naming Emotions from Faces. When psychology became an empirical science, one of the first topics it investigated was people's ability to judge emotions from the faces of other people. Pictures, either drawings or photographs, were presented, and the subject was requested to identify the emotion they showed, either from a list prepared by the experimenter or by giving her or his own label. In an early experiment, 11 subjects were shown photographs and tried to guess the emotions an actor was trying to convey (Langfeld, 1918). The best subject was correct 58 percent of the time; the worst was graded as being in close agreement only 17 percent of the time. These data were hardly encouraging to those who claimed the face is the major communicator of emotions.

It is possible that the facial expressions of an *actor* are not as communicative as a person's real expressions. Another psychologist photographed people subjected to an incredible set of situations, each situation designed to elicit a particular emotion (Landis, 1924). One of the 16 situations had the subjects witnessing the beheading of a white rat. Many subjects responded to this sight with a sickly smile, the same sickly smile that appeared in many other situations. The psychologist concluded that in ordinary people there was no significant relationship between emotions and facial expressions.

Other psychologists, puzzled at the negative results for what appeared to be a quite reasonable hypothesis, looked for flaws in the design of prior experiments. One psychologist concerned himself with the problem of *naming* an emotion (Woodworth, 1938). It was clear that in many experiments judging the facial expression of actors, subjects were penalized for using odd words; if the actor intended anger, for example, and

the subject guessed rage, is this a hit or a miss? By carefully examining the judgments of 100 subjects judging 86 poses, Woodworth devised a crude scale, as follows:

1. Love, Happiness, Mirth
2. Surprise
3. Fear, Suffering
4. Anger, Determination
5. Disgust
6. Contempt

This is a scale; it is not simply six categories. If every judgment is placed in one of these six categories—both rage and anger go into category 4—subjects agree with each other extremely well. And, if they disagree, the disagreements almost invariably fall into neighboring categories. If most subjects call a particular expression *fear* (category 3), the few who don't are most likely to call it *surprise* (2) or *anger* (4).

Once the scale was devised, it was used in a typical face-judging experiment. This time both the emotion intended by the actor and the emotion guessed by the subject were listed by one of the broad categories, not by the specific emotion. For example, if the actor intended to show anger—category 4—and the subject guessed rage—also category 4—the subject was given credit for a correct judgment. Using this method, subjects were nearly perfect in their judgments.

Sources of Facial Expressions. In his book *Expressions of the Emotions in Man and Animals*, Charles Darwin (1872) suggested that expressing emotion in bodily, primarily facial, gestures was related to important behaviors in animal life. Baring its teeth has a very practical purpose for an angry dog, and we usually assume that a dog with its teeth bared is angry. Humans rarely bite each

Figure 7.8   *Chimps and humans smile in similar situations. Members of both species smile nervously in the presence of a superior and, of course, when they're enjoying themselves.*

other in a fight; still, they often bare their teeth or pull their lips back tight when they are angry.

Darwin believed that all an animal's emotional expressions could be related to practical habits in its personal or evolutionary history. Another example is the facial gesture many people use when they are disgusted; they look as though they were about to spit something out, which would be a practical reaction to offensive material. Similarly, the adult expression of sadness—"she looks as if she were about to cry"—is related to actual crying.

The smile is another facial expression believed to be related to primitive behaviors, but scientists disagree about what behavior pattern it is connected with. Some believe the smile is related to the grimace of attack, some believe it is related to the grimace of fear, and some think it derives from grooming gestures in which the teeth are exposed to bite the fleas and ticks off a good friend (Eibl-Eibesfeldt, 1972). Perhaps the last hypothesis is the most appealing.

Whether or not all facial communications really have some prominent heritage in important behavior patterns is uncertain. In any case, the face certainly is used to convey important emotional messages. The smile, whatever its origin, communicates appeasement and friendship in all known human cultures; it is used appropriately even by people blind from birth. A smile is disarming, sometimes literally. During the war in Vietnam, there was a report of an American who came face to face with two Vietcong. His gun misfired and he smiled, which momentarily stopped the opposing soldiers. A brief moment of human contact followed, eye contact between deadly enemies. Fear swept over the American, however, and he ejected the faulty cartridge and killed the two Vietcong (Eibl-Eibesfeldt, 1972).

Face versus Body. Another series of experiments confirmed that the face is a fairly trustworthy source of information. People delivered verbal messages in which their facial expressions, tone of voice, and the actual words sometimes told different stories. The facial expressions were judged by subjects to carry the most reliable message; the relative weights were computed as 55 percent face, 38 percent vocal tone, and only 7 percent for the words (Mehrabian, 1972). That is to say, if a poker player says her hand is a poor one, but her face says it's a powerhouse, we don't bet; we trust the face.

On the other hand, someone who is controlling her facial expression still may be betrayed by the rest of her body (Ekman and Friesen, 1969). A poker player might be able to keep the thrill of a powerful hand from showing in her face, but she may unconsciously lean forward in anticipation of collecting the chips. This finding stands to reason, for we know that our face is a prime

source of information to others; if we are trying to deceive them, we are careful about our face, while we are less cautious about our legs, feet, and hands, which ordinarily are less communicative.

In other experiments, the face was found to express the *nature* of a particular emotion, but it told subjects less about the *intensity* of the emotion. The face tells you whether it is fear or anger; but whether the emotion is extreme or mild is more directly indicated by other means—body position, for example (Ekman, 1965).

Message Control in the Face

We have been discussing the nonverbal messages about one's emotional state from the point of view of an observer who might be trying to "read" someone's face. This hypothetical "someone," of course, has a point of view, too. She knows full well that her face is a message board, and she is usually in control of the messages she cares to display. There are many ways we *use* our faces in communication. Most of the time we try to supplement the verbal message, showing an angry face to back up our angry words or smiling to emphasize our assertions of happiness.

A number of very specific facial gestures have been identified that convey specific meanings, almost the way words do (Ekman and Friesen, 1975). The eye wink is an example; it is an intentional symbol, and its meaning is usually clear to both sender and receiver. In different contexts, the wink signifies agreement, flirtation, or, in my friend Lewie's eyes, "I am having a *fantastic* time conning this guy." The raised eyebrow is an-

Figure 7.9   *The same facial gesture—an upward jerk of the eyebrows—is used to indicate greeting in widely diverse cultures.*

other common gesture. If it is raised and held, it indicates a questioning attitude. A quick flick of the eyebrows to someone approaching, however, is a sign of greeting; its form and meaning is the same in cultures around the world (Eibl-Eibesfeldt, 1972). Eye-

brows can also "punctuate" a sentence. Watch someone with an animated face talk sometime; you'll see her flick her eyebrows to emphasize certain words or phrases. "The expression accents the spoken word as italics do the written word" (Ekman and Friesen, 1975, p. 39).

Perhaps the best examples of intentional management of the face's message are those involving deception. A salesperson puts on an insincere look of sincerity, an embezzler looks surprised at the empty safe. Not all deceptive faces are put on for evil purposes, however; in many situations, social customs ask us to disguise our true feelings. Traditionally, in the past, men were taught to show no fear, for example, and women were expected to control (disguise) their faces when they were angry. At funerals, it is considered unseemly to display more grief than members of the immediate family.

Psychologists have identified five major types of facial deceit (Ekman and Friesen, 1975). First, one can *modulate* a facial expression; that is, one can adjust the apparent intensity of an emotion, up or down. Someone might be willing to show fear but not as much as she really feels. Or a ho-hum birthday gift might require an exaggerated display of happiness, so the giver's feelings aren't hurt. Second, one can *qualify* a facial expression by taking on an additional expression as a kind of comment on (or qualification of) the basic message. The smile is a frequent qualifier. A very sad person, relating a tale of woe, may add a smile at the end, communicating "I'm in control. I'm not going to kill myself." How the qualifier is used can make a difference in the message. A smile after anger suggests that the person will not go too far with her anger. A smile blended or mixed with anger suggests she is enjoying her rage in a sadistic sort of way.

The remaining three types of facial deceit all involve falsifying a facial expression. You can *simulate* an emotion when in fact you feel nothing, as a child might feign pleasure when her or his birthday presents are all clothing. You can *neutralize* an emotion, that is, show no indication of feeling when in fact you are very happy, sad, angry, fearful, or whatever; this is the widely acclaimed "poker face." Or you can *mask* one emotion with another. Someone trying out for a competitive position in a play or on a sports team does not want to look happy when her chief competitor performs poorly, so she puts on a sad expression, even if she is laughing on the inside.

Psychologists can also say a few things about *detecting* facial deceit (Ekman and Friesen, 1975). Often detection is not a problem, since the "other emotion" is meant to be read; it is part of the message. Qualifications in particular are part of a total communication. Consider two lovers saying goodbye because one has a fantastic job opportunity in another city; the happy-you-got-the-job look is qualified by the sad-you're-going look. Even when someone's intent is to disguise and mislead, a sharp observer often can pick up a clue to the true emotion, or at least a hint that the displayed emotion is not to be trusted. The deceptive person's timing may be off—she may hold a smile too long. Or the true emotion may flicker across her face before she gets it under control. Video tapes often show these true "micro-expressions" preceding a false face; they last maybe 1/25 of a second, but they are visible, if you are looking for them. Another principle of deception is that most people try to control the emotional expression in the lower part of their face, particularly around the mouth. Often the upper face —the eyes, eyebrows, and forehead lines— displays the true emotion in spite of the stiff upper lip.

Looking

The region of the eyes is very important in nonverbal communication, with flickering eyebrows and lids that can tense or relax, open wide or squint. But the eyes themselves—"these lovely lamps, these windows of the soul," as Guillaume de Salluste called them—have their own important role to play (Argyle, 1978). There is a language of looking, for example, that most people learn early in life—in fact, are sometimes taught: "Don't stare; it's not nice," or "Don't look at him; don't encourage him." Eye contact with a panhandler means you're sure to be approached for a handout. Eye contact with a weirdo on the subway . . . well, let's say it isn't the best policy. Eye contact with a lover, however, is heartily recommended; exploring another's soul through the eyes can be an intense, magical moment.

People lie with their eyes, just as they lie with their faces. In one study, people classified as more nearly Machiavellian—more like people who will do anything to achieve their ends; unprincipled people—were compared with normals in a situation in which they had to lie (Exline, 1972). The Machiavellians looked squarely in the eyes of the experimenter while lying; the normals could not maintain eye contact. Since eye contact is typically taken as an indication of sincerity and truth, the Machiavellians were obviously better at making a lie seem truthful,

Figure 7.10   *What does the eye contact tell you about this conversation?*

which of course was their purpose. The stereotyped used-car salesperson is a good example of these abilities.

Threat is one of the common messages conveyed by looking. Simply staring at someone is sometimes enough to provoke an attack. In an interesting study (Ellsworth et al., 1972), one of the experimenters stood at the corner of a busy intersection. As people stopped for the red light, the experimenter stared at them intently, while another experimenter clocked their "escape" across the intersection when the light turned green. These stared-at subjects moved considerably faster than average. Staring at someone is commonly interpreted as a threat, and people who are stared at may react in different ways. In one experiment, someone stared at subjects who were later placed in a position to act aggressively toward the starer. The stared-at subjects appeared intimidated; they delivered less punishment to the starer than other subjects did to someone who had not stared (Ellsworth and Carlsmith, 1973). On the other hand, in my own community, there was recently a case in which a teenaged boy murdered another teenaged boy and raped his girlfriend. Why? "He looked at me," said the defendant.

Another message commonly conveyed by eye contact is attraction or love. In the right circumstances, a meeting of the eyes across a crowded room can be an electric event. Lovers look into the eyes of their beloved more frequently than pairs of people who are not romantically involved (Rubin, 1970). And simple eye contact is not the only way eyes communicate love. Consider an experiment in which male subjects were shown two photographs of a woman's face and asked to state their preference (Hess, 1965). The choice was difficult because as far as the subjects could tell, the two photos were identical: the same picture of the same woman (see Figure 7.11). Forced to choose, most picked the same photograph, although they could not say why. In fact the photo usually selected had been retouched to make the pupils of the woman's eyes slightly larger. Since it had been previously determined that pupil size increases with sexual interest (other factors such as light being equal), the subjects were choosing the woman who was exhibiting more interest in them.

Figure 7.11 *Which of these two photos do you think male subjects would choose as more attractive? Why?*

SUMMARY

1. Language uses symbols according to a set of rules (grammar) in an attempt to communicate meaning. According to this definition, most animal communication systems are not languages.

2. Attempts to teach language to chimpanzees were unsuccessful until sign language instead of speech was used. A chimp named Washoe learned over 150 signs and used them to create "sentences" she had never seen before. Such creative productivity has become a prime indicator of language.

3. A child's first systematic vocalization is cooing, then babbling. Around the age of one, the child begins to speak. In the stage of one-word speech, each word is used to express a complex idea; usually it must be heard in context to be understood. The later stage of two-word speech is characterized by telegraphic communications and the frequent use of certain general-purpose (pivot) words.

4. Young children, like Washoe, exhibit creative productivity, apparently using grammatical rules to create completely novel sentences like "Allgone sticky." Sometimes children overregularize; this misapplication of grammatical rules is additional evidence that they are learning rules as well as forms. Children's speech is more primitive than adult speech mainly in that it is less differentiated.

5. Recent attempts to construct a children's grammar emphasize the *meaning* of children's utterances as well as their format by describing the relationships between words — agent-object, possession, etc. Such descriptions apply to adult speech, too, although adult grammars are more complex.

6. It is still unclear what induces children to progress from primitive to adult speech. Attempts to discover strong effects of imitation and reinforcement on children's acquisition of language have been unsuccessful: Parents reward true statements more than grammatical statements, and childlike forms do not seem to communicate much less effectively than adult forms.

7. Many psychologists believe the important capabilities for language are innate, and only specific words and some localized grammatical rules need be learned. The presence in all known languages of certain essential features called *universals* supports this belief. Learning theorists contend that although children evidently do not learn adult forms of speech through mimicry, they probably do learn grammatical rules through imitation.

8. What we say is normally supplemented by how we say it; voice inflections, facial expressions, and "body language" add a nonverbal message to our communications. A higher than usual pitch to a voice, for example, indicates stress and has been used as a crude lie detector.

9. Many facial expressions are primitive reactions, possibly derived from more complex behaviors — the expression of disgust is probably related to "spitting out," for example. Facial expressions can be intentionally altered to convey the message we want. We can modulate, qualify, simulate, or mask an emotion, or neutralize it with a "poker face."

10. Eye contact can communicate threats, affection, or a number of other messages, depending on the context.

USING PSYCHOLOGY

While you're watching a short emotion-packed drama on television with a friend, you can test your skill at identifying emotions without using verbal cues. Turn the sound down and plug or cover your ears well so that you can't hear the sound at all, but your friend can (or better yet, have your friend use earphones, if they are available, to hear the television). Another way to mask out the TV sound is for you to listen to music via earphones. Have your friend tell you when an emotion is being portrayed by a character in the drama, and guess what it is. Since you cannot hear the sound track, you must rely on facial and body expression and situational cues. See whether your description of the emotion matches that of your friend, who is probably very accurate at recognzing the emotions portrayed because he or she has the benefit of verbal cues as well. From experimental evidence discussed in the text, one would expect your guesses to be quite accurate since facial expression, situational information, and body expression are considered to be revealing cues to the emotion another person is expressing.

SUGGESTED READINGS

Lane, H. *The wild boy of Aveyron.* Harvard U. Press, 1976.
A fascinating account of attempts to teach language to a 12-year-old boy discovered running wild in the forests of France around 1800. You'll learn a lot about language in general.

Ekman, P., & Friesen, W. *Unmasking the face.* Spectrum, 1974.
Written by two of the foremost researchers on facial expressions of emotions, this nontechnical book tells you how to identify emotions and how to tell when people are trying to disguise them.

Clark, H. H., & Clark, E. V. *Psychology and language.* Harcourt Brace Jovanovich, 1977.
An outstanding textbook, covering both language learning in children and language use and comprehension in adults.

Dale, P. S. *Language development.* 2nd ed. Holt, Rinehart & Winston, 1976.
A relatively easy introduction to theories and research on child language. Also covers the relationship between language and thought and Black English.

INTERLUDE

Human Sexuality

Sol Gordon, director of the Institute for Family Research and Education at Syracuse University, was expressing the frustration of many psychologists whose work deals with human sexuality. Much of the research, he claimed, is misdirected: "A psychologist goes to an average couple and says, 'Couple, how many outlets do you have?' And the couple says, '20, 30.' . . . I mean they're talking about electrical outlets until the things get clarified " (Gordon, 1977, p . 13). When the couple understands that the psychologist is talking about sex, they say, "Oh, six or seven outlets per week." But what this means may be that they had one rapturous week in 1978 when they had coitus six or seven times, and (as so often happens in human affairs) they like to think of that maximum performance as their average. Then other couples read the report and feel inferior.

In another study, 300 pregnant teenagers (unmarried) were asked if they had wanted to get pregnant. Many said "Yes, I wanted something to love and care for." A matched group of 300 teenagers was asked if they would like to get pregnant. Not one said yes. They said, "I'm 14 years old! What do you think, I'm stupid?" Suspecting that the first group's pregnancies were caused more by ignorance than a desire for something to care for, Gordon asked those girls why they had not taken precautions. "Oh, I did. I used one of my mother's birth control pills." "I didn't think you could get pregnant the first time." "We didn't think I could get pregnant if we had sex standing up" (Gordon, 1977).

What does this say for sex education? "We think we have sex education in schools," says Gordon. "We have courses on plumbing." Not only is the information on contraception not getting across, but there is practically nothing about affection in sex. "Where is love? Where is caring for another human being?" Why don't we discuss the contrast between exploitation and the mature devotion of two equals, not merely such topics as the difference between vaginal and clitoral orgasms?

It's easy to become frustrated and depressed about human sexuality. It affects people's lives so terribly at times—an underprivileged girl's unwanted pregnancy, a traumatic rape. Sexuality is too often seen in its lowest form—exploitative, selfish, a meaningless flash of pleasure—a particularly depressing picture for an activity that is potentially sublime. Psychological studies of human sexuality, I'm sorry to say, do not add much to our understanding of its potential ecstasy. On the other hand, psychologists are aware that children have sexual ideas, as many people are unwilling to admit, and that people over the age of 70 or 80 do, too.

We will examine, in this interlude, how we feel and act about sex over the course of life. At the end we will briefly examine homosexuality, that striking alternative behavior pattern that psychologists should be able to understand quite well, but don't.

FREUD AND CHILDHOOD SEXUALITY

In 1905, an almost unknown physician named Sigmund Freud published a book entitled *Three Essays on the Theory of Sexuality.* Unlike his earlier book, *The Interpretation of Dreams, Three Essays* was widely read; and it provoked an immediate and violent reaction. Freud's theories had grown from unsubstantiated nonsense to *dangerous* nonsense, according to his critics. For better or for worse, Sigmund Freud became one of the most famous names in psychology.

And what was Freud's offense? He said, "We do wrong entirely to ignore the sexual life of children." Freud pointed out that children are capable of all of the thoughts and many of the physical acts of sex. They are interested in sex, and many of their ideas and behaviors are motivated by the sex drive. In particular, many emotional disturbances in childhood involve the frustration, anger, fear, and anxiety of a sexual being who is too young — too ignorant and incompetent, overly inhibited by parents — to satisfy his or her sexual urges. A society that views the child as innocent, Freud continued, and tries to suppress all sexual expression with severe punishment, will create adults unable to love — or work — effectively.

Perhaps these abstract sentiments by themselves would not have triggered the deluge of destructive criticism that came down on Freud. It was, I believe, his descriptions of individual patients that jangled the nerves of Victorian Europe. Imagine yourself a respectable European scholar in 1905, reading Freud's report of his treatment of Dora, a beautiful teenaged girl. At one point Freud interprets Dora's nervous cough:

> So it is not to be wondered at that this hysterical girl of nineteen, who had heard of the occurrence of such a method of sexual intercourse [sucking at the male organ] should have developed an unconscious phantasy of this sort and should have given it expression by an irritation in her throat and by coughing (Freud, 1959, p. 63).

Freud interpreted the case as a whole in terms of Dora's sexually based love for (1) Mr. K, a married friend of the family, (2) her father, (3) Mrs. K (!), and a few others, some male, some female. In the process, Freud gave direct and meaningful illustrations of his view of the child's sexuality, that the child is — my favorite Freudian concept! — a polymorphous pervert. "Polymorphous" means "many forms"; the child is interested in all forms of sexual pleasure, even those that adults would consider perverted.

This stuff is pretty heavy, even in a liberated society like today's. In 1905, it must have been ghastly. Freud compounded his problems with his abstract theory of childhood sexuality, the theory of sexual stages. The first stage, the *oral stage,* was meant to describe the kind of sexual pleasure an infant one year of age or less can and wants to experience: involving the mouth. Breast-sucking is the favorite activity. The idea that the cuddly little infant, suckling his or her mother's breast, was experiencing sexual satisfaction—well, that idea was not too popular in 1905. The second stage, the *anal stage,* was worse yet; the child is supposed to experience his or her primary sexual pleasures by passing or, in some cases, withholding feces.

But the coup de grace was the next stage, called the *phallic stage.* The young child, aged three to five or thereabouts, is supposed to develop an intense sexual interest in the parent of the opposite sex. The repercussions of such interests on personality development are discussed in Chapters 8 and 10, but here try to sympathize with those scientist-parents who were reluctant to view the love of a father and a daughter as sexual, or the love of the son for the mother as intending sexual intercourse. It was probably too much to accept, for most of Freud's critics.

Freud was indeed shocking, but was he right? Most of the details of Freud's theory—about the specific sexual stages, for example—are practically impossible to test experimentally, and the details of Freud's interpretations—about Dora's cough, for example—are open to alternative interpretations. Nevertheless, Freud must be credited with alerting us to the sexual lives of children. Psychologists universally accept the general notion of childhood sexuality, even though they may disagree with the specifics. There is little doubt that children are interested in sensual pleasures involving various parts of their bodies, including but not restricted to genital organs. Since Freud opened our eyes, we can easily observe that children often act to increase sensual pleasure, and that they are often frustrated and confused in their attempts. These childhood frustrations and confusions, if they result in severe emotional conflicts, can profoundly affect the adult sexual lives of children who suffer them. These are a few of Freud's legacies to the study of human sexuality.

PREMARITAL AND EXTRAMARITAL SEXUALITY

Before Freud, most parents didn't think much about their children's sexuality until puberty, the biological time of sexual maturity. Even today, many people think of prepubertal children as "innocent," or at least inexperienced. But the data show quite a different picture. Even in the 1930s and 1940s, according to the famous Kinsey reports (Kinsey et al., 1948, 1953), 45 percent of all males had masturbated before the age of 13; 15 percent of all females had, too. In a survey published in 1974 (Hunt, 1974), these figures had increased to 63 percent for boys and 33 percent for girls. Similarly, a national survey published in 1973 (Sorenson, 1973) found that 44 percent of boys and 30 percent of girls surveyed had had sexual intercourse before the age of 16. (Kinsey's figures, obtained in the 1940s, were 39 percent for boys and only 3 percent for girls.) Clearly sexual behavior of all sorts is well under way by the time children reach adolescence. And early sexual activity is increasing, especially among females, who now approximate males in their level of sexual activity.

No doubt the increases in sexual behavior, even among prepubertal children in their early teens, reflect what the youth counterculture of the 1960s called "the new morality." This change in sexual attitudes has been damned by some as a libertine hedonism that foreshadows the decline of Western culture; others have praised it as an acceptance of sensuality that will lead to a new age of the Whole Person. A more measured and objective view is given by young people themselves: "When it comes to morality in sex," agreed three-fourths of the American adolescents in one survey (Sorenson, 1973), "the important thing is the way people treat each other, not the things they do together." The new morality, in other words, emphasizes the quality of the relationship, not the sexual acts. "It's all right for young people to have sex before getting married if they are in love with each other" is a statement endorsed by 80 percent of the adolescent boys and 72 percent of the adolescent girls in this country. In contrast, the majority of young people oppose the use of pressure or force in sex, exploitation, and sex solely for physical enjoyment.

Sexual behavior among older teenagers and young adults, generally speaking, corresponds to the sexual attitudes. In a 1972 survey of 18- to 24-year-olds, 95 percent of the men and 81 percent of the women reported

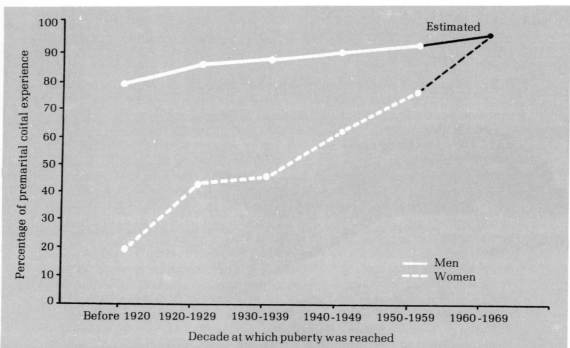

Figure 1 *The percentage of men and women with premarital sexual experience is increasing, and the rate of increase is greater for women. Unless societal standards change, percentages will probably level out somewhat below 100 percent, with few if any differences between the sexes.*

having premarital intercourse (Hunt, 1974). These figures show a dramatic increase from Kinsey's figures for the 1940s, which were 49 percent for men and 25 percent for women. What's more, the figures are still rising; soon, if present trends continue, close to 100 percent of both men and women will have had sexual experience before marriage (see Figure 1). It should be noted, however, that many young people have religious principles that prohibit premarital sex; as a result, premarital sexual activity is very low in certain communities—12 percent among women attending one church-affiliated college, for example (Packard, 1968).

The generally permissive attitude of the new morality toward premarital sex does not extend to extramarital sex. Articles and movies about mate-swapping notwithstanding, both young and old people view sexual fidelity as essential to the marriage contract; infidelity is considered a serious moral offense (Hunt, 1974). About half of married men have at least one "affair" in their lifetime, which indicates that these moral standards are not easily kept. But even the offenders see their behavior as "wrong": The average philanderer experiences considerable guilt. Perhaps for this reason, unfaithful husbands' extramarital encounters bring them less pleasure than marital sex (Hunt, 1974). There has been no noticeable increase in extramarital sex among men since Kinsey's time (the 1940s). Although there has been a significant increase among young married women, this is more an indication of the death of the double standard than a measure of increasing permissiveness toward extramarital sex. The attitudes of most Americans, including young women, are firmly set against it.

MARITAL SEX THROUGHOUT THE LIFE SPAN

If a married couple put a nickel into a jar every time they had coitus during the first year of marriage, and then took a nickel out every time they had coitus after that, the jar would never empty. So said my friend Leo, a road packer for a highway construction crew I once worked on. (Leo didn't use the term "coitus," but a word to that effect.) Leo's theory, that sexual activity decreases dramatically as the marriage grows older, was of course exaggerated for humor's sake. Fortunately, the data show a more gradual decrease in sexual activity. By my estimate, assuming an average age of marriage, no divorce, and an average life span, one would have to put in nickels for the first fifteen years for Leo's joke to work. In fact, fully 20 percent of an average person's sexual encounters occur after the age of 55. Figure 2 shows data on average weekly frequency from two eras, the

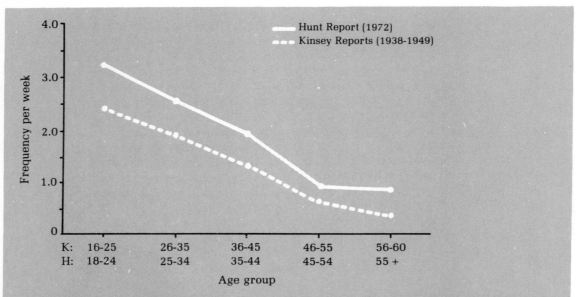

Figure 2 *Sexual intercourse among married couples (male and female estimates combined). Comparing the 1970s to the 1940s, the bad news is that frequency still declines with age. The good news is that frequency for all age groups is up; it's better to be 40 and average today than it was to be 30 and average in the 1940s.*

1940s and the 1970s. The gradual decrease with age is apparent in both curves, and so is the difference 30 years of increasing sexual permissiveness can make, even for the more elderly among us.

Biological factors may account for some of the decline in sexual activity with age. Sex researchers Masters and Johnson (1966, 1970) have found that older men take longer to have an erection when sexually stimulated, ejaculate with less force, and require more time—sometimes up to 24 hours—before they can perform again. Women show age-related decreases in the lubrication and elasticity of the vagina, especially after menopause around the age of 50. Contractions of the vagina during orgasm continue for a shorter average duration as women grow older.

Psychological and social factors also affect the frequency of marital coitus. Psychologically, the fear of losing sexual competence—sometimes called performance anxiety—can cause impotence in men. Some couples become bored with each other, at least sexually. An important social factor affecting the amount of sexual activity is the presence of children; children in the home limit the opportunities for coitus and also the allowable degree of chasing, hollering, and other exciting accompaniments of the sex act. Another social factor, particularly prominent in the middle years of life (35 to 60 or so), is the pressure of work; when one or both members of a couple are working, they spend less time at home, and work they bring home can spoil the few precious hours they do have there (Mussen et al., 1979b).

HOMOSEXUALITY

Although heterosexual behavior is the most popular and socially acceptable expression of sexuality, it is not the only expression. Some of the alternatives are highly respectable, such as celibacy among priests; others are generally scorned—as Leo says, ten years on the farm and the sheep get to looking mighty pretty. One of the most common and controversial alternatives to heterosexuality is homosexuality: sexual behavior involving two members of the same sex.

Until quite recently, homosexuality was severely condemned in our society; it was considered morally wrong and psychiatrically unhealthy, and it was against the law. In the past decade or two, however, there has been accelerating acceptance of homosexuality. Surveys of young people, for example, show rapidly increasing numbers who believe that a homosexual relationship between consenting adults is a private matter, involving decisions that are none of the business of anyone except the individuals involved (Yankelovich, 1974). In 1973 the American Psychiatric Association removed homosexuality from its list of psychiatric disorders. Even a few church officials have called for, if not acceptance, at least tolerance and understanding.

One result of the decreasing suppression of homosexuality is increasing openness among those who practice it. People with a predominantly or exclusively homosexual orientation have been admitting publicly that they are gay—"coming out of the closet." Gay liberation movements demand respect for this alternative sexual preference and equal treatment for gays under the laws. Books, magazine and newspaper articles, plays, and movies about the homosexual experience proliferate.

When attitudes become more permissive, the incidence of the behavior in question usually increases, as we have seen in the case of premarital coitus. Therefore, it is surprising to find almost universal agreement among researchers that there has been *no* measurable increase in homosexual behavior in the United States from the time of Kinsey's survey (the 1940s) to the present. Several investigations have produced the following

average figures: About 20 to 25 percent of adult males have had homosexual experiences, but most of these occurred during childhood and adolescence, in a sort of sex-play, exploratory fashion (Hunt, 1974). About 2 percent of American males are exclusively homosexual, and another 3 percent are "occasionally" so (Gagnon and Simon, 1970). Perhaps a better term for the "occasional" homosexual is bisexual, meaning he can respond sexually to whomever he is presently in love with, regardless of his or her sex. The statistics for females, across the board, are about half of those for males: Around 12 or 13 percent of females have had homosexual experiences, and around 1 percent are exclusively homosexual; another 2 or 3 percent are bisexual (Karlen, 1971; Hunt, 1974; McCary, 1978). These figures in most cases are similar to Kinsey's figures for the 1940s and in some cases are lower (Hunt, 1974).

Why are some people predominantly heterosexual in orientation whereas others are predominantly homosexual? An interesting and thoroughly researchable question, one that psychologists should be able to answer. Alas, such is not the case. There have been a few studies of hormonal differences between heterosexuals and homosexuals, the idea being that perhaps male homosexuals have less of the so-called male hormones or more of the female hormones; these studies have generally found no differences, or they have been inconclusive (but see Kolodny et al., 1971). The same picture appears in the few studies of environmental differences between homosexuals and heterosexuals. Most are inconclusive, although for males the family environment of a dominant mother paired with a weak and detached father appears often (Bieber et al., 1962). There is no generally accepted theory of homosexuality among psychologists today.

SEX AND LOVE

I want to conclude this brief interlude on sexuality with a brief statement about love and intimacy—"hearts and flowers stuff," as Leo called it. Love and sex are separable, to be sure. It is possible to love someone without having sexual relations or even desiring them, and it's certainly possible to have loveless sex. Nevertheless, love and sex together represent one of the highest human experiences. Love become physical is the ultimate protection against isolation and loneliness, a sharing, a caring, an intricate dance of life. Sex become spiritual is, as one young woman put it, "the ultimate, mind-blowing experience, . . . the ultimate human connection" (Gordon, 1974, p. 231). Sex researchers find their subjects keep the goal of loving sex constantly in mind. One investigator concludes,

> The new sexual freedom operates largely within the framework of our long-held cherished cultural values of intimacy and love. Even while it asserts its freedom from marriage, it is . . . considered successful by its participants when it grows, deepens, and leads to ever-stronger commitment, and unsuccessful and a wasted effort when it does not (Hunt, 1974, p. 154).

Masters and Johnson (1975) say, "Sex removed from the positive influence of the total personality can become boring, unstimulating, and possibly immaterial." But I like Leo's comment, when I asked him if he knew anything about aphrodisiacs (sexual stimulants): "Hearts and flowers, kid. Love is the greatest aphrodisiac in the world."

SUGGESTED READINGS

Hunt, M. *Sexual behavior in the 1970s.* Dell, 1974.
    A detailed nationwide survey of sexual behavior in the early 1970s, written for the intelligent layperson.
Peplau, L. A., & Hammen, C. L. (eds.). Sexual behavior: social psychological issues. *Journal of Social Issues,* 1977, *33* (No. 2).
    An entire journal issue devoted to the social psychology of sexuality. Topics include the nature of sexual arousal, the relationship between sex and aggression, and the ethics of research on human sexual behavior.

PART

3

Personality and Development

"Personality" is not easy to define; but (as one psychologist put it) whatever it is, development is what leads up to it. In Chapter 8, we will focus on the cognitive and social development of the personality during childhood. We will look at such notorious Freudian concepts as the Oedipus complex, anal compulsiveness, and penis envy, and at Jean Piaget's fascinating studies of children. But our personalities do not cease to grow and change when we reach adulthood. In Chapter 9 we will examine the formative experiences that shape most of us in later years, from marriage and career choice to aging and the approach of death.

Next, in the chapter on personality, we will discuss three major ways to view an individual's unique identity. Is a person a combination of Freud's impulsive id, realistic ego, and moralistic superego? Or are we humans more like other animals, pulled to create and explore by some kind of cosmic chunk of cheese at the end of the maze? Then there is the third viewpoint, that human motives *are* special and unique, especially the highest motives that lead us to the spiritual mountaintops of self-actualization.

Behavioral Objectives

1. List Piaget's successive stages of cognitive development and describe characteristic behaviors that are learned during each stage.
2. Define what Piaget calls an "operation" and give some examples.
3. Describe a Piagetian "conservation" problem and tell why preoperational children have difficulty with this type of problem.
4. List some ways in which egocentric thought manifests itself in the preoperational child's behavior.
5. Define and give an example of reversibility.
6. Describe how the child's ability to classify or categorize improves as he or she develops.
7. Explain why "mothering" is extremely important to a child's development and tell what happens when a child isn't "mothered."
8. List and describe the Freudian stages of personality development; discuss their presumed effects on later personality and behavior.
9. Define and give examples of accommodation and assimilation.

CHAPTER

8

Child Development

What do you think of when you think of a child? Birth. A bundle of joy. A bright-eyed infant exploring the surrounding environment. The first triumphant step, the first word. Into the world of the Peanuts gang and Dennis the Menace. School. Adolescence and Happy Days. Graduation. The parents cry, they're so happy.

It was not always so. It may be hard to believe, but parents in centuries past, by all accounts, had a profoundly negative attitude toward children. At best, children were considered a nuisance, kept around because they might later contribute to the family pocketbook. At worst, the children were deliberately murdered by their parents; in most societies, it was considered no crime to dispose of one's own "possession." Unwanted children were thrown into rivers and cesspools, stuffed into large pots to starve, or left naked on roadsides as prey for wild animals (deMause, 1974). Daughters, who were of less economic value than sons, often were routinely destroyed, as were illegitimate children, babies with birth defects, and cranky infants. A famous philosopher wrote a treatise on "How to Recognize the Newborn That is Worth Saving."

Children who weren't murdered were kept quiet by various incredible means. Severe beatings were not only permitted, they were encouraged—to break the "evil" will of the child. Opium and liquor were used in such quantities that drug-induced deaths among infants were commonplace. Virtually every known society had some version of "swaddling," which involves wrapping the infant tightly in a bandage-like garment to keep it from moving its hands and legs. Swaddled infants were left, like parcels, in any convenient corner, or hung from hooks and forgotten.

When the children were old enough to be of economic value, they were exploited mercilessly. Many died from work too difficult or work that required more nutrition than they were given. Many were sold outright to other families as domestic servants or, worse yet, to rich landowners as sexual slaves.

Sometime between the fourteenth and seventeenth centuries, attitudes toward children began to change (deMause, 1974). Infanticide began to decrease, and although beatings were still an everyday experience for many children, parents began to speak of "molding" their offspring into acceptable adults. In the late 1600s, we begin to find the very first discussions of "parental affection" as a possible factor in children's development (Kagan, 1977). In a rather drastic turnaround, the "innocence" of children became a popular concept, and clergy began to argue that "evil topics" like sex should not be discussed (much less practiced) in the presence of children. Children were set off from the rest of society as a special group, even dressed differently (Aries, 1962). The modern era of "beloved children" had begun.

How does one properly raise a beloved child? How does one train a child to grow up achievement-oriented and creative, and not rebellious or cruel? These questions, suddenly compelling, triggered new interest in child development. Charles Darwin, for example, published a diary of his observations of his son's early development and called for more scientific research. In this chapter, we will investigate the current status of such research.

This chapter will cover child development, from birth through adolescence; the following chapter will cover the even more recently emerging area of adult development and aging. There are two major areas of developmental psychology. One is cognitive development—how the child's intellect unfolds from its primitive simplicity to the sophisticated complexity of the adult. Language acquisition, which we discussed in Chapter 7, is part of this area. The other aspects of cognitive development are covered in the first half of this chapter.

The other major area of developmental psychology is personality development. Why is Janice trusting and Bonnie cynical? Do these traits have anything to do with early experiences? Questions like these are the focus of the second half of the chapter.

STAGES OF COGNITIVE DEVELOPMENT

The intellectual development of the child is commonly divided into several stages, which are distinguished by major changes in the way intelligence is expressed. The nature of these stages was first described in detail by the Swiss psychologist, Jean Piaget, and it is on Piaget's ideas we will focus our attention.

The Sensory-Motor Period

The first stage of intellectual development is called the *sensory-motor period.* For the typical child, this period extends from birth to the time he or she begins to speak at about 18 months. The use of language is a major break in the continuity of development, so it is natural to view this period, before language, as the first stage.

Although parents can tell you that their infant does grow in intellect, they would be hard pressed to describe the *nature* of the

Figure 8.1 *Jean Piaget (far left) observing some children.*

change; the development of an intelligence without language may be hard for adults to understand. Jean Piaget set out to describe this period of nonverbal intellectual functioning.

Intelligent Acts. In the sensory-motor stage of development, a child's intelligence is manifested in his actions. At birth he has few integrated behavior patterns to use to solve life's inevitable problems. He is an expert sucker, however, and in the early months of infancy, he is likely to explore his environment by sticking every object he encounters into his mouth. Gradually, as the child gains control over his body, he develops more intricate behavior patterns, allowing him to adapt more effectively and in more varied ways to his environment (Figure 8.2).

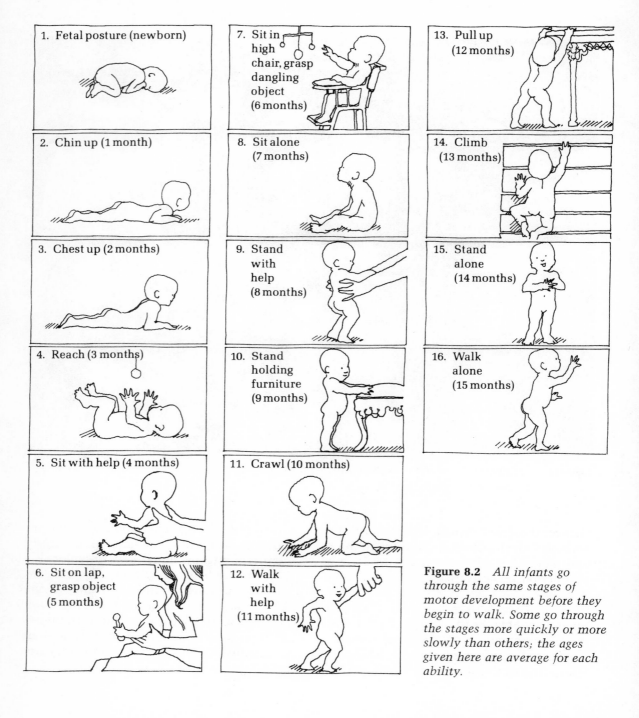

1. Fetal posture (newborn)

2. Chin up (1 month)

3. Chest up (2 months)

4. Reach (3 months)

5. Sit with help (4 months)

6. Sit on lap, grasp object (5 months)

7. Sit in high chair, grasp dangling object (6 months)

8. Sit alone (7 months)

9. Stand with help (8 months)

10. Stand holding furniture (9 months)

11. Crawl (10 months)

12. Walk with help (11 months)

13. Pull up (12 months)

14. Climb (13 months)

15. Stand alone (14 months)

16. Walk alone (15 months)

Figure 8.2 *All infants go through the same stages of motor development before they begin to walk. Some go through the stages more quickly or more slowly than others; the ages given here are average for each ability.*

An example of one of these more intricate actions is reaching. Effective reaching may not seem very complex to an adult, who generally can reach for and grasp an object at will. But as any parent knows who has anxiously watched an infant reach for and knock over a glass of milk, such abilities take a while to develop in children.

The most striking feature of reaching — which one psychologist prefers to call "the intelligent use of the hands" (Bruner, 1968) — is the *integration* of complex sensory inputs and motor commands it requires. On the motor side of the picture, the simple act of reaching involves muscles in the fingers, hand, arm, shoulders, and neck. All of these movements must be integrated — one should not grasp and then extend the arm. And the infant's motor commands must be coordinated with visual and ultimately tactile sensory input if the reaching is to be successful.

At about 12 weeks of age, a human infant will "swipe" at an object close to him. This may be the first voluntary reaching act of his career, and the efficiency of it all is often startling to him; he blinks and shudders as if an unknown object is flying nearby — it is his own fist. Between the third and the fourth month, the infant achieves a certain mastery of the situation, so that he can reach an object, grasp it — and put it in his mouth.

Within the sensory-motor period, Piaget sees the infant's intellectual advances as showing themselves in his or her increasingly adaptive behaviors. Around the age of four to six months, for example, a child might try to make a mobile move by kicking the crib. A child of one year might experiment with different solutions to a single problem; although he knows that he can get to a toy hidden behind a pillow by his usual means — swatting the pillow with his hand —

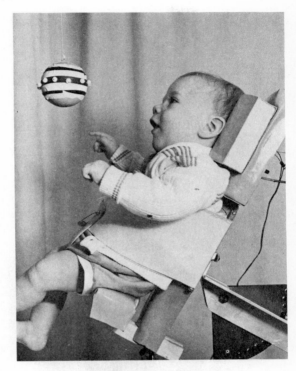

Figure 8.3 *An infant in the seat used for studying integrated sensory-motor actions like reaching.*

he tries using another toy as pillow-swatter, to see what happens, or he tries kicking the pillow away with his foot.

Object Permanence. One of the things children learn during the sensory-motor period is *object permanence*. As Piaget posed the question, how does a child learn that objects do not cease to exist the moment he or she can no longer sense them? Piaget was able to show that very young infants would show interest in an object only as long as they could feel, smell, see, hear, or taste it. Hide the object behind a screen, for example, and the child would think it was gone forever.

Gradually the child develops a sense of object permanence (see Figure 8.4). Piaget has described an incident involving his daughter Jacqueline at ten months; she was just developing the sense of object permanence and could be said to be at an interme-

diate level. Piaget took her toy parrot and twice hid it under her mattress at point *A*.

Both times Jacqueline looks for the object immediately and grabs it. Then I take it from her hands and move it slowly before her eyes to the corresponding place on her right, in (point) *B*. Jacqueline watches this

Figure 8.4 *Before and after the development of a sense of object permanence. The infant in the top pictures loses interest once the object disappears from sight. The child in the lower pictures seeks out the hidden object, demonstrating his understanding of the fact that objects exist apart from his perception of them.*

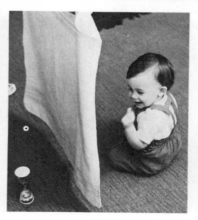

movement, very attentively, but at the moment when the parrot disappears in *B,* she turns to her left and looks where it was before, in *A* (Piaget, 1954, p. 51).

This strange phenomenon has since been observed in several children by several researchers (most of whom were rather skeptical at first); reasonable explanations are still scarce (Gardner, 1978a).

Toward the end of the sensory-motor period (at the age of one and a half or so), the child behaves toward hidden or missing objects much the way an adult would. His actions show that he knows a toy or a shoe continues to exist even if it is not where he expects to find it; and if he wants it, he will search for it. To adults, such behavior is so "natural" that we rarely consider what an intellectual achievement it represents for the developing child.

The Preoperational Period

Around the age of 18 months, the child gains two important new abilities. One is the ability to *imagine* doing things, and imagine the possible consequences of those actions; Freud called this "experimental action in thought." Piaget describes an illustrative incident: "Lucienne tries to kneel before a stool but, by leaning against it, pushes it further away. She then raises herself up, takes it and places it against a sofa. When it is firmly set there she leans against it and kneels without difficulty" (Piaget, 1952, p. 338). Lucienne was able to imagine the consequences of placing the stool against the sofa; thus she solved her problem *before* acting, rather than by trying out different actions as a younger infant might have done.

The second new ability, not unrelated to the first, is language. With language, the child has access to a wealth of symbols which he or she can combine to describe events.

Imagination and language mark the end of the sensory-motor period and the beginning of the *preoperational period.* During this stage, the child's intellectual advances take place primarily in a "conceptual-symbolic rather than purely sensory-motor arena" (Flavell, 1963, p. 121). From the age of one and a half to six or so, the child's ability to think in terms of symbols, such as images and words, grows by leaps and bounds. Consider, for example, the growth in vocabulary, and the progression from simple words ("Dada!") to complex sentences.

As its name implies, however, something is lacking in the preoperational stage. In Piaget's theory, an *operation* is a complex mental routine that enables a person to transform information for some purpose. In a mathematical operation, two numbers might be added together to form a third. Classifying similar things to form a class or concept—"All those are cats; these are dogs"—is another operation. The preoperational child cannot perform these operations; his intelligence is symbolic, but he cannot manipulate symbols in the complex ways an adult can.

Conservation Problems. The preoperational period is one in which organizing operations are absent or weak. In Piaget's famous *conservation* problems, the preoperational child's deficits are clear. In one, Piaget showed the child two beakers of the same size and shape, each containing the same amount of liquid. Before the child's eyes, the contents of one beaker were poured into a third breaker of a different shape, either taller and thinner or shorter and wider. The child was then asked which beaker contained more liquid. Children over the age of seven or so (and adults too, of course) answered that there was the same amount in each; simply pouring liquid from one container to another does not increase or decrease its volume. But younger children said that the taller beaker had more because it was taller; or, less frequently, that the wider beaker had more because it was wider. They could not *integrate* the two dimensions, height and width, and *understand* that an increase in one can *compensate* for a decrease in the other. These operations—compensation, integration, and, ultimately, understanding—are still beyond the intellectual abilities of preoperational children.

Intellect enables us to distinguish between appearance and reality. The taller beaker may appear to hold more liquid, even to an adult, but we *know* that volume is unaffected by transfer. In similar fashion, we know that the earth is round, that the earth spins around the sun, and that a pencil does not bend in water, all in spite of *visual* evidence to the contrary. Children, on the other hand, are more heavily swayed by the perceptual display (see Figure 8.5).

Figure 8.5 *Which cup contains more liquid? Children under seven usually choose the cup in which the level is highest, regardless of the size of the containers.*

Egocentric Thought. The intellect of the child less than six years old is confused by appearances. It also suffers from what Piaget calls *egocentrism*—the tendency to consider only one's own point of view. This is not selfishness in the adult sense, for the child has no choice. He was not born with the ability to know what other people might be seeing or thinking, and his developing awareness of other points of view is one of the most significant advances in his cognitive development.

If you take a preoperational child out for a walk and then ask him where his home is, he is likely to point behind him. It makes no difference where it is in reality, or whether he has just left home or is returning—home was behind him when he left, so why would it change? Likewise, the sun travels around in the sky to stay with him; it is his own personal lighting and heating unit.

Not surprisingly, egocentric children find it difficult or impossible to solve problems in which they must take the perspective of another person. In an early study (Piaget and Inhelder, 1956), children viewed a scale

Figure 8.6 *Young children assume everyone sees the same things they do.*

model of three mountains (see Figure 8.7). Children in the preoperational period could not identify what other people, located on different sides of the mountains, were seeing; they were likely to assume everyone saw what they were seeing. Another example of this difficulty was recently presented to me as I watched the daughters of a friend. One was looking at a book when the other, a three-year-old who was sitting on the opposite side of a small table, shouted, "Your book's not right!" Whereupon she turned it so it was right side up for her—and

upside down for her sister. "Now you can read OK!" the three-year-old announced, with satisfaction. (Her sister, aged seven, smiled at her and then at me. "Kids!" she said, shrugging her shoulders.)

Egocentric thought exhibits itself in egocentric language, too. The speech of a child under the age of six or seven is often remarkably uninformative, for he speaks from his point of view alone. He does not feel a need to define his terms or justify his logic—it's all clear enough to him! The basic problem with egocentric communication is that the speaker does not take into account the requirements of his listener. A vivid demonstration had children explaining things to a blindfolded adult (Flavell et al., 1963). The young children had great difficulty adjusting to the fact that the adult could not see, and they continued with worthless instructions such as "You must pick up this" (pointing) "and you must put it there" (pointing).

Recent research has qualified Piaget's notions of egocentric thought somewhat (Gardner, 1978a). One researcher has shown that even some three-year-olds can solve the three-mountains problem if they are properly motivated and given careful instructions about what they are supposed to be guessing (Burke, 1975). With more familiar scenes (How does a fire engine look from different perspectives?) young children do even better. And several studies have shown that young children can, to some extent, modify verbal instructions and other communications, depending on the needs of the people listening (Shatz and Gelman, 1973; Menig-Peterson, 1975). But this research suggests only that if the situation is a very simple one, involving a familiar task that the child is highly motivated to perform, children below the age of six do not look as egocen-

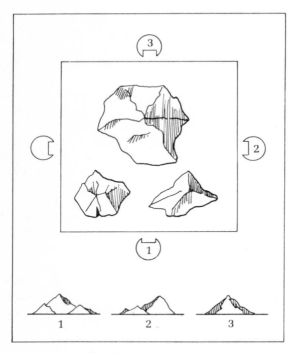

Figure 8.7 *The three mountains test of egocentric perspective. Children sit at position 1 and select from a group of drawings what they think a person would see from positions 1, 2, and 3. The correct answers are shown in the bottom part of the figure. Egocentrism is indicated by the selection of one's own perspective (#1) as the answer for all three positions.*

tric as the sharp discontinuities of Piaget's stage theory would have us believe. In most normal life situations, however, preoperational children do exhibit an egocentric perspective that they find quite difficult to overcome.

In Piaget's view, egocentric thought declines because it encounters social reality. Through interactions with other people, especially arguments and disagreements, children learn that thoughts different from their own exist on the same topic. They learn that important communications are misunderstood unless they take this other perspective into account, and that it is hard to predict what someone else will do unless they take his or her thinking into account. Egocentric thought becomes "socialized thought"—thought that adheres to the usual social requirements of logic, definition of terms, and so on.

Moral Development. Piaget also studied morality as an aspect of cognitive growth (1948). He asked children to compare two stories. In one story, a child accidentally broke fifteen cups; in the second story, a child deliberately broke a single cup. "Which child is naughtier?" Piaget asked. He found that preoperational children judged breaking fifteen cups naughtier than breaking one cup; they focused on the outcome, in other words. The older children judged morality on the basis of intentions and said the deliberate destruction of one cup was the greater evil.

Piaget noted that before a child can make a moral judgment on the basis of another person's intentions, he or she must have progressed beyond the stage of egocentric thought. He or she must be able to think about what other people are thinking. But these cognitive abilities do not develop until the period of concrete operations, after the age of seven. So the preoperational children judge morality on the basis of results and outcomes, the only source of information they can understand.

Thus moral development depends partly on the stage of intellectual development. Some researchers have hypothesized, in fact,

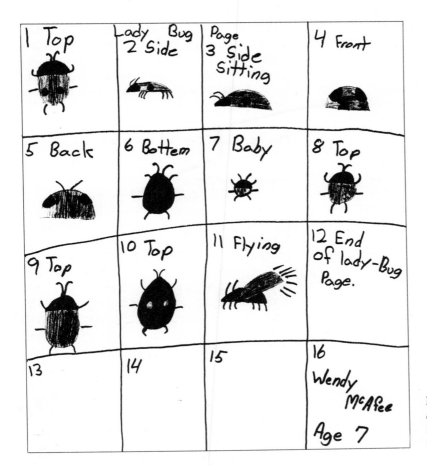

Figure 8.8 *A seven-year-old artist gets some practice in taking different points of view.*

that moral development occurs in stages, just as intellectual and personality development do. (See Interlude: Moral Development, pp. 348–355.)

The Period of Concrete Operations

Around the age of six or seven, the child's intellect reaches a new plateau. The next four years or so Piaget calls the *period of concrete operations*. The child begins to demonstrate abilities not shown before: For example, he knows now that the quantity of liquid does not change when poured from one container to another.

The remarkable advance in intellectual abilities that occurs at this time is due, according to Piaget, to the child's increasing use of mental operations. He begins to *think* about things in logical and organized ways, and is not as easily swayed by appearances. In the conversation of quantity problem, the child can now understand that the height and width of a glass can *compensate* for one another. Or he can see the problem in terms of *reversibility:* If the amount in the two glasses was the same before the contents of one were poured into a taller, thinner vessel, then one can reverse the process, pouring the contents back into the original glass.

Whatever it is that makes for the phenomenal advance in a child's intellectual abilities around the age of seven, one of the results is a marked increase in his ability to categorize or classify things. He can form and use *concepts* in ways he could not before. If children of various ages are given a variety of objects and asked to form categories, the youngest children form *heaps,* collections of totally unrelated objects (Vygotsky, 1962). Older children, between five and seven, form *complexes,* collections in which the various members are related, but often in very strange ways. A complex, for example, might contain all the objects mentioned in a story the child has heard. A boot and a mitten go together, not because they are both clothing, but because, in the story, the heroine puts on her boots and mittens before going sledding. The sled, of course, is also a member of this complex.

After the age of seven, the child begins to classify things as an adult would, by using *superordinate concepts.* Now boots and mittens are together as "articles of clothing," and the sled is over with the bike as "toys" or "toys I can ride on." This development is a very gradual one, with the more sophisticated concepts slowly replacing complexes over a span of years running roughly from age six to the high teens. It parallels the lessening egocentrism of children's thought to some extent, for a child just barely over seven will often classify things on the basis

of what he himself could do with them (Bruner, 1964). He can make noise with both a book and a pencil, so these two are related. Later, he uses the more traditional functions: Bananas and eggs can both be eaten (are foods).

The Period of Formal Operations

Somewhere around the age of 11 or 12, according to Piaget, children enter the final period of intellectual development (Inhelder and Piaget, 1958). Since this is the beginning of thought processes as we adults know them, we do not have much difficulty in understanding the abilities that develop in this stage. For example, thinking about abstract ideas becomes possible. Formal logic and bits and pieces of the scientific method come into play in this, the *period of formal operations.*

Formal operations are concerned more with the form of a problem and less with its content than concrete operations. An 11-year-old can solve a problem like "If a banana can eat two rocks in one day, how many rocks can it eat in three days?" Younger children often have difficulty, for they cannot imagine a banana that eats rocks; they cannot disregard the content of the problem and reason in a purely hypothetical way (Mussen et al., 1979b).

Differences among the various levels of cognitive development show up clearly in intellectual games like "twenty questions" (Mosher and Hornsby, 1966). Younger children, aged six, had no idea of how to proceed with the task of identifying the object the experimenters had in mind. They typically asked questions about specific objects—"Is it a dog? No? Well, is it a spoon?"—until they used up their allotment of inquiries.

Figure 8.9 *Formal operational thought is a big help to teenaged scientists.*

Children in the stage of formal operations, aged 11, systematically narrowed down the possibilities by using fairly abstract concepts — "Is it a toy of some sort?" "Is it bigger than a breadbox?" — much as adults do. Children in the intermediate stage of concrete operations, aged eight, were able to be systematic about narrowing down the possibilities only if the possible correct answers were somehow concretely represented for them. If the experimenters indicated that the "correct" object was represented by one of 42 pictures of animals, toys, machines, and other things, and if the pictures were in view during the guessing, the concrete-operational children could ask questions like the formal-operational children — "Is it a toy?" "Is it an animal?" — and thus home in on the correct answer. But if the pictures weren't available, they couldn't organize a logical series of questions in their head.

Older children become capable of thinking about thought itself. They can reflect on *how* they solved a problem, and often do, intrigued by general procedures for acquiring knowledge. Adolescents are in love with the hypothetical, the future, and the remote. As one adolescent was overheard saying, "I was thinking about my future, and then I began to think about why I was thinking about my future, and then I began to think about why I was thinking about why I was thinking about my future!" (Conger, 1977, p. 183). This kind of preoccupation with thought processes is, according to Piaget, one of the prime characteristics of the stage of formal operations.

INTELLECT AND PERSONALITY

As the child's intellect grows, his personality develops concurrently. These two aspects of psychological development are usually discussed separately, but of course they are interdependent. For example, until the infant develops a sense of object permanence, he cannot distinguish his parents as particularly important objects in his social environment; thus personality development requires a certain degree of cognitive development. Later in life, as certain people become significant in the child's life, he begins to worry about conflicts and disputes with them; his social needs force him to grow intellectually — to give up his egocentric patterns of thought.

With these interdependencies in mind, we now shift our focus from cognitive development to the child's developing social skills and his or her unique, individualized adjustment to the world.

THE FIRST SOCIAL RELATIONSHIP

It is surprising how many people believe babies undergo no personality development in the first few months of life. To them, these wee creatures simply eat and sleep, building strength for the social learning experiences to come later. Actually, however, the world of the child in the first two or three months is a stimulating one: He is learning to perceive. Indeed, he may appear so passive only because his motor capacities mature more slowly than his sensory capacities; he is, in effect, looking before he leaps (Bruner, 1968). What he is learning is very primitive stuff: The leg of the table and his own leg are two different things; when the woman with the breast leaves, she or someone strikingly similar returns after a while.

In most societies, the child's first social relationship is typically with his or her mother. But we should note at the outset of our discussion that what is generally the case is not always the case. Especially in American society (for reasons discussed in Interlude: The Psychology of Sex Differences, pp. 179–193), fathers are more commonly sharing caretaking responsibilities, and some are even taking the primary responsibility. In other cases, children are raised communally, making it difficult to single out any individual as most influential. Much of the research to be described, however, involves mother-child interactions — the typical case.

Children without Mothers

What happens when a very young child is deprived of his or her mother? Some evidence on this question comes from a number of studies done in the 1940s and later.

These studies began in an attempt to understand some terrifying statistics on the infant death rates in orphanages and foundling homes. For example, of the 10,272 children admitted to the Dublin foundling home between 1775 and 1880, 45 survived (Kessen, 1965). As incredible as this statistic may be, it does not represent an isolated case. Mortality rates in institutions for infants have always been high, and figures such as 75 to 90 percent dead in the first year were not uncommon (Spitz, 1945). An obvious explanation, that these institutions were run by greedy proprietors who cared little for their charges and provided less than the necessary health services, was easily shown to be a myth. People who had observed the children said that they were well cared for, in most cases. It was something else; apparently they just lost their will to live.

The Nursery and the Foundling Home. Psychologist Rene Spitz conducted a remarkable study of two infant institutions and gave us a few of the answers (1965). In one, called the Nursery, the babies were cared for by their real mothers, who were in prison. In the other, called the Foundling Home, the infants had been given up by their mothers and were cared for by professional nurses. We have, then, a natural experiment. Our dependent variable is what happens to the infants. And we are going to have problems in interpretation. But data are data, and these data are interesting.

The babies in the Nursery, with only a few exceptions, developed normally. At the end of two years, almost all were happy and healthy.

The babies in the Foundling Home did not fare so well. Almost all of them developed the same pattern of symptoms. At the

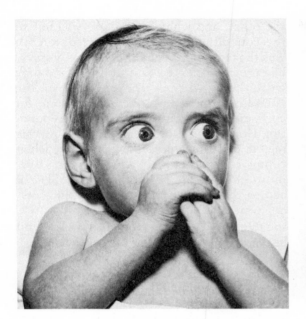 

Figure 8.10 *These two anxious faces attest to the tendency for both children and monkeys raised with little or no contact with their mothers to withdraw from the world as they get older.*

age of six to eight months, their typical smiling behaviors, which had started at about three months, disappeared. The children began to sleep more than is ordinary, and when awake, they seemed lethargic and unresponsive. A researcher described one typical case:

> When approached she did not lift her shoulders, barely her head, to look at the observer with an expression of profound suffering sometimes seen in sick animals. As soon as the observer started to speak to her or to touch her, she began to weep. This was unlike the usual crying of babies, which is accompanied by a certain amount of . . . vocalization, and sometimes screaming. In-

stead she wept soundlessly, tears running down her face. Speaking to her in soft, comforting tones only resulted in more intense weeping, intermingled with moans and sobs, shaking her whole body (Spitz, 1965, p. 270).

Eventually, motor deficits became more pronounced, and the children became more and more passive. Their faces became empty, their eyes focused on nothing, and their facial expression reminded observers of imbeciles. By the second year, tests of social and mental development showed them to be, on the average, 45 percent of normal—the level of idiots. At the age of four, few of them could sit, stand, walk, or talk. That is, if they reached the age of four. Over one of three died before reaching the ripe old age of two years.

I really find these data among the most incredible and heartrending in all of psychology. The children in the Foundling Home simply withered away; the lucky ones died, and the others approached the age when most children enter school without so much as the ability to sit up.

Reasons for the Differences. To what are we to attribute these horrors? Comparing the children in the Foundling Home with the development of the average, normal child is too big a task, so we can instead consider the children in the Nursery. Only two of the over two hundred children there died before the age of two.

The medical care was slightly better in the Foundling Home, where physicians checked on each child each day. In the Nursery, there was a pediatrician "on call," but no daily rounds were made. Both institutions drew from a population below average in several variables related to mental and physical health. Obviously, the delinquent mothers whose children filled the Nursery tended to be maladjusted in some ways, and several apparently were feeble-minded or had physical defects of one sort or another. Similarly, the parents of the children in the Foundling Home, though not criminal, were onto hard times, at least some for reasons of health. Spitz claims the parents of the Foundling Home babies were, on the average, a slightly more respectable lot.

Thus, in comparisons of "innate differences" and medical care between institutions, there was very little to favor one over the other, and what favor there was fell to the Foundling Home. The major difference was the fact that the children in the Nursery had their mothers to care for them and play with them, whereas the children in the Foundling Home had only nurses, one for every eight to ten children. In fact, the Foundling Home was more nearly typical in this regard, and the Nursery exceptional, when compared to other infant institutions — live-in mothers were not common. Also, of course, the happy, healthy babies of the Nursery were not common either, so it is reasonable to attribute the happiness and health to the presence of the mothers.

Love and Learning. But what exactly did the mothers provide? Certainly their emotional involvement — their love — was important. But the mothers also provided a richly varied perceptual environment, which the children may well have needed to develop normally. The children in the Nursery had both these advantages — love, and someone to talk to them, hold and fondle them, play with them, and interact with them in an often educational manner: "See the birdie!"

The Nursery babies also had toys. Very few of the infants in the Foundling Home had a toy of any description. They lived on their backs facing the green-gray ceiling, the only part of the room they could see. To quiet the babies, the nurses hung bedsheets or blankets over the bed railings, to keep them from seeing the "outside world." Not that there was much to see. There was usually no one around except for the other babies, each lying in solitary confinement in its crib, and a usually motionless caretaker.

It seems quite probable that both the

mother's roles, as love provider and as stimulus feeder, are important (Thompson and Grusec, 1970). Probably the perceptual deprivation and lack of stimulation, and the resulting loss of learning experiences, are more important during the first half-year, whereas the loss of mother herself is more important later. The age of six months is the time when the baby first shows signs of recognizing his mother as a distinct and unique person and as a highly valued one, too.

FOCUS

Social Deprivation in Monkeys

If a monkey is raised in isolation for the first six months of its life, it reacts very much like the isolated human infant. It avoids social contact, withdraws extremely, and appears to be constantly frightened (Harlow and Harlow, 1966). Even the postures of monkey and human infants in depression look alike.

The research on social deprivation in monkeys has been done mostly by Harry and Margaret Kuenne Harlow and their colleagues at the Primate Laboratory at the University of Wisconsin. The research originated as an attempt to answer a question that perhaps only a psychologist would ask: Why does an infant love its mother? One possible answer is that the mother provides the basic reinforcements in the infant's life—food, in particular, when it is hungry—and therefore she becomes a giant secondary reinforcement. The Harlows were able to show that this view is too simple at best by demonstrating that young monkeys will choose to associate with a "terry cloth mother" in preference to a "wiremesh mother," even if it is the wire-mesh mother that feeds them (see Figure 1).

The experiment developed as follows. Noticing the devotion young monkeys paid to the gauze-covered pads on the bottom of their cages, the Harlows thought of the stereotype of a child and his "security blanket"— the Linus character in the Peanuts cartoon, for example. They decided that whatever motivations were involved in such behaviors, they seemed strong enough to compete with hunger. So they raised monkeys from birth with two "mothers" that had been built by the researchers. One was an armless, legless cylinder made of wire mesh; this mother fed the infant from a bottle placed in what one might call the breast region of the contraption. The other was similar except for two facts; it did not feed, and it was covered with terry cloth. A mother to cling to. And indeed, that is

Figure 1 *Infant monkeys deprived of their real mothers preferred cuddly "mothers" to wire ones. But their adult behavior was quite abnormal compared to that of monkeys raised with their real mothers.*

what the young monkeys did. They spent almost all their time with the cloth mother, running to it when frightened and using it as home base during exploration of strange objects in the environment. They approached the wire mother only for food.

Of more interest to us in our present discussion is what happened to these monkeys after they grew up. These monkeys were not normal; their social interactions with other monkeys were definitely aberrant. For example, their sexual behavior was so misdirected and incompetent that very few were successful in mating, despite obvious willingness and eagerness. Those few females who were successful in mating made atrocious mothers, beating and generally abusing their unfortunate offspring.

Attachment

It is clear that one of the most important factors in the personality development of infants is the quality of their relationship with their primary caretaker, usually their mother. In particular, the emotional bond between mother and child—called the attachment bond or simply *attachment*—has been widely investigated in recent years.

Research on infants around the world has yielded a general picture of how attachment develops from birth through early childhood, shown in Figure 8.11. (The ages given are typical; variations of a month or two in individual infants are perfectly normal.)

Indiscriminate and Specific Attachment. Human infants seem predisposed to respond with affection to other humans. They are calmed by their presence and upset by their absence. During the first six months of life, however, they show *indiscriminate attachment* to adults; they protest separation from comforting strangers as much as separation from their mothers (Schaffer and Emerson, 1964). Sometime between the sixth and the eighth month of life, an intense *specific attachment* develops between the infant and mother. The infant directs most of his behaviors — smiling, babbling, crying, clinging, following — toward the mother. He is distressed when she leaves (especially in an unfamiliar environment); he is delighted to see her return. She can soothe her child as no one else can. When he is hungry, tired, bored, or afraid, the infant seeks her out (Mussen et al., 1979b).

This intense attachment to the mother was once believed to be a function of her role as "feeder," but the Harlows' monkey stud-ies, among others, showed that hypothesis to be much too simple (see Focus: Social Deprivation in Monkeys, pp. 329–330). Physical contact (hugging, cuddling) is also involved. Also, in the normal course of events, the mother is the primary source of stimulation for the infant. She talks to him, smiles at him, looks into his eyes, kisses his cheek, bathes him. She is the stimulus to which he most often responds, and she is a great fan of his ever-increasing repertoire of social behaviors. It's no wonder he falls in love with her.

There is some evidence that if an infant does not have a mother (or mother-substitute) during a critical period when attachment normally develops (roughly, six to eight months after birth), the psychological effects can be devastating. Spitz, for example, found a few "abnormal" children in the Nursery, which otherwise produced

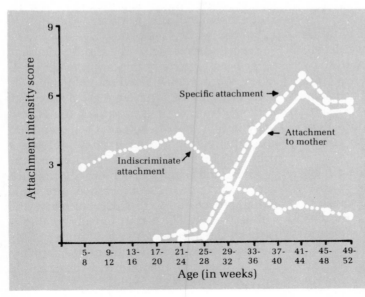

Figure 8.11 *Infant attachments to people during the first year of life. At first an infant protests when separated from whomever he or she is close to at the moment. Around 6 or 7 months, the infant begins to notice mother as a special person, and will protest the most when taken away from her.*

Figure 8.12   *As fathers take increasingly greater roles in infant care, the attachment bonds between father and child will surely grow stronger.*

happy and healthy babies. These children were weepy and demanding and overdependent. Eventually they began to withdraw completely from social interactions. Spitz (1965) checked their records and discovered that every one of these children (34 of them) had been deprived of his or her mother for some time, beginning in the sixth to the eighth month.

John Bowlby (1973) has noted the effects of long-term separation from the mother during the second year of life, after attachment bonds have been formed. First there is a "violent protest" phase, in which the child cries, screams, and exhibits wild and uncontrollable behavior—continually, all day long. This is replaced by a period of "pro-

found despair," in which the child, totally preoccupied with the loss of his or her mother, mopes about in hopeless agony. If reminded of Mother, the child is likely to fly into a rage of frustration and resentment. After several months, the final phase of "detached acceptance" begins, in which the child is able to cope normally with most of the everyday problems of living, but in a cold and aloof manner. Such children are much like the characters in novels who have had an intense love affair that ended in tragedy. They survive, but deep scars prevent them from forming close emotional relationships again.

Multiple Attachments. The period of intense, specific attachments lasts from about 6 months to 18 months of age. Then the child is capable of *multiple attachments.* The affection for, and dependency on, the mother does not decrease, but other people —the father, a grandparent, a babysitter— can become equally significant in the infant's emotional life. In other words, his or her social world is expanding.

Secure attachment to another human being is an extremely important event in infancy. We have discussed some of the problems faced by children who are deprived of the opportunity to form attachments, but the positive aspects of "good attachments" are equally impressive. If an infant has a primary caretaker who is affectionate, supportive, and appreciative of the infant's needs and growing competence, the child will approach life with trust, curiosity, and self-assurance. These traits are observable as early as the age of two years (Sroufe, 1978), and the effects of secure infant attachments can be seen throughout life, even into old age (Lerner and Ryff, 1978).

STAGES OF PERSONALITY DEVELOPMENT

In their efforts to understand child development, psychologists often resort to theories that view change and growth in a series of stages. Piaget's theory is one example. Another is the psychoanalytic theories of Sigmund Freud and Erik Erikson. Freud's general personality theory, of which his development theory is part, will be discussed in more detail in Chapter 10. As shown in Figure 8.13, Erik Erikson, who followed Freud in time, gave Freud's ideas a

Approximate age	Psychosocial crisis	Virtues
I. First year	Trust versus mistrust	Hope
II. Second year	Autonomy versus shame, doubt	Willpower
III. Third year through fifth year	Initiative versus guilt	Purpose
IV. Sixth year to onset of puberty	Industry versus inferiority	Competence
V. Adolescence	Identity versus role confusion	Fidelity
VI. Early adulthood	Intimacy versus isolation	Love
VII. Adulthood	Generativity versus stagnation	Care
VIII. Old age	Integrity versus despair	Wisdom

Figure 8.13 *Erikson's eight stages of psychosocial development. Each stage is marked by a learning situation (crisis) that must be resolved in some way. Preferably the solution will be a balance that favors the positive characteristic without ignoring the negative. The lasting outcome of such a balance at each stage is a basic human virtue.*

more social, less biological, emphasis than they had in the original formulation. Erikson also extended these ideas to adult development and aging and thus his theory will be reprised in Chapter 9.

The Oral Stage

Clearly things are happening in the first year of life, changes that can exert profound influences on later personality. Freud called the first year the *oral stage* of personality development. During this period, much of the infant's interaction with its environment involves its mouth: feeding, burping, spitting up, biting. The infant often explores objects by putting them in its mouth. Research with monkeys (see Focus: Social Deprivation in Monkeys, pp. 329–330) suggests that the infant's relationship with its mother is much more than simply a feeding relationship; however, feeding is important, for hunger is one of the baby's first intense frustrations.

Freud suggested that what the child learns in these oral (or mouth-related) activities are some very basic habits, attitudes, and personality traits. For example, if a baby is consistently frustrated because of too few or too small feedings, it may develop an unusually strong desire to suck on things — its thumb at first, and later in life, perhaps cigarettes. Obviously, this hypothesis is difficult, maybe even impossible, to test. Also, even Freudian theorists believe oral frustrations to be a significant cause of smoking only in some people; there are many reasons people smoke.

More generally, during this stage the child's main attitude is one of passive dependence on external supplies. Most of his or her interactions with other people involve receiving and accepting things from them. As Erik Erikson (1950) said, the child learns the meaning of the verb "to get." And if children get what they need, at least most of the time, they learn to *trust* the world as an essentially benevolent environment. This is their first learning task; its outcome obviously is going to affect their later personality development.

Figure 8.14 *Oral behavior at four stages of life.*

The child also must learn some sense of *mistrust*. Children must learn that one does not always get what one wants, and that the external world will not always provide them with the supplies they desire. Most of our attitudes, like trust and mistrust, require a balance between two opposites. It is to be hoped that the child will be more trusting than not, but a little wariness or mistrust now and then is necessary for survival.

The Anal Stage

In the second and third years of life, a number of significant developments occur. The child begins to speak, for example, a step that is exceptionally important for both cognitive and personality development. He also begins to move around and actively explore his environment, as his motor abilities — walking, climbing — improve. Children seem to take great pleasure in their newly developed manipulative skills. In one study, children of age two were given a clear plastic box with a toy inside (Kagan, 1971). They could get to the toy by opening a couple of latches on the box, and most of the children succeeded in doing so. But they were not very interested in their reward, the toy; instead they kept opening and closing the door and the latches. Apparently they were intrigued by their mastery of the situation.

The child's newly developed motor and manipulative abilities do not meet with universal approval, however. Children enjoy running about, and a good chase is exhilarating, but if the home is filled with expensive furniture, vases, and dishes, the child is taught to be more restricted in his body movements. Blacks were once thought to have more innate rhythm than whites, but as discrimination let up slightly and a few blacks made it to the upper middle class, their children's movements turned out to be just as inhibited as those of upper-middle-class whites. "Rhythm" seems to be a social class difference based on learning, not an innate, racial difference. Children in homes with fewer expensive and breakable possessions are allowed more freedom of movement.

Also, the development of motor abilities brings with it new responsibilities, behaviors that are expected of the children. One of the social responsibilities the parents are most interested in teaching their children, as soon as the children are able, is when and where to urinate and defecate. In middle-class America, toilet training is usually begun around the first birthday and is completed during the second year of life. This learning experience was important enough, in Freud's opinion, to lend its name to the second major period of personality development. Freud called the time from age one to age three *the anal stage.*

The Conflict of Toilet Training. Toilet training is the major learning situation of the anal stage, according to Freud. Consider, first, the event: In the beginning, when a child is born, his body expels feces and urine by powerful, involuntary reflex actions. For several months, he is unable to control these functions because he lacks the necessary sensory and motor abilities. There is some question when he attains all the necessary abilities, but most recent texts put the figure at 18 months (Mussen et al., 1979b). In one study, one twin was given training in bladder control early, beginning in the first months of life, and the second twin was trained in the second year. Both twins achieved control at the same time (McGraw,

1940). The early training didn't help much because control requires mature sensory-motor abilities, not experience.

Sometime around the beginning of the second year (plus or minus six months), the child begins to realize that his parents have become very interested in his ability to control his bladder and bowels. No doubt this is a bit puzzling to him at first. Even if he vaguely perceives what is required, the how and especially the why remain mysteries. And he is expected to develop control even while sleeping! Is that possible?

Toilet training is one of the first real battles of wills. It is one of the first times the child is expected to *do* something, to respond positively, to act in one way and not in another. He cannot do nothing; he cannot be passive, for that means soiling and probable punishment. But he is being asked to do something he would rather not do. It is a case of what his parents want versus what he wants. As the first major conflict of this type, toilet training is viewed by most psychologists as a crucial situation for the development of personal autonomy and independence in the child.

The child soon learns that, in this battle, he is not without weapons. He finds that he can make his parents happy by performing correctly, and he can make them sad by soiling. He plays social-interaction games with his parents: "If you won't let me play with the stereo with my screwdriver, I will lose control of my bowels. And I'll time my 'accident' to coincide with the arrival of your dinner guests." So the battle is cast. It is a battle the child is sure to lose, but in the process he gains skills, ideas, and attitudes that affect most of his later life.

According to Erikson, the child learns what "holding on" and "letting go" mean, in the most basic sense. He learns, too, the meaning of *autonomy*, what it is to be a willful creature separate and distinct from his parents (and from uncontrollable reflex actions), and he also learns the meaning of *shame* and *doubt*. These concepts are interrelated because one must have at least a sense that he is a unique individual before he can experience shame — *I* am ashamed! — and before he can doubt *his own* abilities to comply with requests from others. One would hope, here, for a favorable balance of confidence over shame and doubt. But again we should not desire a child with *no* sense of shame or with *no* doubts about his ability; such a child will encounter great difficulties later in life.

The Anal Character. In Freud's view, a child who does not solve the problems encountered in the anal stage becomes an adult with certain specific character traits. The most commonly discussed are frugality, obstinacy, and orderliness (Blum, 1953). Frugality or stinginess is seen as similar to holding on to feces during toilet training; frugality with money is common, but one may be stingy with time or love or just about anything else. Obstinacy or stubbornness stems from the interpersonal weapons the child uses during toilet training. "I simply refuse to comply" is the message conveyed. And orderliness — "Clean up your mess!" — needs no explanation.

Is the theory true? It is not easy to do research on these relationships. First of all, anal problems may lead to frugality, but frugality can result from other causes as well (Erikson, 1945). In one study, the three traits stressed by Freud — stinginess, stubbornness, and orderliness — were found to be related in a sample of college males (Sears, 1936). If a

Figure 8.15 *Those who feel shame about a "soiled" kitchen—the remnant of early anal conflicts, according to Freudian theory—are willing consumers of cleaning products. (The quarter moon on this product label, suggestive of outhouse symbolism, would interest some psychoanalysts.)*

person was rated stingy, he was more likely to be rated as stubborn and orderly, too, compared to someone rated low in stinginess. These are the kind of guys we used to call "tight-assed," although I never thought then about the Freudian implication of the term.

But the early toilet-training experiences of these fellows were not investigated in this study. My guess is that if they had been, the researchers would have found evidence of premature training, coercive training using a lot of punishment, or both. This has been the experience of clinical psychologists who work with children (Mussen et al., 1979b). Although such evidence would be in line with Freud's theory, it is evidence of a mediocre kind. Consider orderliness, for example: Parents who are unusually neat, for whatever reasons, try to teach their children a sense of orderliness. They will also try to accomplish no-nonsense toilet training as soon as they think the child has any chance of complying. If the children then grow to be orderly adults, who is to say that abnormal toilet training is the prime factor, or even a significant one?

The Phallic Stage

Following the anal stage, according to male Freudian theory, the male child enters the *phallic stage* of personality development. (The Freudian view of female development, which is presumed to be different from the male's at this age, will be discussed later.) "Phallic" derives from "phallus," which means "penis." The term is meant to imply a period in which the first glimmerings of normal sexual relationships appear.

The Oedipus Complex. The major learning situation of the phallic stage is called the *Oedipus complex,* after the tragic Oedipus Rex (King Oedipus), who, in Sophocles' play, unknowingly killed his father and married his mother. In the Freudian theory of personality development, the young male (aged between three and five) is dimly aware of his sexuality. He chooses his favorite girl—his mother (or whoever plays that role for him)—as his first great love object. But she is already taken! He discovers that he has a rival—his father. He dreams of running off

Figure 8.16 *The attraction children have for the parent of the opposite sex is the basis of several Freudian concepts, including the Oedipus complex and penis envy.*

with his mother and of violent "accidents" that eliminate his father. These dreams elicit guilt, however, because he loves his father. The dreams also inspire fear, for if he can plot against his father, then his father can plot back. Surely, the child thinks, my father knows what I am up to. He begins to have *castration anxiety,* a fear that his father will cut off his penis to eliminate competition. This fear arises whenever the boy thinks about his mother, so eventually the boy does not think "that way" about his mother any more. He *represses* the naughty thoughts. And he begins to see his father in a new light, as a powerful figure he would like to imitate. He begins to identify with the father and, coincidentally, with the male role in society. He may even decide that girls are no good for anything.

My initial reaction to this description of my life from age three to five was that it was nonsense, totally foreign to my experience, and I wondered how anyone could have come up with such a theory. Reading more of Freud convinced me that reading more of Freud is necessary to understand what he was trying to say. Let me attempt to present the theory of the Oedipus complex in terms that are oversimplified, but somewhat more reasonable to the modern American mind.

Freud was describing the beginnings of social interactions that require the child to take into account not only his relationships with other people but also *their* relationships with other people. The anal stage involves a battle of wills between two people. The phallic stage and the Oedipus complex involve three people: child, mother, and father. The social relationships are more complicated than simply child-parent, as in the anal stage. Now they are child-mother and child-father, plus the very difficult to understand relationship between mother and father. This last relationship does not even involve the child. The child is in a prelogical stage of thinking, as we know from the work of Piaget and others, and thus he can only *sense* the interpersonal dynamics. He may well develop a vague sense of fear because his desires in this matter involve relationships he is too young to understand. With increasing pressures to "act like a male," he may well put his confusion about the Oedipal triangle out of his mind and concentrate on becoming a man, a task that is fun and receives the blessings of the family.

A poor "solution" to the Oedipal problem may affect the child's later personality. If he was extremely attached to his mother, if his father was an unloving, harsh man, or if some other aspect of the family romantic triangle was extremely atypical, it is not difficult to imagine these repressed desires — which are at least partly sexual, in a childlike, primitive sense — and the repressed fears, vague and foreboding, arising again to influence behavior in later life. When he must take a young girl from her father, in marriage, for example, the similarity of the situation to the original Oedipal period might dredge up long-forgotten attitudes.

Penis Envy. In the Freudian theory of personality development, males and females proceed in roughly similar fashion through the oral and anal stages. While the boys are involved in the Oedipal intrigue, however, girls are supposedly trying to deal with *penis envy.* One of the most controversial concepts in all of psychoanalytic theory, penis envy was intended to explain why girls idenity with the female role, just as the Oedipus complex with its castration anxiety was conceived to explain a boy's desire to be a man.

Formulated with the aid of prominent female psychoanalysts (for example, Helene Deutsch), the Freudian theory of personality development is based on the envy little girls (aged three to five) are presumed to have for the genital organ of the male. It is bigger and more versatile. Their own genitals appear to be wounds; they feel mutilated and inferior. They blame their mother (turning away from her) and desire a penis of their own (turning toward the father). Gaining a penis becomes symbolically equated in the little girl's mind with gaining a husband and, eventually, having children. Thus, healthy adjustment to the natural penis envy involves living vicariously through one's husband and children. Unhealthy adjustments include giving up, which produces a meek, frigid spinster, and overreaction, which produces masculine women who enter male areas of endeavor and who may be lesbian.

Again, one's initial reaction to this theory is likely to be that it is complete nonsense. It should be pointed out in Freud's defense that he was using the penis as a symbolic representation for *activity* of a certain kind: an active, *intrusive* mode of behavior, as Erikson conceptualized it. In contrast, the vagina was viewed as representing a generally *passive* attitude toward life. The envy of the little girl, therefore, was not simply for a male organ, but for all that maleness represented biologically: strength, speed, aggressiveness, activity. According to the theory, the little girl learns that if she is to get her way, she must use her wits. And she always faces the possibility of "rape" — the violation of her rights by brute force — in nonsexual arenas as well as sexual ones.

Most psychologists find the concept of penis envy of little or no value today, especially when questions of which sex differences are biological and which are social are still being debated (see Interlude: The Psychology of Sex Differences, pp. 179–193). If they speak of envy at all, they consider *privilege envy* — a *socially* induced envy of privileged male status — to be a more useful concept than penis envy, a biologically based concept.

Latency, Puberty, and the Genital Stage

In Freud's theory, the phallic stage is followed by a period of *latency,* which means very few advances in sexual wisdom occur until puberty. Having worked out the complicated problems of the Oedipus complex, the child begins a long period of peace and quiet before pubertal storms again raise up disquieting thoughts of sexual adventure. But this does not mean that the period between roughly six and puberty is without significance. The child of six and above is busy identifying with various people he or she desires to impersonate, for one reason or another, seeking his or her own identity.

According to Erik Erikson, this is a time when the child is exposed to the technology that she or he is expected to master as an adult. In our society, this exposure is formal: The child is sent to school.

But then comes *puberty.* The girl's breasts grow and menstruation begins. The boy's voice breaks, hair starts growing in strange places, and he becomes capable of fathering a child. Biologically, puberty is a point of demarcation between the child and the adult; in particular, puberty means the person is now ready to procreate. But whether the teenager is psychologically adult is quite another question.

The Identity Crisis. This is the time of the *identity crisis,* in the term for which Erikson is most famous. It is a difficult period. Not only is the person half-child, half-adult, with stormy passions rising within that he doesn't know how to handle, but society now announces that it would like him to make decisions about his future career that will affect the rest of his life. Do you want vocational-technical courses or college-preparatory courses? Speak. What do you want to be when you grow up? Decide.

One of the major sources of information on one's identity is the *peer group*—people the same age with whom the person has some interaction. They are experts on what is dumb or cool or whatever the current phrases of evaluation might be. Because what is desirable—in dress, hobbies, idols, values, goals, and such—is usually determined by group consensus, adolescents tend to form in-groups bound together by fierce loyalties to the truth as they see it.

Eventually the balance must be struck between identity and role confusion. With luck, the ratio will be in favor of identity but with enough confusion to keep one's options open.

The Genital Stage and Beyond. If the major problems of growing up—from frustration at the breast to the crisis of personal identity—are resolved adequately, the child (now adult) can enter what Freud called the *genital stage.* In the genital stage, the individual is capable of what Freud viewed as the ideal love affair: an erotic relationship between two equals, filled with love and mutual respect (see Interlude: Human Sexuality, pp. 300–309). Freud was generally more concerned with the earlier stages, which he considered fraught with great significance for personality development. He discussed the genital stage almost as an aside; he did not think circumstances permitted most people to reach such an ideal state.

Erikson, on the other hand, was quite concerned with personality development in the later years of life. He did not discount the importance of the early years, and the conflicts of the oral, anal, and phallic stages, but he felt that significant change in personality was possible in both the adolescent and the adult years. One of his contributions was to reformulate Freud's genital stage in terms of a crisis of intimacy. Just as conflicts about toilet training create a crisis about personal autonomy in the anal stage, conflicts about marriage create a crisis for young adults about how to deal with intimate relationships—how many of one's deepest secrets to share, for example. More about this in the next chapter.

Imitation, Modeling, and Identification

The stage theories of Piaget, Freud, and Erikson approach psychological development in terms of *periods* of the child's life. An alternative approach is to focus on psychological *processes* that might account for changes within several stages. A prominent example is *imitation*, the process by which children produced behaviors strikingly similar to those of parents, siblings, playmates, or other people important to them in some respect. A daughter may imitate her mother in different ways at different times of her life: As a tyke, she might mimic her mother's way of walking; as a teenager, she might take up similar sports; as a young adult, she might favor her mother's preferred political candidates.

Imitation makes it possible for children to learn quite complex behavior patterns rather quickly. For example, throughout our life span, each of us is engaged in attempts to act properly in the different social roles we are asked to play. These roles may be as small and insignificant as "the dinner guest," in which the major problem may be a choice among forks, or as all-encompassing as a sex role: "male" or "female." If all the details—including not only behaviors but also the proper attitudes and ideals—had to be taught, one by one, it is doubtful any of us would have progressed much beyond properly executed temper tantrums. We do

Figure 8.17 *Imitating her father, this young girl is learning about sex differences as well as shaving.*

better, however, because we learn a lot by imitation.

Imitative learning has sometimes been called *identification*, which implies that children (and adults) imitate others they want to be like, in some aspect at least. Children identify with and imitate their parents. But, also, children might imitate someone they despise—a bully or tyrant perhaps—because they value his power.

Imitation is most often discussed today in the context of *modeling* (Bandura, 1969). One person does something—he is called the *model*—and he is observed by someone else, called the subject or the observer. The observer may or may not imitate the model; the investigation of what determines whether he does or not is an important current line of research.

One of the advantages of using the term modeling is that we get away from the idea that imitation has to be a direct mimicking of the model. Research has shown that children are quite capable of imitating an attitude, a rule, or a moral principle even though the behaviors involved are different. If a boy sees his older sister sharing her toys with friends, for instance, he might share his candy with his parents. If many models are observed, the observer's behavior is likely to contain elements from several, organized in a new, unique pattern. This situation is perhaps the most common in real life.

The amount of research on identification, imitation, and modeling is staggering (Bandura, 1969; Mussen et al., 1979b), and well it should be. The transition from stumble-footed, ignorant child to graceful, brilliant adult is made vastly easier by imitation. One psychologist calls it "no-trial learning" (Bandura, 1969). We will focus our discussion on a small bit of the research, on three factors that have been hypothesized to be related to identification and imitation: power, nurturance, and similarity.

Powerful Models

It is a widely held theory that children (and everyone else) want to be like a powerful model. Freud's view was that the young male identifies with his father because of the father's obvious power, a perception based on the dynamics of the Oedipus complex.

In one carefully designed experiment, nursery school children were randomly assigned to various conditions involving an adult male and female—a "family" situation (Bandura et al., 1963). In some conditions, the male had the power, controlling who played the games and who got the treats; in other conditions, the female had the power. The children, both boys and girls, imitated the male or female with the power much more frequently than they imitated the other adult.

In some conditions the adult without power was a "consumer": The goodies the powerful person had at his or her disposal were all given to the other person. Nevertheless, the child imitated the controller, not the lucky recipient. The child chose power.

One of the most interesting features of power theories of identification is the idea that people imitate people who frighten them. This is called *identification with the aggressor*. According to Freudian theory, children identify with threatening people in order to handle their fears. For example, Anna Freud reported a case of a young girl who dreaded ghosts to the extent that she had difficulties crossing the dark hall at night:

> Suddenly, however, she hit on a device which enabled her to do it: She would run across the hall, making all sorts of peculiar gestures as she went. Before long, she triumphantly told her little brother the secret of how she had got over her anxiety. "There's no need to be afraid in the hall," she said, "you just have to pretend that you're the ghost who might meet you" (1946, pp. 118–119).

But identification with the aggressor is not always a child's game. Descriptions of the life in Nazi concentration camps during World War II offer several examples of this unfortunate means of coping with severe threat, even among adults (Bettelheim, 1958). Some of the prisoners who had been in the camp for a long time would begin to act, and even to look, like the Gestapo guards. They would torture and kill the other prisoners for being "unfit." They took pride in their toughness, as the guards did, and they played "toughness games" learned from the guards. One such game sought to determine who could stand pain for the longest time before showing discomfort.

Nurturant Models

Another variable supposedly related to identification and imitation is *nurturance.* Related to "nurse," it refers to the acts of caring for someone dependent. The parents, and the mother in particular, nurture the child. Many psychologists have emphasized these rewarding qualities of the parents as a basis for identification and imitation (Mowrer, 1960). In learning-theory terms, the parent-models come to have the properties of a secondary reinforcement because they are so often associated with primary reinforcements. Thus, imitating the acts of the parent becomes rewarding in itself.

Plenty of research supports the hypothesis that nurturance is responsible for increased imitation. Boys who describe their relationship with their father as warm and nurturant tend to be more like their fathers in attitudes and behaviors than those who do not (Payne and Mussen, 1956; Mussen and Distler, 1959), and a similar relationship can be observed between girls and their mothers (Mussen and Parker, 1965). These, of course, are natural, correlational experi-

Figure 8.18 *Are children more likely to identify with a warm, nurturing parent?*

ments subject to several alternative explanations. It may be that parents who are warm and nurturant spend more time with their children and that the greater similarity in actions and attitudes results from the greater opportunity for observation, not from nurturance at all. True experiments tend to produce ambiguous results (for example, Bandura and Huston, 1961; Mischel and Grusec, 1966). Albert Bandura, who has conducted much of this research, is unwilling to make a general statement. Instead he says that nurturance "enhances the reproduction of some responses, has no effect upon others, and may actually diminish the adoption of still others" (1969, p. 131). Such a conclusion may be a bit too cautious. The evidence as a whole seems to support the conclusion that nurturant models are more likely to be imitated in most cases. But power appears to be a stronger factor, generally speaking.

Similar Models

If a child perceives a model as similar to himself, will he then be more likely to imitate this model? I imagine you are well enough along in the psychology game to suspect that the effect of similarity between model and child will be mixed. Similarity, after all, is a broad concept, encompassing similar physical attributes (skin color, height, sex), similar social categories (Catholic, Republican, college-educated), and similar personal characteristics (attitudes, ideals, temperament). We can expect that similarity will have a positive effect when the likeness is valued, something the child is proud of, and probably a negative effect if the likeness is embarrassing. In one study, children often imitated models of a dissimilar social class, if that social class was one they aspired to (Maccoby and Wilson, 1957). In another study, people who perceived themselves as similar to a model were more likely than average to imitate him if he was also perceived as a generally competent person, but less likely if he seemed incompetent (Baron, 1970).

PSYCHOLOGICAL DEVELOPMENT: CHANGE AND CONTINUITY

As a child grows, his intellect becomes more complex, more effective, more useful; his personality becomes more complex, more integrated, more individualized. Through the various developmental processes such as imitation, identification, and other forms of learning, the child develops a personal style of coping with the world and a sense of "self" that reflects that unique adjustment. Children have a distinct personality of their own very early in life, based on both the temperament they inherit from their parents and their earliest experiences with life.

Once formed, a child's developing personality provides a foundation on which new achievements grow. How the child has adapted to the conflicts of the oral stage, for example, determines in part his response and eventual adaptation to the conflicts of the anal stage; if he has no trust in his parents, he will probably experience more conflict in toilet training.

In the intellectual sphere, too, earlier adaptations determine responses to new situations. Piaget spoke of the developmental processes of *assimilation* and *accommodation*. Assimilation, in simple terms, is the use of habitual ways to cope with new experiences. An infant, when presented with an object he has never seen before, is likely to shake it or bite it, as he does with familiar objects. As an adolescent encountering a new object, he may try more complex ways of coping—he may try to classify the object, for example, by analyzing its features.

When assimilation does not work, accommodation is necessary. Accommodation refers to the development of new ways of coping when the old ones are inadequate. A two-year-old child presented with a magnet might initially interact with it in habitual ways—bouncing it or trying to make it produce a sound. But once he discovers the unique qualities of a magnet, he will accommodate to those qualities; he will touch the magnet to a variety of other objects, to see if they stick.

Assimilation is an attempt by the child to remain the same in the face of new experiences, new problems. Accommodation represents change and growth. In both the intellectual and the personality realms, human development may be most efficiently viewed as a series of encounters with life experiences in which the child (or adult) tries to make do with present abilities and present values. When assimilation fails, the child is, in a sense, *forced* to accommodate — to grow, to replace part of his developing "identity" with a new ability, a new value. But the child changes grudgingly, trying to retain as much of the "old me" as possible; like government bureaucracies, the more children change, the more they remain the same. There is a personal identity apparent amid growth, a continuity in spite of change.

Let me say the same thing in terms of psychological research on change and continuity in personality. In two major studies correlating various personality traits assessed in childhood (before the age of three) with the same traits assessed in late adolescence or adulthood — traits such as shyness, aggressiveness, and compulsiveness — the investigators found very few significant relationships. In one, only 4 of 174 correlations were statistically significant (Kagan and Moss, 1962), and in the other, 44 of 784 correlations were significant (Schaefer and Bayley, 1963). These results do not indicate a high degree of stability in personality; they indicate considerable change.

On the other hand, evidence of a different kind suggests a basic continuity between early and later personality. In a follow-up of an intensive earlier study of 25 children, personality sketches at age 17 were compared with similar sketches of the same children at age 2 (Neilon, 1948). A number of people were given the set of early sketches and the set of late sketches, and they were asked to match each child's early description with his or her later description. They could do this quite well, although no one, not even they, could say why. In the judgment of one review, people can get some sense of the person in very gross terms, but this sense is hard to dissect and analyze into specific traits like shyness, aggressiveness, and compulsiveness (Kessen et al., 1970).

In summary, early personality development may be the foundation of adult personality, but personality is by no means "locked in" by the age of 6 or 16 or even 60. And (in spite of the often contrary opinions of their children) adults are capable of significant intellectual growth. These are the topics of the following chapter.

SUMMARY

1. Developmental psychologists are concerned with the physical, intellectual, and personality changes that occur over each person's life span. Early development, from birth to the late teens, has been most intensively studied. Theories of development often postulate stages of growth that are relatively distinct, even though the overall process is continuous.

2. In Jean Piaget's theory of intellectual development, the first stage is the sensory-motor period — from birth to the advent of language. The child learns perceptual skills like identifying objects, and motor skills like reaching and grasping; he or she also develops a sense of *object permanence*.

3. In the preoperational period (from about one and a half to six years of age), children are unable to integrate, compensate, and perform other logical operations adults take for granted. Because of their egocentric point of view, children find it difficult to imagine what someone else is thinking. They judge morality on the basis of the outcome of a behavior rather than its intention.

4. Children aged six to eleven or so are in the period of concrete operations. They can mentally operate on sensory input, for example, to conclude that a higher level of liquid in a thinner glass does not necessarily mean that there is a greater amount than in a wider glass with a lower level (Piaget's problem of *conservation*). Around the age of seven, children learn to classify objects using *superordinate concepts.*

5. Around the age of eleven or twelve, children reach Piaget's period of formal operations, in which abstract thought and hypothesis testing are possible.

6. The first year is crucial to normal personality development. Infants apparently require varied stimulation as well as love from their parents or caretakers; if they do not get it, they exhibit extremely abnormal behaviors and may die. Because much of the learning in the first year involves feeding situations and other mouth activities, Freud called this the oral stage. According to Erik Erikson, this is the time when the child learns trust in "the world out there."

7. Specific *attachment* bonds between infants and their caretakers develop between the sixth and eighth months of life. At first the infant directs most of his behavior toward his primary caretaker — usually his mother — and is distressed when she leaves. By 18 months or so, the social world of the infant expands as he forms multiple attachments.

8. In the second and third years the child learns how to use language and which body movements are acceptable. Toilet training, in what Freud called the anal stage of personality development, is a battle of wills between parent and child. Disturbing experiences at this time may produce a frugal, obstinate, and orderly adult; a successful resolution teaches the child self-control.

9. Years three to five and above, according to Freudian theory, mark the *phallic stage,* the time of the Oedipus complex for boys and penis envy for girls. The Oedipal situation involves a boy's adjusting to his desire to have his mother all to himself (in a primitive sexual sense). Penis envy is a rather archaic Freudian concept describing a young girl's desire to be biologically male (aggressive, strong, fast, with a penis).

10. Between roughly age six and puberty Freud postulated a *latency stage,* followed by the *genital stage* of biological adulthood. According to Erikson, adolescence is the time of the *identity crisis,* as the young person is faced with making his or her first adult decisions.

11. Imitation accounts for a significant amount of human learning, especially among young people. People tend to identify with models who have power and who are similar to them, at least if the similar models are otherwise reasonably admirable. The model's nurturance has an ambiguous effect, but it may be a factor also.

12. Piaget's concepts of *assimilation* (understanding a new object or idea in terms of previous experience) and *accommodation* (learning a new concept from a new object or idea) help explain how we grow and change while maintaining our individuality.

USING PSYCHOLOGY

If you are able to spend about five minutes with a child from three and a half to seven years of age, you can observe two phenomena from the preoperational period: conservation and egocentric thought.

Conservation: You will need two identical glasses and another glass of a very different shape and size. Use glasses that you can see through, so that the child can see the water level inside. Pour exactly equal amounts of water into the two identical glasses so that the water levels in the two glasses are exactly the same. Have the child help you judge when both glasses have the same amount of water in them. Then, with the child watching, pour all the water from one of the glasses into the differently shaped glass (make sure ahead of time that this glass will hold all the water you will pour into it). Ask the child, "Do both glasses have the same amount of water, or does one glass have more water?" If the child can-

not yet conserve, he or she will probably say the glass with the tallest level of water has more water in it. The preoperational child is overwhelmed by the appearance of the different water levels in the glasses.

Egocentric thought: Get a book with attractive, easy-to-identify pictures on the front and back covers. There should be a different picture on each cover. Show the pictures to the child, have him or her identify them, and talk about them briefly. Sit facing the child and hold the book up with the front cover facing the child and the back cover facing you. Ask the child what picture he or she sees, and what picture you see. A child in the preoperational period of cognitive development will probably tell you that you see the same picture he or she sees. The child cannot yet understand that other people have thoughts and points of view different from his or her own. This is egocentrism.

SUGGESTED READINGS

Mussen, P. H., Conger, J. J., Kagan, J., & Geiwitz, J. *Psychological development: a life-span approach.* Harper & Row, 1979.
I don't mind recommending my own textbooks, especially when the co-authors are distinguished development psychologists. It's a quality book, covering psychological development in the adult years, too.

Conger, J. J. *Adolescence and youth.* 2nd ed. Harper & Row, 1977.
The leading textbook on the personal and social problems of adjustment during the teen years and early adulthood.

Evans, R. I. *Jean Piaget: the man and his ideas.* Dutton, 1973.
An interview of the famous Swiss psychologist; an interesting introduction to his theories of cognitive development.

Erikson, E. *Childhood and society.* 2nd ed. Norton, 1963.
The best introduction to Erikson's ideas about personality development; see especially Chapter 7 on the eight stages of life.

INTERLUDE

Moral Development

In 1843, Henry Thoreau, the philosopher of Walden Pond, was jailed because of his opposition to slavery. One day in his cell, peering out the jail's barred window, Thoreau spotted his old friend Ralph Waldo Emerson, and called to him. Emerson was amazed. "What are you doing in jail?" he asked. Thoreau was equally amazed. "What are you doing out there?"

All our lives we face moral dilemmas and through them refine our moral principles. Must we obey unjust laws? Is the moral individual inside prison and the immoral outside? What right does the individual have to "take the law into his or her own hands"? When does the individual have an obligation to do so?

Children face similar dilemmas on their own level. Is it ever OK to lie? The teacher wants the name of the student who wrote dirty words on the blackboard; should I tell on my friend? my enemy? Why should I share my candy with my brother?

Psychologists have posed such moral dilemmas for children and adults in research on moral development. How people think about morality, how they reason to reach their conclusions in matters of morality—these are the processes under study. These issues in psychology have been defined largely by the work of Lawrence Kohlberg; this interlude will focus on Kohlberg's theory and the research, pro and con, related to it.

DILEMMAS AND CHOICES

In his initial research, Kohlberg presented ten stories involving moral dilemmas to subjects aged 7, 10, 13, and 16. One of the ten was the following:

> In Europe, a woman was near death from a special kind of cancer. There was one drug that the doctors thought might save her. It was a form of radium that a druggist in the same town had recently discovered. The drug was expensive to make, but the druggist was charging ten times what the drug cost him to make. He paid $200 for the radium and charged $2000 for a small dose of the drug. The sick woman's husband, Heinz, went to everyone he knew to borrow the money, but he could only get together about $1000, which is half of what it cost. He told the druggist that his wife was dying and asked him to sell it cheaper or let him pay later. But the druggist said: "No, I discovered the drug and I'm going to make money from it." So Heinz got desperate and broke into the man's store to steal the drug for his wife. Should the husband have done that? (Kohlberg, 1963, pp. 18–19).

Other dilemmas were similar in structure, but with different content. One involved a doctor faced with a patient about to die, in great pain, and begging for a mercy killing. Another portrayed a military leader who must send someone (himself?) on an almost certainly fatal mission.

In each dilemma, a case can be made for either course of action: "Yes, Heinz should have stolen the drug" or "No, Heinz did wrong." Kohlberg was not interested in the positions the subjects took on the issues, but in the reasoning they used to justify their positions. From the subjects' answers to the dilemmas and, in particular, the reasons they gave for their answers, Kohlberg arrived at six stages of moral reasoning. The six stages are divided into three levels of two stages each (see Table 1).

The first level is called *preconventional*. At this level, the person responds to popular notions of what is right and what is wrong, but he or she has no sense of any underlying reasons. In Stage 1, the *punishment and obedience orientation*, the *outcome* is the only consideration, especially if it is unpleasant. One does what is "moral" because if one does not, one gets hurt by others more powerful than oneself; these others are the people who define what is and what is not "moral." In the Heinz story, such reasoning would go something like, "No. Heinz shouldn't have done that. It's against the law, and he'll get put in jail."

In State 2, moral reasoning is based on *self-interest*. This stage represents the *instrumental relativist orientation:* All instructions are interpreted *relative* to the person's own desires—"I'll do it if I feel like it"—and obeyed if *instrumental*, which means that the behavior satisfies the personal desire. The major advance is that other people are sometimes considered, but only in the sense of "If you'll scratch my back, I'll scratch yours." Most of Kohlberg's seven-year-old subjects gave answers at Level I, most of them at Stage 2.

The second level of moral development, a level many never pass, is called the *conventional level*. The traditions and "social contracts" of families, groups, and nations are perceived as important, deserving of loyalty even if the immediate personal outcomes are not favorable. In Stage 3, the *good boy, good girl orientation*, the *intention* of the actor becomes a major factor, and conforming to group standards becomes significant. In the Heinz story, Heinz can be seen as good because he can't be blamed for doing something out of love for his wife. Or he can't be blamed for refusing to break the law. In Stage 4, the *law and order orientation*, subjects recognize the need for some kind of order and obedience to fixed rules, even if the rules are not those the subject would prefer. Heinz might want to steal the drug, but if we let Heinz steal, then we would have to let all unfortunate souls steal. Most of Kohlberg's oldest subjects, aged 16, scored at this level, most at Stage 4.

Table 1
KOHLBERG'S STAGES OF MORAL DEVELOPMENT AS SEEN IN THE HEINZ DILEMMA

Level I   Preconventional

Stage 1: Punishment and obedience orientation

Pro: It isn't really bad to take it—he did ask to pay for it first. He wouldn't do any other damage or take anything else and the drug he'd take is only worth $200; he's not really taking a $2,000 drug.

Con: Heinz doesn't have any permission to take the drug. He can't just go and break through a window or break the door down. He'd be a bad criminal doing all that damage. That drug is worth a lot of money and stealing anything so expensive would really be a big crime.

Stage 2: Instrumental relativist orientation

Pro: Heinz isn't really doing any harm to the druggist, and he can always pay him back. If he doesn't want to lose his wife, he should take the drug because it's the only thing that will work.

Con: The druggist isn't wrong or bad, he just wants to make a profit like everyone else. That's what you're in business for, to make money. Business is business.

Level II   Conventional

Stage 3: Good boy, good girl orientation

Pro: Stealing is bad but this is a bad situation. Heinz isn't doing wrong in trying to save his wife; he has no choice but to take the drug. He is only doing something that is natural for a good husband to do. You can't blame him for doing something out of love for his wife. You'd blame him if he didn't love his wife enough to save her.

Con: If Heinz's wife dies, he can't be blamed in these circumstances. You can't say he is a heartless husband just because he won't commit a crime. The druggist is the selfish and heartless one in this situation. Heinz tried to do everything he really could.

Stage 4: Law and order orientation

Pro: The druggist is leading a wrong kind of life if he just lets somebody die. You can't let somebody die like that, so it's Heinz's duty to save her. But Heinz can't just go around breaking laws and let it go at that—he must pay the druggist back and he must take his punishment for stealing.

Table 1 *(continued)*

Con: It's a natural thing for Heinz to want to save his wife, but it's still always wrong to steal. You have to follow the rules regardless of how you feel or regardless of the special circumstances.

Level III   Postconventional

Stage 5: Social contract-legalistic orientation

Pro: Before you say stealing is wrong you've got to really think about this whole situation. Of course the laws are quite clear about breaking into a store. And even worse, Heinz would know there were no legal grounds for his actions. Yet, I can see why it would be reasonable for anybody in this kind of situation to steal the drug.

Con: I can see the good that would come from illegally taking the drug, but the ends don't justify the means. You can't say Heinz would be completely wrong to steal the drug, but even these circumstances don't make it right.

Stage 6: Universal ethical principle orientation

Pro: Where the choice must be made between disobeying a law and saving a human life, the higher principle of preserving life makes it morally right—not just understandable—to steal the drug.

Con: There are so many cases of cancer today that with any new drug cure, I'd assume that the drug would be scarce and that there wouldn't be enough to go around to everybody. The right course of action can only be the one which is consistent to all people concerned. Heinz ought to act, not according to his particular feelings for his wife, nor according to what is legal in this case, but according to what he conceives an ideally just person would do in this situation.

From James R. Rest, The Hierarchical Nature of Moral Judgment: The Study of Patterns of Comprehension and Preference with Moral Stages. *Journal of Personality,* 41, no. 1 (1974), pp. 92–93. Copyright 1974 by Duke University Press. Reprinted by permission.

The third level of moral development is called *postconventional* and also *principled*. People at this level try to formulate moral principles independently of social groups, traditions, and authorities. Stage 5 is called the *social contract-legalistic orientation,* which Kohlberg describes as the official morality of the U.S. government. What is right is that which the majority of citizens agree on and set into law. If any aspect of this morality by general agreement (social contract) is shown to be ill-advised, then the contract can be revised—the laws can be changed, using proper procedures. Heinz would be wrong to steal the drug, but the subject might suggest changing the laws to provide for such emergencies.

In Stage 6, the *universal ethical principle orientation,* morality is defined by abstract ethical principles based on logic. An example is the Golden Rule. Subjects with this orientation might argue Heinz should steal the drug because the higher principle of saving a life is involved. Or they might argue that by stealing it, he would keep it from another, perhaps more deserving patient. (Note that both the pro and con arguments do not mention the fact that his wife is involved. One must not be selfish in Stage 6; one acts according to impersonal values, objectively derived.) In Kohlberg's opinion, very few people ever achieve Stage 6.

A FOLLOW-UP AND A SLIGHT FOUL-UP

Kohlberg's original subjects were between seven and sixteen years of age when first tested. Fifty males from this group have been retested every three years for a period of fifteen years, to follow the progression of stages within each individual's life. Their pattern of development regularly followed Kohlberg's stages—with one exception. Stage 4 (law and order) high school students who did not go on to college developed as Kohlberg expected, but several students who did go to college *declined* in their level of moral reasoning during their first years of college! Most of those who "fell back" went from Stage 4 to Stage 2, and although the decline was only temporary, it appeared to be a serious contradiction of Kohlberg's theory, which postulates an invariant sequence. Here is an example of the kind of reasoning that many of these college students used:

> [Heinz] was a victim of circumstances and can only be judged by other men whose . . . subjective decisions . . . are neither permanent nor absolute. The same is true of the druggist. I'd do it. As far as duty, a husband's duty is up to the husband to decide, and anybody can judge him, and he can judge anybody's judgment. If he values her life over the consequences of theft, he should do it.

Asked if the druggist had a right to refuse selling the drug, this same 20-year-old answered:

> One can talk about rights until doomsday and never say anything. Does the lion have a right to the zebra's life when he starves? When he wants sport? Or when he will take it at will? Does he consider rights? Is man so different? (Kohlberg, 1972, Table 3.)

The reasoning seems to be Stage 2 "instrumental" morality, in which right and wrong are determined by self-interest. But careful investigation led Kohlberg to conclude that these responses were actually a transition between Stages 4 (law and order) and 5 (social contract and democracy). The students had come to question the Stage 4 orientation of strict conformity and obedience to law, duty, and authority, so they did not feel bound by "the rules" or what is conventionally "the right thing to do." But at the same time, they had not fully accepted a Stage 5 morality which respects the will of the majority, as this may express itself in laws, and grants certain universal rights to all. As a result, these students expressed a moral relativity ("Who can say what's right or wrong? It's up to each person to decide for himself.") which appears similar to Stage 2, but is really quite different. One difference may be seen in the quotation given above. The student indicates that *he* would steal the drug—but that he can't say what would be right for Heinz. The reasons such subjects give for their *personal* actions frequently had characteristics of Stage 5 or even Stage 6 reasoning.

MORAL REASONS AND MORAL ACTIONS

Up to this point we have discussed Kohlberg's theory strictly in terms of moral *reasoning*. Moral *actions*, especially in the dilemmas posed in Kohlberg's tests, have been irrelevant. At each stage, for example, subjects might logically approve or disapprove of Heinz's action; their *reasons* were what Kohlberg was after.

Most life situations are more clear-cut than Kohlberg's dilemmas, and a clearly moral choice is often available. Thus, very often it is possible to predict the moral action someone will take from his or her stage of moral development, according to Kohlberg. Who is for gun-control laws, and who is opposed? Who supported the war in Vietnam and who did not? Kohlberg's theory should be able to make predictions on such issues, because the reasons for support and opposition are often at very different stages.

For example, in one study, college students were given a vocabulary test which they were allowed to score themselves, giving them a prime opportunity to cheat. Only 11 percent of subjects who previously had been assessed at the highest level (III) of moral reasoning cheated, whereas 42 percent of those assessed at lower levels did (Schwartz et al., 1969). Apparently, Stage 3 and 4 subjects cheated because they felt that in the experimental situation they did not really harm anyone by cheating and there was no indication that anyone disapproved of their action, since others in the experiment and even the figure of authority, the experimenter, did not seem to care. On the other hand, subjects at Stages 5 and 6 appeared to feel that they had an obligation not to cheat and take advantage of the experimenter or others. For these subjects, the more trusting the experimenter appeared, the more they felt obliged not to cheat.

A second source of evidence indicating that people act in accordance with their moral judgment is a study of the Berkeley Free Speech Movement. In 1964 the University of California in Berkeley decided to enforce a rule forbidding certain kinds of political activities on campus which had previously been allowed. Students organized protest activities against the administration's decision to limit freedom of speech. In addition, the students felt that the university had shown itself unsympathetic to student interests by giving in to outside pressures to halt the previously accepted activities. The protests led to confrontations with the school administration, and reached a high point with a sit-in at the administration building, where over 800 students were arrested. Some time later a study of Kohlberg's stages happened to include many students who had been at the university during the period of free speech protests. The researchers found that students who made moral judgments at the principled level (Stages 5 and 6) were much more likely to have taken part in the protests and been arrested than students at lower levels of moral reasoning (Haan et al., 1968).

KOHLBERG AND OTHERS

Kohlberg's work is extensive and important, but of course his is not the only significant theory of morality. The psychoanalytic theory of the superego is one other (see Chapter 10). Social behavior theories can be applied easily to moral behavior and moral development (for example, Mischel and Mischel, 1974). Here are some primary differences between Kohlberg's theory and the others: (1) Kohlberg places less stress on situational factors than the others do. A social behavior theorist would expect many people to steal in a situation that offered great rewards for very little risk, regardless of their level of moral reasoning. (2) Kohlberg gives less consideration to a child's early interactions with his parents—what acts they praise, what acts they punish, and what they do while the child observes. (3) Only Kohlberg makes the claim that moral stages develop in the same invariant sequence in all children in all cultures.

Kohlberg's work has stimulated a lot of thinking and research on moral development, and he has clarified many of the issues. As he and others continue to investigate this area, we can expect more data—and more controversy. For example, Kohlberg (1973) has now begun a program for raising people's level of moral reasoning through group discussions of his moral dilemmas. As you might expect, this project and others have drawn criticism (Brown and Herrnstein, 1975). Do we know enough about moral development to be able to change it for the better? Is it always a good thing for someone to move to a higher stage of moral reasoning? Who is qualified to say? We can expect more questions like these, and more tentative answers, as research goes on.

SUGGESTED READINGS

Kohlberg, L. Moral Stages and Moralization. In T. Lickona (ed.), *Moral development and behavior.* Holt, Rinehart & Winston, 1976.
Until Kohlberg's long-awaited book is published, his shorter works are a good source for information on his theory and research.

Damon, W. (ed.). Moral Development. *New directions for child development,* 1978, No. 2. (Jossey-Bass, publishers.)
A collection of fine articles, including one by Kohlberg, presenting several different views on moral development.

Behavioral Objectives

1. List and define the "filters" used in selecting an appropriate mate.
2. Describe some recent changes that have occurred related to children in the typical American family.
3. Describe the psychological effect on the spouses of the two ways in which marriages end, divorce and widowhood; state the general likelihood of these two events.
4. List at least four factors that contribute to our choice of a career, and identify the one often used in psychological tests for career counseling.
5. Define "mid-life crisis" and tell when it occurs.
6. Describe the types of person who adjust best and poorest to retirement, and generally how most people react to retirement.
7. Discuss the relationship between intellectual abilities and age, and describe some methods used to study this question empirically.
8. Describe the cross-sectional and longitudinal methods of developmental research and discuss their advantages and disadvantages.
9. Identify and describe the biological changes that affect or often affect females and males at about age 50.
10. List and describe the five stages of attitudes that have been identified in people who are dying; identify the one most consistently observed.

CHAPTER

9

Adult Development and Aging

What is it like to grow old? I asked my friend Sarah, age 70, a patient in a mental institution. Sarah suffered from brain damage, caused largely by excessive use of alcohol, but most of the time she was happy and completely lucid. In reponse to my question, she wrote a short story:

When I was young, the whole world opened up to me. I felt like a child in a candy store, with brightly colored peppermints here, with richly flavored chocolates there, all there for the taking.

"Didn't you realize that each candy had a price?" I said to myself when I was older.

"Not at the time," I replied. "It was too exciting. I had a good job—I was a high school teacher of mathematics, about as good a job as a woman of my era could hope for. I was dating a handsome young businessman. . . . There were hints of marriage."

"I don't understand why you weren't frightened. You were about to make some very serious decisions, decisions that would give you chocolate perhaps, but forever forbid the peppermint."

When I was older, I said, "The candy store was an illusion. I didn't have many options." I asked myself, "Why did you start drinking?"

"I got married and had three children. I had to quit my job. My life was going nowhere. I was starved for intellectual stimulation."

"So you drank? You fool! I don't understand why you didn't see that alcohol just added to your problems."

"It was the fault of the young me. She didn't understand. She had too many hopes."

The older me wouldn't accept that. "Youth is a time for hope. You should have been more responsible."

When I was very, very old, the whole

world opened up to me again. I saw it more clearly. For the young me, it was a place of illusions, a candy store of opportunities, a reason for hope. For the older me, it was bound to be disappointing, a reason for despair. But now I am very, very old, and I have no regrets. My life was interesting, fascinating, satisfying; how could a human life be otherwise? I wouldn't have changed a minute of it. I wouldn't trade my life for anybody's.

What is it like to grow old? Sarah's story aptly decribes the three main divisions of adult life: young adulthood—a time of decisions, a time of hope; middle age—a time of reevaluation and, for some, a time of midlife crisis; and old age—a time for review. The chronological age ranges for these periods are not distinct. Some people seem middle-aged at 30, others seem youthful until 50. People will tell you that a "young adult" is under 30, that "middle age" runs from 40 to 50, and that your 65th birthday means you have become "old" (Neugarten et al., 1968a). Perhaps more useful are the overlapping categories one social psychologist has proposed: 17 to 45 is early adulthood, 40 to 65 is middle adulthood, 60 and up is late adulthood (Levinson, 1978).

In this chapter we will examine several facets of the human life cycle. *Family* is one topic we will follow from young adulthood, when most people are busy choosing a mate, to old age, when widowhood and remarriage are common possibilities. *Careers* too are a recurring concern for most of us, from our first decisions to our eventual retirement. And then there is *intellectual development:* Do we really grow "too soon old and too late smart," or does our brain power recede along with our hairline and eyesight? *Biological changes* preoccupy us more and more as we

become middle-aged and then elderly: Do our teeth and our muscles really disintegrate with age, or is disease and not age the important factor? Finally, we will look at *death*, and what it is like to die—a fitting end to a discussion of the human life span.

FAMILIES

In the normal course of events, a family reproduces itself when the children reach maturity, split off from the family that nurtured them, and organize new families by getting married and having their own children. As this social process repeats itself generation after generation, each person involved must make decisions about love, marriage, and parenthood. In doing so, she or he usually gets a lot of free advice from other people; parents are notorious for their attempts to "guide" their young-adult children into "proper" marital unions. Occasionally the decision about a marriage partner turns into a battle of wills, somewhat similar to an earlier one that occurs with toilet training. The parents are struggling to maintain their control over their child, while the child is fighting for independence.

There is nearly always a sense of urgency about these affairs, as if you will face a meaningless life of misery if you don't marry (the right person) and generate grandchildren, as if society will crumble without "your family" to support it. Although certainly exaggerated, these claims are not without an element of truth. For many people, the family is the major source of intimate relationships, a strong foundation that can provide security and encouragement in good times and a refuge in times of trouble. Society relies on the family for most biological reproduction, for much of the generation-to-generation transmission of cultural values, and for much of the consumption that powers its economic motors.

Choosing a Partner

By the early twenties, nearly everyone has at least thought about getting married. An individual may decide that marriage should be postponed or that the institution is obsolete, but, one way or another, each young adult must confront the issue. According to Erik Erikson (1963), young adulthood is the period of the "intimacy crisis." Although one may develop a close emotional relationship with a friend, the need for intimacy is most deeply fulfilled in a loving sexual relationship. As Erikson describes the ideal case, such a relationship is affectionate and sensual; the sex is free of fear and guilt; it is not selfish, as much juvenile sex tends to be. Mutual respect and trust are required. On this basis, an intimate alliance is formed "with a loved partner . . . with whom one is able and willing to regulate the cycles of work, procreation, and recreation" (Erikson, 1963, p. 266). Such a relationship is usually proclaimed publicly in some sort of marriage ceremony.

Although more and more young people are choosing to remain single or to live together "without benefit of clergy," about 96 or 97 percent marry eventually (Carter and Glick, 1976). The average age of first marriage for men in the United States is 23, for women 21.

Choosing a mate, in this country, is usually up to the young people involved. That they should have any say in the matter whatsoever is a recent development in human history, one that even today many cultures view with alarm. A marriage partner is much too important a choice to be made by people so young, according to these cultures. And that the choice is made on the basis of "love"! What a shallow, hedonistic foundation for a union with such important social, religious, and economic implications! These cultures believe that love should come *after* marriage, not before (Mace and Mace, 1960).

Filtering Potential Partners. How do we choose a husband or wife (or a partner outside of the legal institutions of marriage)? In many theories the selection process is seen as a series of filters that screen out unacceptable candidates at various stages of a developing relationship (Udry, 1971, 1974). As Figure 9.1 shows, the pool of all possible dating partners is first screened through a *propinquity* filter. "Propinquity" means "closeness" in a geographic sense; this "screen" refers to the simple fact that people tend to marry people who live near them. Not only are you more likely to meet someone from your own neighborhood, but also, once begun, a romance carried on in person usually wins out over a romance carried on long-distance, by letter, phone, and occasional visit (Mussen et al., 1979b).

Next there is an *attractiveness* filter. Among the people you know, some strike you as more attractive (as potential mates) than others. Why? Your individual notion of "good looks" enters here, along with your preferences on a number of physical dimensions. An otherwise acceptable partner might be rejected because he or she is too fat for your tastes, or too thin, too tall or too short. A factor that enters the selection process in subtle ways is age: In the United

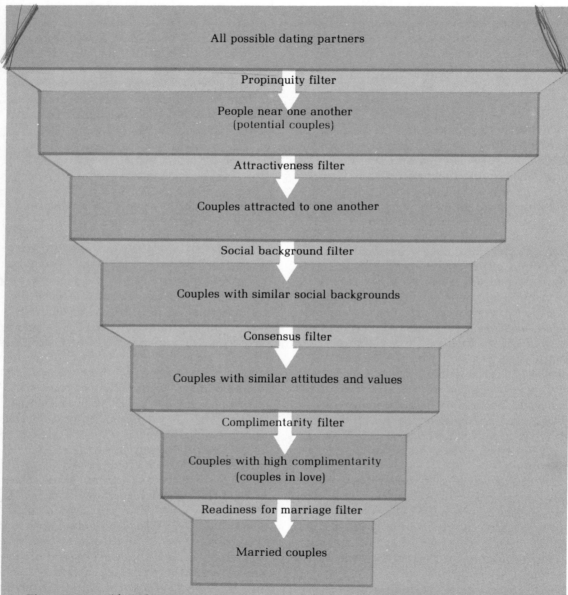

All possible dating partners

Propinquity filter

People near one another
(potential couples)

Attractiveness filter

Couples attracted to one another

Social background filter

Couples with similar social backgrounds

Consensus filter

Couples with similar attitudes and values

Complimentarity filter

Couples with high complimentarity
(couples in love)

Readiness for marriage filter

Married couples

Figure 9.1   *A filter theory of mate selection. The "filters" represent variables that predict whom one will choose as a marital partner; they do not necessarily reflect conscious decisions.*

States, the groom is expected to be slightly older than the bride, and typically is, by two or three years (Carter and Glick, 1976). According to custom, the husband can be up to ten years older or three years younger than the wife without much problem. If these limits are exceeded, parents and friends are likely to apply pressure to break up the relationship. On the other hand, the basis of this custom is the notion that the man is the "breadwinner" of the family and should "establish" himself before marriage. As women develop careers of their own, we can expect more marriages in which the woman is as old or older than her husband.

The third filter in Figure 9.1 is *social background*. People tend to marry people who are similar to themselves in religion, race, political affiliation, education, occupation, and social class. In the past these factors were nearly absolute: Strong pressure from parents and society at large nipped most interracial and interfaith relationships in the bud, and frowned on those that persisted. Today attitudes are more tolerant, but social background is still important. Occupational and educational similarities, for example, are *more* predictive of marriage (and of marital success) than they used to be. This is largely because marrying someone "of like mind"—someone who shares similar values and is striving for similar goals in life—is still important, and social background factors like occupation, religion, and level of education remain among the clearest indicators of such similarities.

Narrowing the Choice. As the relationship continues, the two people involved move from broad indicators of attitude similarity to more specific screening. Joe might be a white Methodist Republican with a B.A.

from a respected Midwestern college, but June, another white Methodist Republican with a Midwestern B.A., may still find Joe's values and goals quite different from hers. The *consensus* filter screens marriage candidates on the basis of their specific attitudes and values. Potential marriage partners who have similar attitudes are attracted to one another; they are more likely than others to date, to enjoy the date, to proceed toward serious courtship, and finally to marry (Udry, 1974). Then comes a *complementarity* filter, to ensure that beyond similarity of attitudes, values, goals, and needs, we find a partner who *complements* us. We want someone who "completes" us, someone who is strong where we are weak. If we are quiet and unassertive, perhaps a talkative, feisty person will make a partner in life.

It is important to realize that these filters operate in very subtle ways. People do not ordinarily make conscious, deliberate decisions about the social background and the attitude similarity of a potential wife or husband. Instead, in the typical case, the individual feels comfortable in the presence of someone with similar views on life: "He understands me; we have fun together." Only when we look back on the process, analyzing several thousand successful marriages, does the filtering process become apparent.

There is one more filter—the *readiness* filter. Most people tend to get married within a very limited age range. Below the age of 18 or 20 is "too young," and people unmarried by the age of 30 are often viewed with suspicion. Over three-quarters of all people who marry do so before they reach 25 (Carter and Glick, 1976). Thus, there is a certain tendency for a person to marry whomever he or she happens to be dating when the time seems right. For example, many people marry the person they are dating in their senior year of college. Graduation from college often means it's time to settle down—to get a job, and to choose a mate. Not surprisingly, many people who find themselves in this position choose the person they love at the moment.

And Baby Makes Three . . .

Once two people decide to marry, other decisions quickly present themselves. What kind of marriage shall we have? An old-fashioned marriage with the husband as patriarch? An equalitarian marriage, sharing rights and responsibilities? Perhaps even a communal family or some other sort of group marriage would suit us best.

And shall we have children? When? How many? Although 60 percent of married couples have their first child sometime in the first two years of marriage, this "typical American family" is becoming less and less typical. More couples are childless by choice than ever before—their number increased by 23 percent in the three years from 1971 to 1974 alone (Van Dusen and Sheldon, 1976). Couples who have children are having them later than ever, and they are having fewer children, on the average, than their parents and grandparents did. Still, almost all married couples have at least one child.

It is probably impossible for a couple to imagine how vastly their lives will change with the arrival of their first child. Every moment is somehow affected. Children bring profound joys and satisfactions that cannot be adequately described in words; they also bring new obligations that disrupt relationships with friends and even between

spouses. In one survey (LeMasters, 1957), 83 percent of the middle-class couples interviewed called the arrival of their first child a "crisis." The new mothers complained of chronic tiredness, decreases in outside social activities, and sharp increases in household duties; many of them had to give up satisfying jobs. The new fathers also complained of chronic tiredness and decreases in social activities, and they were amazed at the cost of babies, both before and after birth; the loss of the mother's income made matters even worse. The mothers felt they had suddenly become less sexually attractive, while the fathers felt that the mothers had suddenly become less sexually responsive. No doubt decreases in sexual opportunities were at the heart of both complaints.

The Postparental Family

In spite of the sacrifices a child entails, most people view their children as the "greatest satisfaction" in their marriage (Luckey and Bain, 1970). Some parents, both mothers and fathers, go so far as to define their family life—even their personal identity—in terms of their children. For these people, the middle years of adulthood can be a traumatic time. It is then, typically when the mother is between the ages of 45 and 50, that the youngest child leaves the home. Once again the couple is childless; "postparental" is the term sociologists use for this stage, which is also often called the "empty nest."

Although some middle-aged couples resent or resist the emptying of the nest, most find the postparental period not particularly difficult. In one study (Deutscher, 1968), over half of the couples rated their life *better* than it had been with children in the home;

most of the rest rated their life about the same as before. Only 6 percent saw their lives "sliding downhill."

Why is life in the empty nest better for most people? Among the specific reasons mentioned were an improved financial situation and a startling decrease in housework. Wife and husband have time for each other again, with more money and opportunity to do things together. Their satisfaction with their marriage in general, which declines from the time the first child arrives, increases sharply after the last child leaves home (see Figure 9.2). And, last but not least,

happy postparental couples cite the "satisfaction" and "contentment" that come from having successfully completed what they see as one of life's most important tasks: raising children. It was often fun; there were miseries and heartbreaks to go with the joys and the vicarious thrills; but now it's finished, and they can relax and enjoy life.

Divorce

For many couples, the family life cycle is never completed; the basic husband-wife unit splinters in divorce. The divorce rate is

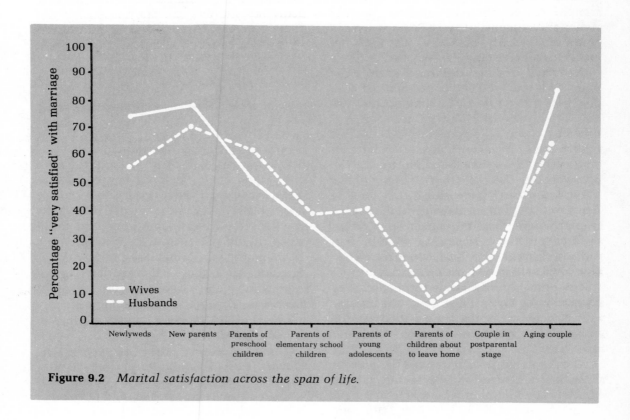

Figure 9.2 *Marital satisfaction across the span of life.*

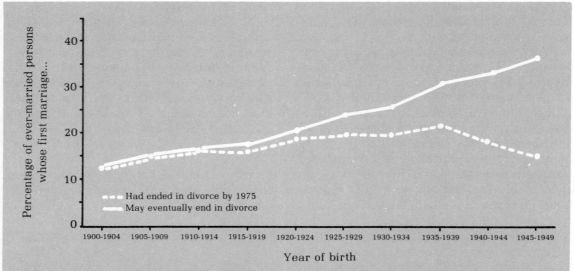

Figure 9.3 *The probability that an individual's marriage will end in divorce. For men and women born in more recent years, the likelihood of divorce in their lifetimes (which still have a long time to run) is estimated from the divorce rates of older generations and, thus, is probably an underestimate.*

high, around 50 percent for people who married in the 1970s (Glick and Norton, 1973). Some observers (Toffler, 1970) have suggested we are witnessing a new form of marriage: *serial marriage*, in which most of us marry more than one person—in a series, of course, not all at once. A few young people have begun to anticipate such a progression of spouses by writing marriage contracts that specify the terms of any separation or divorce. These contracts may even specify a limited time period for the union—say, five years—with options for renewal!

Most of us think of divorce as the bottom of the marital barrel; but it is not always the least successful marriages that end in divorce (Mussen et al., 1979b). Many unhappy

people stay married for religious or economic reasons, or "for the sake of the children." And many relatively contented couples divorce, for a variety of reasons. Perhaps one spouse has found someone she or he loves *more*. Careers sometimes lead to divorce, if the wife gets a new job in New York and the husband chooses to stay in Los Angeles. An easing of divorce laws or increases in public assistance to divorced parents of dependent children is generally followed by an increase in the number of divorces (Moles, 1976).

The psychological effect of divorce on the spouses is usually negative, even if the marriage was not a happy one. Often both partners come away feeling depressed, lonely, and anxious; usually there is a sense of failure. For some people, the stress of divorce is so great that it results in physical or mental disorders (Kimmel, 1974). Almost all known illnesses are more common among the divorced than among the married. Alcoholism rates are higher among divorced people; so are suicide rates. Admissions to mental institutions are much higher. Perhaps in some cases the problem—alcoholism, mental disorder—preceded the divorce, even caused it; but there is no doubt that divorce itself is a very stressful event.

The Later Years

For those couples which stay intact into the later years of life, family life generally consists of the central relationship between husband and wife, plus relationships with their children, who by now are middle-aged. Usually there are grandchildren, maybe even a great grandchild or two. For the aging couple, grandchildren are a whole new adventure—a chance to relive some of the excitement and fun of their earlier years from the secure vantage point of maturity.

Much has been made lately about the breakdown of the extended family. Certainly it is true that the traditional (extended) household comprising several generations and branches of the family has largely given way to the "nuclear family" of one set of parents and their children. Still, the change is not as stark as it is painted. Although it is getting rarer to find three or four generations in the same house, family members still keep in fairly close contact. Approximately 85 percent of American parents over 65 report having seen at least one of their children in the previous week (Shanas et al., 1968). Letters and phone calls make it possible for even the most distant of kin to stay in touch. And it is not infrequent for an "empty nest," just recently deprived of children, to be filled again when an aging parent moves in. About a third of all people over 65 who have living children live with them (Troll, 1971). Even if they don't live together, adult children and their aging parents can benefit from sharing their resources, with each providing at least emergency financial support for the other. Grandparents also are called on to do their share of baby-sitting and other duties left over from the days of the all-in-one-house extended family.

Widowhood. Generally husbands are older than wives, and generally women live longer than men. As a result, most women can expect to live several years at the end of their lives as widows. Statistically, over half of the women over 65 are widowed; in comparison, less than 15 percent of men over 65 have lost their wives (Carter and Glick, 1976).

Widows face a myriad of economic, social, and psychological problems, particularly in the first year or so after the death of their spouses.[1] Grief over the loss of a loved one, especially one who played such a central role in one's life for so many years, may affect the widow's health; the death rate rises sharply (Parkes et al., 1969). One research finding that you might not expect is that older women who have lost their husbands seem to adjust better than younger women (Blau, 1961). Apparently the younger widows' friends are still occupied with their husbands; an older widow is more likely to

[1] The term "widow" is used here to refer both to women and to men who are traditionally known as "widowers."

have a friend or two in the same situation, and they can help each other adapt to this great change in their lives.

Remarriage. Many widowed persons over 65 remarry. These late-life marriages often face extreme opposition and disapproval from friends and family. A marriage so late, they say, is childish. Remarriage, they say, shows a lack of respect for the dear departed. Such

Figure 9.4   *Marriages later in life tend to involve happy, satisfying relationships.*

objections often reflect the almost mystical awe felt by the adult children for the marriage that produced and nurtured them. How could Mom possibly love any man but Dad? In addition, and less tenderly, the adult children of the bride- and groom-to-be are often afraid their inheritance will be lost or complicated.

Despite the opposition, marriages in old age tend to be highly successful (McKain, 1972). Old people have fewer illusions about what marriage is and is not. They don't expect romance; they don't expect marriage to change them or their spouses. They want "the pleasure and satisfaction of having someone nearby, someone to talk to, someone to make plans with." They may enjoy having a sexual partner again, contrary to the myth that sex is not important to old people. In general, the widow who chooses to remarry feels she or he can make the new spouse a little happier, a little more content. And it's nice to feel useful; "the need to be needed does not fade in the later years" (McKain, 1972, p. 65).

CAREERS

Like our families, our careers affect and concern us throughout our lives. Their significance is somewhat different at different life stages, of course. As young adults, one of our most crucial decisions is choosing a career, or, for some, opting for some temporary or permanent alternative. In the middle years, we often reevaluate our career and, especially in today's rapidly changing society, choose a new line of work. The later years of life confront us with at least the possibility of retirement.

Choosing a Career

Choosing a career is similar in many respects to choosing a marriage partner. You're looking for the "right" job, one that will satisfy your individual needs and interests. At the same time, employers are looking, too, trying to decide whether or not you fulfill *their* needs. If the job relationship turns out to be unsatisfactory to one or both of the participants, it may end in "divorce," in the form of quitting or firing.

For the psychologist, choosing a career is similar to choosing a husband or wife in that we can use social and personal factors to

"This place is all right. Two more weeks, and I'll be a molecular biochemist."

© 1971 by Sidney Harris/American Scientist Magazine

predict to some extent the choice a person will make. Propinquity (geographic nearness) plays a role; people are obviously more likely to choose a career available in their home town than one that requires moving to an unfamiliar place (Mussen et al., 1979b). People also tend to choose careers in line with the social class of their families. There is more crossing of social class boundaries in the United States than in most other countries, but even if a child chooses a career of greater status than her or his parents', it tends to be a rung or two up the ladder, not several rungs. Certain ethnic groups provide a subculture for their children that may slightly predispose them to choose certain occupations; the Jewish subculture values education highly, which leads a large number of Jews to choose academic professions.

Certain careers are chosen for negative reasons such as widespread discrimination. For example, because many business firms discriminate against women for sales and executive positions, a woman's choices may be limited to secretary or clerk; this state of affairs is currently changing. Similarly, black workers often have been forced to accept the lowest-paying, lowest-status jobs, because these jobs were the only ones open to them. Workers over 40 or 50 years of age frequently find it difficult to find employment of any kind. The picture for black and aged workers is brightening somewhat, although it can hardly be called rosy.

Personality also can be used to predict career choice in some instances. Small but consistent relationships show up, for example, between measures of the need for achievement and the choice of a scientific career. The need for affiliation—friendliness—correlates slightly with the choice of a sales career; and the need for power is modestly related to the choice of a career that leads to a supervisory position (Veroff and Feld, 1970). One investigator found that actors, as a group, have a slightly less developed sense of personal identity than average (Henry, 1965). This finding was interpreted as meaning that some people find acting attractive because it gives them a chance to take on a vicarious identity from the playwright's pen. Interestingly, the more confused the actor's identity was, the greater her or his talent.

Vocational Interests and Values

One of the best predictors of a person's career choice is her or his interests — the activities she or he likes and dislikes. Typically psychologists gauge people's interests by their scores on vocational interest tests such as the Strong-Campbell Interest Inventory or one of the Kuder preference tests, tests familiar to anyone who has had career counseling in high school and college. The general theory behind these tests is that people who share a number of interests with successful members of a particular occupational group will probably like that occupation. (We will discuss these tests in more detail in Chapter 11.)

People's scores on these inventories do tend to correlate with their job choices. A study of men who had earned their highest scores on the Engineer scale of a vocational interest test found that, 18 years later, fully a third of them had become engineers. Another third were working in engineering-related jobs (Strong, 1955). Vocational interest tests also predict who will be happiest with their jobs (Perry, 1955), and who are likely to change occupations in later life

(Strong, 1943). Thus, just as similar interests are important for a stable marriage, attitude similarity is an important factor in the successful matching of person and occupation.

People's values, like their interests, have a strong relation to the kind of work they choose. In the past two decades or so, many young people — and quite a few older ones — have rejected the notion of choosing a job on the basis of "material success." They view businesses as exploitative, unjust, and concerned with profit at the expense of human needs and the physical environment. During and after the war in Vietnam, college students chased a number of corporate job recruiters off campus, particularly those known to be involved in war-related activities such as manufacturing napalm. These values translated into nontraditional job choices: social work, public interest, the Peace Corps. Traditional occupations were seen as too impersonal; young adults wanted a chance to be creative and to do something of benefit to society.

With the end of the Vietnam war and the onset of high unemployment and inflation, this trend has reversed to some extent. Young people today are still less willing than the older generation to put up with arbitrary, authoritarian, or impersonal treatment by employers, and they still view American business and industry with considerable cynicism. On the other hand, the majority of today's youth believes in the "work ethic"; they believe, for example, that hard work leads to success and wealth, and that these goals are worth striving for (Yankelovich, 1969, 1974). The percentage of college students whose major goal is training for a career, as contrasted with goals like "self-discovery" or general education, has been increasing steadily since the late

1960s. "The money you earn" is becoming one of the most important criteria for an acceptable job (Yankelovich, 1974). In general, today's youth seem to be trying to integrate the human concerns that emerged in the 1960s with a more realistic view of jobs as primarily a source of income.

Women and Work

We mentioned that sex is a factor in career choice: Certain jobs, notably elementary school teaching, nursing, and secretarial work, are widely considered "women's work." Occupations that employ a sizable majority of women generally are characterized by low prestige and low pay. On the average, women earn about 62 percent of what men earn, even after we adjust for differences in length of employment, education, and other income-related factors (Suter and Miller, 1973). Although this situation is changing—both job opportunities and pay for women have been improving in many areas—discrimination against women is still fairly widespread. The average woman scientist, for example, has to be better qualified and more productive to receive the same professional rewards as a man (White, 1970).

Much of the discrimination against women is based on employers' traditional assumption that the typical female worker is either a young woman killing time until she meets Mr. Right, or an older woman whose children are grown and who has been forced back into the labor market to supplement her husband's income. They believe that the older woman need not be paid well or offered a creative job because both her interest and her job opportunities are limited —all she wants is a few extra dollars and something to occupy her time. As for the young woman, it would be a waste of company time and money to train her for a position of any importance, because she will undoubtedly quit soon to marry and have children. Some employers also assume that young women are getting financial support from their parents until they find husbands to support them.

These stereotypes were not entirely accurate 50 years ago; today they are highly inaccurate. Most working women today are married and have children. The labor force includes about half of all American women in their "child-rearing years" (25 to 34 years old)—an increase of nearly 40 percent since 1960 (Van Dusen and Sheldon, 1976). Most of these women do not view their work as stopgap or supplemental; it is, for better or for worse, their career.

In spite of these changes in the character of the average female worker, most women in the labor force are still to be found in "women's work." Sociologists have computed an index of occupational segregation that estimates the percentage of people who would have to switch from a job commonly held by a member of the opposite sex—a man could become a nurse, a woman could become a truck driver—in order to eliminate segregation completely (Fuchs, 1975). In 1960, this index was 66 percent; by 1970, it was 59 percent, a decline but a surprisingly slight one. Much of the decline could be accounted for by (1) an influx of men into nursing and elementary school teaching; (2) women's taking jobs as engineers, accountants, and science technicians; and, most prominently, (3) a large increase in jobs that have never been highly segregated—high school and college teaching, computer technology, health services.

Recently a number of psychologists have

Figure 9.5 *Once it was rather difficult to find a picture of a woman doing a "man's job," but today very few occupations totally exclude women.*

studied the backgrounds of women who have chosen careers not traditionally associated with women. What leads such women to break with tradition? Support and encouragement from parents, teachers, friends, and boyfriends generally are identified as among the most significant factors (Cartwright, 1972; Tangri, 1972). There is very little evidence that achieving women identify more strongly than average with their fathers. Instead, the role of the mother, typically a high achiever herself, is found to be particularly important (Hoffman, 1973). The achieving mother provides a model for successful accomplishment. She also tends to reward independence and achievement strivings in her daughter, from birth on. And she usually has a loving husband who is proud of her accomplishments; from this the daughter learns that competition and achievement do not make her less attractive to men, as many women fear (Horner, 1970). Quite the contrary, the daughter sees that a relationship between two self-actualizing people can be very satisfying indeed.

The Mid-Life Crisis

It was not so long ago that, at this point in our discussion of careers, we would have shifted to a discussion of retirement. For many years, social scientists more or less ignored the years between young adulthood and the age of 65. It was as if nothing much happened between the fires of youth and the warm glow of the sunset years, as if one made her or his career choice and then slowly moved up to manager, supervisor, president, or whatever lay at or near the top of the particular heap the individual had chosen to ascend. And then she or he retired with a gold watch.

In recent years, however, there has been an upsurge of both popular and academic interest in career development in the middle years (Sheehy, 1974; Levinson, 1978). The research has focused mainly on middle-class men, so we should be cautious in generalizing the results. Most current theories, though, see the age of 30 or thereabouts as a time of commitment to one career. For

Figure 9.6 *Patricia Harris, Secretary of Housing and Urban Development and Secretary of Health, Education, and Welfare in Jimmy Carter's Cabinet, is a model for successful accomplishment.*

some, this is the age of finally getting a foothold in law or medical practice, or winning tenure, or being promoted to a supervisory position. For many others, for whom the years since high school and college have been a time of experimentation with various occupations, 30 is when one is expected to settle down. Either way, the years around 30 may be a time of anxiety: It seems like the last chance to make radical changes in one's career.

The period between the ages of 32 or so and 40 is generally devoted to "rooting," as people work on the careers to which they have made their commitments. Around the age of 40, another career crisis develops, part of a general reevaluation of life's goals and dreams that has been termed the *mid-life crisis* (Jacques, 1965). This is a time when most people find themselves comparing their dreams to the reality they have achieved. In the comparison, reality almost invariably suffers, and extreme depression may result. We may have to accept the fact that we are not going to become company president or an acclaimed novelist; indeed, even a vice-presidency or publication in the local newspaper may seem out of reach. Although most people eventually accept their state in life and go on to a new stability and personal contentment in their forties, some do make spectacular career changes. Paul Gauguin left a respectable job and family at 35, and at 43 took off from Paris for Tahiti, where he spent most of the rest of his life as a painter. Dorothy Sayers abandoned a successful career as a mystery novelist in her forties to become a translator and writer of religious works.

It should be pointed out that in an advanced technological society like ours, many of us should expect to have more than one career (see Interlude: Future Shock, pp. 385–391). We may begin one type of job only to see it disappear as a result of automation, or change radically in response to social or political change. My friend Carol recently quit her job as a nurse when she took stock and discovered that she was spending most of her time filling out forms and very little time with patients; the aspects of the profession that had attracted her were no longer present, so she began looking for a new career.

Retirement

The concept of retirement is fairly new in human history. In the past, few workers lived to old age, so the concept had little meaning or usefulness. Not until the late nineteenth century, when Chancellor Otto von Bismarck of Germany established a state pension for people over 65, was there any institutional support for retirement. In the United States, the Social Security Act of 1935 confirmed the idea that when one reached 65, it was time to retire. Before Social Security, most men over 65 continued to work—68 percent of them, for example, in 1890 (U.S. Bureau of the Census, 1976). Even after Social Security, working after 65 was common—46 percent of men over 65 in 1950 still worked, and 26 percent in 1970. Today we are again seeing significant changes in the concept of retirement. Government and business both are trying to move away from policies of mandatory or forced retirement for everyone at a certain age, and toward retirement based on individual competence and merit. The able-bodied elderly who want or need to continue working—and who may be as good or better at their job as they have ever been—will probably find more job opportunities in the future.

One of the many myths of old age is that our work is central to our self-concept, and that retirement, therefore, is a severe shock. In fact, there is very little evidence that this is true for the average American (Dubin, 1956; Mussen et al., 1979b). Most workers are quite happy to quit working; the only shock they experience is a severe drop in in-

come. There are exceptions, of course. Most of these are high-salaried executives and professionals with high-status jobs that are interesting and involving, and therefore hard to give up. It's a bit paradoxical that "the very individuals who, half a century ago, were considered to be candidates for a leisure class characterized by conspicuous leisure may now be the unexpected candidates for a 'working' class characterized by conspicuous occupational involvement" (Maddox, 1968, p. 360).

Those who adjust best to retirement are psychologically healthy people who have an overall view of the life cycle, and who see retirement as the final state of an orderly career (Bischof, 1976). Some workers, however, meet retirement with anger and resentment; typically these are people who feel bitter about having failed to reach their goals in life, and are unwilling to accept the idea that their attempts to reach their goals are over (Reichard et al., 1962). In between the two extremes are the women and men who manage to get along with retirement. These include both people with generally passive personalities, who like being freed from responsibility, and those defensive types who ward off anxiety and feelings of uselessness by plunging into frenzied activity—social organizations, hobbies, home improvement projects, and the like.

INTELLECTUAL DEVELOPMENT IN ADULTHOOD

What happens to our intellectual skills during the adult years? Do we gain in experience and wisdom as we grow older? Or does our brain become fat and flaccid like our bodies, less functional, so that our intellect declines with age? There are several ways to investigate these questions. Most notably, some researchers have studied age-related changes in scores on intelligence tests. Another approach is to look at the products of intellect—the great works of art and science—to see if these works occurred consistently in the early, middle, or late years of those who created them.

Age and Intelligence

The relationship between age and intelligence is the area of study that, perhaps best in all of psychology, shows how scientists using inadequate research methods can come to absolutely the wrong conclusions. The story begins with the development of intelligence tests early in this century (see Chapter 11). IQ (intelligence quotient) tests were devised to show an individual's intelligence relative to a group of her or his peers. The raw scores for each individual (essentially, the number of questions answered correctly) was adjusted so that the average score for every age group would be 100. Thus all age groups, from 20 to 102, have the same average IQ—by definition, 100. But if we look at the unadjusted raw scores, we see quite definite differences among age groups. Apparently people increase in intelligence (as operationally defined by these tests) up to the age of 20 or so (Wechsler, 1944). What happens after the age of 20, of course, is the topic of our story.

The early studies of the relationship between intelligence and age in the adult years employed what is called the *cross-sectional method* of developmental research (see Figure 9.7). The researchers would give an intelligence test to a group of 20-year-olds, a group of 30-year-olds, a group of 40-year-

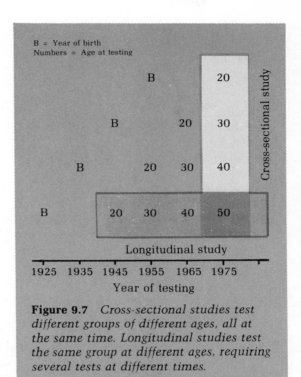

Figure 9.7 *Cross-sectional studies test different groups of different ages, all at the same time. Longitudinal studies test the same group at different ages, requiring several tests at different times.*

olds, and so on, maybe including a group of 80-year-olds or even 90-year-olds. Their (unadjusted) scores would be average and plotted on a graph, something like Figure 9.8. These studies, almost without exception, led to one conclusion: Intelligence, after the age of 20, gradually but inexorably declines with the years. Theorists began to speak of intellect as if it were a biological capacity, subject to the same deterioration with age as hair or muscle tone.

In the early 1950s, a new method of developmental research—the *longitudinal method*—became possible. Longitudinal research follows the same people as they grow

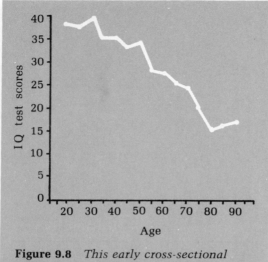

Figure 9.8 *This early cross-sectional study would lead us to believe that intelligence test scores decline with age; later longitudinal studies told us otherwise.*

older, so that the average score for 20-year-olds involves the same people as the average score for 30-year-olds. Longitudinal research, as you can imagine, is costly and difficult, and few academic psychologists can afford to wait several years to complete a study that might aid their chances for promotion. Fortunately, by the 1950s, there were a number of people around who had taken intelligence tests back when they were first given to college freshmen, around 1920. By retesting these people, investigators had themselves a longitudinal study of the change in intelligence test scores between the ages of 20 and 50.

The results were astonishing. Instead of a steady decline in intelligence with age, the longitudinal studies showed a sizable *in-crease* in average test scores (e.g., Owens, 1966).

Most of the early longitudinal studies tested college-educated people who went on to professional careers involving extensive reading and the use of academic skills such as mathematics and abstract reasoning. Later longitudinal studies, using subjects more representative of the population as a whole, indicated that the *increase* in intelligence was unique to the special subjects used in the early investigations. But the absence of decline was confirmed again and again (see Figure 9.9). We can now conclude that there is essentially no change in the average person's intellectual abilities during her or his adult years, at least up to the age of 65 or so (Schaie and Labouvie-Vief, 1974).

Generational Differences in Intelligence

How can we account for the differences in results of the cross-sectional and longitudinal studies? How could psychologists have been so misled by the results of the early cross-sectional investigations? The answers appear to lie in unexpected, but quite large, differences in average intelligence test scores between generations. At least until very recently, each generation has had higher scores than the one before. For example, when the average scores of armed service recruits in World War I were compared to those of soldiers in World War II, the World War II men scored much higher (Tuddenham, 1948). In fact, only 17 percent of the World War I recruits would have made it into the top 50 percent of World War II recruits.

Consider the typical cross-sectional results shown in Figure 9.8. Along the bottom

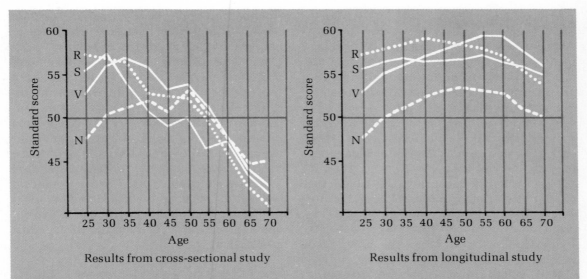

Figure 9.9 *How average mental ability scores change with age. The tests used were designed to measure reasoning (R), spatial ability (S), number or mathematical ability (N), and verbal ability (V). Notice the difference between the results of the cross-sectional and the longitudinal study.*

of the graph are listed the *ages* of the various groups. Suppose instead we list the *year of birth* (which defines one's generation). This particular study was done around 1930, so the 20-year-olds were born around 1910, the 30-year-olds around 1900, and so on to the 90-year-olds, who were born around 1840. Our reconstructed graph would show a decline of average intelligence test scores from the most recent generation to the least recent generation. This is what the cross-sectional studies mean: People are scoring higher and higher with each succeeding generation.

If we took any one generation, however, and followed its members across their life span, we would find their average test scores to be quite stable. This we know from the longitudinal studies. The longitudinal studies tipped us off to the fact that generation and not age was operating in the cross-sectional studies — that generation, not age should be listed along the bottom of cross-sectional graphs.

The obvious next question is: *Why* is the measured intelligence of each succeeding generation increasing? Better education? More familiarity with tests? Better nutrition? Nobody knows for sure. In recent years, the steady upward march of intelligence test scores has slowed, maybe even started on a downward course. Average scores for high-school seniors on the Scholastic Aptitude Test have been declining since 1962 (Zajonc, 1976); we will look at this recent decline in Chapter 11.

Age and Achievement

Another way to study intellectual development in the adult years is to investigate the creative works of scientists, philosophers, artists, innovative business executives, politicians, chess players, and other people who rely primarily on their intelligence to make a living. Do they do their best work when they are young and sharp-witted, or when they are old and wise?

Most people's most notable work—the one or two major accomplishments for which they are justly famous—tends to occur at a relatively young age (Lehman, 1953). There are exceptions, of course, such as Goethe's *Faust,* written after the author was 80. And the most notable works in some fields—philosophy, for one—occur a little later in life than in other fields. But most scientists, scholars, and artists tend to produce their most famous works in their thirties.

If we look at the total output of creative people, however, rather than simply one or two major works, the picture is quite different (see Figure 9.10). Then we find the sixties to be the most productive of all decades for several groups: historians and philosophers (as shown in the figure), botanists, and inventors (Dennis, 1966). Scientists in general are most productive in their forties, fifties, and sixties, with artists slightly earlier, in their thirties, forties, and fifties.

Clearly, creative people are capable of producing high-quality work through their lives. Although their most significant contributions may come relatively early in life, this does not necessarily mean that their intellects are better at the younger age. Youth is a time of ambition, a time to make one's mark. After achieving notable success, the need for achievement may diminish; the individual may not be willing to do the hard work and make the sacrifices necessary to achieve another scientific, scholarly, or artistic "breakthrough." Early achievement, therefore, may be based on age differences in motivation, not in age differences in intellect. Furthermore, a person's first presentation of a new, creative set of ideas is often viewed as her or his most significant work, even though the later elaborations of those ideas may be equally brilliant. Sigmund Freud's early publication, *The Interpretation of Dreams,* is generally considered his most important work, but he continued to expand and improve his psychoanalytic theory until his death at the age of 83.

BIOLOGICAL CONCERNS ACROSS THE LIFE SPAN

One does not usually discuss the biological concerns of young adults, because people think you're going to talk about sex. Of course, there's more to it than that. Most young adults are at the peak of their physical powers, able to run and play all day and all night. But sometimes after the age of 30 or 40, most people begin to notice the loss of some of their physical abilities. Little things at first: A 30-year-old woman discovers that her reactions on the tennis court are not as sharp after drinking a lot of wine the night before. A 40-year-old university professor realizes that she has lost her former capacity to go a day or two without sleep if necessary for an important project. A 35-year-old executive notices lines in his face and bulges in his stomach, so he buys a skin cream (which he hides in a drawer) and a book on jogging.

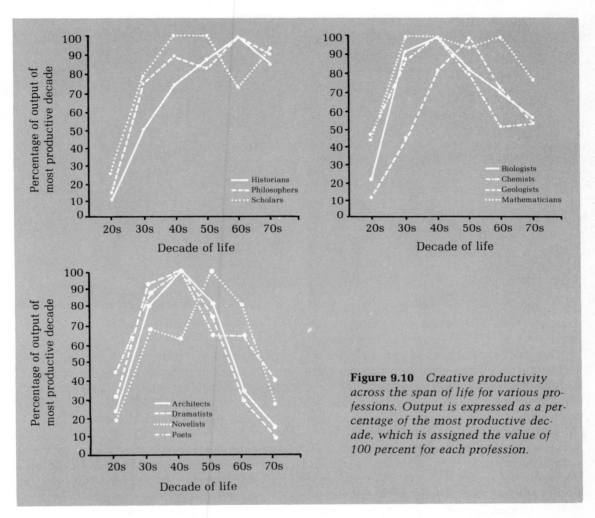

Figure 9.10 *Creative productivity across the span of life for various professions. Output is expressed as a percentage of the most productive decade, which is assigned the value of 100 percent for each profession.*

As people enter middle age, they become increasingly concerned with what they see as declining physical attractiveness and physical strength. It can be very painful when you realize that person in the mirror is no longer the tough, shapely creature you were always so proud of! The loss of physical stamina is less often discussed, but in many respects it has an even greater influence on one's life. Many middle-aged people complain of constant tiredness, a depressing condition that robs them of the motivation they need to overcome their declining abilities. This lack of stamina is especially frustrating to somewho who has made a reputation by being "hard-driving," working 80-hour weeks. There comes a time when one simply has to slow down—or burn out.

Figure 9.11   *What clues do you use to determine a person's age?*

The lack of stamina is a factor even in occupations that, on the surface, don't seem to require much stamina. In a study of great artists, for example, almost every one showed some kind of dramatic change in creativity around the age of 35 or 40 (Jacques, 1965). Usually the change was one of intensity— impulsive brilliance giving way to mellowed and more deliberate style as the artists evidently realized they simply could not maintain the constant high energy of their youth. Thus it is not only those who earn their keep with physical labor who are affected; decreasing stamina affects the ability to perform sustained mental activity as well.

The Fifties: Menopause and Heart Attacks

Menopause is an inevitable biological event that affects women around the age of 50.

Heart attack is a preventable, disease-related event that most often strikes men around the age of 50. Together these two events occupy a good share of middle-aged people's thoughts about biological issues.

Menopause. Menopause is the time of life when the female's ovaries stop producing a monthly ovum (egg). Along with the end of fertility, menstruation ceases. For most women this happens between the ages of 48 and 52 (Berger and Norsigian, 1976). For a year or two preceding menopause, menstruation may become increasingly irregular, and a number of physical symptoms may occur, notably "hot flashes" (the skin suddenly feels hot) and vaginal dryness. If the physical symptoms are particularly severe, a doctor may prescribe a hormone (estrogen), which generally relieves or eliminates the symptoms. About 20 percent of women experience no unusual symptoms at all during menopause.

The reality of menopause is quite different from most women's expectations, for the myths of menopause are many, and most of them frightening. "I was afraid we couldn't have sexual relations after the menopause," said one woman (Neugarten et al., 1968b), "and my husband thought so, too." Another woman thought "menopause would be the beginning of the end . . . gradual senility closing over, like the darkness." A number of women express fears about "losing their minds." Almost every woman has a few mythical beliefs about menopause which cause her anxiety. A group of women who had begun or finished menopause were asked what was the "worst thing" about it. The most frequent reply was, "Not knowing what to expect."

The reality of menopause, therefore, comes as a pleasant surprise to most women. Not only are the symptoms less severe than they expected, but also the benefits are more numerous. Simply not menstruating is nice, and so is not worrying about pregnancy; many women report a more satisfying sex life. Increased physical vigor is an unexpected benefit for many. In one study (Neugarten et al., 1968b), almost half of the women aged 45 to 55 agreed with the statement, "Many women think menopause is the best thing that ever happened to them."

Heart Attack. About one of every five males in the United States will have a heart attack before the age of 60 (Taylor, 1976). For reasons that appear to relate to male hormones, male victims of heart attack outnumber female victims by about four to one. Around the age of 50 is the danger period. The hormone level is still reasonably high, and the body is . . . well, for most men, in pretty bad shape. If a man makes it to 60 without an attack, the probability he will have one actually decreases, presumably because the amounts of male hormones decrease.

One of the best predictors of whether or not a man will have a heart attack is his life style. Some researchers have identified a life style called "Type A," which is marked by highly competitive achievement strivings, constant feelings of "not enough time," and general hostility toward a world that doesn't move fast enough in the direction the individual wants it to (Friedman and Rosenman, 1974). In contrast, "Type B" people are easygoing and patient. Type A men have more than twice as many heart attacks as Type B men (Rosenman et al., 1975). Their hard-driving style is a stressful one, and stress leads to heart disease in two primary ways: It is associated with heavy cigarette smoking, one of humanity's most deadly habits. More directly, stress is known to increase the level of blood cholesterol, which jams up the veins and arteries and overburdens the heart.

Biological Changes in Old Age

It is of course in the later years of life that biological concerns become most prominent for most of us. Hair falls out or turns gray. Skin wrinkles. More than two-thirds of all people over 75 have lost all their teeth (Bischof, 1976). One's voice is slightly higher in pitch than it used to be, and weaker, softer. Muscles atrophy and bones degenerate, so agility decreases and a stooped posture may develop. Vision and hearing losses are common, although with compensatory devices such as eyeglasses and hearing aids, most old people can lead a fairly normal sensory life.

The chances of disease increase dramatically over the age of 65. Over 80 percent of old people have at least one chronic disease, such as high blood pressure, arthritis, diabetes, or heart disease (Butler, 1975). Although they constitute only 10 percent of the population, the elderly consume 25 percent of all legal drugs, fill a third of the nation's hospi-

tal beds, and account for 40 percent of physicians' office visits.

The illnesses of age have many different effects on the lives of old people. Some diseases, such as arthritis, can be very painful. There are financial difficulties, in spite of Medicare. Many diseases restrict activity, sometimes to the extent of making the person dependent on others—often a blow to her or his self-concept. Reduced blood flow

Figure 9.12 *Extreme competitiveness, impatience, and hostility mark a man as a likely heart-attack victim. Taking it easy can save your life.*

to the brain because of cerebrovascular diseases is believed by many to account for most of the observed decline in intellectual functions like memory after the age of 65. In fact, many of the changes we see in old people we know, changes we commonly attribute to "getting old," are actually the effects of disease, and not aging at all.

Biological Aging

Why do people grow old? This question has intrigued scientists for centuries, yet "the fundamental causes of biological aging are almost as much a mystery today as they have ever been" (Hayflick, 1975, p. 36). Aging has been defined as "a decline in physiologic competence" (Timiras, 1972)—meaning simply that as we grow older, biological changes in our bodies weaken us generally and affect our ability to fight off disease. Death eventually occurs when our bodies fail to regain the physiological balance that disease disrupts.

But what makes our bodies more susceptible to disease? There are a vast number of theories. Probably the most likely one is that the genetic apparatus begins to use inaccurate, distorted information because the essential "information molecules" are damaged (Mussen et al., 1979b). As a result, the body replaces and repairs cells less rapidly and efficiently than before—or produces abnormal (cancerous) cells instead. The weakened body cells rob the body of its ability to react to stress, increasing the probability of disease. In many old people, death is due to relatively mild stress—for instance, a change in fluid balance caused by diarrhea—to which the aging body can no longer adapt.

The potential life span of the average human has been estimated as between 70 and 100 years, probably around 90 (Hayflick, 1975). Although life expectancy in the United States has been increasing fairly rapidly—from 47 years in 1900 to about 72 today—living longer appears to be due entirely to decreases in the illnesses and injuries that formerly brought many people to an "untimely" end. There is no evidence that the "normal" life span, uninterrupted by disease or accident, has increased in the slightest (Kimmel, 1974). In other words, when your time has come, something will get you; if cancer and heart disease have been eliminated by then, it will most likely be a lesser ailment that your body no longer has strength to resist (Hayflick, 1975).

DYING

The approach of death affects many people, including the dying person's spouse, children, friends, creditors, and many others. But most of all, dying is an intensely personal process, as the individual contemplates the biological end of life.

Elisabeth Kübler-Ross (1969), a psychiatrist who has interviewed hundreds of dying patients, has identified five stages in dying, each characterized by a particular attitude. The first stage is *denial,* a refusal to believe either obvious symptoms or medical opinion, insisting there must be some mistake. Denial ordinarily cannot be maintained for very long, however, and gives way to *anger.* The patient seeks someone to blame: She or he may vent hostility on doctors, nurses, family, even God.

In the third stage of dying the patient takes a *bargaining* attitude, seeking to postpone the event she or he now sees as inevitable. The patient may carefully follow the doctor's orders, in the hope of gaining a few months for "good behavior." God—even, in some cases, Satan—is inundated with pleas for more time.

The fourth stage of dying is *depression*, marked by a deep sense of loss as the patient realizes there is no hope of recovery. Finally, however, depression dissipates and she or he moves to the last stage, *acceptance*. This is not a happy stage nor a sad one. "It is almost void of feelings. It is as if the pain had gone, the struggle is over" (Kübler-Ross, 1969, p. 100).

Kübler-Ross's theory of dying has awakened quite a bit of scientific interest in the psychological aspects of dying, but not all of her conclusions have been supported by later research. Although most researchers find several stages in dying, the only one found by nearly everyone is depression (Schultz and Alderman, 1974). It seems likely that future investigations will show that people's reactions to approaching death are affected by several variables (Kastenbaum, 1975). For example, the nature of the disease: Dying of cancer, many physicians note, is different from dying of heart disease. Members of different ethnic groups often face death in different ways. A person's religious beliefs are obviously an important factor in how she or he views death.

Personality is also important. Someone's approach to death is likely to reflect, to some extent, the type of person she has been all her life—reflective or impulsive, warm or aloof, etc. (Kastenbaum, 1975). As Erik Erikson noted, this is a time of *ego integrity versus despair*. For some people, death is simply the last in a lifelong series of frustrations. For others, people with integrated egos, death is a part of the life cycle, and they are not afraid.

Figure 9.13 *The late Senator Hubert Humphrey with his wife, Muriel. "He taught us all how to hope and how to love, how to win and how to lose," said Walter Mondale at Humphrey's funeral. "He taught us how to live and, finally, he taught us how to die."*

The elderly person with integrity provides a model of successful personality development. Such women and men personify the goal of a life worth living; they offer hope to our children. As Erikson said, "Healthy children will not fear life if their elders have integrity enough not to fear death" (Erikson, 1963, p. 269).

SUMMARY

1. Most research on human development has focused on children, but recently the adult years have come under study. Young adulthood is a time of hope and making decisions; during middle age we reevaluate; and in old age we review. Major preoccupations during adulthood include the family, career, intellectual development, biological changes, and finally death.

2. A major decision for the young adult is whether and whom to marry. Most Americans do marry. The process of choosing a partner can be viewed as a series of filters that screen potential mates on the basis of propinquity, attractiveness, social background, consensus of attitudes and values, complementarity, and readiness. Around half of all marriages nowadays end in divorce.

3. Nearly all married couples have at least one child, though a growing number are choosing to remain childless. Children place enormous demands of time, energy, and money on their parents, as well as causing changes in the couple's relationship; still, most people consider their children the greatest satisfaction in their marriage. Although some parents have trouble facing the "empty nest" when their children are grown, this phase allows the couple new freedom and resources.

4. In late middle and old age, family life may mean grandchildren, widowhood, moving in with one's grown children, or remarriage. Most aging parents still keep in touch with their children and grandchildren.

5. Choosing a career, like choosing a marriage partner, involves matching talents and interests with needs. Career choice also is influenced by many of the same social factors — such as propinquity and family background — as marital choice. Vocational interest tests can be helpful in predicting what careers a person is likely to be happy with.

6. Discrimination also is a factor in job choice. For instance, most women in the labor force still are found in occupations traditionally viewed as "women's work," though their goals, skills, and commitment generally are not notably different from their male counterparts'. Women who break into career fields traditionally dominated by men usually have had strong support and encouragement from parents, teachers, and friends.

7. By the age of 30, most people are settled into one career. Around 40 often comes the *mid-life crisis,* in which dreams are compared to real achievements; this period of reevaluation may lead to depression and eventual resignation, or to a career change. Career change at all ages has become increasingly common in recent years. Retirement, though resented by some workers, means the beginning of an enjoyable new phase of life for most.

8. Longitudinal studies indicate that whereas average IQ is increasing with each succeeding generation, individual IQ does not generally change with age until one reaches 65 or so. Creative people typically do their most notable work in young adulthood, but continue and often increase their productive output with age.

9. Sometime after the age of 30, many people begin to notice a decrease in some physical abilities, particularly stamina. Around 50, women face menopause, the end of fertility and menstruation, and men confront an increased probability of heart attack. In old age, biological changes may include deterioration of muscles, skin tone, and sensory abilities, as well as loss of teeth and

hair. Susceptibility to disease increases dramatically beyond age 65; many of the changes we think of as "old age" are actually results of disease, as the body's information and cell replacement systems apparently become less efficient.

10. Some theorists believe a dying person passes through several psychological stages before death. Elisabeth Kübler-Ross has identified five such stages: denial, anger, bargaining, depression, and finally acceptance. Attitudes toward death also are influenced, though, by the nature of the disease, the person's ethnic background and religious beliefs, and her or his personality.

USING PSYCHOLOGY

You can study people's views of human development by asking people of different ages (over a large age range) to separate the human life span into the following categories:

1. childhood
2. adolescence
3. young adulthood
4. middle age
5. old age

Ask your subjects to give an age range for each period of life listed above.

Try to include at least one subject whose age falls within each of these six ages: 10–20, 20–30, 30–40, 40–50, 50–60, and 60–70.

After you have collected all your data, answer these questions: Do most people agree fairly closely in their age ranges for each period? What is the average age range your subjects reported for each period? Is there a tendency for younger people to shift all life periods to lower age ranges and for older people to report older age ranges for these life periods (for example, people under 30 might report the age range of the old age period to be over 55, whereas people over 40 might report old age to occur after age 70)? If so, how would you explain this difference of opinion?

SUGGESTED READINGS

Butler, R. N. *Why survive? Being old in America.* Harper & Row, 1975.
A scholarly call for recognition of the problems of aging in America by the director of the National Institute of Aging.

Levinson, D. J. *The seasons of a man's life.* Knopf, 1978.
The best of the books on adult life stages; the research on which other books (such as Gail Sheehy's *Passages*) were largely based.

Kimmel, D. C. *Adulthood and aging.* Wiley, 1974.
An excellent textbook, comprehensive and thoughtful, with several case histories.

Birren, J. E., and Schaie, K. W. (eds.). *Handbook of the psychology of aging.* Van Nostrand, 1977.
Readable, authoritative articles on the most important topics in adult development.

INTERLUDE

Future Shock

"To prophesy is extremely difficult—
especially with respect to the future."
—Old Chinese proverb

If you were to divide the last 50,000 years into "lifetimes" of between 60 and 65 years, there would be about 800 such lifetimes. Humans spent at least 650 of these lifetimes in caves. Only in the last four lifetimes have humans been able to measure time accurately. Only in the last two have humans had the use of electric motors. The vast majority of things we use today were developed in the latest lifetime.

New products are being introduced at an extremely rapid rate, and so are varieties of older products. Twenty years ago, you had to face the decision whether to buy a Ford, a Chevy, or a Plymouth. Now that decision is only a first step. If you choose a Ford, will it be an LTD, a Pinto, a Thunderbird, a Fairmont, a Fiesta, a Mustang? What color? Do you want the special options? At one time, Philip Morris made only one cigarette; now you have a choice of several from this one manufacturer alone, as well as various lengths, filters (or not), and flavors. I have trouble in some gas stations deciding which of the several blends is right for my car. A study of soaps and detergents showed that the average consumer could choose among 200 brands in 1963, compared with only 65 brands in 1950.

Of all the scientists who have ever lived, over 90 percent are alive now. They try to keep abreast of close to 100 million pages of scientific and technical reports published each year.

Not long ago there was virtually only one option for two people in love: the traditional marriage. Today there are several possibilities, ranging from traditional marriages to decidedly untraditional group marriages, and there is growing acceptance of unions between two people of the same sex. Public opinion about what used to be called pornography has changed so rapidly that it is rather boring to watch the "skin flicks" of the early 1960s or to look at issues of *Playboy* from that period.

Social and technological changes are coming so fast, they boggle our minds. Traditions pass away so quickly that there is some question whether we are capable of adapting. We may suffer from *future shock*, a term coined by Alvin Toffler to describe the stress brought on by too much change occurring in too little time. In 1970, Toffler published a book called *Future Shock*, in which he documented some of the changes causing the stress and from which most of the examples in this interlude are taken.

THE THROW-AWAY SOCIETY

Despite recent conservationist trends, America continues a relentless march toward a world of impermanent things. Toffler calls it the throw-away society. When I was in high school, people had one pen for years, often for life. Now I go through several pens a year. People don't use handkerchiefs; tissues are so much handier. Cloth diapers are being replaced by paper, disposable diapers. There are throw-away cigarette lighters, disposable flashlights, one-shot toothbrushes, even paper wedding gowns. Even many permanent items skid in and out of our life quickly, because we rent instead of buy them. Cars, garden tools, homes, party supplies, and graduation robes are among the many things that are often rented.

It is easy enough to believe that the impermanence of things is a business trick. Cars, some say, are built to fall apart in a few years so the owner has to buy another. "Planned obsolescence," they warn us, is the goal of greedy American capitalists. This view is at least oversimplified; usually it is advancing technology that makes things obsolete, not corporate decisions.

Advancing technology has two primary effects. First, it tends to make older things less desirable to the consumer. Toffler relates the case of some apartment buildings torn down after ten years of existence. After they had been built, new methods of air-conditioning were developed, and people refused to rent the hot, stuffy old apartments. To modify the old buildings would have been more expensive than to tear them down and rebuild. This is the second effect of advancing technology: The costs of manufacture are typically much less than the costs of repair. Manufacturing, in today's world, is largely automated or assembly-lined, but repair is still a "craft." It is much cheaper to manufacture a pen than to repair one, so we throw away old pens. The cost of a new Timex watch is about the same as the cost of cleaning an old watch, so I buy a new Timex every two years or so and throw it away when it starts faltering. The cost of repairing a TV set often exceeds the cost of a new set.

THE NEW NOMADS

My parents lived their entire married life in one place. I have lived in over 15 different places since I graduated from college. I am one of what Toffler calls the "new nomads," people who live in the highly mobile world of today. And the mobility of Americans is incredible. About one-quarter of the United States population changes its address every year. People are

moving around, constantly. People in management in particular move often, sometimes to better jobs with different companies and sometimes to better jobs within the same organization. Advancement often means moving; an executive in New York might have to wait years to be promoted in the New York office, but she can become a vice-president now if she is willing to move to Phoenix, where there is an opening.

What are the psychological effects of being continually uprooted? Members of a family who have left their home for a new one face many problems of adjustment. First, they feel a sense of loss of old friends and old familiar places and activities. This is a reaction common enough to have a name: homesickness. Then, too, they must adapt to other new surroundings. They have to find a doctor they like and trust, a good dentist, and a service station with a good mechanic. They must meet their new neighbors; the parents have new coworkers, and the children are the "new kids" in school.

Once someone has made several moves, the trauma of moving may become somewhat less threatening. One learns to cope with constant change; but again, the psychological cost may be high. The sense of security and "belonging" that comes of living in a familiar place vanishes. And without roots, it is difficult for people to develop interest and concern for any place where they live. Why plant a tree if you aren't going to see it grow? Why paint the living room or fix the sink? Why vote in local elections if the results will not affect you? Why bother to make friends in the neighborhood?

LOVERS AND OTHER STRANGERS

As a highly mobile nomad who has lived much of his life in apartments, I have often been puzzled by the effect of such a life on relationships among people. One would expect that as population density rises, increasing the number of people who live close together, the number of friends would also increase. Instead, the reverse is more common. Many people in the apartment buildings I have lived in were virtual hermits, often by choice. To be a "neighbor" is to be obliged to do certain things: to help in times of need, to invite to an occasional dinner or party, to divulge at least some intimate secrets. To do this in a high-density apartment setting, where the number of neighbors might reach 50 to 100, is out of the question. In reaction, the apartment-dweller often retreats into total isolation.

It's a paradoxical situation. The more people we encounter daily, the more selective we are forced to be in our friendships, and often even these relationships become less personal. Involvement with another person becomes limited to some minor aspect of her or his life. We know someone as our dentist, or as a waiter in a favorite restaurant. Does she or he believe in God? play the flute? have children? Typically we don't know, and often we don't care. How different this is from interactions between people in the past or, even today, in small towns. In the town where I was born and raised—total population around 1000 people—my dentist was also my Sunday School teacher and a close friend of my parents.

THE DISPOSABLE PERSON

As friends come and go, so do occupational associates—people with whom we work. In the technological and professional occupations in particular, moving is common. (IBM, it is said by some, stands for "I've Been Moved.") Some of the rapid shifting involves promotions and demotions, but some is of a completely different type, involving the use of what we might call "disposable people." Many people in the aerospace industries, for example, work on "projects" that have an end, at which point the people are no longer needed, and they leave.

A "project" orientation to jobs has been partly responsible for the rapid increase in what Toffler calls "rent-a-person" agencies. These agencies provide temporary employees to serve urgent but fleeting needs. Secretarial help is the best known temporary service, but it is possible to hire unskilled laborers, butlers, plumbers, and even—or should I say "of course"?—aerospace engineers. It has been estimated that one out of

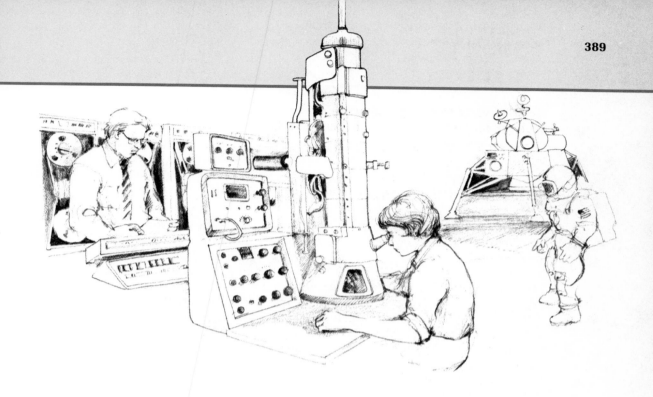

every hundred workers has been a "rent-a-person" at one time. The effect of this trend has been to decrease the employee's loyalty to or sense of association with any particular company. Most people in these mobile professions think of themselves in terms of their vocation—"I'm a psychologist"—rather than in terms of their employer—"I teach at Stanford." Or they may not even feel that they have a vocation. Young people, especially, may take a secretarial job to make enough money to travel for a while, then wait tables at a ski resort or work on a construction project until they get bored and try something else. The job is not a career or even part of their identity—it's just a way to make money and pass some time.

Another effect of technological advance is to change the jobs that are available. Old jobs are eliminated by automation or by improved technological systems. Once there was a job called "airline flight engineer"; it had a total lifespan of about 15 years (Toffler, 1970, pp. 94–95). New jobs come into being at a rapidly increasing rate. Look at the "help wanted" section of a newspaper and ask yourself how many of the listings would have been possible 30 years ago. A survey of a thousand young executives uncovered the remarkable fact that fully one-third had jobs that never existed before they took the positions (Guzzardi, 1966).

The notion of one career in life is virtually obsolete. The average American can be expected to change jobs between five and ten times in a lifetime. A good percentage (maybe 25 percent) of you who read this book will, 25 years from now, be holding a job that does not exist today; you will hold it about 5 years; then you will take a new job, another one that does not exist today.

"TEACH YOUR PARENTS WELL . . ."

Impermanent things, places, people, and jobs—this is the environment of rapid change in which we must live and cope. It is likely that some of the anxiety, depression, violence, and apathy of the American people has grown from our frustration in trying to adjust to a constantly changing environment. Psychologists are just now beginning to explore the effect of an increasingly fast pace of life on an individual's mental health.

One effect of rapid change, according to anthropologist Margaret Mead (1970), is to increase the generation gap. Mead distinguishes between *postfigurative* cultures, in which children learn from their parents—these include almost all known civilizations—and *prefigurative* cultures, in which the children must teach their parents. Because of rapid technological change, we live in what must be considered closer to a prefigurative culture than any that has ever existed. The past is no longer a true indication of the future, and the "experience" of the parents was in an environment that no longer exists. Young people know and expect change and impermanence in a way their parents cannot quite fathom. So the children must teach the parents. When the parents get divorced after 25 years of marriage, it is their children who support them, tell them it is not the end of the world, and give each of them advice on how to live as an individual. When a parent loses her or his job after 25 years, the children can suggest new opportunities.

Toffler (1974) emphasizes the need for changes in our educational system. Not only should we have courses on futurology—the study of the future—to cushion the jolt of future shock; traditional courses, too, should include discussions of future trends. "Marriage and the Family," for example, should mention what the student can expect to happen to these institutions. Career counselors should anticipate the job-switching that is highly probable in the future of their students. Instead of "What do you want to be when you grow up?" it should be "What do you want to do first?" and "What jobs will offer you the most flexibility for later occupations?"

Whatever we do, the future will continue to arrive at what will appear to be a more and more rapid rate as changes keep coming faster and faster. Coping will become more and more difficult. Anticipation will become more important. Keep this in mind: The year you were born is the middle of human history, technologically speaking. Almost as much will happen in your lifetime as happened before you were born (Boulding, 1964). That's future shock!

SUGGESTED READING

Toffler, A. *Future shock.* Random House, 1970.
  This interlude is an advertisement for Toffler's book, I hope.

Mead, M. *Culture and commitment.* Natural History Press, 1970.
  A short and scholarly book that contains the informed and humane views of Margaret Mead on the past, the present, and the future.

Behavioral Objectives

1. Describe Freud's development of psychoanalytic theory and the methods he used to explore personality.
2. Identify and describe the three aspects of personality according to psychoanalytic theory and tell how they interact.
3. Define "defense mechanism"; list the types of defense mechanisms discussed in the text and give an example of each.
4. Discuss the major shortcoming of psychoanalytic personality theory.
5. Tell how a person develops self-control and why self-control is important.
6. List some cognitive variables that are incorporated into many social behavior theories.
7. Explain why radical behaviorists refuse to admit cognitive variables into their theories and what implications this has for their theories.
8. Define the organismic premise of humanistic personality theory.
9. Briefly describe Carl Jung's personality theory and define the terms "collective unconscious" and "archetypes."
10. Define "self-actualization" and describe what may prevent people from achieving it.
11. Compare psychoanalytic, social behavioral, and humanistic approaches to personality.

CHAPTER

10

Personality

Five years before David was born, his mother suffered a serious miscarriage and was told she would not be able to have children (Weiner, 1973). Consequently, David's birth was viewed as a miracle, a hopeless dream somehow come true. His mother lavished him with attention. She was overly concerned about his health and safety, forbidding most of the vigorous things young boys do. In return for her maternal devotion, she expected obedience and love. And success; when David was two years old, she opened a savings account, in preparation for his medical school expenses.

Personality psychologists have the task of describing each individual's unique adjustment to the world. It is a very challenging task. There are so many details in a person's life. Which among them are the most important? Where should we focus our attention?

David was a bright child and learned quickly that academic success pleased his parents. He knew, at some level of knowledge, that he had to be good at school, witty but well-behaved at home; it was a payment to his parents, even a requirement for their affection. He was called the "miracle boy," the "genius," the "star." His mother was able to bear two more sons, but his status did not seem to diminish. He perceived, however, that his younger brothers were able to lead more normal lives, and he envied them.

What is happening to David? Is he headed for trouble? How can we describe his individuality?

David was a top student, as much a star among teachers as he was in his own family. He was witty; he had a flair for words; he became the editor of the high school newspaper and the school literary magazine. He was accepted at an expensive private university, where he did well. He was accepted at a prestigious medical school.

In medical school, David's life began to crumble. He found the laboratory courses "a grind," a regimen unsuited to his talents for words and wit. He met a young woman, a free-spirited individual with a very independent attitude toward her parents. He responded to her freeness and her independence, but his parents perceived the same qualities as a threat to their relationship with their son. They gave him an ultimatum: break off with her, or they would not pay his way in medical school. David stopped seeing the only woman he ever loved. He also failed a course in medical school and was dropped from the program.

David was growing resentful of his parents' influence — in his private life, on his career. How can we describe such resentment? How can we describe the conflicts between what an individual desires and what other people — his or her parents or society in general — desire?

David retook the course in medical school he had failed, but, as he did, he embarked on a career of thievery, stealing stereo equipment and records from local stores. He convinced his parents that his "purchases" were made possible by a part-time job. But his thievery was rather transparent, and the police arrested him. He cut his wrists in an obviously phony attempt at suicide.

His family perceived his problems as those of a very talented person under great pressure to succeed. They continued to support and encourage him. For his legal offenses, David was given a suspended sentence, provided he begin psychotherapy. After six months of therapy, David enrolled

in graduate school, in biochemistry. He dreamed of a Nobel prize. As a research assistant to an internationally famous professor, he falsified data to support a dramatic hypothesis he had proposed. He was discovered and dismissed from the university.

Could all of this have been predicted? What will happen next?

David's parents still perceived him a fragile "miracle boy"; their support and encouragement seemed impervious to real-life events. David eventually got a job as a copywriter in an advertising agency, where his bright wit and eagerness to please his superiors were highly regarded. He married an older woman, who supported his desperate ambitions but who also made most of the important family decisions. (A substitute mother?) He had few friends — even his brothers disliked him — and his business colleagues considered him talented but treacherous and overly competitive. He was quite successful in his profession, earning many awards. He attributed his success to his family.

Theories of personality represent attempts to pinpoint the factors that are important in understanding a person's unique personality, David's or anyone else's. In this chapter, we will explore the three most prominent approaches to personality. The first is *psychoanalytic theory*, created by Sigmund Freud; this theory focuses on emotions and unconscious mental processes. The second is called *social behavior theory* and emphasizes learning and behavior in social environments. Finally, we will discuss the *humanistic* theories, which get their name from their championing of the so-called higher or human motives involved in personal growth.

THE PSYCHOANALYTIC THEORY

Sigmund Freud was 44 years old when his monumental treatise, *The Interpretation of Dreams*, was published in 1900. Within a few decades, Freud's theory of personality, the psychoanalytic theory, swept through Europe and America. It entered literature, philosophy, and dinner-table conversation as well as psychology, and became perhaps the most influential psychological theory ever constructed.

But let us go back a little, to some happenings before 1900, to glimpse some of the reasons Freud put together his theory the way he did.

Hysteria and Hypnosis

The story begins in 1880 with Bertha Pappenheim, an attractive and witty young woman who was suffering from an unusual collection of symptoms. She was having difficulties with her vision, three of her limbs were paralyzed, and she had a bad cough. The family called Dr. Joseph Breuer, an eminent Viennese physician, to treat her cough. Breuer immediately diagnosed her illness as *hysteria*, which meant that her symptoms had no organic or physical cause—it was a "nervous" disease—and also that no treatment was possible. But Bertha had another symptom, a double personality, flip-flopping from "normal young woman" to "naughty little child." Breuer was intrigued, and decided to take her as a patient in spite of the poor prognosis.

Bertha herself provided the key to unlock the mystery of some of her symptoms. She typically put herself into a hypnotic state during the transition between her two per-

Figure 10.1 *Sigmund Freud strolling with his daughter, Anna.*

sonalities. Once, while in this hypnotic transition state, she told Breuer how one of her symptoms first occurred. Later, to Breuer's surprise, the symptom disappeared. Breuer hypnotized her deliberately and asked her about other symptoms; these, too, disappeared or improved.

Unfortunately, Breuer's wife became jealous of all the time he was spending with Bertha, and Breuer was forced to tell Bertha that he could no longer continue treatment.

She was much better, anyway. Bertha reacted hysterically to this news—as hysterics are likely to do—and went into imaginary labor. As Breuer watched with a combination of fear and fascination, she gave birth to an imaginary child. His child, of course. Stunned, Breuer hypnotized her, told her she would feel better in the morning, and ran from her house. The next day he and his wife left for Venice for a vacation (Jones, 1961).

When Breuer returned, he told his friend Sigmund Freud about the treatment he had devised for hysteria. Freud was impressed, both by the treatment and by the account of Bertha's imaginary childbirth. He began using hypnosis with his own patients, with some success. He found that having them relive experiences (in their minds) often resulted in a sudden *release* of strong emotions. This release of tension, which Freud called *catharsis*, was frequently followed by an improvement in the patient's condition.

Free Association

Freud soon became dissatisfied with hypnosis, for a number of reasons. Many people are not hypnotizable. In addition, Freud discovered, many of the people he did hypnotize could describe an emotional experience while in a hypnotic trance but soon forgot it again when awakened. So when a young woman named Elisabeth, who was not susceptible to hypnosis, asked for therapy, Freud decided to try something new. He made her lie on a couch. He asked her to concentrate on one of her symptoms and to recall the moment of its origin. If she could not, which was usually the case, he pressed his finger on her forehead and told her an important memory would come to mind. In short, Freud was trying direct suggestion,

similar to the suggestion he used with someone under hypnosis, but without the hypnotic trance.

Freud's new method was a miserable failure at first. Elisabeth remembered nothing. Freud pressed her forehead again and again. Finally Elisabeth said something, but it seemed totally unrelated to the symptom. She apologized and said she could have come out with it earlier, but it didn't seem to be what Freud had wanted.

But Freud believed that every event has a cause, even if the cause is not conscious. Elisabeth's statement, he reasoned, though seemingly unrelated to her problem, was probably highly related. If only he could uncover the lines of association between her words and the deep, hidden conflict that was causing her surface symptoms, then perhaps he could cure her. So he encouraged Elisabeth to continue, adding a new rule: She was not to hold anything back, even if it seemed unimportant.

Elisabeth had a few requests herself. Would Freud please stop pressing on her forehead? It was distracting her. So was his stream of questions. These requests Freud granted immediately, since what he wanted was free and uninterrupted associations.

Freud called his new technique *free association*. It was to become the major diagnostic technique in psychoanalysis.

Repression and the Unconscious

The technique of free association was designed to get at the emotional ideas that, in Freud's developing opinion, were responsible for his patients' surface symptoms. Take the example of the young boy who had been required to sit in the bedroom of his ailing father. The boy fell asleeep and the father

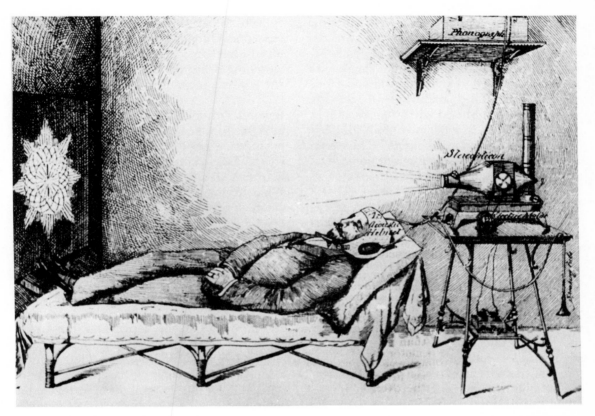

Figure 10.2   *Before Freud, physicians did little more than try to calm their "nervous" patients. One doctor in the late 1800s used "headphones" (an acoustic helmet) and a soothing slide show to lull patients into a relaxed state.*

died. Could he have saved his father? Had he failed in his sentry duty? His arm, slung over the chair as he slept, was numb. It remained numb, paralyzed, a hysterical symptom.

Freud believed this hysterical paralysis was due to an idea that the boy could not bear to express or even think. Perhaps the idea was that he had in effect killed his father, or that he had desired his father's death, and he was unconsciously punishing himself by paralyzing one of his limbs. Freud saw his own task as discovering the *unconscious mental activity* underlying the boy's symptom. He had to discover the traumatic event (in this case, the death of the father) and what the patient unconsciously thought about it. He used free association to "psychoanalyze" these unconscious thoughts.

Freud used the term *repression* for the psychological process of driving ideas out of consciousness. Ideas that are too threatening or too anxiety-provoking, such as the thought the boy might have had about being responsible for his father's death, are quickly repressed — excluded from conscious thought and later memory. (Repression should not be confused with *suppression,* in which someone is conscious of an idea but refuses to tell anyone about it.) Repression and the unconscious were major constructs in both the early and the later theories.

The Trauma Theory. Originally, Freud believed that most psychological disturbances were traceable to the effect of some particularly disturbing event, called a *trauma.* By means of hypnotic inquiry or free association, Freud was able to find traumas in the life history of every patient. He was surprised at how many of these traumas were sexual — the patient, when a child, had been molested or raped, often by a parent. Surely such assaults were enough to disturb someone emotionally!

But doubts entered Freud's mind. He knew the parents of many of the patients, and to find so many of his friends accused of incest was a bit hard to accept. There was another problem with his "trauma theory," this one the opposite of the first: Some of the traumas were not sensational enough! Many patients described the death of a parent, for example; but such an experience, although certainly unpleasant, is commonplace, and most people do not break down over it. Similarly, some patients would describe being frightened by a horse, or by the dark — reasonable, but again, so commonplace! Freud began to suspect that in these cases the patients must have been predisposed, somehow, to react with very strong emo-

tions to the event. It is like saying "Boo!" to someone: Outside in the sunshine it has no effect, but at night, when the person is watching a horror movie and thinks he or she is alone, it can be extremely frightening.

Beyond Traumas. Freud concluded that his next step must be to look for these predisposing factors. He decided not to stop at the trauma but to continue analysis into the life histories of his patients, digging deeper. What he discovered were traumas back of traumas and then traumas deeper still. If Freud had difficulty accepting the idea that a young girl, the daughter of family friends, had been raped by her father at the age of 16, it was even more difficult to accept the girl's report that, when she was 4, her father had violated her through the anus. Freud began to suspect the truth: The acts his patients described had never happened; they were fantasies.

Can you imagine how Freud felt at this point? He had a theory of some repute which was based on the trauma as the cause of the nervous ailment, and now the whole empirical basis for the theory had disintegrated. The reported traumas were lies. He had a theory based on lies.

Freud became thoroughly depressed. He considered giving up theoretical medicine.

The Interpretation of Dreams

Freud decided he needed help: therapy. Since he considered other psychologists incompetent — they would have prescribed perhaps a warm bath in those days — he decided to try to analyze himself. This is not an easy task, of course. Self-analysis requires that the same person function as the therapist, who

"Frankly, Doctor, I don't believe in Freud's theory of childhood sexuality."

Freud began to see that the "lies" he and his other patients had told were not the ordinary kind. They were not deliberate or even conscious attempts to deceive, for the patients themselves believed the stories to be true. They were fantasies—but fantasies that had evidently had a profound influence on the personality development of the children who created them.

To illustrate, recall the Freudian theory of psychosexual stages presented in Chapter 8. The Oedipus complex is the male child's fantasy of his love-relationship with his mother and threats of violence (castration) from his father. Many years later, fighting against his own unconscious resistances to remember these ideas, a patient might vaguely recall that when he was three or four, he was severely beaten by his father. But it is a fantasy, or, better, a distorted memory of a childhood fantasy.

must be critical, and the patient, who is required not to be.

Freud decided to analyze his dreams. Freud, the critical, analytic scientist, would use the uninhibited dream activities of the sleeping Freud and maybe get to the soul of both men.

Again, he encountered material not to his liking. Using dreams as clues, he tracked his memories of his childhood. He found them full of sexual desires for his mother and aggressive feelings—hatred—for his father. According to his analysis of his dreams, his father had committed some atrocious acts, and young Sigmund had been the victim.

Startled and incredulous, Freud went to his mother and asked her about some of these events. They had not occurred. Freud, too, had been lying to his therapist.

Id, Ego, and Superego

Neuroses are those relatively mild forms of mental illness in which the patient has not lost touch with reality. Freud's early view of neuroses was that they resulted from conflicts between ideas in the conscious mind and ideas in the unconscious mind. Most of us have mild forms of such conflicts—consciously you might like and respect someone, but unconsciously your liking and respect are mixed with dislike and contempt. The result might be one of the so-called "Freudian slips"—slips of the tongue or the pen that betray attitudes hidden "under the surface." An example given by the English translator of Freud, Joan Riviere, concerns a newspaper reporter's account of an interview with a famous general who was better known for his presence in bars than in wars. In the first report, the general was described as "this battle-scared veteran." The next day a hurried apology read, "The words of course should have been 'this bottle-scarred veteran"! (Freud, 1924).

Some individuals have severe conflicts between attitudes, which can result in crippling symptoms. An unconscious hostility toward a loved one could result in symptoms as different as physical paralysis ("If I can't move, I can't hit her") and exaggerated love ("How can you say I hate him, when I love him so much?").

But as Freud encountered a wider range of neurotic problems in his patients, he soon realized that he could not maintain a theory of conflict simply between the conscious and the unconscious. Often the conflict appeared to be between two processes, *both* unconscious. For example, some compulsively neat people might be using constant cleaning to defend against an unconscious desire, retained from the anal period, to smear feces around (at least symbolically). But they might also be totally unaware of their compulsiveness and of their unconscious guilt about wanting to commit such a socially unacceptable act.

To represent conflict, then, Freud decided he needed more than the simple division into conscious and unconscious. So he constructed his theory of the *id*, the *ego*, and the *superego*.

The Id. The id is the power system of the personality, providing energy (sexual and aggressive) for the individual's actions. It operates on the *pleasure principle*, which states that all unpleasant events should be avoided, regardless of cost. The id cannot tolerate tension and seeks immediate relief.

If the person is hungry, the id wants to eat immediately, no matter what else the person might be busy doing.

In thought, the pleasure principle produces *primary process* thinking, in which the everyday restrictions on thought—logic, reasonableness—do not hold. A bizarre dream is a good example of the primary process, as are many hallucinations. In babies, the pleasure principle produces primary process thinking in a very direct way: When babies are hungry, they cry and cry, but their crying is frequently interrupted by moments in which they suck and seem almost pleased. Psychoanalysts believe they are hallucinating a warm, full breast.

Hallucinating a desired goal object is not a very effective way of reducing one's tensions, so the id must delegate some of its energy to the ego, to be used to locate and obtain resources.

The Ego. The ego is the strategist of the personality. It operates on the *reality principle*, which focuses on the distinction between the real and the unreal rather than the distinction between pleasure and pain. In other words, it moves to satisfy the desires of the id in a realistic manner. The kind of thought involved is called *secondary process*—rational, logical, purposeful, critical. Generally, it is the kind of thought we think we do as adults, at least while we are awake and alert.

The ego is concerned only with what the person *can* do. It does not make decisions about what to look for, only how to look for it and what to do when it is found. The id makes the decisions about what the person wants, and the ego does its best to get it. The ego has no morals; unless arrest were probable, it would just as soon steal food as work for it. Morals are the province of the superego.

The Superego. The superego has two aspects, corresponding essentially to "good" and "bad," rewards and punishments. The positive, nonpunitive aspect of the superego approves of unselfish acts that accord with the highest moral principles; this aspect is sometimes called the *ego ideal*. If we rescue a pig caught in the mud, even though we are in our fine clothes, we experience a burst of personal pride. It is the superego rewarding the ego, according to Freud.

The critical, punitive aspect of the superego corresponds to what we call *con-*

science. It makes us feel guilty when we do or think things against our internalized moral standards—when we steal or cheat or kick a dog.

The superego develops from interaction with parents. Typically the moral principles of a society are interpreted to a child by his or her parents, by several means. Parents reward moral acts and punish immoral acts as a kind of external superego. They also (for the most part) act in accord with these moral principles, so that the child learns by observation and imitation (Bandura, 1969). And of course some principles are transmitted by direct instruction, often combined with threats and promises of punishments and

Figure 10.3 *Inner conflicts are the basis for Freud's concepts of id, ego, and superego. The id craves immediate pleasure, whereas the superego orders continued studying.*

rewards: "You should never do *X*; if you do, you'll get a spanking."

Eventually the child internalizes these moral principles and no longer depends on external rewards and punishments—he can feel proud or guilty all by himself.

Defense Mechanisms

The *defense mechanisms,* which we have mentioned once or twice already, are simply unconscious maneuvers the ego uses to keep the id and the superego under control. For example, a student who secretly feels hostile toward a teacher may defend against this aggressive impulse by thinking it out of his or her own mind and into the teacher's: "That teacher hates me!" This defensive tactic—unconsciously attributing your feelings to others—is common enough to have a name: *projection.*

There are numerous defense mechanisms that do not have names, because they are used with individual flair or in uncommon situations. Perhaps you can think of some as we discuss the common, named ones.

Repression. *Repressing* an idea—driving it out of consciousness—is a very basic defense mechanism. Often it is used in combination with others: In projection, the threatening impulse is projected into somebody else, *and* the idea that the impulse is in you is repressed.

Reaction Formation. Repression is also involved in the defense called *reaction formation,* which reflects the old idea that the best defense is a good offense. First an objectionable idea is repressed; then it is replaced by its opposite. The student who hated the teacher

Figure 10.4 *Self-denial is a meaningful religious practice for many; for a few, it can be a defense mechanism against unacceptable sexual impulses.*

now loves the teacher. Reaction formation is a part of compulsive neatness, discussed before; an unconscious desire for dirt and disorder is repressed and replaced by a conscious passion for cleanliness.

Undoing. *Undoing* involves an act designed to correct an earlier action. A very common (and normal) undoing is acting especially nice to a friend you had angrily "snapped at" a bit earlier. A more neurotic manifestation might be someone's attempting to undo an act that never actually occurred, such as a fantasy left over from the Oedipal drama. Such a person might seek a religious cure, joining a cult that emphasizes self-sacrifice and frequent cleansing rituals such as fasting. (I hope it is needless to say that not all members of rigorous religious organizations are neurotic or involved in undoing.) Even simple atonements such as saying "Hail Marys" can be undoings, and exorcism rites are a kind of ultimate undoing.

Regression. *Regression* is a reaction to anxiety or frustration in which the person reverts—goes back—to less mature behaviors.

Many of us, when we do not get what we want, act somewhat childishly. A business executive may work hard and well to get that big contract for his company and, in honest competition, finish second. Then he pouts, claims he has no ability at all, accuses his competitors of cheating and of ganging up on him; and to complete a near perfect regression, he spends several hours in the neighborhood bar, sucking on a bottle.

Isolation. A very common defense involves *isolating* an idea from its emotional significance. Sometimes the isolation has a basis in time and place, as with a salesman who is the perfect husband, father, and churchgoer

Figure 10.5 *According to Freud, overeating is often a regression to behavior characteristic of early childhood. Infants in the oral stage of development do little but eat.*

at home and a vulgar, lustful reprobate while away on trips. More general among us is the tendency to isolate the sensual from the tender components of love, so much so that some men and women enjoy sex more outside of marriage. Many analysts relate this tendency to the sensual love of the child for the parent of the opposite sex (Fenichel, 1945). The sensual aspect is frustrated but not the tender aspect, which divides the two in the child's mind; later the person may feel very loving (tender) toward his or her spouse, but not very sexual (sensual).

Isolation of ideas from emotional associations is a respected ability in many areas of society. Scientists are supposed to be "objective," not letting their feelings interfere with their interpretations of data. A judge and members of a jury are similarly asked to review the facts of a case without letting the emotional significance of the facts distort their judgment. These manifestations become neurotic only when they are overdone and even situations that should have emotional significance are viewed "intellectually": "I am killing this man, but it is not murder, because his life would have been miserable and he would have been a bad influence on everyone around him."

Sublimation. Sometimes the ego develops defensive tactics that allow for the discharge of id tensions *and* satisfy the moral standards of the superego (even gain its approval) *and* are acceptable to society. These defenses are called *sublimations.* Art is often used for examples, since it affords so many analogies to anal activities. You want to smear feces on the wall, so you smear paint on a canvas instead. Painting a picture kills whatever was painted, in a sense, as it cap-

tures its look at one moment in time, so aggressive instincts too may be involved. Almost any occupation or vocation can be viewed as a sublimation of id instincts. The wine taster may enjoy his or her work because of oral interests. Some members of antipornography groups may unconsciously enjoy all the "filth" they must examine in order to censor it. (It must be emphasized again, however, that there are numerous reasons for choosing any occupation or hobby; a wine taster may hold that job simply because he or she has superior taste discrimination.)

Evaluating Psychoanalytic Theory

As old and influential as psychoanalytic theory is, there is little solid evidence in support of it. Most of the evidence comes from observations made by therapists during analysis. Rarely are systematic records kept of data bearing on specific hypotheses; appropriate control or comparison groups are hard to find or even define; and the therapist's observations and conclusions are biased by his or her belief in the theory. There have been a few laboratory investigations of psychoanalytic hypotheses (for example, Blum and Miller, 1952), but the Freudian concepts are often too complex and ambiguous to put into operational definitions.

Is psychoanalytic theory true? Perhaps the most severe criticism one can make of it is that nobody knows. And nobody knows how to find out. A single concept—say, penis envy—may be discredited by a wealth of contrary indications, but the effect on the theory as a whole is minor. Scientific attacks on psychoanalysis have always reminded me of attacking a slab of gelatin with a sword: It slices easily, but then it coalesces again, and no signs of damage remain.

In spite of its invulnerability to scientific testing, many of the concepts and the hypotheses of psychoanalysis have been accepted by almost all psychologists. Most accept the notion of unconscious mental activity and a process something like repression, which today's psychologists view as a kind of active and deliberate forgetting. Many therapists generally antagonistic to psychoanalytic theory still look for defensive processes of the type the analysts described.

SOCIAL BEHAVIOR THEORIES

Social behavior approaches to personality, often called social learning theories, emphasize behavior. They are based on the notions described in Chapter 4: that the working of the human mind are best understood in terms of how people behave, and that behavior is directed by stimuli and reinforcements. Social behaviorists typically express their goals as the prediction and control of behavior, and they evaluate both their own theories and contrasting ones by how well they do this. Unlike psychoanalytic theory, which is based on observations in the clinical (or therapy) setting, the data for learning theories come mostly from laboratory experiments.

The differences between psychoanalytic and behavioral theorists are clear from the questions each asks in a situation. Suppose a child is wetting the bed well beyond the normal age. A social behaviorist would ask, "What is maintaining this behavior? What is keeping it going? What reinforcements is the child responding to?" To treat the undesirable habit, the behaviorist might use rewards and punishments, rewarding dry nights or directly punishing wetting with mild electrical shock.

A psychoanalyst would be appalled by this behavioral therapy. In his view, a bed-wetting problem is merely a symptom of a much deeper conflict. He would ask, "What is the underlying problem? What are the child's unconscious ideas?" Perhaps the child wets the bed because he feels he lost all autonomy and free will during toilet training; wetting, to him, is an act of defiance. To apply simple punishments to control the symptom closes off the single avenue of expression of the child's independence. Even worse symptoms may result.

We will discuss the disagreements about therapeutic procedures in Chapter 13. Our purpose here is to note the differences in approach. The psychoanalyst sees undesirable behavior as a symptom of an unconscious, underlying conflict—the behavior is only a clue to the real problem, not the problem itself. But the psychologists who emphasize behavior take a different view. They feel that the real problem is the abnormal behavior itself, and that their task is to do something about it. Social behaviorists would, of course, judge any procedure that resulted in the substitution of a worse problem to be ineffective and undesirable. But they feel that psychoanalysts become so concerned with underlying conflicts, which are often very difficult to identify, that they don't help the patient with his or her problem behavior.

Outcome Control of Behavior

The concept of reinforcement is central to all social behavior theories. The core idea is fairly simple: Behaviors that lead to positive (pleasant) outcomes are more likely to be learned and performed than behaviors with neutral or negative consequences. This is the Law of Effect, and it is also common sense. If someone did not respond to the positive or negative incentives in the environment, he or she would not live long.

To understand a particular action from the point of view of social behavior theory, one tries to discover the environmental outcomes that are reinforcing the behavior. These rewards and punishments are often social: They involve praise, attention, and other human rewards, rather than simply food or the like. Often people are unaware of the rewards involved in a situation. Take the common example of the child who doesn't want to go to bed. To get his parents to stay around, he cries and makes a general nuisance. The parents unintentionally reward this behavior by running to his room, comforting him, and playing with him until he falls asleep from exhaustion. The next night the behavior is more likely than before. If this schedule of reinforcement is maintained, the parents may have to seek professional help.

A therapist with a behavioral approach would probably suggest removing the rewards for the behavior. The parents would be instructed to put the child to bed (with loving attention), close the door, and then totally ignore the screams and cries that follow. It is not an easy task. But in one reported case the procedure worked well (Williams, 1959). The first night the child cried almost an hour. The second night he was much better, and by the end of the week, he didn't cry at all, but played happily by himself until he dropped off to sleep.

Learning Self-control. If we had to rely on rewards administered by social agents such as parents, teachers, and the police, socially acceptable behavior would happen only in the presence of such people. How is it that people develop self-control and give *themselves* rewards and punishments in the appropriate circumstances?

It appears that we develop our own standards for self-reward and self-punishment in a number of ways, including imitation, direct reinforcement by social agents, and instruction. In each, we are influenced by someone else's standards. In one laboratory investigation, children played buyer and seller in a toy store game (Ross, 1962). One of the children was a confederate or stooge of the experimenter. When the children finished the game, each was allowed to select one toy to keep. They made their selections while the adult experimenter was out of the room — no social agent around — and the stooge chose first. If he took three toys, thus violating moral standards in this situation, the subject was also more likely to take more than the allowance, compared to control subjects whose stooges followed the instructions. In short, one of the factors influencing self-control at an early age is what one's peers are doing.

But what about the rewards and punishments one gives to oneself? These too seem to be affected by other people. In another study, children played a bowling game after watching a model bowl first (Bandura and Kupers, 1964). Candy in a dish near the bowler was free for the taking, but the model did not allow himself any unless he achieved

Figure 10.6 *Many people allow themselves a small reward after a job well done.*

a certain score. In one condition, the score had to be very high before he praised himself and took candy, and in another, the score was quite low. When bowling, the children's standards of self-reward were similar to those of whichever model they had observed. Children with no model ate freely of the candy, not using it as a self-reward at all. Thus, children imitate not only the self-control of models but also their level of self-reward.

Internal versus External Regulators. Often our self-control mechanisms complicate the task of the social behavior theorists, who must consider the possibility that these mechanisms are working against environmental incentives. Behavior related to achievement is apt to involve self-control, even in very young children. In one experiment, boys and girls were allowed to set their own standards of achievement in a task that was demanding but not very rewarding in itself. All of the children required themselves to work quite hard to earn the small favors offered. Not one chose the least effort and about half chose the highest possible achievement level as their goal (Bandura and Perloff, 1967). This result makes no sense without the notion of self-rewards and self-punishments.

Similarly, a teenager in a peer group that offers reinforcements for the use of dangerous drugs and punishments for abstinence will not necessarily abuse drugs. Worried parents must sometimes rely on "inner strength," "will power," or a properly tuned superego—the self-control mechanisms—to guide their children through temptation and peer pressure.

Stimulus Control of Behavior

At the other end of the conditioning model from outcomes are stimuli, and these too are important to behaviorists. The theory behind stimulus control of behavior is that variation in the stimuli presented to a subject, either by the natural environment or by the psychologist, produces variation in the subject's response. For a child who often misbehaves, the variation in stimuli might be the presence or absence of a parent. One such case involved a boy who had terrible fits of hostility and aggressive behavior, almost always when his father was absent. When his father was home, the boy was a model child, for the father punished any misbehavior quickly and dispassionately. But as soon as the child saw his father's car pull out, he would run to his mother's closet and tear up her clothes, or smash furniture, or chew on the walls (Moser, 1965).

Obviously this boy was using information from the environment to gauge the probable outcome of his tantrums. The stimulus of particular importance was something about his father—but what? The father's maleness? Would the boy respond to all adult males in the same way? Is it the nonmother

Figure 10.7 *Do you think this is an effective stimulus for controlling parking behavior?*

aspect of the father? Is the boy aggressive only when alone with his mother, never in the presence of anybody else? To use the notion of stimulus control in understanding personality, one must have some way of determining exactly what the stimulus is. Very often one can do this by careful observation, and sometimes even by asking the subject.

Once the stimulus has been identified, it can be manipulated so as to change the response. In this case, the psychologist probably would try to develop the mother's control of the child, making her a stimulus more similar to the father in that respect. The boy then should generalize his response of good behavior to include the stimulus of his mother as well as his father.

Cognition in Behavioral Theories

From the point of view of the observer, stimuli and outcomes can be used to predict a subject's behavior. This does not mean, of course, that the subject is responding automatically, like a machine, or that his thoughts play no role in his behavior. In fact, when we speak of self-rewards and self-punishments, we are already moving from discussion of publicly observable stimuli, responses, and outcomes to private events that occur inside the head of the subject.

A number of experiments have pitted the effects of relatively powerful external rewards against the effects of what the subject is thinking. For example, a stream of cool air was used as a reinforcer for subjects in an almost unbearably hot room (110°). Shown a series of pairs of similar sentences, subjects were to choose one in each pair. (The "correct" sentences all had some common element arbitrarily chosen by the experimenter.) If they picked the right one, they were rewarded with a cooling breeze. If the experimenter *told* them that the stream of cool air meant they had guessed correctly, then the subjects soon increased their proportion of correct responses. But if subjects were told the cool air had nothing to do with the correctness of their responses, they showed no improvement, even though correct responses actually were still rewarded by cool breezes. The reinforcement was not effective unless the subjects *thought* it was a reinforcement (Dulany, 1968).

Expectancies and Subjective Values. Two cognitive variables that social behavior theorists are using more and more are expectancies and subjective values (Mischel, 1973). An *expectancy* is a person's belief that if he or she behaves in such and such a way, then such and such an outcome will result. Knowing someone's expectancies is important if you are trying to predict his or her behavior, especially if the expectancies do not match what is actually likely (see Figure 10.8). We would wonder why a friend tried to pet a snarling Doberman unless we knew he *expected* kindness to overcome hostility.

The value an individual places on a particular outcome is often very personal, and knowledge of these *subjective values* is also important in predicting behavior. In many achievement tasks, such as class quizzes, some students place a high value on doing well, no matter how the other students do. Others value scoring higher than someone else, even if their actual scores are low (McClintock, 1972). The first type of student would perform equally well in a group or alone, but the second type needs the presence of competitors to do his best.

Figure 10.8 *Will expectations affect the interaction between these two people?*

Self-efficacy. In a further refinement of the cognitive variable of expectancy, Bandura (1977a) distinguishes between *efficacy expectations* and *outcome expectations*. I may believe that a particular act of mine will lead to a particular outcome—that a carefully constructed argument will convince the person from the Internal Revenue Service that my taxes are in order, for example; this is an outcome expectation (see Figure 10.9). I may have doubts, however, about my ability to construct and deliver such an argument; this is an efficacy expectation. ("Efficacy" means

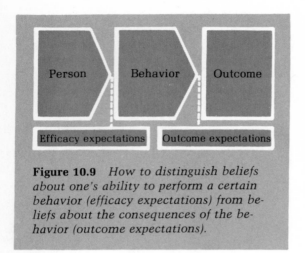

Figure 10.9 *How to distinguish beliefs about one's ability to perform a certain behavior (efficacy expectations) from beliefs about the consequences of the behavior (outcome expectations).*

"the power to have an effect.") In Bandura's view, it is through changes in our efficacy expectations—in our feelings of *self-efficacy* —that most important personality changes occur.

Our notions of our self-efficacy can change in several ways. The first and foremost influence on these feelings is our real accomplishments. If we try something— give a speech, organize a fund-raising drive— and we are successful, our feelings of self-efficacy quite realistically increase. Failure, on the other hand, lowers our efficacy expectations. Thus, in behavioral therapy, someone with a fear of water might be led to attempt and to master a series of encounters with water; first he might simply stand in shallow water, then gradually try more difficult tasks, like diving or swimming underwater (Sherman, 1973). Presumably the reason this sort of therapy is effective is that it raises the person's sense of self-efficacy.

Although our own accomplishments are usually the most powerful source of changes in our self-efficacy (and the resulting changes in our behavior), other factors also can have an effect. Watching someone else do something successfully—seeing that riding a bike is not so difficult, for example— can increase our feelings of self-efficacy. So can simply talking to someone; when you have doubts about your ability to meet a challenge, a friend may be able to persuade you that "you can do it." Psychoanalytic therapy and other "talking therapies" must rely on this sort of change, that is, verbal interpretation and persuasion. Finally, the various means an individual (or a therapist) uses to reduce emotional arousal, particularly anxiety, probably owe their effectiveness to two things. First, they allow the person to cope with a situation that normally would be disturbing in a setting where the undesirable emotion is not aroused, or is aroused less strongly than usual. Second, this absence of anxiety signals to the person that he or she need not be so afraid of failing, and thus increases his or her self-efficacy.

Cognition, Behavior, and Manipulation. The stimuli that precede a response, the outcomes that follow the response, and the respondent's thoughts about these stimuli and outcomes (his or her cognitions) are the primary factors in human behavior, according to most social behaviorists. The third factor—cognitions—is not acceptable to some radical behaviorists, who admit only observable data. And, of course, cognitions grow out of stimuli and outcomes. As Bandura puts it, "Analysis of cognitive control of behavior is . . . incomplete without specifying what controls the influential cognitions" (1971, p. 39). One's expectation of the probable outcome of a given behavior is not a blind guess; it comes from experience with the same or similar situations in the past. Thus, if we know something about an individual's previous experiences, of what results behavior X has had for him before, we can make a reasonably good prediction of what his cognitions are now. The more radical behaviorists, therefore, recommend ignoring cognitions altogether and predicting behavior directly from prior experience instead (Skinner, 1953).

It was this determination to leave out cognitive variables that aroused so much concern when the radical behaviorists first expressed it some 30 years ago. Experiments like Watson's conditioning of little Albert (see pp. 154–155) raised frightening questions about behavior manipulation. Were people now to be considered no more than helpless machines, controlled by the stimuli and the reinforcements set before them by harsh and unsympathetic psychologists?

Social behaviorists would certainly say no. Whether or not they admit cognitive variables, behaviorists do not subscribe to a "helpless machine" view of human nature; they view human beings as controlling the environment as much as the other way around (Bandura, 1977b). We can choose the environment in which we want to perform, for example, and once in an environment, our behavior can change it. If an animal is placed in a situation in which shocks are delivered unless it presses a lever in a certain amount of time, its lever pressing changes the aversive environment to a neutral one (Sidman, 1966). If it were not for the fact that each person partially creates his or her own environment, behavioral therapies would be of little use; the patient would be "cured" in the therapist's office, but "sick" again as soon as the office door opened, letting in the old environment. Lasting changes do occur because people can control the environmental influences they want to expose themselves to.

THE HUMANISTIC APPROACH

Perhaps the best way to define the humanistic approach to personality is to consider the relationship between psychoanalytic theory and social behavior theories. In the view of one thoughtful reviewer, psychoanalytic theory was an attempt to show that humans are, in many respects, like lower animals, whereas behavioral (learning) theories began in the attempt to explore the opposite premise, that animals are, in many respects, like humans (Atkinson, 1964). Both theories were strongly influenced by Darwin's theory of evolution. Before Darwin, the uniqueness of the human species, its differences from other animals, was exaggerated. Humans were conscious, rational, and free, but animals were unconscious automatons, unthinking reactors to the environment and to their internal needs or instincts. Darwin destroyed these notions. Freud began to look for the unconscious sexual and aggressive instincts (animal tendencies) in humans, and Thorndike and Pavlov began to investigate associative processes (thinking) in lower animals.

Now we can place the humanistic psychologists in this scheme. They are the watchdogs of human status who object when the psychoanalytic theorists paint us as too animalistic; they do not object to concepts of animal motives in humans, but they want to list our higher, more spiritual motives too. They also object if a behaviorist claims that research on rats can lead to an understanding of most human behavior. In short, a humanistic psychologist is one who wants to study humans in their most human (least animal) aspect.

The Organismic Premise

If you were to observe the actions of a single football player, totally disregarding the movements of the other ten players, you would be getting an unusual and distorted picture of the game. Watching a lineman hit forward, fall down, get up, and do it again, the picture would be of some extremely puzzling antics of an oddly clad behemoth. One cannot understand a functioning part of a football team without understanding the interrelated actions of the whole team. Applied to human personalities, this is called the *organismic premise:* Single acts cannot be understood in isolation from the activities of the total organism.

Kurt Goldstein's organismic approach to the study of brain-injured soldiers is a classic in the humanistic tradition (Goldstein, 1939, 1940, 1942). Goldstein was the director of a hospital for World War I soldiers and thus was in a good position to observe the effects of brain injuries first-hand. Extremely often, he noted, these patients were unusually neat and orderly, and they conformed well to the rigid hospital routine. In fact, because they were so manageable, brain-injured patients were the most popular with the hospital staff.

But these effects were not the direct result of the patients' brain injuries. Direct results included partial or complete blindness, partial or complete paralysis, difficulties in speaking, difficulties in understanding, and the like, each related to the extent and location of the injury. Almost all patients, however, were abnormally orderly.

Goldstein realized that these neatness behaviors were defensive maneuvers designed to avoid situations in which the patients could no longer cope as well as they used to.

One of Goldstein's patients tied a string to his bed to identify it; without the string, he could not remember which was his, because all the beds looked so much alike. He could not remember the way to the dining hall, so he followed the other patients. He could not distinguish fact from fiction and became extremely agitated if someone told a story. If the story had it raining and in fact the day was sunny, the patient would shout, "It is not raining!" and refuse to listen to any more nonsense. This man's routine was his salvation. Any deviation from a neat and orderly life was a potential nightmare.

If we are to understand this man, said Goldstein, we must consider all of him: his body (his brain is injured), his mind (it functions less adequately than formerly in some respects), his strivings (he wants to cope; he wants to avoid anxiety-causing situations), and all the other facets of a multifaceted personality. If we do not consider the whole man, we are likely to be misled. For example, Goldstein observed that brain-injured patients scored low on several tests. This was not because they were unable to do better, but because they were unwilling to take the risk of failure associated with an all-out attempt at success.

In addition to the direct effects of brain injury and the secondary, defensive tactics, there were also changes in behavior that could be classified as *compensatory.* Blind soldiers for example, worked to develop their other senses. In this regard, Goldstein made another remarkable discovery: Patients who *completely* lost a psychological or physical function adjusted more quickly and fared better than those whose loss was only *partial*. The reason was that those with a partial loss kept trying to recover, to regain their former level of ability, which in most cases was impossible. Those with a complete loss tried instead to compensate by developing other means of coping, with considerably more success.

Finally, there were other changes that are best described as growth behaviors. The soldiers were trying to become better people, better than before if possible, but at least the best they could be. Goldstein called these *self-actualization* behaviors.

For many of the brain-injured patients, the best they could be was somewhat limited. In one case, a boy learned to perform exceptional feats of computation and amazing reproductions of musical tunes he had heard. He focused all his energies on these two potentials, growing in the few directions open to him.

Maslow and Self-Actualization

If the term "self-actualization" sounds familiar, it is because you recall Chapter 6 and the discussion of Abraham Maslow. Although Maslow's most important contribution was his insightful comments on human motivation, as discussed earlier, we cannot have a section on humanistic theories of personality without at least mentioning this great man. Maslow named the approach "humanistic psychology" in 1962 and designated it a "third force," different from psychoanalysis and behaviorism (Bühler and Allen, 1972). His hierarchy of needs refined Goldstein's notions of the organismic motivations that drive an individual, related the various needs to one another, and, above all, described in detail the need "to be the

Figure 10.10   *Self-actualization in action. Half an arm and half a foot would seem to be a major handicap in sports, but kicker Tom Dempsey holds the record for the longest field goal in the National Football League.*

best one can"—the need to self-actualize. In particular, Maslow showed us how peak mystical experiences are part of the cause and part of the effect of self-actualization; he showed us why self-actualizing people laugh at absurdities, not at other people's failings; and he showed the efficacy of self-actualization—its fearless drive to perceive reality accurately, its creativity. Why not, in his honor, reread the section on Maslow in Chapter 6 (pp. 258–261)?

FOCUS

Carl Jung and the Collective Unconscious

Carl Gustav Jung (1875–1961), some say, is in the psychoanalytic tradition; he was a disciple of Freud's for a while, and his theory of personality is similar to Freud's in many respects. Others put him in the humanistic tradition; he was one of the first to talk about self-actualization, and his split with Freud was essentially over what he saw as Freud's preoccupation with animal instincts (like sex) and unwillingness to discuss the higher human instincts (like spirituality). But Jung does not fit well in any tradition. He was unique, surely one of the most innovative thinkers psychology has ever produced.

One of Jung's most innovative thoughts was the concept of the *collective unconscious*. In Jung's theory of personality, there is a *personal unconscious* which, like Freud's unconscious, contains ideas repressed because they were too painful to acknowledge. But in addition, claimed Jung, there is a collective unconscious that contains "mythological" images, ideas, and emotions that have developed in the course of human evolution. Everyone has essentially the same collective unconscious — which is why it is called "collective," as contrasted with the "personal" unconscious. It is supposedly the "deposit of ancestral experiences," reflecting evolutionary changes in the human brain as generation after generation of humans experienced the same events. For example, people of all centuries have had mothers, experienced birth and death, feared the dark, and worshiped a god or gods (Schultz, 1976). Because of these repeated experiences, a "universal memory" (the collective unconscious) develops, and each individual is born with certain "ideas" about what it is like to be a human being — certain "predispositions" to interact fondly with a mother, to fear darkness, and to worship something.

The contents of the collective unconscious are *archetypes* (which means "an original form" of something). Archetypes include thoughts, images, and feelings about objects (like "brother" or "the sun") or events (like "danger"). Archetypes influence the way we perceive and react to the experiences they represent, just as repressed material in the personal unconscious does (Geiwitz and Moursund, 1979). For example, the archetype of "mother" predisposes us to behave in certain ways (and not in others) toward our real mothers. Archetypes inspire awe, and thus they are apt to inspire poets and artists, who try to express the archetypes in verbal or pictorial form — the "mother" archetype is reflected in paintings

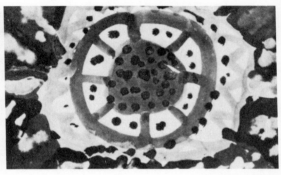

Figure 1 *The artful circle, or mandala, which Jung saw as the expression of the archetype of "unity" or "wholeness," is found in great cathedrals and children's scrawls.*

and other images of the madonna, for example. In fact, one of the reasons Jung began to believe in universal images was his discovery of the same symbols and pictures in almost every country he investigated, some civilized and some primitive. The mandala or magic circle is a universal symbol for unity, not only in the art of various cultures but in the drawings of children and in dreams, too.

To illustrate how archetypes might affect one's life, consider those for members of the opposite sex. The *anima* is the archetype of the female in men, and the *animus* is the archetype of the male in women. These archetypes generally facilitate interactions between the sexes, according to Jung, because they allow each sex to understand something of the nature of the other. On the other hand, interactions that violate the archetypes may lead to conflict. For example, in a case of real or imagined infidelity, the offender's behavior is discrepant from the general image of a "proper" intimate relationship, and the other person in the relationship may react with an intense emotion (sexual jealousy, hostility). Or a relatively minor dispute might lead a man to say, "I will never understand women!" What he really means is, "I don't understand why she is not like my anima."

One of the key features of Jung's theory of personality is the notion of *balance*. In the healthy personality, there is a balance between the conscious and the unconscious, so that each contributes, each plays its role.

Jung looked with disfavor on societies that prescribed sharply distinct sex roles for men and women (as our society has traditionally done), claiming that men suffer when they cannot express the feminine side of their personalities and that women, too, experience conflict between their conscious sexual identity and their animus (the unconscious masculine tendencies). He claimed that one's archetypical tendencies cannot be suppressed forever, that sooner or later they will come out. Since society usually requires the strongest allegiance to sex-role stereotypes among *young* adults, Jung predicted that older men would become more feminine and older women would become more masculine. Whether or not it occurs for the reasons Jung believed, there is research evidence for such a shift in sex roles beginning in middle age (Neugarten, 1977). Similarly, Jung's assertion that the healthiest personalities give equal weight (balance) to "masculine" and "feminine" tendencies has found support from studies of "androgynous" college students (Bem, 1974; see pp. 192–193).

The Need for Positive Regard

The drive to self-actualize, according to most humanistic theories, is in constant danger of being inhibited. In Maslow's hierarchy, the lower drives can preempt the higher ones; only when all our lower drives are satisfied do our self-actualizing tendencies exhibit themselves. In particular, the class of motives ranked just below self-actualization — the esteem needs — present real problems for humans trying to become the best they can be.

Carl Rogers is the humanistic psychologist who has written most extensively on the conflict between self-actualization and what he calls the *need for positive regard* (1959). A homely illustration of this conflict, one experienced by us all, is the process of learning a new leisure skill such as skiing or playing the piano. At first our movements are awkward and our performance is embarrassing; people may laugh at us. Only after much practice do we achieve a level that brings us esteem and positive regard, where people are impressed. During the early stages, we elicit negative regard, which is painful. Many people do not put in the effort, therefore, to get through these early awkward stages; their drive to better themselves — to learn a new skill and a new means of self-expression and creativity — is inhibited by their need for positive regard.

The need for positive regard, in Rogers's view, is not necessarily incompatible with self-actualization but becomes so because of certain childhood experiences. As a child grows, he or she becomes aware of an "I" or a "self," a "something" that is perceived as distinct from everything else (nonself). These perceptions include awareness of *being* or existence (I *am*) and awareness of *function* (what I *can do*).

The child also begins to perceive that other people, his parents in particular, are *evaluating* his functional abilities (his be-

havior, in other words). They call some behaviors "good" and others "bad," and it is
clear that "good" wins more approval than
"bad." Eventually the child begins to evaluate his own behaviors, calling some "good"
and some "bad." There is nothing particularly threatening about this process (threatening to self-actualization needs, that is); in
fact, positive and negative regard of behavior
is probably necessary to self-actualization.

The problem is that the child does not
(because he cannot) distinguish between
being and function. He takes criticism of his
behaviors as criticism of his existence, and
this perception, needless to say, is *very*
threatening. He experiences what Rogers
calls *conditional positive regard:* He sees his
parents as saying, "We will love you if and
only if you behave in the ways we value."
The child develops conditional self-regard;
he likes himself if and only if he behaves in
the ways he values, becoming elated and
proud after doing good, and depressed, with

Figure 10.11 *The first stages of learning a skill
are usually embarrassing. Some people quit
trying.*

profound feelings of unworthiness, after
doing bad.

As a result of conditional positive regard,
both by self and by others, the child begins
to be selective in his thoughts and behaviors
so as to satisfy these "conditions." The result is quite different from a personality
striving only to self-actualize. The person
puts himself in what Rogers calls a state of
incongruence, which means there is some
discrepancy between the way he perceives
his deepest true self and the way he sees
others perceiving him. He believes himself
to be a warm and sympathetic person, but
his interactions with other people suggest to
him that this is not how he appears. He
doesn't know what to do or say that will
convey his true friendly, loving self. This
makes him anxious at times, or depressed.

A person trying to self-actualize approaches or avoids activities depending on
whether or not he or she expects the resulting experience to lead to personal growth.
Someone motivated by the need for positive
regard, on the other hand, evaluates activities on the basis of whether or not they will
meet with the approval of other people (or
the self, once the standards of others have
been internalized). We encounter many situations in which one need says "go" while
the other says "stop." In the conflict between these two basic needs—to self-actualize and to achieve positive regard—is the
drama of an individual's life story, according
to Rogers.

The Concept of Self

The concept of *self* has been a prominent
one in this section of humanistic personality
theories. We have discussed *self*-actualiza-
tion, *self*-regard, and a number of other re-

lated topics. It is appropriate, I think, that we turn our attention directly to the concept of self.

Definitions of self are about as numerous as selves (Wylie, 1968). Allport listed seven aspects of selfhood that deserve consideration: (1) bodily self: a sense of one's body as different from "other things" (perhaps the first aspect to develop); (2) self-identity, the sense of continuity through time; (3) self-esteem, the sense of wanting to do things for oneself and to take all the credit; (4) self-extension, the sense of possessions: that some other people are "my people" and some are not; that some things are mine and some are not; (5) self-image, a sense of how others view me; (6) self-as-rational-coper, the idea that "I" have intellectual abilities suitable for solving problems; (7) self-values, the things and events the person esteems most highly (Allport, 1961).

The self as a whole is some sort of organization of ideas and percepts, an organization that includes at least those seven components. It is helpful to think of organizations of people—political parties, businesses, committees—as similar in some ways to the organization we call the self. All organizations come into being for some purpose—to gain power, to make a profit, or whatever. Once formed, however, the organizations develop new motives. Two very prominent organizational motives are *defense* and *growth*. Any organization will try to protect itself from outside attack (or criticism); like individuals, businesses and political parties have been known to deceive themselves, claiming social value for some of their most selfish activities. And organizations, once formed, tend to strive for growth; they tend to continue and grow larger even after their original purpose has been completed (see Figure 10.12).

The self is like such organizations in many respects. In particular, many of the motives exhibited by humans are motives of the self-organization, as distinct from those for which the self-organization was formed. The self, in its ego-like aspects, is formed to satisfy the basic drives of the human animal, but once formed it develops its own values and goals. The self defends itself; it does not take criticism lightly. It strives to grow, to self-actualize.

PSYCHOANALYTIC, BEHAVIORAL, AND HUMANISTIC THEORIES

There is truth in the psychoanalytic, the social behavior, and the humanistic traditions of personality theory. Many psychotherapists are eclectic, borrowing from each approach and following none religiously.

But integrating the major approaches to personality is hardly an easy task. The degree of conflict among approaches may be debatable, but conflict among the *people* advocating the different approaches is unquestionable. Bandura, a prominent behaviorist, sees psychoanalytic concepts (for example, repressed impulses) as "somewhat akin to the pernicious spirits of ancient times" (1969, p. 2). The great psychoanalyst David Rapaport said of behavioral theorists that "the more they try to make [their theories] neat and pat, the more cavalier they become in their disregard of clinical fact" (1953, p. 207). The humanist Abraham Maslow included both behavioral and psychoanalytic traditions in his indictment of "analytic-dissecting-atomistic-Newtonian" theorists

Figure 10.12　*The March of Dimes Foundation won its fight against polio, but it didn't stop there. Like any other successful organization it continued to grow and seek new directions, taking birth defects as its next enemy.*

who ignore the "higher levels of human nature" (1970, p. ix).

I don't know. It seems to me that these statements, which are typical, simply repeat the different emphases of the different approaches. The social behaviorists put their money on *behavior* and ridicule the behavior-predictors of other theorists; the psychoanalytic theorist challenges others to beat his or her ability to explain distorted *thought* processes; and the humanist cries out for attention to the higher *purpose* of humanity. All three traditions have made some valuable points; it is time for an integration, and I think we can expect one soon.

SUMMARY

1. There are three major types of personality theory. *Psychoanalytic* theories emphasize emotional conflicts and unconscious mental processes. *Social behavior* theories emphasize behavior and its environmental causes. *Humanistic* theories emphasize motives, especially the "higher" human motives.

2. Psychoanalytic theory was constructed by Sigmund Freud. As a physician treating nervous ailments with no obvious physical cause, he had some success initially by hypnotizing patients and having them relive traumatic experiences.

3. Freud soon developed a new and better technique for "analysis of the psyche" — *free association.* A patient was required to report any and all thoughts that came to mind in connection with another thought or idea. Freud was trying to uncover the emotional thought processes responsible for the observable symptoms; many of these thought processes turned out to be unconscious. Freud defined *repression* as the process by which these ideas were pushed out of consciousness.

4. Freud discovered childhood memories

to be frequently sexual in nature; disbelieving, he psychoanalyzed himself by analyzing his dreams. He found that the early *traumas* he had thought were responsible for many later conflicts often were *fantasies,* dramatic events invented by the mind in response to unconscious struggles.

5. A later revision of Freud's theory divided the personality into the id, ego, and superego. The *id* represents the energy system, striving always for immediate gratification (the *pleasure principle*); its thought processes are chaotic and illogical (*primary process thinking*). The *ego* uses logical planning (*secondary process thinking*) to achieve satisfaction of id desires in a real world that does not always allow immediate gratification; the ego operates on the *reality principle.* The *superego* represents internalized moral standards taught by parents and society. It functions as the *conscience,* punishing "bad" deeds by making the person feel guilty, and as the *ego-ideal,* rewarding "good" deeds with pride.

6. The ego's *defense mechanisms* against threats from the id, the superego, and the world include projection, repression, reaction formation, undoing, regression, isolation, and sublimation.

7. Social behavior theories emphasize environmental events — stimuli and outcomes — that affect learning and performance. Reinforcements often control behavior in ways not readily apparent. A cranky child may increase cranky behavior because of the loving care or attention it elicits. Self-control by means of rewards and punishments one gives to oneself is something we begin learning as children, largely by imitating our peers and our elders. Self-rewards can counteract the effects of environmental out-comes, and must be considered in a behavioral theory.

8. *Outcome control of behavior* involves the Law of Effect: We tend to learn and repeat actions that have favorable outcomes. By *stimulus control of behavior,* we usually mean that a person "reads" a situation for stimuli on which to base his or her response.

9. Social behavior research on cognitions indicates that what subjects *think* is being reinforced is often more important than the actual state of affairs. A person's expectancies and subjective values are important variables that help us predict his or her behavior. Feelings of self-efficacy — our sense of our own ability to influence outcomes — are one significant type of expectancy.

10. Humanistic psychologists emphasize motivation, human purpose, goals, and values. The *organismic premise* asserts that one cannot understand the whole simply by summing knowledge about its parts. Brain-injured patients show direct effects of their injuries but also many indirect effects, including defensive, compensatory, and growth behaviors.

11. Abraham Maslow, who conceptualized a *hierarchy of needs* ranging from our basic physiological needs to *self-actualization,* was a major contributor to humanistic psychology. Carl Jung was a disciple of Freud's whose orientation later became more humanistic; he originated the concepts of the *collective unconscious* and *archetypes,* among others.

12. Carl Rogers focused on the tendency of lower needs to interfere with self-actualization. In particular, the need for positive regard often conflicts with one's desires to better oneself. A state of incongruence can develop between what a person thinks

he is and how he believes others perceive him.

13. We can conceptualize the *self* as the organization within the personality that per- forms many of the internal administrative functions of the personality. It directs behavior in ways that defend the organization and promote its growth.

USING PSYCHOLOGY

This is an activity you can perform the next time you watch a television program or movie or read a play or novel that deals with interpersonal relationships. Unlike the activity involving viewing a drama described in Chapter 7, this activity should actually enhance your enjoyment and understanding of a drama. It will also improve your understanding of the psychoanalytic concept of the ego's defense mechanisms. The defense mechanisms of projection, repression, reaction formation, undoing, regression, isolation, and sublimation are described in the text. Read over these descriptions and the additional material covering defense mechanisms in the study guide until you feel you have a good understanding of each and can think of your own example of each. Now simply watch or read a drama and look for examples of defense mechanisms in the personal interactions you see or read about. If you enjoy this activity or have a particular interest in it, you might even choose to keep a simple record of the defense mechanisms you observe. Such a record could tell you which defense mechanisms are the most common (in dramas at least) or perhaps whether there are any sex-differences frequently portrayed (do men tend to use certain defense mechanisms and women, others?).

SUGGESTED READINGS

Bandura, A. *Social learning theory.* Prentice-Hall, 1977.
A concise statement of the social behavior approach by one of its most highly respected proponents.

Bühler, C., & Allen, M. *Introduction to humanistic psychology.* Brooks/Cole, 1972.
A concise statement of the humanistic approach by two of its most highly respected proponents.

Hall, C. S., and Lindzey, G. *Theories of personality.* 3rd ed. Wiley, 1978.
The acknowledged classic on theories of personality.

Geiwitz, J., & Moursund, J. *Approaches to personality.* Brooks/Cole, 1979.
A slightly irreverent look at the lives of the major personality theorists and their ideas.

INTERLUDE

Sleep and Dreams

A third of life is spent in sleep. This mysterious and unavoidable state of consciousness so impressed our ancestors that they spun myths about "temporary death" or "the time when the spirit leaves the body." (The latter theory was preferable because at least it accounted for dreams—as nocturnal adventures.) You would think that such an intriguing phenomenon as sleep, one we all experience about eight hours every day, would attract an enormous amount of attention from researchers and that, by now, we would have an adequate theory.

Alas, it is not true. We have made great progress, as we shall see, but the essential answers still elude us. For example, take the most essential question—why do we sleep? What is the purpose of sleep? One biological psychologist admits we do not have an adequate answer: "There is little significant change in energy consumption by the body between quiet waking and sleep. We have yet to discover any metabolic poisons or toxins that require the occurrence of sleep to be dissipated. In short, the reasons for sleep to occur at all and to seem necessary remain a complete mystery" (Thompson, 1975, p. 413). One psychologist even suggested we stop asking why we sleep and ask instead, why do we wake up? That is a bit easier to answer.

Perhaps the purpose of sleep is to afford an opportunity to dream. Don't laugh; many psychologists believe this is a distinct possibility. The basic hypothesis, which can be expressed on several levels, is that dreams represent the organism's attempt to reorganize thought processes in such a way that yesterday's emotional traumas can be more adequately handled tomorrow. Freud, as we have seen in Chapter 10, considered dreams to be the "royal road to the unconscious." In his view, they are attempts to deal with important personal conflicts that cannot be expressed openly. Contemporary psychologists with an information-processing approach think of dreams as mental activity "that both prepares the organism for future learning and facilitates consolidation of prior learning" (McGrath and Cohen, 1978, p. 25). On a biological level, it has been discovered that the effects commonly attributed to the lack of sleep may be in fact the result of missed opportunities for dreaming. If you let a person sleep but do not let him dream (with methods we will shortly discuss), he will suffer almost all of the ill effects of prolonged lack of sleep.

And, ah, dreams! What do these mysterious night movies mean? Do they predict the future? Do they reflect our unconscious desires? How can they be interpreted? These questions too resist easy answers, though considerable research has been done on them, as we shall see.

THE BIOLOGY OF SLEEP AND DREAMS

Although the most basic questions remain without adequate answers, we have learned a good deal about biological changes that occur in sleep. There is every indication that sleep is a highly integrated activity, involving many systems of the body, chemical as well as neurological. The idea that sleep is an "activity" by itself reflects scientific progress, for sleep was once considered a very passive state: One slept when there was nothing else to do, when sensory stimulation was reduced, and the like. This clearly is not the case. If you deprive a human of most sensory stimulation, he does not sleep; he gets very anxious and may begin to hallucinate (Heron, 1961), but he sleeps only when he is ready to sleep— which is once every 24 hours or so, like everybody else. Also, you can induce sleep by stimulating part of the thalamus (Thompson, 1975); this suggests that sleep is just as "stimulated" as waking, and that the difference lies more in *which* brain parts are active than in the general level of neural activity.

Whatever the brain mechanisms involved, our cycle of sleep and wakefulness follows a 24-hour schedule called a *circadian rhythm* (from *circa,* meaning "around," and *dia,* meaning "day"). There are over a hundred biological functions in humans that cycle from a minimum to a maximum value once a day; examples are blood pressure, various hormonal secretions, and body temperature. On a more behavioral level, our moods, our performance on mental or physical tasks, and of course our sleeping habits have distinct circadian rhythms. These behaviors are no doubt influenced in complex ways by our underlying biological cycles.

Disrupting one's habitual rhythm of sleep and wakefulness can have unusual effects. People who travel by air to different time zones experience "jet lag," which manifests itself in an inability to sleep and an inability to perform at peak capacity during the waking hours. If a person flies from San Francisco to Boston and tries to go to sleep at 11 P.M., he will probably find it difficult; it's only 8 P.M., California time. If he has people to see, they are waiting bright-eyed and bushy-tailed at 8 A.M.—5 A.M. his time. The decline in mental and physical performance, however, is only partly attributable to lack of sleep. More important is the disruption of the bodily rhythms that directly affect such processes as alertness, concentration, and planning. Even simple motor behavior is affected. In one study, people who had just arrived in Europe from the United States (experiencing a six-hour time difference) performed miserably on a simple task that had them place different-sized objects in different-sized holes (Klein et al., 1972). Their performance still followed a circadian rhythm, but their best showing occurred at midnight! Performance does not return to normal levels and habitual cycles for a week or two in the new time zone, which is about the same length of time it takes the biological functions like body temperature to recover their usual rhythm.

The circadian rhythm of sleep is obviously related to the earth's 24-hour rotation around its axis. Does this same 24-hour cycle remain in the absence of day and night changes in illumination? What happens if you put people in a deep dark cave, for example, and let them sleep whenever they want to? The answer, strangely enough, is that the rhythm continues, but in a 25-hour cycle in the average person (Dement, 1974). With deliberate planning, people can train themselves to live on rhythms between about 23 and 27 hours. Variations greater than this are apparently impossible to maintain, even in a cave, for long periods; you could not train yourself, for example, to sleep 12 hours and stay awake for 24. There is one exception to these limits: About one person in twenty has the ability to adapt to a 48-hour cycle, with a 16-hour sleep period followed by 32 hours awake.

The more or less unalterable circadian rhythm should not be interpreted as meaning that all people need the same amount of sleep each night. Although everyone sleeps on a 24-hour schedule, the percentage of that schedule devoted to sleep varies considerably. Infants sleep on and off all day and night, logging an average of about sixteen hours, but individual infants may sleep as little as four or five hours. Teenagers sleep between ten and eleven hours, on the average, and adults put in seven to nine hours (Dement, 1974). There are scattered but documented reports of individuals who sleep no more than three or four hours a night, apparently with no loss of alertness during the day. A single individual's sleep patterns may vary, too; for example, he or she may sleep more when ill or after a fatiguing period of work (like "finals week").

THE BRAIN'S ALL-NIGHT BROADCAST

Research on sleep and dreams was given a big boost by the discovery that the brain is continually broadcasting. The electrical waves from the brain were first noted by an Englishman named Caton in 1877. Poor Caton was trying to detect an electrical impulse in the cortex following a specific sensory input, but he could not; his galvanometer was recording constant fluctuations. The brain was sending off signals on its own, and Caton's puny messages were lost in the "static" of the cortex. Caton gave up.

Berger (1929) rediscovered brain waves and made several technological advances, one of which was the design of an apparatus sensitive enough to record brain waves from the surface of the skull rather than from the surface of the cortex. For human subjects, who dislike having their cortex exposed, this was an improvement. With human research thus made practicable, the search for an understanding of these mysterious signals began in earnest. The recordings from electrodes attached to the scalp were called electroencephalograms, or EEGs for short.

When the subject is awake, the EEG record usually shows one of two types of waves. The first, called *beta* waves, is characterized by a more or less random pattern of low-voltage waves, about what you would expect if you were recording the total activity in millions of brain cells. But sooner or later a new and puzzling pattern emerges, typically when the subject is sitting quietly with his or her eyes closed. The waves are slower (8 to 13 cycles per second) and higher in voltage, as if large groups of cells are firing in unison: Boom . . . Boom . . . Boom. These are called *alpha* waves. Even today they are a bit of a mystery. We do know they are not reflecting merely the total voltage of a group of cells firing in unison; the waves continue in the absence of recordable cell discharges in the cortex (Jasper, 1960). Their biological significance is similarly unknown.

When the subject falls asleep, the wave pattern changes again. The waves get slower and slower and higher in voltage: BOOM!! . . . . . . BOOM!! . . . . . . BOOM!! *Delta* waves are the slowest (one or two booms per second) and the highest voltage, and are found in the deepest stage of sleep. These waves are shown in Figure 1.

This description may be a bit misleading, for it sounds as if the EEG will show one of three wave patterns—alpha, beta, or delta—and no other. In sleep, in particular, the EEG often shows combinations of patterns, with the deepest sleep defined by a pattern that shows delta waves more than 50 percent of the time. Various weird "explosions" called spindles, spikes, and K-complexes occur at unknown times for unknown reasons. "BOOM . . . . . . BOOM . . . . . . boom . . . boo, boo, boo, boo . . . boom . . . KA-BOOOOM!!!"; this is a more typical recording.

PARADOXICAL SLEEP AND DREAMS

Whatever brain waves represent, they show a clear progression from alert, waking attention (fast, low voltage) to deep sleep (very slow, very high voltage). During sleep, brain waves become slower and slower and slower, to a point. At that point, during what by some measures can be considered a very deep stage of sleep (it is very difficult to awaken the person), the brain waves become fast and irregular and of low voltage again. This is called *paradoxical sleep,* a paradox because the EEG is like that of an alert, waking subject but the person is sound asleep.

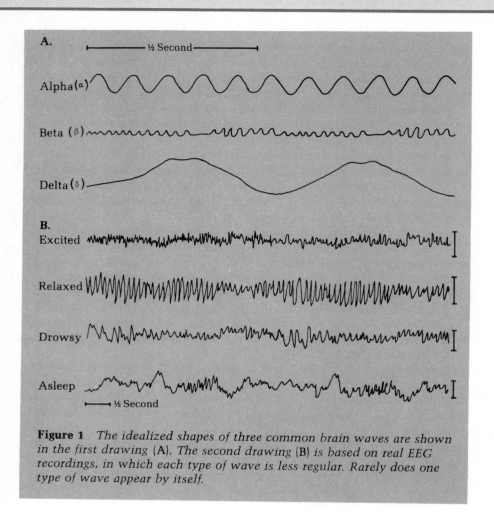

Figure 1   *The idealized shapes of three common brain waves are shown in the first drawing (A). The second drawing (B) is based on real EEG recordings, in which each type of wave is less regular. Rarely does one type of wave appear by itself.*

In most cases, paradoxical sleep is also characterized by rapid eye movements (called REMs), irregular breathing and heartbeats, and erection of the penis in male subjects. If you awaken the sleeper at this point, he will almost always report a dream; he will rarely do so in other stages of sleep. For this reason, paradoxical sleep is also called D-sleep (D for "dream"). Because of the characteristic eye movements, it is also called REM sleep, perhaps its most common name.

Researchers have been able to plot the course of sleep for an average person during an average evening. Sleep begins peacefully in a non-REM (NREM) state. About 70 or 80 minutes after the person falls asleep, the first REM period begins, lasting about 10 minutes (Dement, 1974). Thereupon follow several cycles of NREM and REM periods, each cycle lasting about 90 minutes; in other words, you dream about once every 90 minutes all night long. The REM periods become progressively longer as the evening wears on, lasting up to an hour. Thus, your night's entertainment typically consists of a few "short subjects," capped by a "feature film" toward the end. Typically an individual dreams four or five times a night (Luce and Segal, 1966). Some people remember dreams, some do not; but everybody dreams.

Although dreaming and REM sleep are highly correlated, cognitive activity (like "thinking") goes on all night long. In other words, if subjects are awakened right after fast EEG and REM, they report having had a dream. If they are awakened at other times, they may report that they were thinking about something ("It's not a dream," they say. "It's . . . you know, just thinking."). Of course, this set psychologists to work on the proper distinction between "dreaming" and "just thinking." What would you say, from your own experience? The theorists said that dreaming is, among other things, less controllable, more visual, and more emotional. Do you agree?

Is there a need to dream? Psychologists tried to answer this question by waking their subjects as soon as they began to exhibit rapid eye movements, effectively keeping them from dreaming (Dement, 1960). After several nights of this irritating procedure, they were allowed to sleep, and dream, as much as they wanted. The subjects showed a dramatic increase in their "dream time" for the next few nights. Just as a person who is deprived of the opportunity to eat will eat more heartily than usual when given free access to food, people deprived of the chance to dream will dream more frequently than usual when they are allowed.

One of the practical implications of dream-deprivation research concerns alcoholics who are trying to kick their habit. Alcohol, among its other effects, suppresses dreaming. When the alcoholic stops drinking, he is in for a few nights of almost constant dreaming, with more than a few nightmares. And delirium tremens, the terrifying daytime hallucinations of severe alcoholics, may be a kind of spill-over of nightmares into waking mental activity (Dement, 1974).

Newborns spend 50 percent or more of their sleep time in REM sleep, a figure that decreases to the adult level — 22 percent — around the age of ten or so (Webb and Cartwright, 1978). No one knows what this means. Are the infants dreaming? Of what? In what form? Animals other than humans also show paradoxical-sleep patterns. Does your dog or cat dream? How could you know for sure? Many people assume that a sleeping dog who is whimpering and making leg movements is chasing a cat in a dream, but such an interpretation is probably false; in humans, talking and walking during sleep typically occurs in NREM sleep. In REM sleep, the dream time, the motor apparatus is shut off almost completely; the person is motionless.

One group of researchers (reported in Dement, 1974) trained monkeys to press a switch whenever they saw a certain common visual pattern. During REM sleep, they discovered, the monkeys often made the same finger movements, the same switch-pressing movements, indicating they were viewing the same visual pattern—in a dream? Food for thought, fuel for research.

THE MEANING OF DREAMS

"An island of somethingness in an ocean of nothingness"—that's the way one person defined a dream. We have been describing research on how often dreaming occurs, when, and with what effect, but the dream itself— what does it mean? Throughout recorded history, there have been people willing to answer that question—oracles, or dream interpreters. In Egypt, great temples were built to house the oracles. Outside one room in one of these temples, constructed about 3000 B.C., anthropologists deciphered a little professional advertising: "I interpret dreams, having the gods' mandate to do so. Good luck! The interpreter present here is Cretan" (Van de Castle, 1971, p. 3).

A major breakthrough in the understanding of dreams came in 1900, when Sigmund Freud published his book *The Interpretation of Dreams.* Freud distinguished between the *manifest content* of a dream—the dream as it is reported—and the *latent content,* the true meaning of the dream. In between the latent and the manifest content, *dream work* occurs, transforming a straightforward "message" into a bizarre and often puzzling visual experience. To interpret a dream, therefore, Freud would have us do the dream work in reverse, translating the manifest content into its original form (Freud, 1924, 1938).

One mechanism of the dream work is *condensation,* which refers to the combining of several ideas into one. You might dream of a person who looks like one of your friends, dresses like your father, and has the

occupation of someone you dislike, and yet you have a vague feeling that it is really a fourth person; probably all four people are being represented. Another major dream mechanism is *displacement*, in which the original object or idea is represented by some other object or idea. Euphemisms people use in waking life — "rolling in the hay" for sexual intercourse — are displacements of sorts; a person who dreams of rolling in hay might thus be suspected of "meaning" a quite different activity, although dreams do not frequently let themselves be so easily decoded.

Some displacements are so common that they are called *symbols* and can often be translated directly. Fire, for example, is said to symbolize sexual passion; snakes often represent the penis; and the color yellow can stand for urine.

Another kind of displacement changes the emphasis in a dream. The major characters and important ideas of the latent content become minor characters and passing thoughts in the manifest content. People you hardly know and ideas of no personal relevance are elevated to center stage, giving the dream a foreign appearance: "I wonder why I dreamed of a meeting with Sally Evans, of all people, and at a botany lecture, of all places!"

An important feature of dreams is that they are *visual* representations; the latent ideas may not be visual at all. Translating ideas into visual forms can be quite difficult, and the results therefore quite puzzling. Imagine trying to communicate the ideas in this paragraph to someone else, using only pictures and drawings; or look at a rebus, a puzzle or picture-riddle in which you try to guess a sentence represented by visual forms—the word "I" by an eye, the word "can" by a can, etc. Dreams, as visual representations, are bound to be a little bizarre for this reason alone. In its attempt to represent a difficult concept like "breaking marriage vows," the dream work might choose the breaking of something more easily pictured, such as an arm or a leg.

And finally, after condensing, displacing, symbolizing, and translating into pictorial forms the ideas of the latent content, the dream work performs a final operation called *secondary elaboration*; the now chaotic collection is rearranged to give it some semblance of logical progression and coherent organization. It is as if you were given pictures of a snake, a rainbow, your grandmother, and someone cutting toenails, and asked to make up a story with all these elements. The organization imposed in secondary elaboration may have little to do with the latent content and thus may be further misleading. Just because your snake is interacting with your grandmother does not mean that your fantasies regarding a penis involve your grandmother; they may be two distinct ideas, thrown together simply because your mind is too embarrassed to offer up a dream in which a snake and a grandmother stand side-by-side, ignoring each other.

In line with his general theory of personality, Freud believed that the latent content of most dreams consists of unconscious wishes and fantasies. These desires cannot be expressed directly, even in dreams, for admitting them would result in overwhelming anxiety and guilt. Thus, in Freud's view, the purpose of the dream work is to disguise or mask the true meaning of the dream, something like a network censor who will not allow direct expression of dirty words on television but will permit allusions, euphemisms, and other indirect forms.

Freud's dream theory is very hard to test experimentally. But his description of the mechanisms of translation from latent to manifest content is a major contribution to dream research. It is a model that can aid dream interpreters whether or not they accept Freud's theory of unconscious desires or his notion that distortion is the aim of all dream work.

Modern Research on Dreams

Modern research on the content of dreams typically tries to avoid speculations about the nature of dreams, and focuses instead on the manifest content. For instance, modern research can provide answers to such questions as: In how many dreams, on the average, is the dreamer the sole human character? (15 percent.) Are there more dreams involving unpleasant emotions than pleasant emotions? (Yes; see Hall, 1966; Hall and Van de Castle, 1966.) Often these simple descriptions of manifest content have obvious theoretical significance. An example is the discovery that swimming (which Freud considered a symbol for sexual intercourse) occurs with unusual frequency in males' dreams in which orgasm also occurs.

The content of dreams varies with such factors as the sex, age, and social background of the dreamer. Men dream more frequently of other men, whereas women dream of both sexes about equally (Hall and Domhoff, 1963). Women's dreams have more "close-ups" of heads, providing more detail on face, hair, and eyes; more home-and-family themes; more emotion; more moral judgments. Men's dreams have more physical aggression and more sexual activity; more unfamiliar outdoor settings; more success-and-failure or achievement themes; more automobiles, tools, weapons, and money (Van de Castle, 1971; Winget et al., 1972). These dream differences seem to reflect stereotyped sex roles—one would probably obtain almost identical results by analyzing the content of waking conversations or magazines designed for one or the other sex—and thus can be expected to change as the roles of women and men in society change.

People's dreams also are heavily influenced by their situation. The dreams of pregnant women, for instance, are significantly different from those of nonpregnant women. The dreams do not usually contain references to pregnancy and childbirth until the fourth or fifth month (Van de Castle, 1971); however, in the second half of pregnancy, such themes progressively increase. Most pregnant women have several frightening dreams, in which their baby is born deformed or dead or turns out to be the devil's child (the theme of *Rosemary's Baby*). Many women dream of delivering a litter of animals. Without the knowledge that such dreams are common, many women suffer needless anxiety and guilt; they keep their terrifying dreams to themselves, fearing that others will think they resent their pregnancy.

People suffering from mental illness tend to dream in ways that reflect their particular disorder. Schizophrenia, a relatively severe disorder, results in dreams that, compared to normal dreams, have more stress, more aggression against the dreamer, and more themes such as being choked, impaled, or crushed by walls slowly coming together (Carrington, 1972). The dreams of severely depressed patients are notably bland and barren (Webb and Cartwright, 1978).

Some researchers have tried manipulating subjects' experiences before or during a dream, to see what effect the experiences will have on the dream. Typically these experiments are not very successful. Subjects deprived of water for 24 hours prior to sleep did not dream about liquids or thirst (Dement, 1974). In another study, a violent television show right before bed had no effect on the content of dreams (Foulkes and Recht-schaffen, 1964). Dreams following movies of childbirth and circumcision were no more explicitly sexual in nature than dreams following a pleas-ant travelogue, although they did contain more sexual symbolism (Wit-kin and Lewis, 1967).

Events that can affect the individual personally seem to have much greater impact. We have mentioned the dreams of women during preg-nancy. Another example is the dreams of subjects in sleep experiments, who must sleep in strange beds with wires attached to their heads. About a third of first-night dreams clearly depict the laboratory situation. Apprehension about being electrocuted during sleep is a common theme (Dement, 1974).

Your Dreams Reflect You

The one conclusion repeatedly encountered in current research literature is that, although dreams might sometimes take rather bizarre forms, they "accurately reflect the waking personality"; they are "remarkably faith-ful replicas of waking life"; they "correctly reflect waking emotional con-cerns and styles." Our dreams are not usually difficult to interpret, for most of the personal anxieties and conflicts they represent can be iden-tified in our waking lives as well.

But dreams are as individual as personality. What a particular dream element means varies from person to person, and from dream to dream for the same person. Attempts to control the content of dreams are generally unsuccessful, and even when the experimenter's manipulation is repre-sented in a dream, it is usually in a very personal way. Freud was right in assuming that dreams are clues to important *personal* concerns. Your dreams reflect you.

It is possible to use your dreams to understand yourself a little better. Obviously, dream books with a standard interpretation for each dream element are essentially worthless, for each dream is unique. But if you relate your dreams to personal conflicts and problems you are facing, the meaning of many dreams will become clear. You can use Freud's method of dream interpretation: Explore the dream characteristics and events by seeing what comes to mind when you think about them. For example, a clown appeared in one of my dreams. My mental associations to "clown," at the time, were variations on the theme of embarrassment and ridicule. I was anxious about a public-speaking engagement the next day, afraid of doing poorly. Later that same month, a clown appeared again, but this time my associations were "carefree" and "carnival," most likely in anticipation of (and in some conflict about) a long-awaited but sinfully indulgent vacation.

SUGGESTED READINGS

Hall, C. S. *The meaning of dreams.* McGraw-Hill, 1966.
   A thoroughly reasonable introduction to the personal and scientific study of dream content.
Dement, W. C. *Some must watch while some must sleep.* Freeman, 1974.
   A fascinating account of EEG-based sleep and dream research by one of its most respected practitioners.

PART

4 Psychology in the World

In this section we will look at intelligence tests, personality tests, abnormal psychology, psychotherapies, and social psychology. Although this collection may strike you as a mixed bag, all of these topics concern the person as he or she is directly influenced by psychology in the real world. You have a memory that you use every day, of course, and a personality that affects your every action, but most of the time you are not aware of them. A test, however—a college entrance exam, for example—is something that you are very much aware of when you have to take it, something you are forced to deal with in one way or another.

In Parts 1–3, we have concentrated mostly on psychology's insights into what makes people tick—how they react to their environment, how they got to be the way they are. Part 4 takes us through the looking glass, so to speak. We will see how psychology is of practical use in describing and comparing groups of people, identifying and helping people with "problems of living," and interpreting the ways people interact.

Behavioral Objectives

1. Discuss the early development of intelligence tests; distinguish between individual and group tests, and give important examples of each.
2. Explain what is meant by the term "IQ" and know how to compute one in the original way.
3. List and describe the three measures of test reliability and the two general categories of test validity.
4. Discuss what is known about the stability of IQ scores throughout the human life span.
5. Explain on what grounds some psychologists criticize IQ tests.
6. Describe what the Scholastic Aptitude Test attempts to predict, how it is used in our society, what changes have occurred in SAT scores in the past 20 years or so, and what the reasons are for this change.
7. Describe the four categories of personality tests on the basis of the needs they were designed to meet and give an example of each.
8. Compare projective and objective personality tests, giving an example of each; tell which kind is primarily used today and why.
9. Discuss the use and possible misuse of personality tests.
10. Explain in what ways test bias is a problem.

CHAPTER

11

Testing Intelligence and Personality

Today we are tested in so many ways, so many times, that it is almost impossible to imagine someone who has never taken a test. I once knew an old man who had taken very few, and none of the paper-and-pencil variety. Born in a foreign country, he had no formal schooling; his parents had taught him to read and write. He was nearly 80 years old and was about to take his first written examination, a driver's test. Terrified at the thought, he came to me for advice.

He asked, "What will be on this test? What kind of questions?"

I told him there would be some true-false questions and some multiple-choice. This made no sense to the old man. He asked me what a true-false question was. How can it be, he pondered, that something can be both true and false at the same time? I told him what a true-false question was, and he looked even more bewildered. He said that he had read the driver's manual and had seen many statements that he thought were true, but none that seemed to him false. Well, they make up false statements for the test, I said. No, he didn't think the government would do that, not on purpose.

Desperate, I tried a new approach, an example: "There is a sign on the side of the road. The sign says, 'Fresh Oil Ahead.' This means that there will be a gas station in the next mile or so. True or false?"

He thought for a while and then replied, "Well, there could be. You never know."

My wise old friend died before he could take his test, but I am certain he would have failed. He knew the rules of the road as well as anyone else, but he did not know tests. And he was very anxious besides.

But we know tests, don't we! There are achievement tests, of the type we take during and after a course to determine how well we have mastered the course content. There are intelligence tests. There are college entrance exams, graduate record exams, medical entrance exams. Vocational interest tests may help us decide what careers we should follow. Personality tests tell us what we are like and sometimes whether we would be better off in a mental institution. When we apply for a job, we may take another set of tests. There are tests to be passed before we can drive a car or a truck, and many people think there will soon be tests to get married or have children. Our lives are full of tests, and the scores are used, usually by others, to make momentous decisions about us.

In the first part of this chapter we will focus on intelligence tests, along with some of the general issues relevant to all testing—how we know a test measures what it presumes to measure, for example. Personality tests will be discussed later in the chapter, including those fun types in which we get to answer True or False to such items as "I am afraid somebody may cut off my nose." (Believe it or not, that's a real item on a real personality test!) The questions in Table 11.1 were written by humorist Art Buchwald. Created to poke fun at those who make up items for actual tests, Buchwald's questions are very close to the originals he satirizes. (See Goldberg, 1974.)

EARLY ATTEMPTS AT MEASURING INTELLIGENCE

When Charles Darwin published his theory of evolution in 1859, it was a milestone in human knowledge that had significant repercussions in psychology. Some psychologists, like Freud, began thinking about the animal nature in man; others, like Thorndike, began thinking about the human-like

Table 11.1
ANSWER "YES," "NO," OR "DON'T BOTHER ME, I CAN'T COPE!"
The sight of blood no longer excites me.
It makes me furious to see an innocent man escape the chair.
When I was a child, I was an imaginary playmate.
I am bored by thoughts of death.
I become homicidal when people try to reason with me.
I don't like it when somebody is rotten.
Most of the time I go to sleep without saying goodbye.
Frantic screams make me nervous.
Reprinted by permission of Art Buchwald.

intelligence of animals. This chapter is about those psychologists who picked up a third important feature of Darwin's theory, the assumption of wide individual differences among the members of a species. Survival of the fittest could hardly occur if some were not more fit than others.

Ten years later, a half-cousin of Darwin's named Francis Galton published a book applying Darwin's theory to human intelligence. His book was entitled *Hereditary Genius;* in it, he tried to show that genius runs in families. From an investigation of 1000 geniuses, he concluded that intelligence is mostly inherited, not learned. He advocated a program of *eugenics:* By selective breeding, allowing the more intelligent people to have most of the babies, he reasoned, the race would get smarter and smarter, evolving to even greater heights in Darwin's phylogenetic tree.

Galton campaigned for a national program of eugenics for the English. But there was a fatal flaw in Galton's program and Galton knew it: There was no way to identify the people who were highly intelligent. To be sure, there were some people whose genius was readily apparent and agreed on by all, but they were too few for the task Galton had in mind. Were the obvious geniuses called on to populate the British Isles, they would have had precious little time for their art or writing or whatever made them famous in the first place. No, a test must be devised, an intelligence test, one that would measure individual differences in in-

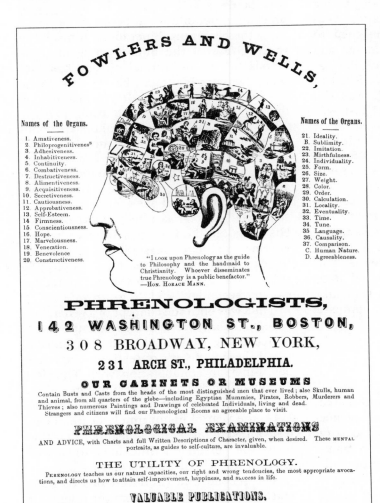

Figure 11.1 *The now-discredited "science" of phrenology postulated that an unusual amount of a mental ability was indicated by a bump in the skull where the ability was presumed to be located in the brain.*

telligence and allow Galton to substitute his program of selective breeding for Darwin's natural selection.

In 1883, Galton published the first intelligence test—it was called a "mental test"—and it was woefully inadequate. Influenced by British philosophers who considered intellect to be directly related to the ability to process sensory information, Galton devised a series of tasks designed to measure how well a person could see and hear and smell and taste and feel. For example, in one task the person was asked to lift two weights and say which was the heavier. We can be thankful this test was never used to select intelligent breeders!

Still, Galton's test and others like it prevailed for several years. The tests were used primarily to *describe* a person or group; rarely were they used for prediction or selection. In the 1890s, incoming freshmen at Columbia were required to take them; the results, again, were published simply to describe the classes, but these tests were the forerunners of today's entrance exams. The tests were also popular at county and state fairs, probably because people are generally interested in finding out how they compare to others.

BINET AND
THE INTRODUCTION OF IQ

A French psychologist by the name of Alfred Binet developed the first "real" intelligence test. Binet placed little faith in the sensory aspects of intelligence. He took a more traditional view (one might even say a more cultured view), believing that playing chess indicated intelligence better than smelling vinegar. Binet also was given a very practical problem to solve: The French Minister of

Public Instruction pleaded with him to construct a test that would enable school officials to distinguish between students of low ability (such as the feebleminded) and those of high ability but low motivation. Different programs of study would be proposed for the two types of students, so Binet was being asked to help in a *selection* procedure, not simply in description.

At the beginning, Binet found himself "in the position of the hunter going into the woods to find an animal no one has ever seen. Everyone is sure the beast exists, for he has been raiding the poultry coops, but no one can describe him" (Cronbach, 1970, p. 200). There was a great deal of debate about how many "animals" were involved; was there a general ability we can call intelligence, or were there several independent abilities, each deserving the name? Binet tended to the view of one general ability and so devised his test as a hodgepodge of tasks. His tasks, unlike Galton's, were verbal, involving judgments, reasoning, and the like. Instead of lifting weights, for example, the subject was asked to tell the difference between "yesterday" and "tomorrow."

Thus was born the concept of a general intellectual ability and its assessment by tests of reasoning, judgment, and imagination, which began the era of testing in psychology. Binet, in collaboration with Theodore Simon, published his first test in 1905; a second version came out in 1908 and a third in 1911, the year of his untimely death. These tests all were *individual,* meaning that they tested one person at a time, in contrast with *group* tests, which we will discuss later.

The second and third versions of Binet and Simon's test differed from the original in that they used the concept of *mental age* for the first time. The original test had 30 questions or problems arranged roughly in order of difficulty, and Binet had some rough estimates of how many problems a child of any given age could be expected to pass. By 1908, the items had been arranged into age scales running from age three to age thirteen. Each separate age scale had within it four to eight "subtests," problems that, as Binet had determined from previous testing, 60 to 90 percent of children that age could solve. Thus, if a child passed all the items on the age six scale and none higher, she had a mental age of six. If she was chronologically (that is, really) five years old, this meant she was brighter than average, and if her chronological age was eight, it meant she was dull. Teachers and administrators who used these tests found the notion of a mental age intuitively satisfying, and Binet's tests soon spread around the world.

The Stanford-Binet

In the United States, several adaptations of Binet's test were quickly put to use. Several psychologists translated or revised Binet's test, but the most famous revision by far was by Stanford University psychologist Lewis Terman in 1916. Ever since, the test has been called the *Stanford-Binet.* Revised twice again in later years (Terman and Merrill, 1937, 1960), the test remains one of the most commonly used individual tests of intelligence.

Terman's first revision introduced the *intelligence quotient,* or IQ. This was the subject's *mental age* (MA) divided by her or his *chronological age* (CA): IQ = MA/CA. In Terman's test, the mental age could be calculated with considerable precision because each age scale had six problems or items. (See Figure 11.2 for some examples.) Each

item was given a score of "two months." Imagine then a child of eight years and four months (her chronological age) who passes all the items for age eight, four out of six at the nine level, and even one at the ten-year-old level. She gets a mental age score of eight years, plus two months for each correct answer at the nine level (4 × 2 = 8 months), plus two more months at the ten level, for a total mental age score of eight years and ten months. Her IQ would be her mental age, expressed in months, divided by her chronological age, expressed in months: IQ = 106/100 = 1.06. The IQ is then multiplied by 100 to eliminate the decimal point. This child has an IQ of 106. Since an IQ of 100 is *by definition* average, this child is slightly brighter than average.

In 1960, the method of computing the IQ was changed. The simple division of mental age by chronological age, however reasonable and appealing, was a rather crude statistical procedure. Today, more sophisticated techniques are used, and each individual is given a score that indicates his or her position relative to other people of the same age. The average score for any age group is, by agreement, called 100, the same as on the old Stanford-Binet IQ scores. Scores above 100 still indicate above-average intelligence, as before. The newer procedures use straightforward measures like "number of items passed," and then convert them to "IQ-type scores," with an average of 100—something like converting the number of items passed on an exam to a percentage score.

In spite of the change in the computation of intelligence test scores, the name IQ stuck. IQ is a bit of a misnomer. By today's definitions, it means, simply, "intelligence test score," not "intelligence quotient." Per-

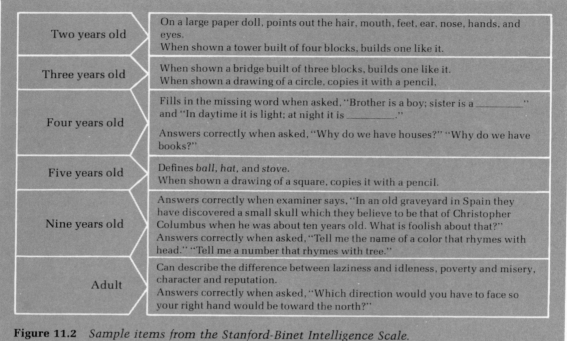

Two years old	On a large paper doll, points out the hair, mouth, feet, ear, nose, hands, and eyes. When shown a tower built of four blocks, builds one like it.
Three years old	When shown a bridge built of three blocks, builds one like it. When shown a drawing of a circle, copies it with a pencil.
Four years old	Fills in the missing word when asked, "Brother is a boy; sister is a _____" and "In daytime it is light; at night it is _____." Answers correctly when asked, "Why do we have houses?" "Why do we have books?"
Five years old	Defines *ball*, *hat*, and *stove*. When shown a drawing of a square, copies it with a pencil.
Nine years old	Answers correctly when examiner says, "In an old graveyard in Spain they have discovered a small skull which they believe to be that of Christopher Columbus when he was about ten years old. What is foolish about that?" Answers correctly when asked, "Tell me the name of a color that rhymes with head." "Tell me a number that rhymes with tree."
Adult	Can describe the difference between laziness and idleness, poverty and misery, character and reputation. Answers correctly when asked, "Which direction would you have to face so your right hand would be toward the north?"

Figure 11.2 *Sample items from the Stanford-Binet Intelligence Scale.*

haps it survives as a kind of honor to Binet, Terman, and the others who worked so hard to develop the most successful psychological test of all—the intelligence test.

Other Individual Intelligence Tests

Through the doors of Bellevue Hospital in Manhattan pass people with individual differences of an extremely wide range. The staff at Bellevue needed a test that could distinguish among types including illiterates, psychotics, mentally retarded people, people with brain damage, and of course relatively normal people. David Wechsler developed the Wechsler-Bellevue Test for use with adult patients (Wechsler, 1939); the test was revised in 1955 and is now known as the Wechsler Adult Intelligence Scale (WAIS). It is the most commonly used individual test for adults. Two versions for children, the Wechsler Intelligence Scale for Children (WISC), for ages seven to sixteen, and the Wechsler Preschool-Primary Intelligence Scale (WPPIS), are also widely used. The WAIS correlates around .85 with the Stanford-Binet (Wechsler, 1955); this is a high degree of relationship, which is as it should be, since both tests purport to measure the same thing.

The WAIS is different from the Stanford-Binet in several ways. Many of the specific items or tasks are similar, but WAIS items are arranged in ten *subtests*. These consist of two groups of five subtests each, one of *verbal* and one of *performance* tests. Each subtest has its own score, each subgroup (verbal and performance) generates an IQ score, and there is also a total overall IQ score.

Wechsler hoped to use all this information to diagnose patients. For example, he believed that brain damage lowered the overall IQ but did so primarily on certain subtests. Psychosis (serious mental illness) might show up with a different pattern. Research has not been kind to Wechsler's hope in this regard (Cronbach, 1970). The scores on the subtests are used today mostly to develop hunches about certain intellectual problems, which must then be examined much more closely in other ways.

The difference between verbal and performance tests, however, has been very valuable. A performance test is one in which the response is not verbal. For example, in one of the subtests the subject is asked to copy a design made with blocks. In another he or she is asked to arrange pictures in their proper sequence; the pictures may show several stages in building a house, and the subject must not put the finished house before the laying of the foundation.

In contrast, verbal subtests call for verbal responses. The subtests have names like Information (Who wrote *War and Peace*?), Similarities (How are bottles and cans alike?), and Vocabulary (What is a neurosis?). These are more familiar to you, no doubt, for they are more like the verbal items on the group intelligence tests you have taken.

The performance tests are very useful for testing the IQs of certain kinds of subjects. People who cannot understand or speak English well generally do better on the performance scale. This includes people for whom English is a second language, people who

have not had very much education, deaf people, and others. In one school system, bilingual children classified as mentally retarded by a verbal IQ test were retested in their other language, Spanish; 45 percent scored average or above (Ruch and Zimbardo, 1971). A performance test of IQ would have been useful in such a situation. A different study of bilingual preschool children showed them 7 IQ points higher (from 91 to 98) on the performance test than on the verbal test (Darcy, 1946).

Group Tests of Intelligence

Lewis Terman, the Stanford part of the Stanford-Binet, had a student named Arthur Otis who was working on an intelligence test that could be given to groups of people (the Stanford-Binet had to be administered to one person at a time). In April 1917, the need for such a test became urgent. The United States Congress had declared war on Germany and had passed a draft law, and the Army was preparing to induct large numbers of young men in a hurry. Terman was one of a seven-member committee appointed by the American Psychological Association to create a group intelligence test for draftees, a test the Army hoped would enable it to place men in jobs appropriate to their intellectual abilities without taking too much time to administer. Otis turned his test materials over to the committee, and they created the first major group IQ test, the *Army Alpha*.

Alpha was a written test of the type you know well, a series of multiple-choice, true-false, and short-answer questions. The fact that one had to be able to read and write English in order to take it presented problems, because nearly one-third (!) of the draftees were illiterate (Garrett, 1957). A group non-

Figure 11.3 *The United States Army tries to find round pegs for its round holes. The Army was the first organization to use group intelligence tests.*

verbal test called the *Army Beta* was constructed for testing these soldiers. In many respects it was a more remarkable accomplishment that the Alpha. Giving a performance test to a group was difficult: The examiner had to read aloud all the instructions, examples had to be given, and the examiner had to be adept at gesture and pantomime because some of the draftees couldn't even speak English. The subtests included solving mazes and analyzing patterns of *X*s and *O*s.

The Army released the Alpha for civilian use in 1919, and a number of colleges and high schools began to use it immediately. Arthur Otis, whose material was the basis for the Alpha, put his own test on the market in 1918; 500,000 copies were sold in the first six months, which gives us some idea of society's need for such a test.

The latest edition of the Otis group test, called the *Otis-Lennon Mental Ability Test,*

is still among the most widely used. Several versions are available, each for a particular age group.

Scholastic Aptitude Tests

One of the things IQ tests do best is predict success in schools. The Stanford-Binet, the Wechsler Adult Intelligence Scale, and the well-constructed group tests like the Otis-Lennon all correlate around .50 with college grades (Cronbach, 1970). It is not surprising, therefore, to find IQ-like tests playing a major role in the admission procedures of colleges and universities. Most schools use either the Scholastic Aptitude Test (SAT) or the American College Testing Program test (ACT). Graduate schools use a kind of advanced SAT called the Graduate Record Exam (GRE). Unlike IQ tests, which claim to be measuring general intelligence, these "scholastic aptitude" tests are specifically geared to their task of predicting academic performance. Many of the items are more "school-like": reading a paragraph and then taking a little test on it. Nevertheless, the scores correlate very highly with the traditional IQ tests (Cronbach, 1970).

Since ACT and SAT both measure the same trait—scholastic aptitude—and are used to select students in often highly competitive situations, a comparison of the scores of students who took both tests is informative. There is a high correlation between these tests; but let us look further: What does this correlation mean in terms of people? In Figure 11.4 we can see that *most* of the students who scored in the top 25 percent of the ACT also scored in the top 25 percent of the SAT, which is as it should be;

this is essentially what "high correlation" means. But a great number of people did well on one test and less well on the other. They might have been accepted by a college that used their good test scores but rejected by a college that relied on their "poor" tests. Nineteen people actually scored in the *top* quarter on one test and in the *bottom* quarter on the other! Figured as a percentage of the total number of taking the tests, 19 is a very small number; but if you were one of the 19, percentages would not seem important.

The reason tests like these continue to exist, even though nobody claims they are error-free, is that college administrators do have to make practical decisions about admissions, one way or another. As you can see in Figure 11.4, most students would re-

	ACT score		
	Bottom 25%	Middle 50%	Top 25%
Top 25%	14 (1%)	287 (13%)	820 (73%)
Middle 50%	404 (36%)	1555 (69%)	303 (27%)
Bottom 25%	711 (63%)	416 (18%)	5 (0%)

(SAT score)

Figure 11.4 *ACT scores compared with SAT scores.*

ceive about the same rank by either test. And the tests do correlate quite well with performance in college. Considering some of the criteria colleges have employed in the past—sex, skin color, family status—the scholastic aptitude tests are a clear advance.

The Decline in SAT Scores. Since 1963, there has been a steady drop in average scores on the Scholastic Aptitude Test (SAT), one of the most widely used college entrance examinations (see Figure 11.5). To some people, the SAT decline suggests that Americans are growing less intelligent—a frightening possibility! What is causing the decline? It has been blamed on everything from permissiveness toward pornography to subversive political activity by Communists. In October 1975, the College Entrance Examination Board commissioned a blue-ribbon advisory panel to investigate the reasons for the decline; in 1977 the panel issued its report (Advisory Panel, 1977).

The first task of the panel was to investigate the test itself. New items replace old ones each year, so it is possible that over the years the SAT has become more difficult and that this simple fact accounts for the decline. But, horror of horrors, studies showed just the opposite! Subjects who took both the 1973 and the 1963 version of the test scored eight to twelve points higher on the newer test, on the average, than on the older one. This suggests that the test has become not harder but easier—which means the decline in SAT scores is actually *greater* than the figures indicate.

Investigating further, the advisory panel discovered two distinct factors at work, each seeming to account for a major portion of

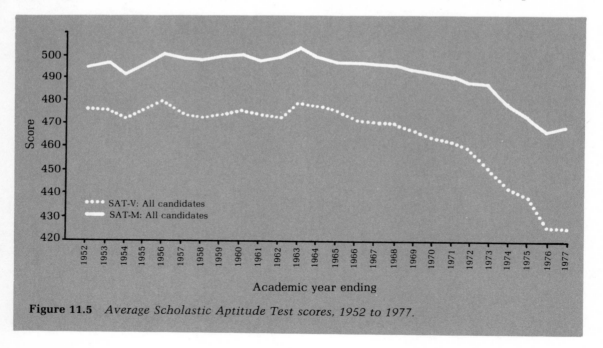

Figure 11.5 *Average Scholastic Aptitude Test scores, 1952 to 1977.*

the decline at a different time. From 1963 to 1970, there was a dramatic change in the *composition* of the group who finished high school and wanted to attend college — the group taking the SAT. In particular, far more students from lower socioeconomic classes and minority ethnic groups took the test than in previous years. For a variety of reasons, these students typically score lower on tests like the SAT, so the average score was pulled down. Similarly, increasing numbers of women, who normally score lower than men on the mathematical half of the test, pulled down the average for that portion (but not for the "verbal" half). Also there were more students wanting to enter two-year colleges and schools with a technical or vocational emphasis, instead of what the panel referred to as the "prestigious and selective four-year, liberal arts colleges and universities." All told, the *compositional shift* was estimated to account for two-thirds to three-fourths of the SAT decline between 1963 and 1970. Rather than being frightening, this decline is an encouraging sign that our educational ideals — opening up educational opportunities for all people — are having some effect.

Pervasive Change. Since 1970, however, the composition of the group taking the SAT has not changed as much. Seventy to 80 percent of the recent decline must be blamed on something else, some pervasive change in American students as a whole. High scorers are affected as much as low scorers; the average SAT score for high school valedictorians, for example, is declining at about the same rate as the scores in general.

Certainly there are many causes at work, and the causes overlap; the evidence is correlational, circumstantial, never conclusive.

Making "informed" guesses, the panel identified several suspicious-looking social trends. They noted that in the high schools, fewer "basic" courses are being required or offered; attractive but insubstantial electives are replacing them at a rapid rate. Consider English courses, where students have typically learned how to read the often complex questions on the SAT. Enrollment in expository classes in one state dropped by 77 percent between 1972 and 1975, while enrollment in frothy courses on mysteries, science-fiction, and television and film doubled. Students in schools that bucked this trend and stayed with the old reading-and-writing curriculum did not show SAT declines.

Many other potential causes of the SAT decline were also examined. The panel noted with disfavor the increasing use of classroom tests that require no writing, only the putting of *X*s in boxes. Lower school standards are having an effect, resulting in more absenteeism and less homework. Changes in the family, such as sharp increases in single-parent families and households with working mothers, probably are influencing educational experiences in the home. The cynicism among young people after the turbulent 1960s may have lowered their motivation to pursue traditional goals like a college education. One psychologist has suggested that the decline is due to a temporary decrease in the percentage of firstborn children among those applying to college, on the basis of data showing that the eldest children typically score higher on IQ tests (Zajonc, 1976).

A few suspected causes were dismissed for lack of evidence: For example, "grade inflation" — giving more high grades and fewer low grades — does not seem to be a factor in SAT decline, nor do "experimental, innovative teaching methods."

One of the major influences on students' intellects these days is television. The effects are not all bad; educational programs like Sesame Street seem to be improving students' performance in the early grades. Thereafter, however, it is hard to find positive effects from television. If nothing else, TV is a thief of time, stealing hours that were once used for homework, reading, and writing. (By age 16, the average child has watched between 10,000 and 15,000 hours of television!) In addition, TV-watching is a passive experience, usually entertaining, and largely visual. Many psychologists believe that it destroys watchers' incentive, and eventually their ability, to read and write—active, verbal experiences that yield their satisfactions only with a struggle.

FOCUS

Biased Tests

I once missed an item on a test because I didn't know what a "comfort station" was. In my area, the equivalent term was "rest room." Every IQ test has some items that discriminate against people of a certain subculture. For example, one item in an IQ test requires schoolchildren to choose the word that does not belong in the following group of five: cello, harp, drum, violin, guitar. The correct answer is supposed to be "drum," the only instrument without strings. Psychologists looking at the results of the tests discovered that 85 percent of students in the higher social class answered correctly. But only 45 percent of lower-class students chose "drum." Most of them chose "cello," a word unfamiliar to their culture, whereas the other four were all clearly musical instruments (Eells et al., 1951).

In order to test "pure" intellectual ability rather than the effect of living in a certain home and neighborhood, several psychologists have sought to construct "culture-free" IQ tests (for example, Cattell, 1949). The original culture-free tests were like (or identical to) the nonverbal or performance subtests on the general IQ tests (see Figure 1). The idea, of course, was that a child from an "underprivileged environment" might not happen to know who our fourteenth president was or what the word "assume" means, but education and culture in general do not contribute to the ability to find a figure hidden in camouflage. Performance tests are supposedly measures of *pure* intelligence, not acquired knowledge.

Unfortunately, disadvantaged children did not do well on these tests either (Jensen, 1969). Some psychologists took this as evidence that IQ is largely inherited and affected little by environment. (See Interlude: Is IQ

Inherited?, pp. 468–479, for a more complete discussion.) But there is also evidence that scores on performance tests can be improved with practice (Vernon, 1969). In fact, with practice, black schoolchildren improve rela-

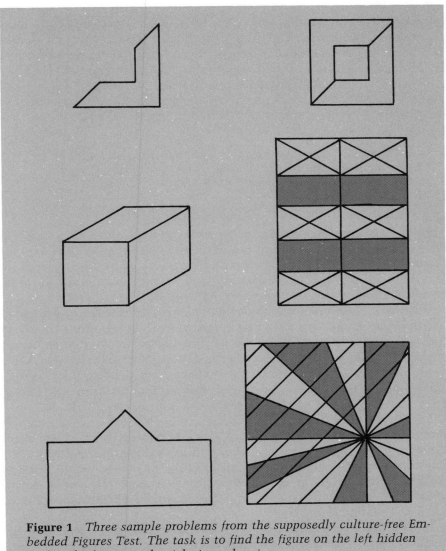

Figure 1   *Three sample problems from the supposedly culture-free Embedded Figures Test. The task is to find the figure on the left hidden within the figure on the right in each pair.*

tive to whites on nonverbal tests but never overcome their average disadvantage on the culturally loaded vocabulary, information, and other verbal tests (Coleman et al., 1966). Probably, black children are at a disadvantage in nonintellectual factors such as "test-taking": In general, white children are exposed to tests more often and they are less afraid of the room, the situation, and the test-giver. Whites probably have more experience with the "toys" used in performance tests, too, which are like the jigsaw puzzles and toy blocks often found in middle-class homes. So, it seems, the culture-free tests were not free of culture at all.

The task of being fair in testing presents real problems. A black social worker, Adrian Dove, constructed an "IQ test" with ghetto words and definitions to show whites what it's like to take a culturally unfair test (Aiken, 1971). Here are two sample items:

> A "Gas Head" is a person who has a: (a) fast moving car; (b) stable of "lace"; (c) "process"; (d) habit of stealing cars; (e) long jail record for arson.
> Which word is out of place here? (a) splib; (b) Blood; (c) grey; (d) Spook; (e) Black.

The correct answer, for you greys, is (c) in both.

Lately, psychologists have begun to focus on the major issue — *bias* — in different ways. Bias is a major issue because tests are so often used for selection; on the basis of test scores, people are chosen or rejected for jobs, schools, or programs of various sorts. Unfair selection or rejection based on a biased test is what we want to avoid.

In terms of selection for a job or a school, a biased test can be defined as one that consistently predicts a higher or lower level of performance than the level the person would actually achieve if he or she were given the job or the slot in the freshman class (Cleary, 1968). Another definition: A test is fair (unbiased) only if it selects the same percentage of a minority group that would be selected on the basis of their actual performance (Thorndike, 1971).

You may have to reread the two definitions to notice any difference. They seem almost identical, or at least conceptually equivalent. But using the first definition, the common college admissions test, the Scholastic Aptitude Test (SAT), can be shown to be biased *in favor of* black students; using the second definition, the same test can be shown to be biased *against* black students! (See Schmidt and Hunter, 1974, for the rather technical details.)

Psychologists will generate a great deal of research on test bias in the next few years. It's an exciting area of research, with great practical significance. Laws on all levels of government are becoming much stricter in regard to testing; it is the law now, for example, that selection tests must have a *demonstrated* relationship with job performance, and test bias is also illegal in many areas. But what is test bias? We have seen that two reasonable definitions lead to opposite conclusions. The scientific controversy will force society to define its goals and values more precisely, and this result is certainly desirable.

ARE IQ TESTS DEPENDABLE?

We have reviewed the reasons why IQ tests were developed, along with several examples of individual and group forms. But are these tests dependable? Do they do the job they were designed to do? To answer these questions, assessment psychologists rely heavily on two measures of test dependability: reliability and validity. We will discuss these concepts in the context of IQ tests, but they are equally appropriate to the evaluation of personality tests, as we will see later in the chapter.

The Reliability of IQ Tests

Reliability is a technical concept defining the degree to which a test gives the same subject the same score whenever it is used. We do not want a test that estimates someone's IQ as 100 one day, 137 the next, and 75 next week; it cannot be relied on. Unless the person being tested changes drastically, we expect approximately the same score each time she or he is tested.

Reliability is usually measured by one of a number of statistics, all of which somehow reflect the correlation of the test with itself. The same test may be given to the same people on two different occasions, say a week apart, and the scores correlated. This *test-retest* reliability for the Stanford-Binet is .91, a very high correlation (Terman and Merrill,

1960). If many items in a test are similar, say 100 of them, we can take the score on 50 randomly chosen items and correlate it with the score on the other 50 items, giving us a kind of test-retest measure on the same day. This correlation measures *internal consistency*. If we have 200 roughly equivalent items and divide them into two tests of 100 items each, then we have two *forms* of essentially the same test, giving us a coefficient of *equivalence*.

There is a point at which a correlation between two takings of the same test stops being an estimate of reliability and becomes an investigation into the stability of IQ itself. Thus the test-retest reliability is often called the coefficient of *stability*. When we ask how similarly people score on the same test over a period of a few days, a week, or even a month, we are asking reliability questions, but when we ask whether the scores remain similar over a period of years, we are asking how stable IQ is.

The Stability of IQ. Most psychologists consider an individual's intelligence to be a fairly stable characteristic, and they do not expect measured IQ to change much over the years. There are notable exceptions, of course. A child from a severely deprived environment could change in IQ considerably when given remedial treatment or when placed in a richer environment. Sometimes a person's IQ jumps dramatically because her or his motivation to do well on the test increases for some reason.

But despite unusual cases, psychologists expect that people's IQ scores will remain fairly similar over the years. And a number of studies show this to be a highly reasonable expectation. In one, with IQ measures by the Stanford-Binet, scores at age four correlated .70 with scores at age sixteen, a very high relationship considering how young the children were when first tested. Scores at age eleven correlated .92 with scores of the same people six years later (Bayley, 1949).

No test yet devised has been able to measure IQ below the age of two with much success. IQ scores determined for three-month-old babies using the California First Year Test (Bayley, 1949) correlated −.13 with those children's Stanford-Binet scores six years later. A negative correlation! This result is extreme, but it justifies the general statement that until a child is at least two years old, her measured IQ is not highly related to her IQ later in life. The most likely reason for this is that until the child is two or more, her intellectual abilities are primitive and sensory-motor in nature; after the age of two, her symbolic and language skills are more fully developed. It is these verbal skills that we are usually judging in adult tasks supposed to define brightness—for example, can she read a paragraph and understand it?

Adult IQ Changes. The high correlations in measured IQ after the age of two do not mean that no changes occur in our intelligence from early childhood to old age. If we disregard the adjustments normally made for chronological age and look at "raw" IQ scores—the number of items peo-

Figure 11.6 *A person's intelligence test scores are usually quite stable over the years, but special training, especially among the young, can result in striking increases in measured IQ.*

ple answer correctly—we note a general increase in intelligence up to the age of 15 or 16. (The high correlations mean that, even though the typical 12-year-old is more intelligent than the typical 6-year-old, the rank order of the children remains highly similar. The brightest kids at age 6 are still the brightest at age 12.) After the age of 16, average intelligence test scores do not change much until the later years of life, after the age of 65 or so (see Chapter 9). And there are indications that the decreases in measured intelligence in later life are not due to aging per se, but to diseases that affect the flow of blood to the brain or other biological bases of intellectual ability.

The Validity of IQ Tests

In addition to high reliability, a test must have *validity* to be useful. Validity is another technical concept with several meanings, but most of the meanings can be gathered into two general categories: construct validity and predictive validity. *Construct validity* involves the claim that test X is a measure of the theoretical construct Y: What evidence is there that the test is indeed measuring what it is said to measure? In trying to prove construct validity, one often correlates the test in question with other measures of the same trait, in hopes of finding a high correlation. If I develop a new technique for estimating intelligence, it had better correlate highly with the Stanford-Binet, or I'm in trouble. On the other hand, if my test is supposed to measure creativity, then a high correlation with IQ tests might well *invalidate* my claim to be measuring something that is distinct from intelligence.

Predictive validity defines validity in its broadest sense of "usefulness." If a test predicts a certain behavior, it has predictive validity for that behavior. For example, a personality test might be able to predict whether a mental patient will commit suicide. IQ tests were originally developed to predict scholastic achievement, and this they do reasonably well.

The Case against IQ Tests

Recently IQ tests have come under severe attack from several psychologists who claim that the apparent predictive validity of the tests is misleading. These dissident psychologists do not deny the reasonably high correlation between the tests and school grades. Rather, they claim that neither IQ scores nor school grades (which they sometimes use as roughly equivalent terms) have much predictive validity for "grades in life" (McClelland, 1973). For example, a review of many studies correlating college grades with later earnings (adjusted for age) found almost all correlations near zero (Hoyt, 1965). Most college graduates listed in *Who's Who* averaged C+ to B in school (Blum, 1976).

IQ and Job Success. Most psychologists would allow that the importance of intelligence for job success varies with the job, and that IQ tests should therefore have more validity for, say, research scientists than for, say, unskilled laborers. But studies show that school grades and amount of education are unrelated to success in a wide range of occupations: factory worker, bank teller, air traffic controller, and a number of other professions (Berg, 1970). And the same picture emerges for the research scientist! One study rated the merit of the work of several scientists doing basic research in engineering (Taylor et al., 1963). The top-rated researchers averaged 2.73 (B−) in college; the second-ranked group averaged 2.60 (B−); the low-rated investigators averaged 2.69 (B−).

In another review, the careers of 493 scientists were rated by a panel of judges seeking to determine who was most worthy of an award. Correlations between college grades and scientific competence ranged from −.20 to +.14; all the correlations were statistically no different from a true zero correlation plus random error (Harmon, 1963).

Two psychologists correlated high school grade point averages with achievements in college other than grades (Holland and Richards, 1965). Examples were success in theater, special science projects, musical talents, and, in general, the areas of endeavor

Figure 11.7   *What do IQ scores really tell us about a person? According to his IQ score, James D. Watson (left) was not an unusually intelligent person. However, he and Francis H. C. Crick discovered the cornerstone of modern genetics, the double helix, a breakthrough which won them the Nobel Prize. John Kirtley (right) has an IQ of 174, and belongs to Mensa, an international association of exceptionally intelligent people. He prefers to do custodial work rather than risk having his superior intellect "used" by our technology-hungry society.*

called extracurricular. Over 75 different correlations were computed; the average was .03 for men and .06 for women.

IQ and Job Status. The correlations between IQ and job status, on the other hand, are considerably higher. People in high-status occupations (those with higher prestige and usually higher income) score higher on IQ tests, on the average, than people in lower-status jobs. Correlations between job status and IQ are in the range from .40 to .60 (Dun-

can et al., 1972). The "obvious" interpretation is that high-status jobs require more intelligence, of the kind measured by IQ tests. Thus, IQ tests do have predictive validity for something other than school grades.

The critics reply that any correlational study (that is, any natural experiment) is not so easily interpreted. People who score high on IQ tests are also different in several other ways from people whose measured IQ is less: They usually have more formal education, for one thing, and many high-status positions *require* a degree of some sort—a Ph.D., an M.D., a B.A., or whatever—even when the relevance of the degree may be questionable. People who score high on IQ tests often have helpful family backgrounds. Their families teach them the etiquette that is considered appropriate in high-status occupations, introduce them to the "right connections," and frequently have the money to bankroll their careers (see Figure 11.8).

All of these variables—IQ, amount of education, and family background—are corre-

Figure 11.8 *George Bernard Shaw's play,* Pygmalion, *and the musical version,* My Fair Lady, *give an example of the considerable advantages of status-appropriate speech and manners. With instructions from Professor Higgins, Eliza Doolittle is transformed from an ill-spoken street vendor into an accepted member of high society.*

lated in the .40 to .60 range with occupational status. Who is to say which variable is the most important? There are many who argue that education and background are the important factors (for example, Bowles and Gintis, 1973), and that IQ is irrelevant.

Are IQ Tests Valid or Not? In the last few paragraphs I have presented the views of those who believe IQ tests are overrated. Most psychologists, however, believe that the tests are useful in predicting a wide range of behaviors, from scholastic performance to performance in various occupations. In the course of this debate, the concept of intelligence is bound to be refined further—and that's good. There is little question that we have been overusing IQ tests for selection, promotion, and other purposes. Let's hope the critics will help avoid abuse of the potentially useful IQ tests.

PERSONALITY ASSESSMENT

If the Binet test of intelligence can be said to be the first important IQ test, probably the *Personal Data Sheet* is the first important test designed to assess a personality characteristic (Woodworth, 1920). The Personal Data Sheet was used by the Army during World War I to identify the emotionally unfit among draftees and volunteers. The test was simple in theory and in practice. The author, psychologist Robert Woodworth, made a list of symptoms generally considered to indicate emotional maladjustment ("psychoneurotic tendencies" was what the test was said to measure). From the list, he constructed 116 questions, such as "Do you usually feel well and strong?" which could be answered yes or no (Ferguson, 1952). The total number of questions answered in the direction Woodworth thought of as maladjusted constituted the psychoneuroticism score; a soldier scoring high enough was seen by a psychiatrist.

A soldier had to be fairly well along the road to mental disaster to flunk this test, if he really wanted to pass. (Most World War I soldiers did want to pass!) To questions like "Do you daydream all day long?" who would answer yes? But, as naive as the items sound today, the test worked quite well (Cronbach, 1970), and certainly it was better than nothing; individual examination of every soldier was out of the question.

The Personal Data Sheet was constructed in response to a social need. Most tests, both of personality and of intelligence, are constructed for this reason; remember that Binet's test was developed to identify the mentally retarded for the schools. Within this broad category of social needs, we can identify three major subclasses (Goldberg, 1971): (1) the need to measure a person's "adjustment," especially when he or she enters the Army, a mental institution, a school, or the like; (2) the need to predict satisfaction and success in one's choice of career; probably most of you have taken "vocational interest tests" in high school; and (3) the desire to predict academic achievement from factors other than intellectual—motivations, for example. There is also another category of personality tests, much less directly related to societal needs and practical applications. These tests are typically designed by academic psychologists to measure some trait (or traits) of theoretical interest—for example, masculinity-femininity and introversion-extraversion. Thus, another reason for assessing personality is to provide an operational definition—a test score—for some theoretical construct.

PROJECTIVE TESTS

Once we have decided to assess a personality trait, we must decide *how* to measure the trait. There are two basic types of personality test: projective and objective (Butcher, 1971).

Objective tests, which we will discuss in following sections, generally have straightforward questions to which the possible answers are also clear. Q: Do you wet your bed? A: Often; occasionally; never.

A *projective test* is one in which the stimuli, which are comparable to questions in objective tests, are deliberately made vague and ambiguous. For example, an item on a projective test might be a request to "tell a story." Outside of the vaguely defined term "story," there is no clear definition of what the response should be. The theory behind such tests is that the test-taker will have to "project" her own personality onto the stimulus in order to organize a coherent response. The story she tells in response to the interviewer's request will presumably reflect a lot about her—her interests, values, fears.

The Rorschach Test

The best-known projective test and the most widely used is the Rorschach Inkblot Test.[1] Herman Rorschach, the Swiss psychiatrist who published this test in 1921, made the first inkblots by dropping ink on papers, then folding them in half. The result was a set of symmetrical blots explicitly chosen, from among the many blots Rorschach created, to be "suggestive." (What do the choices tell us of Rorschach's personality, I wonder?)

[1] Pronounced "Roar-shock."

The subject is shown each blot and asked what it makes her think of (see Figure 11.9). After going through all ten blots in the test, the examiner goes through them again, this time questioning the subject about the source, nature, and meaning of her replies.

When the questioning is finished, the subject's responses are coded into categories on such bases as which part of the inkblot is involved—the whole blot? large details? small details?—and content (the topic of the response)—humans? animals? fire? From these codes, the examiner makes an *interpretation* about a number of personality characteristics, ranging from intelligence and creativity to hostility and general maladjustment (see Table 11.2).

The validity of these interpretations is questionable (Mischel, 1968). About half of the studies relating Rorschach interpretations to other criteria have failed to support the test. For example, responses to inkblots suggesting human movement—"It's a man running"—are supposed to indicate in-telligence. But studies correlating the frequency of this type of response with objective IQ tests found the relationship to be essentially zero (Barron, 1955). Studies that do support Rorschach interpretations involve correlations with objective measures that are too low (.20 to .40) to be used safely when dealing with individual cases (see p. 464).

The TAT

The Thematic Apperception Test (TAT) is made up of 20 pictures of people who appear to be involved in some kind of event. The subjects are told that the test is one of "creative imagination"; they are shown the pictures and are requested to tell a story about each one. What led up to this scene? What will be the outcome? What are the people in the picture thinking and feeling? The answers to these questions are not provided by the pictures; the subject must make them up out of her own knowledge and experi-

Figure 11.9 *A clinical psychologist giving the Rorschach test. What does this retouched inkblot make you think of?*

Table 11.2
EXAMPLES OF INTERPRETATIONS OF RORSCHACH RESPONSES

Response	*Inkblots*	*Nature of interpretation*
This is a butterfly. Here are the wings, feelers and legs.		Using the whole blot in this way is considered to reflect the subject's ability to organize and relate materials.
This is part of a chicken's leg.		Referring to only a part of this inkblot is usually interpreted as indicative of an interest in the concrete.
This could be a face.		The use of an unusual or tiny portion of this blot may suggest pedantic trends.
Looks somewhat like a spinning top.		Persons who reverse figure and ground in this manner often are observed as oppositional, negative, and stubborn.

Reprinted by permission of the publisher from Benjamin Kleinmuntz, *Essentials of Abnormal Psychology.* Harper & Row, 1974. Page 78.

ence. She must project her own hopes and fears into her story (so the theory goes) and thereby expose characteristics of her personality. The TAT is a projective test, for these reasons.

The TAT can be used to judge an individual's general level of adjustment, but it is most often used to assess the particular psychological needs that interested its creator, Henry Murray (see pp. 254–256). In regard to these needs—examples are the needs for aggression, achievement, and dominance—the validity picture is not the best. For example, research on the relationship between highly aggressive stories on the TAT and aggressive behavior in real life is discouraging, with most correlations near zero (Murstein, 1963; Zubin et al., 1965).

An enormous amount of research was done on achievement motivation in the 1960s, using the TAT measure of the need. But toward the end of the decade, as critics began questioning both the validity and the reliability of the TAT measure (Katz, 1967; Weinstein, 1969; Entwisle, 1972), its use in achievement research declined considerably. This was a blow to the use of projective tests in general, as the TAT was certainly one of the most sophisticated attempts to use projective tests in a scientifically mean-

Figure 11.10 *Some projective tests use ambiguous pictures similar to this one (*Christina's World, *by Andrew Wyeth) as stimuli. The subject's story about a scene supposedly reveals his or her own feelings.*

ingful way. Researchers today much more commonly use objective tests.

OBJECTIVE TESTS

We have discussed several reasons and uses for personality tests. Another purpose such tests have been designed for is to help guide people into careers in which they can be satisfied and productive. Ability tests, including the general ability or IQ test, are useful for this. The more specialized aptitude tests assist by assessing people's manual dexterity, their ability to perceive spatial arrangements, or, more directly, their ability

to perform a particular job. But ability is not the only important factor in wise career choices. One should also be interested in one's job, at least to some extent. Some people like to work outdoors, some hate it; some like the organizational structure of military life, some hate it; some are happy as long as their income is high, whereas others are motivated by different interests.

The Strong-Campbell Interest Inventory

The Strong-Campbell Interest Inventory (SCII) is the latest version of a test which, until 1974, was called the Strong Vocational

Interest Blank (SVIB). The test was designed to measure career likes and dislikes, and to relate them to probable success in various fields. Most of the items request a response of "like," "dislike," or "indifferent" to various occupations (e.g., architect), school subjects, activities (e.g., repairing a clock), amusements (e.g., movies), and types of people (e.g., old people, or daredevils). The resulting scores indicate the degree of similarity between the subject (usually a high school senior) and satisfied members of various professions: psychologist, engineer, musician, farmer, salesperson, lawyer, and many others. To illustrate, almost all men who are satisfied engineers dislike the idea of being a stage actor, an activity that men in general like much more. So males who say they dislike acting are given one point for being similar to engineers, and those who like acting get one point subtracted from their engineer score. There are almost 325 items like this; not all are scored for engineer, but enough are to give a good picture of the individual's general similarity — in interests only, not ability — to people already in that profession (Campbell, 1974).

Sex and the SCII. One of the major reasons for the 1974 revision of the SCII was complaints by feminists, who felt that interest tests in general and the SVIB in particular were often used to discriminate against women (Sundberg, 1977). Vocational interest tests do not work as well for women as for men. This is no doubt due to the fact that women have been less able than men to choose careers suited to their particular tastes and talents, not only because of job discrimination but also because many have subjugated their personal interests to the needs of their husbands and families. As more career fields open up to women, and as more women enter them, this state of affairs will surely change.

In the meantime, however, there is a danger of ignorant employers' refusing to hire a capable woman whose pattern of interests does not match that of successful women (or, worse yet, successful men) in that field. The new SCII has 124 occupational scales, 67 for men and 57 for women, with scores based on similarity to updated samples of successful men and women in the various occupations. But even with these careful validation procedures, the predictions for women are not as strong as for men, and the scores should not be weighed as heavily in screening women as they are for men. In most fields, we simply do not know what interest patterns will lead to job satisfaction and success for women; we know merely that the patterns are not the same as for men.

Validity and Reliability of the SCII. For men who have taken the SVIB twice, the correlation between scores is around .90 if the two tests were 30 days apart and around .75 if the interval was 20 years (Cronbach, 1970). The first statistic is a reliability coefficient, because there is no reason to expect significant change in these basic attitudes in a month, but the second statistic is a reasonable estimate of the stability of the interests being measured. And the stability is quite remarkable: These correlations rival those of IQ.

In addition to these reliability and stability statistics, the author of the SVIB, E. K. Strong, presented impressive evidence of his test's validity, that is, that test scores are related to actual job satisfaction (1943, 1955). Five times as many men had very high interest scores for their own occupa-

Figure 11.11 *A person's basic interests are remarkably stable throughout life and can be used to predict the occupation the person will find most satisfying.*

tions as did men in other professions. Men who remained in an occupation for ten or more years had higher average scores for that occupation than for any other. In one study, office clerks were classified as satisfied or dissatisfied (Perry, 1955); the average SVIB score for Office Worker for the satisfied clerks was 48, and for the unhappy ones, 21.

Of course, high interest in an occupation is no guarantee of success; interest cannot make up for a lack of ability. Many psychologists have suggested that interests will be most highly correlated with job success for jobs that depend largely on motivation and perseverance, like sales jobs. Strong (1943) studied insurance agents and reported that those with very high scores on his Sales subtest wrote an average of $169,000 in new policies per year, whereas those with very low scores wrote an average of only $62,000 per year.

The MMPI

The MMPI is easily the most widely used personality test. Its full name is the Minnesota Multiphasic Personality Inventory. Developed at the University of Minnesota in the 1930s and 1940s (Hathaway and McKinley, 1943), the MMPI is called multiphasic because it was designed to include several subtests or scales, like the SVIB. It consists of 566 items of the form: "I am frightened to read of prowlers in my area." The subject is to answer True or False, or, if the statement simply does not apply, she or he can skip it. The MMPI is easy to use; scoring and even interpretation can be done by computer (Butcher, 1971).

The MMPI originally was designed to aid in the diagnosis of psychiatric patients. The scales were developed by comparing responses made by normal subjects to the responses of various patients in psychiatric hospitals. For example, the test was given to a large group of patients diagnosed as schizophrenic and to a large group of normal people; the patients answered some of the items differently, and these items are thus scored as part of the Schizophrenia scale. About 35 percent of the schizophrenics answered True to the item "I hear strange things when I am alone," whereas only 5 percent of the normals did, so someone answering True to this item is scored one point for schizophrenia. The total Schizophrenia scale includes 78 items. There are eight such scales for psychiatric abnormalities. In addition, there is a scale for masculinity-femininity, one for social introversion (uneasiness in dealing with others), and three supplementary scales to detect lying, carelessness or misunderstanding, and defensiveness.

The MMPI and Personality Research. Although developed for psychiatric diagnosis, the MMPI is often used in personality research on normal subjects. A psychologist may hypothesize that "normal" people with drinking problems will score higher on, say, the Depression scale than normals without drinking problems. The psychologist is not looking for scores in the severely depressed range — those which might require hospitalization — just for higher scores among the drinkers than among nondrinkers. (See Goldberg, 1974, for a review of research on the MMPI and other objective tests.)

I arranged for my friend Bob to take the MMPI. The results, plotted in a multiscale form called a *profile,* are shown in Figure 11.12. To make it possible to compare scores from different scales, all MMPI scores are transformed so that 50 is average and 20 points above or below 50 is quite unusual.

Scores above 70, in particular, are considered dangerously unusual — few people are concerned if the subject scores below 30 and is thus "abnormally" happy or trusting.

You will notice that all of Bob's scores are within the normal range except one, on the Fake (F) scale, which we will discuss in a moment. Although not abnormally so, he is high on Depression, Femininity, and Schizophrenia. High scores on Femininity (Mf) are characteristic of males who admit to liking such things as poetry, cooking, flowers, and Lewis Carroll's books, and disliking reading car magazines and teasing animals. The high score on Depression (D) is characteristic of patients who are in mental hospitals because they are pessimistic and suicidal, feel hopeless and worthless, and are so "tired" and unmotivated that they cannot function in society. But normal men with high D scores have been rated by objective observers (fellow students, psychologists) as modest, sensitive, reserved, and highly emotional (Hathaway and Meehl, 1951). Later studies confirmed this picture of someone who is wary of life, known by only a few good friends, and dissatisfied with himself (Dahlstrom et al., 1972). He has aesthetic interests, like high scorers on Femininity.

Schizophrenic patients score high on the Schizophrenia scale, but certain normals do, too. The normals have been described by their peers as prone to worry, dissatisfied with themselves, with aesthetic interests; they are *not* perceived as deviant and withdrawn. They have wide-ranging interests, which they like to discuss (Hathaway and Meehl, 1951).

Bob's elevated score on the Fake (F) scale is the most interesting of all, especially because it is the only one in the "abnormal" range. The original interpretation of such a

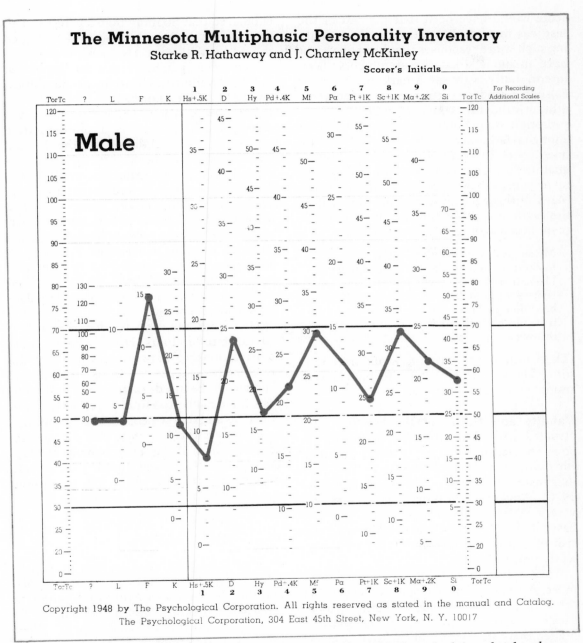

Figure 11.12 *MMPI profile. The transformed scores can be found along the left and right edges.*

score would have been that the rest of the test was invalid, that the subject was making such weird responses that he or she must have misunderstood the statements, been intentionally careless (marking True or False in a random pattern), or pursued some other invalidating course of action. This assumption was shown to be incorrect soon enough (Hathaway and McKinley, 1951); by now, some 30 years later, it seems almost quaint. The Fake scale was designed to pick up responses that were unusual in the 1940s. Many of these responses are less unusual in the 1970s and 1980s. Bob got an abnormal F score because of replies such as these:

> My sex life is satisfactory — False
> My soul sometimes leaves my body — True
> I have had periods in which I carried on activities without knowing later what I had been doing — True
> It would be better if almost all laws were thrown away — True

(These four responses *alone* would have put him "above average"; but he had eleven more "abnormal" answers.)

Validity and Utility of the MMPI. Constructed with the utmost care, the MMPI soon showed itself to be relatively useless for doing just the task it was created for: diagnosing psychiatric illness (Cronbach, 1970). Anyone classifying a person as severely depressed or schizophrenic on the basis of MMPI scores alone would run a high risk of pinning an incorrect label on a perfectly normal person.

This is true in spite of the fact that, by most standards for personality tests, the MMPI has reasonably good validity. If one uses a certain score to say, "Anyone scoring higher than this is X" (depressed, schizophrenic, or whatever), setting the score high

enough so that no more than 5 percent of all normals are incorrectly diagnosed as X, then she or he will correctly identify about 70 percent of the patients previously diagnosed as X by psychiatrists (Hathaway and McKinley, 1943). That's not bad.

But now consider using this test on a group of people. If it is a representative sample of the population of the United States, there will be 85 schizophrenics in every 10,000 people (Anastasi, 1968). Using the cutting score as before, 5 percent of the 9915 normals — that is, 496 citizens — will be wrongly labeled schizophrenic, and 70 percent of the 85 true schizophrenics — that is, 60 people — will be so classified. To put it another way, of the 556 called schizophrenic, barely 10 percent will be correctly classified (see Figure 11.13). This is an obviously dangerous social practice.

There are two reasons for this unfortunate state of affairs. First, although there is a relationship between the test and the psychiatric categories, it is not strong enough to be used safely with individuals — there is just too much overlap between X people and non-X people. The second reason involves the *base rate* of the X characteristic, which, if X is a psychiatric category, is very low (Meehl and Rosen, 1955). There just aren't that many schizophrenics around.

INSTITUTIONAL VERSUS INDIVIDUAL NEEDS

Psychological tests are often used by institutions such as business corporations, schools, and the United States Army in an effort to predict whether or not an individual will be successful in a certain position or job. Very often the correlations of the test scores with what they are meant to predict (like "job

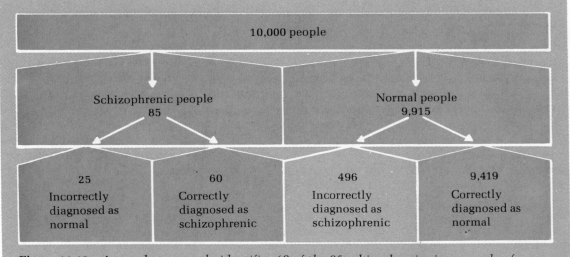

Figure 11.13   *A test that correctly identifies 60 of the 85 schizophrenics in a sample of 10,000 people will unfortunately misdiagnose close to 500 normal people.*

success") are low but consistent. If the institution hires or selects a large number of people each year, the correlation need not be large for the test to be of great economic benefit. It has been estimated, for example, that a simple personality questionnaire with modest predictive validity could save the military up to $4 million per month (Dunnette, 1967).

Because small correlations can be useful to large institutions, tests like the ones we have discussed are widely used. From the point of view of the individual, however, this practice seems unfair. She or he is told, in essence, something like this: "You will not get the job because person *X* got a higher score on The Test than you did. A higher score on The Test means that person *X* is likely to perform better than you."

"How likely?"

"About one chance in a thousand."

One chance in a thousand is a good bet for a corporation that hires hundreds of thousands of employees, but it means that several extremely capable applicants will be incorrectly, and thus unfairly, rejected.

It's easy to say there must be a balance between the needs of the institution and the rights of the individual, but that balance is not easily defined. By law, institutions cannot "assess" age, sex, and skin color and use those "tests" in their hiring procedures, even if they did predict job performance. But there are other kinds of "discrimination." In 1971, the United States Supreme Court ruled that tests or other selection devices must have *demonstrated* validity in predicting job performance (*Griggs* v. *Duke Power*, 1971); however, a correlation as low as .01 can satisfy the legal requirements. The situation is like that of the young male driver who must pay extraordinarily high car insurance premiums even if he himself is an extremely safe driver because his group is a bad risk in terms of probability.

I see the area of psychological testing as one of the most exciting in psychology today. Perhaps I have been overly critical of testing because it affects so many people's lives, but that same fact makes it important and relevant and of great potential benefit. Consider the past. People were chosen for jobs or schools on the basis of family background, religion, race, or the general impression they created in unstructured interviews. Tests are an improvement. Furthermore, institutions are not likely to start choosing among applicants by putting all names in a hat; whatever the alternative is, it will be a test of some sort. As the tests now in use are refined, great issues will be aired — bias, discrimination, heredity versus environment, the nature of intelligence, the nature of personality. And the ethics of great organizations — political, economic, and educational — will be reviewed and, we hope, improved.

SUMMARY

1. The first intelligence test, published in 1883, tested sensory abilities. The types of reasoning and vocabulary problems found in today's tests were incorporated in a test developed by Alfred Binet in 1905. A later version introduced *mental age,* estimated by the number of items a child could answer relative to others in his or her age group.

2. Lewis Terman at Stanford University translated and adapted Binet's test for American use; it has since been called the *Stanford-Binet.* Terman also introduced the *intelligence quotient* (IQ), a figure obtained by dividing mental age by chronological age.

The term IQ is still used today, though more sophisticated statistical techniques are used to compute it.

3. David Wechsler devised several tests of intelligence for both children and adults, including the WAIS, WISC, and WPPIS. These have various subtests and so can reveal a pattern of intellectual abilities. The subtests include *verbal tests,* in which the response can be spoken or written, and *performance tests,* which involve nonverbal behaviors such as copying and arranging. Performance tests are very useful for subjects who cannot understand English well.

4. The *Army Alpha,* used in World War I, was the first important intelligence test that could be administered to large groups. The *Army Beta* was a group intelligence test of the performance type.

5. *Scholastic Aptitude Tests* are often used in college admissions. These tests correlate well with grades in college, although neither the tests nor the grades correlate well with job performance after college, according to some critics. Since 1963, average SAT scores have been declining, apparently at first because of changes in the population taking the test and later because of pervasive changes such as an increase in TV watching and a decrease in basic-skills courses in schools.

6. IQ tests are highly *reliable* in that they give approximately the same score each time they are taken by the same individual. Yielding the same score over a long period of time might better be said to show the *stability* of the quality being measured. IQ scores are remarkably stable after the age of two.

7. A test with *construct validity* measures what it says it does. A test with *predictive validity* is able to predict other behaviors; IQ tests have predictive validity for

school performance. Critics of the tests claim that although scores do correlate with school performance and later job status, much of what the tests attribute to intelligence is actually due to the subject's education and family status.

8. The *Personal Data Sheet* was the first major personality test, used in World War I to screen out draftees with serious mental problems. Adjustment, vocational interests, motivations, and general personality traits are the qualities personality tests are most often designed to evaluate.

9. *Projective tests* present an ambiguous stimulus (like an inkblot) to a subject, who then has to project her own personality onto the stimulus to organize a coherent description of it. The Rorschach Inkblot Test and the Thematic Apperception Test (TAT), which uses pictures, are the most common projective tests. Their usefulness has been criticized, and their use is declining.

10. *Objective tests* have clearly defined questions (Do you smoke?) with clearly de-fined answers (yes or no). The Strong Campbell Interest Inventory (SCII) gives scores on career interests based on the similarity of the test taker's answers to those of people already in various professions. It has good reliability, stability, and validity for men, but less for women.

11. The *Minnesota Multiphasic Personality Inventory* (MMPI) is the most widely used objective personality test. It gives scores on a number of scales originally designed to relate to psychiatric diagnoses, though it is also much used in personality research. Although the diagnostic validity of the test is quite good compared to that of other personality tests, it should not be used (by itself) to diagnose an individual.

12. Psychological testing is a fact of life, and it will probably increase. We must work to balance the needs of large institutions, for which low correlations between a test and successful performance can be useful, and the needs of individuals, who may be treated unfairly on the basis of such tests.

USING PSYCHOLOGY

If you were going to construct a test to predict whether a person would be a successful parent, how would you go about it? What would be your major difficulties?

SUGGESTED READINGS

Tyler, L. E. *Individuality.* Jossey-Bass, 1978.
    An important statement by a noted researcher on how we should assess individuality. The subtitle describes the scope of the book: "Human possibilities and personal choice in the psychological development of men and women."

Blum, J. M. *Pseudoscience and mental ability.* Monthly Review Press, 1976.
    A sociologist, an attorney, and a radical, Blum presents the case against IQ testing with clarity.

Wiggins, J. S. *Personality and prediction.* Addison-Wesley, 1973.
    Lewis Goldberg said of this book, "If you read only one book in this field every ten years, the choice for you has now been made easy." It's a bit technical, though.

Anastasi, A. *Psychological testing.* 4th ed. Macmillan, 1976.
    An excellent and comprehensive textbook.

Is IQ Inherited?

Lenny Bruce had a joke about a boy who was lost in a wilderness area and raised by a pack of wild dogs. Found by humans when he was in his teens, the boy quickly learned the ways of his natural species. Eventually he went to Harvard, where he earned a Ph.D. This, said Lenny, shows how important heredity is; the kid spent all his formative years with the dogs, but once back with humans, his strivings and achievements became human ones. But one should never disregard the effect of environment: This Ph.D. was killed chasing a car.

Heredity or environment? It's an age-old question. Yet if you think about the uses of tests we discussed in Chapter 11, it's clear that the question is more urgent now than ever. Colleges, employers, and many other organizations are increasingly interested in assessing individual differences. If the ability measured by an important test can be learned — if it is *environmental,* in other words — then we can expect that a wide range of people will be able to do well on the test, and will get the job or get into the college or whatever. But if the ability is *hereditary,* then only people whose parents and grandparents had it will be able to do well on the test. The individual's own hard work and unique personality will not make much difference.

IQ tests, as you know, were designed to predict someone's ability to do well in school. At the time, it was assumed that "ability to do well in school" was essentially the same thing as "intelligence," so IQ tests were said to measure intelligence. Now we are not so sure how valid that assumption is. But IQ tests are still widely used to decide who is considered for what job, who is accepted by what college, and so on.

Is IQ inherited? It's a question that is still being hotly debated. In this interlude we will look at recent research and current viewpoints, and try to draw some conclusions.

WHAT IS HERITABILITY?

How do you tell if a characteristic is inherited? Scientists look for similarities between people who are related biologically. These people share *genes,* the basic units of heredity transmitted in the sperm of the father and the egg of the mother. More specifically, scientists use statistical correlations to measure similarities. The higher the heritability of a trait, the higher the correlation between two related people who share it.

But a high correlation does not *necessarily* mean high heritability. We must remember that parents and children, and relatives in general, share much of their environment as well as genes, so many similarities may have no genetic basis at all. The children of parents who like broccoli will probably tend to like broccoli too, but environment is likely to be the important factor in this case. Correlations are necessary *but not sufficient* to establish heritability.

The heritability of many characteristics is unquestioned. Height, for example, is inherited to a large extent. So is susceptibility to tooth decay. What this means is that one's height and decay-susceptibility are related to the same characteristics in one's parents. It means that taller parents will *tend* to have taller children and that parents with poor dental records will *tend* to have children with the same. It does *not* mean the environment has no effect. Nutrition is one of the many environmental factors that can affect height, and brushing teeth after meals with a good fluoride toothpaste can make a sizable difference in the number of cavities.

THE CASE FOR HEREDITY

Table 1 gives a summary of the correlations of IQ between various relatives along with correlations between unrelated people for comparison. These correlations have been averaged from the results of over 50 different studies in 8 different countries using a wide variety of IQ tests (Erlenmeyer-Kimling and Jarvik, 1963; Jensen, 1969). The correlations are close to what one would expect if genetic factors played the major role in intelligence.

For example, the correlation of unrelated children reared together is .24. This can be taken as a very rough estimate of the percentage of variation in IQ due to environment alone, since these children share no genes. Subtracting from 100 percent, this leaves 76 percent for genetic factors. Now look at the correlation for identical twins reared apart. Identical twins have absolutely identical genetic makeups, so any differences between them must come from environment. Since these twins were separated early in life and brought up in different homes, any similarity between them should reflect heredity. Thus the correlation is a very rough estimate of the percentage of IQ variation due to genetic factors: 75 percent. This leaves 25 percent for environment. Note the striking agreement between the two methods of making these estimates.

One could continue making comparisons like these, but there are more sophisticated mathematical formulas for estimating the heritability of

Table 1
CORRELATIONS FOR INTELLECTUAL ABILITY

Correlations between	Number of studies	Average correlation
Unrelated persons		
Children reared apart	4	−.01
Foster parent and child	3	+.20
Children reared together	5	+.24
Collaterals		
Second cousins	1	+.16
First cousins	3	+.26
Uncle (or aunt) and nephew (or niece)	1	+.34
Siblings, reared apart	3	+.47
Siblings, reared together	36	+.55
Fraternal twins, different sex	9	+.49
Fraternal twins, same sex	11	+.56
Identical twins, reared apart	4	+.75
Identical twins, reared together	14	+.87
Direct line		
Grandparent and grandchild	3	+.27
Parent (as adult) and child	13	+.50
Parent (as child) and child	1	+.56

From A. R. Jensen, How much can we boost IQ and scholastic achievement? *Harvard Educational Review,* 39 (1969), pp. 1–123. Copyright © 1969 by the President and Fellows of Harvard College. Reprinted by permission.

IQ. This *heritability* we can now define technically as the percentage of variation in IQ due to genetic factors. From the correlations in the table, this figure has been computed as around 80 percent (Jensen, 1969). This is a very high heritability, comparable to estimates for the heritability of height (94 percent) and weight (88 percent) found in a study by Burt (1966).

THE NATURE OF HERITABILITY

One must use this statistic, heritability, with caution. It does not mean anything like "80 percent of Jane's IQ is accounted for by her genes and 20 percent by her environment." What it *does* mean is this: In a *group* of people, IQ scores vary. Heritability estimates the percentage of the total variation that can be accounted for by genetic factors. It's something like other group statistics: The population of the United States is about 8 percent Irish. This does not mean *you* are 8 percent Irish. The most that one can say about an individual's IQ is that it will be probably somewhere around the average of her parents' IQs. As groups, bright parents will tend to have brighter children than dull parents.

An interesting feature of heritability is that it is not constant. For example, tuberculosis used to be highly heritable. This sounds strange because we know that the disease is caused by bacteria (which is an environmental factor). What the heritability meant is that *susceptibility* to the disease is probably inherited. At one time, tuberculosis bacteria were virtually everywhere—everyone was exposed—so the only thing that determined whether or not you got the disease was some kind of inherited susceptibility. Modern medicine (an environmental factor) has killed off most of these bacteria, so now whether or not you get the disease depends mostly on whether or not you are exposed to the few remaining bacteria. So the heritability—the importance of genetic factors—has gone down. Similarly, heritability figures for tooth decay probably have gone down since the discovery of fluoride treatments.

Also, heritability is different for different groups. In homogeneous (nonmixed) groups like, say, Norwegians, skin color is due more to environment (for example, whether or not the person works outdoors in the sun) than to heredity. In heterogeneous (mixed) groups like Americans, skin color is due more to heredity. The figure of 80 percent heritability for IQ applies only for whites in the United States and Europe; it may not be the figure for other groups. In fact, estimates of IQ heritability for American blacks place the figure much lower (Scarr-Salapatek, 1971a). Environmental factors apparently play a greater role in IQ test scores for blacks than for whites, but we can only guess what these factors might be: educational facilities? nutrition?

HERRNSTEIN AND THE MERITOCRACY

One of the implications of the concept of heritability is that if environmental variation is reduced, heritability will increase. Genetic factors will become more important. (If everyone's environment were exactly the same, *all* individual differences would be inherited.) Harvard psychologist Richard J. Herrnstein proposed that we had better consider the implications of this fact in relation to the values we hold in a democratic society. He asked us to think about the following four-step logical sequence:

1. If differences in mental abilities are inherited, and
2. If success requires those abilities, and
3. If earnings and prestige depend on success,
4. Then social standing (which reflects earnings and prestige) will be based to some extent on inherited differences (Herrnstein, 1971, pp. 58–63).

In our democratic society, we value social equality; we look down on political systems like aristocracies with rigid classes or castes. We want to give everyone equal opportunity. We desire a system we could call a *meritocracy*, in which each person is rewarded for merit instead of for social position. It is clear we have not achieved such a system yet; many people still are not able to obtain the education, the health care, and other environmental advantages that would allow them to develop their full potential. But Herrnstein warns us that if we could remove all environmental obstacles — if we could achieve the goals of a democratic society, in other words — individual differences in ability would not disappear. In reaching democratic goals, we would create a much more rigid caste system based on genetic factors.

One of the reasons for this state of affairs is that people tend to marry people with similar IQs. Thus, the bright will marry the bright and have bright children. If environment plays little or no role in their achievement, these children will become the doctors, lawyers, and business executives who make most of the money. (Singers, athletes, and other people with special talents will remain exceptions to the general rule; they may be brilliant or dull.)

Is this the society we desire? If not, what are the alternatives? You, the readers of this book, probably will have more to say about the answer in the long run than either Herrnstein or I.

RACE DIFFERENCES IN INTELLIGENCE

Arthur R. Jensen, a Berkeley psychologist, is one focal point in the current storm of controversy surrounding the IQ and heredity issue. In a long article published in the prestigious *Harvard Educational Review* (1969), Jensen considered three bits of information: (1) The heritability of IQ is high; 80 percent, he claimed, is a reasonable estimate. (2) Numerous studies have shown that blacks score between 10 and 20 points below whites on IQ tests, on the average. (3) A number of special remedial programs have been designed to increase the IQ of poor, disadvantaged children (usually black) by enriching their environment and by giving them direct training; these programs have been unsuccessful. Therefore, Jensen concluded, it is very likely that blacks, on the average, are genetically inferior to whites in those genes related to intelligence. This is not a fact, said Jensen, but a distinct possibility, one that would have wide-ranging implications if it were true. It is a topic deserving of much research attention.

Well, the topic gained attention. Jensen expected some difficulty from radical student groups, but his life since the Review article has apparently been a nightmare (Rice, 1973). The sign "Jensen Must Perish" appeared around the Berkeley campus, and anti-Jensen rallies were held. The university hired two bodyguards. His lectures were disrupted. During one speech, demonstrators rushed the platform, tore up his notes, and threw the pieces of paper in his face. Police were required for Jensen to leave the building.

THE ACADEMIC FREEDOM CONTROVERSY

The race-IQ-heritability controversy thus generated its own sideshow, a controversy over the rights and the responsibilities of a scholar or scientist dealing with an inflammatory issue. Many teachers found themselves torn between their feelings that Jensen speculated a little too freely in an area that involves the rights of other human beings, and their equally strong feelings that everyone has a right to free thought and free speech. Jensen wasn't helped when William Shockley, a Stanford physicist, suddenly went on a crusade to keep those he considered the constitutionally dumb from having big families. He proposed a plan whereby anyone — black or white — with a low enough IQ would receive a cash bonus for voluntary sterilization. Shockley, unlike Jensen, has described blacks as clearly "genetically inferior" (Rice, 1973).

Even Herrnstein, who didn't discuss the racial issue at all — except to say that black-white differences in IQ were probably environmental — was barraged with threats, both verbal and physical (Holden, 1973).

What is the stand to take on the matter of free inquiry versus the rights or at least the feelings of others? Some say that no restrictions on free speech are to be tolerated. Others would limit free speech by at least condemning the person who falsely shouts "Fire!" in a crowded theater. One psychologist critical of Jensen expressed precisely this view: "To assert, despite the absence of [conclusive] evidence, and in the present social climate, that a particular race is genetically disfavored in intelligence is to scream 'FIRE . . . I think' in a crowded theater" (Scarr-Salapatek, 1971b, p. 1228). This is probably the opinion of most psychologists.

It is clear that racial bigots and others who desire discrimination against blacks are using Jensen's article to keep blacks at a social and economic disadvantage.

> A scant five days after Arthur Jensen made headlines in Virgina papers regarding inferiority of black people as measured by IQ tests, defense attorneys and their expert witnesses fought a suit in Federal District Court to integrate Greensville and Caroline County schools. Their main argument was "that white teachers could not understand the Nigra mind" and that the Nigra children should be admitted to the white school on the basis of standardized tests. Those who failed to make a certain score would be assigned to all-black remedial schools where "teachers who understood them could work with them." The defense in this case quoted heavily from the theories of white intellectual supremacy as expounded by Arthur Jensen. (Brazziel, 1969, p. 200.)

It is because of the role of Jensen's theory as ammunition against blacks, for which Jensen claims he cannot be held responsible, that some people think the topic should not be discussed at all, even if Jensen is right.

The most sensible position, in my opinion, was expressed by a society of psychologists interested in the psychological study of social issues (SPSSI). In a statement released after Jensen's article was published, SPSSI reaffirmed its "long-held support for open inquiry on all aspects of human behavior." But the society also called for scientific responsibility: "When research has bearing on social issues and public policy, the scientist must examine the competing explanations for his findings and must exercise the greatest care in his interpretation" (Raven, 1974).

THE CYRIL BURT AFFAIR

One of the most bizarre consequences of the race-IQ-heritability controversy was the discovery that some of the most impressive data on the side of genetic influences was completely untrustworthy, and that the researcher involved, British psychologist Cyril Burt, had probably fabricated the data to fit his genetic theories. Burt, who died in 1971 at the age of 88, was perhaps the major figure on the genetic side; he was the greatest single source of data on IQ correlations among relatives, which included the best data (or so it seemed) on identical twins reared in separate homes. Both the Herrnstein and the Jensen papers relied heavily on his studies. In 1946, Burt became the first psychologist to receive a knighthood. In 1971, Sir Cyril was awarded the prestigious Thorndike prize by the American Psychological Association.

In 1972, psychologist Leon Kamin (1974) began to draw public attention to some remarkable features of Burt's data. For example, Burt's studies of identical twins reared apart were first published in 1955; for 21 pairs of twins, he reported a correlation of 0.771. By 1958, he had accumulated over 30 pairs; the correlation was still 0.771. By 1966, 53 pairs had been found; the correlation was still exactly 0.771. A remarkable coincidence? The correlation for identical twins raised together stayed at 0.944 through three reports, though the sample size for these pairs was also growing. There were several other statistical abnormalities of this sort.

In 1976, the London *Times* reported another mysterious feature of the Burt studies (Gillie, 1976). Several of Burt's later publications were coauthored by Margaret Howard or J. Conway. The *Times* could find no record of Howard or Conway at London University, the address given on their scientific publications. Nobody seemed ever to have met or even heard of them. The *Times* suggested that Burt's coauthors were figments of his imagination. The story unraveled further: the names of Howard and Conway had frequently appeared over book reviews in the 1950s in the *British Journal of Statistical Psychology,* which Burt edited. Writing in a style practically indistinguishable from Burt's, Howard and Conway panned the work of Burt's critics and praised Burt. When Burt quit as editor, the Howard and Conway reviews ceased (Wade, 1976). Although it turns out there was a Burt assistant named Margaret Howard at London University in the 1930s (Cohen, 1976), there is little doubt that by the 1950s "Howard" and "Conway" were merely pseudonyms for Sir Cyril Burt.

But then how are we to explain the data Burt gathered after 1950? In 1969 Burt wrote that when travel was necessary to test twins, "The job was delegated to Miss Conway or Miss Howard" (Wade, 1976, p. 918). If Howard and Conway were figments of Burt's imagination, who administered the tests?

At first, the statistical abnormalities were dismissed by some as carelessness, and the pseudonyms as silly but not particularly evil. But it soon became apparent that many of the data Burt reported (after 1950 at least) were simply made up, deliberately concocted to support his theories of genetic influence on intelligence (Dorfman, 1978; Hearnshaw, 1979). All of Burt's data are now suspect.

What happens to estimates of heritability if we discard the Burt studies? In general, they must be reduced by a considerable amount. Jensen

(1977) has reduced his estimate of the genetic contribution to variation of IQ scores among whites from 80 percent to 65 percent. Many other researchers, using somewhat different sets of data and different mathematics, have arrived at a similar figure (Vernon, 1979). Even these reduced estimates inspire less confidence than before, when they were supported by Burt's supposedly mammoth and carefully designed investigations.

Burt's study of identical twins reared apart is probably the most significant loss, since his sample (53 pairs) constituted almost half of the pairs ever tested (122 pairs). In addition, Burt's data were a major piece of evidence against those who claimed that identical twins reared apart still experienced largely similar environments. Typically, separated twins are placed in two related families, or at least in families with similar socioeconomic status. But a table Burt published in 1966 showing the socioeconomic levels of the two homes for each of his 53 pairs of identical twins revealed no correlation in environment whatever. At the time, this table lent strong support to the notion that the correlation between twins in IQ is due to underlying genetic similarities. It now seems clear that these data were bogus.

THE CASE AGAINST HEREDITY

Is IQ highly heritable? Is it becoming increasingly so, as Herrnstein suggests? Are there genetic differences between races? Inflammatory or not, these are topics on which relevant empirical data can be gathered. Jensen reviewed some of these studies, and he is strongly on the side of heredity. Now we will present the opposite case, the evidence against the role of heredity, especially in the measured difference in IQ between races.

First, let us make clear some important conceptual considerations. As we have mentioned, heritability estimates come almost entirely from studies of whites, and the few, imperfect estimates indicate that heritability is lower among blacks (for example, Scarr-Salapatek, 1971a). But even if heritability of IQ were known to be 65 percent among both whites and blacks, one could not conclude that the measured difference between whites and blacks was mainly genetic. Consider a collection of corn seeds with varying genetic characteristics. We *randomly* divide these seeds into two groups, thereby making sure that the two groups are approximately equal in their genetic quality. We plant one group in rich soil and the other in poor soil. Up come the plants. The corn in the rich soil varies in height, and these differences *within* the group are almost entirely genetic. The same is true for the plants in the poor soil. But the average corn stalk in the rich soil is much higher than the average stalk in the poor soil. This difference *between* groups is *entirely* environmental. We know that because we *randomly* divided the seeds at the beginning of our experiment. So plant height, highly heritable within each plot, is not related to genetic factors *at all* when we compare the difference between groups. Many psychologists consider the difference in the "soil" (environment) of American blacks and whites large enough to make this analogy relevant.

Black Children in White Soil

Studies of black children adopted by white families lend strong support to environmental theories of race differences in IQ. In an extensive investigation of 130 such children (Scarr and Weinberg, 1976), the average IQ was 106, well above the national average. Had these children been raised by their natural parents in poor black neighborhoods, they could have been expected to score about 90 on IQ tests. Even children adopted fairly late in childhood scored significantly higher than expected, although children adopted early did better, averaging 110. "In fact, the *lowest* score of an early adopted child, 86, was close to the average for all black children in the nation" (Scarr-Salapatek and Weinberg, 1975, p. 81).

Another group of black children who scored significantly higher on IQ tests than would have been expected from the IQs and socioeconomic status of their natural parents were those taking part in well-planned remedial programs (Garber and Heber, 1977). Black children from the poorest areas of Milwaukee, from the age of three months on, attended a training center for seven hours a day, five days a week, where psychologists made an all-out effort to improve their perceptual and intellectual skills. Simultaneously, the mothers were given training in homemaking, childrearing, and vocational skills. By the age of 18 months, the children were pulling away from comparable children who received no special training. Around the age of three, their average IQ was 123! Although the IQ scores of these children began to drop when they entered school—when special training was discontinued—they are maintaining a lead of approximately 25 IQ points over the children of the control group. This is, by any standard, a whopping difference.

Studies that show a strong effect of environmental enrichment on IQ do not necessarily mean that genetic influences are not also important, any more than Crest's studies of the beneficial effects of brushing with fluoride toothpaste means that susceptibility to tooth decay is not inherited. But the striking gains made by environmentally deprived black children when they are placed in more stimulating circumstances certainly lead one to question genetic interpretations of racial differences in average IQ. If we were to discover that black children had 15 percent more cavities than white children, for example, but that brushing with Crest eliminated the difference between races, we would certainly suspect that poor dental hygiene among the black children was responsible for the initial difference, not genetic differences in susceptibility to decay. The same reasoning can be applied to IQ.

CONCLUSIONS

What are we to conclude from all of this? We don't have enough data to conclude anything with certainty. If I sense majority opinions among psychologists on Jensen's two main points, they are these:

1. *Is IQ highly heritable among whites?* Probably most psychologists believe the evidence indicates that it is, although most would set the figure lower than Jensen does. However, there have been some telling attacks on Jensen's data and assumptions (for example, Light and Smith, 1969; Kamin, 1974), and several psychologists who had accepted the conclusion without much thought are thinking it through again.

2. *Are blacks genetically disadvantaged in IQ, compared to whites?* Very few psychologists would take this position publicly, though some might hold it privately. Jensen's arguments actually may have *decreased* the number who agree with him, because of the many well-reasoned rebuttals. Probably the majority opinion is that, scientifically speaking, there simply is not enough evidence available to make a judgment on this issue. Geneticists (Bodmer and Cavalli-Sforza, 1970; Dobzhansky, 1973) as well as psychologists (Loehlin et al., 1975; Vernon, 1979) have expressed this view.

Finally, one remarkable effect of Jensen's article has been to focus both scientific and popular attention on IQ tests and the nature of intelligence. The IQ test is clearly overused today; it is applied in situations where it plays no useful role but simply discriminates unfairly against people who score low. And intelligence probably is overvalued among the range of human abilities. New research is coming out of this controversy, and new ideas are being generated. This result, at least, has been a healthy one.

SUGGESTED READINGS

Loehlin, J. C., Lindzey, G., & Spuhler, J. N. *Race differences in intelligence.* Freeman, 1975.
> The authors of this book, whose royalties all go to minority-group scholarships, were "commissioned" to write it as the "definitive" work on the topic. The Social Science Research Council, which arranged for its publication, has a long history of producing authoritative works.

Vernon, P. E. *Intelligence: heredity and environment.* Freeman, 1979.
> The magnum opus of a major researcher who works hard to present both sides of the issue as fairly as possible.

Behavioral Objectives

1. Tell how society has viewed and treated mental illness at different ages in history.
2. Define "abnormal behavior"; identify the criteria that are used to define mental illness and explain why some psychologists dislike the term "mental illness."
3. Name and describe the two major categories of mental disorders.
4. Describe the two main types of psychosis and give an example of each.
5. Identify the most common form of psychosis and describe its primary symptoms.
6. Discuss the evidence for the heritability of schizophrenia.
7. Compare the effects of large doses of hallucinogenic drugs with schizophrenic symptoms.
8. Review the evidence that suggests schizophrenia may be caused by a biochemical imbalance.
9. Describe two kinds of treatments that seem to be beneficial to schizophrenics.
10. Identify and describe some common forms of neurosis.
11. Discuss the relationship between environmental variables and neurosis.

CHAPTER

12

Abnormal Psychology

My friend Lewie, like many of us, was fascinated by the topic of abnormal psychology. He had done some volunteer work in a mental hospital, and he was struck by how sane most of the "inmates" seemed. "The only way I could tell they weren't normal was that they were in the hospital," he said once. "So how does anybody know they're mentally ill?"

Only half-joking, I told him my foot-chewing, eye-gouging theory of mental illness. "Suppose we go up to a person and ask him what time it is. His response is to start chewing on his foot. What would you think?"

"This is one strange fellow!" said Lewie.

"Would you be frightened?"

Lewie thought for a minute. "Yes. I would be frightened."

"Why?"

"I'm not sure. I guess because I wouldn't be sure of what he might do next."

"Maybe his next response would be to gouge out your eyes, right?"

"Well, maybe not that. But who knows? I guess that's your point, isn't it?"

"Exactly. The people who get *labeled* mentally ill and are put away someplace are people who are *unpredictable.* Someone's chewing on his foot is not a threat to us, but how do we know what he'll do the next time we ask him a question? So we lock him up."

Unusual behavior that is unpredictable by ordinary standards is nearly always the reason someone is labeled mentally ill. Sometimes a psychiatrist does the labeling; sometimes an individual is so anxious, so depressed, so fearful, that he presents *himself* to a psychologist, psychiatrist, police officer, or hospital admissions clerk as mentally ill. His behavior may not be unusual, but he describes his inner world of thoughts and needs as full of turmoil and out of control. The agent of society he contacts decides that this inner state might soon result in dangerous external behavior, so the person is put away because he too might soon gouge an eye.

There are many flaws in my foot-chewing, eye-gouging theory of mental illness, needless to say. Often people are placed in institutions, not because others are afraid of them, but because it appears that is the best place for them to receive the care they need. Some people enter institutions because there is no alternative: They have no family, no friends, nowhere else to go, and they cannot function by themselves. The chief virtue of the foot-chewing, eye-gouging theory is that it emphasizes the fact that "mental illness" is defined primarily by *social* criteria. When we say that someone is mentally ill, we are saying that someone else has observed his or her behavior or mental state

and judged it unusual *enough* to be called mental illness. This is not the same as diagnosing a physical disease, like the measles.

This chapter is about abnormal psychology, which is about "unusual" behaviors and self-reports of unusual inner states. In our culture, scientists have set up categories of unusual behaviors, and much of the chapter will be devoted to describing people who fit these categories. We will also discuss views on what causes the unusual behaviors.

A BRIEF HISTORY OF INSANITY

The history of the treatment of the insane has been, until recently, a history of inhumanity and cruelty. Until the 1800s, there were no real mental hospitals. There were a few "zoos," such as the infamous Bethlehem asylum in London, where citizens could watch the antics of the inmates for a slight

Figure 12.1 *Early apparatus for treating the mentally ill. The wooden cage (Belgium, 1889) did little more than restrain the patient. The centrifuge bed (Germany, 1818) was considered relaxing and, by driving blood to the head, it cleared the cobwebs of the mind—or so it was believed.*

fee; the word "bedlam," meaning wild and disorganized activity, derives from the common pronunciation of Bethlehem. The theory of insanity[1] most popular among both the educated and the uneducated was that mild forms of it were caused by moral inferiority, whereas particularly bizarre behavior was the result of possession by demons. (Roughly speaking, the mild forms would today be called neuroses and the more severe manifestations would be labeled psychoses.)

Treatment was based, as always, on theories of the cause. If the person was lucky enough to have loving friends and relatives, they could use prayer to drive out the evil spirits. If not, chances were good that the person would end up in prison, in chains for life. Or, if the person was female, she might be thrown into great fires used to rid the community of witches. A French judge bragged of burning 800 women in 16 years; in another town, 7000 were burned over several years (Bromberg, 1937).

The Idea of Mental Illness

The Paris physician Philippe Pinel, in the early 1800s, took the view that "The mentally sick, far from being guilty people deserving of punishment, are sick people whose miserable state deserves all the consideration that is due suffering humanity" (Zilboorg and Henry, 1941, pp. 323–324). His humane treatments met with great success,

[1] Over the years, a number of different labels have been applied to the phenomena we have been calling mental illness — madness, insanity, mental disorder, behavioral disorder, and problems of living are only a few. There are reasons for and against the use of each of these terms, and we will discuss some of them. Throughout this chapter, I will try to use the term that is most appropriate for the time, place, or viewpoint being examined.

especially compared to burning, chaining, and whipping; but more than that, he succeeded in labeling people with behavior disorders as "ill," which is quite different from "morally inferior" or "possessed." True *hospitals* for the insane then became possible.

In America, a Massachusetts school teacher named Dorothea Dix almost single-handedly roused the nation to respond to the needs of the insane. In 1840, mental hospitals housed about 15 percent of those who needed care. In 1843, Dix published her famous *Memorial in Behalf of the Pauper Insane and Idiots in Jails and Poorhouses Throughout the Commonwealth*, a stinging indictment of the treatment of the insane: "confined in cages, closets, cellars, stalls, pens . . . chained, naked, beaten" (p. 4). In the years following, Dix traveled the country, pressuring reluctant state legislatures into building humane institutions. By 1890, 50 years later, almost 70 percent of the insane were in mental hospitals.

Problems with the Idea of Illness. Defining insanity as mental illness and constructing mental "hospitals" for the care and treatment of the insane were great advances over the theories and therapies of the preceding eras. Recently, however, many psychologists have entered strong objections to the use of the term "mental illness" and have worked to get mental patients out of hospitals and back into the community.

The original effect of defining insanity as mental illness was tranquilizing to the public. To think of your neighbor as possessed was probably frightening; but to think of him as ill . . . well, illness is something we know about. Put him in a hospital.

But the insane are not ill in the usual, medical sense. A belief that one is Napoleon

Figure 12.2   *Philippe Pinel supervises the unchaining of mental patients in a Paris asylum in 1795.*

is not the same as a broken bone or a spastic colon. The strongest connection we can make is to say that in some cases, some neurological or biochemical defect produces abnormal behavior. The "myth of mental illness" (Szasz, 1961) was useful because it replaced other, more dangerous myths, such as possession and moral inferiority. The idea that unusual behaviors were caused by an illness drew a more favorable reaction from the general public, because ill people are not *personally* to blame for their malady, and they need *help.*

Unfortunately, the myth came to be treated as a reality. Psychologists began ex-plaining unusual behaviors by saying the person was mentally ill:

"Why is that person behaving oddly?"
"Because he is mentally ill."
"How do you know he is mentally ill?"
"Because he is behaving oddly."

Theories of mental *illness* are said to be based on a medical model, meaning that medical science is the source of their form and much of their content; hence, such terms as "illness," "psychopathology," and "symptom." The medical model may not be a good one for the description and treatment of "problems of living" (Szasz, 1960), and the social consequences of calling behavior disturbances "diseases" must be considered (Bandura, 1969, Chapter 1). For example, many people who could benefit from a few sessions with a clinical psychologist refuse to label themselves as sick. And sometimes people who face simple problems in living are forced to label themselves as potentially sick in order to solve the problems. At one time, women who wanted an abortion in California had to get certificates from two psychiatrists, saying birth would be dangerous to the mother's mental health, and final approval of the certification from a hospital board.

Away from Mental Hospitals. The trend toward housing people in institutions is also reversing. Many who would have been in hospitals are now being treated in the community, as out-patients; halfway houses have been established in many cities, for out-patients to live in or visit during their adjustment to "real" life. It is the view of almost all psychologists that living (and working) in the community is highly desirable for the patient. Someone who has problems of living should have the chance to solve those problems, with help, where they exist. The hospital environment is often radically different from the community environment, and even with the best of intentions, overworked hospital staff often find themselves inadvertently rewarding passivity and punishing patients who make demands on their time. Still, the new community programs would probably be impossible if it were not for vast changes in the public's attitude toward people with psychological problems. In addition, new drugs enable many patients to face their problems without overwhelming anxiety or depression.

What Is Abnormal Behavior?

When we say someone is behaving in an unusual or abnormal way, what exactly are we saying? As the words "*ab*-normal" and "*un*-usual" imply, we are saying first of all that his or her behavior is different from the average. But what is average? Average for a middle-class psychologist or psychiatrist may not be average for a working-class patient, and the evidence is that differences like this often affect judgments of "unusual behavior" (Hollingshead and Redlich, 1958). What is usual in one subculture may be unusual in another. Blacks, for example, score abnormally high on some MMPI scales, which would ordinarily indicate severe maladjustment, because they say True to items indicating great cynicism about society, its laws, and its government (Gynther, 1972). For whites, a lot of such responses often indicate paranoia, but for blacks this cynicism is a more realistic attitude.

Assuming that we can establish a non-biased average for behavior—a large assumption—we next need to examine how abnormal behavior differs from normal. Very often the difference is one of *frequency*, not of the nature of the behavior itself. Or it might be the *timing* of the behavior that is unusual. Normal people exhibit many of the same symptoms we use to define the various categories of mental illness—depression, anxiety—but usually only now and then, in response to particular situations.

Noting differences from the average is unsuitable as a complete definition of abnormality, however, because it includes the exceptionally gifted, the extremely friendly, the unusually adjusted, the totally unprejudiced, and the extraordinarily cheerful along with the people who have problems in living. We could add a social value criterion to the deviation criterion and say that abnormal behaviors are those which depart from the norm or average *and* which have no social value. The genius is socially valuable, so the fact that he or she is not average does not detract from his or her high standing in society. These criteria again force us to be aware of the social definition of mental illness. But they too are unsuitable, because social value is often defined politically. Rebels, revolutionaries, and just plain outspoken citizens often have been called mentally ill and placed in confinement simply because their behavior offended the powers that be.

Most clinical psychologists use criteria of

Figure 12.3 *In many countries, political rebellion is classified as abnormal behavior, and the rebel is confined in a mental institution.*

abnormality that stress chronic *inability to cope with one's environment.* This is essentially what we mean by problems of living. More specifically, the inability to cope includes the inability to use logic and reason; it may also involve uncontrolled emotions such as violent tempers and deep depression. Impulsive behavior or its opposite, rigid, overcontrolled behavior, is common, and so is the inability to relate to other people because of extreme egocentrism, distrust, or the like. These criteria too can be misused, of course; but if we emphasize the inability to cope, whatever the environment and the specific behaviors, then a lot of the social and political relativism is taken out of the definition.

Classifying Abnormal Behaviors

Abnormality comes in many forms; every case is unique. But there are similarities that enable scientists to classify cases into general categories. Someone with an erotic interest in feet would be classified, along with others who have erotic attachments to inanimate objects or parts of the body, as suffering from *fetishism;* this case would involve a foot fetish. All fetishes are examples of *sexual deviations,* a more general category that also includes voyeurism (for example, Peeping Toms) and exhibitionism. All sexual deviations are *personality disorders,* a category that includes all deeply ingrained, maladaptive behavior patterns such as alcoholism and drug addiction. All personality disorders, along with the neuroses, the psychoses, and others, are *mental disorders.* These are diagnostic categories of the American Psychiatric Association (1968), shown more completely in Table 12.1.

We will focus our attention on the two

Table 12.1
CATEGORIES OF MENTAL DISORDERS

1. Mental retardation
2. Brain damage
   a. Organic psychoses (e.g., general paresis)
   b. Nonpsychotic disorders: mental capacity to cope not severely impaired
3. Functional psychoses
   a. Schizophrenia
   b. Emotional disorders
   c. Paranoid states
4. Neuroses
5. Personality disorders and certain other nonpsychotic disorders
   a. Personality disorders: maladaptive behaviors that are intricately bound up in the whole personality
   b. Sexual deviations (e.g., fetishism)
   c. Alcoholism
   d. Drug dependence
6. Psychosomatic disorders
7. Special symptoms (e.g., nervous tics)
8. Temporary disturbances: extreme reaction to a real crisis
9. Disorders of childhood and adolescence (e.g., the hyperkinetic, or overactive, child)
10. Maladjustments (e.g., marital or occupational problems)

Adapted by permission of the American Psychiatric Association from *Diagnostic and Statistical Manual of Mental Disorders*, 2nd Ed. 1968.

(White, 1964). Individuals with *neuroses*, although anxious and unhappy, can often function reasonably adequately in their environment, outside of a hospital. They are frequently treated as clients or outpatients.

Reprinted by permission of the Chicago Tribune — New York News Syndicate, Inc.

major classifications of "mental illness": the psychoses and the neuroses. A *psychosis* is a major disturbance characterized by loss of contact with reality and often requiring hospitalization, at least for a time. The two major psychoses, schizophrenia and manic-depressive psychosis, account for about two-thirds of all patients in mental institutions

F O C U S

DSM-III Is Coming

Probably about the time this book is published (early 1980), the American Psychiatric Association's third edition of the Diagnostic and Statistical Manual of Mental Disorders (DSM-III) will become official, replacing DSM-II, whose categories are shown in Table 12.1. DSM in any edition is an important document, defining for example those mental disorders for which an insurance company will be willing to fund treatment or provide disability benefits. In addition, since any category list is based in part on theory, the creation of DSM-III has been watched carefully and critically by warring camps in theoretical psychology.

The one feature of DSM-III that will set the most tongues to wagging is the absence of the term "neurosis." Can you believe it? The disorders that were called neuroses in DSM-II are still around, of course, but in DSM-III they are reclassified into several new categories, such as "anxiety disorders." Essentially what has happened is that the framers of DSM-III have decided that all the disorders previously called neuroses do not have enough in common to deserve a single general label. To psychoanalysts, abandoning the term "neurosis" is a direct insult to Freud, who formulated the theory of neurosis and included the many "superficially dissimilar" disorders on the ground that all involved anxiety as the basic disruptive process (Goleman, 1978). To social behavior theorists, on the other hand, the change is for the good; it represents a shift in focus toward behavior and away from "unsubstantiated theoretical assumptions" about underlying, causative processes (Davison and Neale, 1977).

Another major change in DSM-III is what is called "multiaxial diagnoses." Instead of assigning a single diagnostic label, patients are evaluated on five dimensions or axes. The first is the single diagnostic label of old. The second axis is called "personality disorders and developmental disorders," which is included "to insure that consideration is given to the possible presence of long term disturbances which are frequently overlooked when attention is directed to a current episode of illness" (Task Force on Nomenclature and Statistics, 1977). In other words, for a person suffering from severe depression, Axis 1 would probably be a diagnosis of a depressive disorder of some sort, and Axis 2 would be an attempt to identify the general personality problems, if any, that led to or aggravated the primary symptoms—perhaps he has a terribly inflated view of his own abilities and this is why he is constantly frustrated and depressed.

The third axis is for (nonmental) medical disorders, such as diabetes or high blood pressure, that might be relevant to planning treatment for the patient.

The remaining two axes require judgments, on seven-point scales, about the "severity of stress" and the "highest level of adaptive functioning" in the year preceding the disorder. If the person has recently experienced a business failure, for example, or a divorce, he would be rated high on stress (Axis 4). If he has been floundering around, not coping well with major or minor stresses, he would be rated low on adaptive functioning (Axis 5).

Multiaxial diagnoses, combined with careful description of the "operational criteria" for each diagnosis—the behaviors that must be present for the diagnosis to be assigned—make DSM-III a significant improvement over DSM-II. Nevertheless, controversy over the new diagnostic and statistical manual remains heated. Some psychologists are talking about writing their own alternative diagnostic manual (Davison and Neale, 1977). This is largely because of fears that psychiatrists, who are medical doctors, are trying to define mental disorders in such a way—as *medical* disorders, for example, and as "organismic dysfunctions"—that only people with M.D. degrees will be allowed to treat them. Clinical psychologists, who tend to view mental disorders in terms of environmental influences and who generally have Ph.D. degrees, worry that the manual's medical bias will work against them (Schacht and Nathan, 1977).

Special interest groups have been watching DSM-III to see if their interests are handled fairly. Feminist groups, for example, were able to change a category called "gender-identity disorder of childhood," which was designed to describe people with compulsive desires to dress and act like the opposite sex (transsexualism) but which originally could have been interpreted to include tomboys as well. Women also objected to the "sexual sadism" category, which they perceived could be used by rapists to escape criminal prosecution. Because of the changes, a rapist now must demonstrate a history of compulsive violence to qualify for a psychiatric loophole in the criminal law (Goleman, 1978).

Homosexuality, which was deleted from DSM-II in 1974, is still missing. There is a "homosexual conflict disorder," however, for homosexuals who feel a distressing amount of guilt and shame. A similar category has been created for cigarette smokers who feel "distress at the need to repeatedly use the substance," that is, people who want to kick the habit but can't. One psychiatrist, tongue firmly in cheek, expressed hope that DSM-IV will recognize his particular disorder: distress over missing three-foot putts on the 18th hole (Goleman, 1978).

Much of the controversy over DSM-III has been political, with radical feminists, radical homosexuals, and even mainline Democrats and Republicans arguing over what is to be considered "normal" and what "disordered." The politicization of DSM-III disturbs some psychiatrists, who consider bending to the demands of special interest groups tantamount to giving up psychiatry's scientific birthright. But psychiatric diagnoses have always been influenced by societal values, and to write a DSM that is not political in this sense is probably impossible. Were it possible, it would probably be worthless for the categorization of the mental disorders of people who live in a real world.

THE ORGANIC PSYCHOSES

An *organic psychosis* is a major mental disturbance that has an identifiable physical cause, usually brain damage. The brain damage can result from a number of causes: too many years of excessive drinking, which produces an alcoholic psychosis; untreated syphilis, which can produce a rapid and serious deterioration 10 to 20 years after initial infection; old age, which produces senility in some people; and others.

General Paresis

Even in the bedlam of the zoo they called Bethlehem Hospital, a careful observer could note a group of patients different from the others (Haslam, 1798). These patients were silly, boasting of great capabilities though they could hardly stand up. They had delusions of grandeur, thinking themselves grand when they were in fact pathetic. And they never recovered. They always got worse and worse until they died.

Later observations and statistical tabulations produced more data on this strange syndrome. The patients were rarely women, and the disease rarely appeared earlier than age 30. The deterioration was clearly progressive, beginning with barely perceptible abnormalities and ending with general paralysis of mind and body, and death. The pupils of the eyes did not reflexively close to light, and the knee jerked extremely when tapped, suggesting damage in the brain and spinal cord. Examination of the brain tissue after death showed widespread destruction.

Around the beginning of the twentieth century, two major breakthroughs occurred. First, in 1894, a scientist named Fournier compiled statistics showing that 65 percent of the patients suffering from *general paresis,* as it had now been named, had syphilis when younger, compared to 10 percent of other patients. Fournier advanced the hypothesis that general paresis was caused by syphilitic infection of the brain and spinal cord. This hypothesis was supported by the results of an incredible experiment in 1897 by a physician named Krafft-Ebing (who later became famous for writing books on sex) in which nine paretic patients who denied ever having syphilis were injected with the microorganisms that cause the disease. None developed syphilis, suggesting that most and maybe all of the 35 percent of Fournier's subjects who didn't admit to the disease were covering up past indiscretions (Zilboorg and Henry, 1941).

In 1913, the microorganism that causes syphilis was identified in the brain tissue of dead paretics, further substantiating Fournier's hypothesis. Today there is no question of the facts. Syphilis organisms first cause immediate symptoms—a large sore at the point of infection and a rash; these disappear without treatment, but the organisms remain. They later attack in various places in the body: the heart, the liver, and, in about 10 percent of the cases, the central nervous system. If they do end up in the brain and spinal cord, the result is general paresis (Kleinmuntz, 1974).

Poisons

Lead and mercury poisoning can lead to brain damage and psychotic symptoms. If the poisoning is slight, the symptoms may be hard to detect. It's possible that the irritability of automobile commuters isn't just frustration, but partly a result of inhaling lead from the exhaust of the cars surrounding them. Severe lead poisoning, which occurs in some industries where workers are exposed to lead in dusts and fumes, can lead to delusions, hallucinations, and a lack of emotional control. In short, lead poisoning can lead to organic psychosis, with progressive mental deterioration. Another unfortunate situation exists in many old houses and apartment buildings, where children eat leaded paint that is peeling off the walls; the result may be mental retardation (Kleinmuntz, 1974).

Mercury poisoning has similar effects. Several years ago there was a rash of concern over the high level of mercury found in fish, especially swordfish. A case was reported in

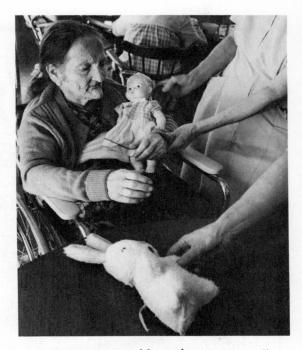

Figure 12.4   *Many old people given up as "senile"—meaning they are presumed to be suffering from irreversible and progressive brain disease—are in fact suffering from functional disorders such as schizophrenia or neurosis or from reversible organic disorders such as malnutrition or alcoholism.*

Newsweek (May 31, 1971) of a woman who, in an attempt to lose weight, ate practically nothing but swordfish for almost two years. She lost weight, but she gained a few unusual symptoms: dizziness, memory loss, difficulty in focusing, and others. She saw a doctor, who told her that the symptoms were the result of "nerves." She saw a psychiatrist for two and a half years, with no benefits. Finally the State Health Depart-

Figure 12.5   *The Mad Hatter from* **Alice in Wonderland** *could blame mercury poisoning for his mental condition—hatters once used a dangerous mercury compound to treat felt for hats. The March Hare, equally mad (according to the Cheshire Cat), had no such excuse; he got his name by acting as if it were always March, the breeding season, when all hares are "wilder."*

ment tested a sample of her hair and found that she was suffering from mercury poisoning.

With the level of pollution in our food, water, and air today, it is possible that some of us have been poisoned enough to have symptoms like mild irritability and occasional depression. Of course, these are symptoms everyone experiences, poisoning or no, and only thorough examination by a physician can determine the exact causes. However, we can and should work for an environment that does not expose us to these poisons.

THE FUNCTIONAL PSYCHOSES

The *functional psychoses* are those which have no known organic cause. Many psychologists believe that organic causes eventually will be discovered, although the cause probably is not brain damage, as it is in most of the organic psychoses. There is evidence that many of the functional psychoses involve biochemical abnormalities that affect the brain (Snyder et al., 1974).

There are three main categories of functional psychosis. One group of illnesses involves *depression,* which is characterized by feelings of sadness and worthlessness. *Manic-depressive psychosis* is probably the best-known member of this group. It is characterized by violent swings of emotion, from excessive joy and excitement (mania) to extreme depression.

The second group involves *paranoia,* which is identified by delusions (false beliefs) of persecution. Paranoid people often manage to avoid hospitalization, for they are extremely suspicious and rarely let others know what is going on in their minds.

The third group of functional psychoses are the *schizophrenias.* This group, by far the most common, will be our major focus in this chapter.

The Nature of Schizophrenia

More than 3000 years ago, the symptoms of schizophrenia were identified as different from other mental abnormalities (Hoch and Zubin, 1966). The term "schizophrenia" was first used in 1911, replacing the older term, *"dementia praecox,"* which replaced "stupidity." Like most names of diseases, each suggested a theory of the illness. Stupidity was used by physicians who thought the syndrome reflected an extreme lack of intelligence. Dementia praecox suggested a progressive disturbance in thinking (dementia) that begins to show itself in children (praecox, related to "precocious"). The early onset and progressive deterioration, however, are not universal features, so most psychologists use the term schizophrenia, which suggests a splitting up (schizo-) of the mind, a loosening of associations, and general disorganization in thought and behavior. (It does *not* mean split or multiple personality—more on this later.)

Primary Symptoms. The man who named schizophrenia, Eugene Bleuler, claimed that it has three primary symptoms: unusual emotions, social withdrawal, and thought disturbance. *Unusual emotions* are those expressed at inappropriate times—laughing when the situation is sad, crying for no reason—or those not expressed at all—the patient is emotionless while describing how his pet dog was run over by a car. *Social withdrawal,* or *autism* as it is often called, is a lack of interaction with other people, believed by some to be a result of a vivid fantasy life going on inside the patient's head. *Thought disturbance* means simply that the thought processes of the schizophrenic are often odd, uninterpretable. This shows up in disorganized speech, as in this brief example from an essay written by a schizophrenic:

> And is fulfilling the Nature Identification in a like Weaker Material Identification creation in which Two Major Bodies have already fulfilled ratio body balances, and embodying a Third Material Identification Embodiment of both. (From White, 1956, p. 550.)

Figure 12.6 *Schizophrenia is marked by a loss of contact with reality, a frustrating and highly unpleasant experience.*

dramatic, though they are not present in all cases. *Hallucinations*—perceptions of what is not really there—are common. Schizophrenic hallucinations almost always involve "hearing voices," and thus are unlike the mostly visual hallucinations of normal subjects under the influence of drugs. Another set of common secondary symptoms is *delusions*—beliefs in something that is not so. *Paranoid schizophrenics* typically believe they are being controlled by external forces or that they are being persecuted.

Table 12.2
TYPES OF SCHIZOPHRENIA

I. Classification according to unique symptoms

A. Hebephrenic schizophrenia: impulsive conduct, silliness, sudden laughing or crying, infantile behavior, lack of control of body functions.

B. Catatonic schizophrenia: wild swings of mood; while depressed may stay in one position for hours.

C. Paranoid schizophrenia: hostility, delusions of persecution.

D. Simple schizophrenia: no distinguishing features other than those shared by all schizophrenics.

II. Classification according to life history

A. Process schizophrenia: gradual onset of symptoms, long history of bizarre behavior; complete recovery rare.

B. Reactive schizophrenia: sudden onset of symptoms, often associated with a particularly disturbing event (for example, death of spouse), a not particularly unusual life history; prognosis for recovery usually good.

In vocabulary, at least, this sentence could almost as easily have been created by a great writer or philosopher. Remember, though, that the "creations" of schizophrenics are much less controlled. For instance, it is more difficult for them to vary their speech or prose according to the circumstances; the writer of the sentence you read above might use the same kind of intricate, convoluted phrases to order morning coffee.

Secondary Symptoms. The so-called secondary symptoms of schizophrenia are more

With *delusions of grandeur,* the patient pictures him- or herself as a great person about to do some great thing.

Bizarre behavior is also common in schizophrenia. In *catatonic schizophrenia,* patients undergo long periods of depression or apathy and become totally unresponsive to the outside world. They are known for their ability to hold one posture for hours, even days. It was once thought that patients heard and saw nothing in a catatonic phase, but this turns out not to be the case. They hear and otherwise perceive, but they do not respond, often because they *dare* not; "something catastrophic" might happen (Kleinmuntz, 1974).

As you can see, more than one kind of schizophrenia has been distinguished by psychologists. Table 12.2 describes the most common types.

Figure 12.7 *Joan of Arc listening to her guiding voices in the garden. Was she a visionary leader? Or were her visions the hallucinations of mental illness?*

FOCUS

A Conversation with a Schizophrenic

A purely clinical description of symptoms, even combined with case reports of actual people fitting the classic types, gives a poor picture of schizophrenia. One must remember that these patients are typically very much the same as anyone else; *most* of the thought and speech of the average schizophrenic is quite intelligible. A good friend of mine was diagnosed as a simple schizophrenic. He was being treated as an outpatient at the time we had the following conversation. (There are a few changes, to protect his identity.)

Me: I need a title for the book.
Him: Why don't you call it, *Dr. Spock's Wife Writes Another Novel, Her First.* (*I laugh; he does not; he seems puzzled by my response.*)
Him: Of course, there's a little bit of green there! (*He laughs and seems puzzled that I do not.*)

Him: Green with envy, you. She's green; first novel.

Me: You know, Bob, a lot of times you say things that seem nonsense to me. But sometimes I see your associations. Do you always have an association?

Him: No. Sometimes I just talk. Nonsense.

Me: Why?

Him: People say something to me. I don't get their meaning, but they obviously want me to say something. Questions are bad. So I just say anything.

Me: Doesn't sound like much fun.

Him: I used to love books.

Me: Books?

Him: I can't understand them anymore. I tried to read one by John Steinbeck, about Monterey, California. I used to live there, you know.

Me: Cannery Row.

Him: Right. I read a little bit each night for, oh, it must have been six months or so. Sometimes I thought I was understanding but then the story would go off in a direction I didn't expect. . . . You know, it gets pretty frustrating. . . . Sometimes I get angry, too. I can't understand other people and they can't understand me. . . . Why did you laugh at my book title?

Me: Well, it was good. "Another novel, her first" is a contradiction; it's funny.

Him: I suppose you're right. I just said it. It doesn't make any sense to me.

Me: You were diagnosed schizophrenic, weren't you?

Him: Yes.

Me: What do you think schizophrenia is?

Him: When somebody thinks crazy. When his thinking is all screwed up.

Me: What causes it?

Him: I don't want to answer questions. You sound like the shrink.

The Development of Schizophrenia

There are three main lines of research into the causes of schizophrenia, which can be put in the form of three questions: Is schizophrenia inherited? Is schizophrenia the result of biochemical abnormalities somewhere in the body that affect the brain? Is schizophrenia a result of a very poor environment in which the person learned ineffective ways of thinking and acting?

Heredity and Schizophrenia. A former president of the American Psychological Association, in his presidential address, asked his audience to consider a bet (Meehl, 1962).

Suppose they were to wager a thousand dollars that they could find someone who would be diagnosed schizophrenic by a psychiatric staff. They could not use any symptoms displayed by the individual; but they could use all the information they could gather on his family environment, his life history, the personality of his relatives, and the like. What would they do?

If one defines a good bet as having better than 50:50 odds of winning, then there is only one possible answer. The audience would have to find a diagnosed schizophrenic who has an identical twin, and choose the twin. The largest study that has been done on schizophrenia and heritability found 174 sets of identical twins and 296 fraternal twins for comparison (Kallman, 1946). One member of each set was a diagnosed schizophrenic. The question was, What percentage of the other twins were, also? Of the identical twins, 69 percent were schizophrenic. For the fraternal twins (only those of the same sex were used, because identical twins are always the same sex), the figure was 11 percent. These data indicate considerable heritability.

Later studies have found the percentages for identical twins somewhat less (Gottesman and Shields, 1972). Using data from over a dozen different investigations, the average figure is about 50 percent (an even bet, so don't waste money on it). Still, the average for identical twins is much higher than that for fraternal twins of the same sex — about 12 percent.

Other relatives of schizophrenics also are more likely than the average person to be schizophrenic. Children of schizophrenic mothers who are placed in homes with normal foster parents are much more likely to become schizophrenic or to exhibit schizo-phrenic-like behavior patterns than foster children of nonschizophrenic mothers (Heston, 1970).

All of these statistics indicate that something about schizophrenia, some kind of susceptibility to it, is inherited; probably most psychologists believe this. The heritability data for mental illnesses, however, have not received the close scrutiny that comparable data for IQ have. One could make a good case for the position that schizophrenia is not inherited at all, if all we had to consider were the studies of twins and other relatives. But, as we shall see, biochemical evidence makes the twin data more convincing.

The Chemistry of Schizophrenia. There has been no lack of biochemical studies of schizophrenia. Anyone with equipment can measure the differences between schizophrenics and normals in one or another body fluid, and several thousand scientists have done so. Several hundred have found — "discovered" is the word typically used — significant differences. Almost every discovery has a typical course: Someone makes the discovery; other investigators fail to confirm it; then there are a few replications; and, finally, it is established that the difference was due, not to schizophrenia, but to some trivial characteristic of schizophrenics, such as their lack of exercise or the hospital diet.

When scientists discovered the hallucinogenic (hallucination-producing) drugs, LSD and the amphetamines (speed) in particular, a new wave of research began under the assumption that these drug states resembled psychoses. The drugs, in fact, were sometimes called "psychotomimetic," implying that they mimicked the effects of psychotic agents — whatever those might be — inside the body. This basic assumption, however,

Figure 12.8 *The "psychedelic" effect of schizophrenia. This artist's paintings of cats moved from realism to almost total fantasy as he became more and more schizophrenic. The intricate formal patterns of his late works seem to reveal a frantic attempt to organize his thought processes.*

has been challenged (Hollister, 1968). In the case of LSD and certain related drugs (mescaline, psilocybin), heavy doses produce psychotic-like behavior in that logical thought is disrupted, inappropriate emotions (laughing, crying) are common, and the subject often withdraws from social interactions: He or she may sit for hours staring at a wall. But the differences between true psychotic states and an LSD trip are many. To mention a few: Hallucinations are usually visual on LSD, usually auditory (voices) in psychoses; observers in mental institutions have no difficulty distinguishing schizophrenia from drug-induced psychosis; and schizophrenics who take LSD claim the drug experience is totally unlike their psychotic experiences. Drug experiences can be pleasurable, but psychotic experiences are not.

However great the apparent differences,

some scientists are reluctant to give up so easily (Snyder et al., 1974). They point out that drug users usually know the reason for their unusual experience and expect to return to normal in a short time, whereas schizophrenics are, in essence, on LSD all their lives—not a pleasant prospect. Schizophrenics who become psychotic suddenly, often under stress, after a relatively normal life, frequently experience a "psychedelic phase" of intense joy, visual hallucinations, and a feeling of heightened awareness and creativity. But this phase apparently cannot be tolerated very long; either the patient becomes normal again or he or she degenerates into the sad, withdrawn type we associate with chronic schizophrenia.

A much stronger case can be made for amphetamine psychosis as a model for schizophrenia. In large doses, speed produces a reaction that is indistinguishable from acute paranoid schizophrenia. Auditory hallucinations are common. Schizophrenics who take amphetamines simply become more schizophrenic (Snyder et al., 1974). The major drawback to assuming that schizophrenia and amphetamine psychosis are essentially identical is that amphetamines produce only one kind of schizophrenia—the paranoid kind.

Another link in the chain of associations between schizophrenia and amphetamine psychosis is their treatment. Someone who enters a hospital suffering from amphetamine psychosis is usually given one of a class of drugs known as the phenothiazines. These drugs are also effective in the treatment of schizophrenia, reducing cognitive confusion, anxiety, and social withdrawal.

In fact, the effectiveness of the phenothiazines in relieving the symptoms of schizophrenia is in itself a major reason for the belief, among many psychologists, that schizophrenia is based on a biochemical imbalance in the brain. The reduction in the disorganization of thoughts and emotions is dramatic, allowing many patients to leave the hospital and lead relatively normal lives in the community. These drugs are largely responsible for the striking drop in the number of people housed in mental institutions in this country. It is sometimes said that these drugs, which are called tranquilizers, simply stupefy the patient, but when they are properly administered, quite the opposite is the case: Patients become able to think clearly and respond to other people without fear, often for the first time in memory.

Environmental Factors in Schizophrenia. Many psychologists believe that schizophrenia's main cause is not biochemical imbalances or brain damage, but growing up in a poor environment. Even psychologists who believe that schizophrenia is caused almost entirely by nonenvironmental factors must take the environment into account to understand the precise symptoms that develop in each individual. Environmental factors also clearly affect what happens to the patient after he or she leaves the hospital. In a good family and community environment, chances of a successful life are good, whereas a poor environment can reverse the therapeutic gains made in the hospital.

Psychoanalytic theorists emphasize early family interactions as causes of schizophrenia. One such theorist claims that all cases of schizophrenia, without exception, involve poor family relations and unhappy childhoods resulting in severe conflicts (Arieti, 1960). The anxiety generated by these conflicts is simply too much to bear, so the individual retreats into his or her own private world, with its own private logic. This social isolation, in turn, allows the schizophrenic to develop unique, idiosyncratic thought patterns, unrestricted by the normal, everyday human contacts most people experience. In short, because of the way they isolate themselves, schizophrenics and preschizophrenics lack the social feedback necessary to keep their ideas and behavior in line with reality.

Similar notions have been developed by nonpsychoanalytical theorists. One popular theory suggests that the preschizophrenic child is placed in a *double bind* by his parents, in particular by his mother (Bateson et al., 1956). The double bind is a situation in which the communications of the other person mean different things at different levels. Usually, at one level there is a request to "stay away!" (usually unspoken) and, at the other level, to "come forward, love me!" Here is a reported example:

> A young man who had fairly well recovered from an acute schizophrenic episode was visited in the hospital by his mother. He was glad to see her and impulsively put his arms around her shoulders whereupon she stiffened. He withdrew his arms and she asked, "Don't you love me anymore?" He then blushed and she said, "Dear, you must not be so easily embarrassed and afraid of your feelings." The patient was able to stay with her only a few minutes more and following her departure he assaulted an aide and was put in the tubs. (Bateson et al., 1956, p. 144.)

The double bind, in this situation, is clear. The mother's words say "Love me" and her actions say "Stay away." A fully rational adult, of course, would see and possibly point out the discrepancy, but the dependent child cannot. He withdraws, gradually, into a world where he can ignore what he cannot deal with—his private, schizophrenic world.

British psychiatrist R. D. Laing talks of the *position of checkmate*, a notion comparable to the double bind. Laing views schizophrenia as an understandable reaction to the terrible environment in which the patient lives (1967, 1970). "Normal" people often perceive the behavior of the schizophrenic as disorganized and his thought and language as nonsensical, but if they examined the family situation in which he grew up, they would find that his thoughts and behaviors make much more sense. This point Laing supports in a study of eleven families of schizophrenics (Laing and Esterson, 1970).

Unfortunately, there is not a lot of research on early interactions in the families of schizophrenics, and what there is does not

Figure 12.9 *This fortunate infant senses the love underlying the scolding. If the situation is reversed and the child senses hate beneath surface affection, he or she is in a double bind. The child cannot respond to the affection (because it is not real) or to the hostility (because it is not "out in the open").*

suggest that such early interactions have a strong influence. One of the problems has been lack of comparison groups. A psychiatrist may be struck by how many schizophrenics come from impoverished and broken homes, not realizing that impoverished and broken homes are not uncommon in the lower social classes from which most of the patients come. In one well-controlled study, investigators found that poverty and divorce were *less* common in the families of schizophrenics than in families of "normals" matched on age, sex, and marital status (Schofield and Balian, 1959). Even more damaging to the hypothesis is the evidence that the children of schizophrenic mothers who have been raised from birth in foster homes (by normals) are just as likely to become schizophrenic as children raised in the chaotic environment provided by their own schizophrenic mothers (Page, 1971).

On the other hand, as evidence accumulates for some kind of biochemical imbalance in schizophrenia, the environment cannot be ignored as a contributing factor. A poor environment is difficult for the most insightful normal to cope with, and it is doubly threatening and confusing to the schizophrenic. By the time the schizophrenic arrives at a mental institution, he is often so fearful that he is unwilling to try anything that might help.

This *unwillingness* to try effective action is often interpreted, incorrectly, as an *inability* to perform. There was a time when a psychologist could publish a scientific paper simply by hypothesizing and showing that schizophrenics did worse than normals in X, where X equals just about any behavior imaginable: crossing out Es in printed material, throwing darts, whatever. But it soon became clear that most of these findings did not result from inability but from lack of will. Under proper conditions, with a familiar and encouraging experimenter, schizophrenics did as well as normals on most tasks (Shakow, 1963).

Perhaps schizophrenics need a simpler, more benevolent environment than most people, if they are to perform as effectively as others. In one experiment that involved turning a hospital ward into a miniature society, patients were paid for their work on the ward with tokens they could exchange for various favors (Ayllon and Azrin, 1965). In contrast with the typical slow, unwilling work habits of schizophrenics, these people were regular and responsible. It's apparent that in a simple, logical environment in which effective actions are clearly defined and rewarded, the behavior of schizophrenics can be very nearly normal.

THE NEUROSES

A neurosis, at least according to DSM-II, is a mental or behavioral maladjustment involving severe anxiety or reactions to anxiety. It is typically a milder disorder than a psychosis, and hospitalization is much less likely. Probably everyone is a little neurotic—it's normal to be anxious about some things. The afflictions we call real neuroses are unusual, and go beyond the bounds of normal hang-ups. Most neurotics eventually seek the help of a psychologist or psychiatrist, not because they cannot function in society (they usually can), but because there is little joy in life for them. They realize that they have a problem and are unable to do anything about it, so they seek aid.

Anxiety Neurosis

All the neuroses are characterized by anxiety or a reaction to anxiety, but none more clearly than *anxiety neurosis*. The person suffering from an anxiety neurosis lives in fear, convinced that something terrible is going to happen. But he or she is not sure what that something is. *Anxiety* is sometimes distinguished from fear in that fear is specific, has an object—I fear X—but anxiety is nonspecific, free-floating, with no definable object.

It's easy to see why there is not much joy in the life of an anxiety neurotic. Without a specific object to fear, everything is suspect, and he is constantly alert (he sleeps poorly), easily distracted (he cannot concentrate), and concerned about his health, for every irregularity in body function is, to him, an indication of impending death. Panic at being faced with everyday life is the fate of the anxiety neurotic—not all the time, but enough of the time to make life miserable.

A typical anxiety neurosis involved a young man who sought help because he thought he was losing his mind. This idea is not uncommon among anxiety neurotics because they cannot see any logical reason for their extreme fears. This man's periods of severe panic came on when he had the attention of his fellows—while he was lecturing troops in the army, for example, or whenever someone teased him. The most severe attack began when something seemed to snap in his ears and everything became louder and louder. He held his hands over his ears and fell to the ground. On the ground, he became afraid that he would never be able to rise again, so he jumped up and told everyone that everything was fine. He thought to himself, however, that he was going crazy, and he went to the Veterans Administration outpatient clinic soon thereafter (Kleinmuntz, 1974).

Obsessions and Compulsions

If anxiety neuroses involve the disrupting effects of anxiety itself, *obsessive-compulsive neuroses* are the ill effects of trying (unconsciously) to keep anxiety within bounds. An *obsession* is a repetitive and constantly intruding thought or idea. A normal person may become obsessed, temporarily, with a

tune he can't get out of his mind, or with the idea that he forgot to turn off the stove before he left home. Usually the serious obsessions are more threatening. Death is a common theme: The obsessive thought might be that the person is going to kill his mother or father or child. The image hangs in his mind like a premonition, which he fears it is, and severely disrupts other intellectual activity.

A *compulsion* is an act (or series of acts) that a person feels compelled to do. Compulsions are often related to obsessions, as in the case of the relatively normal person who, obsessed with the idea that the stove is on, compulsively checks each knob before

Figure 12.10 *Lady Macbeth's constant hand-washing—an attempt to cleanse herself of guilt for taking part in a murder—is a typical compulsive behavior.*

he or she leaves the house. Some of the more common severe compulsions include *cleansing rituals*—the person takes a bath or washes his hands, or cleans house, several times a day—and *undoing* behaviors, which often betray the underlying obsession because they are opposite to it in some sense—a child with a recurring thought of murdering his father acts overly friendly to him.

Obsessions and compulsions, it is generally agreed, are bad habits that develop in response to strong anxiety or fear. Imagine yourself walking through a cemetery at night, deathly afraid but trying to show courage. To combat the fear, you might try to distract yourself by thinking of other things or by doing something ritualized like a hopscotch step. If it works, you reinforce these thoughts and behaviors, making them more likely to occur again in the future. Crossing cemeteries regularly might result in obsessions and compulsions, in that setting at least.

Hysteria

The prime characteristic of hysterias is the individual's unconscious mental isolation of some part of his or her body or mind to avoid anxiety. In *conversion hysteria*, some bodily function is stopped: The patient might become paralyzed, blind, or deaf. The psychological cause is usually fairly clear. There is something the patient does not want to do or see or hear (or do or see or hear *again*). Hysterical paralysis on a wedding day, for example, is usually the result of sexual fears or uncertainties.

We know these hysterias are psychological in origin because the symptoms are different from the symptoms of true physiological deficits. People who are hysterically blind will still avoid objects in their path. Paralyses correspond to what people think of as a bodily unit—a hand, an arm—instead of what is physiologically a unit. If some sort of nerve damage resulted in the paralysis of a hand, for example, it would surely affect the wrist and arm as well; but a hand hysteria typically affects only the "glove area."

Dissociative hysterias involve an unconscious mental isolation of some part of the personality. One form of such mental isolation is *amnesia*, memory loss that is caused by an unconscious wish to forget (not by physical causes); amnesia is a frequent theme in novels and films. *Fugue states* are much more complicated, involving a person with amnesia for his or her life history, who wanders off and begins an entirely new life someplace else.

Multiple Personality. The most dramatic of the dissociative hysterias is the multiple personality, where two or more intricately organized personalities exist side by side in the same body. Multiple personalities are extremely rare, but when they occur, they are exciting both to scientists and to the public. Two of the most famous cases have been made into movies—*The Three Faces of Eve* and *Sybil*.

Like the archetypical story of Dr. Jekyll and Mr. Hyde, many cases of multiple personality represent a split between "good" and "evil" selves. As such, they represent an exaggeration of a normal developmental process, in which children create notions of a "good self" and a "bad self." Normally, these two selves are eventually integrated into one personality with good and bad aspects, but sometimes the two are isolated from one another and develop independently. The individual cannot accept the bad self into an integrated personality, so it lurks, Hyde-like, at the boundaries of consciousness—sometimes taking control of consciousness (Gruenewald, 1977). In therapy, a third personality often appears, one that incorporates the other two. This personality denies neither its good nor its bad impulses; it simply tries to avoid acting on the basis of its less healthy tendencies.

The Three Faces of Eve. The "three faces of Eve" are a case in point (Thigpen and Cleckley, 1957). The early Jekyll and Hyde division was between Eve White, the saintly, reserved young thing, and Eve Black, wild, impetuous, carefree woman of the world. Here are some of the adjectives the therapists used to describe Eve White: neat, colorless, demure, poised, superlatively calm, utterly self-controlled, delicate. Here are some adjectives for Eve Black: reckless, intimate, careless, playful, provocative. Many people sympathize with the devilish personalities in accounts like this, partly because saints are usually dull; but devilish, immoral personalities, although vivacious, lack the simple human virtues of love and compassion. Eve Black's sexual encounters, for example, were motivated primarily by anger or disgust. Eventually a third, more integrated personality, called Jane, emerged; Jane was described as mature, vivid, capable, interesting. The third personality was, according to the therapists, the combination of the good parts of Eve White and Eve Black, with their major faults eliminated.

Although the small number of documented cases precludes definitive answers, many interesting research questions are raised by multiple personalities. Why do most cases involve females (Page, 1971)? Is it because cultural norms prohibit women from expressing "evil" tendencies? No one knows for sure. How distinct are the personalities? Eve reports, "If I had learned to sew as one personality and then tried to sew as another, I couldn't do it" (Santa Barbara *News-Press*, September 15, 1975). In more systematic tests on an individual who exhibited four personalities, each personality

Figure 12.11 *Chris Sizemore, who acknowledged that she is the woman in* The Three Faces of Eve, *designed her painting to symbolize her multiple personalities.*

learned a short list of paired associates (e.g., basket-orange); the other three personalities showed no recall of the learned lists (Ludwig et al., 1972). Each of the four personalities showed a distinct pattern of responses on personality tests, indicating distinctive personality organizations.

Hypochondria and Phobias

Neuroses in which the anxiety becomes attached to something very specific, even though that something clearly doesn't deserve all the attention, include hypochondria and the phobias. The *hypochondriac* is convinced he or she has a defective body that is about to give out. The *phobias* are unrealistic and disrupting fears of particular objects or situations, often classified under colorful names. Examples are acrophobia—fear of heights; claustrophobia—fear of closed-in spaces; and even pathenophobia—fear of sermons. Except for acrophobia, claustrophobia, and a few other common phobias, these names are rarely used; it seems senseless to coin a Greek word for every object and situation a human can be afraid of.

Causes of Neuroses

It is generally believed that environmental factors play a more significant role in the neuroses than in the psychoses. This does not mean that genetic, biochemical, and neurological factors play no role at all; they almost certainly do. It is the balance between the two that is different here, as we shall see.

Physiological Factors. Many psychologists suspect that neurotics have nervous systems that are more active or sensitive in some

"Leave us alone! I am a behavior therapist! I am helping my patient overcome a fear of heights!"

© *1980 by Sidney Harris*

way than those of normal people (Eysenck and Rachman, 1965); neurotics "spook" easily. Such a nervous system might be inherited (Eysenck and Prell, 1951). But we must be cautious in discussing biological influences in neuroses, because they are not of the same type as those in psychoses. There is a world of difference between an inherited deficit that affects your ability to think straight and one that makes you nervous. Whereas the biological deficit in a psychosis directly diminishes the individual's ability to cope with reality, the deficit in a neurosis simply makes his or her life unpleasant. A neurotic may function poorly because he or she constantly has to deal with fears and anxieties, but some neurotics function better than average. We all know obsessive-compulsive types who work long hours with complete concentration and are extremely productive. Not all artists are neurotic, but many are and were; their creations, which give us so much pleasure later, may be painful and in some sense therapeutic for them.

Another important point about possibly inherited tendencies toward neurosis is one Freud made back in 1924: Inborn tendencies and environmental factors interact in different proportions for every individual. To reach a high level of anxiety, person *X*, who is nervous by nature, requires only a little stress from the environment. Person *Y*, who is calm by nature, requires a great deal of stress to reach the same level. The inborn predisposition and the environmental pressures work together; if one factor is low, a high level of anxiety still can result if the other is high. Thus, a person who is under great stress for a long period could become neurotic even if he or she is not unusually nervous.

Stress from the Environment. There once was a situation to which many people were exposed that produced neurosis in 95 percent of them: being a member of a heavy bomber crew during World War II (Hastings et al., 1944). Considering the probability of death in some of these combat units (well over 50 percent), one would have to say extreme fear was realistic, and certainly neurosis was normal in the statistical sense. The bomber crews' targets, the people below, were also likely to become neurotic, especially if they were predisposed ("nervous" before). Single traumatic events, such as the A-bomb attacks on Hiroshima and Nagasaki, had much less effect than frequent attacks. Also, children tended to copy their

parents; if their parents showed great fear, the children were more likely to become emotionally disturbed (Janis, 1951).

The stress of war, which often includes problems like lack of sleep and food as well as the threat of death, elicits anxiety in almost everyone. When the environment returns to normal, most of the "war neuroses" disappear (Brill and Beebe, 1955). Also, from studies of earlier wars, psychologists have discovered ways to lessen some of the anxieties war produces. For example, setting a time limit on a tour of combat duty makes it easier for soldiers to endure till the date they know their stress will end (Brill, 1967).

Figure 12.12 *War is hell. Few people can stand the stress of prolonged combat, but most recover quickly in a normal environment.*

Childhood Experiences and Neurosis. The stress of war and other situations in which extreme fear is realistic can cause anxiety in nearly anybody. But in less severe situations, individual differences appear in people's reactions to stress. Most often, situations cause stress without the victim knowing exactly why. I find public speaking extremely anxiety-provoking, much more than most people do, but I can't give a reason. I have absolutely no fear of airplanes and find it strange that others do.

For explanations of these and other stresses of unknown origin, psychologists look to early childhood experiences. Childhood conflicts that turn up repeatedly in case histories of neurotics include the following: (1) The father is either very dominant (authoritarian) or extremely weak and passive. (2) Parents are overprotective and indulgent, leading the child to become dependent and insecure when alone. (3) Parents are impulsive and inconsistent, making it difficult for the child to learn rules for proper living and also modeling neurotic behaviors for the child to imitate.

Interpretations based on childhood experiences often depend on psychoanalytic theory. As we discussed in Chapter 10, research evidence for psychoanalytic hypotheses almost always comes from natural experiments involving correlations, and the results are difficult to interpret. It is quite possible to come to two (or more) equally reasonable conclusions from the same data. But by any theory, the behavioral symptoms that make up a neurosis are learned.

FOCUS

Six TV Myths about Mental Illness

TV detectives Ufindem and Ihitem have a "psychopath" on their hands, a deranged maniac who is murdering middle-aged women. The police psychologist tells them to look for a young man who drinks bloody marys and wears suspenders. He explains that the murders are probably the work of a college dropout who harbors deep resentment toward his mother, which he expresses by murdering middle-aged women who remind him of her. Bloody marys remind him of murdered mothers, and suspenders bolster his failing masculine self-image. Ufindem catches a young business executive with his suspenders down, so to speak, and a few slaps from Ihitem reduce the murderer to a babbling madman.

Plots like this are not uncommon on TV; in fact, the preposterous script just described is a thinly disguised version of one that actually played in prime time. The simplistic and distorted ideas about mental illness that people gain from TV are not only inaccurate but sometimes dangerous, leading to public attitudes that make life for the mentally ill even harder. Psychologist Otto Wahl, writing in *TV Guide*, listed six of the most common TV myths (Wahl, 1976).

Myth 1: *Psychiatric omnipotence*. Given the slightest evidence, the TV psychiatrist or psychologist seems able to describe a person in detail, including not only sex, age, personal habits, and unconscious motives, but also life history and probable future behavior. Diagnosis and assessment are neither as easy nor as accurate as portrayed on the tube. Public beliefs about the exceptional analytic powers of psychologists lead to fears about exposing oneself in their presence. I and every psychologist I know, including those who are interested in nothing but the retina of a frog, have experienced meeting someone who, when told of our profession, shies away nervously as if we had x-ray eyes. At cocktail parties, such defensive postures are simply annoying; in therapy, they can reduce the psychologist's chances of helping the individual.

Myth 2: *Confrontation equals cure*. On TV, what happens when the humanitarian meddlers observe destructive patterns of behavior in an individual? Why, they confront the person, pointing out how he is injuring not only himself but his spouse, his children, and his friends as well. As a result, the individual changes his ways and begins acting like a model citizen. Fade out. . . . In real life, confrontation rarely leads to beneficial change. Most people react to confrontation with rationalizations and other defensive maneuvers that further insulate the problem, and hostility toward the humanitarian meddler. (If you don't believe it, try telling your roommate about his or her personal problems!)

Myth 3: *Schizophrenia is split personality*. No, it is not.

Myth 4: *Conversion hysteria is as common as the measles*. Betty sees a crime and becomes hysterically blind. Joe learns that his wife is having an affair and becomes paralyzed from the waist down. Although the frightening or psychologically painful origins of hysterical symptoms are not inaccurately represented, this mental disorder is, in real life, quite rare. In addition, hysterical symptoms almost never erupt in the life of someone who has had no mental problems before.

Myth 5: *The psychopathic killer*. Typically two sorts of killers are labeled "psychopathic" on TV. One distorts reality, lives in a dreamworld, and kills those who have the misfortune to become involved in his fantasies; he is not killing them, he is killing his mother, his father, or his girlfriend. The other sort suffers from a compulsion to kill; he knows it is wrong, but he cannot help himself. As Wahl states, "Both labels are grossly inappropriate."

Psychopaths—or "antisocial personalities," as they are now called—do not suffer from obsessions and compulsions, nor do they exhibit delusions and other distortions of reality. Instead, they are "grossly selfish, callous, irresponsible, impulsive, and unable to feel guilt or learn from experience and punishment" (American Psychiatric Association, 1968, p. 43). They seem to have no sense of morality, no sense of compassion or remorse. They are often criminals, for obvious reasons, but their offenses are usually burglary, fraud, and other crimes against property. If they kill, it is a murder of convenience, not one of passion or compulsion. The cool and calculating "hit man" for the mob may be a psychopathic killer, but not the madman in the streets.

Myth 6: *Mentally ill means dangerous.* Perhaps the most pernicious TV myth is that mentally ill people are dangerous. The homicidal maniac and the deranged rapist may make for exciting drama, but in real life they are very uncommon. The typically mentally disordered person is "inert, *not* assaultive; afraid, *not* hostile; submissive, *not* aggressive" (Wahl, 1976, p. 8). Although a small (but well-publicized) proportion of the mentally disordered are dangerous, the vast majority are harmless. Former mental patients as a group have a much *lower* rate of violent crime than the general population (Pollock, 1938; White et al., 1969; Ekblom, 1970). Other people's fears of mental illness obviously make it difficult for former patients to adjust to life outside mental institutions, and these are people who can do without another straw on their camel's back.

CATEGORIES AND INDIVIDUALS

The categories of mental disorder are not as distinct as we make them appear in textbooks. The broad categories can be distinguished fairly easily—most observers can agree on "neurosis" versus "psychosis"—but the more detailed the diagnosis, the more disagreement among clinicians (Schmidt and Fonda, 1956). One rarely finds pure cases. The anxiety neurotic often has several compulsions, and the catatonic schizophrenic may also be paranoid. Mental retardation is often mistaken for schizophrenia (formerly called "stupidity," remember), and vice versa. Symptoms of depression are common in almost every category of disorder.

Because of the unreliability of diagnostic categories at the detailed level, many psychologists have called for abandoning the traditional classification system. But most continue to use the system, though they may do so with caution, allowing for the possibility that a patient has been misdiagnosed. There is an increasing tendency for practicing psychologists to treat their patients or clients as individual cases, and thus to be less influenced by the label they formerly might have attached.

No individual is identical to another. Each has his or her own unique set of learning experiences and peculiar biological imperfections. We should expect, in these circumstances, a range of mental and behavioral disorders, with clear distinctions rare. If there is a collection of symptoms we can call schizophrenia, then there is a schizophrenia dimension on which all of us can be placed—you and I place low, we hope. Using the noun "schizophrenic" is a gross generalization, defining an individual in terms of only one deficit among the many gifts and deficits that constitute his or her whole personality.

SUMMARY

1. A person is usually judged to be mentally ill when his or her behavior is unpredictable by ordinary standards. A less socially based definition of mental illness is inability to cope with one's environment.

2. Until fairly recently, people with mental disorders were treated not much differently from criminals. To regard them as "ill" and treat them in hospitals was a significant advance. However, because mental problems do not reflect an illness in the usual sense, the medical model is less than ideal; treatment within the community is gaining favor.

3. The major division in the classification of mental disorders is between psychoses and neuroses. *Psychoses* are generally much more severe. The *organic psychoses* involve brain damage due to alcohol, syphilis (general paresis), aging (senility), poisons (often introduced by pollution), and other causes.

4. *Functional psychoses* have no known organic cause, although many psychologists believe that biochemical imbalances may be involved. The three main categories of functional psychosis are those which involve depression (including manic-depressive psychosis), paranoia (delusions of persecution), and schizophrenia.

5. *Schizophrenia* is characterized by three primary symptoms: thought disturbance, unusual emotions, and social withdrawal. Secondary symptoms often present are hallucinations, delusions, and bizarre behaviors such as maintaining one posture for several hours.

6. There is significant evidence that susceptibility to schizophrenia is at least partly inherited. Its resemblance to amphetamine psychosis suggests that schizophrenia may involve chemicals in the brain similar to amphetamines. Drugs useful for treating amphetamine psychosis, such as the phenothiazines, have also been effective with schizophrenia.

7. Environmental theories of schizophrenia emphasize unhappy childhood experiences. The *double-bind* hypothesis suggests that children faced with contradictory demands from their parents may in effect flee into schizophrenia. Similarly, R. D. Laing bases his *position of checkmate* theory on family interactions which he says leave the schizophrenic little or no alternative to the behaviors he displays. Research on environmental factors like broken or conflict-filled homes, however, indicates that such factors are not a direct cause of schizophrenia, though they may encourage its development.

8. Although the term *neurosis* has been dropped from the American Psychiatric Association's current diagnostic and statistical manual, it remains useful as a general category for less severe maladjustments characterized by anxiety or reactions to anxiety. Common neuroses include *anxiety neurosis,* in which anxiety is experienced directly; *obsessions* (repetitive thoughts) and *compulsions* (compelled behaviors), which apparently serve to reduce anxiety; and *hyste-*

rias, which can convert mental conflicts to physical symptoms like paralysis or which can isolate parts of the personality, causing *amnesia* (forgetting due to repression) or *multiple personalities.*

9. Genetic and biochemical factors are not insignificant in the origin of neuroses, but learning is believed to play a more important role. Normally, innate nervousness combines with environmental stress to cause neurosis. However, extreme stress, such as that experienced in war, can produce neurotic behavior in nearly anyone.

10. Trained psychologists can distinguish among normals, neurotics, and psychotics with some reliability, but the more precise diagnostic categories seem to be useful generalizations rather than distinct realities. There is a healthy trend toward treating each individual as unique, without labels.

USING PSYCHOLOGY

Many communities have local mental health associations composed of nonprofessionals that are involved in volunteer work with the mentally ill. Their volunteer activities typically include visiting and aiding in mental hospitals or clinics, or working on a one-to-one basis with an adult or child in the community. They are also active in programs intended to inform the public about mental illness and to train volunteers in some basics of psychological counseling and therapies. If you are interested in learning more about mental illness and what your community is doing about it, call your local mental health association and see what kind of information they can give you. They will probably have pamphlets, discussion groups, and public lectures on the subject. If this additional information arouses your interest further, you might consider becoming a volunteer worker with the organization. Make sure when you deal with patients or others with mental problems that you do not behave toward them as the gawking, amused public did to the unfortunate inmates of London's Bethlehem asylum. Individuals with mental problems are often sensitive, intelligent human beings. As the text points out, their mental disorders are deficits among many other aspects—both positive and negative—of their personalities. They deserve to be treated with as much dignity as other human beings.

SUGGESTED READINGS

Davidson, G. C., & Neale, J. M. *Abnormal psychology.* 2nd ed. Wiley, 1978.
    One of many excellent textbooks. The authors are most closely associated with the social behavior approach, but their discussions are fair and comprehensive.

Laing, R. D. *The politics of experience.* Ballantine, 1967.
    A truly different view of "mental illness," one that treats it as essentially normal—possibly even beneficial.

Reed, D. *Anna.* Basic Books, 1976.
    A tragic story of a mentally ill young woman who . . . You must read it; it can't be summarized.

Maser, J. D., & Seligman, M. E. P. (eds.). *Psychopathology: experimental models.* Freeman, 1977.
    An exceptional collection of reviews of laboratory research on clinical disorders (anxiety, depression, obesity, etc.).

INTERLUDE

Drugs

As anyone knows who has ever walked into a drugstore, the word *drugs* covers a multitude of products. Technically, a drug is any chemical substance that changes the structure or function of the body, even food (Nowlis, 1971). For the purposes of this interlude, we will consider only the drugs that people take for escape — to forget their problems — or for recreation — to "get high." After a few comments on the definition of "addiction," we will take a brief look at the more common drugs now in use in the United States, and then focus on two of them: alcohol and marijuana.

WHAT IS ADDICTION?

One of the first questions one asks about a drug is, "Is it addictive?" It is not an easy question to answer. Scientists now prefer the term "drug dependence," and they distinguish between two types, physical and psychological (Kleinmuntz, 1974).

Physical dependence is what was formerly called addiction. It is characterized by *tolerance* and *withdrawal. Tolerance* means that more and more of the drug must be taken to achieve the same effect, as use continues. *Withdrawal* means that if use is discontinued, the person experiences unpleasant symptoms. When I quit smoking cigarettes, for example, I went through about five days of irritability, depression, and restlessness. Withdrawal from heroin and other narcotics is much more painful, involving violent cramps, vomiting, diarrhea, and other symptoms that continue for at least two or three days. With some drugs, especially barbiturates, cold-turkey (sudden and total) quitting can result in death, so severe is the withdrawal.

Psychological dependence refers to a need that develops through learning and other nonphysical means. One forms the habit of using the drug, and, like nail-biting, the habit may be hard to break. For example, after my five-day withdrawal from nicotine, I found my battle against cigarettes had just begun. What should I do with my hands? I had used cigarettes as a reward for working hard over a long stretch; now what? It took several months to break the habit of smoking.

AMERICA'S CHEMICAL COMFORTS: AN OVERTURE

As we mentioned, alcohol and marijuana will be discussed in detail later. The other chemical substances commonly called drugs (not including food) will be noted only briefly.

The *narcotics* include opium, morphine, heroin, and methadone. The source of most narcotics is the opium poppy. *Opium* is the dried juice taken from the seed pods, and *morphine* is the active ingredient, extracted by chemical processing. In 1874, scientists discovered that combining morphine with acetic acid (the acid in vinegar) resulted in a chemical compound two or three times stronger than morphine by itself; this new compound was called *heroin* (Davison and Neale, 1978). *Methadone* is a synthetic narcotic, used to treat heroin addicts because it's cheaper and available by prescription. All narcotics are highly addictive, and tolerance develops quickly. Death by overdose is common. Medical uses include pain relief, sedation and sleep, and suppression of coughing (codeine).

The two most common drugs that are legal and do not require a prescription are caffeine and nicotine. *Caffeine* is the active ingredient in coffee, tea, and many cola drinks. It stimulates the central nervous sytem and heart and therefore is often used to stay awake. Heavy use—say, seven to ten cups of coffee per day—has toxic effects, that is, acts like a mild poison. Prolonged heavy use appears to be addicting. *Nicotine* is the active ingredient in tobacco. One of the most addicting of all drugs and one of the most dangerous, at least when obtained by smoking, it has been implicated in lung cancer, emphysema, and heart disease.

The drugs most users call "uppers" are the *stimulants*, including cocaine and the amphetamines. *Cocaine* is extracted from the South American coca plant. It stimulates the central nervous system and its primary effect is euphoria (feeling good). The *amphetamines* (speed) include benzedrine, methedrine, and dexedrine. They increase alertness, which is why many students use them to get through final exams, and they decrease appetite, which is why they are often prescribed for overweight patients. Heavy use leads to paranoia and, often, violent and aggressive reactions to imagined insults. The potential of these stimulants for physical dependency (addiction) is unclear, but habitual use, especially of amphetamines, is extremely dangerous and may result in a mental condition indistinguishable from paranoid schizophrenia (see pp. 498–499).

The "downers" or *depressants* include barbiturates and tranquilizers. Like alcohol, they depress (slow down) central nervous activity, and the effect is generally relaxing. The popular barbiturates are known by their brand names: Nembutal and Seconal, for example. Their effects are similar to alcohol's, and they are highly addictive. The *tranquilizers* (Miltown, Equanil, Librium, Valium, and others) have similar effects but are considered less addicting.

The *hallucinogens* are so named because they often produce hallucinations, usually visual. *LSD* (lysergic acid diethylamide) was discovered in 1943 by a research scientist who extracted it from a fungus and inadvertently tasted it. "Fantastic visions" forced him to interrupt his laboratory work. LSD also can be made synthetically, manufactured from pure chemicals. Its effects include wild, chaotic perceptions and unusual sensations, lasting up to 12 hours; panic reactions (bad trips) are not uncommon (see pp. 99–100). There is some evidence that LSD may have therapeutic use for alcoholics and the mentally ill. *Peyote,* a spineless cactus native to central and northern Mexico, has effects similar to those of LSD. So does *mescaline,* a chemical derived from peyote. None of the hallucinogens is considered addicting.

Two recreational drugs that have become increasingly popular in the last few years are Quaaludes and PCP. Quaaludes (a brand name for methaqualone) seem to fall between barbiturates and tranquilizers in terms of their effects and the potential for physical addiction. After early notoriety as an aphrodisiac, Quaaludes are now considered "just another downer" (Julien, 1975). PCP (phenylcyclidine), sometimes called "angel dust," is used legally as an animal tranquilizer and anesthetic, but its effects on humans are closer to those of hallucinogens. In moderate doses, PCP usually results in a pleasant dreamlike state, but in larger doses and even sometimes, unpredictably, in small doses, it produces panic, paranoia, violent or psychotic behavior, severe depression, and spastic body movements, which users call the "moon walk" (Smith, 1978). Most heavy drug users I know consider PCP a very dangerous drug.

Speaking of dangerous drugs, ordinary drinking water joined the list in 1977, when a young Florida woman died of an overdose (*Newsweek,* March 14, 1977). In an obsessive-compulsive attempt to rid her stomach of imaginary "poisons," she stopped eating and began drinking four gallons of water a day. Her kidneys failed, and she died of "internal drowning" when her lungs filled with fluid. It goes to show that even the safest substance can be dangerous if taken in large quantities over a long enough period.

With this brief introduction to some of the common drugs in America, we will turn to two others: alcohol, a legal drug that is often used and often abused, and marijuana, an illegal drug with a similar record of use and abuse.

ALCOHOL

The alcohol we drink is ethyl alcohol, which manufacturers produce by fermenting the sugar in barley (to make beer), grapes (to make wine), or apples (to make "hard" cider). Some alcohols are then distilled to increase the percentage of alcohol. Most alcoholic beverages—whiskey, gin, vodka, etc.—contain between 40 and 50 percent alcohol. The alcohol content is indicated by the "proof" number, which is twice the percentage. Thus, 100 proof gin contains 50 percent alcohol. This is a much higher percentage of alcohol than is found in beer (usually between 3 and 5 percent) or wine (usually between 10 and 12 percent). On the other hand, gin, whiskey, and the other strong liquors are often served in mixed drinks—an ounce or two of the liquor combined with water or some other non-alcoholic beverage. The result is no more intoxicating than a can of beer or a glass of wine. However, some mixed drinks, like the martini, use another form of alcohol as a mixer, which makes them much stronger.

Alcohol: Who Uses It?

Alcohol is the most widely used drug of all, with one exception—nicotine. The heaviest drinkers are men between 21 and 39 years of age; the lightest drinkers are women over 60. Drinking habits do not vary much with social class (Cahalan et al., 1969), but they do vary with sex, religion, and ethnic group. Protestants are less likely to drink than Catholics or Jews. Italians and Chinese have a very low rate of alcoholism, but Anglo-Saxons and blacks have a high rate.

One particularly interesting thing about the relationship between ethnic background and alcoholism is that it is *not* related to differences in consumption—the actual *amount* of alcohol used. Italians and Jews, for example, have a high rate of consumption but comparatively few alcoholics. There are probably several reasons for this. One is that the children in the ethnic groups less likely to produce alcoholics are taught how to drink at home, usually at a family or religious celebration. They learn early to discriminate between "good drinking" (festive) and "bad drinking" (escapist). It is significant that alcoholics are much less likely than normals to have had their first drink at home (Ullman, 1960).

Alcohol: How Does It Work?

The immediate effect of a small amount of ethyl alcohol, the amount contained in one or two mixed drinks, is to depress the parts of the brain associated with judgment and criticism (Greenberg, 1953). Thus, after a drink or two, many people become less inhibited. They relax, they talk more freely, and their actions are less guarded.

If more is consumed, say the equivalent of five to ten drinks (or beers or glasses of wine), more of the brain is depressed, and motor (behavioral) functions are affected. The drinker cannot walk a straight line, and his or her speech begins to slur.

If the equivalent of a pint of whiskey is consumed quickly, motor behavior may deteriorate to the point where the person is "falling down drunk." Violent shifts in emotion, from euphoria to extreme depression, are also common. With even higher levels of alcohol in the blood, the drinker will probably "pass out"—become unconscious—and there is a chance he or she may even "pass away"—die. "Intoxicated," you know, means "poisoned."

Alcohol's Long-Term Effects

If a person drinks heavily for several years, he or she may suffer damage to the brain and other parts of the body. (Some of these effects may be due to the generally poor diet of most chronic alcoholics.) The liver, which has the job of breaking down alcohol in the body, is strained and develops cirrhosis, a dangerous disease that can cause death. Brain cells are destroyed by alcohol, too, and if enough of them are destroyed, certain mental and behavioral abnormalities result. Hand tremors are common. Whole body tremors have a name: "the shakes." Then there is the scourge of the chronic alcoholic: the feared DTs. DT is short for *delirium tremens*. The condition is characterized by the shakes (*tremens*) plus frightening hallucinations (*delirium*), often of little attacking animals. The person with the DTs often panics, and he may injure himself trying to escape his imaginary hell.

Eventually the chronic alcoholic might end up in a mental hospital. Typically around 25 percent of the males admitted to a mental institution for the first time are diagnosed as alcoholics.

Alcohol's Social Effects

Alcohol may be the worst social problem in the United States. It has been estimated that alcohol abuse costs American industries $10 billion a year in sickness benefits, lowered productivity, and absenteeism (Wolman, 1974). Of every ten arrests made in this country, at least four are for drunkenness (disorderly conduct while drunk, driving while intoxicated, etc.). About half of all homicides are committed by people who have been drinking; about a third occur in bars, cocktail lounges, and other watering holes; and many of the victims (69 percent in a Baltimore study) had alcohol in their blood (Brecher et al., 1972).

The detrimental effect of alcohol on driving is well documented (McCarroll and Haddon, 1962). A driver who has been drinking is about three times as likely to be involved in a fatal automobile accident; all told, drinking drivers kill about 25,000 people a year.

Helping Alcoholics

Alcoholism—alcohol addiction—is usually defined as repeated drinking in amounts that exceed those considered reasonable by the community and that interfere with the person's job, health, or interpersonal relations (Keller, 1962). By conservative estimate, there are over 5 million alcoholics in the United States today (Brecher et al., 1972). Like most addicts, the alcoholic finds it difficult to solve his or her problem alone. Among the many helping agencies, Alcoholics Anonymous (AA) is the most famous. Started in Akron, Ohio, AA is now a nationwide organization of alcoholics who have banded together to help each other keep sober. When a drinking alcoholic joins AA for help, a nondrinking alcoholic becomes his "sponsor," helping him day and night to avoid liquor. Weekly meetings of AA build a new circle of friends who have been through it, people who respect and care about the drinker—and who know all the little tricks, such as, "I'll just cut down to one drink a day."

Psychotherapy also can help the alcoholic. In particular, a type of therapy called *behavior modification* seems to be quite effective (see Chapter 13). The main ingredient in this approach is the pairing of the sight, smell, and taste of alcohol with some unpleasant event—usually an electric shock or chemically induced vomiting. This will usually stop the alcoholic from drinking for a while. Then other forms of therapy can be used to teach the alcoholic how to relax in stress situations that led him to drink before. And, if his drinking was in part caused by the fact that he felt like a general failure in life, he can be taught how to be more assertive and self-confident.

The effectiveness of these treatments often depends on the social environment the alcoholic returns to. Skid Row bums who return to Skid Row because their friends are there are unlikely to remain abstainers for long. Wealthy alcoholics, who live in a world that discourages such "weakness" and that warmly supports those who have "licked their problem," are much less likely to slide back into drinking.

MARIJUANA

Marijuana is a drug that usually consists of the dried leaves and flowering tops of a plant called *Cannabis sativa*. The stalk of the plant contains long, strong fibers used to make linen, canvas, and rope. For this reason the hemp plant, as it used to be called, was grown on farms in the Midwest for many years. Even after marijuana was made illegal in 1937, hemp farming continued to supply rope needed in World War II. And even today the hemp plant flourishes, as a weed, in the Midwest; 156,000 acres of Nebraska is covered by this "evil weed," according to an estimate made in 1969 (Brecher et al., 1972).

Hashish is the dried resin from the Cannabis plant. It is from five to eight times as strong as marijuana. The chemical ingredient in marijuana and "hash" that is responsible for most of the effects is *tetrahydrocannabinol,* abbreviated THC. THC has been produced synthetically; because its dosage is easier to control, it is used in much marijuana research.

Marijuana: Who Uses It?

The number of Americans who have used marijuana at least once was estimated to be about 50 million in 1976 (Zinberg, 1976). Among adults, the increase in use has been dramatic: In 1969, according to a nationwide Gallup survey, only 4 percent had tried pot; by 1973, that figure had tripled, to 12 percent; by 1977, the percentage had doubled again, to 24 percent (Gallup, 1977). Most marijuana users are young: 59 percent of Gallup's respondents between the ages of 18 and 24 had tried it, but only

5 percent of those over 50. Increases among adolescents have also been striking, from 29 percent in 1972 to 40 percent in 1976 among 16- to 17-year-olds, from 10 to 21 percent among 14- to 15-year-olds; the percentage of 12- to 13-year-olds has been stable at 6 percent since 1971 (National Institute on Drug Abuse, 1976). From various national surveys, the increase among college students can be plotted: In 1967, 5 percent said they had tried marijuana; in 1969, 22 percent; in 1970, 42 percent; in 1972, 51 percent; in 1975, 63 percent (Conger, 1977). Most people who use marijuana do so infrequently—once or twice a month, or less (Johnston and Bachman, 1975).

These nationwide averages disguise wide variations from one geographical area to another. Heavy use of marijuana is concentrated on the West Coast and in the Northeast, although these differences are diminishing as marijuana use becomes more widespread (National Institute on Drug Abuse, 1976). In different high schools, use may be as low as 6 percent or as high as 65 percent. Sex differences are also apparent: Males are more likely to smoke pot than females, even among adolescents.

We should not close this section without a historical note. Before 1937, when pot was outlawed, many Americans used it for both medicinal and recreational purposes. There were at least 28 medicinal products containing marijuana on the market in 1937, and the law making possession and use illegal was actively opposed by the American Medical Association. Marijuana was considered an excellent treatment for migraine headaches,

among other ailments. George Washington, our first president, is believed to have kept a little patch of marijuana for "medicinal purposes" (Andrews, 1967).

Marijuana: How Does It Work?

The immediate effects of an average dose of marijuana—one-fourth to two "joints," or marijuana cigarettes, depending on the strength—are euphoria, a sense of time passing more slowly, and a general increase in sensory functioning, so that sights, sounds, tastes, touches, and smells are more pronounced (Hollister, 1971). The increase in sensory functioning probably accounts for the use of pot at rock concerts, which sound better, before meals, which taste better, and before sexual intercourse, which feels better. But, for the same reasons, pot also can amplify a bad situation. Poor food served to someone stoned would probably taste worse. And fear or depression under the influence of pot often becomes panic or despair.

At high doses of THC, hallucinations and fears of "losing control" are more likely. Although marijuana is sometimes classified as a hallucinogen (hallucination-producer), along with LSD, current evidence indicates that hallucinations only result from an overdose of the drug, as they do with alcohol (Brecher et al., 1972).

A number of studies have been done to determine the effect of marijuana on thinking and behavior. Compared to control subjects who had been given a placebo (a neutral substance that looks and tastes like marijuana or THC), subjects who have taken marijuana or THC generally do worse at complex mental tasks, such as mentally multiplying two-digit numbers; but the pot subjects show no deficit at simpler tasks, such as repeating a short list of numbers (Kleinmuntz, 1974).

The effect of marijuana on complex activities such as driving a car is, surprisingly, unclear. Subjects who are not experienced users of pot do poorly in simulated driving tests, but probably because they are so distractible and less able to concentrate on the task at hand. Experienced users are not bad drivers and certainly are much better than drunk drivers (Crancer et al., 1969). Some drivers seem to do better stoned on pot than sober, probably because they are frightened and overcompensating (Klonoff, 1974). It's an interesting research issue, but nobody has good evidence on the effect of marijuana on high-speed freeway driving or in emergency situations. Since a single lapse in concentration is enough for a serious accident, the best recommendation is that one should not drive under the influence.

Marijuana's Long-Term Effects

Almost every hypothesized long-term effect of marijuana use is highly controversial. One of the main reasons is that good research is hard to do. Most of the early studies were natural experiments, in which psychologists compared a group of experienced smokers to a group of subjects who had never smoked. If the smokers showed a higher frequency of some trait—say, abnormal body cells—it was concluded that marijuana caused abnormal body cells. But the smokers differed from the nonsmokers in an infinite number of ways; more of them took other drugs, for example, and the abnormal cells could be as easily attributed to the stronger drugs.

The answer to such confusion is to run a true experiment, comparing the reactions of two randomly formed groups (smokers and nonsmokers) to a certain amount of THC per day for a year or so. However, many scientists would be reluctant to run this study even if they had the time and the funds; with even a slight possibility of brain damage in the pot-smoking subjects, how could they justify it ethically?

So scientists stumble along, trying to do their best with a combination of natural experiments, a few short-term true experiments, and various studies using chimps and rats. We will discuss a few of the major areas of research concern, along with some of the controversial findings (Maugh, 1974a, 1974b; National Institute on Drug Abuse, 1976; Zinberg, 1976).

First, there is some evidence that frequent and prolonged use of marijuana may be hazardous to one's health. Several studies have shown that by altering certain characteristics of body cells, pot seems to affect immune reactions, making the user more susceptible to infection and disease. Several other studies, however, failed to show this effect. Some researchers have noted that the subjects in many of the studies that show no effect have not been "heavy users," where heavy use is defined as smoking several marijuana cigarettes a day for several years; perhaps this can account for the lack of results. But in one carefully controlled investigation, subjects had averaged two joints a day for over three years. During the 18-day study, they were given an oral dose of 210 milligrams of THC a day—the equivalent of 50 to 100 cigarettes! No effect on immune response, compared to control subjects, was observed (Lau et al., 1976).

Prolonged smoking of pot appears to have an adverse effect on the user's throat, bronchial tubes, and lungs. Marijuana tar causes cancer in mice. A study of the lungs of heavy users, average age 21, showed that many had reached a state characteristic of the early stages of cancer. Emphysema also has turned up among young pot smokers. Some scientists have concluded that not only does smoking pot cause the same diseases as smoking cigarettes, but it does so much more quickly, for some reason.

There is also some evidence that prolonged use of marijuana may be hazardous to one's sex life. In studies of male users, frequent use was correlated with less of the male sex hormone; with a diminished number of sperm in the semen; and with sexual problems such as the inability to maintain an erection. Other investigations show no such effect. Like the studies of the immune response, the reasons for the different results in different experiments are unclear.

Finally, there is the highly controversial *amotivational syndrome*. After heavy use over a long period of time, according to several psychologists, pot smokers become sluggish and apathetic ("amotivational" means "without motivation"). Subjects show signs of mental confusion, tiredness, and an inability to describe a complete train of thought. At first, most scientists disregarded these reports as moralistic pronouncements of up-tight physicians who disliked the "freak culture" and didn't understand it; the freaks just weren't motivated to make money. But other researchers claimed it was a valid syndrome, caused by partial brain damage. In support of their claims, they cited a British study showing a decrease of the amount of brain tissue in ten heavy marijuana users. However, the subjects in this study had also used other drugs, including LSD, amphetamines, and alcohol (which is known to cause brain damage), so the results were hardly definitive. Several more recent and more carefully designed studies show no evidence of brain damage, even with heavy use of marijuana. Thus, the bulk of the evidence on this issue so far is clearly and consistently on the side of the pro-marijuana forces.

Three studies of marijuana use in foreign countries (Jamaica, Costa Rica, and Greece) show practically no effects after many years of frequent indulgence (National Institute on Drug Abuse, 1976). In the Jamaica study, for example, the subjects had smoked 7 to 25 cigarettes of relatively powerful Jamaican marijuana per day for between 10 and 25 years. Compared to carefully matched nonusers, the users were no less motivated; they showed no evidence of brain damage; and they had no greater history of infection and disease (as we might expect if their immune reactions were impaired). Marijuana use did not seem to affect heart, liver, or kidneys. There was no evidence of chromosome damage, another claim that often surfaces in discussions of marijuana and other drugs. Mental disorders were equally prevalent among users and nonusers. In sum, frequent use of marijuana over long periods of time had essentially no influence on mental or physical health (Rubin and Comitas, 1976).

From the research so far, it seems fair to say that marijuana is one of the least toxic drugs ever studied. Caution is still indicated, however, as research continues. It would seem a reasonable course of action to consume in moderation, if one must consume at all.

Marijuana's Social Effects

According to the National Commission on Marijuana and Drug Abuse, marijuana is not a major social problem (1972). About the only serious social effects are due to the fact that smoking pot is illegal. Users have no respect for these laws and break them frequently. Sometimes they get caught, and then they are criminals. The police spend a lot of their time and budget busting users and pushers; and many of the lawbreakers lose respect for police and the legal system in general.

SUGGESTED READINGS

Zinberg, N. E. The war over marijuana. *Psychology Today.* December 1976.
   Zinberg, a respected psychiatrist, summarizes the research findings and finds little evidence of harmful effects.

Marihuana and health. Sixth Annual Report to the U.S. Congress from the Secretary of Health, Education, and Welfare, 1976.
   Ordinarily I wouldn't recommend a government publication when "public morality" is an issue — such publications are usually biased and often patent nonsense — but this one tries to be fair and is a good summary of the research. Your congressperson can obtain a copy for you.

Behavioral Objectives

1. List the three major approaches to therapy and identify their goals.
2. Describe the techniques used in psychoanalytic therapy.
3. Describe the techniques used in behavior therapy.
4. Describe the techniques used in humanistic therapy.
5. Define "directive therapy" and identify which therapeutic approaches are directive and which are not.
6. Discuss the advantages and disadvantages of group therapy as compared to individual therapy.
7. Describe some of the problems that are involved in evaluating the effectiveness of therapy.
8. Discuss the tentative conclusions about the effectiveness of various therapies.
9. Define "eclectic psychotherapy" and identify its primary advantage.

CHAPTER

13

Therapies

Fanny was a "doctor" of the Yurok Indian tribe, treating both physical and psychological complaints for a fee. If the ailment was diagnosed as psychological, the entire family of the patient was asked to attend the "psychotherapy" session, to be held in Fanny's living room.

Fanny smokes her pipe "to get into her power." Then she puts her mouth above the navel of the patient and sucks away "the pain"—the physiological cause of the problem, in her theory. Every pain has a mate, so the second pain must be located and also sucked away.

Then Fanny smokes again and dances; she goes into a trance, has a vision. She speaks to the family, accusing one or more of its members of practicing sorcery or perversion. This is the interpersonal cause of the problem, according to Fanny's theory. She will say something like, "I see a man and a woman doing business [having sexual intercourse], although the man has just prayed and should not touch a woman." Invariably, the father, an uncle, or some male of the family confesses it was he. There is much crying and forgiving and hugging all around, and the patient is usually cured (Erikson, 1963).

It's easy enough to see how this method of psychotherapy worked. Fanny, having high social status, was privy to most of the tribal gossip. From this information and from expert readings of facial expressions during her magic act, her accusations were rarely off target. She truly believed that she was pinpointing family disturbances related to the neurotic behavior of the patient, and who can say that she was wrong? The public confession and forgiveness no doubt helped, and the general expression of family solidar-

Figure 13.1   *Belief in the powers of the medicine man is an important part of the healing process. The Navajo child is seated on a "magic" sand painting, which has at least a placebo effect.*

ity was also therapeutic. The sucking of the pains probably functioned as a placebo, effective because the patient thought it would be.

What makes psychotherapy effective? The therapy Fanny practiced seems primitive, even ridiculous, by today's standards—until we consider the healing power it had in that culture. In our culture, what makes psychotherapy effective? In this chapter we will review some of the answers to this question. Some psychologists claim that very few therapies are effective, whereas others view

all therapies as effective at least in the placebo aspects.

Generally speaking, there are three broad traditions of therapy, which, not surprisingly, correspond to the three traditions in personality theories (Chapter 10). Psychoanalytic theory strives for insight and understanding—cognitive goals. Behavior modification intends to change the actions of the individual—behavioral goals. And humanistic therapists work toward self-actualization, which they consider the highest of the motivational goals.

PSYCHOANALYSIS

The primary goal of psychoanalysis is to promote insight into the patient's total personality. In particular, unconscious conflicts are to be brought into consciousness, so they can be integrated with the needs and motives the person is aware of. Also, therapist and patient work to understand the defense mechanisms (pp. 402–404) the patient has been using to help control the anxiety stemming from unconscious conflicts.

In psychoanalysis, two people, the therapist and the patient, are trying to understand one individual, the patient. Usually the therapist perceives conflicts in the personality of the patient before the patient does, and then she or he tries to explain them to the patient, in the form of an *interpretation*. Interpretations, based on the psychoanalytic theory of personality, are made primarily from four types of data gathered from the patient: free associations, dreams, resistances, and a type of interpersonal interaction called transference.

Free Associations

As we have discussed, the method of free associations grew out of Freud's developing the psychoanalytic theory of personality. To review briefly, the patient is asked to put into words whatever comes into her or his mind, even if it seems trivial or disgusting. Free association requires practice, since we are taught from birth not to talk about trivia and vulgarities. It may come to mind that the doctor's ceiling needs painting—the patient is, after all, usually lying on a couch staring at the ceiling—but the patient says nothing, figuring this thought is not about the neurosis, not what the doctor wants. But it *is* what the doctor wants. True enough, in some cases, thoughts about the ceiling may be simply a way of unconsciously avoiding more threatening thoughts, but even this is useful information for the therapist.

Typically, the psychoanalyst uses free associations to form tentative hypotheses about the patient's unconscious conflicts and childhood experiences. Then she puts forward these hypotheses (interpretations) to gather more data. For example, the therapist may begin to suspect that the patient's father was absent for a period of time when the patient was young; she might check this hypothesis simply by asking. If the therapist suspects that the patient unconsciously hates a sister or brother, she may suggest it, looking for verification in a too vigorous denial; the patient "doth protest too much," as Shakespeare put it.

Dreams

Often the therapist asks the patient to report dreams she or he can remember. The interpretation of dreams was one of Freud's major skills, and it was the title of his first major book. As described in the interlude on sleep and dreams (pp. 422–433), Freud's theory of dreams begins with the dream as reported by the patient, called the *manifest content*. Behind the manifest content are the *latent thoughts*, which produce the manifest content in complex ways. The latent thoughts are the target of analysis. Sometimes the latent and manifest content are virtually the same, especially in children, who have not learned to disguise their socially unacceptable impulses. Freud reports a dream of a small boy who was forced to

Figure 13.2 *The Wolf Man's dream. One of Freud's most famous patients recalled a childhood nightmare and drew this scene from memory. In the dream, several wolves were sitting in a tree, silently staring at him. Free association indicated fears of being eaten by wolves and, underlying those fears, castration anxiety.*

give away some of his cherries as a gift; that night the boy dreamed that he had eaten all the cherries by himself (1924).

In adults, however, the distortions that occur between latent and manifest content are many. Some material is simply eliminated in dreams. Other information is modified, pointing indirectly to the true material; the more prohibited the thought, the more severe the distortion. Certain symbolic representations are frequent, perhaps even universal: Kings and queens regularly translate into fathers and mothers. The penis is represented by objects that resemble it in form— poles, trees—or in its penetrating functions —knives, guns. (As a teacher of mine once put it, anything longer than it is wide can be a phallic symbol.)

In practice, the analyst develops a guess about the latent meaning of part of the manifest content and then tests this hypothesis in various ways. She or he can have the patient free associate to the dream element to see if the associations are in line with the interpretation: The series, "Knife."—"Stab. Gun. Cowboy. Hurt. Rape." would be seen as quite different from "Knife."—"Fork. Dinner. Fireplace. Wine." Or the analyst can state her or his hunches to test the patient's reaction to them.

Resistances

Ideas are repressed for a reason. Anxiety and neurotic fatigue may have driven the patient to seek help, but this does not mean her or his unconscious mind will immediately cough up its deepest and darkest secrets. Resistances to therapy are therefore prime clues to the nature of the underlying conflict.

Resistance can take many forms. It can be a blank, something missing from memory or in the middle of an otherwise logical sequence. It can be an overly vigorous denial of an interpretation by the analyst. It can be a too easy, unemotional acceptance of an interpretation. At the extreme, the patient might reject therapy, leave, and never return. Often patients rationalize their resistances: One patient kept hidden a heated love affair because "that sort of thing is private."

If a patient objects to an interpretation offered by the analyst, how can the analyst tell whether this is a resistance, covering some unconscious conflict, or a legitimate objection, indicating simply that the interpretation is wrong? A skilled psychoanalyst is always wary of making quick judgments and constantly tests her hypotheses in the ongoing therapy. Only as she gathers evidence from several sources does the analyst gain confidence in her interpretations.

Transference

Transference refers to an emotional attachment of the patient to the analyst that cannot be easily explained. Most psychoanalysts believe that the emotion and other characteristics of the relationship are transferred from a relationship in the patient's past. Recall the extreme emotional attachment of Breuer's patient, Bertha, who went so far as to "give birth" to an imaginary child for him. In less extreme cases, the patient commonly believes that she or he is simply feeling a normal attraction to—or dislike for—the analyst as a person. In fact, the attraction or dislike often is reasonable in its character, but not in its intensity. Young girls act like daughters to elderly male therapists; older women play the lover. Male patients want to be the "buddy" of the male analyst, the lover of the female analyst. Or the emotion may be negative, hostile in the extreme.

When psychotherapists first encountered transferences, they considered these emo-

"...and the reason I hated my father was because he always expected little favors from me."

tional reactions nuisances, impediments to therapeutic progress. It soon became evident that quite the opposite was the case: The very conflict the therapist was trying to unearth by free association, dream analysis, and other techniques was being enacted in real life before her or his eyes. The therapist was suddenly thrown into the role of mother or father or sibling (or all three at once) and made the target of the patient's hopes and fears, lovings and hatings. Once psychoanalysts realized what was happening, transference reactions became a rich source of clues for analysis and interpretation.

Transference involves emotions that are not easily mistaken. They seem so out of line with reality that the therapist would have to be very egotistical to imagine that she or he has earned all that affection (or hostility). The patient may even slip and call the therapist by the name of her or his father or mother. The therapist must be careful to respond to this love or hate in a neutral way —not an easy task. It is nice to be loved, and it hurts to be the target of hostilities, whatever the source of the emotions. In addition, the therapist, like all of us, has her or his own conflicts, and may transfer them to the patient (countertransference). To avoid these problems, among others, every psychoanalyst is required to undergo analysis before treating patients.

Interpretations, Right and Wrong

Psychoanalysts are often accused of making interpretations that are impossible to verify. It is worthwhile, therefore, to present Freud's view on the validity of psychoanalytic interpretations, one with which you may agree or disagree. Freud agreed that any single interpretation could easily be wrong, in part or in total; that is why the analyst must continually test her or his interpretations in further exchanges with the patient. The whole personality, however, is unique and like a jigsaw puzzle: Once all the fragments are in the right place, you *know* you have the solution (Fenichel, 1945). This is an interesting approach to truth, holding that how well statements fit together (cohere) is the important consideration, rather than how well each statement alone corresponds to the "real" world (the usual scientific approach). The coherence approach is a respectable position, one that every scientist uses, consciously or not, in addition to the traditional correspondence approach (Rychlak, 1968). Psychologists, for example, tend to disbelieve the empirical and experimental evidence for ESP because they cannot make ESP fit (cohere) with their other theoretical notions about the universe.

BEHAVIOR THERAPIES

The primary goal of behavioral therapies is to modify the behavior patterns of the subject. Derived from social behavior theories of personality (see Chapter 10), behavior therapies concentrate on the stimuli that precede a response and on the outcome or consequences of the response. To modify these response patterns, behavior therapists first examine the individual and her or his environment to determine the conditions responsible for the present behaviors. Then, more importantly, they decide on procedures to change the behaviors that led the person to seek help.

Behavior therapy is very effective with fairly specific problems. I had a friend who was relatively normal except for the fact that he panicked whenever he took a major examination in school. He was very bright, always able to write "A" term papers, but final exam situations were so anxiety-provoking for him that he could not concentrate, and he often failed. He sought help from a local behavior therapist, who trained him to relax in test situations. Within three months, my friend was matching the As of his term papers with As on his exams. The method used in treatment, desensitization, will be discussed later in this chapter under Counterconditioning.

Behavior therapies involve many different methods. We will discuss briefly five of the most common: positive reinforcement, extinction, counterconditioning, aversive control, and modeling.

Positive Reinforcement

If a choice is possible, the carrot is more effective than the stick in getting the donkey to move. As we saw in Chapter 4, *positive reinforcement*, rewarding good behavior, is generally preferable to *aversive control*, punishing bad behavior.

Positive reinforcement is most appropriate when desired behaviors are not occurring: The child does *not* play with the group. The patient *won't* cooperate with the therapist. The criminal *won't* identify "Mr. Big." Very often, in these situations, the rewards for undesirable behavior are stronger than the rewards for more desirable acts. The withdrawn child elicits the attention and

Figure 13.3 *What rewards or punishments have made this child withdraw? What would you do to get her back into the group?*

comforting responses of her or his parent or teacher and is thus reinforced for withdrawing; the criminal wins the respect of peers. The goal of behavioral therapy is to decrease reinforcement for undesirable behavior and increase it for desirable behavior.

In one case, psychologists observed an extremely withdrawn boy to determine the rewards he was getting in his nursery school environment (Harris et al., 1964). This child spent about 80 percent of his time alone. His teacher took no particular notice of the few times he did join in the activities of other children, but tried to console him when he was withdrawing. The psychologists in-

structed the teacher to reinforce social behavior instead of isolation: to ignore the boy when he was by himself, and when he joined a group, to give the group full attention. The effect was immediate. The child soon spent 60 percent of his time in interaction with others, compared to only 20 percent before. Gradually, the teacher played less of a role, as the child began to find rewards in the group interaction itself.

Sometimes the positive reinforcements a client is to receive, and for what, are discussed at length by therapist and client and then written up in the form of a contract (see Figure 13.4). Such a procedure, called *contin-*

Figure 13.4   *A contingency contract designed to encourage responsible behavior by a father and a son. Spelling out the details of an agreement and getting it in writing are often more effective than vague promises and threats, for mental patients as well as anyone.*

Son agrees to:
1. Carry out garbage pail each day.
2. Work six hours on Saturday every week. Work will consist of anything that he is capable of doing, such as hoeing, weeding, washing the car, or helping father, and so forth.

Father agrees to:
1. Pay $4 per week for above work each week (Saturday).

Both parties agree to the following conditions:
1. Penalty for failing to carry out garbage after being reminded will be reduction of 25¢ for each failure.
2. Penalty for not working on Saturday when work is available will be 40¢ per hour unless condition is covered by another condition.
3. When no work is available due to bad weather or father unable to supervise, $1 per Saturday will be paid.
4. Reevaluation after a trial period of three weeks.
5. If son is sick, there will be no penalty reduction on garbage detail, and $1 will be paid for Saturday. A total of $2 will be paid under this condition.

Signed: _____   Signed: _____
　　　　　　　　(Father)　　　　　　　　　　　　　　　　(Son)

From Dinoff, M., and Richard, H. D. Learning that privileges entail responsibility. In I. D. Krumbaltz and C. E. Thoresen (Eds.), *Behavior counseling: Cases and techniques.* New York: Holt, Rinehart and Winston, 1969.

gency contracting, has the advantage of specifying clearly the goals of therapy and the consequences (positive or negative) of achieving those goals (Harmatz, 1978). A juvenile delinquent, for example, might sign a contract in which certain behaviors — attending school, observing a curfew — will bring privileges agreed to by her or his family — money, use of the family car.

Extinction

Extinction occurs when one stops reinforcing a behavior one wants to eliminate. This technique is particularly suitable for patients whose problems include obnoxious, criminal, self-destructive, or otherwise undesirable behaviors. One schizophrenic patient was a "talker"; she blabbed on and on in jumbled speech filled with her generally uninteresting personal delusions. Other patients found her so obnoxious that they threatened her and, on occasion, beat her severely. The nurses, on the other hand, rewarded her talking with sympathy and attention, in an effort to understand her psychosis. Psychologists instructed the nurses to ignore the woman's psychotic speech. Again the effect was dramatic. In a short time, the woman reduced her psychotic verbal output to about 25 percent of its former level, while increasing her "sensible" speech (which the nurses were careful to reward). This happened in spite of the long-standing nature of her problem — three years of relentless, psychotic babbling (Ayllon and Michael, 1959).

Counterconditioning

Counterconditioning is the process by which a patient learns a new response to a stimulus, one that is incompatible with the unwanted response. If you decide that every time you want a cigarette, you will chew a stick of gum instead, you are attempting a form of counterconditioning. This technique is often used to treat patients who suffer from abnormal learned fears in certain stimulus situations. Phobias, for example, are effectively treated by counterconditioning; you remember my friend with his great fear of taking exams. That particular kind of counterconditioning, where the response of fear or anxiety is replaced by the incompatible response of relaxation, is called *desensitization* (Wolpe, 1958, 1969).

A common counterconditioning procedure begins with a careful assessment of situations in which the patient experiences anxiety. Someone with an extreme fear of snakes, for example, might fear most a snake crawling on her. She would be slightly less fearful of simply touching a snake; better would be looking at a snake from across the room; and touching a toy snake made of cotton would hardly bother her at all.

The incompatible response the therapist hopes to attach to these situations is usually relaxation. In this desensitization procedure clients are first taught how to relax, often with the aid of machines that measure bodily signs of relaxation (see Focus: Biofeedback, pp. 52–53). Once the client knows how to relax, she is exposed to the situations that usually make her anxious. First she is exposed to a situation that might make her just a little anxious, and she is told to try to relax. If she can be calm in the presence of a toy snake made of cotton, she is told to imagine looking at a real snake from across the room. Then she imagines touching a real snake, and so on, up the line to her greatest fears. Surprisingly, if the patient can relax while imagining these potentially traumatic events, she usually finds that she can then relax while actually experiencing them.

Counterconditioning can be applied in situations other than those involving anxiety or fear, and it can use incompatible responses other than relaxation. (These cases are not called desensitization.) Unusual sexual practices are often treated in this manner. Consider an abnormal sexual response to some object, say a handbag. (This behavior pattern is called fetishism.) The stimulus (fetish) is a handbag; the response is sexual arousal. In place of the pleasurable sexual response, the therapist will try to attach aversive responses such as nausea or avoidance of shock. One such patient was "cured" by being presented with a collection of handbags while experiencing chemically induced nausea (Raymond, 1956).

Behavior therapists often use counterconditioning to treat addictions of various kinds, including drug addiction, cigarette addiction, and alcoholism. Typically, either the patient is caused to vomit soon after taking the undesirable drug, or she or he is given a chemical that interacts with the drug to produce very unpleasant side effects (Bandura, 1969; Stolz et al., 1975).

Assertiveness Training

Many people are unable to express their desires or feelings openly to other people because of nervousness (anxiety), shyness, or a lack of self-confidence. As a result, they feel incompetent, exploited, and generally miserable. Many behavior therapists conceive of this as a situation calling for counterconditioning: The timid response usually

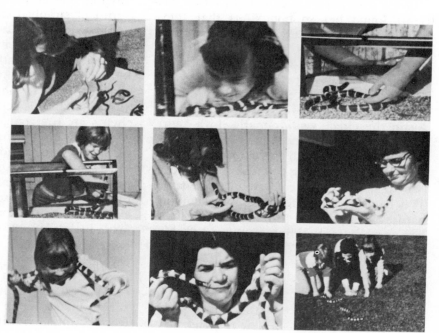

Figure 13.5 *People with extreme fears (phobias) of snakes were treated by desensitization. First they were asked to touch rubber snakes, then to look at live snakes in a glass enclosure, then to handle snakes while wearing rubber gloves. Eventually they were able to interact with snakes without fear.*

elicited by an encounter with another person needs to be replaced by an assertive response that states the client's feelings honestly and straightforwardly (Korchin, 1976).

Assertiveness training often begins with a discussion between therapist and client of threatening situations and the behavior that would be effective in such situations. You have ordered a steak rare, for example, and a gloomy waiter brings you a piece of meat burned beyond recognition. What do you say? Reasonable and unreasonable replies are discussed. The client might be asked to play a role in a mini-drama, with the therapist as waiter. Or the client might watch the therapist play the diner while someone else plays the waiter. Perhaps both therapist and client will venture forth to a real restaurant, to test new ideas, new assertive responses. Other situations that elicit submissiveness are similarly explored: Someone cuts in line in front of you at the supermarket. Someone you dislike asks you for a date. A friend asks you to do a favor you'd rather not.

With training, shy people gain in feelings of self-efficacy (personal power). As they become more assertive, they find that people do not hate them simply because they stand up for their rights or express their feelings. They experience the rewards of effective interpersonal interaction. A few become so assertive that they become absolute bores.

Aversive Control

If a response is followed by negative consequences, it is unlikely to be repeated. This fact of human nature is the basis for the use of punishment to control behavior, a practice more widespread than it deserves to be. Punishment is rewarding to the person doing the punishing because its effects are usually immediate, but the effects are generally less enduring than those of other techniques. There also can be undesirable side effects on the person punished, such as unspoken hostility or guilt. Administered with knowledge and compassion, however, punishment can be an effective procedure for modifying behavior, especially if used in conjunction with other techniques.

Aversive control (the behaviorist's technical term for using punishment to control behavior) is the most humane method of treatment for some problems. Schizophrenic children, for reasons not clearly understood, often seem to try to injure themselves. (Normal children sometimes do this too, but not as often.) At the extreme, some children have been known to bang their heads on sharp objects or bite off pieces of their own flesh. There is a serious risk of permanent injury in such cases, and therefore the children must be constantly restrained.

Aversive control has been used to eliminate these harmful behaviors and allow the children to move about freely. It was demonstrated that if people around such a child reacted to her or his self-destructive behavior with affection and sympathy, the child generally increased such acts, but children who were punished suppressed the behavior (Lovaas et al., 1965). If the child was punished for self-destructive behavior and simultaneously rewarded for other, more socially acceptable acts like talking to the therapist or playing with other children, then the punishment had an enduring effect, not simply a temporary suppressive one.

Often the punishment need be little more than brief social withdrawal—the therapist stops interacting with the child for a time if she starts banging her head. If this doesn't

Figure 13.6 *Aversive control of drinking. As the problem drinker takes in the sights, smells, and tastes of a bar, he receives an electric shock at his left hand. Eventually the whole bar environment becomes associated with unpleasant feelings.*

work, painful shocks sometimes help. One such case involved a boy who had had occasional periods of self-destructive behavior for five years. He was treated in the midst of one of these periods, when he would hit himself at a rate of about thirty times a minute for an hour and a half (Bucher and Lovaas, 1968). To modify this behavior, a shock was delivered whenever the boy hit himself. In just four therapy sessions, involving a total of twelve shocks, the boy's self-destructive behavior was essentially eliminated.

Contingency contracts can be written to threaten aversive consequences for "bad" behavior just as easily as to promise positive reinforcement for "good" behavior. In one study (Boudin, 1972), a drug abuser agreed to a contract with her therapist which directed him to send $50 of *her* money to the Ku Klux Klan (an organization she hated) whenever she failed in her attempts to give up amphetamines. After two years under this contract, she was still clean as a whistle.

Aversive control should always be used with care. The therapist must be sure that the punished response is not the only way the patient or client can gain a desired and acceptable reward, because then punishment is likely to be totally ineffective (Herman and Azrin, 1964). If a child's only means of gaining the attention of her parents is by cranky, obnoxious behavior, then punishment will more likely lead to an increase in crankiness than to a decrease. If punishment is the only kind of attention she can get, then she will work to achieve it.

"Today we'll try aversion therapy. Every time you say something stupid, I'll spill a bucket of water on your head."

© *1980 by Sidney Harris*

Modeling

One of the most significant recent contributions to behavior therapy is the technique of *modeling*, largely defined and developed by Albert Bandura (1969, 1977b). In modeling, one person (the model) does something, and another person (the observer or client) watches, learning by observation. Bandura claims that virtually everything people learn from direct experience can also be learned through observation. Practice is still necessary to develop one's skills, of course, such as in playing golf, but even for skill learning, watching an accomplished model is highly instructive (see Figure 13.7).

Modeling offers several advantages as a therapy. For one, a *group* of patients can watch a filmed model and benefit as individuals, without the high cost of individual therapy or the demands on the therapist. Also, patients can be exposed to and can learn new behaviors that they would not be likely to learn otherwise. A patient can observe someone else in a situation she or he has learned to avoid because of fear and can

Figure 13.7 *Teaching by example. Having seen how it is done and that no unpleasant consequences result, the next child will be more skilled and less fearful when her turn comes.*

see that the natural consequences of trying the activity are nothing to be afraid of. A good illustration of this is a case that involved children who were abnormally afraid of dogs. When they watched another child playing happily with a friendly dog, their fears were significantly reduced (Bandura et al., 1967).

Children who are severely withdrawn from human contacts — often they are called *autistic*, which means self-oriented (see p. 493) — usually lack the behavioral skills of other children their age. People normally learn these skills largely through interactions with others, so it is no wonder that autistic children are deficient. Behavior therapists see their primary task in such a case to be teaching these various skills. Modeling appropriate behaviors — how to talk, how to brush one's hair or put on one's clothes, for example — works well in many of these cases. One group of therapists used a combination of modeling and positive reinforcement to teach mute autistic children to speak (Lovaas et al., 1966). First the therapist would make a sound and reinforce the child for imitating it; then she or he would speak actual words for the child to imitate. A similar procedure has been used to teach children how to play by themselves or with others, and how to get along with other children (Lovaas et al., 1967).

Relapses and Self-control

Behavior therapists often lead patients to the point where they are behaving normally, without much anxiety, only to find them lapsing into their previous tense and bizarre life style when they return home. Since the behavior therapist believes that the patient's undesirable behaviors were originally learned in her or his home environment and were maintained by it, some recurrence of symptoms is to be expected when the patient returns home. The problem is how to make relapses less likely or less serious — a problem that has not received the research attention it deserves (Kazdin, 1978).

One obvious way to deal with relapses is to change the patient's home environment. In some cases, this is possible, at least to some extent. Parents of a child undergoing behavioral therapy can be taught the basic principles of behavior modification so that they can reward desirable behaviors and extinguish obnoxious behaviors. Married couples treated together have a better chance than those treated individually, because the therapist can observe their interactions and point out dangerous aspects. But typically the environment is much too broad to control adequately. Most juvenile delinquents, for example, have a poor family situation and a street scene that rewards aggressive if not criminal behavior. In these cases, the therapist must try to teach the patient self-control.

To teach a patient self-regulation, the therapist begins by using ordinary rewards and punishments to encourage the desired behavior. Then she or he teaches the patient to evaluate her own performance so she knows when she deserves a reward, even if she is not yet the person who delivers it. Finally the patient takes control of delivering the reward, too. To illustrate, consider a boy learning to play the piano. At first the teacher and parents must reward his improvements with lavish praise and sometimes material benefits. Eventually the boy learns to distinguish good notes and passages from poor, sloppy performance; he learns to identify those instances which deserve a reward. He takes pride (a self-reward) in a well-played piece, and feels shame (a self-punishment) when he performs below what have become his own *internal* standards. Eventually, too, good performance will bring other rewards—he will be able to play more different pieces, and perhaps even earn money and prestige by playing with an orchestra or a rock band.

HUMANISTIC THERAPIES

Although a variety of definitions is possible, I am using the term *humanistic* to refer to therapies that focus on self-actualization. Self-actualization, in turn, has been defined as "becoming the best you can be" (Maslow, 1970). To illustrate the kinds of therapy practiced with such views, we can begin with the *client-centered therapy* developed by Carl Rogers.

Client-Centered Therapy

Humanistic therapists in general, and Carl Rogers in particular, assume that human beings have powerful tendencies to cure their own psychological problems if given half a chance. The therapist, therefore, does not seek out the history of the individual's problem, as the psychoanalyst does, nor does she or he concentrate on replacing a particular unsatisfactory behavior pattern, as the behavior therapist does. Instead, the client-centered therapist attempts to set up conditions in which the individual's innate self-actualizing tendencies can express

Figure 13.8 *In client-centered therapy, the therapist tries to "reflect" the conflicts and feelings of the client, and avoids giving direct advice.*

themselves. These conditions are part of the therapeutic environment the client-centered therapist tries to establish, an environment we will examine in a moment.

According to Rogers's theory, people seek help from a therapist when they are in a state of *incongruence* (Rogers, 1959). Incongruence means there is a discrepancy between the way the client perceives herself and the reactions she gets from other people. Perhaps she sees herself as a liberal, easy-going person, but others respond to her as if she were very moralistic and easily offended. She finds these puzzling reactions to her well-meaning behavior both unpleasant and threatening, because she cannot understand them. She is anxious and often depressed.

The goal of therapy and the outcome of successful therapy is congruence, with its by-products: less anxiety, less depression, and a clearer path to self-actualization. But how is this goal to be achieved? By instituting the conditions that promote self-actualizing processes.

The Therapeutic Environment. To allow clients to help themselves, the therapist should provide an environment with three essential characteristics. First, the therapist should be able to perceive accurately what is happening in her own interactions with a client; she should not go along with the client's defensive distortions. In Rogers's terms, she should be *congruent,* instead of *incongruent,* as the client is. For example, if the client starts criticizing her for unethical behavior, the therapist should recognize this as part of the client's problems and not react indignantly.

Second, the therapist should have *empathetic understanding* of the client's thoughts and feelings. (*Empathy* means

thinking and feeling like the other person.) She should understand that her client's self-doubts and even self-pity represent an honest and earnest attempt to become a better person, even if this attempt comes off as an irritating self-centeredness.

The third condition is that the therapist feel *unconditional positive regard* for the client. By this Rogers means that the client is to be considered a human being, something of great value, no matter what she or he thinks or does. The positive regard does not depend on "good" behavior. This does not mean all behaviors are accepted as of great value; a particular act may be noted as evil or stupid, but, nevertheless, the client as a person remains highly valued. (This respect for the person is why humanistic therapists use the term "client" rather than "patient." "Patient," according to Rogers, sets up the doctor as an authority figure, and he prefers a "person-to-person" interaction.)

If the therapist can set up an interpersonal interaction with these characteristics, the client will begin to express her or his feelings more openly. Perceiving the therapist's unconditional positive regard, the client will let secret thoughts and feelings come out; it is like talking to a very close friend, someone you feel able to expose yourself to without fear of being condemned or disliked. The therapist's congruence (accurate perceptions) and empathy (perceptions of the client's inner thoughts and feelings) allow her to participate positively in the process of therapy. Together the therapist and the client discuss and clarify the problems and review possible solutions.

The Role of the Therapist. The therapist's role in this process is very nondirective. She is to listen carefully to understand the content of what the client is saying and also the feelings conveyed. She gives her impression of how the client feels about a topic and points out discrepancies that may occur between content and feelings—"Why do you feel no pride at your promotion?"—but she refrains from offering insight, advice, disapproval, or direction to the flow of conversation. The client is to manage her or his own cure—this responsibility is made clear at the outset—and it is the client who decides the topic of discussion, the length of time spent exploring it, and the interpretations to be made from it. To illustrate, here is a brief therapeutic exchange between Rogers and a client. The client has expressed the view that she doesn't need to come in for therapy as often as before.

Rogers: By and large, you feel you are getting close to the end.
Client: I think so. How does one determine?
Rogers: Just the way you are determining.
Client: Oh, is that so? Just by feeling that you don't have to come as often?
Rogers: When you are ready to call it quits, why, we'll call it quits.
Client: Uh huh, and then no return, uh?
Rogers: Oh, yes, if you feel you want to. (Rogers, 1951, pp. 85–86.)

Notice that the responsibility is placed squarely on the shoulders of the client. Although she has been in therapy for quite a while, she still throws out feelers to see if she can get Rogers to give more direction and explicit advice, but he remains slippery; it is up to her.

Results of Client-Centered Therapy. Rogers has always had the admirable trait of doing and encouraging research on his therapy. Not many therapists do this. Research on therapies is costly and time-consuming, and it is difficult to define a reasonable dependent variable. What is a "cure"? What is "personal growth"? But Rogers believes that some data, even with these problems, are better than none at all.

Most of the research has attempted to trace how well various parts of clients' personalities were integrated at various points in therapy. The idea of this approach is that reorganization and increased integration of the personality are the major goals and outcomes of successful therapy. Often therapy sessions have been recorded, and researchers have analyzed the tapes to see how and when the clients referred to themselves. A number of studies found that early references were mainly negative or ambivalent, but clients made increasingly positive statements about themselves in cases judged to be successfully resolved (Raimy, 1948).

Another typical study had clients categorize statements about themselves (Butler and Haigh, 1954). The statements were usually of the form, "I am _____," with endings such as "a hard worker," "likable," and "often anxious" to fill in the blank. The categories ranged from "Most like me" to "Least like me," and the client had to put a certain number of statements in each category. In the study cited, this was done twice, once for "My real self" and once for "My ideal self," defined as the person the client would most like to be. In a normal, control group, the average correlation between real- and ideal-self sortings was .58, but in the group seeking therapy, it was zero. After therapy, this figure rose to .34, indicating, in Rogers's terms, a greater congruence between the clients' reality and their wishes about their selves.

Group Therapy

Therapy in group settings is possible with any approach to treatment, but the humanistic therapies are particularly suitable for it. Group therapy for people with psychiatric problems became widespread after World War II; neurotic soldiers were returning in numbers simply too great to be treated in individual sessions. Since the soldiers had had roughly similar experiences, group discussions under the watchful eye of a clinical psychologist or psychiatrist were more than usually useful.

The advantages of group therapy go beyond economy and convenience, however. There are diagnostic advantages: Many people exhibit their "problems of living" only in interpersonal settings, especially when interacting with someone who is not an authority figure like the therapist, but simply another person with problems. In groups, people have more chance to express hostility and dependence, and an individual's typical reaction to frustration or insult often can only be observed directly in group interactions.

Another advantage of the group setting is that it acts as a miniature version of society, where clients can try out new modes of adapting to reality with less threat than in the real world. A timid woman can express indignation and discover that the world does not therefore come crashing down around her ears. A belligerent male can cry and show compassion, and his fears that he will be laughed at turn out to be untrue.

Origins of Group Therapy. Traditional group therapy involves groups whose members have come to find solutions to mental or emotional problems. The goal in these groups is normal adjustment. Another major category includes groups whose members share a specific problem—drug addiction, alcoholism, or obesity, for example.

Figure 13.9 *For therapy, problem solving, and personal growth, people get together to "get it together." Sometimes groups communicate with words, sometimes with touching, sometimes with shared experiences.*

Perhaps the largest number of groups, however, are made up of people who have no urgent problem; they join such groups to self-actualize, to improve themselves in some way. Along with Carl Rogers, Abraham Maslow has provided much of the philosophical basis for such groups (pp. 258–261). It is indeed characteristic of humanistic therapies that they do not stop at "normal," but go onward (and upward?) to try to achieve the truly *healthy* personality.

Self-improvement groups had their beginnings after World War II, like the therapeutic groups, but their main purpose was to aid big business. Big corporations had come to rely more and more on committees for major decisions, and they turned to psychology for advice on how best to solve problems in the committee (group) situation. It was soon discovered that personal rather than logical factors were responsible for most breakdowns in problem-solving processes. One member would propose a very good solution, but other members would reject it simply because they were unwilling to accept any suggestion from such a pompous SOB.

The original problem-solving groups were called "training groups," or *T-groups,* for short. When they began to focus on people's reactions to each other, they were called "sensitivity T-groups" or just plain *sensitivity groups.* Members of sensitivity groups learn, usually by interaction and interpretation, how to recognize the emotional reactions their actions provoke in other people.

Encounter Groups. *Encounter groups* developed partly from the sensitivity groups and partly from the therapeutic groups run with a humanistic point of view. An *encounter,* in the humanistic definition, is "real" interaction with another human being: open and honest, not "playing games," not hiding behind polite behavior and social roles. In terms of Rogers's theory, people should enter an encounter with unconditional positive regard, empathy, and congruence.

Most encounter groups begin by establishing social rules that are usually different from those in everyday social interactions. You must be honest and open. Express your feelings. Touching is permitted. Crying is permitted. Hostility is permitted. Think about these rules (or social norms, as they are often called). Being open about your emotions doesn't sound radical, but in most of our ordinary interactions—say with a banker or even a casual friend—such behaviors are taboo, not allowed. We get so used to keeping our true feelings under cover that we are often afraid to show them even in situations where they are appropriate, as when a woman finds she cannot be open and honest even with her best friend. Many people have a vague fear that if they tell the truth about their feelings, other people will despise them. In the encounter group, they discover not only that other people can be sympathetic, but that many of them share the same fears and emotions.

There are potential disadvantages to group therapy. Many psychologists feel that the interactions in group situations are too superficial to be of much benefit. A patient with deep-seated conflicts may be better treated by a psychotherapist in individual therapy; the therapist can exert consistent pressure, refusing to let the patient avoid the crucial issues, and she or he can control the therapeutic environment more effectively. Another criticism of groups is that they are too powerful. If the group starts to focus on one individual's defense mechanisms—which are used for a reason, remember—

that individual might break down. If no trained therapist is present — which is often the case in encounter groups — the result can be disastrous.

(You might note that the two major criticisms — too superficial, too dangerous — are incompatible. Incompatible criticisms are often a sign that research is necessary; in the case of encounter groups, research is sadly lacking.)

F O C U S

A Brief Encounter

In an exchange that occurred in an actual group session, two men — call them Sam and Harry — squared off. Sam said, "Harry, I've been listening to you and watching you for a day and a half, and I think you're a phony."

This remark is dangerous. It is honestly expressed, but it is a judgment about Harry, not an admission of Sam's feelings. How can Harry reply? "You're full of bananas!"? He is boxed in, with no reasonable response.

A good group leader senses the problem and asks Sam about the feelings that led him to make the judgment. He thus puts the focus on Sam, relieving Harry. But Sam does not know how to express feelings. He says, "Well, I *feel* that Harry is a phony." The leader presses: How does his phoniness make you feel? "It annoys the hell out of me." Another member of the group jumps in: "What kinds of things has Harry done that annoyed you, Sam?"

A potentially dangerous remark has now become interesting and potentially valuable to both Harry and Sam. Harry is about to learn about behaviors that led at least one person to think of him as a phony. Sam is learning to distinguish his feelings from evaluations, and his answer to the last question will elicit group reactions. Does Harry's behavior annoy others? Is it Harry's problem? Sam's problem? Or both?

Several additional questions were necessary to get all of Sam's answer, but finally it came out that he was annoyed by Harry's "smooth ways" with women and especially with the apparent success of these ways. In a word, Sam was jealous. He couldn't admit this feeling, however, without group analysis and group support; instead he tried to bolster his own ego by seeing himself as a "sincere" person and Harry as a "phony."

How about Harry? Harry learned a lot, too, from this brief encounter. Further discussion of Harry's interaction with women turned up admissions from other men in the group that they too felt jealous and competitive toward Harry. The group setting is especially useful for learning whether one person's reaction is or is not unique. Harry was thus faced with a decision about his interactions with women, interactions that were rewarding to him but that produced jealousy and hostility in other men. He could modify his behavior—the group would help him—or, of course, he could choose to do nothing. The important thing is that he has the choice to make; before joining the group Harry did not know how others saw him. Becoming aware of choices may be the most valuable outcome of encounter group experiences. (Adapted from Aronson, 1976.)

IS PSYCHOTHERAPY EFFECTIVE?

There's an old saying that, left untreated, a cold will last two weeks, but, treated with medicine *X*, it will be gone in 14 days. Many illnesses, left untreated, clear up by themselves, and mental illnesses are no exception. Most people are first seen by a therapist when they are at their worst, and normally occurring changes in their body chemistry, home environment, and ability to cope often result in some improvement, no matter what the therapist does.

A patient's improvement is of course reinforcing to the therapist, whether or not she or he had anything to do with it. The patient or client came in with certain complaints, the therapist provided treatment, and the patient improved. It is only human nature for the therapist to think she or he was influential in the process of change. But human nature is not always good science. In this section we will examine some of the research bearing on the question, Is psychotherapy really effective? It is a *very* controversial topic.

The Eysenck Paper

Hans Eysenck, a British psychologist, reviewed a number of studies on the effectiveness of therapies, including psycho-analysis and humanistic therapies but not behavioral therapies (1952). He found that about one-half to two-thirds of the patients (mostly neurotics) improved, regardless of the particular therapy. He then reviewed other studies to estimate the rate of improvement in people who received no psychotherapy at all. He discovered that about two-thirds of these people improved. Is psychotherapy effective? Eysenck's answer was a resounding no!

The Eysenck paper was immediately challenged, of course. Most critics attacked his use of one particular study (Denker, 1946) as a primary source of data on improvement rates in untreated neurotics. These data came from the files of an insurance company. The subjects, around 500 total, claimed disability benefits because of neurosis; they were given what was called "superficial" therapy by general-practice physicians: sedatives, tonics, suggestion, and reassurance. "Cure," to an insurance company, is clearly defined: They stop paying benefits! To the individual involved, this usually meant she or he had recovered sufficiently to return to work. Within one year, 45 percent had been cured, and, in the next year, another 27 percent returned to work, leading to the estimate of "72 percent cured" in two years with no more than superficial treatment.

The critics complained that no evidence was (or could be) presented on how superficial the therapy of a general practitioner was. Certainly these were not *untreated* patients who recovered *spontaneously*. And if the amount and depth of therapy is unclear, the quality of the "cure" is even less so. Although most of the cured patients returned to work, some were called cured simply because they "relinquished compensation"; we can only guess what that means. Those who went to work did not necessarily return to their previous jobs. One psychologist pointed out that the people under study became neurotic during an economic recession and were cured during a period of economic recovery (Cartwright, 1955). In any case, many full-blown neurotics can function in society, so a return-to-work definition of "cure" is not acceptable to most psychotherapists. At least we can say that a 72 percent spontaneous cure rate in two years is exaggerated.

Eysenck replied, saying he agreed the data were questionable. He agreed there were no good data to support the claim that therapy is ineffective; but also, he asserted, there are no good data to support the opposite claim, that psychotherapy is effective. The only studies available suggest that psychotherapy is ineffective. But the real need is for good research on the effectiveness of therapy.

The Controversy Continues

Before Eysenck's broadside against the psychoanalytic and humanistic therapies, most psychologists had simply assumed that psychotherapy was effective. They had, after all, seen their patients improve, in about 65 percent of the cases at least. The shocking statistic was that a similar percentage of so-called untreated patients also improved. Psychotherapists found their judgment questioned and their livelihood threatened by Eysenck's paper, and more and better studies on the effect of psychotherapy were quickly forthcoming. Periodic reviews of these studies by advocates of one point of view or the other fueled the continuing controversy. Eysenck kept watch, and by 1966 he had concluded that his earlier (1952) opinion was all but proved. Another review claimed that, looking at all the old and new research, one would have to conclude that there is absolutely no difference on the average between groups treated by psychotherapy and control groups receiving no special treatment (Truax and Carkhuff, 1967). (Behavioral therapies were excepted from this conclusion.) Bandura's assessment of the research is essentially the same (1969).

On the other side were reviews that are favorable to psychotherapy. One discussed 101 different studies and found that 81 of these showed positive results from psychotherapy (Meltzoff and Kornreich, 1970). Looking only at what they called the "adequate studies"—those with control groups and free from major flaws in experimental design—48 of 57 studies (84 percent) showed positive results.

Finally, some puzzling reviews (for example, Bergin, 1966, 1971) presented evidence suggesting that psychotherapy clearly has an effect, but it makes some people better and some people worse! According to this view, comparing *average* rates of improvement between treated and untreated groups might show no difference, because the patients who improve significantly because of psychotherapy are balanced by the few who get significantly worse.

Some Tentative Conclusions

What is one to conclude from this bewildering array of arguments and counter-arguments? As one reviewer states, "Controversy continues as to the conclusions which can be drawn from a quarter century of research and polemic." And he adds, "Anyone with the patience of Job and the mind of a bank auditor is cordially invited to look again at the cumulated mass of material and settle the issue for himself" (Korchin, 1976, p. 433). I have neither of those attributes, but I have formed a few of my own conclusions.

First, the rate of improvement of untreated neurotics — the rate of spontaneous remission, as it is called — was almost certainly overestimated by Eysenck. Instead of the two-thirds (65 percent) Eysenck claimed, probably closer to 40 percent of neurotic control subjects improved without treatment (Lambert, 1976). This alone would make the rate of improvement with most therapies (around 65 percent) significantly higher than the rate of spontaneous remission. On this evidence it seems reasonable to conclude that psychoanalytic and humanistic psychotherapies are effective. The conclusion is weakened, though, by the fact that spontaneous remission rates vary wildly from study to study, from 0 percent to 90 percent, depending on the type of neurosis, the criterion of improvement, and other factors (Lambert, 1976). This means that there is no stable "spontaneous remission rate" for us to compare to improvement rates with various therapies. Again, it is clear that we need good untreated control groups in each and every experiment on therapeutic outcomes.

Investigations of therapeutic effectiveness that do include an untreated or minimally treated control group mostly support the hypothesis that psychotherapy is effective (Meltzoff and Kornreich, 1970; Luborsky et al., 1975). One intensive statistical analysis of 375 controlled studies showed that the average patient receiving therapy is better off than 75 percent of the control group (Smith and Glass, 1977). The summary statements of such reviews are impressive; but again we should realize that it is very difficult to do research on therapy — to find an adequate control group, to measure "improvement," etc. Several hundred imperfect experiments do not necessarily filter out truth (Rachman, 1971).

It is my impression that most researchers are turning away from the broad question "Is psychotherapy effective?" to a more specific question: "*When* is psychotherapy effective?" They too have concluded that the evidence, such as it is, indicates that psychotherapy is generally effective but that there is great variation in its effectiveness; indeed, as we noted, its effect may sometimes be detrimental (Bergin, 1966). Characteristics of the patient (especially her or his expectations about the effectiveness of therapy), characteristics of the therapist (how much experience, how much openness), and, most interestingly, the match between patient and therapist (do they see the world in the same way?) — these are the variables under study today. Such research promises to make psychotherapy even more effective.

However, the continuing controversy must be noted. Politics enter the issue, for often the reviews concluding that traditional therapies are ineffective are written by behavior therapists eager to have you accept their point of view (e.g., Kazdin, 1978). The reviews favoring the traditional therapies, on the other hand, are written by traditional psychotherapists, eager to justify their vocation (e.g., Korchin, 1976).

This does not mean the reviewers distort facts to suit their purposes. But just as the theories of personality behind the different therapies focus on different aspects of human functioning, the different reviewers look at different kinds of data. Behavior therapists are interested in behavior modification, and they favor studies showing clear changes in behavior (before, the patient avoided snakes; now she can touch them). Behavior therapists discount perhaps too readily simple statements from patients who say they "feel better" after therapy. Many neurotic people are functioning reasonably well and suffer mostly from depression and anxiety, so "feeling better" is for them a big achievement.

Behavior therapists can be criticized, too, for asking too little (Wolberg, 1967). Too often they take the position that if an offending behavior disappears in response to treatment, the patient is cured: If the child stops wetting the bed, she or he is OK. In many cases, they may be right, but they do not often ask *why* the child was wetting the bed. The research indicates that in most cases, this question is not important (Bandura, 1969). But in a few cases, it is significant; bed-wetting may be the child's only way of expressing "free will."

How Effective Is Behavior Therapy?

Behavior therapists claim that their methods are highly effective in producing meaningful behavioral change. One early claim had 90 percent of the neurotics treated by counterconditioning therapy cured or improved (Wolpe, 1958). Other reports seem to suggest almost 100 percent success with a range of methods (for example, Krasner and Ullman, 1965). Broad reviews of research are impressive (for example, Bandura, 1969; Sherman, 1973; Kazdin and Wilson, 1978). To cite a typical experiment, clients whose main problem was a lack of assertiveness were treated by behavioral therapy and by two other therapies, not behavioral. Of the 25 clients in each of the 3 groups, 23 were significantly improved in the behavior therapy group, with 8 and 11 improved in the others (Lazarus, 1966).

The research and the case studies can be criticized (Stevenson, 1964; Meltzoff and Kornreich, 1970), but the evidence is accumulating that behavior therapy is superior to other treatments, at least in cases that involve only one of a few symptoms, such as a phobia or lack of assertiveness.

This is not to say that behavior therapy is less effective than other therapies in dealing with other mental and behavioral problems; these more complex collections of symptoms make research more difficult and less clearly interpretable. There is every indication that behavior therapies will be effective with multisymptom complaints as well. In fact, behavior therapists are now trying to analyze complex complaints into more specific, behavioral problems (Mischel, 1971; Kazdin, 1978). A patient enters treatment, for example, complaining, "I am just so depressed all the time." The behavior therapist first tries to discover the specific situations in which the patient feels depressed. In one case, a young man was frustrated and depressed by (1) academic failure, (2) lack of social acceptance by his peers, (3) the breakup of his engagement, and (4) indecision about his future career. Each of these problems was treatable: The generality "I am so depressed" was too global to give much direction to the behavior therapist.

The Eclectic Psychotherapist

Most of the psychotherapists I have known, some working in clinics or hospitals and some in private practice, quickly evolve an *eclectic* approach to therapy. ("Eclectic" means to select from among various possibilities, without being dogmatic about any.) Trained as behavior therapists, client-centered therapists, or psychoanalytically oriented therapists, they soon take on the methods of other approaches too where appropriate. There are very few "pure" clinical psychologists who use one approach to the exclusion of others (Garfield and Kurtz, 1974, 1977). In an indirect way, even the observations of advocates of one theory or another confirm this. Behavior theorists, for example, suggest that behavioral controls are used in humanistic and psychoanalytic therapies (Bandura, 1969). Psychoanalysts observing behavior therapy suggest that the transference relationship between patient and therapist is used by behavior therapists in much the same way as in psychoanalysis (Breger and McGaugh, 1965; Klein et al., 1969).

The job of the psychotherapist is to serve the patient or client. The best of the eclectic psychotherapists keep up with scientific developments in all traditions—psychoanalytic, behavioral, and humanistic—as well as with new research in psychology more generally. They hope to find something on group processes that might help their group therapy, something on brain damage that might enable them to better understand the strengths and weaknesses of such patients, or some new breakthrough in the under-

Figure 13.10 *The eclectic psychotherapist uses the methods of psychoanalysis, behavior therapy, and humanistic therapy whenever the problems of the patient seem to require them.*

standing of human speech. They try to apply the best available knowledge to each patient's problems.

One eclectic psychotherapist made the point clearly: There is no "best" therapy except that which suits the patient's needs at the time she or he comes for treatment (Wolberg, 1967). One patient with a sound and well-organized personality may have gone to pieces in exceptionally trying circumstances. If the circumstances are temporary, all this patient needs is support during the traumatic period: "Listen. It's going to work out. It's going to be OK." Trying to reconstruct her or his entire personality with lengthy psychoanalysis would be ill-advised. A second patient might have a hard time relating to other people, and behavior modification techniques might be indicated. A third patient applies for treatment because of a minor disturbance at work, but it is soon clear that the minor disturbance is part of a radically disorganized personality structure; major reconstructive therapy, such as psychoanalysis, might therefore be indicated.

> When we examine critically what successful psychotherapists do, we find that, irrespective of the school to which they belong, and in spite of what they say they do, methods are modified to suit the needs of particular patients and situations. The more experienced the therapist, the more flexible he becomes in the kinds of techniques he utilizes. This eclecticism in approach is of the greatest significance if the therapist really wants to help each patient achieve effective relief from symptoms and as extensive a personality growth and development as is within his potential. (Wolberg, 1967, p. 312.)

SUMMARY

1. The primary goal of *psychoanalytic theory* is to help the patient understand her or his problems by uncovering the unconscious ideas and conflicts that underlie them. These ideas and conflicts the therapist infers and interprets from the patient's dreams, free associations, resistances, and transferences. Although the psychoanalyst's hypotheses cannot usually be tested experimentally, the validity of each interpretation is bolstered when they all *cohere*, or fit together in a logical pattern.

2. *Free associations* are thoughts reported without inhibition; they provide the therapist with clues to the patient's unconscious conflicts and childhood experiences. *Dreams* are considered to conceal *latent thoughts* beneath their *manifest content*; these latent thoughts also reveal aspects of the patient's unconscious mental processes. *Resistances* — gaps in memory or vigorous opposition to the therapist — often indicate points of stress and conflict. *Transferences* are the patient's projections of emotions related to a previous important relationship onto her or his relationship with the therapist.

3. *Behavior therapists* try to modify the stimuli and outcomes that are controlling the patient's behavior. One method of behavior modification uses *positive reinforcement* to increase desired behaviors. *Extinction* procedures eliminate undesirable behaviors.

4. *Counterconditioning* replaces an offensive response with a preferred one. In the form of counterconditioning known as *desensitization*, relaxation responses replace anxious behaviors. Assertiveness training is a form of counterconditioning that replaces timid responses in social interactions with more confident behavior.

5. *Aversive control* involves using punishment, such as electric shocks, to suppress the patient's undesirable behavior. *Modeling* (learning by watching) is a relatively new form of therapy that uses filmed or other examples of desired behavior to expose a patient to experiences she or he might not have otherwise.

6. *Self-control* — a personal sense of pride or shame — also can be taught by behavior-modification therapists. This is often necessary when the patient is about to return to a home environment that reinforces the un-

desirable behaviors the therapist has been treating.

7. *Humanistic therapies,* such as Carl Rogers's *client-centered therapy,* focus on self-actualization. In Rogers's view, the client (never called a patient) is responsible for her own cure. Problems are seen as arising mainly from the client's *incongruence* — her perception of a significant difference between the way she sees herself and the way others see her.

8. The therapist's role in client-centered therapy is to be *congruent* (to perceive the meaning of interactions accurately), to be *empathetic* (to understand what the client is thinking and feeling), and to have *unconditional positive regard* for the client (to value her essential self, regardless of what her actions might be). In this supportive environment, the client can work out her own problems. Research, which Rogers has encouraged, confirms that client-centered therapy increases patients' congruence.

9. *Group therapy,* which involves one therapist and several patients, became popular after World War II. In addition to the advantages of economy and convenience, group therapy allows the therapist to observe patients' interactions directly; it also gives patients a chance to try out new behaviors in a kind of miniature society.

10. Groups in therapy include those for people with serious emotional problems, people with a common problem (for example, fatness), and individuals whose only goal is to become a better person. The last is often called an *encounter group.*

11. Is psychotherapy effective? Many psychologists think the research evidence indicates that only one therapy — behavior modification — can claim to have a beneficial effect. This statement is one of the most controversial in this book, and much more research will be necessary before most psychologists will be willing to take a stand. However, it is clear that behavioral therapies are useful with several common behavioral disorders.

12. *Eclectic* psychotherapists use the techniques of the psychoanalyst, the humanist, and the behaviorist; their only concern is to help their patients. Evidence indicates that an eclectic approach may be the best; different people present different problems, and each traditional therapy handles a particular range of personal problems particularly well.

USING PSYCHOLOGY

If you have not done so before and are interested, participate in an encounter group or a sensitivity group once. Ask your college counseling service or similar knowledgeable community organization to recommend a group that is responsibly handled and has a good reputation.

After the group session (or, if you have already experienced a group situation like this, in recalling it) ask yourself these questions: Do you feel your group succeeded in its goals of making you more aware of the reactions other people have to you, and of the reactions you have to other people's behavior? What did you learn from the group? How did you react to the group situation? How did the others react? Do you think the group was well led? Why or why not? All in all, do you feel the group session was a valuable experience?

SUGGESTED READINGS

Korchin, S. J. *Modern clinical psychology.* Basic Books, 1976.

The standard, comprehensive work on psychotherapy. As one reviewer comments, students will now be operationally defined as' "knowledgeable" or not, depending on whether or not they have read Korchin's book.

Kazdin, A. E. *History of behavior modification.* University Park Press, 1978.

History and latest findings of the behavior-modification approach to psychotherapy, beautifully presented by a major proponent and researcher.

Rogers, C. R. *On becoming a person.* Houghton Mifflin, 1970.

A classic in the humanistic tradition.

Kesey, K. *One flew over the cuckoo's nest.* Viking Press, 1962.

An "underground" psychiatric novel that describes psychotherapy from the point of view of the patients. Radical, haunting, and magnificently written.

Life in Mental Hospitals

A mental hospital is supposed to be a place for the mentally ill to reside during critical periods of their illnesses. Doctors treat them, and nurses and other staff members minister to them, so that what was wrong gets corrected, and convalescence begins. That's the theory. What actually happens in a mental hospital is our present topic of discussion.

No two hospitals are run exactly alike. No doubt some are dismal, poorly kept "jails" for people society doesn't want to see on the outside; these hospitals turn up in the news now and then. And others are true "therapeutic communities," with pleasant, well-planned environments in which interactions between patients and staff are warm, friendly, and caring. The average hospital falls somewhere in between the ideal and the nightmare.

Admission involves information-gathering—life history, medical history, personality tests, physical examination, and so on. Then the patient is assigned to a ward, an area of the hospital where several patients live, on the basis of her or his diagnosed illness. Potentially violent patients and those who cannot care for themselves at all are usually assigned to special wards; the other wards contain a grab bag of reasonably self-sufficient people with a variety of problems.

Once on the ward, patients have very little to do. Many watch television all day long, some read, and some just sit, staring at a blank wall for hours. Some have minor chores in the ward, such as sweeping the hall, and some have jobs in the laundry, kitchen, or elsewhere. Besides the patients, the ward is populated by nurses and ward attendants, sometimes by hospital volunteers and nurses' aides, and by an occasional psychologist, psychiatrist, or social worker. Therapy depends on a number of considerations, such as the ratio of patients to doctors, but in most large public hospitals, individual psychotherapy is rare. Group therapy is more common, and drug therapy is almost always prescribed. For special cases, electroschock treatments or other severe interventions are used.

Hampered by lack of funds, the average mental hospital falls far short of the ideal therapeutic community. The patients spend very little time with psychiatrists and not much more with the nurses. Their most frequent contact is with ward attendants, who have very little training in psychology. A patient can most easily obtain rewards (going on trips, more privacy) by being cooperative and conforming to routine (Korchin, 1976). The humanitarian intentions of the hospital personnel cannot withstand the odds—too many patients—and, like a mother with 15 children, they sag, buckle, and finally thank the Lord for TV. Saturday morning cartoons are not educational, but they are absorbing.

PATIENTS AS ROLE PLAYERS

A number of social scientists and their associates have been admitted to mental hospitals posing as mental patients. The staffs of the wards did not know these people were not real patients, and thus several reasonably normal people have observed hospital routine from the inside out. A sociologist focused on the social structure within the hospital (Goffman, 1961). His theory of both normal and abnormal people views them as actors playing roles in society. In the hospital, Goffman noticed how carefully the admitted patients were *taught* their proper roles. They had failed in real life, they were given to believe, and like children they would do best to behave as they were told.

The patients quickly picked up these cues. In one study, a number of experiments were carried out in a hospital setting (Braginsky et al., 1969). In one, patients who had been in the hospital a long time and expressed no desire to leave were compared to newcomers who wanted to leave as quickly as possible. All subjects were given a 30-item test, with items chosen from the MMPI. The items were fairly neutral—"I gossip a little at times." Half of each group was told that the test would be used to determine "mental illness" and that each item marked "true" would be scored one point. The want-to-stay group averaged 18.8, while the want-to-leave group averaged 13.0. The other half of each group was told that this was a "self-insight" test: Each item marked "true" would indicate that the patient was realistic and ready to face life on the outside. The want-to-stay group averaged 9.7 points on this scale, while the want-to-leave group averaged 18.8. Clearly both groups were trying to achieve their respective goals.

A second study in the same series (Braginsky et al., 1969) involved want-to-stay subjects randomly assigned to two groups. Each subject was interviewed for two minutes in a standard manner. Half of the subjects were told that the interview would be used to determine whether or not they should be discharged from the hospital. The other half was told that the interview would be used to determine whether they were to live in an open ward (much freedom) or a closed ward (little freedom). Later, psychiatrists who knew nothing about what any subject had been told listened to the tape recordings of the interviews and rated how "mentally ill" each patient was. The patients in the stay-or-leave interviews were rated as quite ill, much more so than the patients in the open-or-closed-ward interviews. Clearly the patients could go into their "illness act" when it was to their advantage, and they could turn it off when to act ill might lead to a restriction on their freedom in the hospital.

THE SCHIZOPHRENIC PSEUDOPATIENTS

A second study of hospital routine used a number of pseudopatients who got admitted to various hospitals across the country (Rosenhan, 1973). Eight reasonably normal individuals, three women and five men, most of them professional people, went to the hospitals complaining of "hearing voices." The people were asked what the voices said, and the uniform reply was that the words were often unclear, but as far as they could make them out, the words were "empty," "hollow," and "thud." This report of auditory hallucinations was the only lie they told about their psychological experiences. Because some of the pseudopatients were psychologists or psychiatrists, these people also lied about their profession, in order to avoid professional courtesies that might be extended to them. All used false names, to avoid carrying the label of "mental patient" for the rest of their lives. Beyond this, every pseudopatient described her or his life as it actually had been lived—a normal life marred only by this sudden attack of hallucinations.

All eight individuals were admitted to hospitals, diagnosed, with one exception, as schizophrenics. The one exception was diagnosed as a case of manic-depressive psychosis. Once on the ward, the pseudopatients acted as normally as they could, no longer claiming they heard voices. A psychiatric ward is a bit frightening, at least at first, and unceasingly boring and unpleasant, so the pseudopatients had great incentive to act normal, so they could leave as soon as possible. They wrote down their observations of the ward life, secretly until they found that no one cared; then they wrote openly.

The average stay in the hospital was 19 days. The "schizophrenic" pseudopatients were discharged with the diagnosis of "schizophrenia, in remission," which means, "Once a schizophrenic, always a schizophrenic, but right now the disease is not acting up." In no case did the hospital staff recognize a pseudopatient as sane. Many of the other patients did: By one count, 35 of 118 patients spontaneously accused a pseudopatient of being sane, and many also guessed the reason—spying— for his being in there.

In order to view normal people as psychotic, the hospital staffs had to deal with an enormous bulk of contrary evidence. The patients' life histories were normal, and their ward behavior was normal. How did the staff reconcile this with the official diagnosis? Mostly they operated on the assumption that the behavior of a crazy person is crazy, even if normal people sometimes act that way, too. In the case of one pseudopatient, for example, "writing behavior" turned up as a suspicious symptom on his case reports. In other words, the diagnosis affected how the staff perceived his behavior, rather than his behavior affecting the diagnosis. Normal life histories were miraculously transformed into the morbid experiences of a preschizophrenic:

> This white 39-year-old male . . . manifests a long history of considerable ambivalence in close relationships, which begins in early childhood. A warm relationship with his mother cools during his adolescence. A distant relationship to his father is described as becoming very intense. Affective stability is absent. His attempts to control emotionality with his wife and children are punctuated by angry outbursts and, in the case of the children, spankings. And while he says that he has several good friends, one senses considerable ambivalence embedded in those relationships also. . . . (Rosenhan, 1973, p. 253.)

PATIENT-STAFF INTERACTIONS

The room in which most patients spend their daytime — the dayroom, which has the TV sets, the ping-pong tables, etc. — typically has a glassed-in area that pseudopatients in various hospitals quickly nicknamed "the cage." This is where most staff members spend their working hours, isolated from the patients. Nurses on the most active (daytime) shift left the cage, on the average, less than twice an hour; their total time out of the cage was too little to measure reliably. Physicians were seen on the ward an average of 6.7 times a day. Only the ward attendants were outside the cage much, and they averaged 89 percent of their time *inside* the cage. The 11 percent outside was not all interaction with patients; it included folding laundry and other nonsocial activities.

The most striking thing the pseudopatients ran into was the staff's reactions to requests they made. The pseudopatients asked standard questions at appropriate times — "Pardon me, Dr. *X*, could you tell me when I will be eligible for ground privileges?" or "When I will be presented at the staff meeting?" or "When I am likely to be discharged?" Unbelievably, only 4 percent of the psychiatrists queried stopped and talked; 71 percent walked on by, with their gaze averted to avoid eye contact (the rest at least looked at the patient). Of nurses and ward attendants, 88 percent walked on by, and less than 1 percent stopped to talk. When the staff member did stop, the interaction was typically brief and uninformative. Here is a sample:

Patient: "Pardon me, Dr. *X*. Could you tell me when I will be eligible for ground privileges?"

Psychiatrist: "Good morning, Dave. How are you today?" (He strides on by, ending communication.)

DEPERSONALIZATION

Almost all pseudopatient studies are full of anecdotes about how degrading and impersonal the experience is. The patients are not treated as human beings but as objects. They have very little privacy. Staff members discuss a patient's problems in his presence, as if he were deaf or incapable of understanding. Patients have few rights. The pseudopatients observed several patients being physically beaten by ward attendants for minor offenses — talking too much, for example. One patient was beaten for telling an attendant, "I like you."

Ken Kesey's brilliant novel, *One Flew Over the Cuckoo's Nest*, describes the reality of a poor (and all too common) ward in ways no case report can. Big Nurse ran the ward, a constant force unchanged by dif-

ferent psychiatrists or different patients. "Routine" was her goal: "What she dreams of . . . is a world of precision efficiency and tidiness like a pocket watch with a glass back, a place where the schedule is unbreakable and all the patients . . . are wheelchair Chronics with catheter tubes running direct from every pantleg to the sewer under the floor" (Kesey, 1962, p. 30). There are probably people like Big Nurse in mental hospitals, but it is more the system that is at fault. So little money, so few personnel, what else can one do?

Once, during Rosenhan's study, a nurse unbuttoned her uniform to adjust her bra in a room full of male patients. She was not trying to be sexy. Quite the contrary—she did not consider these people men, in the sexual sense. The patients found it offensive and degrading.

DIFFERENT APPROACHES

The average mental hospital seems bound by its design to create the not-too-pleasant environment described by the pseudopatients. For this and other reasons, psychologists have been trying new approaches designed to be more therapeutic and allow patients more personal dignity without increasing the cost of mental health services. Most of these programs rely on positive reinforcements for responsible behavior and often use patients to help other patients.

One approach, called the *token economy* (Ayllon and Azrin, 1968), uses the same principles of behavior modification as our free-enterprise society. Patients are paid with tokens for various activities, such as cleaning up their own area and working at jobs both on and off the ward. Patients respond very well to these programs. They begin to behave more responsibly almost immediately, and they learn many skills and ideas that will help them adjust to their eventual reentry into the world outside. Most patients like these programs, too, because they have some control over what happens to them. They can exchange their tokens for such things as cigarettes, candy, a pass to leave the ward, a room divider screen to increase personal privacy, or a chance to interact with the staff. (More privacy was the reinforcer they chose most often.)

Moving patients back into the community is a national trend (see Chapter 13), but this move can be too abrupt, especially for patients who have spent years in mental hospitals. A program designed to make the transition easier began with a group of patients who had been in hospitals for so long that their chances of ever living successfully in the community were essentially zero (Fairweather et al., 1969). First, they were assigned to a special ward. Each patient was given the greatest amount of freedom possible in managing his own life and, in addition, he was expected to function responsibly as a member of this little society, adding his share to group decisions about group activities. The better adjusted members helped the less able patients.

Eventually the group moved en masse to a lodge in the community. The men organized a janitorial and yard service, run completely by themselves, from the work to the bookkeeping. Individually, they had responsibility for their own health care, clothing, recreation, and the like. Psychologists overseeing this operation soon became unnecessary, and they left. Within three years, this group of patients were completely on their own; they stayed together (of their own free will, of course) as a kind of free-enterprise commune.

SUGGESTED READINGS

Rosenhan, D. L. On being sane in insane places. *Science,* 1973, *179,* 250–258.
The classic study of life in mental hospitals, as observed by normal patients. There is much in this article not covered in this interlude, and it is fascinating, though saddening reading.

Goffman, E. *Asylums.* Anchor, 1961.
A sociologist, Goffman focuses on social roles that society forces people to play. Goffman was admitted to a mental hospital as a pseudopatient; in this book, he reports his observations of how one must act if one is to be a "proper" patient.

Behavioral Objectives

1. Define "social psychology."
2. Compare social psychology and personality theories.
3. Define "aggression" and discuss ways in which it is expressed.
4. Discuss the relationship between frustration and aggression.
5. Describe ways in which group cohesiveness can be instilled and conflict between groups can be reduced.
6. Discuss several factors that affect persuasion.
7. Identify several factors that affect why and how readily people help others.
8. Identify some factors that tend to make people like us.
9. Discuss the psychological findings regarding the effect of watching television violence on aggressive behavior.
10. Describe the techniques involved in "brainwashing," and discuss how permanent brainwashing is.

CHAPTER

14

Social
Psychology

"Here's the situation," said Lewie. "Two people—call them Bonnie and Clyde—have robbed a bank together, but there isn't enough evidence to convict them. The district attorney goes to see each of them in their separate cells. First he visits Bonnie. 'Listen,' he tells her, 'If you confess, I'll get you off easy. If Clyde confesses too, you'll both get light sentences—say, five years. If Clyde *doesn't* confess, you'll be set free because you cooperated, and Clyde will get the maximum sentence—say, ten years. But if Clyde confesses and you don't, he goes free and *you* get the maximum.' Then the DA goes to Clyde and offers him the same deal."

Ron had the wary look of someone about to be led into a logical error that would make him look foolish.

"Naturally," said Lewie, "both of them will confess."

"You're crazy!" Ron protested. "You just said there wasn't enough evidence to convict them. If they say nothing, both of them go free!"

"I forgot to mention what happens if neither one confesses," said Lewie. "Then the DA will prosecute both of them for some minor crime like carrying a gun. They'll get a year in jail for sure."

Ron sensed that Lewie's trap had been set. "Let's see. If I'm Clyde, what do I do? If Bonnie confesses, and so do I, I get five years. If she confesses, and I don't, I get ten years. If Bonnie doesn't confess, and I do, I'm free. If she doesn't confess and I don't either, I get one year. So no matter what Bonnie does, I'm better off confessing."

"Right!" Lewie said triumphantly.

"Wait a minute," I said. "What happens if both of you confess?"

Ron thought. "We both get five years."

"And what happens if you both keep your mouths shut?"

"Aha! We both get one year. So it's better not to confess."

"But how can you be sure your partner's going to decide the same thing?" objected Lewie. "Your only sure bet is to confess, Ron."

Ron was totally confused. "I don't know," he said. "It's enough to keep you from robbing banks."

The confusion Ron felt in this situation — called the Prisoner's Dilemma — stems from the fact that if a person considers *only his own welfare,* Lewie's solution is clearly the best — to confess. But if the person considers both his welfare and his partner's — *the joint welfare of the pair,* in other words — he will choose the opposite solution. These two choices represent the major social behaviors of human beings: competition and cooperation. Like life among real people, the Prisoner's Dilemma has no correct solution — or, at least, no *one* correct solution.

Social psychology is the study of how people interact. Sometimes they compete, fight, and develop hostile attitudes toward each other; sometimes they cooperate, help, and love one another. Often they try to persuade others that their view is superior; but perhaps just as often they conform without question to someone else's view. Why and how human beings relate to each other is the topic of this chapter.

AGGRESSION

Why does one person sometimes want to hurt another person? Violent, intentional aggression is a puzzle social psychologists would very much like to piece together. There have been many fine studies of aggres-sion, and they have provided some pieces of the puzzle. Some are simple. For example, when people desperately need something (food, heroin), they will do practically anything to get it. This fact underlies many violent crimes. Too much use of alcohol also encourages violent behavior (see Interlude: Drugs, pp. 512–523).

In Chapter 1 we considered the hypothesis that frustration leads to aggression. This hypothesis is more than a showroom model; quite a bit of real research has been done on it. Let's take another look at it and see how it fits into social psychology.

Frustration and Aggression

In 1939, a group of psychologists at Yale University proposed that aggression is always the result of frustration (Dollard et al., 1939). Whenever there is aggression, they hypothesized, frustration must have gone before, and whenever frustration occurs, some form of aggression will surely follow. They defined frustration as encountering an obstacle to some desired goal, and aggression as behavior intended to injure the person at whom it is directed. (*Intention* was an important part of the definition. A deliberate swing at my jaw is aggressive even if I duck in time, but an accidental punch in the jaw from a hand gesturing in animated conversation is not.)

Research on Frustration and Aggression. Since its formulation, the frustration-aggression hypothesis has generated a lot of research. In an interesting study of aggression in the real world, the price of cotton in the Southern states from 1882 to 1930 was used to estimate frustration (Hovland and Sears, 1940). High cotton prices meant generally

Figure 14.1 *The Regulators —a white extremist group in the South in the late 1800s— lynch a black man. The number of lynchings seems to have been related to the amount of frustration induced by low cotton prices.*

good times for Southern farmers, business-people, and workers, whereas low cotton prices meant frustration. The particular form of aggression studied was lynching, the illegal hanging of a person for some real or imagined crime. The psychologists correlated the cotton prices with the reported number of lynchings, year by year, and found a high relationship.

Notice that the target of aggression in this instance is not the frustrating agent. Ordinarily, according to the hypothesis, a frustrated individual will attack whoever is responsible for the frustration. (Or *what*ever, if the frustrating agent is not human: People have been known to attack candy or soft drink machines that won't deliver.) In this instance, however, the victims of the aggressive Southern farmers were usually helpless blacks. This illustrates two additional features of human aggression. First, once the aggressive tendency is aroused, it can be *displaced* from its original target to another, more convenient target. If a worker is frus-

trated by his boss or by a police officer, he may aggress against his dog or his children when he gets home, rather than (foolishly) insult the true target of his anger. Second, when people are frustrated and angry and the cause is not clearly defined, they often try to define it clearly for themselves, even if that definition is objectively false. Frustrated people often choose *scapegoats* on which to vent their anger.

Modifying the Hypothesis. The hypothesis that frustration *always* leads to aggression and that aggression *always* follows frustration—the "strong form" of the hypothesis—was soon damaged by research. In particular, a number of psychologists claimed, with good evidence, that frustration very often produces behavior other than aggression. In children, for example, frustration often leads to immature behavior or *regression* (Barker et al., 1941). The framers of the hypothesis therefore modified it to say that aggression is a "highly probable" response to frustration (Dollard and Miller, 1950). This phrasing turned researchers' attention to the factors that determine *when* and *how much* aggression will follow frustration.

The *type* of frustration is one variable that has been found to be important. Preventing people from reaching a desired goal — the original definition of frustration — is just one way among many that have been used to create frustration. Others include causing subjects to fail at some task or to lose something of value. Some researchers verbally insult or electrically shock subjects and consider them frustrated, under the assumption that an insult interferes with the goal of a pleasant self-image and a shock interferes with the desire to feel good. These latter frustrations, which we can call "attack" forms, are generally much more potent in eliciting aggression than the other, "blocking" forms (Buss, 1966; Bandura, 1973).

An *unintentional* frustration typically elicits less aggression than an intentional one, as we would expect, although the differences are not as great as we might expect (Nickel, 1974). "Mitigating circumstances" — a good excuse — can sometimes dampen our aggression, too, especially if we know those circumstances before the frustration occurs (Zillman and Cantor, 1976). If we know a friend's mother has just died, we are unlikely to hit him because he forgot to get us tickets to the Bruce Springsteen concert. (Change that to "the college choir concert"; I'm not so sure about Springsteen fans!)

Another factor that helps determine whether aggression will follow frustration is *stimuli in the environment*. If the stimuli are somehow related to aggression, aggression is more likely. One experiment was run once with a few guns lying around (though weapons had nothing directly to do with the experiment) and once with a couple of badminton rackets lying around; the gun-cluttered room drew more aggression from the frustrated subjects than did the room with the sports-related stimuli (Berkowitz, 1969). Similarly, subjects who had previously learned a list of aggressively toned words like "fist," "punch," and "smash" were more aggressive than others who had learned neutral words (Turner and Layton, 1976). In another experiment, the frustration consisted of subjects' being insulted by an accomplice of the researchers, who was introduced as either a physical education major interested in boxing or a speech major; guess who elicited more aggression. Another variation had the insulting accomplice introduced as either Kirk Anderson or Bob Anderson. The insulted subjects then watched a film clip from a boxing movie (*Champion*) in which Kirk Douglas gets the daylights beaten out of him. Given the opportunity to give shocks to the accomplice in a socially acceptable manner, subjects gave Kirk significantly more of them than Bob (Berkowitz, 1969; Geen, 1972).

Group Aggression: The Robbers Cave Conflict

Frustration, at least by the modified hypothesis, is only one potential cause of violent behavior. Most of the research has involved frustrating individual subjects, whose aggressive behavior is then tested. Much less is known about the frustrations a whole group of people inflicts on another, or why two groups compete, or what causes dislike and hostility between groups.

Rarely do psychologists get the opportunity to study conflict and aggression between groups in as much detail as in the classic Robbers Cave experiment (Sherif et al., 1961). A team of researchers carefully selected 22 boys, age 11, for a 3-week camp at Robbers Cave, Oklahoma. None of the boys knew any of the others before the camp; all were physically and mentally healthy, from stable, white, Protestant, middle-class families.

Phase I: Forming Cohesive Groups. In the first phase of the experiment, the boys were divided into two groups, camped at two sites far enough apart that neither group knew another was around. Each group spent the first week developing the organized all-for-one and one-for-all spirit that psychologists call *group cohesiveness*. The researchers, posing as camp counselors or maintenance workers, carefully maneuvered the camp activities to encourage the boys to form closely knit groups. The boys were given most of the responsibility for planning and carrying out their own activities; they had to make group decisions about how best to have fun. Two prime requirements for cohesive group formation were involved here: *Interdependent actions* were needed to achieve *highly appealing goals.*

Soon each group had created internal structures—leaders and followers, status systems—and other signs of group solidarity, such as slogans and flags. Now it was time to begin Phase II; it was time for the Rattlers, as one group named itself, to confront the other group—the Eagles.

A few contacts between the two groups had been arranged during Phase I: They passed each other on a hike, and members of different groups met while gathering water at the spring. Each group began to insist on competition with the other group—a tournament of games, baseball, tug-of-war, and others, each sport having one winner, one loser. The counselors "gave in" to the demands of the campers. The competition began, and with it began Phase II: intergroup conflict.

Phase II: Conflict Development. The tournament started in a spirit of good sportsmanship in defeat, modesty in victory—the American ideal—but it quickly degenerated into just the opposite. The winners bragged, lording it over the losers, and the losers accused the winners of cheating. After losing a tug-of-war, the Eagles burned the Rattlers' flag. The Rattlers retaliated by stealing their opponents' flag. Name calling, a few fights, and a number of raids on each other's cabins followed. Finally, a few days later the Rattlers lost the tournament. In frustration they once again raided the Eagles' cabin, making all previous raids look very mild indeed.

The researchers knew hostility between groups would develop because of previous experiments of the same type (see Sherif and Sherif, 1969, for an overview). Now, when intergroup conflict was at a peak, the psychologists had a chance to study its effects. One effect was that in various ways, members of each group consistently overrated themselves and underrated members of the other group. This happened even when rewards were given for accurate judgment. In-group members were seen as "nice guys," whereas out-group members were rated very unfavorably. Both groups wanted no more contact with each other, and, by all measures, each was more internally cohesive than ever before.

An individual's status within a group

Figure 14.2 *Conflict and cooperation at Robbers Cave. Games like tug-of-war generated conflict between the two groups of campers. The resulting hostility was reduced by cooperative efforts like pushing the food truck to get it started.*

sometimes changed radically from Phase I to Phase II. The top Eagle during the peaceful first week lost his leadership role when the conflict intensified, because he was reluctant to lead combat. A bully in the Rattlers had very low status until he turned his aggressive tendencies toward the out-group, and then he became a hero.

Phase III: Conflict Reduction. In the third week, in Phase III of the experiment, the psychologists tried to reduce the conflict. They knew from earlier studies that the adult staff's preaching about "good will" would not have much effect. Another previous attempt had been to bring in a third group so that the two battling groups would unite against the new, common enemy. This tactic worked briefly (while the common enemy was around), but the old conflicts returned when the third group left.

After trying a number of logical but ineffective procedures, the researchers planned a series of events set up so that goals desired by both groups could be reached only if the two groups worked together. When the camp's shared water supply broke down, the two groups had to work together to find and fix the trouble. A movie requested by both groups, they were told, was too expensive for either group alone; they pooled their resources and watched it together. On an outing together, a truck that was supposed to go for food wouldn't start; all the boys pulled together to start the truck.

Slowly the campers formed friendships that cut across group lines. They requested a joint campfire. One of the groups spent a five-dollar prize won in previous competition on refreshments for both groups. A few diehards remained hostile at the end of the third week, but, by and large, the attempts at reducing conflict by introducing cooperative goals were successful.

Conclusions. Two conclusions from the Robbers Cave experiment are particularly worth noting. First, the experiment showed that intergroup conflict does not always grow out of social differences or personal problems. These campers were deliberately chosen from a single racial and socioeconomic group, and all were judged psychologically healthy. The conflict developed because two cohesive groups were placed in win-lose situations in which each group's desired goal could be achieved only at the expense of the other group. So, though differences in language, culture, and skin color can add to intergroup hostility, they are not necessary factors.

The second important conclusion is that the only effective means of reducing conflict was to set up situations in which either *both* groups won or both lost. Such cooperative situations are the opposite of the competitive situations that started the conflict in the first place.

It is possible that other procedures the researchers didn't try would have worked; but it is important to realize that once intergroup conflict has developed, several methods immediately become ineffective. Any individual who tries to be friendly with members of the opposing group is suspected by them of being a spy and by his own group of being a fink. Shared experiences other than the necessarily cooperative ones serve only as a chance for the rivals to attack each other. As mentioned before, the "common enemy" approach worked only temporarily; and if we consider what it means in real life, substituting a broader conflict for a lesser one, it is a dangerous solution at best. A national leader might be able to reduce conflicts between groups within his country by proclaiming national emergencies and stirring up conflicts with other nations, but he risks a far greater conflict in the long run.

FOCUS

TV and Violence

Scenes of violence are common on television. By one estimate there is a fairly stable rate of about eight acts of violence per hour (Gerbner, 1972). A survey of Saturday morning cartoons showed that 95 percent had some violence, according to the National Commission on the Causes and Prevention of Violence. By age 16, the average American child will have witnessed more than 13,000 killings on TV (Waters and Malamud, 1975). Another study found that of all items on American news broadcasts, *excluding* items about wars in progress, 36 percent concerned violent topics (Singer, 1970). (In comparison, the figure for Canadian news broadcasts was 18 percent.)

What effect does all this violence have on the viewer? Some psychologists hold that it results in an increase in aggressive behavior. Others say just the opposite, suggesting that TV violence is an outlet, draining off aggressive energy and thus making violence less likely. Finally, there is always the possibility that TV violence has no effect one way or the other.

Several government committees have studied the issue, and almost all have concluded that there is a "modest relationship" between TV violence and aggressive behavior (for example, Surgeon General's Advisory Committee, 1972). This also seems to be the majority opinion of psychologists who have reviewed the relevant evidence. Laboratory subjects consistently show greater aggression after viewing filmed aggression (Wrightsman, 1977). As you might imagine from our discussion of modeling in Chapters 8 and 13, watching TV violence can teach people how to be violent (observational learning); and it also weakens social norms against aggressive behavior by showing that "other people do it." There have been numerous reports of directly imitative acts among children. One child asked his father to help him poison a box of chocolates for a teacher he disliked; he had seen it on TV. Another child was caught sprinkling ground glass into the family's dinner, to see if it worked as effectively as on TV (Bandura, 1973).

There is one major exception to the evidence suggesting an increase in

Figure 1 *A psychologist monitors the emotional response of a subject watching a violent movie segment. Frequent television viewers showed little emotion compared to infrequent watchers, who apparently had not yet become insensitive to such scenes (Cline et al., 1972).*

aggression after TV violence. This study examined the relation between real-life violence and TV watching in the format of a true experiment (Feshbach and Singer, 1971). The subjects were several hundred boys, aged 8 through 17, enrolled in boarding schools. They were randomly assigned to an aggressive TV schedule (*Gunsmoke, FBI, Wild, Wild West,* and others) or to a nonaggressive schedule (*Gilligan's Island, Dick Van Dyke, Ed Sullivan,* and others).

The controlled TV watching continued for six weeks. Surprisingly, the students on a diet of violent TV shows came out significantly *lower* in most measures of aggression. The students watching nonaggressive TV were involved in roughly twice as many fistfights; they pushed and shoved almost twice as often; they were involved in "angry verbal interchanges" more than twice as often; and, well over twice as often, they were observed with a "sullen, angry facial expression." (I am tempted to say that I would probably react the same way to six weeks of Gilligan's Island!) The authors of this study concluded that exposure to TV violence does not result in an increase in aggressive behavior and may in fact reduce it.

Psychologists who believe that TV violence is harmful to children attacked the boarding-school study on methodological grounds (Ball-Rokeach, 1971; Liebert et al., 1972), a not-too-difficult task for a field study in which experimental controls were difficult. One of the most telling attacks pointed out that there was a sizable difference in aggressive behavior between groups *before* the controlled TV watching began; the group that eventually watched nonaggressive TV was initially more aggressive, just as they were later. (This is unlikely with randomization procedures but not impossible.) The investigators tried to control for this difference by comparing the effects of TV schedule on subgroups of subjects equated for initial level of aggressive behavior, and violent TV still produced less aggressive behavior. But such after-the-fact manipulations always weaken the validity of research conclusions.

A similar real-life experiment was done in Belgium with boys aged 14 to 16 (Leyens et al., 1975). Movies were used instead of TV. For one week, half the boys watched violent pictures, including *Bonnie and Clyde* and *The Dirty Dozen,* and half watched nonviolent films, such as *Lili.* The boys who watched the violent movies showed more physical aggression, much of it directly imitative of the activities portrayed in the movies.

A number of studies have shown no effect of violent TV shows (Middlebrook, 1974). And sometimes weird results turn up: One study found that, for children of higher social classes, watching violent TV resulted in significantly more cooperative, sharing, and helping behaviors (Stein and Friedrich, 1971)! The researchers suspected guilt was involved.

The consensus among psychologists seems to be that watching violence on TV probably has no effect on most people. For some—people with a generally high level of aggression to begin with—it increases slightly the probability of aggressive behavior. But research findings are not consistent, which points to uncontrolled factors introducing variability into the data. Tracking these unknown factors will intrigue many a psychologist in the years to come.

PERSUASION, CONFORMITY, AND OBEDIENCE

To *persuade* originally meant to advise, though it now implies a somewhat more urgent attempt to change another person's opinion or belief. To *conform* means to be in agreement or in harmony, although it has a somewhat negative, passive connotation, as if someone had persuaded you to do something not quite in line with your own wishes. To *obey* has an even stronger sense of submission to the opinion of an authority figure.

How people try to persuade, why they conform and obey, or resist—these are the topics we will review in the following sections.

Persuasion

Persuasion can be aggressive: It is possible to coerce someone physically into doing something you want done. Such forms of persuasion are fairly common, especially between parent and child. But the more civilized forms of persuasion involve verbal communication. A car salesperson tries to convince me this automobile is the best. Ralph Nader tries to convince me the automobile is "unsafe at any speed." The Surgeon General tries to convince me smoking is hazardous to my health. Do all—or

any—of these messages have an effect? What makes a communication persuasive?

Before we look at some possible answers to this question, we should ask another one: What are the goals of persuasion? Obviously, one goal is to make someone change his or her mind. The car salesperson wants me to believe his car is the best. Why? Because he gets a commission if I buy one. In other words, his persuasive speech is an attempt to change both my *attitude* and my *behavior*. He concentrates his attack on my attitude, figuring that if he is successful I will change my behavior accordingly. This is not always the way it works, as we will see later in this chapter. But for the moment, let us focus on attitude change—the salesperson's first goal—and how it is accomplished.

Most of the research on persuasion has used changes on simple attitude scales as the dependent variable. First, subjects indicate their attitude toward, say, abortion by picking a number on a scale ranging from 1 (Abortion should be left up to the woman alone) to 10 (Abortion is clearly murder). Then they are exposed to some propaganda from one side or both, and their attitudes are measured again. Or two randomly composed groups (assumed to have similar attitudes) are exposed to different communications, and their attitudes are assessed only once.

This kind of measure can give us a good

Who Says It? The *source* of the communication—who says it—is one important factor in attitude change. In general, the *credibility* of the communicator, how *attractive* he or she is, and how *powerful* he or she is are factors known to determine the effectiveness of the message (McGuire, 1972).

The *credibility* of the communicator—how believable he or she is—involves characteristics such as expertise and trustworthiness (see Figure 14.4). To illustrate, one experiment randomly divided subjects into four groups (Walster et al., 1966). Two groups read an argument that police and judges should be given more power to deal with criminals, and the other two groups received the opposite message, that police and judges should have their power reduced. One of each pair of groups was led to believe the source of the communication was G. William Stephens, a prominent prosecuting attorney. The other group in each pair was informed that they were reading the opinion of Joe "The Shoulder" Napolitano, a notorious convict.

The greatest amount of attitude change occurred when "The Shoulder" was arguing for *more* police and court power and when the prosecuting attorney was arguing for *less*. That makes sense, doesn't it? Both men were seen as reasonably expert in all four cases, but when they argued *against* what you would expect to be their selfish interests, subjects believed them. (It is particularly interesting that people who ordinarily would consider "The Shoulder" to be totally disreputable could still be swayed by him in a situation where his unique knowledge made him believable.)

What Is Said and How? The message itself is of course a factor in whether on not an atti-

Figure 14.3 *This man leaves little doubt of his opinion and what he thinks yours should be.*

idea of subjects' attitudes; but bear in mind that it does not tell us how strongly the subjects feel about these attitudes, which is often an important factor in attitude change. Nor does someone's pro-abortion attitude mean he or she will march in a demonstration supporting abortion-on-demand, or have an abortion should the occasion arise.

The independent variables in persuasion are many, but they can be summarized as *who* says *what* to *whom* and *how* (Lasswell, 1948).

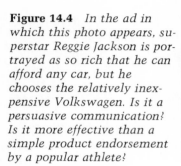

Figure 14.4 *In the ad in which this photo appears, superstar Reggie Jackson is portrayed as so rich that he can afford any car, but he chooses the relatively inexpensive Volkswagen. Is it a persuasive communication? Is it more effective than a simple product endorsement by a popular athlete?*

tude or opinion is changed by a persuasive communication. Numerous characteristics of what the message was and how it was delivered have been found important (McGuire, 1969). Some of these variables are:

1. *Type of appeal.* Is it intellectual or emotional? Does it stress the rewards for obedience or the punishments for disobedience? Is it serious or humorous?
2. *Omissions.* Is the conclusion stated directly or left for the reader or listener? Are opposing arguments discussed or ignored?
3. *Ordering.* If an opposing argument is also presented, is it better to go first or last?
4. *Discrepancy from the receiver's initial position.* Is it better to ask the reader or listener for a little change when a lot is desired?

No one has been able to come up with a model of *the* most effective kind of message for every situation, but we can discuss a few

specific findings. One popular *type of appeal* is the warning that plays on the listener's fears. Mutilated bodies dramatize the dangers of drunk driving. Movies of lung surgery are shown in high schools to prevent smoking. How effective is fear as a motivation to change an attitude? An early study varied the fear-arousing properties of a recommendation about dental hygiene (Janis and Feshbach, 1953). The high-fear message emphasized pain and included pictures of severe dental decay and infection. The low-fear message emphasized the health and beauty of good teeth. A moderate-fear condition was in between these extremes. This study used behavior change to measure effectiveness, and found that the most effective, by far, was the low-fear condition, with a 36 percent net change in dental-care behaviors. The moderate-fear condition produced 22 percent change, and the gruesome high-fear condition yielded only 8 percent.

This study should convince us that creating high degrees of fear is not the best way to persuade us. But the research findings are not consistent. In other studies (for example,

Leventhal and Niles, 1965), greater fear arousal led to increased attitude change. Such inconsistent results usually mean other factors are involved. Many psychologists believe that the most persuasive amount of fear is enough to get you concerned but not enough to make you avoid the issue altogether (Janis, 1967). The "proper amount of fear," in turn, depends on a number of other variables. For example, high fear is more effective than low fear if the person can respond quickly to reduce it — "there is polio around, get a shot" — than if the coping response is less clear.

The effect of most other message characteristics is just as complex, or even more so. A one-sided argument is effective if your listener already agrees with you, but to convince a neutral or opposed audience you do better to present both sides (Hass and Linder, 1972). Whether to go first or last in a debate seems to depend partly on your audience's point of view, partly on timing. The first argument is likely to get more attention, especially if your listeners agree with it. Also, it may be remembered better than the second — remember *interference* of earlier learning with later material? But if your listeners have to act on one of the arguments right after they hear both, the second one is more likely to stick in their minds — the *recency effect.*

Who Is Listening? Other things being equal, are some people more susceptible to persuasion than others? One would imagine so. Don't you know a few people you consider gullible, easy marks for any con artist who comes along?

One logical hypothesis is that people with low self-esteem are comparatively easily persuaded, because they do not value themselves or their own opinions very highly and thus are more willing than average to accept the views of someone else. This hypothesis has been tested in many experiments, with wildly mixed results (McGuire, 1972). William McGuire, an astute social psychologist who views simple relationships with profound suspicion, has tried to make some sense of this muddled research picture. McGuire hypothesizes several *steps* in the process of persuasion: To be persuaded, one must first pay attention to and comprehend the persuasive message; then one must yield. An intelligent person, for example, might attend and comprehend better but yield less readily than other people, so the factor of intelligence would have complex effects. So, too, would self-esteem. People with high self-esteem should be likely to pay attention to a message and comprehend it, because self-esteem indicates confidence and a willingness to consider new possibilities. But it also implies a tendency to hold on to one's own beliefs. The prediction might be, then, that those easiest to persuade would be people with moderate self-esteem, enough to listen and comprehend but not to be totally resistant to argument.

Conformity

To many people, conformity implies lack of independence, lack of backbone. But there is not much pleasure in deviance, and there are many rewards in conformity. Generally conformity is socially valuable; consider the scene at the stoplight if most people didn't conform most of the time. And, as it has often been said, it is truly difficult not to conform to the standards of *some* group; even rebels group together and set social norms for proper rebellion.

Figure 14.5 *Conformity. What is bad about it? What is good about it?*

A simple but ingenious group task devised by a psychologist named Solomon Asch has been used in many studies of the effects of group pressure on conforming behaviors (Asch, 1956). In what is described as a test of perceptual judgment, several subjects are asked to say which of three comparison lines match another line (called the standard). This they can do easily enough. But in one variation of the task, only one of the subjects is a real subject; the others are all confederates of the experimenter. Again the task is not difficult: On each of several trials, only one of the comparison lines clearly matches the standard. During the first two trials, each subject in turn calls out the correct answer, the real subject last. The third trial, however, is a shocker. All the subjects before the real subject agree on the same comparison line, but it clearly does not match the standard line.

The subject feels disturbed and puzzled. It happens again and again, on over half the trials: Other subjects say "line C," but the real subject sees line A as correct. The real subject feels like an outcast, and he begins to doubt his senses. The question is, Will he conform? Will he *say* "line C" when he *sees* line A?

In Asch's experiments, 80 percent of the subjects conformed on at least one of the seven test trials, although only one out of ten conformed on all trials (or all but one). Combining subjects and trials, subjects conformed 33 percent of the time.

A number of variations were tried on this same basic task. At least three confederates were needed to get a high degree of conformity, but more than three did not add much to the extent of conformity. If the situation was set up so that the subject knew the others' judgments but could respond in writing, rather than by speaking, conformity dropped sharply; apparently group pressures are much less effective if the group does not know what the individual is doing (which is one good reason for the secret ballot in elections).

In other variations, the subject was given a "friend," also a confederate, who agreed with the subject against the majority. One friend reduced conformity significantly. But if the friend deserted the subject later in the series of trials, conformity increased to its previously high levels.

Obedience

Like conformity, obedience has more of a bad name than it deserves. The kind of obedience we dislike is blind obedience in which someone obeys another person instead of higher values or his own personal moral standards. At the trial of Adolf Eichmann, the Nazi responsible for exterminating 6 million Jews during World War II, Eichmann argued that he was innocent because he was ordered to do what he did. Many of the people involved in the famous Watergate scandal of the early 1970s also claimed that they had obeyed instructions without thinking, though they regretted their actions later.

The Milgram Studies. In a series of laboratory studies of obedience, psychologist Stanley Milgram had subjects report for the experiment in pairs (1963). One member of each pair was a confederate of the experimenter. The pair was informed that this was a learning experiment involving the use of shock as punishment. To determine who was to be the learner and who the teacher, the subjects drew lots, but of course the drawing was fixed: The confederate always became the learner.

The confederate was strapped into a chair in the next room, an electrode attached to his hand, with the subject watching. The visual effect was not unlike watching someone being strapped into an electric chair. The subject then went to his teaching machine, a shock generator supposedly capable of delivering from 15 to 450 volts of electricity. If the confederate got an answer wrong, the subject was to deliver a shock. With each wrong answer, the subject was to increase the level of shock by 15 volts. The voltage was clearly marked, and verbal descriptions indicated the severity of shocks in a certain range: "Slight shock" for 15–60 volts, "Very strong shock" for 195–240, "Danger: Extreme shock" for 375–420, and, for the last two intensities, 435 and 450, the level was simply "XXX." The subject was given a sample shock of 45 volts (see Figure 14.6).

The learner never received any shocks, of course, but he pretended he did. He gave wrong answers frequently, and the subject "shocked" him accordingly. When the shock level hit 300 volts, he kicked on the wall, and then gave no more answers. However, the experimenter told the subject to consider "no answer" as a wrong answer and to continue increasing the shock. At 315 volts, the learner pounded again. Then complete silence.

Most subjects hesitated at one point or another. But the experimenter told them to continue; if necessary, he insisted, "You have no other choice, you must go on."

How long would the subject continue? He was obviously causing pain to another human being, and, for all he knew, the learner had fainted, or worse, around 300 volts. He could have stopped, just as Eichmann could have refused to follow orders. Five of Milgram's 40 subjects quit at 300 volts, when the first pounding sounded. Another 9 subjects quit before reaching the maximum, 450 volts delivered to a silent learner. But 26 (65 percent) went all the way.

What Determines Obedience? Later studies using the same obedience situation proved that a number of factors can influence the degree of obedience (Milgram, 1974). In addition to the basic condition described above, one condition added a few vocal effects: At 75 volts, the learner began to moan. At 150 volts, he asked to quit. At 180 volts, he cried that the pain was too great. At 300 volts and above, the kicking and silence routine was repeated. This reduced the number who continued to give shock only slightly, to 62 percent.

In another condition, the learner was placed in the same room with the teacher-subject, so the subject not only heard the moans and cries, he saw the grimaces of pain. Obedience (continuing to 450 volts) dropped to 40 percent. Fewest subjects of all obeyed when the learner refused to keep his hand on a shock-plate after 150 volts, and the subject was required to physically place the victim's hand on the shock-plate and deliver the shock, while the victim struggled, moaned, and grimaced. Still, almost one of three subjects completed their session with total obedience.

The directness with which the authority figure gave his orders also affected the degree of obedience. If the experimenter gave instructions by telephone or by tape recorder, not only did obedience decrease as the dis-

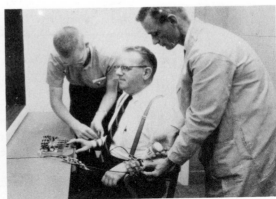

Figure 14.6   Top left: *The fake shock generator used for the Milgram obedience studies. Each switch supposedly increases the shock level by 15 volts; half the switches are down already.* Top right: *The learner, a confederate of the experimenter, is strapped into the chair and electrodes are attached to his wrist.* Bottom left: *The teacher (subject) receives a sample shock of 45 volts.* Bottom right: *A subject quits rather than continuing to raise the shock level to maximum voltage. Copyright 1965 by Stanley Milgram. From the film* Obedience *distributed by the New York University Film Library.*

tance of the authority figure increased, but also the subjects began to cheat. They administered lower-voltage shocks than the instructions called for. This is a fairly common response to the conflict between injuring another person and disobeying authority—pilots drop bombs in empty pastures "by mistake" and sympathetic prison guards slip books to a prisoner in solitary confinement.

FOCUS

Brainwashing

The ultimate form of persuasive communication is *brainwashing.* This term has been used to explain everything from minor changes in a person's political beliefs to Patty Hearst's unusual behavior after her kidnapping. Religious cults like those at Jonestown are sometimes said to brainwash their followers. Whatever the validity of these claims, the specific definition of "brainwashing" and the only solid empirical evidence of its effects come from studies of certain methods used by the Chinese Communists around the time of the Korean War (Lifton, 1956, 1961). The Communists' goals were (1) to get their prisoners to "freely" confess to war crimes against the people of Korea, and (2) to inspire them to believe in Communism. Several means were used for these ends.

The Communists used a minimum of physical torture, at least of the violent type portrayed in American movies during World War II. Instead, a captive's life was made extremely uncomfortable, and improvement depended on his giving in to the demands of the captors. The prisoner was stripped of all personal dignity. He was addressed by his prison number, never his name. He was chained around the ankles and handcuffed, his hands behind his back. He had to ask fellow prisoners (who were further along in the reformation of their thinking and therefore not chained) to open his pants to urinate and to wipe him after defecation.

Social pressure was intense. Placed in a cell with several "reformed" prisoners, the captive was constantly abused. Both jailers and fellow prisoners ridiculed his defiance, pointed out faults in his arguments, and spat on him. He slept infrequently, when there was no one awake to badger him.

Interrogation was grueling, lasting for hours. The prisoner was asked how he could deny crimes "against the people"—Had he never consumed resources foolishly? Had he never acted selfishly? Always, rewards were promised for compliance. Change your mind, and the chains will come off. Your food will be better. Your fellow prisoners will like you. The interrogations will become "lessons."

Most of the prisoners eventually said anything their interrogators wanted. Both sides recognized this yielding as superficial. The next stage of brainwashing was an attempt to turn superficial compliance into sincere beliefs. The social group—the group of prisoners who lived together in one cell—was a major instrument. The group's main activities were discussion of morality and criticism of others, and its language system was Marxist. Everything one said had to be said in Marxist terms, and thus the captive got used to thinking in those terms. The criticisms from the other prisoners (phrased in Marxist terms) were often justified, or at least well intended. The new prisoner began to wonder, "Maybe these guys are right! Maybe the whole Communist system is preferable to my own country's." Each sign of change toward the Communist position was carefully noted and rewarded, usually with further acceptance by the group. Warm and friendly companionship, in that setting, was an extremely powerful reinforcer. Backsliding (reversion) was also noted and punished.

After two or three or even four years of this kind of treatment, most of the prisoners had been brainwashed and gave reasonably sincere confessions, often in the presence of American news reporters. Many were then released. Some chose to stay in China, where they participated in the fellow-prisoner groups that were used to persuade new captives. Some returned to the United States, a source of concern both to American authorities and to the brainwashed prisoners themselves. Most prisoners were bewildered and afraid, with vague thoughts of hooking up with the American Communist Party when they got home. The typical result, however, was that, once back in a capitalistic environment, they changed their minds again, reverting to their old attitudes, opinions, and beliefs. Many began to despise Communism when they looked back at their experiences in prison.

The techniques of brainwashing are powerful, largely because they manipulate a person's total environment. The effects, however, require that environment for support, and cannot withstand the opposing pressure of another total environment, such as the United States culture. The main danger was that a brainwashed prisoner would intentionally place himself in a situation that would continue to support his beliefs. The men who stayed in China, for example, and those who made immediate contact with the American Communist Party, were much less likely to revert to their old beliefs.

HELPING

Much of the research on why people help others was stimulated by a series of incredible real-life incidents in which people ignored others in need. Perhaps the most famous was the case of Kitty Genovese, a young woman who was stabbed to death in New York City in 1964. No less than 38 people witnessed the murder from apartment windows. From beginning to end, the murder took over 30 minutes, with screaming, running, stabbing—the killer was frightened off and came back to finish the job—

and finally death. Not one of the 38 people did a thing to help Kitty Genovese, not even call the police. Asked why they didn't respond, most of them said they were afraid. Of what? They couldn't say (Rosenthal, 1964).

One of the factors in "innocent bystander" situations is the *number* of bystanders. Some psychologists have argued that the presence of several witnesses tends to spread out the responsibility for giving aid, making it less likely that any of them will take action (Darley and Latané, 1968). In the Genovese case, witnesses may have thought that, since there were so many people watching, *someone* would do something; someone would call the police. If they all thought this, of course, then no one would call, which is what happened.

In a laboratory experiment similar to the Genovese case, subjects were asked to discuss college life over an intercom system (to avoid recognition and embarrassment, supposedly) with other students. Actually, the "other students" were tape-recorded confederates. There were three conditions: In one, the real subject discussed life with just one other "student"; in a second, with two others; and in the third, with five others. During the group discussion, which the subject had been told was not being monitored by the experimenters, one of the confederates staged an epileptic-like seizure. The subjects who thought they were alone with the confederate responded quickly to the cries for help. The subjects in the group with the victim plus one other "subject" were a bit slower and a bit less reliable. In the six-person group, over a third of the real subjects never even reported the seizure. These nonreporting subjects, however, were obviously concerned and in apparent conflict

when the experimenter entered the lab later, and they seemed to have assumed that someone else had reported the seizure.

Is It an Emergency?

Most emergencies are ambiguous. Maybe I have a fertile imagination, but I run into several potential emergencies every day. A man is shouting at the cashier at the supermarket, and I get ready to respond to a robbery in progress, but the man, it turns out, is complaining about the price of cottage cheese. Another man shuffles and stumbles on the street. I ask him if he needs help. He says, "No, but I could use a quarter."

An observer of a developing emergency first has the task of identifying the situation as one that requires help (see Figure 14.7). It is an unfortunate individual who has a heart attack on a city street, stumbles, and falls, for he very well might die without aid; passers-by would probably think he's drunk.

In a study of cues that reduce the ambiguity of the situation, psychologists had a confederate stagger and fall to the floor of a subway car in New York (Piliavin et al., 1969). Strategically placed observers watched the response of the other passengers. In some trials, the confederate smelled of liquor and was carrying a liquor bottle wrapped in a brown paper bag. In others, he appeared sober and was carrying a cane. The "cane" victim was helped over 95 percent of the time. The "drunk" victim was helped 50 percent of the time. Clearly the cues—the cane and the liquor—were important in determining the response to a fallen stranger who differed in no other respects.

In a variation of this experiment, the victim with the cane staggered and fell and then either did or did not bleed from the

Figure 14.7 *A drunk sleeping it off, right? Or is it a person who needs help?*

mouth. Bystanders were much slower to help the bleeding victim (Piliavin and Piliavin, 1972). Presumably other attitudes are also involved, such as nervousness at the sight of blood, which might lead the observer to fear that trying to help may make matters worse; blood, after all, defines the situation as an extreme emergency.

Why Do People Help Others?

Experiments designed to study helping behaviors have given good cause for optimism. The rate of helping is generally high, sometimes so high that differences among conditions can be measured only by the quickness of the helping response. This is true even on New York subways, which many people who live outside of Manhattan think of as perhaps the most impersonal setting in the world. Occasions when people don't help other people, as in the Kitty Genovese case, make news for two reasons: (1) They are *exceptional*, not common; and (2) they arouse the passions of readers, who would have helped—or so they think, and probably a

good percentage are right. A friend of mine living in Washington, D.C., told me that shortly after the Genovese case, a woman in his neighborhood had her purse stolen. As she pursued the thief, screaming, nearly 200 people from nearby apartments joined the chase—became physically involved—because "this neighborhood is not like Genovese's neighborhood."

But why do people help other people, generally? Although this question has no quick answers, it is encouraging a significant amount of research in psychology today, and several answers are being suggested (Sigelman, 1977).

Let us consider a concrete example, one that involves most of the important factors. In my hometown, a farming community in the Midwest, every so often a farmer would break a leg or come down with pneumonia or some damn thing would happen just as spring seeding had to be done or right in the middle of fall harvest. In such cases, his friends and neighbors—usually about twenty or thirty farm families—would get together, do all the work of two or three weeks in one day, and get their picture in the *Mascot,* our local weekly newspaper (see Figure 14.8).

Why do these people help? One reason is the *social norms* (generally agreed-upon rules for behavior) that govern helping behavior. One such norm, the *social responsibility norm,* states that we should help those who need help. Another, the *reciprocity norm,* states that one should return a favor, even in advance: Do unto others as you would have them do unto you. These norms were often expressed directly in the farm-helping situation: "Tom needed help, so here we are!" (social responsibility). "Tom would do the same for me, I'm sure of that" (reciprocity). Norms define proper behavior

in a society, and organize it: The farther away from Tom's farm one lives, the less the requirement to go to his aid, so only his neighbors, relatives, and perhaps a few close friends help out. The norms thus keep poor Tom from being surrounded by a thousand tractors all at once, and enable people to know when they should help without having to worry about it every time some farmer in the county breaks his leg.

A second way of looking at helping behavior is to consider the rewards and costs facing an individual. As a neighbor, what does it gain you to help Tom? You get in on a big party, for typically a huge feast is prepared for the end of the day's work. There is fun and companionship, good times. Helping

Figure 14.8   *These friends and relatives gathered to help a disabled farmer plow his fields.*

people also makes you feel good, as the superego dispenses its internal rewards. The costs include a day of hard labor with no return in your family's own produce, plus the expenses of operating your machines for a day; and the cost of the party must be shared.

On the other hand, if you didn't help there still would be costs. Your superego would make you feel guilty, and if your superego wasn't working too well, your neighbors would shame you. If you needed help, some would refuse to give it, on the grounds that you had previously violated the reciprocity norm, and they would be seen as justified.

LIKING

Interpersonal attraction is psychologists' jargon for liking. Interpersonal attraction is one of the most investigated topics in all of psychology, which does not mean we know all there is to know but at least gives the lie to the occasional claim that psychologists study only the morbid aspects of human behavior.

Why do you like the people you like? You would probably answer, "For different reasons." Some of your friends may be gentle, kind, and humane, and you couldn't imagine anyone disliking them. Others may be rather abrasive and generally offensive, but you like them because they are interesting, ready to attack life. Some of your friends hold the same social and political views you do, but some do not.

Factors in Liking

The experiments of psychologists have uncovered several factors related to interper-

sonal attraction (Wrightsman, 1977). Not surprisingly, perhaps, most of these are the same factors that operate in our choice of a marriage partner (see pp. 359–362). One is *propinquity*, which means closeness — other things being equal, you like people who live closer to you. *Need complementarity* refers to needs that are different but fit together — if I am quiet and interested, and you are talkative and interesting, we would probably get along fine. *Reciprocity* means that we tend to like those who like us.

Another widely studied factor is *attitude similarity* (Byrne, 1971). Typically, in experiments on attitude similarity, a subject is given an attitude questionnaire filled out by another subject and is asked to say how much he or she would like, and enjoy working with, this person. (Often there is no "other subject," of course, and the questionnaire is filled out by the experimenter.) If the questionnaire shows similar attitudes to the subject's on topics like the legalization of marijuana and the general superiority of the color red, then the chances are very good that the real subject will like and want to work with the "other subject." This effect is so strong, in fact, that it is often used to study the effects of friendship or attraction on other variables. In the Prisoner's Dilemma discussed at the beginning of the chapter, for example, subjects who are led to think that their opponent has attitudes similar to their own are more likely to cooperate and less likely to compete (Tornatzky and Geiwitz, 1968).

A Few Surprises

Most of these factors related to liking are what one might expect. But psychologists have uncovered a number of relatively unexpected factors as well. In one experiment, subjects were found to like a person with different attitudes from their own more than someone with similar attitudes (Jones et al., 1972). The subject overheard two people (confederates) describing him favorably to another person before he rated them; he indicated that he liked them both, but he liked the one with dissimilar opinions more. It has also been found that subjects dislike obnoxious people with similar opinions to their own more than ordinary people with dissimilar opinions (Taylor and Mettee, 1971). These studies suggest that it is pleasing to be liked by someone different from you and unpleasant to have someone who is similar to you doing things of which you disapprove.

Another surprising finding is the way liking for people of superior ability is affected by stupid and clumsy behavior (Aronson et al., 1966). Subjects believed they were listening to a tape recording of a candidate for a college quiz bowl. The candidate heard by one group of subjects answered a set of extremely hard questions almost perfectly. The candidate heard by another group answered only about a third correctly. In each case, toward the end of the session, the candidate clumsily spilled coffee over himself. The effect of this blunder was to decrease liking for the poorer candidate but to *increase* it for the better candidate. Apparently people who are too nearly perfect seem more human and thus more likable if they blunder.

Romantic Love

When science attempts to grapple with something as vague yet as often discussed as romantic love, one wonders if either science or love can hope to survive the encounter. I remember reading an account of one study in which love was operationally defined as the tendency to exaggerate virtues and minimize faults in another person. Although this definition allowed easy measurement with paper-and-pencil questionnaires, it struck me as rather like using a balloon dotted with paper stars to represent the universe. A small bit of a poem by e. e. cummings has a similar thought: "While you and i have lips and voices which are for kissing and to sing with who cares if some oneeyed son of a bitch invents an instrument to measure Spring with?"

Nevertheless, in recent years, a number of undaunted psychologists have done interesting research on romantic love. We may never capture the full meaning of love in our scientific apparatus, but we are learning more about some aspects of it.

For example, psychologists have measured the Romeo-and-Juliet effect (Driscoll et al., 1972), a term that refers to the intensification of a love affair as a result of parental disapproval and interference. In a study of unmarried couples, the correlation between measures of parental interference and romantic love was +.50, a rather strong relationship considering the range of possible influences on romantic love. In a follow-up study, changes in the degree of parental interference were found to result in changes in the degree of romantic love. Among other things, it would appear that increasing parental approval is generally related to decreasing affection!

You probably remember from Chapter 6 the general theory about emotions that says we often use situational cues to interpret

Figure 14.9 *Excited by danger, Bogey and Betty may interpret their emotional arousal as love.*

our emotions; that is, depending on where we are and what we are doing, we may interpret our state of emotional arousal as fear, love, disgust, or something else. One prediction of this theory is that people are somewhat more likely to "fall in love" while they are aroused. Thus, sex may contribute to love by increasing physiological arousal. Biographies are full of intense love affairs begun during emotional times like war. The Roman poet Ovid noted that an excellent time to express one's love for a woman was while the gladiators were disemboweling each other in the arena (Rubin, 1973).

In a more recent observation, a female psychologist interviewed male subjects as they stood on a narrow wooden bridge that tilted and wobbled over a 230-foot chasm (Dutton and Aron, 1974). The control group consisted of men interviewed on a sturdier bridge only ten feet off the ground. The subjects on the wobbly bridge responded to ambiguous stimuli (the TAT; see p. 457) with more sexual imagery than the control group. Also, many more of them contacted the attractive interviewer later "for more information" (and a possible date?). They had apparently interpreted at least part of their fear arousal as attraction to the interviewer.

FOCUS

Personal Space

Does it make you nervous if someone stands too close to you during a conversation? If so, how close is "too close"? If you had sat in the same seat for fifteen class sessions, would it bother you to find someone else sitting there when you arrived for the sixteenth? How do you "save your seat" at the library or in a theater, if you have to leave it temporarily?

Figure 1   *Like birds on a telephone line, people space themselves around a fountain (left). Extreme physical closeness is a sign of emotional closeness. People often stake a temporary claim to personal territory by leaving books or other personal items to mark the space (right).*

Social psychologists have begun to study these questions of *personal space*, as they are often called, where behavior is related somehow to a space that an individual considers his or her own. Personal space includes an area surrounding the body, and also other spaces or areas, like chairs, that people temporarily or permanently adopt as their own and will often defend against intruders.

The physical closeness aspect of personal space has been studied in several ways. In one experiment, students working for the experimenters intentionally sat down a foot or less from other students in a library. The reactions of the subjects (the other students) were varied. Some turned their heads in the opposite direction, some changed body position so that an elbow or similar "space divider" stood between the subject and the invader, and most (over 20 out of 30) left before the half-hour observation period was up. In a randomly chosen control group who encountered no "invaders," only 4 out of every 30 left within half an hour (Felipe and Sommer, 1966). In a similar study, standing "too close" to another person waiting to cross the street at an intersection resulted in far speedier crossings than normal (Konecni et al., 1975).

The aspect of personal space involving an area that "belongs to me" has been studied in experiments on what some psychologists call *territory* (Middlebrook, 1974). Urban gangs defend their own "turf." Groups of friends tend to establish "their" table at college dining halls or in university libraries, and an unsuspecting intruder may be told directly that this is not his "place."

Individuals also have areas they think of as their own. A young person who lives in his parents' house resents any snooping around "his" room. The possessiveness may be only temporary, as when one lays claim to a seat in a library or theater. If the "owner" must leave temporarily, he stakes his claim by leaving a sweater or some similar marker. If space is at a premium (the library is crowded), a personal marker, like a sweater, is more effective than a less personal one, like an opened book (Sommer and Becker, 1969). Or the person may ask a "neighbor"—someone sitting next to him—to protect his personal space, even if it is someone he has never seen before and has no particular reason to trust. Our respect for personal space is great enough that such "neighbors" will almost always watch out for one another's territory.

THEORIES IN SOCIAL PSYCHOLOGY

Since social interactions and the attitudes and opinions that go with them include almost everything humans do, one might expect that theories of social psychology would be among the most general of all theories—broader, say, than theories of perception or memory. Quite the opposite is the case. Perhaps because the field is so broad, theories in social psychology tend to focus on a small slice of it, such as attitude change, cooperation, aggression, or leadership.

Cognitive Dissonance

One prominent theory that has encouraged and given direction to a great deal of research in social psychology is the theory of *cognitive dissonance*. Formulated in 1957 by Leon Festinger, the theory defined cognitive dissonance as a "nonfitting relation among cognitions." For example, a wife's belief that the man should handle the family finances does not fit with her awareness that she is better at budgeting than her husband. Such dissonance between cognitions in the same mind, according to the theory, is unpleasant. The person is therefore motivated to change one or the other of the clashing ideas. In our example, she will either take a hand in balancing the checkbook or convince herself that her husband is really better at it.

The theory of cognitive dissonance became immediately popular because it made a number of correct predictions that weren't obvious. In a classic experiment, subjects worked for an hour at a very boring task. Then they were each asked to lie to the next subject and tell him the task was actually interesting and fun. One group of subjects was offered $1 to do this and another group was offered $20 to do it. Subjects in both groups later rated how interesting they really thought the job was (Festinger and Carlsmith, 1959). What would you predict?

The obvious prediction, so most psychologists thought at the time, was that the subjects rewarded with $20 would find the task

"I suppose I shouldn't admit this, but I liked it better at three-fifty."

Drawing by Frascino; © 1975 The New Yorker Magazine, Inc.

more interesting than the $1 group. Instead, the opposite happened. Those paid $1 rated the job fairly interesting; but the $20 subjects, like the control subjects who were not asked to lie about it, thought the task was boring.

This was exactly the nonobvious prediction of the theory of cognitive dissonance. According to this theory, the issue was one of justification. To tell a lie for $20 is reasonable. But to do it for just $1 is dissonant, and requires changing the cognition that the job was boring.

Attribution Theory

A second theory that is useful in much of social psychology is *attribution theory* (Heider, 1958; Kelley, 1973). As we noted in Chapter 6, attribution theorists believe that the reasons we interpret a situation in one way and not another have to do with the causes to which we *attribute* behavior—both our own and other people's. To illustrate with examples from the topics in this chapter, how aggressive you feel toward someone who has insulted you depends partly on whether you believe the insult was intentional—whether you attribute hostility to the offender. Whether you help someone who falls down in a subway depends similarly on how you interpret the situation—as an emergency or as public drunkenness, for example—which has to do with whether you attribute the fall to illness or overindulgence. People may interpret the same emotional arousal as love, anger, or fear in different cirumstances. Thus, much research in social psychology today is directed toward determining an individual's attributions in various situations.

Much of the older cognitive dissonance research has been reinterpreted in terms of attribution theory (Bem, 1967, 1972). For example, in the experiment described earlier, subjects who were paid $1 to lie about their feelings believed their own lie more than did subjects who were paid $20. According to attribution theorists, the subjects were examining their own behavior to judge how they felt about the boring task. "I said the job was interesting, for a measly dollar, so it must have been more interesting than I thought." In other words, they could attribute their statement that they liked the experiment to one of two "causes": (1) They actually did like it more than they thought, or (2) they were paid $1. Cause 2 is too weak —why would I say that for only $1?—so it must be cause 1.

One of the main findings of attribution research is that people tend to overestimate the importance of personal motivations and abilities in behavior, and to underestimate situational factors (Freedman et al., 1978). We tend to view the failures of fat people to reduce as due to lack of individual effort, even if we have definite evidence to the contrary; we tend to view the improving mental health of a sick friend as a considerable personal achievement, even if a new drug appears to be mostly responsible. Such attributional bias can have bad consequences. For example, people tend to attribute rape, at least in part, to some hidden desire and provocative action by the woman victimized (Jones and Aronson, 1973). Similarly, the victims of severe accidents or diseases are often held partly to blame for circumstances usually entirely beyond their control.

Social Psychology Tomorrow

Like every aspect of psychology we have considered in this book, social psychology is not an island but a part of the continent. In particular, the fields of social psychology and personality are so closely related that few people care to take the time to try to draw a line between them. Individual personality factors have begun to influence social psychology—for example, attribution of causes to another person's behavior. And social factors like stimuli and outcomes have had a strong effect on modern personality theories, as we saw in Chapter 10. Thus, we can expect an increasing alliance between the two fields, as psychologists work to integrate individual life histories with the effects of changing situations.

Still, personality and social-psychological theories have different purposes. In the future, personality researchers will continue to focus on individual differences. Social psychologists will trace the common characteristics of diverse people placed in the same situation. We can expect each field to come up with new ideas that are particularly suited to its own viewpoint, while the two continue to interact and help each other move forward.

SUMMARY

1. The Prisoner's Dilemma confronts two people with a choice between protecting their individual welfare and acting for the welfare of the pair. It illustrates the basic poles of research in social psychology: competitive and cooperative behavior.

2. *Aggression* (a competitive behavior) occurs for many reasons, one of which is *frustration*. Research on the relationship between frustration and aggression suggests that aggression is a probable but not inevitable response to frustration. Violence is more likely in response to aggressive frustrations, such as insults, than to simple interference with goal-directed behavior. A violent environment—one with stimuli like guns around—leads to aggression more often than less provocative environments.

3. The Robbers Cave experiment showed how competition can be created and then replaced with cooperation. The experiment first created two cohesive groups, then developed competition between them by pitting them against each other in a number of winner-loser contests. The psychologists then practically eliminated the intergroup conflict by creating situations in which the

subjects were forced to cooperate to achieve common goals.

4. Research on *persuasion* includes studying the variables of *who* said it, *what* was said and *how*, and *to whom* it was said. Credibility, attractiveness, power, and apparent objectivity work in a communicator's favor. Messages phrased to play on the audience's fears are popular but not always effective; other *what* and *how* factors also vary in their effect. How easily someone can be persuaded depends partly on complex interactions among variables such as intelligence and self-esteem. To be persuaded by a message, one must pay attention to it, comprehend it, and finally yield to it.

5. *Conformity* is doing what others do. In the Asch experiments, many subjects echoed the majority opinion instead of voicing their own in a simple perceptual judgment. Conformity was greatest when the subject would have had to disagree with the united opinion of three or more others in a direct confrontation.

6. In the Milgram experiments on *obedience*, most subjects followed the orders of an authority figure and delivered what they thought were severe shocks to a "learner," in spite of the learner's moaning and other indications of possible serious effects. Such obedience declined as interaction with the learner became more direct and as the instructions of the authority figure became less direct.

7. Research on *helping* behavior indicates that people will usually help someone in trouble. The more bystanders in an emergency, the less the probability that any single one will help. People are most likely to help a stranger who is clearly the victim of an emergency.

8. People help other people for several reasons, including two important *social norms* (unwritten laws): the *social responsibility norm*, which states that we have an obligation to help those in need, and the *reciprocity norm* — the Golden Rule — which says that we should do for others what we would have them do for us. Helping also brings rewards, including pride and the admiration of the community, and refusing to help can sometimes bring punishments, like community disapproval.

9. Factors that encourage *interpersonal attraction* (liking) include *propinquity, need complementarity,* and *reciprocity:* We tend to like people who are near us, whose needs complement ours, and who like us. We like people who have similar attitudes to ours, but if people who are different from us like us, we find them particularly attractive. Obnoxious people who are similar to us seem particularly obnoxious. But a seemingly "perfect" person becomes more likable if he or she is caught in a blunder.

10. Studies of romantic love suggest that love is often encouraged by parental disapproval (the Romeo and Juliet effect), and that people frequently interpret emotional arousal as love even if it is actually caused by something else.

11. Two major theories in social psychology are *cognitive dissonance* and *attribution.* The first suggests that people find it intolerable to hold two contradictory ideas at once, and that we act to eliminate the dissonance between such conflicting cognitions by changing one of them. Attribution theory posits that the way we interpret a situation depends on the causes to which we attribute our own and others' behavior.

USING PSYCHOLOGY

You can do some "experimenting" on your own about personal space. First, spend some time observing such things as how close to each other people stand or sit when they are talking, and how frequently they maintain eye contact under different circumstances. Then purposely violate these social conventions a bit by standing closer or farther away than is conventional when you are speaking with a person. What is the effect? Does the person you are talking with move farther away or closer to you to adjust the distance to the "correct" one? How is eye contact affected? Do you notice the farther away people are, the more they maintain eye contact?

SUGGESTED READINGS

Bandura, A. *Aggression: a social learning analysis.* Prentice-Hall, 1973.
   An analysis of social aggression written by a former president of the American Psychological Association.

Milgram, S. *Obedience to authority.* Harper & Row, 1974.
   The complete discussion of Milgram's studies of obedience.

Freedman, J. L., Sears, D. O., & Carlsmith, J. M. *Social psychology.* 3rd ed. Prentice-Hall, 1978.
   An excellent textbook.

Aronson, E. *The social animal.* 2nd ed. Freeman, 1976.
   A reviewer says, "The book reads like a novel. . . . It is a succinct, enthusiastic, and quite accurate representation of social psychology." I agree.

correlation coefficient in light of what is known about the variability of such coefficients in general. We can evaluate our computed correlation in terms of what is essentially the standard deviation of all correlations like ours. If ours is two or more standard deviations away from the estimated mean of all such correlations (usually zero), we sit up and take notice; we call our correlation "significant" (trustworthy).

Let me provide the formula for estimating the standard deviation of correlations, without getting into the complex mathematical theory behind it:

The standard deviation of correlations (σ_r) equals the square root $(\sqrt{\ })$ of the correlation we obtained, squared and subtracted from 1, divided by the number of subjects minus 2.

$$\sigma_r = \sqrt{\frac{1 - r^2}{N - 2}}$$

* If N is large (say, over 30), a simpler formula can be used:

$$\sigma_r = \frac{1}{\sqrt{N - 1}}$$

Using the numbers from our math-philosophy illustration,

$$\sigma_r = \sqrt{\frac{1 - (0.63)^2}{5 - 2}} = .45$$

Now, what we want to know is whether our correlation is significantly different from a zero correlation. Our coefficient of .63, though high, does not reach two standard deviations (.45 × 2 = .90), so it is not statistically significant. With so few subjects, it is almost impossible to obtain a correlation significantly greater than zero.

Note again the importance of the number of observations—or, in this case, the number of subjects. As N increases, the standard deviation decreases. If we had observed 50 subjects instead of 5, for example, the standard deviation would have been .11.

$$\sigma_r = \sqrt{\frac{1 - (0.63)^2}{50 - 2}} = .11$$

Our correlation of .63, with 50 subjects, is over five standard deviations away from zero, a very noteworthy result.

SUGGESTED READING

There are several fine introductory statistics textbooks. I recommend:

Horowitz, L. M. *Elements of statistics for psychology and education.* McGraw-Hill, 1974.

Glossary

absolute threshold: the minimum stimulation necessary to activate a sensory *receptor* so that it will transmit a signal.

achievement motivation: the need to succeed or do well and accomplish something of importance.

acquisition: the state during which a new *response* is learned and gradually strengthened.

adaptation: a change in the sensitivity of a sense organ; following stimulation sensitivity is lessened and following an absence of stimulation sensitivity is increased.

addiction: see *dependence.*

adrenalin: see *epinephrine.*

affiliation need: the need for association and friendship with other people.

aggression: *behavior* intended to harm the target (usually a person) at whom it is directed.

aging: biologically, the decline in the ability of the body to avoid or fight off the effects of accidents, disease, and other types of stress.

alarm reaction: the first phase of the *general adaptation syndrome,* in which the body responds vigorously to something stressful.

alcoholism: repeated drinking in amounts that exceed those considered reasonable by the community and which interfere with the person's job, health, or interpersonal relations.

all-or-none principle: the principle that a *neuron* always fires with the same intensity when it is triggered.

alpha waves: a *brainwave* pattern typical of quiet restfulness with the eyes closed. The waves have a cycle of about 8 to 13 per second.

amnesia: lack of memory for past events.

amniocentesis: the surgical process of inserting a hollow needle through the abdominal wall and uterus of a pregnant female to obtain amniotic fluid, which is analyzed for chromosomal abnormalities in the fetus.

amotivational syndrome: a *syndrome* found by some researchers in those who indulge in heavy *marijuana* use over a period of time, characterized by sluggishness, apathy, and mental confusion, possibly reflecting partial brain damage.

amphetamine: any one of a group of *stimulant* drugs which increase alertness and decrease appetite.

amplitude: the height of a sound or light wave, which roughly corresponds to our experience of loudness or brightness, respectively; also called intensity.

anaclitic depression: despondency in infants deprived of their mothers between the ages of six and eight months.

anal stage: Freud's term for the *psychosexual stage* marked by parental emphasis on toilet training (ages 1 to 3).

androgens: male sex hormones.

androgyny: having both masculine and feminine personality traits.

anima: in Jung's theory, the archetype of woman in males.

animus: in Jung's theory, the archetype of male in females.

anxiety: vague, nonspecific fear.

anxiety neurosis: a type of *neurosis* characterized by nonspecific and pervasive dread.

aphrodisiac: that which excites sexual desire.

aptitude test: a test designed to measure and predict someone's ability to learn and perform certain skills.

archetype: in Jung's theory, the basic unit of the collective unconscious, consisting of inherited ideas, symbols, and predispositions.

Army Alpha: the first major group *IQ* test used to classify soldiers in World War I.

Army Beta: a group nonverbal *IQ* test used to classify illiterate soldiers in World War I.

arousal: a state of bodily excitement, including rapid pulse rate, flushed face, dry mouth.

association: a relationship between two ideas learned through previous experience.

association value: a numerical value indicating meaningfulness of *nonsense syllables* and words, determined from *subjects'* reports of the *associations* they form to the nonsense syllables or words.

attachment: in developmental psychology, the emotional bond between child and parent or caretaker, evidenced by such behaviors as distress with separation.

attention: the focusing of *perception* on certain aspects of current experience to the neglect of others.

attitude: a positive or negative orientation toward some object, concept, or situation.

attribution theory: a *theory* concerned with the psychological processes by which individuals assign causes to *behavior.*

audition: the sense of hearing.

autism: severe avoidance of social interaction with other people.

autokinetic effect: the apparent movement of a stationary spot of light in an otherwise dark room.

autonomic nervous system: the part of the peripheral nervous system that regulates bodily activities over which we do not ordinarily exert conscious control; the sympathetic division tends to dominate in times of stress, increasing arousal and preparing the organism for activity; the parasympathetic division tends to dominate in quieter times, promoting general maintenance (e.g., digestion).

aversive control: the use of *punishment* to control *behavior.*

axon: the part of a *neuron* which transmits nerve impulses to other neurons.

backward conditioning: in *classical conditioning,* presenting the *conditioned stimulus* after the *unconditioned stimulus;* little or no *learning* results.

bait shyness: learned avoidance of poisoned bait, characterized by one-trial *learning* with the *negative reinforcer* (nausea) occurring long after the *response.*

barbiturates: highly addictive drugs which slow down the *central nervous system.*

behavior: any observable action of an organism.

behaviorism: the viewpoint associated with John B. Watson, who proposed that psychology be limited to the study of observable *behavior.*

behavior therapy: a type of *psychotherapy*, based on *learning* principles, which works to change *behavior*.

beta waves: a more-or-less random pattern of low voltage *brainwaves*, typical of wakefulness.

binocular cue: a cue to the *perception* of depth or distance which depends on the use of two eyes.

biofeedback: information given to a subject about his measured biological state (e.g., a tone signifying the presence of *alpha brainwaves*).

bipolar cells: *neurons* in the *retina* which relay messages from the *receptor cells* on to other cells whose *axons* form the *optic nerve*.

blind spot: the area of the retina where the optic nerve leaves the eye; it has no receptor cells and is not sensitive to light.

blood-brain barrier: a special barrier existing between blood vessels and brain tissue which prevents diffusion of some substances from the blood to the brain.

brain stem: evolutionarily the oldest part of the brain, directly above the uppermost part of the spinal cord, important in such essential *behaviors* as breathing and the beating of the heart.

brainwashing: a method of changing *attitudes* and beliefs, usually by completely controlling the individual's environment.

brainwaves: rhythmic fluctuations of electrical voltage in the brain.

Broca's area: an area in the left cerebral hemisphere thought to regulate speech production in right-handed individuals.

B-values (values of being): the highest goals of human activity, according to Maslow.

caffeine: the stimulant present in coffee, tea, and many cola drinks.

Cannon-Bard theory: the view that primitive subcortical brain structures are central in the control of *emotions* in that they send information on to the *cortex* and also send signals to the internal organs, preparing them for responding to the situation.

castration anxiety: the male child's fear that his father will cut off his penis to eliminate competition for the mother, a component of the *Oedipus complex*.

cat: one hell of a nice animal; frequently mistaken for a meatloaf (Kliban).

catatonic schizophrenia: a type of *schizophrenia* in which patients undergo long periods of *depression* or apathy, become totally unresponsive to the outside world, and at times remain in one posture for long periods.

catharsis: sudden release of strong *emotions* with an emotionally cleansing effect.

cell body: the part of the *neuron* containing the nucleus, to which *dendrites* conduct information and from which the *axon* conducts information.

central nervous system: the brain and spinal cord.

cerebellum: the part of the brain located to the top and back of the brain stem, primarily concerned with coordinating movements.

cerebral cortex: the surface layer of the cerebrum. It is the most recently evolved portion of the brain and is involved in intellectual activities.

chromosomes: the chain-like structures of genetic material found in the nuclei of cells; see *genes*.

chunking: recoding individual items of information into groups to facilitate remembering.

circadian rhythm: a cycle of biological activity that has a maximum and minimum value once every 24 hours.

clairvoyance: a form of *extrasensory perception* in which events are perceived without direct sensory input.

classical conditioning: a form of *learning* in which a formerly neutral stimulus consistently precedes an *unconditioned stimulus*, with the result that the formerly neutral stimulus, now called the *conditioned stimulus*, elicits the *response* originally given to the unconditioned stimulus.

client-centered therapy: a *humanistic psychotherapy* developed by Carl Rogers, emphasizing *self-actualization*, in which clients learn to take responsibility for their actions and to use their own abilities to solve their problems.

clustering: the tendency in *free recall* for *subjects* to recall items in categorical groupings.

cocaine: a *drug* extracted from the South American coca plant which stimulates the *central nervous system*; its primary effect is *euphoria*.

cochlea: the part of the inner ear containing the hearing receptors.

codability: the ease with which an idea can be phrased in words.

cognition: a thought or idea.

cognitive: having to do with mental activity, as opposed to, for example, observable behavior.

cognitive dissonance: awareness of inconsistency between simultaneously held beliefs, or between a belief and a *behavior*; in such a condition a person acts to reduce the inconsistency by changing his or her behavior or belief.

cognitive theory: a *theory* that emphasizes *perception*, memories, and other thought processes; often contrasted with *behavior* theory.

coitus: sexual intercourse.

collective unconscious: in Jung's theory, a part of the individual's unconscious which develops through evolution and is shared by all humans; each individual also has a nonshared, personal unconscious.

color blindness: partial or total inability to distinguish one color from another; the most common forms involve an inability to distinguish between two complementary colors.

color constancy: the tendency to perceive a color as unchanging despite varied situations or illuminations.

color detector cells: *neurons* in the visual system which without stimulation fire at a certain rate, but change their rate of firing when stimulated depending on the *wavelength* of the stimulating light. Typically one wave length increases the rate and another decreases it.

common fate: a Gestalt principle of perception in which stimuli which act together are seen as part of the same form.

complementarity filter: in theories of mate selec-tion, the process of screening candidates on the basis of needs and values that complete or "go with" one's own; for example, dominance with submissiveness.

complex: a collection of items related in an arbitrarily rather than objectively logical way. For instance, a child 5 to 7 years old might group all the objects mentioned in a story in one complex.

compulsion: an act or series of acts a person feels that he or she must do.

concept: an idea or relationship common to a class of ideas or objects.

condensation: in the psychoanalytic theory of dreams, the fusion of two or more elements into a single dream image.

conditioned response (CR): the learned or acquired *response* to a *conditioned stimulus*.

conditioned stimulus (CS): an originally neutral *stimulus*, which, after pairing with an *unconditioned stimulus*, elicits a *conditioned response*.

conditioning: see *classical conditioning*, *operant conditioning*.

cone: a retinal *receptor cell* which registers differences in *wavelength* in light and differences in intensity in bright light, and also provides *visual acuity*.

confederate: an experimental *subject* who is actually an agent of the experimenter; a stooge.

conformity: the tendency to change opinions or *behavior* as a result of group pressure, and to accept the group *norms*.

congruence: a state in which one is able to perceive accurately the meaning of interactions between oneself and others; in *client-centered therapy*, one of the three essential characteristics of the therapeutic environment (see *empathetic understanding*, *unconditional positive regard*).

conscience: the critical, punitive aspect of the *superego* (contrast *ego ideal*).

consensus filter: in theories of mate selection, the process of screening candidates on the basis of similarity of attitudes and values.

conservation: the principle that essential qualities such as volume remain constant in spite of changes in form.

construct validity: the ability of a given test to measure what it was designed to measure.

contingency contract: a type of behavior therapy that sets down in writing the rewards or punishments an individual can expect with certain behaviors.

continuation: a Gestalt principle of perception in which stimuli that continue a pattern are seen as part of that pattern.

control group: in an *experiment*, the group of *subjects* not given the treatment whose effect is being studied.

conversion hysteria: a type of *neurosis* in which some bodily functions stop; symptoms include paralysis of limbs, blindness, or deafness.

cornea: the transparent outer covering of the eye's lens and iris.

corpus callosum: the band of nerve fibers connecting the two cerebral hemispheres of the brain.

correlation: a statistical estimate of the degree to which two variables are related; it ranges from a value of -1.00 to $+1.00$, with -1.00 indicating a perfect negative relationship, $+1.00$ a perfect positive relationship, and zero no relationship between the variables.

correlation coefficient: the numerical value assigned to a *correlation*.

cortex: see *cerebral cortex*.

cortical detector cells: *neurons* in the visual *cortex* which respond to a very specific *stimulus*; e.g., one type responds to lines with a certain tilt.

counterconditioning: the process by which a new, incompatible *response* is attached to a *stimulus* in order to counter the unwanted response previously attached (see *desensitization*).

countertransference: in *psychoanalysis*, the transference by the therapist of his own conflicts onto the patient.

critical period: a stage in the development of an animal in which it is most ready for the *acquisition* of certain *response* patterns.

cross-sectional method: a study of groups of people comparing individuals in different stages of development (contrast *longitudinal method*).

decay theory of forgetting: a *theory* of forgetting which states that the more time elapsed since *learning*, the more forgotten.

defense mechanism: an unconscious maneuver of the *ego* to control the *id* and the *superego*. It enables people to maintain a satisfying self-image by transforming offensive feelings into acceptable ones.

deficiency needs: motives to satisfy a lack or incompleteness in one's life.

delirium tremens (DTs): a condition of tremors of the whole body and frightening *hallucinations*, found in some chronic alcoholics.

delta waves: the slowest type of *brainwaves* (one or two per second) and the ones with the highest voltage, found in the deepest stage of sleep.

delusion: an irrational, groundless belief, often of grandeur or persecution.

dendrite: the part of the *neuron* that receives impulses from other neurons and passes them to the *cell body*.

deoxyribonucleic acid (DNA): a complex molecule found in the nucleus of cells which contains the genetic information determining the basic structure and functioning of the organism.

dependence: a physical or psychological need for a drug, also referred to as addiction, created by repeated use (see *physical dependence*; *psychological dependence*).

dependent variable: a *behavior* or condition which changes as a result of changes in the *independent variable*.

depressant: any of a class of drugs which slow down the *central nervous system* and whose effect is generally relaxing.

depression: feelings of sadness and worthlessness.

depth perception: the ability to judge the relative distances of objects from the observer.

depth of processing theory: a theory of memory which predicts that the deeper a person delves into the meaning of a word or event, the more likely he or she is to remember it.

desensitization: *counterconditioning* in which the *response* of fear or *anxiety* is replaced by the incompatible response of relaxation.

development: the sequence of physical, behavioral, and mental changes that takes place in a maturing organism.

deviance: *behavior* not considered acceptable by the individual's group or culture.

difference threshold: the minimum amount of *stimulus* change necessary for a *subject* to detect a change in his or her psychological experience.

discrimination: *learning* to make different *responses* to a reinforced *stimulus* and to similar nonreinforced stimuli.

discriminative stimulus: in operant contexts, the *stimulus* which allows the *subject* to discriminate between situations in which a *response* will and will not lead to *reinforcement*.

displaced aggression: *aggression* against a person or object other than the source of one's anger.

displacement: in the psychoanalytic theory of dreams, a substitution of one image for another, usually to reduce anxiety; or a shift in emphasis, such as giving major characters minor roles.

dissociative hysteria: a type of *neurosis* involving an unconscious mental isolation of some part of the personality; e.g., *amnesia* and *multiple personality*.

distractor technique: a procedure in *memory* experiments in which the *subject* performs a task between presentation of the *stimulus* and *recall* which prevents *rehearsal*.

distributed practice: *learning* sessions separated by periods of rest; a more efficient way of learning than *massed practice*.

DNA: see *deoxyribonucleic acid*.

dominant gene: a gene carrying traits which will show up in offspring regardless of the gene from the other parent.

double bind: a situation in which the subject faces the impossible task of responding to verbal and behavioral demands which conflict.

Down's syndrome: a form of mental retardation caused by genetic abnormality (an extra chromosome); physical correlates include extra eyelid folds, which is why the syndrome used to be known as mongolism.

dream work: in the psychoanalytic theory of dreams, the process of converting the underlying thoughts (latent content) to the actual dream (manifest content); includes condensation, displacement, translation of thoughts into visual images, and secondary elaboration.

drug: any chemical substance that changes the structure or function of the body.

DSM-III: abbreviation for the third edition of the *Diagnostic and Statistical Manual of Mental Disorders*, published by the American Psychiatric Association.

DTs: see *delirium tremens*.

echo: the facsimile of an auditory *stimulus* which persists for a very brief period following presentation of an auditory stimulus.

eclectic psychotherapy: an approach to *psychotherapy* using different methods (*behavior therapy, client-centered therapy*, or *psychoanalytic therapy*) as appropriate.

educational psychology: a specialized field of applied psychology concerned with the psychological aspects of teaching and the formal learning processes in schools.

EEG: see *electroencephalogram*.

ego: according to Freud, the part of the personality corresponding most closely to the perceived *self*. The ego is the strategist of the personality; it distinguishes between reality and unreality (see *id, superego*).

egocentric speech: speech which apparently is not designed for communication with another person.

egocentrism: the tendency to consider only one's own point of view.

ego ideal: the positive nonpunitive aspect of the *superego* which approves of unselfish acts that accord with the highest moral standards (contrast *conscience*).

electroencephalogram (EEG): a record of

brainwaves from electrodes attached to the scalp.

electroshock treatment: a treatment for mental illness in which high-voltage current is passed briefly through the head, producing temporary unconsciousness and convulsions.

emotion: a feeling accompanied by characteristic physiological and behavioral events.

empathetic understanding: the ability to identify intelligently with the difficulties and problems of another person; in *client-centered therapy*, one of the three essential characteristics of the therapeutic environment (see *congruence, unconditional positive regard*).

empirical data: information (data) gathered through the senses; particularly, data gathered in an *experiment.*

empty nest: a home which all the children have left.

enactive memory: *learning* retained in the muscles which is easily retrieved after periods without practice, like the ability to ride a bicycle.

encoding: what is done to information to prepare it for storage in *memory.*

encounter group: a group of individuals who meet together to try to understand and improve interpersonal interactions and communications, emphasizing openness and honesty.

endocrine system: the blood, bloodstream, and system of glands that send hormones into the bloodstream.

epinephrine (also called adrenalin): a hormone released by the adrenal gland that causes bodily *arousal.*

ESP: see *extrasensory perception.*

estrogen: a female sex hormone.

ethologist: a scientist who studies the *behavior* of animals in their natural habitats.

eugenics: a selective breeding program allowing only superior people to become parents.

euphoria: a feeling of unusual joy and well-being.

excitement: a condition in which a *neuron* has been stimulated not enough to fire, but enough to fire easily when it receives other impulses.

exhaustion: the third phase of the *general adaptation syndrome,* in which body resources are depleted and the body can no longer fight a stressful situation.

expectancy: a person's belief that a certain *behavior* will lead to a certain outcome.

experiment: a carefully designed situation set up by a scientist to test a hypothesis (see *natural experiment, true experiment*).

experimental group: in an *experiment,* the group of *subjects* given the treatment whose effect is being studied.

extinction: the procedure of presenting the *conditioned stimulus* without reinforcement to an organism previously conditioned; also, the reduction in *response* resulting from this procedure.

extrasensory perception (ESP): reception of information through channels other than the sensory systems; it includes *telepathy, clairvoyance,* and *precognition.*

feature analysis theory: a theory that *perception* is based on analyzing the component features of *stimuli.*

feedback: information about previous responses used to guide future responses, as in knowledge of results in tests.

fetishism: an erotic attachment to inanimate objects or parts of the body.

figure-ground perception: perceiving a visual pattern in terms of a figure (the primary interest) and a background.

fixed-interval schedule: a schedule of *reinforcement* in which each *response* made after a certain interval of time is reinforced.

fixed-ratio schedule: a schedule of *reinforcement* in which a certain ratio of *responses* is reinforced; for instance, every n^{th} response is reinforced.

forgetting curve: a curve measuring the progress of *memory* loss, in which some measure of remembering is on the vertical axis and elapsed time is on the horizontal axis. The curve usually decreases very rapidly at first and then levels off.

fovea: the central region of the *retina*, packed with *cones*, which is most sensitive in daylight for detail and color.

fraternal twins: siblings born at the same time who have developed from two different ova (eggs); genetically, fraternal twins are no more similar than any pair of siblings.

free association: a diagnostic technique in *psychoanalysis* in which the patient reports whatever comes into his or her mind.

free recall: retrieving items stored in *memory* without attention to the order in which they were learned.

frequency: how often a sound or light cycles from maximum to minimum intensity, which corresponds roughly to our experience of sound pitch and color, respectively; also called wavelength.

frustration: encountering an obstacle to some desired goal.

fugue state: a condition in which a person has *amnesia* for his or her life history, wanders off, and begins a new life somewhere else.

functional autonomy: the idea that *motives* may become independent of their origins.

functional psychosis: a *psychosis* having no known organic cause.

future shock: a term coined by Alvin Toffler to describe the stress brought on by too much change in too little time.

galvanic skin response (GSR): rapid changes in the electrical conductivity of the skin, indicating emotion.

general adaptation syndrome: a sequence of physiological reactions to sustained stress, consisting of three phases: *alarm reaction, resistance, and exhaustion.*

general paresis: a type of organic *psychosis* caused by syphilitic infection of the brain and spinal cord.

generalization: in conditioning, the principle that once a *conditioned response* has been established to a certain *stimulus*, similar stimuli will also elicit that response.

genes: the basic units of heredity, located in the chromosomes of every cell.

genetic: pertaining to the genes, the units of hereditary transmission.

Gestalt psychology: a system of psychological *theory* emphasizing the overall relationship among elements, the pattern of the whole.

gradient of texture: a *monocular cue* of *depth perception* in which the individual features of distant objects appear closer together, making the texture appear denser.

grammar: the set of rules that describes the ways the classes of words in *language* may be combined.

group therapy: a psychotherapeutic technique involving a therapist providing guidance and a small group of patients discussing their problems.

growth needs: motives to develop the *self* from a solid stable base.

GSR: see *galvanic skin response.*

hallucination: a *percept* with very little relationship to the actual *stimulus.*

hallucinogen: any of a group of nonaddictive *drugs* which produce *hallucinations*, usually visual.

hashish: a dried resin from the *Cannabis* (marijuana) plant, five to eight times stronger than *marijuana.*

Hearsay: a computer program designed to recognize human speech.

hebephrenic schizophrenia: a type of *schizophrenia* characterized by impulsive conduct, silliness, sudden laughing or crying, infantile behavior, and lack of control of body functions.

hemisphere: one of the two halves of the brain, connected by the *corpus callosum.*

heredity: the characteristics genetically derived from one's ancestors.

hermaphrodite: an individual who has both male and female sex organs.

heroin: a highly addictive *narcotic* derived from *opium.*

hierarchy of needs: Maslow's model of human *motivation* in which the most basic needs (e.g., physiological and safety needs) must be satisfied before one progresses to higher-order needs (e.g., esteem and self-actualization needs).

homeostasis: the tendency of an organism to maintain a constant state, as in temperature control or blood sugar level.

hormones: internal secretions of the endocrine system into the bloodstream that affect internal bodily functions.

humanistic theory: a view of personality concerned with distinctively human *motives, purposes, goals, and their interrelations, as contrasted with people's animal *motivations.*

humanistic therapy: a type of *psychotherapy* focusing on *self-actualization.*

hypnosis: a relaxed state characterized by heightened *suggestibility* to the directions of the hypnotist.

hypnotic induction: the procedure of putting a person into a hypnotic state; it usually involves having the subject relax and concentrate on the hypnotist's instructions.

hypochondria: a type of *neurosis* in which a person is excessively concerned about ailments and the condition of his or her body.

hypothalamus: a part of the brain lying between the *brain stem* and the cortex, whose functions include regulating sleep, temperature, thirst, sex, hunger, and *emotion.*

hypothesis: a tentative statement about events, or relationships between events, in the real world.

hysteria: a neurosis marked by the psychological isolation of part of the body (see *conversion hysteria*) or part of the mind or personality (see *dissociative hysteria*).

icon: a facsimile of the visual *stimulus* which persists for a very brief period (usually less than a second) following presentation.

id: according to Freud, the part of the personality which desires immediate gratification of primitive needs regardless of the consequences; it seeks to avoid all unpleasantness (see *ego, supergo*).

identical twins: twins developing from a single ovum (egg) and who thus have identical heredities.

identification: seeing oneself as like someone else and wanting to increase the similarity, often leading to imitation of the person or group identified with.

identity crisis: the period in adolescence when the individual must make major decisions about the future of his life while also confused by the biological changes between childhood and adulthood.

illusion: an inaccurate *percept* caused by a misleading *stimulus.*

impossible figure: a *stimulus* which cannot be organized into a meaningful *percept.*

imprinting: *learning* certain social *responses* (e.g., following) to something (usually the mother) in a short *critical period* after birth.

incongruence: a state in which there is a discrepancy between the way a person perceives him or herself and the way others react to him or her.

independent variable: the *variable* which is manipulated in an *experiment* in order to see how it affects the *dependent variable.*

industrial psychology: a specialized field of applied psychology concerned with methods of hiring, training, counseling, and supervising personnel in business and industry. Sometimes it is also concerned with increasing work efficiency and redesigning machines to suit better the capacities of the worker.

information processing approach: a view of psychological processes in terms of how information is handled in, for example, perception, memory, and problem solving; contrasts with behavioral approaches and others; often uses computer as analogy to human thought.

inhibition: a condition of the *neuron* in which firing is less likely than usual (contrast *excitement*).

insight: the sudden discovery of a solution to a problem or of a new *concept.*

instinct: unlearned, patterned, goal-directed *behavior* which is species-specific; for example, nest-building in birds.

instinctive drift: interference in *learning* a *behavior* from instinctive behaviors characteristic of the animal in its natural habitat.

intelligence: a person's abilities over a wide range of tasks involving vocabulary, numbers, problem solving, *concepts,* etc.

intelligence quotient (IQ): a numerical representation of intelligence as measured by certain tests. As originally defined, the IQ was the *mental age* divided by the chronological age and multiplied by 100; now it is a score indicating position relative to other people the same age.

interactive theory of perception: a theory that depicts perception as an interaction between sensory input and states of readiness for certain kinds of information.

interference theory (of forgetting): a *theory* of forgetting which postulates that other information makes it difficult or impossible to retrieve the desired information.

intermittent reinforcement: the *reinforcement* of a given *response* only some of the times it occurs.

interpersonal attraction: liking between people.

interpretation: in *psychoanalysis,* the analyst's explanations of conflicts in the patient's personality, primarily based on data from *free associations,* dreams, *resistances,* and *transference.*

intimacy crisis: in Erikson's theory, the young adult's conflict between newfound independence and his or her need for an intimate emotional relationship.

introspection: reporting inner experiences.

IQ: see *intelligence quotient.*

iris: the colored part of the eye around the *pupil.* The muscles of the iris narrow or enlarge the pupil to control the amount of light entering the eye.

isolation: a *defense mechanism* in which an idea is separated from its emotional significance.

James-Lange theory: the view that *emotion* is the *perception* of reactions and changes in the body.

just noticeable difference (j.n.d.): a measure of the *difference threshold.* The ratio of the j.n.d. to the standard is approximately constant over a wide range of stimulation.

language: a form of communication in which symbols are combined according to a set of rules (*grammar*) to convey meaning.

latency stage: Freud's term for the *psychosexual stage* following the *phallic stage,* when sexual and aggressive impulses are somewhat subdued and the child turns his *attention* outward toward his environment (ages 6 to 12).

latent content: in dream *interpretation,* the underlying significance or real meaning of a dream, usually not apparent from the dream's *manifest content.*

latent learning: *learning* that occurs without obvious *reinforcement* and without behavioral demonstration until later, when there is an incentive.

law of effect: Thorndike's principle stating that *behavior* will be influenced by its effect (outcome): A satisfying outcome to a *response* increases the likelihood that the response will be repeated; an unsatisfying one decreases it.

learned helplessness: a condition in which an organism has learned that it can do nothing to escape an aversive situation.

learning: a general term referring to a relatively permanent change in *behavior* that is the result of practice.

learning curve: a graphic representation of progress in *learning* in which *performance* is plotted on the vertical axis and trials or time are plotted on the horizontal axis.

lens: the focusing element of the eye.

lesion: localized damage to an organ or tissue.

lie detector (polygraph): an apparatus usually

measuring heart rate, breathing rate, and the *galvanic skin response*. Comparison of these measures at the time of the investigatory questions with a base rate determined by other questions is used to judge whether the subject is lying or not.

limbic system: a set of structures in the brain located on the underside of the *cerebral cortex*; concerned with *emotion* and *motivation*.

linear perspective: a *monocular cue* of *depth perception* in which distant objects appear closer together than near ones.

localization: in biological psychology, the view that a limited area of the brain is crucial to and primarily responsible for a particular biological function.

longitudinal method: the study of an individual at different stages of his or her development (contrast *cross-sectional method*).

long-term store (LTS): the storage system of *memory* that has an unlimited capacity and is the relatively permanent component of the memory system.

LSD: lysergic acid diethylamide, a powerful *hallucinogen* which appears to have some therapeutic use in the treatment of alcoholics and the mentally ill.

LTS: see *long-term store*.

Machiavellian: the quality of people who believe in interpersonal manipulation without regard to moral standards; after Machiavelli's book on politics, *The Prince*.

manic-depressive psychosis: a *functional psychosis* characterized by violent swings of *emotion* from *euphoria* and excitement to extreme *depression*.

manifest content: in dream *interpretation*, the dream as reported by the patient (contrast *latent content*).

marijuana: a drug consisting of the dried leaves and flowering tops of the *Cannabis sativa* plant. Smoking or otherwise consuming it may enhance sensory experiences and produce a state of *euphoria*.

massed practice: a long, continuous *learning* session, less efficient than *distributed practice*.

mean: a measure of central tendency calculated by dividing the sum of a set of scores by the number of scores.

median: in a set of scores, the score above which half the scores fall and below which half the scores fall.

memory: the retention of learned *behavior* or information over time.

memory span: the amount of material which can be retrieved after a single presentation, usually seven items plus or minus two.

menopause: the time of a woman's life when her ovaries cease producing eggs; menstruation also ceases; usually occurs in the woman's late forties or early fifties.

mental age: a scale unit used in *intelligence* testing; the age level at which a child is performing (for example, a child of 5 who can do things an average 7-year-old does has a mental age of 7).

mental disorder: a general term referring to *personality disorders, neuroses, psychoses,* and others.

mescaline: a *hallucinogenic* drug derived from *peyote*.

methadone: a synthetic *narcotic* used in the treatment of *heroin* addicts because it is cheaper and available by prescription.

method of loci: a type of *mnemonic device* in which a person imagines a series of locations and then integrates to-be-remembered information into these loci.

mid-life crisis: in adult developmental psychology, a time of intense reevaluation of family and career goals which may lead to disruptions such as divorce or radical career change.

Minnesota Multiphasic Personality Inventory (MMPI): the most widely used personality test, which includes several subtests or scales measuring different traits.

mnemonic device: a method of introducing meaning into an unrelated series of items to be learned (such as, Thirty days hath September . . .).

mode: in a set of scores, the most frequent score.

model: a description or interpretation of events in terms of a particular theory; or, a person imitated by another (see *modeling*).

modeling: the observation of one person (the *model*) by another person, who may thereby *learn* the *behavior* modeled (or some aspect of it).

monocular cue: a cue to *depth perception* not dependent on the use of two eyes, such as *linear perspective, gradient of texture,* changes in color, shadows, and relative movement.

moral reasoning: the mental processes a person uses to evaluate the morality of a situation and, presumably, to reach decisions about how to behave in the situation. According to L. Kohlberg, there are six invariant stages of development through which an individual's moral reasoning can pass.

morphine: the *narcotic* ingredient in the *opium* poppy, extracted by chemical processing.

motivation: a general term referring to an organism's tendency toward need-fulfilling and goal-seeking *behavior*.

motive: a need directing *behavior* toward a goal.

motor messages: impulses the *central nervous system* sends to the muscles, initiating relaxation or contraction.

multiaxial diagnosis: in DSM-III, patients will be evaluated in several ways (axes), including the primary mental disorder, complicating personality and physical problems, and degree of life stress and coping ability.

multiple personality: an extreme form of *dissociative hysteria* in which two or more intricately organized personalities exist in the same person.

narcotic: any of a group of highly addictive drugs whose medical uses include pain relief, sedation, and sleep inducement.

natural experiment: an *experiment* in which the difference between the *experimental* and *con-trol groups* are not created by the psychologist; the groups are formed on the basis of some characteristic the *subjects* had before they were studied.

natural language material: psychologists' jargon for sentences and stories and similar material, in contrast to nonsense syllables and lists of unrelated words.

need complementarity: the fitting together of two people's different needs in such a way that each person may be able to satisfy the other's needs; a factor involved in *interpersonal attraction.*

negative correlation: a *correlation* between zero and −1, indicating a negative relationship between two *variables:* if one variable goes up, the other is likely to go down.

negative hallucination: the absence of *perception* in spite of the availability of information to a sense organ.

negative reinforcer: a stimulus whose removal after a given *behavior* increases the likelihood that the behavior will be repeated; for example, electric shock.

negative transfer: the detrimental effect of previous *learning* on later learning, believed to occur because incompatible *responses* are required in the old and the new situations.

nerve: a bundle of fibers each composed of many *neurons.*

nervous system: the brain, the spinal cord, and the *nerves* serving the muscles, sense organs, and glands.

neuron: a nerve cell, the basic unit of the *nervous system,* which consists of *dendrites,* a *cell body,* and an *axon.*

neurosis: the relatively mild form of *mental disorder* in which a sense of reality is maintained in spite of excessive *anxiety;* often characterized by exaggerated *defense mechanisms.*

nicotine: the addictive active ingredient in tobacco, implicated in lung cancer, emphysema, and heart disease.

nonsense syllable: a meaningless combination of three letters, two consonants separated by a vowel.

nonverbal communication: transmission of ideas without the aid of words, by using (not necessarily intentionally) facial expressions, tone of voice, body posture, etc.

norm: a standard or *model* for behavior in a group.

NREM: non-REM sleep, that is, sleep without Rapid Eye Movements; generally, nondreaming sleep.

nurturance: caring for someone who is dependent.

object constancy: the tendency to perceive an object as the same recognizable figure in varied situations.

objective test: a measure posing straightforward questions which call for factual, noninterpretive answers, such as true-false, multiple choice, or completion questions (contrast *projective test*).

obsession: a repetitive and constantly intruding thought or idea.

obsessive-compulsive neurosis: a *neurosis* characterized by *obsessions* or *compulsions* or a combination of both.

Oedipus complex: Freud's term for the male child's fantasy love for his mother, accompanied by fears of his father's violence toward him. It may refer to the sexual attachment of a child of either sex to the parent of the opposite sex.

olfaction: sense of smell.

one-word speech: the first stage of speech, in which a single word is used to express a complex idea.

open words: words other than *pivot words*, used by young children in combination with pivot words to form two-word sentences.

operant conditioning: the process of strengthening a *response* by reinforcing it all or some proportion of the times it occurs.

operation: a mental routine enabling a person to transform information for some purpose.

operational definition: a definition of a term or concept in terms of the observable activities considered to indicate its presence.

opium: a *narcotic* consisting of the dried juice from the seed pods of the opium poppy.

optic nerve: the bundle of neural fibers transmitting messages from the *retina* to the brain.

oral stage: Freud's term for the first *psychosexual stage,* when much of the child's pleasure and interactions with its environment involves its mouth (the first year).

organic psychosis: a *psychosis* having an identifiable physical cause, usually brain damage.

organismic premise: the view that single acts cannot be understood in isolation from the activities of the whole animal.

overregularization: in the development of language skills, the child's generalization of the rules of *grammar* to situations where they are inappropriate; for example, "hisself" instead of "himself."

paired-associate learning: the *learning* of items arranged in pairs so that an *association* develops between the first item of each pair (the *stimulus*) and the second (the *response*).

pandemonium model: Selfridge's *model* of *perception* in which sensory input and feature extraction by various "demons" lead to perception and recognition of visual patterns.

paradoxical sleep: the type of sleep in which the *brainwaves* are like those of an alert, waking subject, but the *subject* cannot be awakened readily. Dreaming occurs during paradoxical sleep.

parallel processing: the simultaneous utilization of several streams of incoming information.

paranoia: a *functional psychosis* characterized by *delusions* of persecution.

paranoid schizophrenia: a type of *schizophrenia* in which the patient has *delusions* of persecution or believes he or she is controlled by external forces.

parapsychology: the study of psychic phenomena such as ESP.

parasympathetic division: see *autonomic nervous system.*

peak experience: a mystical experience involving

a *euphoric* feeling of the unity and harmony of everything in the world.

penis envy: in Freudian psychosexual theory, the envy of girls aged 3 to 5 for the male genital organ, accompanied by attraction to the father.

percept: an organized image received through one of the senses.

perception: the process of becoming aware of and interpreting the environment through use of the senses.

perceptual contrast: the relationship between a *stimulus* and preceding or surrounding stimuli, emphasizing the differences between them; examples are size contrast, shape contrast, and color contrast.

perceptual cycle: a unit of perceptual activity that includes processing sensory input, trying to identify it by forming hypotheses, anticipating what the next sensory input is likely to be, and actively exploring the environment for crucial stimuli.

perceptual defense: the tendency of people to form *percepts* of unpleasant *stimuli* less quickly than of neutral or positive stimuli.

performance: overt *behavior,* as distinct from, for example, knowledge or information.

performance test: a method of evaluation based on behavior rather than verbal activity.

period of concrete operations: Piaget's term for the ages 6 through 10 when the child begins to think about things in logical and organized ways.

period of formal operations: Piaget's term for the time around age 12 when the child begins to think as adults do, becoming capable of thinking about abstract ideas and using formal logic and the scientific method.

peripheral nervous system: all of the *nervous system* outside the brain and the spinal cord.

Personal Data Sheet: the first important personality assessment questionnaire, used during World War I to identify emotionally unfit soldiers.

personal space: the space or area around a person which he or she is inclined to protect from outsiders; it also includes spaces or areas a per-son permanently or temporarily adopts as his or her own, such as a specific chair (see *territory*).

personality: all the patterns of thought and behavior that characterize an individual.

personality disorder: a category of abnormal behavior including all deeply ingrained maladaptive behavior patterns, such as *alcoholism,* drug *dependence,* and *sexual deviations.*

persuasion: the procedure, usually in the form of verbal communication, of trying to change another person's beliefs or opinions.

peyote: a *hallucinogen* found in the *peyote* cactus of northern and central Mexico.

phallic stage: Freud's term for the *psychosexual stage* in the male following the *anal stage,* when the boy's gratification is associated with his penis and he becomes sexually attracted to his mother (ages 3 to 6) (see *Oedipus complex, castration anxiety*).

phi phenomenon: the *perception* of one event moving into or becoming another; usually, the perception of movement between two successive presentations of separate points of light.

phobia: an unrealistic and disrupting fear of particular objects or situations.

physical dependence: addiction; the body's *dependence* on a *drug* to the extent that not having the drug would cause *withdrawal;* also characterized by *tolerance* (contrast *psychological dependence*).

pituitary gland: the so-called master gland of the endocrine system, located at the base of the brain; controls many of the other endocrine glands.

pivot grammar: a *grammar* proposed to explain the two-word sentence stage of language development in which the child combines *pivot words* with *open words* to form sentences.

pivot words: frequently used general purpose words in the two-word sentence stage of a child's development of language.

PKU (phenylketonuria): a genetically based metabolic disorder that results in mental retardation unless the child's diet is carefully controlled.

placebo: a fake pill or other biologically ineffective treatment given to *subjects* as a control in *experiments*. Often the subjects' belief that it is a real treatment causes a positive effect.

pleasure principle: the *id's* avoidance of unpleasantness and seeking for immediate gratification of desires.

polygraph: see *lie detector*.

positive correlation: a *correlation* between zero and +1, indicating a positive relationship between two *variables*: if one variable goes up, the other is likely to go up.

positive reinforcer: a *stimulus* which, if presented to a *subject* after a response, increases the *probability* that the *response* will be repeated.

positive transfer: the beneficial effect of some previous *learning* on later learning, believed to occur because similar *stimuli* and *responses* are required in the two situations.

postfigurative culture: a culture in which children learn from their parents, the pattern typical of most cultures (contrast *prefigurative culture*).

postparental family: a family after the children have left home.

precognition: knowledge of an event before it happens; a form of *extrasensory perception*.

predictive validity: the usefulness of a test determined by its ability to predict *behavior*.

prefigurative culture: a culture in which children must teach their parents, the pattern modern American society is approaching with its rapid technological change (contrast *post-figurative culture*).

premenstrual syndrome: symptoms many women feel in the few days before their menstrual period, including tension, pain, irritability, bloating, and others.

preoperational period: Piaget's term for the ages 2 through 7 when the child's mental organizational functions are absent or weak.

primary process thinking: thought production characteristic of the operation of the *pleasure principle* in which normal logic does not operate (e.g., *hallucinations* of something desired).

primary reinforcer: in *operant conditioning*, a stimulus whose natural effect, if presented immediately after the operant *response*, is to make the recurrence of that response more likely (see *secondary reinforcer*).

privilege envy: the female's socially induced envy of privileged male status, a *concept* which many psychologists consider more useful than its older counterpart, Freud's concept of *penis envy*.

proactive interference: the negative effects of information previously stored in *memory* on *learning* and *recall* of new material.

probability: likelihood; particularly, the estimate of the likelihood that some event will occur based on previous observation of the same or similar events.

profile: a graphic representation of a person's scores on a number of psychological tests.

projection: a *defense mechanism* in which a person remains unaware of his undesirable traits and attributes them to others.

projective test: a personality test in which the *subject* is presented with ambiguous *stimuli* and asked to describe them or tell stories about them, the idea being that the subject's responses will reveal aspects of his or her self (contrast *objective test*).

propinquity: closeness; a factor involved in *interpersonal attraction*.

proximity: the Gestalt principle of psychology in which objects near each other are seen as going together.

pseudonym: a false name.

psychoanalysis: a *psychotherapy* based on Freud's *psychoanalytic theory* emphasizing insight into the patient's total personality.

psychoanalytic theory: Freud's comprehensive view of personality, emphasizing the effects of early experience and including the concepts of the *id, ego,* and *superego*.

psychokinesis: the hypothetical ability to control physical events by mental means; mind over matter.

psychological dependence: learned *dependence* on a *drug* such that the idea of not having the drug is intolerable (contrast with *physical dependence*).

psychophysics: the study of the relationship between environmental changes and psychological experience at the point of sensory contact between person and world.

psychosexual stage: one of the phases of growing up, according to Freud; each stage is characterized by the part of the body with which pleasure is associated.

psychosis: a *mental disorder* characterized by loss of contact with reality, often requiring hospitalization.

psychosomatic illness: an ailment with physical symptoms attributable to emotional disturbance (such as ulcers, or high blood pressure).

psychotherapy: the treatment of *mental disorders* and mild adjustment of problems by means of psychological techniques.

psychotomimetic drug: a *drug* that produces psychosis-like symptoms.

punishment: a negative incentive capable of producing pain or annoyance, or the process of applying it after a *response.*

pupil: the hole surrounded by the *iris* through which light passes into the eyeball.

randomization: the procedure by which two (or more) groups are selected on a chance basis so as to be as nearly equal as possible.

rapid eye movements (REMs): eye movements that usually occur during dreaming in *paradoxical sleep.*

reaction formation: a *defense mechanism* in which an objectionable motive is replaced with its opposite.

reality principle: the characteristic of the *ego* distinguishing between the real and the unreal and operating to satisfy desires on that basis.

recall: the type of remembering in which the *subject* retrieves from memory information that was learned earlier.

recency effect: the tendency of items at the end of a list to be more easily remembered than items earlier in the list.

receptor cells: cells specialized to respond to particular kinds of changes in physical energy, which provide the organism with information about its environment.

recessive gene: a gene carrying traits which will show up in offspring only if both parents transmit the gene to the child.

reciprocity: in interpersonal attraction, the tendency for people to like those who like them.

reciprocity norm: the standard for social *behavior* stipulating that people should give and return favors to others.

recognition: the type of remembering in which the *subject* chooses or recognizes previously encountered material presented along with new material, as in true-false or multiple choice questions on an examination.

reflex: elementary, direct, unthinking *behavior* executed at the spinal cord level without involving the brain.

regression: a reaction to *anxiety* or *frustration* in which a person reverts to more primitive or childish *behavior.*

rehearsal: mental repetition of information to be remembered.

reinforcement: the presentation, once or periodically, of a *reinforcer.*

reinforcer: in *operant conditioning*, a *stimulus* which, when it follows any *behavior*, increases the *probability* that the behavior will be repeated; in *classical conditioning*, the *unconditioned stimulus.*

reliability: the degree of self-consistency of a method of measurement; for instance, a test on which a test's subject gets about the same score whenever the test is given to that subject.

REMs: see *rapid eye movements.*

repression: a *defense mechanism* in which unpleasant or unacceptable thoughts or *motives* are not permitted to enter consciousness.

resistance: 1. in *psychoanalysis*, a subject's psychological barrier against becoming aware of unconscious impulses and discussing them with the analyst; 2. the second phase of the *general adaptation syndrome*, in which the body endures a continuing stressful situation.

response: a *behavior* elicited by a *stimulus.*

retention: keeping in *memory* what has been learned; this is measured by the *recall, recognition,* or *savings methods.*

reticular formation: a network of cells and fibers extending through the *brain stem* and up into the *thalamus,* important as an arousal mechanism.

retina: the back lining of the eyeball on which light rays are focused and which contains the visual receptors (*rods* and *cones*).

retinal disparity: the slight difference of the image on the *retina* of one eye from that on the other; an important *binocular cue* of *depth perception.*

retrieval: the process in which information stored in memory is brought back into conscious thought.

retroactive interference: the negative effect of new *learning* on the retention of older material.

reversible figure: a *stimulus* that lends itself to two equally valid *percepts.*

reward: a stimulus which arouses pleasure or satisfies a drive; a positive reinforcer.

rhodopsin: the light-sensitive chemical contained in the *rods* of the eye which enables the eye to adjust to varying levels of light by changing in composition.

rod: a retinal *receptor cell* which registers the intensity of light energy (perceived as brightness) but not the wavelength (color); especially important in dim illumination.

Rorschach Inkblot Test: a widely used *projective test* using symmetrical inkblots as the *stimuli.*

same-subject control: form of control in an *experiment* in which the same *subjects* are used for both the experimental and control groups.

sample: the group of *subjects* used in an *experiment,* understood to come from a larger population of possible subjects.

SAT: abbreviation for Scholastic Aptitude Test.

savings method: a way of measuring *memory* in which the *subject* relearns material previously learned; the difference between the number of trials required in each situation represents the savings.

scalloping: in fixed *reinforcement* schedules, the way that after a reinforcement, the rate of responding decreases slightly and increases again before the next reinforcement.

scapegoat: an innocent object of *displaced aggression.*

schedule of reinforcement: some specified sequence for reinforcing a given *response* only some proportion of the time it occurs.

schema: a general plan or framework for perception or action.

schizophrenia: a *functional psychosis* characterized by general disorganization in thought and *behavior,* a loosening of *associations,* and lack of harmony between aspects of personality functioning. Primary symptoms are unusual or inappropriate *emotions,* social withdrawal, and thought disturbance; common secondary symptoms include auditory *hallucinations, delusions,* and bizarre behavior.

scholastic: pertaining to school and education.

scholastic aptitude test: an *aptitude test* used to predict academic performance.

school psychology: guidance and counseling psychology in schools.

scientific method: a systematic way of seeking knowledge consisting of three essential features: stating a *hypothesis* to be tested, gathering evidence which relates to the hypothesis, and interpreting and drawing conclusions about the results.

secondary elaboration: in the psychoanalytic theory of dreams, the final arrangement of dream images to give the dream some semblance of logic and coherence.

secondary process thinking: thought production characteristic of the operation of the *reality principle;* it is rational, logical, purposeful, and critical in nature.

secondary reinforcer: a *stimulus* that has acquired a reinforcing effect by being associated with a *primary reinforcer.*

self: an individual's *perception* of his or her own personality.

self-actualization: Maslow's term for an individual's striving toward realizing his or her greatest potential, in accord with the highest ideals of humanity.

self-efficacy: in Bandura's theory, a belief that one can have an effect.

sensitivity group: a type of self-improvement group in which members learn through interaction and discussion how to recognize the emotional reactions their actions provoke in others.

sensory message: a nervous impulse *receptor cells* send to the *central nervous system.*

sensory-motor period: the first stage of intellectual development (birth to 18 months) when proficiency in sensory-perceptual and motor-behavior acts increases without any mediation by *cognitions.*

sensory store (SS): the first stage of *memory* storage, in which information from the environment is preserved in rather literal form for a very brief period (half a second or so).

separation anxiety: the infant's fear that its mother will leave; it first appears when the child is about 6 months old.

serial processing: handling bits of information one-by-one, in order; contrast with *parallel processing.*

sex-role stereotypes: societal beliefs about differences in what *behavior* is natural or appropriate for men and for women.

sexual deviation: sexual arousal and satisfaction from unusual objects or behavior; e.g., *fetishism* and exhibitionism.

shape constancy: the tendency to perceive a familiar object as always the same shape regardless of the actual visual *stimulus* it presents.

shaping: teaching a desired *response* by reinforcing a series of actions successively more similar to it.

short-term store (STS): the second storage system of *memory,* which is impermanent (limited to about twenty seconds) and of limited capacity (seven items plus or minus two), and in which material is encoded for *long-term storage.*

significance: the trustworthiness of an experiment's result; the level of *probability* that events measured did not occur by chance.

similarity: a Gestalt principle of psychology in which objects in a group that resemble each other are seen as going together.

size constancy: the tendency to perceive a familiar object as of its actual size regardless of its distance from the observer.

social behavior theory: a *theory* of personality that emphasizes *stimuli, responses,* and outcomes in its description of *learning* and performance.

social norm: a widely shared set of views of what constitutes proper *behavior.*

social responsibility norm: the standard for social *behavior* stipulating that people should help those who need help.

socialization: the processes whereby an individual learns those characteristics and *behavior* that are appropriate to his or her social environment.

spontaneous recovery: the return in strength of a *conditioned response* after an interval following *extinction.*

standard deviation: a number indicating the range over which a set of scores varies.

Stanford-Binet test: a widely used individual test of *intelligence.*

state-dependent learning: after learning something in a particular state of consciousness (e.g., while drunk), memory for that information is sometimes better if that state is reinstituted at the time of retrieval.

stimulant: a type of *drug* which increases alertness and heightens the activity of the *central nervous system;* habitual use is dangerous although the potential for *physical dependence* is unclear (see *amphetamine, cocaine*).

stimulus: any object, event, or energy change in the environment that excites a sense organ.

stimulus feeding: providing a child with sensory stimulation.

stooge: see *confederate.*

storage: the *memory* process in which information is stored or saved for future use.

Strong Vocational Interest Blank (SVIB): a questionnaire designed to measure the degree of similarity in things liked and disliked between the *subject* and satisfied members of various occupations, and thus to judge what occupations the subject seems best suited to.

STS: see *short-term store.*

subject: a person participating in an *experiment.*

subjective: reflecting the viewpoint of a particular individual.

sublimation: a *defense mechanism* in which socially unacceptable motives (*id* instincts) are expressed in socially acceptable forms.

suggestibility: a greater-than-normal willingness to accept the statements of another person.

superego: the part of the personality concerned with moral standards; the superego has positive, nonpunitive as well as critical, punitive aspects.

superordinate concept: a class or category that is more abstract than another and includes it; "animal" is a superordinate concept for "dog," "cat," etc.

SVIB: see *Strong Vocational Interest Blank.*

symbol: something that stands for something else, as words are symbols for the objects and events they represent.

synapse: the junction between the *axon* of one *neuron* and the *dendrite* or *cell body* of another, where a nerve impulse is transmitted from one cell to the other.

syndrome: a collection of symptoms characteristic of a particular ailment or condition.

tag question: a short confirming question placed at the end of a declarative sentence; for example, "She can swim well, can't she?"

TAT: see *Thematic Apperception Test.*

telegraphic speech: the abbreviated form of speech of young children.

telepathy: a form of *extrasensory perception* in which one person's thoughts are received by another person.

template matching: the process in which a *stimulus* is compared with a template or model; similar to early theories of human *perception.*

territory: "home turf," an area an individual defends as his or her own (see *personal space*).

testosterone: a male sex hormone which influences not only sex drive but also aggressiveness.

T-group: a training group; a type of *encounter group.*

thalamus: a part of the brain sitting on top of the *brain stem,* which functions as a relay station for impulses coming up from the spinal cord and down from the *cerebral cortex.*

THC: tetrahydrocannabinol, the active ingredient in *marijuana* and *hashish.*

Thematic Apperception Test (TAT): a *projective test* consisting of a series of pictures of people involved in various activities; the *subject's* stories about the pictures are presumed to reveal his or her own hopes and fears.

theory: a set of assumptions used to explain a number of facts and to predict future events.

token economy: a type of *behavior therapy,* often used with mental patients; patients are paid for various kinds of activities with tokens, which can be exchanged for privileges.

tolerance: one of the characteristics of *physical dependence* on a drug in which, as use continues, more and more of the drug must be taken to achieve the same effect.

transfer of training: the effect of previous *learning* on present learning (see *positive transfer, negative transfer*).

transference: in *psychoanalysis,* the patient's emotional attachment to the analyst, either positive or negative, believed to reflect past interpersonal relationships.

tranquilizer: a type of *depressant drug* which slows down the *central nervous system* and leads to relaxation.

trauma: in Freud's early theories, a disturbing event in a patient's life history that was responsible for later psychological problems.

trial-and-error learning: *learning* or problem-solving in which alternative possibilities are tried and those which do not produce desirable results are gradually eliminated.

trigram: a three-letter set of consonants, used in some memory research.

true experiment: an *experiment* in which randomized groups are compared with respect to differences between them created by the experimenter (contrast *natural experiment*).

Type A, Type B lifestyles: from a theory originally designed to predict heart attacks; Type A lives are highly stressful, full of competition, impatience, and frustration; Type B lives are easy-going.

unconditional positive regard: in *client-centered therapy*, the therapist's positive attitude toward the client regardless of his *behavior*; one of the three essential characteristics of the therapeutic environment in client-centered therapy (see *congruence, empathetic understanding*).

unconditioned response (UR): in classical conditioning, the unlearned *response* originally elicited by an *unconditioned stimulus*.

unconditioned stimulus (US): in classical conditioning, a *stimulus* which consistently elicits an unlearned response.

unconscious: Freud's term for the part of the mind whose contents the person is unaware of.

undoing: a *defense mechanism* in which a compensatory act is used to correct an earlier action (such as being especially nice to someone one had been angry with before).

universals: certain essential features of *language* found in all known languages; for example, nouns and verbs.

UR: see *unconditioned response*.

US: see *unconditioned stimulus*.

validity: the degree to which a method of measurement measures what it is intended to measure.

variable: one of the conditions controlled or measured in an *experiment*.

variable-interval schedule: a schedule of *reinforcement* in which *subjects* are reinforced after an interval of time which varies around a specified average.

verbal test: a test requiring spoken or written responses.

visual acuity: sharpness of vision; ability to see one thing as clearly distinct from another.

WAIS: see *Wechsler Adult Intelligence Scale*.

wavelength: the distance from one crest of an energy wave to the next. With light waves, wavelength determines perceived color; with sound waves, it determines pitch.

Weber's Law: a law stating that the ratio of the *just noticeable difference* for any *stimulus* magnitude is relatively constant.

Wechsler Adult Intelligence Scale (WAIS): the most widely used individual *intelligence test* for adults.

Wernicke's area: an area in the left cerebral hemisphere thought to regulate speech comprehension in right-handed individuals.

withdrawal: one of the characteristics of *physical dependence* on a *drug*, in which stopping use of the drug leads to unpleasant symptoms such as irritability and nausea, and, in extreme cases, death.

XYY males: men who have an extra Y sex chromosome; evidence about violence by these men is inconclusive.

References

Most references given here are books and journal articles. The listings provide the following information:

Book

Smith, J., & Jones, R.   *The last purple cow.*
(author or authors)   *(title of book)*

Hapless, 1973.
(publisher) (year of publication)

Journal article

Smith, J.   Unusual fears of college seniors.
(author)   *(title of article)*

Journal of Abstract Ideas,   1976, *28,* 426–433.
(name of journal)   *(year) (volume) (pages)*

Abramson, L. Y., Seligman, M. E. P., & Teasdale, J. D. Learned helplessness in humans: Critique and reformulation. *Journal of Abnormal Psychology,* 1978, *87,* 49–74.

Advisory Panel. *On further examination: Report of the advisory panel on the Scholastic Aptitude Test score decline.* College Entrance Examination Board, 1977.

Aiken, L. R., Jr. *Psychological and educational testing.* Allyn & Bacon, 1971.

Allport, G. W. *Pattern and growth in personality.* Holt, Rinehart & Winston, 1961.

American Psychiatric Association. *Diagnostic and statistical manual of mental disorders.* 2nd ed. American Psychiatric Association, 1968.

Anastasi, A. *Psychological testing.* 3rd ed. Macmillan, 1968.

Anderson, J. A. D., Basker, M. A., & Dalton, R. Migraine and hypnotherapy. *International Journal of Clinical and Experimental Hypnosis,* 1975, *13,* 48–58.

Andrews, G. Comments. In G. Andrews & S. Vinkenoog (eds.), *The book of grass.* Grove Press, 1967.

Argyle, M. The laws of looking. *Human Nature.* January 1978.

Aries, P. *Centuries of childhood.* Knopf, 1962.

Arieta, S. Etiological considerations of schizophrenia. In S. C. Sher & H. R. Davis (eds.), *The outpatient treatment of schizophrenia.* Grune & Stratton, 1960.

Aronson, E. *The social animal.* 2nd ed. Freeman, 1976.

Aronson, E., Willerman, B., & Floyd, J. The effect of a pratfall on increasing interpersonal attractiveness. *Psychonomic Science,* 1966, *4,* 157–158.

Asch, S. E. Studies of independence and conformity: A minority of one against a unanimous majority. *Psychological Monographs,* 1956, *70,* No. 416.

Asher, J. Geller demystified? *APA Monitor,* February 1976.

Atkinson, J. W. *An introduction to motivation.* Van Nostrand, 1964.

Atkinson, J. W., & Birch, D. *An introduction to motivation.* 2nd ed. Van Nostrand, 1978.

Atkinson, R. C., & Shiffrin, R. M. Human memory: A proposed system and its control processes. In K. W. Spence & J. T. Spence (eds.), *The psychology of learning and motivation,* Vol. 2. Academic Press, 1968.

Ax, A. F. The physiological differentiation between fear and anger in humans. *Psychosomatic Medicine,* 1953, *15,* 433–442.

Ayllon, T., & Azrin, N. H. The measurement and reinforcement of behavior of psychotics. *Journal of the Experimental Analysis of Behavior,* 1965, *8,* 357–383.

Ayllon, T., & Azrin, N. H. *The token economy.* Appleton-Century-Crofts, 1968.

Ayllon, T., & Michael, J. The psychiatric nurse as a behavioral engineer. *Journal of the Experimental Analyses of Behavior,* 1959, *2,* 323–334.

Azrin, N. Pain and aggression. *Readings in Psychology Today,* 2nd ed. CRM Books, 1972.

Baddeley, A. D., & Hitch, G. Working memory. In G. H. Bower (ed.), *The psychology of learning and motivation.* Vol. 8. Academic Press, 1974.

Bakan, P. Dreaming, REM sleep, and the right hemisphere: A theoretical integration. Paper presented at the International Congress of Sleep Research, June 30, 1975.

Ball-Rokeach, S. J. Review of *Television and Aggression* [by S. Feshbach & R. D. Singer]. *Public Opinion Quarterly,* 1971, *35,* 501–504.

Bandura, A. *Principles of behavior modification.* Holt, Rinehart & Winston, 1969.

Bandura, A. *Social learning theory.* General Learning Press, 1971.

Bandura, A. *Aggression: A social learning analysis.* Prentice-Hall, 1973.

Bandura, A. Self-efficacy: Toward a unifying theory of behavioral change. *Psychological Review,* 1977a, *84,* 191–215.

Bandura, A. *Social learning theory.* Prentice-Hall, 1977b.

Bandura, A., Grusec, J. E., & Menlove, F. L. Vicarious extinction of avoidance behavior. *Journal of Personality and Social Psychology,* 1967, *5,* 16–23.

Bandura, A., & Harris, M. B. Modification of syntactic style. *Journal of Experimental Child Psychology,* 1966, *4,* 341–352.

Bandura, A., & Huston, A. C. Identification as a process of incidental learning. *Journal of Abnormal and Social Psychology,* 1961, *63,* 311–318.

Bandura, A., & Kupers, C. J. Transmission of patterns of self-reinforcement through modeling. *Journal of Abnormal and Social Psychology.* 1964, *69,* 1–9.

Bandura, A., & Perloff, B. Relative efficacy of self-monitored and externally-imposed reinforcement systems. *Journal of Personality and Social Psychology,* 1967, *7,* 111–116.

Bandura, A., Ross, D., & Ross, S. A. A comparative test of the status envy, social power, and secondary reinforcement theories of identification learning. *Journal of Abnormal and Social Psychology,* 1963, *67,* 527–534.

Baratz, J. C., & Shuy, R. W. (eds.). *Teaching black children to read.* Center for Applied Linguistics, 1969.

Barber, T. S. *Hypnosis: A scientific approach.* Van Nostrand, 1969.

Bard, P. The neuro-humoral basis of emotional reactions. In C. Murchison (ed.), *A handbook of general experimental psychology.* Clark U. Press, 1934.

Bardwick, J. M. *Psychology of women.* Harper & Row, 1971.

Bardwick, J. M., & Behrman, S. J. Investigation into the effects of anxiety, sexual arousal, and menstrual cycle phase on uterine contractions. *Psychosomatic Medicine,* 1967, *29,* 468–482.

Barker, R. G., Dembo, T., & Lewin, K. Frustration and regression: An experiment with young children. *U. of Iowa Studies in Child Welfare,* 1941, *18,* No. 386.

Barland, G. H. Detection of deception in criminal suspects: A field validation study. Unpublished doctoral dissertation. U. of Utah, 1975.

Barland, G. H., & Raskin, D. C. Detection of deception. In W. F. Prokasy & D. C. Raskin (eds.), *Electrodermal activity in psychological research.* Academic Press, 1973.

Barland, G. H., & Raskin, D. C. An evaluation of field techniques in detection of deception. *Psychophysiology,* 1975, *12,* 321–330.

Baron, R. A. Attraction toward the model and model's competence as determinants of adult imitative behavior. *Journal of Personality and Social Psychology,* 1970, *14,* 345–351.

Barron, F. Threshold for the perception of human movement in inkblots. *Journal of Consulting Psychology,* 1955, *19,* 33–38.

Bartlett, K. It's been a long search for the dean of ESP. *Santa Barbara News-Press,* Sunday, August 13, 1978.

Bateson, G., Jackson, D. D., Haley, J., & Weakland, J. Toward a theory of schizophrenia. *Behavioral Science,* 1956, *1,* 251–264.

Bayley, N. Consistency and variability in the growth of intelligence from birth to eighteen. *Journal of Genetic Psychology,* 1949, *75,* 165–196.

Bem, D. J. Self-perception: An alternative interpretation of cognitive dissonance phenomena. *Psychological Review,* 1967, *74,* 183–200.

Bem, D. J. Self-perception theory. In L. Berkowitz (ed.), *Advances in experimental social psychology,* Vol. 6. Academic Press, 1972.

Bem, S. L. The measurement of psychological androgyny. *Journal of Consulting and Clinical Psychology,* 1974, *42,* 155–162.

Bem, S. L. Beyond androgyny. Some presumptuous prescriptions for a liberated sexual identity. In J. Sherman & F. Denmark (eds.), *Psychology of Women: Future Directions of Research.* Psychological Dimensions, in press.

Berg, I. *Education and jobs: The great training robbery.* Praeger, 1970.

Berger, H. Über das Elektrenkephalogramm des Menchen. *Arch. Psychiat. Nervenkr.,* 1929, *87,* 527–570.

Berger, P. C., & Norsigian, J. Menopause. In Boston Women's Health Book Collective (eds.), *Our bodies, ourselves,* 2nd ed. Simon & Schuster, 1976.

Bergin, A. E. Some implications of psychotherapy research for therapeutic practice. *Journal of Abnormal Psychology,* 1966, *71,* 235–246.

Bergin, A. E. The evaluation of therapeutic outcomes. In A. E. Bergin & S. L. Garfield (eds.), *Handbook of psychotherapy and behavior change.* Wiley, 1971.

Berkowitz, L. (ed.). *Roots of aggression: A reexamination of the frustration-aggression hypothesis.* Atherton Press, 1969.

Berlyne, D. E. Behaviorism? Cognitive theory? Humanistic psychology? — To Hull with them all! *Canadian Psychological Review,* 1975, *16,* 69–80.

Bernstein, I. L. Learned taste aversions in children receiving chemotherapy. *Science,* 1978, *200,* 1302–1303.

Berscheid, E., & Walster, E. A little bit about love. In T. L. Huston (ed.), *Foundations of interpersonal attraction.* Academic Press, 1974.

Bersh, P. J. A validation of polygraph examiner judgments. *Journal of Applied Psychology,* 1969, *53,* 399–403.

Bettelheim, B. Individual and mass behavior in extreme situations. In E. E. Maccoby, T. Newcomb, & E. Hartley (eds.), *Readings in social psychology.* Holt, Rinehart & Winston, 1958.

Bettelheim, B. *The informed heart.* Free Press, 1960.

Bever, T., & Chiarello, R. Cerebral dominance in musicians and nonmusicians. *Science,* 1974, *185,* 537–539.

Bieber, J., et al. *Homosexuality.* Vintage Books, 1962.

Birch, H. G. The relation of previous experience to insightful problem-solving. *Journal of Comparative and Physiological Psychology,* 1945, *38,* 367–383.

Birnbaum, I. M., Parker, E. S., Hartley, J. T., & Noble, E. P. Alcohol and memory: Retrieval processes. *Journal of Verbal Learning and Verbal Behavior,* 1978, *17,* 325–335.

Bischof, L. J. *Adult psychology,* 2nd ed. Harper & Row, 1976.

Black, C. The fundamental things apply. *APA Monitor,* August 1977.

Blanchard, E. B. Biofeedback and the modification of cardiovascular dysfunctions. In J. Gatchel & K. P. Price (eds.), *Clinical applications of biofeedback: Appraisal and status.* Pergamon, 1978.

Blau, Z. S. Structural constraints on friendships in old age. *American Sociological Review,* 1961, *26,* 429–439.

Bleuler, E. *Dementia praecox.* International Universities Press, 1950.

Bloom, L. *Language development.* M.I.T. Press, 1970.

Blum, G. S. *Psychoanalytic theories of personality.* McGraw-Hill, 1953.

Blum, G. S. A model of the mind. Wiley, 1961.

Blum, G. S., & Miller, D. R. Exploring the psychoanalytic theory of the "oral character." *Journal of Personality,* 1952, *20,* 287–304.

Blum, G. S., & Porter, M. L. The capacity for selective concentration on color versus form of consonants. *Cognitive Psychology,* 1973, *5,* 47–70.

Blum, G. S., Porter, M. L., & Geiwitz, P. J. Temporal parameters of negative hallucination. *The International Journal of Clinical and Experimental Hypnosis,* 1978, *26,* 30–44.

Blum, J. M. *Pseudoscience and mental ability.* Monthly Review Press, 1976.

Bodmer, W., & Cavalli-Sforza, L. L. Intelligence and race. *Scientific American,* October 1970.

Boring, E. G. *A history of experimental psychology.* 2nd ed. Appleton-Century-Crofts, 1950.

Boudin, H. M. Contingency contracting as a therapeutic tool in the declaration of amphetamine use. *Behavior Therapy,* 1972, *3,* 604–608.

Boulding, K. *The meaning of the 20th century.* Harper & Row, 1964.

Bousfield, W. A. The occurrence of clustering in the recall of randomly arranged associates. *Journal of General Psychology,* 1953, *49,* 229–240.

Bower, T. G. R. The visual work of infants. *Scientific American,* December 1966.

Bowers, K. S. *Hypnosis for the seriously curious.* Brooks/Cole, 1976.

Bowlby, J. *Attachment and loss.* Vol. 2: *Separation: anxiety and anger.* Hogarth, 1973.

Bowles, S., & Gintis, H. *I.Q. in the U.S. class structure.* Warner Modular Publications, 1973.

Braginsky, G. M., Braginsky, D. D., & Ring, K. *Methods of madness.* Holt, Rinehart & Winston, 1969.

Braine, M. D. S. The ontogeny of English phrase structure: The first phase. *Language,* 1963, *39,* 1–13.

Brazziel, W. F. A letter from the South. *Harvard Educational Review,* 1969, *39,* 348–356.

Brecher, E. M., & the editors of *Consumer Reports. Licit and illicit drugs.* Little, Brown, 1972.

Breger, L., & McGaugh, J. L. Critique and reformulation of "learning theory" approaches to psychotherapy and neurosis. *Psychological Bulletin,* 1965, *63,* 338–358.

Breland, K., & Breland, M. The misbehavior of organisms. *American Psychologist,* 1961, *16,* 681–684.

Breland, K., & Breland, M. *Animal behavior.* Macmillan, 1966.

Brill, N. Q. Gross stress reactions: Traumatic war

neurosis. In A. M. Friedman et al. (eds.), *Comprehensive Textbook of Psychiatry.* Williams & Wilkins, 1967.

Brill, N. Q., & Beebe, G. W. *A follow-up study of war neuroses.* U.S. Government Printing Office, 1955.

Bromberg, W. *The mind of man.* Harper 1937.

Broverman, I. K., Vogel, S. R., Broverman, D. M., Clarkson, F. E., & Rosenkrantz, P. S. Sex-role stereotypes: A current appraisal. *Journal of Social Issues,* 1972, *28,* 59–78.

Brown, R. Development of the first language in the human species. *American Psychologist,* 1973a, *28,* 97–106.

Brown, R. *A first language: the early stages.* Harvard U. Press, 1973b.

Brown, R., & Fraser, C. The acquisition of syntax. In C. N. Cofer & B. S. Musgrave (eds.), *Verbal behavior and learning.* McGraw-Hill, 1963.

Brown, R., & Hanlon, C. Derivational complexity and order of acquisition in child speech. In J. R. Hayes (ed.), *Cognition and the development of language.* Wiley, 1970.

Brown, R., & Herrnstein, R. J. *Psychology.* Little, Brown, 1975.

Brown, R., & McNeill, D. The "tip of the tongue" phenomenon. *Journal of Verbal Learning and Verbal Behavior,* 1966, *5,* 325–337.

Brucker, B. S. Learned voluntary control of systolic blood pressure by spinal cord injury patients. Doctoral dissertation. New York U., 1977. Cited in Miller (1978).

Bruner, J. S. The course of cognitive growth. *American Psychologist,* 1964, *19,* 1–15.

Bruner, J. S. *Processes of cognitive growth: Infancy.* Clark U. Press, 1968.

Bruner, J. S., & Goodman, C. C. Value and need as organizing factors in perception. *Journal of Abnormal and Social Psychology,* 1947, *42,* 33–44.

Bruner, J. S., & Potter, M. C. Interference in visual recognition. *Science,* 1964, *144,* 424–425.

Bucher, B., & Lovaas, O. I. Use of aversive stimulation in behavioral modification. In M. R. Jones (ed.), *Miami symposium on the prediction of behavior. 1967: Aversive stimulation.* U. of Miami Press, 1968.

Bühler, C., & Allen, M. *Introduction to humanistic psychology.* Brooks/Cole, 1972.

Burke, H. Piaget's mountains revisited: Changes in the egocentric landscape. *Developmental Psychology,* 1975, *11,* 240–243.

Burt, C. The genetic determination of differences in intelligence: A study of monozygotic twins reared together and apart. *British, Journal of Psychology,* 1966, *57,* 137–153.

Buss, A. H. Instrumentality of aggression, feedback, and frustration as determinants of physical aggression. *Journal of Personality and Social Psychology,* 1966, *3,* 153–162.

Butcher, J. N. Objective personality assessment. *General Learning Corporation,* 1971.

Butler, J. M., & Haigh, G. V. Changes in the relation between self-concepts and ideal concepts consequent upon client-centered counseling. In C. R. Rogers & R. F. Dymond (eds.), *Psychotherapy and personality change.* U. of Chicago Press, 1954.

Butler, R. N. *Why survive?* Harper & Row, 1975.

Byrne, D. *The attraction paradigm.* Academic Press, 1971.

Cahalan, D., Cisin, I. H., & Crossley, H. *American drinking practices.* Monograph No. 6, Rutgers Center for Alcohol Studies, 1969.

Campbell, D. P. *Manual for the Strong-Campbell Interest Inventory.* Stanford U. Press, 1974.

Cannon, W. B. The James-Lange theory of emotion. *American Journal of Psychology,* 1927, *39,* 106–124.

Cannon, W. B. Again the James-Lange and the thalamic theories of emotion. *Psychological Review,* 1931, *38,* 281–295.

Cannon, W. B. "Voodoo" death. *American Anthropologist,* 1942, *44,* 169–181.

Carlson, N. R. *Physiology of behavior.* Allyn and Bacon, 1977.

Carrington, P. Dreams and schizophrenia. *Archives of General Psychiatry,* 1972, *26,* 343–350.

Carter, H., & Glick, P. C. *Marriage and divorce.* 2nd ed. Harvard U. Press, 1976.

Cartwright, D. S. Effectiveness of psychotherapy: A critique of the spontaneous remission argument. *Journal of Counseling Psychology,* 1955, *2,* 290–296.

Cartwright, L. K. Conscious factors entering into decisions of women to study medicine. *Journal of Social Issues,* 1972, *28,* 201–215.

Cattell, R. B. *The culture free intelligence test.* Institute for Personality and Ability Testing, 1949.

Cermak, L. S. *Improving your memory.* McGraw-Hill, 1975.

Chomsky, N. *Language and mind.* Harcourt Brace Jovanovich, 1968.

Clark, H. H., & Clark, E. V. *Psychology and language.* Harcourt Brace Jovanovich, 1977.

Cleary, T. A. Test bias: Prediction of grades of Negro and white students in integrated colleges. *Journal of Educational Measurement,* 1968, *5,* 115–124.

Cohen, J. Heredity and intelligence. Letter to the London *Times,* November 10, 1976.

Coleman, J. S., et al. *Equality of educational opportunity.* U.S. Government Printing Office, 1966.

Conger, J. J. *Adolescence and youth.* 2nd ed. Harper & Row, 1977.

Constantinople, A. Masculinity-femininity: An exception to a famous dictum? *Psychological Bulletin,* 1973, *80,* 389–407.

Corcoran, J. F. T., Lewis, M. D., & Garver, R. B. Biofeedback-conditioned galvanic skin response and hypnotic suppression of arousal: A pilot study of their relation to deception. *Journal of Forensic Sciences,* 1978, *23,* 155–162.

Craik, F. I. M., & Tulving, E. Depth of processing and the retention of words in episodic memory. *Journal of Experimental Psychology: General,* 1975, *104,* 268–294.

Crancer, A., Jr., Dille, J. M., Delay, J. C., Wallace, J. E., & Haykin, M. Comparison of the effects of marijuana and alcohol on simulated driving. *Science,* 1969, *164,* 851–854.

Cronbach, L. J. *Essentials of a psychological testing.* 3rd ed. Harper & Row, 1970.

Dahlstrom, W. G., Welsh, G. S., & Dahlstrom, L. E. *An MMPI handbook.* Vol. I. U. Minnesota Press, 1972.

Dale, P. S. *Language development.* Dryden, 1972.

Dalton, D. *The menstrual cycle.* Pantheon, 1969.

Darcy, N. T. The effect of bilingualism upon the measurement of the intelligence of children of preschool age. *Journal of Educational Psychology,* 1946, *37,* 21–44.

Darley, C. F., Tinklenberg, J. R., Roth, W. T., Hollister, L. E., & Atkinson, R. C. Influence of marihuana on storage and retrieval processes in memory. *Memory and Cognition,* 1973, *1,* 196–200.

Darley, J. M., & Latané, B. Bystander intervention in emergencies: Diffusion of responsibility. *Journal of Personality and Social Psychology,* 1968, *8,* 377–383.

Darwin, C. *The expression of the emotions in man, and animals.* Philosophical Library, 1872.

Davidson, P. O. Validity of the guilty-knowledge technique: The effects of motivation. *Journal of Applied Psychology,* 1968, *52,* 62–65.

Davison, G. C., & Neale, J. M. *Abnormal psychology.* 2nd ed. Wiley, 1978.

Davison, G., & Neale, J. *Abnormal psychology newsletter.* Wiley, Fall 1977.

DeLaguna, G. *Speech: Its function and development.* Yale U. Press, 1927.

deMause, L. The evolution of childhood. In L. deMause (ed.), *The history of childhood.* Harper & Row, 1974.

Dement, W. C. The effect of dream deprivation. *Science,* 1960, *131,* 1705–1707.

Dement, W. C. *Some must watch while some must sleep.* Freeman, 1974.

Denker, P. G. Results of treatment of psychoneuroses by the general practitioner—a follow-up of 500 cases. *N.Y. State Journal of Medicine,* 1946, *46,* 2164–2166.

Dennis, W. Creative productivity between the ages of 20 and 80 years. *Journal of Gerontology,* 1966, *21,* 1–8.

Deutscher, I. The quality of postparental life. In B. L. Neugarten (ed.), *Middle age and aging.* U. of Chicago Press, 1968.

Dewson, J. H. Inside every monkey sits a little bit of man. *The Stanford Magazine,* 1976, *4*(1), 50–54.

Diaconis, P. Statistical problems in ESP research. *Science,* 1978, *201,* 131–136.

Dix, D. L. *Memorial in behalf of the pauper insane and idiots in jails and poorhouses throughout the commonwealth.* Monroe & Francis, 1843.

Dobzhansky, T. Differences are not deficits. *Psychology Today,* July 1973.

Doering, C. H., Brodie, H. K. H., Kraemer, H. C., Becker, H. B., & Hamburg, D. A. Plasma testosterone levels and psychologic measures in men over a 2-month period. In R. C. Friedman, R. M. Richart, & R. L. Vande Wiele (eds.), *Sex differences in behavior.* Wiley, 1974.

Dollard, J., Doob, L. W., Miller, N. E., Mowrer, O. H., & Sears, R. R. *Frustration and aggression.* Yale U. Press, 1939.

Dollard, J., & Miller, N. E. *Personality and psychotherapy.* McGraw-Hill, 1950.

Dooling, D. J., & Christiaansen, R. E. Episodic and semantic aspects of memory for prose. *Journal of Experimental Psychology: Human Learning and Memory,* 1977, *3,* 428–436.

Dooling, D. J., & Lachman, R. Effect of comprehension on retention of prose. *Journal of Experimental Psychology,* 1971, *88,* 216–222.

Dorfman, D. D. The Cyril Burt question: New findings. *Science,* 1978, *201,* 1177–1186.

Driscoll, R., Davis, K. E., & Lipetz, M. E. Parental interference and romantic love: The Romeo and Juliet effect. *Journal of Personality and Social Psychology,* 1972, *24,* 1–10.

Dubin, R. Industrial workers' world. *Social Problems,* 1956, *3,* 131–142.

Dulany, D. E. Awareness, rules, and propositional control: A confrontation with S-R behavior theory. In T. R. Dixon & D. L. Horton (eds.), *Verbal behavior and general behavior theory.* Prentice-Hall, 1968.

Duncan, O. D., Featherman, D. L., & Duncan, B. *Socioeconomic background and achievement.* Seminar Press, 1972.

Dunnette, M. D. *Personnel selection and placement.* Wadsworth, 1967.

Dutton, D. G., & Aron, A. P. Some evidence for heightened sexual attraction under conditions of high anxiety. *Journal of Personality and Social Psychology,* 1974, *30,* 510–517.

Eccles, J. C. *The understanding of the brain.* McGraw-Hill, 1973.

Eells, K., Davis, A., Havighurst, R. J., Herrick, V. E., & Tyler, R. W. *Intelligence and cultural differences.* U. of Chicago Press, 1951.

Eibl-Eibesfeldt, I. *Love and hate.* Holt, Rinehart & Winston, 1972.

Eich, J. E. State-dependent retrieval of information in human episodic memory. In I. M. Birnbaum & E. S. Parker (eds.), *Alcohol and human memory.* Erlbaum, 1977.

Ekblom, B. *Acts of violence by patients in mental hospitals.* Svenska Bokfoerleget, 1970.

Ekman, P. Differential communication of affect by head and body cues. *Journal of Personality and Social Psychology,* 1965, *2,* 726–735.

Ekman, P., & Friesen, W. V. Nonverbal leakage and clues to deception. *Psychiatry,* 1969, *32,* 88–106.

Ekman, P., & Friesen, W. V. *Unmasking the face.* Prentice-Hall, 1975.

Ellsworth, P., & Carlsmith, J. M. Eye contact and gaze aversion in an aggressive encounter. *Journal of Personality and Social Psychology,* 1973, *28,* 280–292.

Ellsworth, P., Carlsmith, J. M., & Henson, A. The stare as a stimulus to flight in human subjects: A series of field experiments. *Journal of Personality and Social Psychology,* 1972, *21,* 302–311.

Engel, G. Emotional stress and sudden death. *Psychology Today,* November 1977.

Entwisle, D. R. To dispel fantasies about fantasy-based measures of achievement motivation. *Psychological Bulletin,* 1972, *77,* 377–391.

Erdelyi, M. H. A new look at the New Look: Perceptual defense and vigilance. *Psychological Review,* 1974, *81,* 1–25.

Erikson, E. H. Childhood and tradition in two American Indian tribes. *Psychoanalytic Study of the Child,* 1945, *1,* 319–350.

Erikson, E. H. *Childhood and society.* Norton, 1950.

Erikson, E. H. *Childhood and society,* 2nd ed. Norton, 1963.

Erlenmeyer-Kimling, L., & Jarvik, L. F. Genetics and intelligence: A review. *Science,* 1963, *142,* 1477–1479.

Estes, W. F. An experimental study of punishment. *Psychological Monographs,* 1944, *57,* No. 263.

Exline, R. Visual interaction: The glances of power and preference. In J. Cole (ed.), *Nebraska Symposium on Motivation 1971.* U. of Nebraska Press, 1972.

Eysenck, H. J. The effects of psychotherapy: An evaluation. *Journal of Consulting Psychology,* 1952, *16,* 319–324.

Eysenck, H. J. *The effects of psychotherapy.* International Science Press, 1966.

Eysenck, H. J., & Prell, D. The inheritance of neuroticism. *Journal of Mental Science,* 1951, *97,* 441–465.

Eysenck, H. J., & Rachman, S. *The causes and cures of neurosis.* Knapp, 1965.

Fairweather, G. W., Sanders, D. H., Cressler, D. L., & Maynard, H. *Community life for the mentally ill.* Aldine, 1969.

Felipe, N. J., & Sommer, R. Invasions of personal space. *Social Problems,* 1966, *14,* 206–214.

Fenichel, O. *The psychoanalytic theory of neurosis.* Norton, 1945.

Ferguson, L. W. *Personality measurement.* McGraw-Hill, 1952.

Feshbach, S., & Singer, R. D. *Television and aggression.* Jossey-Bass, 1971.

Festinger, L., & Carlsmith, J. M. Cognitive consequences of forced compliance. *Journal of Abnormal and Social Psychology,* 1959, *58,* 203–210.

Flavell, J. H. *The developmental psychology of Jean Piaget.* Van Nostrand, 1963.

Flavell, J. H., et al. 1963. Reported in Brown, R. *Social psychology.* Free Press, 1965, pp. 342–343.

Forgus, R. H., & Melamed, L. E. *Perception: A cognitive-stage approach.* McGraw-Hill, 1976.

Foulkes, D., & Rechtschaffen, A. Presleep determinants of dream content. *Perceptual and Motor Skills,* 1964, *19,* 983–1005.

Freedman, J. L., Sears, D. O., & Carlsmith, J. M. *Social psychology.* 3d ed. Prentice-Hall, 1978.

Freud, S. *A general introduction to psychoanalysis.* Boni & Liveright, 1924.

Freud, S. *The interpretation of dreams.* Modern Library, 1938. (First published in 1900.)

Freud, S. Fragment of an analysis of a case of hysteria. In *The Collected Papers of Sigmund Freud,* Vol. 3. Basic Books, 1959.

Friedman, M., & Rosenman, R. H. *Type A behavior and your heart.* Knopf, 1974.

Fuchs, V. R. A note on sex segregation in professional occupations. *Explorations in Economic Research,* 1975, *2,* 105–111.

Gagnon, J. H., & Simon, W. *The Sexual Scene.* Aldine, 1970.

Gallup, G. Gallup poll. *San Francisco Chronicle,* May 16, 1977.

Garb, J. L., & Stunkard, A. J. Illness-induced food aversions in man. *American Journal of Psychiatry,* 1974, *131,* 1204–1219.

Garbarino, M. S. *Native American heritage.* Little, Brown, 1976.

Garber, H., & Heber, R. The Milwaukee project. In P. Mittler (ed.), *Research to practice in mental retardation.* U. Park Press, 1977.

Garcia, J., & Ervin, F. R. Gustatory-visual and telereceptor-cutaneous conditioning-adaptation in internal and external milieus. *Communications in Behavioral Biology,* 1968, *1,* 389–415.

Gardner, B. T., & Gardner, R. A. Two-way communication with an infant chimpanzee. In A. M. Schrier & F. Stollnitz (eds.), *Behavior of nonhuman primates,* Vol. 4. Academic Press, 1971.

Gardner, H. *Developmental psychology.* Little, Brown, 1978a.

Gardner, H. The loss of language. *Human Nature,* 1978b, *1*(3), 76–84.

Gardner, R. A., & Gardner, B. T. Teaching sign

language to a chimpanzee. *Science*, 1969, *165*, 664–672.

Gardner, R. A., & Gardner, B. T. Comparative psychology and language acquisition. In K. Salzinger & F. Denmark (eds.), *Psychology: The state of the art*. Annals of the New York Academy of Sciences, 1977.

Garfield, S. L., & Kurtz, R. A survey of clinical psychologists: Characteristics, activities, and orientations. *The Clinical Psychologist*, 1974, *28*, 7–10.

Garfield, S. L., & Kurtz, R. A study of eclectic views. *Journal of Consulting and Clinical Psychology*, 1977, *45*, 78–83.

Garrett, H. E. *Great experiments in psychology*. 3rd ed. Appleton-Century-Crofts, 1957.

Gates, A. I. The mnemonic span for visual and auditory digits. *Journal of Experimental Psychology*, 1916, *1*, 393–403.

Gazzaniga, M. S. The split brain in man. *Scientific American*, 1967, *217*, 24–29.

Geen, R. G. *Aggression*. General Learning Corporation, 1972.

Geiwitz, J. Another plea for "E." *APA Monitor*, 1978, *9*(8), 3, 17.

Geiwitz, J., & Moursund, J. *Approaches to personality*. Brooks/Cole, 1979.

Gerard, H., & Miller, N. *School desegregation*. Plenum, 1975.

Gerbner, G. Violence in television drama: Trends and symbolic functions. In G. A. Comstock & E. A. Rubenstein (eds.), *Television and social behavior*, Vol. I. Government Printing Office, 1972.

Geschwind, N. Language and the brain. *Scientific American*, 1972, *226*, 76–83.

Gill, B. *Here at the New Yorker*. Random House, 1975.

Gillie, O. Crucial data was faked by eminent psychologist. London *Sunday Times*, October 24, 1976.

Girden, E. A review of psychokinesis. *Psychological Bulletin*, 1962, *59*, 353–388.

Glass, D. C. *Behavior patterns, stress, and coronary disease*. Erlbaum, 1977.

Glaze, J. A. The association value of nonsense syllables. *Journal of Genetic Psychology*, 1928, *35*, 255–269.

Glick, P. C., & Norton, A. J. Perspectives on the recent upturn in divorce and remarriage. *Demography*, 1973, *10*, 301–314.

Goddard, G. V. Functions of the amygdala. *Psychological Bulletin*, 1964, *62*, 89–109.

Goffman, E. *Asylums*. Anchor, 1961.

Goldberg, L. R. A historical survey of personality scales and inventories. In P. McReynolds (ed.), *Advances in psychological assessment*, Vol. 2. Science and Behavior Books, 1971.

Goldberg, L. R. Objective diagnostic tests and measures. *Annual Review of Psychology*, 1974, *25*, 343–366.

Goldstein, K. *The organism*. American Book Co., 1939.

Goldstein, K. *Human nature in the light of psychopathology*. Harvard U. Press, 1940.

Goldstein, K. *After-effects of brain injuries in war*. Grune & Stratton, 1942.

Goleman, D. Who's mentally ill? *Psychology Today*, January 1978.

Golub, S. The effect of premenstrual depression and anxiety on personality and cognitive function. Unpublished doctoral dissertation, Fordham U., 1973.

Gordon, S. *Lonely in America*. Simon & Schuster, 1974.

Gordon, S. But where is sex education? *APA Monitor*, November 1977.

Gottesman, I. I., & Shields, J. *Schizophrenia and genetics*. Academic Press, 1972.

Greenberg, L. Alcohol in the body. *Scientific American*, 1953, *189*, 66ff.

Gregory, R. L. *The intelligent eye*. McGraw-Hill, 1970.

Gross, C. G. Inferotemporal cortex and vision. In E. Stellar, & J. M. Sprague (eds.), *Progress in physiological psychology*. Academic Press, 1973.

Gruenewald, D. Multiple personality and splitting phenomena: A reconceptualization. *Journal of Nervous and Mental Disorders*, 1977, *164*, 285–393.

Gustavson, C. R., Kelly, D. J., Sweeney, M., & Garcia, J. Prey—lithium aversions: I. Coyotes and Wolves. *Behavioral Biology* 1976,*17*, 61–72.

Guzzardi, W. *The young executives.* New American Library, 1966.

Gynther, M. D. White norms and black MMPIs: A prescription for discrimination. *Psychological Bulletin,* 1972, *78*, 386–402.

Haan, N., Smith, M. B., & Block, J. Moral reasoning of young adults: Political-social behavior, family background, and personality correlates. *Journal of Personality and Social Psychology,* 1968, *10*, 183–201.

Haber, R. N., & Hershenson, M. Effects of repeated brief exposures on the growth of a percept. *Journal of Experimental Psychology,* 1965, *69*, 40–46.

Hall, C. S. *The meaning of dreams.* McGraw-Hill, 1966.

Hall, C. S., & Domhoff, B. A ubiquitous sex difference in dreams. *Journal of Abnormal and Social Psychology,* 1963, *66*, 278–280.

Hall, C., & Van de Castle, R. *The content analysis of dreams.* Appleton-Century-Crofts, 1966.

Hansel, C. E. M. *ESP: A scientific evaluation.* Scribner's, 1966.

Hardyck, C., & Petrinovich, L. F. Left-handedness. *Psychological Bulletin,* 1977, *84*, 385–404.

Harlow, H. F. The formation of learning sets. *Psychological Review,* 1949, *56*, 51–65.

Harlow, H. F., & Harlow, M. K. Learning to love. *American Scientist,* 1966, *54*, 244–272.

Harmatz, M. G. *Abnormal psychology.* Prentice-Hall, 1978.

Harmon, L. R. The development of a criterion of scientific competence. In C. W. Taylor & F. Barron (eds.), *Scientific creativity: Its recognition and development.* Wiley, 1963.

Harris, F. R., Wolf, M. N., & Baer, D. M. Effects of adult social reinforcement on child behavior. *Young Children,* 1964, *20*, 8–17.

Haslam, J. *Observations on insanity.* Rivington, 1798.

Hass, R. G., & Linder, D. E. Counter argument availability and the effects of message structure on persuasion. *Journal of Personality and Social Psychology,* 1972, *33*, 219–233.

Hastings, D., Wright, D., & Glueck, B. *Psychiatric experiences of the Eighth Air Force, first year of combat.* Josiah Macy, Jr., Foundation, 1944.

Hathaway, S. R., & McKinley, J. C. *MMPI manual.* Psychological Corporation, 1943.

Hathaway, S. R., & McKinley, J. C. *MMPI manual.* Rev. ed. Psychological Corporation, 1951.

Hathaway, S. R., & Meehl, P. E. *An atlas for the clinical use of the MMPI.* U. Minnesota Press, 1951.

Hayes, K. J., & Hayes, C. Imitation in a home-raised chimpanzee. *Journal of Comparative and Physiological Psychology,* 1952, *45*, 450–459.

Hayflick, L. Why grow old? *The Stanford Magazine,* 1975, *3* (1), 36–43.

Hearnshaw, L. S. *Cyril Burt: Psychologist.* Cornell U. Press, 1979.

Hebb, D. O. *A textbook of psychology.* Saunders, 1958.

Hebb, D. O., Lambert, W. E., & Tucker, G. R. A DMZ in the language war. *Psychology Today,* November 1973.

Heider, F. *The psychology of interpersonal relations.* Wiley, 1958.

Henry, W. E. Identity and diffusion in professional actors. Papers presented at the meeting of the American Psychological Association, September 1965. Cited in Kimmel (1974).

Herman, R. L., & Azrin, N. H. Punishment by noise in an alternative response situation. *Journal of the Experimental Analysis of Behavior,* 1964, *7*, 185–188.

Heron, W. Cognitive and physiological effects of perceptual isolation. In P. Solomon (ed.), *Sensory deprivation.* Harvard U. Press, 1961.

Herrnstein, R. IQ. *The Atlantic,* 1971, *228*(3), 43–64.

Hess, E. H. "Imprinting" in animals. *Scientific American,* 1958, *198*, 81–90.

Hess, E. H. Attitude and pupil size. *Scientific American,* 1965, *212*, 46–54.

Heston, L. The genetics of schizophrenia and schizoid disease. *Science*, 1970, *167*, 249–256.

Hilgard, E. R. *The experience of hypnosis.* Harcourt Brace Jovanovich, 1968.

Hilgard, E. R., Atkinson, R. C., & Atkinson, R. L. *Introduction to psychology.* 6th ed. Harcourt Brace Jovanovich, 1975.

Hilgard, E. R., & Hilgard, J. R. Hypnosis in the control of pain. *The Stanford Magazine*, 1974 (Spring/Summer), *2*, 58–62.

Hinkle, L. E., & Wolff, H. G. The nature of man's adaptation to his total environment and the relation of this to illness. *Archives of Internal Medicine*, 1957, *99*, 442–460.

Hintzman, D. L. *The psychology of learning and memory.* Freeman, 1978.

Hiroto, D. S. Locus of control and learned helplessness. *Journal of Experimental Psychology*, 1974, *102*, 187–193.

Hoch, P. H., & Zubin, J. (eds.). *Psychopathology of schizophrenia.* Grune & Stratton, 1966.

Hoffman, L. W. Early childhood experiences and women's achievement motives. *Journal of Social Issues*, 1972, *28*, 129–155.

Hoffman, L. W. The professional woman as mother. *Annals of the New York Academy of Sciences*, 1973, *208*, 211–216.

Holden, C. R., & Herrnstein, J. The perils of expounding meritocracy. *Science*, 1973, *181*, 36–39.

Holland, J. L., & Richards, J. M. *Academic and nonacademic accomplishment: Correlated or uncorrelated?* American College Testing Program, 1965.

Hollingshead, A. B., & Redlich, F. C. *Social class and mental illness.* Wiley, 1958.

Hollister, L. E. *Chemical psychoses: LSD and related drugs.* Thomas, 1968.

Horner, M. Sex differences in achievement motivation and performance in competitive and non-competitive situations. Unpublished doctoral dissertation, U. of Michigan, 1968.

Horner, M. S. Femininity and successful achievement: A basic inconsistency. In J. M. Bardwick, E. Douvan, M. S. Horner, & D. Guttman, *Feminine personality and conflict.* Brooks/Cole, 1970.

Horowitz, M. J. Hallucinations: An information-processing approach. In R. K. Siegel & L. J. West (eds.), *Hallucinations.* Wiley, 1975.

Horvath, F. S., & Reid, J. E. The reliability of polygraph examiner diagnosis of truth and deception. *Journal of Criminal Law, Criminology, and Police Science*, 1971, *62*, 276–281.

Hovland, C. I., & Sears, R. R. Minor studies of aggression. VI. Correlation of lynchings with economic indices. *Journal of Psychology*, 1940, *9*, 301–310.

Hoyt, D. P. *The relationship between college grades and adult achievement, a review of the literature.* American College Testing Program, 1965.

Hubel, D. H., & Wiesel, T. N. Receptive fields, binocular interaction and functional architecture in the cat's visual cortex. *Journal of Physiology*, 1962, *160*, 106–154.

Hunt, M. *Sexual behavior in the 1970s.* Playboy Press, 1974.

Hyman, R. Uri Geller at SRI. *The Humanist*, May/June 1977.

Inhelder, B., & Piaget, J. *The growth of logical thinking from childhood to adolescence.* Basic Books, 1958.

Jacobs, J. Experiments on "prehension." *Mind*, 1887, *12*, 75–79.

Jacobs, P. A., Brunton, M., Melville, M. M., Brittain, R. P., & McClemont, W. F. Aggressive behaviour, mental subnormality, and the XYY male. *Nature*, 1965, *208*, 1351–1352.

Jacques, E. Death and the mid-life crisis. *International Journal of Psychoanalysis*, 1965, *46*, 502–514.

James, W. *Principles of psychology.* 2 Volumes. Holt, Rinehart & Winston, 1890.

James, W. *Psychology: The briefer course.* Holt, 1892. (Also Harper Torchbooks, Harper & Row, 1961.)

Janis, I. L. *Air war and emotional stress.* McGraw-Hill, 1951.

Janis, I. L. Effects of fear on attitude change. In L. Berkowitz (ed.), *Advances in experimental so-*

cial psychology, Vol. 3. Academic Press, 1967.

Janis, I. L., & Feshbach, S. Effects of fear-arousing communications. *Journal of Abnormal and Social Psychology,* 1953, *48,* 78–92.

Jasper, H. H. Unspecific thalamocortical relations. In J. Field, H. W. Magoun, & V. E. Hall (eds.), *Handbook of physiology: Neurophysiology II.* American Physiological Society, 1960.

Jensen, A. The problem of genotype-environment correlation in the estimation of heritability from monozygotic and dizygotic twins. *Acta Geneticae, Medicae et Gemellologiae,* 1977. Cited in Vernon (1979).

Jensen, A. R. How much can we boost IQ and scholastic achievement? *Harvard Educational Review,* 1969, *39,* 1–123.

Johnston, L., & Bachman, J. *Monitoring the future.* Institute for Social Research, U. of Michigan, 1975.

Jones, C., & Aronson, E. Attribution of fault to a rape victim as a function of respectability of the victim. *Journal of Personality and Social Psychology,* 1973, *26,* 415–419.

Jones, E. *The life and work of Sigmund Freud.* 3 Volumes. Basic Books, 1961.

Jones, E. E., Bell, L., & Aronson, E. The reciprocation of attraction from similar and dissimilar others: A study in person perception and evaluation. In C. G. McClintock (ed.), *Experimental social psychology.* Holt, Rinehart & Winston, 1972.

Julien R. M. *A primer of drug action.* Freeman, 1975.

Kagan, J. *Personality development.* Harcourt Brace Jovanovich, 1971.

Kagan, J. The child in the family. *Daedalus,* 1977, *106*(2), 33–56.

Kagan, J., Hosken, B., & Watson, S. The child's symbolic conceptualization of the parents. *Child Development,* 1961, *32,* 625–636.

Kagan, J., Kearsley, R., & Zelazo, P. R. *Infancy: Its place in human development.* Harvard U. Press, 1978.

Kagan, J., & Moss, H. A. *Birth to maturity.* Wiley, 1962.

Kamin, L. J. *The science of politics of IQ.* Erlbaum, 1974.

Kallman, F. J. The genetic theory of personality. *American Journal of Psychiatry,* 1946, *103,* 309–322.

Kamiya, J. Conscious control of brain waves. *Psychology Today,* April 1968.

Karlen, A. *Sexuality and homosexuality.* Norton, 1971.

Kastenbaum, R. Is death a crisis? On the confrontation with death in theory and practice. In N. Datan & L. H. Ginsberg (eds.), *Life-span developmental psychology: Normative life crises.* Academic Press, 1975.

Katz, I. The socialization of academic motivation in minority group children. *Nebraska Symposium on Motivation,* 1967, *15,* 133–191.

Kazdin, A. E. *History of behavior modification.* University Park Press, 1978.

Kazdin, A. E., & Wilson, G. T. *Evaluation of behavior therapy.* Ballinger, 1978.

Kearns, D. *Lyndon Johnson and the American Dream.* Harper & Row, 1976.

Keller, M. The definition of alcoholism and the estimation of its prevalence. In D. J. Pittman & C. R. Snyder (eds.), *Society, culture and drinking patterns.* Wiley, 1962.

Kelley, H. H. The processes of causal attribution. *American Psychologist,* 1973, *28,* 107–128.

Kellogg, W. N., & Kellogg, L. A. *The ape and the child.* McGraw-Hill, 1933.

Kesey, K. *One flew over the cuckoo's nest.* Viking, 1962.

Kessen, W. *The child.* Wiley, 1965.

Kessen, W., Haith, M. M., & Salapatek, P. H. Human infancy: a bibliography and guide. In P. H. Mussen (ed.), *Carmichael's manual of child psychology,* 3rd ed., Vol I. Wiley, 1970.

Kimmel, D. C. *Adulthood and aging.* Wiley, 1974.

Kimura, D. The asymmetry of the human brain. *Scientific American,* March 1973.

Kinsey, A. C., Pomeroy, W. B., & Martin, C. E. *Sexual behavior in the human male.* Saunders, 1948.

Kinsey, A. C., Pomeroy, W. B., Martin, C. E., &

Gebhard, P. H. *Sexual behavior in the human female.* Saunders, 1953.

Klatzky, R. L. *Human memory: Structures and processes.* 2nd ed. Freeman, 1980.

Klatzky, R. L., & Atkinson, R. C. Specialization of the cerebral hemispheres in scanning for information in short-term memory. *Perception and Psychophysics,* 1971, *10,* 335–338.

Klein, K. E., Wegmann, H. M., & Hunt, B. M. Desynchronization of body temperature and performance circadian rhythm as a result of outgoing and home-going transmeridian flights. *Aerospace Medicine,* 1972, *43,* 119–132.

Klein, M. H., Dittmann, A. T., Parloff, M. B., & Gill, M. M. Behavior therapy: observations and reflections. *Journal of Consulting and Clinical Psychology,* 1969, *33,* 259–266.

Kleinmuntz, B. *Essentials of abnormal psychology.* Harper & Row, 1974.

Klonoff, H. Marijuana and driving in real-life situations. *Science,* 1974, *186,* 317–324.

Klopfer, P. H., Adams, D. K., & Klopfer, F. S. Maternal imprinting in goats. *Proceedings of the National Academy of Sciences,* 1964, *52,* 911–914.

Kogan, I. M. *The informational aspect of telepathy.* Paper presented in absentia at UCLA symposium, A New Look at ESP, 1969.

Kohlberg, L. The development of children's orientations toward a moral order: I. Sequence in the development of moral thought. *Vita humana,* 1963, *6,* 11–33.

Kohlberg, L. *Continuities and discontinuities in childhood and adult moral development.* Paper read at the Life Span Psychology Conference, West Virginia U., 1972.

Kohlberg, L. Implications of developmental psychology for education: Examples from moral development. *Educational Psychologist,* 1973, *10,* 2–14.

Kolodny, R. C., Masters, W. H., Hendryx, J., & Toro, G. Plasma testosterone and semen analysis in male homosexuals. *New England Journal of Medicine,* 1971, *285,* 1170–1174.

Konecni, V. J., Libuser, L., Morton, H., & Ebbesen, E. B. Effects of a violation of personal space on escape and helping responses. *Journal of Experimental Social Psychology,* 1975, *11,* 288–299.

Korchin, S. J. *Modern clinical psychology.* Basic Books, 1976.

Krasner, L., & Ullmann, L. P. (eds.). *Research in behavior modification.* Holt, Rinehart & Winston, 1965.

Krippner, S., & Davidson, R. Parapsychology in the U.S.S.R. *Saturday Review,* March 18, 1972.

Kübler-Ross, E. *On death and dying.* Macmillan, 1969.

Labov, W. *The study of nonstandard English.* National Council of Teachers of English, 1970.

Laing, R. D. *The politics of experience.* Ballantine, 1967.

Laing, R. D. *The divided self.* Pantheon, 1970.

Laing, R. D., & Esterson, A. *Sanity, madness and the family.* Penguin, 1970.

Lambert, M. J. Spontaneous remission in adult neurotic disorders: A revision and summary. *Psychological Bulletin,* 1976, *83,* 107–119.

Lambert, W. W., Solomon, R. L., & Watson, P. D. Reinforcement and extinction as factors in size estimation. *Journal of Experimental Psychology,* 1949, *39,* 637–641.

Landis, C. Studies of emotional reactions: II. General behavior and facial expression. *Journal of Comparative Psychology,* 1924, *4,* 447–509.

Lane, H. *The Wild Boy of Aveyron.* Harvard U. Press, 1976.

Langfeld, H. S. The judgment of emotion by facial expression. *Journal of Abnormal and Social Psychology,* 1918, *13,* 172–184.

Lasswell, H. D. The structure and function of communication in society. In L. Bryson (ed.), *Communication of ideas.* Harper & Row, 1948.

Lau, R. J., Tubergen, D. G., Barr, M., & Domino, E. G. Phytohemagglutinin-induced lymphocyte transformation in humans receiving delta-nine-tetrahydrocannabinol. *Science,* 1976, *192,* 805–807.

Lazarus, A. A. Behaviour rehearsal vs. nondirective therapy vs. advice in effecting behaviour change. *Behaviour Research and Therapy,* 1966, *4,* 209–212.

Lehman, H. C. *Age and achievement.* Princeton U. Press, 1953.

LeMasters, E. E. Parenthood as crisis. *Marriage and Family Living,* 1957, *19,* 352–355.

Lenneberg, E. H. *Biological foundations of language.* Wiley, 1967.

Lerner, R. M., & Ryff, C. D. Implementation of the life-span view of human development: The sample case of attachment. In P. B. Baltes (ed.), *Life-span development and behavior.* Vol. 1. Academic Press, 1978.

LeShan, L. An emotional life-history pattern associated with neoplastic disease. *Annals of the New York Academy of Sciences,* 1966, *125,* 780–793.

Lettvin, J. Y., Maturana, H. R., McCullock, W. S., & Pitts, W. H. What the frog's eye tells the frog's brain. *Proceedings of the Institute of Radio Engineering,* 1959, *47,* 1940–1951.

Leventhal, H., & Niles, P. Persistence of influence for varying durations of exposure to threat stimuli. *Psychological Reports,* 1965, *16,* 223–233.

Levine, R., Chein, I., & Murphy, G. The relation of the intensity of a need to the amount of perceptual distortion: A preliminary report. *Journal of Psychology,* 1942, *13,* 283–293.

Levinson, D. J. *The seasons of a man's life.* Knopf, 1978.

Levy, J., & Reid, M. Variations in cerebral organization as a function of handedness, hand posture in writing, and sex. *Journal of Experimental Psychology: General,* 1978, *107,* 119–144.

Leyens, J. B., Camino, L., Parke, R. D., & Berkowitz, L. Effects of movie violence on aggression in a field setting as a function of group dominance and cohesion. *Journal of Personality and Social Psychology,* 1975, *32,* 346–360.

Liebert, R. M., Sobol, M. D., & Davidson, E. S. Catharsis of aggression among institutionalized boys: Fact or artifact. In G. A. Comstock, E. A. Rubenstein, & J. P. Murray (eds.),

Television and social behavior, Vol. 5, U.S. Government Printing Office, 1972.

Lifton, R. J. "Thought reform" of western civilians in Chinese prisons. *Psychiatry,* 1956, *19,* 173–195.

Lifton, R. J. *Thought reform and the psychology of totalism: a study of "brainwashing" in China.* Norton, 1961.

Light, R. J., & Smith, P. V. Social allocation models of intelligence: A methodological inquiry. *Harvard Educational Review,* 1969, *39,* 484–510.

Limber, J. Language in child and champ? *American Psychologist,* 1977, *32,* 280–295.

Lindsay, P., & Norman, D. *Human information processing.* 2nd ed. Academic Press, 1977.

Loehlin, J. C., Lindzey, G., & Spuhler, J. N. *Race differences in intelligence.* Freeman, 1975.

Loftus, E. F. Leading questions and the eyewitness report. *Cognitive Psychology,* 1975, *7,* 560–572.

Loftus, E. F., Miller, D. G., & Burns, H. J. Semantic integration of verbal information into a visual memory. *Journal of Experimental Psychology: Human Learning and Memory,* 1978, *4,* 19–31.

Lorayne, H., & Lucas, J. *The memory book.* Stein & Day, 1974.

Lovass, O. I., Freitag, G., Gold, V. J., & Kassorla, I. C. Experimental studies in childhood schizophrenia: Analysis of self-destructive behavior. *Journal of Experimental Child Psychology,* 1965, *2,* 67–84.

Lovaas, O. I., Frietag, L., Nelson, K., & Whalen, C. The establishment of imitation and its use for the development of complex behavior in schizophrenic children. *Behaviour Research and Therapy,* 1967, *5,* 171–181.

Luborsky, L., Singer, B., & Luborsky, L. Comparative studies of psychotherapies. *Archives of General Psychiatry,* 1975, *32,* 995–1008.

Luce, G. G., & Segal, J. *Sleep.* Coward-McCann, 1966.

Luckey, E. G., & Bain, J. K. Children: A factor in marital satisfaction. *Journal of Marriage and the Family,* 1970, *32,* 43–44.

Ludwig, A. M., Brandisma, J. M., Wilbur, C. B., Bendfelt, F., & Jameson, D. H. The objective study of multiple personality. *Archives of General Psychiatry,* 1972, *26,* 298–310.

Lunneborg, P. W. What *can* you do with a degree in psychology? Undergraduate Advisory Office, Department of Psychology, U. of Washington. October 1977.

Lykken, D. T. The GSR in the detection of guilt. *Journal of Applied Psychology,* 1959, *43,* 385–388.

Lykken, D. T. Psychology and the lie detector industry. *American Psychologist,* 1974, *29,* 725–739.

Lykken, D. T. The right way to use a lie detector. *Psychology Today,* March 1975.

Maccoby, E. E., & Jacklin, C. N. *The psychology of sex differences.* Stanford U. Press, 1974.

Maccoby, E. E., & Wilson, W. C. Identification and observational learning from films. *Journal of Abnormal and Social Psychology,* 1957, *55,* 76–87.

Mace, D., & Mace, V. *Marriage east and west.* Dolphin, 1960.

Mack, D. Where the black-matriarchy theorists went wrong. *Psychology Today,* January 1971.

Maddox, F. L. Retirement as a social event in the United States. In B. L. Neugarten (ed.), *Middle age and aging.* U. of Chicago Press, 1968.

Maher-Loughman, G. P. Hypnosis and autohypnosis for the treatment of asthma. *International Journal of Clinical and Experimental Hypnosis,* 1970, *18,* 1–14.

Mahone, C. H. Fear of failure and unrealistic vocational aspiration. *Journal of Abnormal and Social Psychology,* 1960, *60,* 253–261.

Mandler, G. Organization and memory. In K. W. Spence & J. T. Spence (eds.), *The psychology of learning and motivation.* Academic Press, 1967.

Mandler, G., & Pearlstone, Z. Free and constrained concept learning and subsequent recall: *Journal of Verbal Learning and Verbal Behavior,* 1966, *5,* 126–131.

Mark, V. H., & Ervin, F. R. *Violence and the brain.* Harper & Row, 1970.

Maslow, A. H. *Motivation and personality.* 2nd ed. Harper & Row, 1970.

Massaro, D. W. *Experimental psychology and information processing,* Rand McNally, 1975.

Masters, W. H., & Johnson, V. E. *Human sexual response.* Little, Brown, 1966.

Masters, W. H., & Johnson, V. E. *Human sexual inadequacy.* Little, Brown, 1970.

Masters, W. H., & Johnson, V. E. *The pleasure bond.* Little, Brown, 1975.

Maturana, H. R., Lettvin, J. Y., McCulloch, W. S., & Pitts, W. H. Anatomy and physiology of vision in the frog *(Rana pipiens). Journal of General Physiology,* 1960, *43,* 129–175.

Maugh, T. H. Marihuana: The grass may no longer be greener. *Science.* 1974a, *185,* 683–685.

Maugh, T. H. Marihuana (II): Does it damage the brain? *Science,* 1974b, *185,* 775–776.

Mayer, J., Marshall, N. B., Vitale, J. J., Cristensen, J. H., Mashayekhi, M. B., & Stare, F. J. Exercise, food intake and body weight in normal rats and genetically obese adult mice. *American Journal of Physiology,* 1954, *177,* 544–548.

Mayer, J., Roy, P., & Mitra, K. P. Relation between caloric intake, body weight, and physical work: Studies in an industrial male population in West Bengal. *American Journal of Clinical Nutrition,* 1956, *4,* 169–175.

McCarroll, J. R., & Haddon, W. Controlled study of fatal automobile accidents in New York City. *Journal of Chronic Diseases,* 1962, *15,* 811–826.

McCary, J. L. *McCary's human sexuality.* 3rd ed. Van Nostrand, 1978.

McClelland, C. C. Testing for competence rather than for "intelligence." *American Psychologist,* 1973, *28,* 1–14.

McClelland, D. C., & Liberman, A. M. The effect of need for achievement on recognition of need-related words. *Journal of Personality,* 1949, *18,* 236–251.

McClelland, D. C., & Watt, N. F. Sex-role alienation in schizophrenia. *Journal of Abnormal Psychology,* 1968, *73,* 226–239.

McClintock, C. G. Game behavior and social motivation in interpersonal settings. In C. G. McClintock (ed.), *Experimental social psychology.* Holt, Rinehart & Winston, 1972.

McDougall, W. *An introduction to social psychology.* Luce, 1921.

McGinnies, E. Emotionality and perceptual defense. *Psychological Review,* 1949, *56,* 244–251.

McGrath, M. J., & Cohen, D. B. REM sleep facilitation of adaptive waking behavior: A review of the literature. *Psychological Bulletin,* 1978, *85,* 24–57.

McGraw, M. B. Neural maturation as exemplified in achievement of bladder control. *Journal of Pediatrics,* 1940, *16,* 580–590.

McGuire, W. J. Nature of attitudes and attitude change. In G. Lindzey & E. Aronson (eds.), *Handbook of social psychology,* 2nd ed. Addison-Wesley, 1969.

McGuire, W. F. Attitude change: The information-processing paradigm. In C. G. McClintock (ed.), *Experimental social psychology.* Holt, Rinehart & Winston, 1972.

McKain, W. C. A new look at older marriages. *The Family Coordinator,* 1972, *21,* 61–69.

McNeill, D. The creation of language. *Discovery,* 1966, *27,* 34–38.

McNeill, D. *The acquisition of language.* Harper & Row, 1970.

Mead, M. *Culture and commitment.* Natural History Press, 1970.

Meehl, P. E. Schizotaxia, schizotypy, schizophrenia. *American Psychologist,* 1962, *17,* 827–838.

Meehl, P. E., & Rosen, A. Antecedent probability and the efficiency of psychometric signs, patterns or cutting scores. *Psychological Bulletin,* 1955, *52,* 194–216.

Mehrabian, A. *Nonverbal communication.* Aldine-Atherton, 1972.

Meltzoff, J., & Kornreich, M. *Research in psychotherapy,* Atherton, 1970.

Menig-Peterson, C. L. The modification of communicative behavior in preschool-aged children as a function of the listener's perspective. *Child Development,* 1975, *46,* 1015–1018.

Michaelson, G. Could a lie detector tell the truth? *Parade,* July 15, 1973.

Middlebrook, P. N. *Social psychology and modern life.* Knopf, 1974.

Milgram, S. Behavioral study of obedience. *Journal of Abnormal and Social Psychology,* 1963, *67,* 371–378.

Milgram, S. *Obedience to authority.* Harper & Row, 1974.

Miller, G. The magical number seven, plus or minus two: Some limits on our capacity for processing information. *Psychological Review,* 1956, *63,* 81–97.

Miller, M. E., Adesso, V. J., Fleming, J. P., Gino, A., & Lauerman, R. Effects of alcohol on the storage and retrieval processes of heavy social drinkers. *Journal of Experimental Psychology: Human Learning and Memory,* 1978, *4,* 246–255.

Miller, N. E. Biofeedback and visceral learning. In M. R. Rosenzweig & L. W. Porter (eds.), *Annual review of psychology.* Vol. 29. Annual Reviews, 1978.

Miller, N. E., & Dworkin, B. R. Critical issues in therapeutic applications of biofeedback. In G. E. Schwartz & J. Beatty (eds.), *Biofeedback: theory and research.* Academic Press, 1977.

Milner, P. M. *Physiological psychology.* Holt, Rinehart & Winston, 1970.

Minard, J. G., Bailey, D. E., & Wertheimer, M. Measurement and conditioning of perceptual defense, response bias, and emotionally based recognition. *Journal of Personality and Social Psychology,* 1966, *2,* 661–668.

Mischel, W. *Personality and assessment.* Wiley, 1968.

Mischel, W. *Introduction to personality.* Holt, Rinehart & Winston, 1971.

Mischel, W. Toward a cognitive social learning reconceptualization of personality. *Psychological Review,* 1973, *80,* 252–283.

Mischel, W., & Grusec, J. Determinants of the rehearsal and transmission of neutral and aversive behaviors. *Journal of Personality and Social Psychology,* 1966, *3,* 197–205.

Mischel, W., & Mischel, H. N. A cognitive social learning approach to morality and self-regulation. In T. Lickona (ed.), *Men and morality.* Holt, Rinehart & Winston, 1974.

Moles, O. C. Marital dissolution and public assistance payments: Variations among American states. *Journal of Social Issues,* 1976, *32,* 87–101.

Moltz, H., & Stettner, L. J. The influence of patterned-light deprivation on the critical period for imprinting. *Journal of Comparative and Physiological Psychology,* 1961, *54,* 279–283.

Money, J., & Ehrhardt, A. A. *Man and woman, boy and girl.* Johns Hopkins U. Press, 1972.

Montague, W. E., Adams, J. A., & Kiess, H. O. Forgetting and natural language mediation. *Journal of Experimental Psychology,* 1966, *72,* 829–833.

Moritz, A. P., & Zamchech, N. Sudden and unexpected deaths of young soldiers. *American Medical Association Archives of Pathology,* 1946, *42,* 459–494.

Moser, D. Screams, slaps, and love. *Life,* May 7, 1965.

Mosher, F. A., & Hornsby, J. R. On asking questions. In J. S. Bruner, R. R. Oliver, & P. M. Greenfield (eds.), *Studies in cognitive growth.* Wiley, 1966.

Moss, T. *The probability of the impossible.* J. P. Tarcher, 1974.

Mowrer, O. H. *Learning theory and behavior.* Wiley, 1960.

Murray. H. A., et al. *Explorations in personality.* Oxford U. Press, 1938.

Murstein, B. I. *Theory and research in projective techniques.* Wiley, 1963.

Mussen, P. H., Conger, J. J., & Kagan, J. *Child development and personality.* 5th ed. Harper & Row, 1979a.

Mussen, P. H., Conger, J. J., Kagan, J., & Geiwitz, J. *Psychological development: A life-span approach.* Harper & Row, 1979b.

Mussen, P. H., & Distler, L. Masculinity, identification and father-son relationships. *Journal of Abnormal and Social Psychology,* 1959, *59,* 350–356.

Mussen, P. H., & Parker, A. Mother nurturance and girls' incidental imitative learning. *Journal of Personality and Social Psychology,* 1965, *2,* 94–97.

National Commission on Marihuana and Drug Abuse. *Marihuana: A signal of misunderstanding.* U.S. Government Printing Office, 1972.

National Institute on Drug Abuse. *Marihuana and health.* U.S. Government Printing Office, 1976.

Neilon, P. Shirley's babies after fifteen years: A personality study. *Journal of Genetic Psychology,* 1948, *73,* 175–186.

Neisser, U. *Cognitive psychology.* Appleton-Century-Crofts, 1967.

Neisser, U. *Cognition and reality.* Freeman, 1976.

Neugarten, B. L. Personality and aging. In J. E. Birren & K. W. Schaie (eds.), *Handbook of the psychology of aging.* Van Nostrand, 1977.

Neugarten, B. L., Moore, J. W., & Lowe, J. C. Age norms, age constraints, and adult socialization. In B. L. Neugarten (ed.), *Middle age and aging.* U. of Chicago Press, 1968a.

Neugarten, B. W., Wood, V., Kraines, R. J., & Loomis, B. Women's attitudes toward the menopause. In B. L. Neugarten (ed.), *Middle age and aging.* U. of Chicago Press, 1968b.

Newman, E. *A civil tongue.* Warner Books, 1976.

Nickel, T. W. The attribution of intention as a critical factor in the relation between frustration and aggression. *Journal of Personality,* 1974, *42,* 482–492.

Noback, C. R., & Demarest, R. J. *The nervous system.* McGraw-Hill, 1972.

Noble, C. E. An analysis of meaning. *Psychological Review,* 1952, *59,* 421–430.

Nourse, A. E., et al. *The body.* Time-Life Books, 1964.

Nowlis, H. H. Perspectives on drug use. *Journal of Social Issues,* 1971, *27,* 7–21.

Nyhan, W. L. *The hereditary factor.* Grosset & Dunlap, 1976.

O'Connor, P., Atkinson, J. W., & Horner, M. Motivational implications of ability groupings in schools. In J. W. Atkinson & N. T. Feather (eds.), *A theory of achievement motivation.* Wiley, 1966.

Ornstein, R. The split and whole brain. *Human Nature,* 1978, *1*(5), 76–83.

Overmier, J. B., & Seligman, M. E. P. Effects of inescapable shock upon subsequent escape and avoidance learning. *Journal of Comparative and Physiological Psychology,* 1967, *63,* 23–33.

Owen, D. R. The 47, XYY male: A review. *Psychological Bulletin,* 1972, *78,* 209–233.

Owens, W. A. Age and mental abilities: A second adult follow-up. *Journal of Educational Psychology,* 1966, *57,* 311–325.

Packard, V. *The sexual wilderness.* McKay, 1968.

Page, J. D. *Psychopathology.* Aldine-Atherton, 1971.

Paige, K. E. Women learn to sing the menstrual blues. *Psychology Today,* September 1973.

Paivio, A. *Imagery and verbal processes.* Holt, Rinehart & Winston, 1971.

Parkes, C. M., Benjamin, R., & Fitzgerald, R. A. Broken heart: A statistical study of increased mortality among widowers. *British Medical Journal,* 1969, *1,* 740–743.

Parlee, M. B. The premenstrual syndrome. *Psychological Bulletin,* 1973, *80,* 454–465.

Payne, D. E., & Mussen, P. H. Parent-child relations and father identification among adolescent boys. *Journal of Abnormal and Social Psychology,* 1956, *52,* 358–362.

Penfield, W. The permanent record of the stream of consciousness. *Acta Psychologica,* 1955, *11,* 47–69.

Perry, D. K. Validities of three interest keys for U.S. Navy yeomen. *Journal of Applied Psychology,* 1955, *39,* 134–138.

Peterson, L. R., & Peterson, M. J. Short-term retention of individual verbal items. *Journal of Experimental Psychology,* 1959, *58,* 193–198.

Phillips, D. *Statistics: A guide to the unknown.* Holden-Day, 1971.

Piaget, J. *The moral judgment of the child.* Free Press, 1948.

Piaget, J. *The origins of intelligence in children.* International Universities Press, 1952.

Piaget, J. *The construction of reality in the child.* Basic Books, 1954.

Piaget, J., & Inhelder, B. *The child's conception of space.* Routledge & Kegan Paul, 1956.

Piliavin, J. A., & Piliavin, I. M. Effect of blood on reactions to a victim. *Journal of Personality and Social Psychology,* 1972, *23,* 353–361.

Piliavin, I. M., Rodin, J., & Piliavin, J. A. Good Samaritanism: An underground phenomenon? *Journal of Personality and Social Psychology,* 1969, *13,* 289–299.

Plutchik, R. *The emotions.* Random House, 1962.

Pollack, I., & Pickett, J. M. Intelligibility of excerpts from fluent speech: Auditory vs. structural context. *Journal of Verbal Learning and Verbal Behavior,* 1964, *3,* 79–84.

Pollock, H. M. Is the paroled patient a menace to the community? *Psychiatric Quarterly,* 1938, *12,* 236–244.

Pratt, J. G. *ESP research today.* Scarecrow Press, 1973.

Premack, D. The education of Sarah. *Psychology Today,* April 1970.

Pribram, K. H. A review of theory in physiological psychology. *Annual Review of Psychology,* 1960, *11,* 1–40.

Pritchard, R. M. Stabilized images on the retina. *Scientific American,* 1961, *204,* 72–78.

Proshansky, H., & Murphy, G. The effects of reward and punishment on perception. *Journal of Psychology,* 1942, *13,* 295–305.

Prytulak, L. S. Natural language mediation. *Cognitive Psychology,* 1971, *2,* 1–56.

Rachman, S. J. *The effects of psychotherapy.* Pergamon Press, 1971.

Raimy, V. C. Self-reference in counseling interviews. *Journal of Consulting Psychology,* 1948, *12,* 153–163.

Randi, J. *The magic of Uri Geller.* Ballantine, 1976.

Rapaport, D. A critique of Dollard and Miller's "Personality and Psychotherapy." *American Journal of Orthopsychiatry,* 1953, *24,* 204–208.

Ratcliff, R. A theory of memory retrieval. *Psychological Review,* 1978, *85,* 59–108.

Raven, B. H. Schemes, schema, and the investigative reporter. *SPSSI Newsletter,* May 1974.

Raymond, M. S. Case of fetishism treated by aversion therapy. *British Medical Journal,* 1956, *2,* 854–856.

Rechtschaffen, A., & Mednick, S. A. The autokinetic word effect. *Journal of Abnormal and Social Psychology,* 1955, *51,* 345–346.

Reddy, R., & Newell, A. Knowledge and its representation in a speech understanding system. In L. W. Gregg (ed.), *Knowledge and cognition.* Erlbaum, 1974.

Reichard, S., Livson, F., & Peterson, P. G. *Aging and personality.* Wiley, 1962.

Reid, J. E., & Inbau, F. E. *Truth and deception: The polygraph ("lie-detector") technique.* Williams & Wilkins, 1966.

Restak, R. The danger of knowing too much. *Psychology Today,* September 1975.

Rhine, J. B. Extra-sensory perception. *Boston Society for Psychic Research,* 1934.

Rhine, J. B., & Pratt, J. G. *Parapsychology: Frontier science of the mind.* Charles C Thomas, 1957.

Rhine, J. B., et al. *Parapsychology from Duke to FRNM.* Parapsychology Press, 1965.

Rhine, L. *ESP in life and lab.* Collier-Macmillan, 1968.

Rice, B. The high cost of thinking the unthinkable. *Psychology Today,* July 1973.

Riggs, L. A., Ratliff, F., Cornsweet, J. C., & Cornsweet, T. N. The disappearance of steadily-fixated objects. *Journal of the Optical Society of America,* 1953, *43,* 495–501.

Roemer, J. Gordon Liddy: He bungled into the White House. *Rolling Stone,* July 19, 1973.

Rogers, C. R. *Client-centered therapy.* Houghton Mifflin, 1951.

Rogers, C. R. A theory of therapy, personality, and interpersonal relationships. In S. Koch (ed.), *Psychology: A study of a science.* Vol. 3. McGraw-Hill, 1959.

Roll, W. G. *Theory and experiment in psychical research.* Arno Press, 1975.

Rosenhan, D. L. On being sane in insane places. *Science,* 1973, *179,* 250–258.

Rosenman, R. H., et al. Coronary heart disease in the Western Collaborative Group Study: Final follow-up experience of 8½ years. *Journal of the American Medical Association,* 1975, *233,* 872–877.

Rosenthal, A. M. *Thirty-eight witnesses.* McGraw-Hill, 1964.

Rosenthal, D. *The genetics of psychopathology.* McGraw-Hill, 1971.

Rosenthal, R. *Experimenter effects in behavioral research.* Appleton-Century-Crofts, 1966.

Rosenzweig, M. R. Biological psychology. In P. H. Mussen et al., *Psychology: An introduction,* 2nd ed. Heath, 1977.

Ross, S. A. The effect of deviant and nondeviant models on the behavior of preschool children. Unpublished doctoral dissertation. Stanford U., 1962.

Rozin, P. The significance of learning mechanisms in food selection: Some biology, psychology, and sociology of science. In L. M. Barker, M. R. Best, & M. Domjan (eds.), *Learning mechanisms in food selection.* Baylor U. Press, 1977.

Rubin, V., & Comitas, L. *Ganja in Jamaica.* Anchor Books, 1976.

Rubin, Z. Measurement of romantic love. *Journal of Personality and Social Psychology,* 1970, *16,* 265–273.

Rubin, Z. *Liking and loving.* Holt, Rinehart & Winston, 1973.

Ruch, F. L., & Zimbardo, P. G. *Psychology and life.* 8th ed. Scott, Foresman, 1971.

Rudy, J. W., & Cheatle, M. D. Odor-aversion learning in neonatal rats. *Science,* 1977, *198,* 845–846.

Rumbaugh, D. M., & Gill, T. V. Language and the acquisition of language-type skills by a chimpanzee. *Annals of the New York Academy of Sciences,* 1976, *270,* 90–123.

Rychlak, J. F. *A philosophy of science for personality theory.* Houghton Mifflin, 1968.

Sachs, J. D. S. Recognition memory for syntactic and semantic aspects of connected discourse. *Perception and Psychophysics,* 1967, *2,* 437–442.

Scarr, S., & Weinberg, R. A. IQ test performance of black children adopted by white families. *American Psychologist,* 1976, *31,* 726–739.

Scarr-Salapatek, S. Race, social class, and IQ. *Science,* 1971a, *174,* 1285–1295.

Scarr-Salaptek, S. Review of *Environment, heredity, and intelligence;* H. J. Eysenck, *The IQ argument;* and R. Herrnstein, *IQ. Science,* 1971b, *174,* 1223–1228.

Scarr-Salapatek, S., & Weinberg, R. A. When black children grow up in white homes. *Psychology Today,* December 1975.

Schacht, T., & Nathan, P. E. But is it good for psychologists? Appraisal and status of DSM-III. *American Psychologist,* 1977, *32,* 1017–1025.

Schachter, S. S., & Singer, J. E. Cognitive, social and physiological determinants of emotional states. *Psychological Review,* 1962, *69,* 379–399.

Schaefer, E. S., & Bayley, N. Maternal behavior, child behavior, and their intercorrelations from infancy through adolescence. *Monographs of the Society for Research in Child Development,* 1963, *28,* No. 3.

Schaffer, H. R., & Emerson, P. The development of social attachments in infancy. *Monographs of the Society for Research in Child Development,* 1964, *29,* No. 3.

Schaie, K. W., & Labouvie-Vief, G. Generational versus ontogenetic components of change in adult cognitive behavior: A fourteen-year cross-sequential study. *Developmental Psychology,* 1974, *10,* 305–320.

Schmidt, F. L., & Hunter, J. E. Racial and ethnic bias in psychological tests. *American Psychologist,* 1974, *29,* 1–8.

Schmidt, H. O., & Fonda, C. The reliability of psychiatric diagnosis. *Journal of Abnormal and Social Psychology,* 1956, *52,* 262–267.

Schofield, W., & Balian, L. A comparative study of the personal histories of schizophrenic and nonpsychiatric patients. *Journal of Abnormal and Social Psychology,* 1959, *59,* 216–225.

Schultz, D. *Theories of personality.* Brooks/Cole, 1976.

Schultz, R., & Alderman, D. Clinical research and the "stages of dying." *Omega,* 1974, *5,* 137–144.

Schwartz, S. H., Feldman, K. A., Brown, M. E., & Heingartner, A. Some personality correlates of conduct in two situations of moral conflict. *Journal of Personality,* 1969, *37,* 41–57.

Scott, J. P. Critical periods in behavioral development. *Science,* 1962, *138,* 949–958.

Searleman, A. A review of right hemisphere linguistic capabilities. *Psychological Bulletin,* 1977, *84,* 503–528.

Sears, P. S. Correlates of need achievement and need affiliation and classroom management, self concept, and creativity. Unpublished manuscript, Stanford U., 1962.

Sears, R. R. Experimental studies of projection: I. Attribution of traits. *Journal of Social Psychology,* 1936, *7,* 151–163.

Segall, M. H., Campbell, D. T., & Herskovits, M. J. Cultural differences in the perception of geometric illusions. *Science,* 1963, *139,* 769–771.

Selfridge, O. G. Pandemonium: A paradigm for learning. In *The mechanization of thought processes.* H. M. Stationery Office, 1959.

Seligman, M. E. P. For helplessness: Can we immunize the weak? In *Readings in Psychology Today,* 2nd ed. CRM, 1972.

Seligman, M. E. P., & Maier, S. F. Failure to escape traumatic shock. *Journal of Experimental Psychology,* 1967, *74,* 1–9.

Seligman, M. E. P., Maier, S. F., & Geer, J. The alleviation of learned helplessness in the dog. *Journal of Abnormal and Social Psychology,* 1968, *73,* 256–262.

Selye, H. *The stress of life.* McGraw-Hill, 1956.

Sevenster, P. Motivation and learning in sticklebacks. In D. Ingle (ed.), *The central nervous system and fish behavior.* U. of Chicago Press, 1968.

Shakow, D. Psychological deficit in schizophrenia. *Behavioral Science,* 1963, *8,* 275–305.

Shanas, E., Townsend, P., Wedderburn, D., Friis, H., Milhhoj, P., & Stehouwer, J. *Older people in three industrial societies.* Atherton, 1968.

Shatz, M., & Gelmen, R. The development of communication skills: Modification in the

speech of young children as a function of the listener. *Monographs of the Society for Research in Child Development,* 1973, *152.*

Sheehy, G. Catch-30 and other predictable crises of growing up adult. *New York,* February 18, 1974.

Sheehy, G. *Passages.* Dutton, 1976.

Sherif, M., Harvey, O. J., White, B. J., Hood, W. R., & Sherif, C. W. *Intergroup conflict and cooperation: The Robbers Cave experiment.* Institute of Group Relations, U. of Oklahoma, 1961.

Sherif, M., & Sherif, C. W. *Social psychology.* Harper & Row, 1969.

Sherman, A. R. *Behavior modification: Theory and practice.* Brooks/Cole, 1973.

Shettleworth, S. J. Constraints on learning. In D. S. Lehrman, R. A. Hinde, & E. Shaw (eds.), *Advances in the study of behavior,* Vol. 4. Academic Press, 1972.

Shucard, D. W., Shucard, J. L., & Thomas, D. G. Auditory evoked potentials as probes of hemispheric differences in cognitive processing. *Science,* 1977, *197,* 1295–1298.

Sidman, M. Avoidance behavior. In W. K. Honig (ed.), *Operant behavior.* Appleton-Century-Crofts, 1966.

Sigelman, C. Prosocial behavior: Cooperation and helping. In L. S. Wrightsman, *Social psychology,* 2nd brief ed. Brooks/Cole, 1977.

Sinclair-Gieben, A. H. C., & Chalmers, D. Evaluation of treatment of wants by hypnosis. *Lancet,* October 3, 1959.

Singer, B. D. Violence, protest and war in television news: The U.S. and Canada compared. *Public Opinion Quarterly,* 1970, *34,* 611–616.

Skinner, B. F. How to teach animals. *Scientific American,* December 1951.

Skinner, B. F. *Science and human behavior.* Macmillan, 1953.

Skinner, B. F. *Verbal behavior.* Appleton-Century-Crofts, 1957.

Skinner, B. F. A case history in scientific method. In S. Koch (ed.), *Psychology: A study of a science.* McGraw-Hill, 1959.

Slovic, P., Fischhoff, B., & Lichtenstein, S. Behav-

ioral decision theory. *Annual Review of Psychology,* 1977, *28,* 1–39.

Smith, B. M. The polygraph. *Scientific American,* January 1967.

Smith, M. L., & Glass, G. V. Meta-analysis of psychotherapy outcome studies. *American Psychologist,* 1977, *32,* 752–760.

Smith, R. J. Congress considers bill to control angel dust. *Science,* 1978, *200,* 1463–1466.

Snyder, S. H., Banerjee, S. P., Yamamura, H. I., & Greenberg, D. Drugs, neurotransmitters, and schizophrenia. *Science,* 1974, *184,* 1243–1253.

Sommer, R., & Becker, F. D. Territorial defense and the good neighbor. *Journal of Personality and Social Psychology,* 1969, *11,* 85–92.

Sorenson, R. C. *Adolescent sexuality in contemporary America.* World, 1973.

Special Presidential Task Force. Report relating to narcotics, marihuana and dangerous drugs. June 6, 1969.

Spence, J. T., Helmreich, R., & Stapp, J. Ratings of self and peers on sex-role attributes and their relation to self-esteem and conceptions of masculinity and femininity. *Journal of Personality and Social Psychology,* 1975, *32,* 29–39.

Sperling, G. The information available in brief visual presentations. *Psychological Monographs,* 1960, *74,* No. 498.

Sperry, R. W. Cerebral function following surgical separation of the hemispheres in man. Paper presented at the meeting of the American Psychological Association, Honolulu, September 1972.

Spitz, R. Hospitalism. *Psychoanalytic Study of the Child,* 1945, *1,* 53–74.

Spitz, R. *The first year of life.* International Universities Press, 1965.

Sroufe, L. A. Attachment and the roots of competence. *Human Nature,* October 1978.

Stein, A., & Friedrich, L. Television content and young children's behavior. In J. Murray, E. Rubinstein, & G. Comstock (eds.), *Television and social learning.* U.S. Government Printing Office, 1971.

Stein, A. H., & Bailey, M. M. The socialization of

achievement orientation in females. *Psychological Bulletin*, 1973, *80*, 345–366.

Stevens, S. S. The surprising simplicity of sensory metrics. *American Psychologist*, 1962, *17*, 29–39.

Stevens, S. S. On the operation known as judgment. *American Scientist*, 1966, *54*, 385–401.

Stevenson, I. Discussion of Chapter 1. In J. Wolpe, A. Salter, & L. J. Reyna (eds.), *The conditioning therapies*. Holt, Rinehart & Winston, 1964.

Stewart, W. A. Urban Negro speech: Sociolinguistic factors affecting English teaching. In R. W. Shuy (ed.), *Social dialects and language learning*. National Council of Teachers of English, 1964.

Stodolsky, S., & Lesser, G. Learning patterns in the disadvantaged. *Harvard Educational Review*, 1967, *37*, 546–593.

Stolz, S. B., Wienckowski, L. A., & Brown, B. S. Behavior modification: A perspective on critical issues. *American Psychologist*, 1975, *30*, 1027–1048.

Strong, E. K., Jr. *Vocational interests of men and women*. Stanford U. Press, 1943.

Strong, E. K., Jr. *Vocational interests 18 years after college*. U. Minnesota Press, 1955.

Sulin, R. A., & Dooling, D. J. Intrusion of a thematic idea in retention of prose. *Journal of Experimental Psychology*. 1974, *103*, 255–262.

Sundberg, N. D. *Assessment of persons*. Prentice-Hall, 1977.

Surgeon General's Advisory Committee. *Television and growing up: The impact of televised violence*, U.S. Department of Health, Education and Welfare, 1972.

Suter, L. E., & Miller, H. P. Components of differences between the incomes of men and career women. *American Journal of Sociology*, 1973, *79*, 962–974.

Szasz, T. The myth of mental illness. *American Psychologist*, 1960, *15*, 113–118.

Szasz, T. *The myth of mental illness*. Harper & Row, 1961.

Tangri, S. S. Determinants of occupational role innovation among college women. *Journal of Social Issues*. 1972, *28*, 177–199.

Tart, C. *Learning to use ESP*. U. of Chicago Press, 1976.

Task Force on Nomenclature and Statistics. *Diagnostic and statistical manual of mental disorders*. 3rd ed. Draft version. American Psychiatric Association, April 15, 1977.

Tavris, C., & Offir, C. *The longest war*. Harcourt Brace Jovanovich, 1977.

Taylor, C. W., Smith, W. R., & Ghiselin, B. The creative and other contributions of one sample of research scientists. In C. W. Taylor & F. Barron (eds.), *Scientific creativity: Its recognition and development*. Wiley, 1963.

Taylor, R. *Welcome to the middle years*. Acropolis Books, 1976.

Taylor, S., & Mettee, D. When similarity breeds contempt. *Journal of Personality and Social Psychology*, 1971, *20*, 75–81.

Terman, L. M., & Merrill, M. A. *Measuring intelligence*. Houghton Mifflin, 1937.

Terman, L. M., & Merrill, M. A. *Stanford-Binet Intelligence Scale*. Houghton Mifflin, 1960.

Thigpen, C. H., & Cleckley, H. M. *Three faces of Eve*. McGraw-Hill, 1957.

Thompson, R. F. *Introduction to physiological psychology*. Harper & Row, 1975.

Thompson, W. R., & Grusec, J. E. Studies of early experience. In P. H. Mussen (ed.), *Carmichael's manual of child psychology*, 3rd ed., Vol. I. Wiley, 1970.

Thorndike, E. L. Animal intelligence: An experimental study of the associative processes in animals. *Psychological Review, Monograph Supplement*, 1898, *2*, No. 8.

Thorndike, R. L. Concepts of culture fairness. *Journal of Educational Measurement*, 1971, *8*, 63–70.

Thorndyke, P. W. Cognitive structures in comprehension and memory of narrative discourse. *Cognitive Psychology*, 1977, *9*, 77–110.

Tiger, L. Male dominance? Yes, alas. A sexist plot? No. *New York Times Magazine*, October 25, 1970.

Timiras, P. S. *Developmental physiology and aging.* Macmillan, 1972.

Titchener, E. B. *A text-book of psychology.* Macmillan, 1910.

Toffler, A. *Future shock.* Random House, 1970.

Toffler, A. (ed.). *Learning for tomorrow.* Random House, 1974.

Tolman, E. C., & Honzik, C. M. Introduction and removal of reward and maze performance in rats. *U. of California Publications in Psychology.* 1930, *4,* 257–275.

Tornatzky, L., & Geiwitz, P. J. The effects of threat and attraction on interpersonal bargaining. *Psychonomic Science,* 1968, *13,* 125–126.

Tresemer, D. Fear of success: popular, but unproven. *Psychology Today,* March 1974.

Troll, L. E. The family of later life: A decade review. *Journal of Marriage and the Family,* 1971, *33,* 263–290.

Truax, C. B., & Carkhuff, R. R. *Toward effective counseling and psychotherapy.* Aldine, 1967.

Tuddenham, R. D. Soldier intelligence in World Wars I and II. *American Psychologist,* 1948, *3,* 54–56.

Tulving, E. Subjective organization in free recall of "unrelated" words. *Psychological Review,* 1962, *69,* 344–354.

Tulving, E., & Thompson, D. M. Encoding specificity and retrieval processes in episodic memory. *Psychological Review,* 1973, *80,* 352–373.

Turnbull, C. M. Some observations regarding the experiences and behavior of the Ba Mbuti Pygmies. *American Journal of Psychology,* 1961, *74,* 304–308.

Turner, C. W., & Layton, J. F. Verbal imagery and connotation as memory-induced mediators of aggressive behavior. *Journal of Personality and Social Psychology,* 1976, *33,* 755–763.

Udry, J. R. *The social context of marriage.* 2nd ed. Lippincott, 1971.

Udry, J. R. *The social context of marriage.* 3rd ed. Lippincott, 1974.

Ullman, A. Ethnic differences in the first drinking experience. *Social Problems,* 1960, *8,* 48–57.

Underwood, B. J. Ten years of massed practice on distributed practice. *Psychological Review,* 1961, *68,* 229–247.

Underwood, B. J. Forgetting. *Scientific American,* March 1964.

U.S. Bureau of the Census. *Statistical abstract of the United States: 1976.* 97th ed. Washington, D.C., 1976.

Valins, S. Cognitive effects of false heart-rate feedback. *Journal of Personality and Social Psychology,* 1966, *4,* 400–408.

Van de Castle, R. L. *The psychology of dreaming.* General Learning Corporation, 1971.

Van Dusen, R. A., & Sheldon, E. B. The changing status of American women: A life cycle perspective. *American Psychologist,* 1976, *31,* 106–116.

Vernon, P. E. *Intelligence: Heredity and environment.* Freeman, 1979.

Vernon, P. E. *Intelligence and cultural environment.* Methuen, 1969.

Veroff, J., & Feld, S. *Marriage and work in America.* Van Nostrand, 1970.

von Senden, M. *Space and sight.* Free Press, 1960.

Vygotsky, L. S. *Thought and language.* M.I.T. Press, 1962.

Wade, N. IQ and heredity: Suspicion of fraud beclouds classic experiment. *Science,* 1976, *194,* 916–919.

Wahl, O. Six TV myths about mental illness. *TV Guide,* March 13, 1976.

Wallace, P. Animal behavior: The puzzle of flavor aversion. *Science,* 1976, *193,* 989–991.

Walster, E., Aronson, E., & Abrahams, D. On increasing the persuasiveness of a low-prestige communicator. *Journal of Experimental Social Psychology,* 1966, *2,* 325–342.

Warren, R. M., & Warren, R. P. Auditory illusions and confusions. *Scientific American,* 1970, *223,* 30–36.

Water, H. F., & Malamud, P. Drop that gun, Captain Video. *Newsweek,* March 10, 1975.

Watson, J. B. John Broadus Watson. In C. Murchison (ed.), *A history of psychology in autobiography,* Vol. 3. Clark U. Press, 1936.

Watson, J. B., & Rayner, R. Conditioned emotional reactions. *Journal of Experimental Psychology,* 1920, *3,* 1–14.

Webb, W. B., & Cartwright, R. D. Sleep and dreams. *Annual Review of Psychology,* 1978, *29,* 223–252.

Wechsler, D. *The measurement of adult intelligence.* Williams & Wilkins, 1939.

Wechsler, D. *The measurement of adult intelligence.* 3rd ed. Williams & Wilkins, 1944.

Wechsler, D. *Wechsler Adult Intelligence Scale.* Psychological Corporation, 1955.

Weiner, B., Frieze, I., Kukla, A., Reed, L., Rest, S., & Rosenbaum, R. M. *Perceiving the causes of success and failure.* General Learning Corporation, 1971.

Weiner, B., & Sierad, J. Misattribution for failure and the enhancement of achievement strivings. *Journal of Personality and Social Psychology,* 1975, *31,* 415–421.

Weiner, M. L. *Personality: The human potential.* Pergamon, 1973.

Weinstein, M. S. Achievement motivation and risk preference. *Journal of Personality and Social Psychology,* 1969, *13,* 153–172.

Weiss, P. Some aspects of femininity. *Dissertation Abstracts.* 1962, *23,* 1083.

Weitzenhoffer, A. M. *Hypnotism.* Wiley Science Edition, 1963.

White, L., Krumholz, W. V., & Fink, L. The adjustment of criminally insane patients to a civil mental hospital. *Mental Hygiene,* 1969, *53,* 34–40.

White, M. S. Psychological and social barriers to women in science. *Science,* 1970, *170,* 413–416.

White, R. W. *The abnormal personality.* 2nd ed. Ronald, 1956.

White, R. W. *The abnormal personality.* 3rd ed. Ronald, 1964.

Whitfield, I. C., & Evans, E. F. Responses of auditory cortical neurons to stimuli of changing frequency. *Journal of Neurophysiology,* 1965, *28,* 655–672.

Winget, C., Kramer, M., & Whitman, R. Dreams and demography. *Canadian Psychiatric Association Journal,* 1972, *17,* 203–208.

Wilcoxin, H. C., Dragoin, W. B., & Kral, P. A. Illness-induced aversions in rat and quail: Relative salience of visual and gustatory cues. *Science,* 1971, *171,* 826–828.

Williams, C. D. The elimination of tantrum behavior by extinction procedures. *Journal of Abnormal and Social Psychology,* 1959, *59,* 269.

Williams, J. H. *Psychology of women.* Norton, 1977.

Witkin, H., & Lewis, H. Presleep experiences and dreams. In H. Witkin and H. Lewis (eds.), *Experimental studies of dreaming.* Random House, 1967.

Wolberg, L. R. *The technique of psychotherapy.* 2nd ed. Part I. Grune & Stratton, 1967.

Wolman, J. Drinking on the job costly. *Santa Barbara, Calif., News-Press,* November 28, 1974, p. H-9.

Wolpe, J. *Psychotherapy by reciprocal inhibition.* Stanford U. Press, 1958.

Wolpe, J. *The practice of behavior therapy.* Pergamon, 1969.

Woodworth, R. S. *Personal Data Sheet.* Stoelting, 1920.

Woodworth, R. S. *Experimental psychology.* Holt, 1938.

Woodworth, R. S. Obituary of John Broadus Watson, 1878–1958. *American Journal of Psychology,* 1959, *72,* 301–310.

Woodworth, R. S., & Schlosberg, H. *Experimental psychology.* Holt, 1954.

Wrightsman, L. S. *Social psychology.* 2nd brief ed. Brooks/Cole, 1977.

Wyatt, D. F., & Campbell, D. T. On the lability of stereotype or hypothesis. *Journal of Abnormal and Social Psychology,* 151, *46,* 496–500.

Wylie, R. C. The present status of self theory. In E. F. Borgatta & W. W. Lambert (eds.), *Handbook of personality theory and research.* Rand McNally, 1968.

Yankelovich, D. *Generations apart.* CBS News, 1969.

Yankelovich, D. *The new morality: A profile of American youth in the 1970's.* McGraw-Hill, 1974.

Yates, F. A. *The art of memory.* U. of Chicago Press, 1966.

Zajonc, R. B. Family configuration and intelligence. *Science,* 1976, *192,* 227–236.

Zellman, G. L. The role of structural factors in limiting women's institutional participation. *Journal of Social Issues.* 1976, *32*(3), 33–46.

Ziegler, H. P., & Leibowitz, H. Apparent visual size as a function of distance for children and adults. *American Journal of Psychology,* 1957, *70,* 106–109.

Zilboorg, G., & Henry, G. W. *A history of medical psychology.* Norton, 1941.

Zillman, D., & Cantor, J. R. Effects of timing of information about mitigating circumstances on emotional responses to provocation and retaliatory behavior. *Journal of Experimental Social Psychology,* 1976, *12,* 38–55.

Zimbardo, P. G. *Psychology and life.* 9th ed. Scott, Foresman, 1975.

Zinberg, N. E. The war over marijuana. *Psychology Today,* December 1976.

Zubin, J., Eron, L. D., & Schumer, F. *An experimental approach to projective techniques.* Wiley, 1965.

(Continued from p. iv)
ing approach," in R. K. Siegel and L. J. West, eds., *Hallucinations.* Copyright © 1975 by John Wiley & Sons, Inc. Reprinted by permission of John Wiley & Sons, Inc.

Chapter 4 *Fig. 4.1* (top): From *Cats in a Puzzle Box* by Edwin R. Guthrie and George P. Horton. Copyright 1946, renewal © 1974 by Edwin R. Guthrie and George P. Horton. Reprinted and adapted by permission of Holt, Rinehart and Winston. (bottom): Tania Mychajlyshyn-D'Avignon. *Fig. 4.2:* From *Animal Intelligence: Experimental Studies* by Edward L. Thorndike. Copyright 1911 by Macmillan Publishing Co., Inc. Reprinted by permission. *Fig. 4.3:* Sovfoto. *Fig. 4.5:* Mimi Forsyth/Monkmeyer. *Fig. 4.6:* From C. B. Ferster and B. F. Skinner, *Schedules of Reinforcement,* © 1957, p. 159. Reprinted by permission of Prentice-Hall, Inc., Englewood Cliffs, New Jersey. *Fig. 4.7:* Russ Kinne/Photo Researchers. *Fig. 4.8:* From B. F. Skinner, *The Behavior of Organisms: An Experimental Analysis,* © 1938, renewed 1966, p. 154. Reprinted by permission of Prentice-Hall, Inc., Englewood Cliffs, New Jersey. *Fig. 4.9:* Josephus Daniels/Photo Researchers. *Fig. 4.10:* From E. C. Tolman and C. H. Honzik, "Introduction and Removal of Reward, and Maze Performance in Rats," University of California Publications in Psychology, 4:17, 1930. Reprinted by permission of the University of California Press. *Fig. 4.11:* Thomas D. McAvoy/© Time Inc.

Chapter 5 *Fig. 5.1:* Cary Wolinsky/Stock, Boston. *Fig. 5.3:* Courtesy of International Business Machines Corporation. *Fig. 5.7:* Michal Heron. *Fig. 5.9:* Erich Hartmann/© 1970 Magnum Photos. *Fig. 5.11:* Courtesy, Dr. W. Feindell, Montreal Neurological Institute.

Chapter 6 *Fig. 6.1:* Dr. Neal E. Miller. *Fig 6.2:* Adapted from J. P. Mayer, P. Roy, and K. P. Mitra, "Relation between caloric intake, body weight, and physical work," *American Journal of Clinical Nutrition,* 4 (1956), p. 172. Reprinted by permission. *Fig. 6.3:* John Veltri/© 1979 Photo Researchers. *Fig. 6.4* (left): Miriam Austerman, © Animals, Animals; (right): Charles Gatewood. *Fig. 6.5:* Jeff Albertson/Stock, Boston. *Fig. 6.6:* From *The Stress of Life* by Hans Selye. Copyright © 1956 by Hans Selye. Used with permission of McGraw-Hill Book Company. *Fig. 6.7:* From R. H. Rahe, "Subjects' recent life changes and their near-future illness susceptibility," *Advances in Psychosomatic Medicine,* 8 (1972), p. 7. Reprinted by permission. *Fig. 6.9:* UPI. *Fig. 6.11:* Wide World Photos.

Chapter 7 *Fig. 7.1* (top): Georgia Historical Society; (left): Philadelphia Museum of Art: Given by Miss William Adger; (right): Courtesy of Museum of the American Indian, Heye Foundation. *Fig. 7.2:* Ylla/Ralpho/Photo Researchers. *Fig. 7.3:* Photos courtesy of R. A. and B. T. Gardner, *Fig. 1, Fig. 2, p. 278, Fig. 3, p. 279:* Photos courtesy of R. A. and B. T. Gardner. *Fig. 7.6* (left): © 1979 Joel Gordon; (right): Harry Kilroy. *Fig. 7.7:* The Bettmann Archive. *Fig. 7.8* (left): Walter Chandoha; (right): Bernard Pierre Wolff/Magnum Photos. *Fig. 7.9:* I. Eibl-Eibesfeldt, *Love and Hate,* Holt, Rinehart and Winston, 1972, p. 16. *Fig 7.10:* © 1976

Joel Gordon. *Fig. 7.11:* Christopher S. Johnson/Stock, Boston. *Fig. 1, p. 304:* From *Human Sexuality,* 3rd edition, by James L. McCary, © 1978 by Litton Educational Publishing, Inc. Reprinted by permission of D. Van Nostrand Company. *Fig. 2, p. 306:* From Mussen, Conger, Kagan, and Geiwitz, *Psychological Development: A Life-Span Approach,* p. 432. Copyright © 1979 by Harper & Row, Publishers, Inc. Reprinted by permission.

Chapter 8 *Fig. 8.1:* Yves de Braine/Black Star. *Fig. 8.3:* Dr. Jerome Bruner. *Fig. 8.4:* George Zimbel/Monkmeyer. *Fig. 8.5:* Dianne Smith Schaefer/Designworks. *Fig. 8.6:* Elizabeth Hamlin/Stock, Boston. *Fig. 8.9:* Leslie Starobin/The Picture Cube. *Fig. 8.10* (left): Dr. Lytt I. Gardner; (right): Dr. Harry F. Harlow, University of Wisconsin Primate Laboratory. *Fig. 1, p. 330:* Dr. Harry F. Harlow, University of Wisconsin Primate Laboratory. *Fig. 8.11:* From H. R. Schaffer and P. E. Emerson, "The development of social attachments in infancy," *Monographs of the Society for Research in Child Development,* 29, 3, p. 23. Copyright 1964 by The Society for Research in Child Development. Reprinted by permission. *Fig. 8.12:* © 1978 Joanne Leonard/Woodfin Camp. *Fig. 8.14* (left): Frank Siteman/Stock, Boston; (left center): Owen Franken/Stock, Boston; (right center): Cary Wolinsky/Stock, Boston; (right): Peter Southwick/Stock, Boston. *Fig. 8.15:* Courtesy, Charlotte Rae and The Drackett Company. *Fig. 8.16:* © Tracy Ecclesine. *Fig. 8.17:* Ruth Orkin. *Fig. 8.18:* Anna K. Moon/Stock, Boston.

Chapter 9 *Fig. 9.1:* From p. 213, "The Multi-Stage Mate Selection Filter," in *The Social Context of Marriage,* 2nd edition, by J. Richard Udry. Copyright © 1971, 1966 by J. B. Lippincott Company. Reprinted by permission of Harper & Row, Publishers, Inc. *Fig. 9.2:* From Boyd C. Rollins and Harold Feldman, "Marital satisfaction over the family life cycle," *Journal of Marriage and the Family,* February 1970, p. 26 (Figure 4). Copyrighted 1970 by the National Council on Family Relations. Reprinted by permission. *Fig. 9.4:* © James Foote/Photo Researchers. *Fig. 9.5:* Abigail Heyman/Magnum Photos. *Fig. 9.6:* Wide World Photos. *Fig. 9.9:* From K. Warner Schaie and Charles R. Strother, "A cross-sequential study of age changes in cognitive behavior," *Psychological Bulletin,* 70, pp. 671–679, figs. 1–5. Copyright 1968 by the American Psychological Association. Reprinted by permission. *Fig. 9.11:* UPI. *Fig. 9.12* (top): David A. Krathwohl/Stock, Boston; (bottom): Robert Schackter/The Picture Cube. *Fig. 9.13:* UPI.

Chapter 10 *Fig. 10.1:* Sigmund Freud Copyrights, Ltd. *Fig. 10.2:* The Bettmann Archive. *Fig. 10.4:* © 1979 Bob Adelman. *Fig. 10.5:* From the MGM release *The Loved One,* © 1965, Metro-Goldwyn-Mayer. *Fig. 10.6:* © 1979 Frank Siteman. *Fig. 10.7:* Charles Dixon/The Boston Globe. *Fig. 10.8:* H. Armstrong Roberts. *Fig. 10.9:* From Albert Bandura, "Self-efficacy: Toward a unifying theory of behavioral change," *Psychological Review,* vol. 84, No. 2 (1977), p. 193. Copyright 1977 by the American Psychological Association. Reprinted by permission. *Fig. 10.10:* Tom Dempsey/Philadelphia Eagles Football Club. *Fig. 1, p. 415* (left): Scala, New York/Florence; (right): The British Museum. *Fig. 10.11:* © 1979 Susan Lapides. *Fig. 10.12:* Courtesy, The National Foundation of the March of Dimes.

Chapter 11 *Fig. 11.1:* The Bettmann Archive. *Fig. 11.2:* From M. L. Terman and M. A. Merrill, *Stanford-Binet Intelligence Scale: Manual for the Third Revision, Form L-M.* Copyright © 1973 by Houghton Mifflin Company. Used by permission. *Fig. 11.3:* Dennis Brack/Black Star. *Fig. 11.4:* Adapted from the *American College Testing Program Technical Report,* 1973, p. 186. Reprinted by permission of the American College Testing Program. *Fig. 11.5:* Reprinted from *On Further Examination* with permission from The College Board. Copyright © 1977 by College Entrance Examination Board. *Fig. 1, p. 449:* Reproduced by special permission from the Group Embedded Figures Test by Herman A. Witkin, Phillip K. Oltman, and Evelyn Raskin. Copyright 1971, published by Consulting Psychologists Press. Reprinted by permission of Consulting Psychologists Press. *Fig. 11.6:* © 1971 Van Bucher/Photo Researchers. *Fig. 11.7* (left): Dr. J. D. Watson; (right): Wide World Photos. *Fig. 11.8:* Museum of Modern Art, Still Archives/Warner Brothers. *Fig. 11.9:* Van Bucher/Photo Researchers. *Fig. 11.10:* Andrew Wyeth, *Christina's World,* 1948, Tempera on gesso panel, 32¼″ × 47. Collection, The Museum of Modern Art, New York; purchase. *Fig. 11.11* (left): UPI; (right): Nina Leen/© Time Inc.

Chapter 12 *Fig. 12.1:* National Library of Medicine, Betheseda, Maryland. *Fig. 12.2:* The Bettmann Archive. *Fig. 12.3:* © Charles Hurbutt/Magnum. *Fig. 12.4:* Susan Meiselas/Magnum. *Fig. 12.5:* New York Public Library Picture Collection. *Fig. 12.6:* Frank Siteman/The Picture Cube. *Fig. 12.7:* Bastien Le-Page, The Metropolitan Museum of Art; gift of E. Davis. *Fig. 12.8:* © Guttman-Maclay Collection, Institute of Psychiatry, London. *Fig. 12.9:* Bob Combs/Ralpho/Photo Researchers. *Fig. 12.10:* Angus McBean Photograph, Harvard Theatre Collection. *Fig. 12.11:* Gerald Martineaux, The Washington Post. *Fig. 12.12:* R. Ellison, Empire News/Black Star.

Chapter 13 *Fig. 13. 1:* Charles W. Herbert/Western Ways. *Fig. 13.2:* Sigmund Freud Copyrights, Ltd. *Fig. 13.3:* Michael Hardy/Woodfin Camp. *Fig. 13.4:* From M. Dinott and H. D. Richard, "Learning that privileges entail responsibility," in *Behavioral Counseling: Cases and Techniques* edited by John D. Krumboltz and Carl E. Thoreson. Copyright © 1969 by Holt, Rinehart and Winston, Inc. Reprinted by permission of Holt, Rinehart and Winston. *Fig. 13.5:* Dr. Albert Bandura, Stanford University. *Fig. 13.6:* Kurt Gunther/Camera 5. *Fig. 13.7:* J. Berndt/Stock, Boston. *Fig. 13.9* (top): Alex Webb/Magnum Photos; (bottom): Hans Stewart/Jeroboam.

Chapter 14 *Fig. 14.1:* The Bettmann Archive. *Fig. 14.2:* From M. Sherif and C. W. Sherif, *Social Psychology,* copyright © 1969 by M. Sherif and C. W. Sherif. By permission of Harper & Row, Publishers, Inc. *Fig. 1, p. 568:* John Telford, *People Magazine,* © 1975, Time Magazine. *Fig. 14.3:* Frank Siteman/Stock, Boston. *Fig. 14.4:* © Volkswagen of America, Inc. *Fig. 14.5* (top): Ruth Orkin; (bottom): Harry Kilroy. *Fig. 14.6:* © 1975 by Stanley Milgram, from the film *Obedience,* distributed by the New York University Film Library. *Fig. 14.7:* Owen Franken/Stock, Boston. *Fig. 14.8:* The Minneota Mascot. *Fig. 14.9:* The Bettmann Archive. *Fig. 2, p. 586* (left): Ruth Orkin; (right): Ellis Herwig/Stock, Boston.

Index

To the owner of this book:

All of us who worked together to produce *Psychology: Looking at Ourselves* hope that you have enjoyed it as much as we did. If you did—or if you didn't—we'd like to know why, so we'll have an idea how to improve it in future editions.

School: _____

Instructor's name: _____

1. What did you think of the book in general, compared to other textbooks you have used? _____

_____

What do you see as its major strengths? _____

_____

Its major weaknesses? _____

2. *Chapters.* Please rate each chapter, using an average chapter in one of your other textbooks for comparison. Please use the following scale: X = not assigned; 1 = poor; 2 = fair; 3 = average; 4 = good; 5 = excellent. If you have comments on the specific chapters—some of the coverage that you particularly liked or disliked, for example, or some topic you would like to see added—please note them in the space provided.

	Rating	Comments
1. The Science of Psychology	____	_____
2. The Biological Framework	____	_____
3. Perceiving	____	_____
4. Learning and Behavior	____	_____
5. Memory	____	_____
6. Motivation and Emotion	____	_____
7. Language and Nonverbal Communication	____	_____
8. Child Development	____	_____
9. Adult Development and Aging	____	_____
10. Personality	____	_____
11. Testing Intelligence and Personality	____	_____
12. Abnormal Psychology	____	_____
13. Therapies	____	_____
14. Social Psychology	____	_____

3. *Interludes.* Please rate each interlude on the same scale. And please comment, if you see fit.

	Rating		*Rating*
Careers in Psychology	____	Moral Development	____
Behavior Genetics	____	Future Shock	____
Parapsychology	____	Sleep and Dreams	____
The Psychology of Sex Differences	____	Is IQ Inherited?	____
Hypnosis	____	Drugs	____
Lie Detection	____	Life in Mental Hospitals	____
Human Sexuality	____		

3a. Can you suggest any topics that you think would make good interludes in a future edition? (For example,

suicide? obesity? creativity? others?) _____

_____

4. Do you feel your instructor should continue to assign this book? _____

Why, or why not? _____

_____

_____

5. Will you keep this book? _____

6. Please add any further comments or suggestions on how we might improve this book:

_____

_____

_____

_____

7. *Optional:* Your name: _____ Date: _____

Address: _____

May we quote you, either in promotion for this book or in future publishing ventures?

____Yes ____No

— —

If you made it this far, we hope you'll follow through and mail the questionnaire to us at:

Psychology: Looking at Ourselves
College Division
Little, Brown and Company
34 Beacon Street
Boston, Massachusetts 02106

Thank you!